MW00759153

COLLUSION

ALSO BY L. BRENT BOZELL III

Whitewash: What the Media Won't Tell You About Hillary Clinton, but Conservatives Will (with Tim Graham)

Weapons of Mass Distortion: The Coming Meltdown of the Liberal Media

COLLUSION

HOW THE MEDIA STOLE

THE 2012 ELECTION——AND HOW
TO STOP THEM FROM DOING IT IN 2016

L. BRENT BOZELL III
& TIM GRAHAM

BROADSIDE BOOKS
An Imprint of HarperCollins*Publishers*
www.broadsidebooks.net

HarperCollins books may be purchased for educational, business, or sales promotional use. For information, please e-mail the Special Markets Department at SPsales@harpercollins .com.

Broadside Books™ and the Broadside logo are trademarks of HarperCollins Publishers.

FIRST EDITION

Designed by J. M. Wispe

Library of Congress Cataloging-in-Publication Data has been applied for.

ISBN: 978-0-06-227472-4

13 14 15 16 17   DIX/RRD   10 9 8 7 6 5 4 3 2 1

To our anonymous benefactors—*we* know who you are.

ACKNOWLEDGMENTS

Finding and organizing the flood of examples of media distortion and omission in this book requires far more than two people. It takes the careful daily record keeping of a whole news-analysis division at the Media Research Center. Brent Baker has directed the MRC's media-monitoring team for more than twenty-five years. Research Director Rich Noyes offered his insights, especially on Benghazi coverage and the avoidance of Obama's economic record. Deputy Research Director Geoff Dickens patiently read through every page of this book to keep us on track.

Our news-monitoring team includes NewsBusters Managing Editor Ken Shepherd and Senior Analyst Scott Whitlock, as well as Matthew Balan, Kyle Drennen, Matt Hadro, and Brad Wilmouth. Clay Waters of the MRC's TimesWatch project helped us expose the *New York Times*. We relied on research from interns Paul Bremmer, Alex Fitzsimmons, Kelly McGarey, Jeffrey Meyer, Ryan Robertson, and Matt Vespa.

We always require extensive use of the MRC video archive for a big book project, so our thanks to Michelle Humphrey.

And then there is Brent Bozell's assistant, the unflappable Melissa Lopez, who coordinates all things with the disposition of an angel.

We thank Adam Bellow and Eric Meyers at Broadside Books for their encouragement and guidance, as well as Jonathan Burnham,

ACKNOWLEDGMENTS

Kathy Schneider, Trina Hunn, Joanna Pinsker, Tom Hopke Jr., and Stephanie Selah.

Tim Graham thanks his wife, Laura, and his children, Ben and Abby, and always thanks God for his parents, Jim and Ann Graham.

L. Brent Bozell III thanks his wife, Norma, for raising five children with sterling values, meaning not a one of them wishes to be a reporter.

CONTENTS

INTRODUCTION

"The Best Campaign Team"

Mitt Romney thought he'd won. So did Paul Ryan. So did we.

With polls set to open in New Hampshire in mere hours, we were working the phones with John McLaughlin, of the McLaughlin Associates polling firm. I've known him for over thirty years. We cut our teeth together at the National Conservative Political Action Committee (NCPAC) in 1980, I in the fundraising operation, John working for the legendary Arthur Finkelstein, who did NCPAC's polling. McLaughlin has a reputation for being as good as anyone in the business. More importantly, he's impeccably honest.

We were on the phone putting finishing touches on some questions the Media Research Center was purchasing from his omnibus Election Night poll. Our desire was to determine the impact the media realized over the 2012 election process. More specifically: Did the public buy the media's "news" reporting during this cycle? Assuming Romney was the victor, would he have won the presidency had the public believed what it was receiving to be objective news reporting?

If the answer was in the negative, one had to ask the frightening question: Can free elections—democracy itself—survive a leftist political onslaught dishonestly packaged as objective news reporting?

I asked John to review with me the polling data for all "battleground" states. So he went to the RealClearPolitics.com website.

Virginia, I began. John walked me through the available media numbers for Northern Virginia v. the southern part of the state versus the mountain region versus the Norfolk/Tidewater area. *Conclusion?* I asked. *Romney.* We moved to the next state. *Florida?* Again the polling analysis, painstakingly. Panhandle, Palm Beach area. In between. *Conclusion? Romney.*

Ohio? Romney. Wisconsin? Romney. North Carolina? Romney. New Mexico? Romney. New Hampshire? Romney. Colorado? Romney. In state after state, after a discussion of polling data, voting trends, and other anecdotal information, the conclusion was unchanged: Romney. Only in Minnesota did McLaughlin hesitate. That state, he suggested, might be just too far out of reach. Give them all the red states and now add in all the battleground states and this was shaping up to be a certain Romney-Ryan victory and quite possibly, a landslide.

Virtually all the GOP-leaning pollsters and virtually all the GOP-leaning pundits (yes, including us) were in agreement. Even the ever-cautious Michael Barone, so learned about every voting backyard in America, was projecting a massive win for the Republicans. The problem was, all the Democratic-leaning pollsters, along with their Democratic-leaning pundits, were calling this one for Obama.

It wasn't unconvincing bravado coming from the Democratic pundits, unchallenged by media pollsters. Obama wasn't like a heavyweight champion who was pounded mercilessly but still smiles, shaking his head to deny the punch had hurt, but whose wobbled legs betray his battered condition. No, they were all confident in his corner. David Axelrod was laughing on national television, pledging to shave his trademark mustache if his boss lost, and his cohorts in the media were chuckling alongside him.

On Election Night the Axelrod lip hair was safe. Michigan. Pennsylvania. Wisconsin. New Hampshire. Minnesota. Florida. Virginia. Colorado. New Mexico. Iowa. One by one the battleground states reported, and one by one they lined up behind the incumbent. Only in North Carolina did the challenger persevere. By 11:30 P.M. there was Karl Rove, the personification of Republican Party politics, the man who raised hundreds of millions from GOP donors while pledging to deliver not just the White House but the Senate as well, desperately waving his hands on national television, the last man standing at the GOP's Little Bighorn, insisting Ohio was not lost.

What had (most) liberals known that (most) conservatives and Karl Rove had failed to grasp?

Yes, the Democrats' turnout machine was as spectacularly successful as the Republicans' was woefully nonexistent. It led the GOP to announce a post-election "autopsy" of their operations, which should have started with firing the idiot who further embarrassed the party by calling the exercise an autopsy.

That was not the concern for my colleague Tim Graham and me. Rather, it was the numbers themselves.

Throughout the campaign, particularly after Labor Day, when pollsters historically switch from the less-efficient "registered voter" to the more accurate "likely voter" formula, a debate raged between media pollsters who consistently found the incumbent enjoying a slight, but solid lead, and those mostly Republican leaners whose pollsters saw the opposite. Conservatives saw a liberal bias: the polling samples consistently were top-heavy with Democrats. Media pollsters defended the skewed samples as reflective of 2008 voting turnout. Republicans rejected this formulation, insisting the more recent 2010 results, which found significant GOP victories, triggered by superior GOP turnout was more accurate. In short, media pollsters saw Virginia as 2008 blue; GOP and conservative pollsters declared the commonwealth 2010 red.

Liberal media bias—that had to be the reason Obama was projected to prevail. But it wasn't. In the end, voter turnout did reflect the 2008 numbers. So the press pollsters were correct, objectively, impartially, truthfully correct.

Arguably it was the only thing about the 2012 elections where the media could be credited as being objective, impartial, and even, when it really counted, truthful.

PRESIDENT OBAMA climbed onstage in front of a raucous crowd in Chicago at 1:45 A.M. on Election Night to pay tribute to those who helped him win a second term. "To the best campaign team and volunteers in the history of politics!" Obama talked gauzily about young field organizers working their way through college, and military spouses sitting in a phone bank dialing away. He spent a lot of time talking about himself, too. He does that mercilessly.

But his praises for all the members of his campaign "family" failed to include his most powerful supporters. There was no love expressed at the lectern for the multimillion-dollar network anchors sitting patiently under the studio lights, preparing each day and night to launch another so-called newscast that would sell Obama and his talking points.

There were no warm words for newsmagazines that would so transparently honor him on their covers, or national newspapers that buried all the worst stories about him. If the "objective" press didn't want to maintain the myth of their nonpartisanship—a myth so easily apparent to anyone who wasn't a "low-information voter"—

Obama would have looked supremely rude by declaring his gratitude publicly.

Some things are better left alone.

The utter failure of Obama's policies and his resulting unpopularity (ratified in the 2010 midterm wave election) barely slowed down the media's reelection propaganda machine. No statistic like a trillion-dollar deficit or a high unemployment rate was going to shake their faith. No presidential candidate in the television era had received the rapturous acclaim that greeted Barack Obama in the Hope and Change election cycle of 2008. They were now invested in his reelection.

The second campaign couldn't be like the first one, where all the Hope and Change chatter painted a gauzy dream of the future. Reality had intruded. Obama promised recovery and delivered only stubborn economic stagnation. Obama promised to cut the deficit in half and instead created dizzying trillion-dollar deficits as far as the eye could see. Obama was handed a Nobel Peace Prize, but kept Guantanamo open and waged deadly drone attacks on terrorism suspects.

All this could have been—*should* have been—disillusioning for Obama's liberal supporters in the press. But so blinded were they by the light of their star that nothing, no fact, no statistic, no storm cloud, no controversy, no scandal—nothing was going to stop them. In 2012 they were doubling down. The national media relentlessly pushed for Obama's reelection with an undisguised affection for Obama-Biden "message discipline." There was an obvious collusion between the president's camp and the "objective" press.

In economics, "collusion" is defined as an agreement between parties to limit open competition by misrepresenting the independence of the relationship between them. The agreement may be set formally, or shared attitudinally. Either way, transparency is necessary but is instead denied. In a collusion, the parties may suppress evidence or even fabricate information to gain a competitive advantage and, ultimately, their economic objective.

This definition certainly fits the media, which utterly failed in 2012 to establish any independence from the Obama machine. While posturing as objective referees of news and information, they suppressed evidence that would mar Obama's personal character or political record, and they allowed the Democrats to invent and project information harmful to the Republicans. If all else failed, the media fabricated it themselves.

National reporters virtually begged their audience to share their desire to keep their man at the national helm. The media's president was a Celebrity President, a charismatic nonfiction TV character with Hollywood swagger. He defined hipness and modernity. And brilliance. And vision. He was History. He was, as Chris Matthews told us, *perfect.*

Mitt Romney's political machine (actually, political junk metal) was oblivious to all this, comfortable in the belief that an electorate searching for a National CEO, a Recovery President, would turn to the Man from Bain. It was a testimony to the singular ineptness of their effort that for the first time a presidential campaign chose to go into a prevent-defense crouch—while losing. When he wasn't being painted as an evil venture capitalist heartlessly stripping innocent Americans of hearth and home, Romney was presented as a pale and corny fifties sitcom dad like Ward Cleaver, someone never real enough to stop appearing in black-and-white.

The 2012 election can be easily cast as what the eighteenth-century English writer Samuel Johnson quipped about a second marriage— "the triumph of hope over experience." John Adams insisted that "facts are stubborn things," but that is now irrelevant. Politicians now are elected on something more slippery—a narrative. The official media-elite 2012 spin pitted a hardworking, compassionate president who was just beginning to show great promise against a soulless capitalist raider who wanted to eviscerate government programs for poor folks. The narrative sold. Voters like stories. Whether or not the official story bore any resemblance to the truth meant nothing to those projecting it.

In a post-election interview with *Politico*'s Mike Allen, campaign strategist Axelrod recounted telling Obama that the media elites hadn't been wrong when they spent much of the first two years of Obama's tenure "reporting" that the Tea Party people were extremists who would quickly ruin the Republican Party. "I said to the President the day after the midterm elections, I thought that the seeds of his re-election had been planted by that election," he remembered. "No Republican candidate was going to be able to get through that process without bowing to the force of the Tea Party and the social conservatives. And a number of very formidable candidates took a pass, in part because they recognized that."

Axelrod could say this because he had confidence that the "objective" media would be his echo chamber. The media coverage of Obama's reelection cycle neatly matched Axelrod's plan. Obama would not be judged based on a balanced and factual evaluation of his dismal record. It would be based on a liberal argument of inclusion— that even if Romney brought his vaunted recovery where Obama had failed, that prosperity would only benefit the "millionaires and billionaires" at the expense of "the people." It was also implied that the racially challenged Republicans, hobbled by their party's overwhelming whiteness, somehow didn't want nonwhite Americans to share in the coming cornucopia.

Axelrod told a crowd after the election at the University of Chicago, "The president's fundamental message was that we need not just to rebuild the economy, but needed to reclaim security. That fundamental compact that we thought of as the American Dream has been shredded." To liberals, welfare-state "security" and the American Dream are very tightly linked. Dependency, unlike recovery, could be guaranteed by government. Romney's vision of free-market solutions was dismissed as discredited top-down economics that benefited only the super-rich.

It was a message fully embraced and projected by the national press.

The media have always been liberal, certainly since TV news erupted in power and influence in the 1960s, but never have they shown such naked bias as they did in the 2012 election. It was unrestrained political agitation. So much of the broadcast networks, their cable counterparts, and the major establishment print media were out of control with a deliberate and unmistakable leftist agenda. The most usable facts about Obama were the positive facts. The most usable quotes about Obama were the positive quotes. The most compelling narratives about Obama were the endearingly personal narratives. The reverse held true for his opponent. Over the last quarter century we have closely monitored national political coverage, and we can say with authority that never has there been a more brazen and complete attempt by the liberal "news" media to decide the outcome of an election.

In 2004, then-*Newsweek* scribe Evan Thomas claimed that a media tilt toward John Kerry would be worth at least five (and "maybe fifteen") percentage points. In a race decided by less than four percentage points, can it be argued that the media's blatant salesmanship for Obama provided his margin of victory in 2012?

We believe the national press corps stole the election for Barack Obama in 2012, and will document the evidence in the pages that follow. We also believe that unless and until this blatant leftist disinformation effort is exposed and neutralized, Republicans—at least conservative Republicans—will not soon recapture the reins of power in this country.

Every conservative in America knows the liberal press has an agenda against them. What they cannot understand is why Republicans are so incapable of solving the problem. We share this frustration. We see the damage done daily, with virtually no GOP countermeasures, ever. Why not? There are several reasons.

Ignorance. Oh, they know there's a problem but they have no idea how serious it is. They take their news from Fox, or the *Washington Times.* Their radios are tuned to Rush Limbaugh, Sean Hannity and Mark Levin. Their favorite websites are Drudge, CNSNews, and Breitbart. The working assumption is that everyone else is there, too. Beyond the news media are the entertainment empires where far more mischief is created. Most Republicans are clueless. I once overheard a man ask the late Jeane Kirkpatrick, former ambassador to the United Nations and our very own force of nature, if she could ever handle watching Michael Moore's movie *Roger and Me.* The man stated with a knowing smile that he could *never* stomach the experience. "I already have, and so should you," she snapped. "You must always know what the enemy is doing."

Arrogance. A few years ago I was visiting with John Moody, then a senior vice president at the Fox News Channel, to talk about his network, which by now had risen to the top of the cable news business. I asked him, at what point did Republicans realize they had a venue that wasn't going to crucify them? I wanted to know. Moody's answer was immediate and emphatic: Democrats were comfortable with Fox far sooner than their counterparts simply because they understood the need to work with the press. When calling down to Washington in search of a GOP guest on Capitol Hill, or at the Bush White House, the Fox booker inevitably would be transferred to some press secretary with no authority to do more than take a message that would or wouldn't be returned by a senior staff member who—yawn—would or wouldn't be interested in delivering his boss. The Democrats? They booked the interview on the spot. Often the member of Congress jumped on the phone to facilitate the interview.

Fear. During the Bush years I was invited to Capitol Hill to meet with a select group of conservatives, from both parties, thoroughly frustrated and intimidated by the national news media over the issue that bound them—tax cuts. Any discussion along these lines invariably became a clarion call for "tax cuts for the greedy rich," when this was never their intent. They still carried the scars of the "Mediscare" campaign of 1995, when the press demolished the nascent Republican majority and buried the Contract with America by stating and repeating endlessly the falsehood that Republicans were abandoning the elderly (along with clean air and water, and the homeless, and the hungry, and blacks and Hispanics, and the children, the children, always the children). "What could they do?" they pleaded. Barring a better answer from me, their (unspoken) solution was to hide.

The answer, I tried to tell them, was otherwise, a three-part exercise. First, present your argument intelligently and cogently. Second, if your message is distorted by the press, give them the benefit of the doubt. Bring the offense to their attention, and give them the opportunity to correct it. Third, if they are in the wrong, and they refuse to correct the error, beat the hell out of them. Make *them* the issue. There was much chest-thumping in return as one by one they gave their speeches endorsing a declaration of war on the media. By and large that never happened. Instead they returned to fretting about what the media might do to them in response and they returned to the tall grass from whence they've not emerged.

That was then. We are in the midst of the most profound communications revolution in history, with extraordinary new opportunities presenting themselves to us, each one making the left-wing news media that much more irrelevant—if we're smart enough, and eager enough, and courageous enough to go there.

First it's critically important to understand the problem fully. Then it's important to correct it. What follows will address both.

CHAPTER 1

From Hope to Hatchets

"He will have to kill Romney."

It is a dirty trick for the national media to decide who's playing dirty. Their support for liberal politicians verges on adoring. Conversely, because the media elite loathes most conservative politicians, almost anything goes in attacking them.

The first thing any conservative should tell his friends about the "news" business is this: reporters, editors, and anchormen are not those characters in your civics textbook, merely interested in telling you what happened in the world while you slept or while you were at work. They're not objective, impartial observers of a political system holding all politicians accountable. They are participants in the process.

The news business in the Obama era has been virtually indistinguishable from the Obama commercials, the official White House videos, and the campaign social-media messages. When they were "reporting" on Obama, reporters weren't offering a news story as much as they were advancing a narrative. They are in the narrative business.

In fact, it could be argued that today's campaign ads are more vetted for accuracy—and in fact, more accurate—than news reports. The 2012 cycle was loaded up with "nonpartisan" fact-checkers with liberal-media backgrounds frisking the candidates and their messages for accuracy. They weren't probing their fellow journalists for lies and inaccuracies. There is often only one difference between a candidate's vicious negative ad and an "investigative" news report: the undeserved patina of media "objectivity" and respectability.

Obama's Republican challengers could be viciously and personally attacked, and the media wouldn't paint the attackers as vicious—especially when they were among the attackers. Team Obama always believed Mitt Romney would be their opponent. In August 2011, *Politico* reported a "prominent Democratic strategist aligned with the White House" speaking bluntly: "Unless things change and Obama can run on accomplishments, he will have to kill Romney." [1]

Imagine the explosion had the Romney camp declared the need to kill Obama. Despite these words appearing in a liberal publication, and despite the Romney camp denouncing the quote as "disgraceful," the words "have to kill Romney" were completely ignored by the major media. They were ignored by the Associated Press, *The New York Times*, *The Washington Post*, and *USA Today*. This phrase wasn't quoted on ABC, CBS, NBC, NPR, PBS, or CNN. As usual, Fox News was the exception to the blackout. Oh wait, there was another. It was relayed once by *Last Word* host Lawrence O'Donnell on MSNBC. He enjoyed it as the "juiciest quote." [2]

The anonymous source was probably not someone like Axelrod, who would never concede Obama had no accomplishments. But it did reflect Team Obama's attitude toward the Republicans. The GOP contenders could all prepare for an historic campaign—defined as an historic level of mud-slinging, the tawdriest, flimsiest attacks of "investigative journalism," and bottom-scraping negative ads.

The architects of Obama's reelection campaign couldn't boast about any reelection mandate. The public was unimpressed by Obama's performance in his first term and reluctant to award him a second one. The Real Clear Politics average of the approval-rating polls in mid-September 2011 measured the president's approval rating at 43 percent approval, and 51 percent disapproval.[3] With these numbers, pundits could have measured his political coffin.

Instead, Axelrod would need to rely on a narrative that the Republicans were all too conservative to offer a serious challenge to Obama. He boasted afterward that he had told the president "the seeds of his re-election had been planted by that [2010] election. The Tea Party movement would need to be marginalized in order to drag all the GOP candidates down. He would need the national media to advance this narrative. In fact, the work was already under way.

Over the summer, the Tea Party wanted the Republicans to vote against increasing the debt limit, as a way to force the Democrats to limit spending. Opposition to Obama equaled hatred, even some form of jihad. *The New York Times* assembled an editorial-page tag team.

Columnist Thomas Friedman warned, "If sane Republicans do not stand up to this Hezbollah faction in their midst, the Tea Party will take the GOP on a suicide mission." Friedman later claimed on NBC that "there's a lot of Republicans who are starved for a candidate" who could debate Obama and attempt to be "as smart and mellifluous as the president."[4]

Times business columnist Joe Nocera claimed the country "watched in horror as the Tea Party Republicans waged jihad on the American people."[5] But columnist Maureen Dowd stood out from

the crowd, sounding like she had swallowed a fistful of hallucino-
genic drugs:

"Tea Party budget-slashers . . . were like cannibals, eating their
own party and leaders alive. They were like vampires, draining the
country's reputation, credit rating and compassion. They were like
zombies, relentlessly and mindlessly coming back again and again to
assault their unnerved victims, [Speaker of the House John] Boehner
and President Obama. They were like the metallic beasts in *Alien*
flashing mouths of teeth inside other mouths of teeth, bursting out
of Boehner's stomach every time he came to a bouquet of microphones."[6]

The New York Times even published a book review by an Ohio
State professor that equated the Tea Party with the Ku Klux Klan.
"Imagine a political movement created in a moment of terrible
anxiety, its origins shrouded in a peculiar combination of manipulation and grass-roots mobilization, its ranks dominated by Christian
conservatives and self-proclaimed patriots, its agenda driven by its
members' fervent embrace of nationalism, nativism and moral re-
generation, with more than a whiff of racism wafting through it. No,
not that movement." Opposing Obama—even if you were Herman
Cain—demonstrated "more than a whiff of racism."

The candidates who jumped in didn't impress Axelrod. So during
the primary season, the media elite treated the emerging Republican challengers as a field of nightmares, a group of pretenders and
has-beens who could not be seriously hoping to defeat Obama. Republican debate audiences were criticized as "bloodthirsty" and demonstrating "bloodlust."[7]

There was no such thing as a loyal or honorable opposition.
Instead, Obama critics were described as assassins. On MSNBC,
Chris Matthews was asserting "the whole shebang, has been elim-
inate this guy's presidency. It's been personal, it's been about him,

and it's about hatred. . . . 'We hate you, want to kill you—[dramatic pause] politically.'"[8]

Republicans on the Chopping Block

From the start of the Republican race in 2011, every candidate who took the lead in the pre-primary polling was subjected to a beating. Even Sarah Palin was slimed in case she decided to run. Outbursts of "investigative journalism" erupted repeatedly against the GOP front-runner of the moment. Republican presidential campaigns were damaged or demolished, one by one.

PALIN. Governor Sarah Palin never declared she was running for president, but she frightened reporters by going on campaign-style bus tours to keep alive the notion that she just might run and her name in the headlines. Journalists feared the voters in Flyover Country might find her more culturally resonant than the globe-trotting sophisticate with the funny name that they preferred. Bill Maher told Piers Morgan on CNN he wouldn't put it past the Republicans. "Somewhere along the line they got on a short bus to Crazy Town, and if someone gets the nomination of one of the two major parties, especially in a bad economy, with a black president, yes, she could become president."[9]

Everyone was qualified to find Palin crazy—even Roseanne Barr. On CNN, she declared "[Palin is] a loon and I think she's kind of a traitor to this country. . . . Her followers are the dumbest people on Earth. . . . They can barely scare up a pulse. I'm serious." MSNBC host Martin Bashir had his own adjectives: "Vacuous, crass, and according to almost every biographer, vindictive too."

Author Joe McGinniss was roundly condemned by liberals as a

smear artist in 1993 for his Ted Kennedy book *The Last Brother*. It was an unreliable, unsubstantiated attack piece, they felt. But when McGinniss wrote *The Last Rogue*, a book attacking Palin, this same maligned scribe was given the red-carpet treatment on *Dateline NBC*. It didn't matter that Palin wasn't running for president. Just the chance that this "mama grizzly" might run inspired NBC's venomous portrayal.

McGinniss called Palin "[a]n utter fraud. An absolute and utter fraud." Rather than challenge that statement, his NBC interviewer, Savannah Guthrie, helpfully added: "You called her a tenth-grade mean girl." McGinniss insisted "those are kind words compared to a lot of what you would hear in Wasilla . . . the people who know her best like her least."

NBC needed no names or documents to prove any smear that McGinniss allegedly was repeating. Guthrie continued: "He accuses the famed hockey mom of using her children as props and reports she was not much of a mother at all." She was "virtually nonexistent as a mother," insisted McGinniss. Guthrie also helpfully relayed the unproven charge that Todd and Sarah Palin were "fighting incessantly and threatening divorce."

The Palins also used cocaine, according to the NBC manure-spreaders. Guthrie touted: "Another bombshell, McGinniss writes that both Todd and Sarah have used cocaine in the past, a claim that has not been verified. How do you substantiate something like that?" A far better, and more important question: Why was this unsubstantiated garbage being repeated on NBC? Are all unverified rumors accepted—if they are salacious enough, and the subject is a conservative?

Guthrie also helped champion McGinniss's claim that Palin slept with a pro basketball star: "McGinniss also quotes friends who speak of a sexual encounter Palin had with basketball star Glen Rice in 1987, while she was a sports reporter for a local Anchorage station, prior to her marriage." Proof of Sarah Heath's bed-hopping with basketball stars at twenty-three? Who needs proof?

Then Guthrie wrapped up: "McGinniss portrays Palin as 'Hands Off' when it came to governing Alaska, but a ruthless political opportunist who crushed her enemies and rarely lived up to the fiscal conservative image she championed." McGinniss said, "At best, she's a hypocrite. . . . At worst, she's a vindictive hypocrite." [10]

Ruthless opportunists . . . vindictive hypocrites who crush enemies—truer words were never spoken . . . if they were applied to the "news" manufacturers at NBC. Guthrie wasn't punished for this exercise in character assassination. She was promoted to her dream job as the cohost of *Today*.

BACHMANN. On July 11, 2011, as Michele Bachmann's popularity was growing (and about a month before she won the Iowa straw poll) ABC's *World News* touted a hidden-camera investigation of the clinic of her therapist husband, Marcus Bachmann. It was a "pray away the gay" scandal, they said. "We begin tonight with an ABC News investigation," oozed anchor Diane Sawyer. "Tea Party powerhouse Michele Bachmann has rocketed to the top of the Republican pack. Tonight, a closer look at the business she and her husband own back home in Minnesota. An outside group filmed undercover video inside the Bachmann's Christian counseling center. Bachmann's husband has said he does not try to turn gay people straight." [11] (The horror!) ABC (and then CNN, and then NBC) claimed otherwise.

But the hidden cameras of this "ABC News investigation" weren't sent in by ABC. They came from a radical homosexual lobby called "Truth Wins Out," a funny name for a group that had lied and faked its way into the Bachmann clinic. No one saw the conflict, apparently.

Mocking Bachmann was easy, and was never seen as sexist. On *The Tonight Show* with Jay Leno, MSNBC host Chris Matthews insisted, "I've always said she's in a trance. I mean, she looks like she's been hypnotized." Former *New York Times* executive editor Bill Keller couldn't stand religious sentiments on the campaign trail. "Rick Perry, Michele Bachmann and Rick Santorum are all affiliated with fervid subsets of evangelical Christianity, which has raised concerns about their respect for the separation of church and state, not to mention the separation of fact and fiction."

In August, *Newsweek* mocked Michele Bachmann on its cover, making her look pale and confused. Nutty. The headline said it all: "The Queen of Rage." The cover story by reporter Lois Romano threw mud. "Bachmann has become the living embodiment of the Tea Party. She and her allies have been called a maniacal gang of knife-wielding ideologues. That's hyperbole, of course. But the principled rigidity of her position has created some challenges for her campaign."

"Obama and his allies are a maniacal gang of knife-wielding ideologues. That's hyperbole, of course." Do you think any editor would ever allow that to stand?

Here's another typical, sneering sentence: "For now, Bachmann revels in the Iowa crowds, which don't fuss about the missing fine print behind her ideas, the perceived contradictions among them, or their radicalism." [12] *Newsweek* claims to loathe contradictions—as they write long, nasty editorials and then claim like complete hypocrites that they were publishing a "news" story.

The liberal website FunnyOrDie.com wrote alternative titles for the Bachmann cover picture, including "The Girl Next Door: Assuming You Live Next to an Insane Asylum" and "Zombies: Michele Bachmann Eats America's Young." [13]

PERRY. Governor Rick Perry looked like a strong contender when he entered the race in August, due to his booming success in the Texas economy and his ability to raise campaign cash. That's when reporters decided to portray him as the worst kind of cowboy bumpkin. ABC anchor Diane Sawyer called him the "human tornado," as reporter Jake Tapper added, "Democrats say that until Perry came along, they never thought they'd meet a candidate who made the other Republican candidates look responsible." [14] CBS ran a wild-haired cartoon image of Perry running with an exploding gun as they explained he believed in "America's right to bear arms—even in a speeding helicopter. Yes, he made it legal to hunt wild boar from the air. After all, he's the kind of governor who would shoot a coyote while he's out jogging." [15]

CNN commentator Jack Cafferty saw his ascent as the End of Brains. "Since Michele Bachmann won the Iowa straw poll and Rick Perry entered the race, these two have been sucking up most of the media's attention, mostly for saying stupid stuff. . . . That's a sad commentary on the state of our politics, isn't it? Here's the question: When it comes to presidential politics, why does America seem to be allergic to brains?"

But his days as front-runner were numbered as the big "investigative bombshell" arrived on October 2, when *The Washington Post* killed trees to report in earthshaking depth how the Rick Perry family had leased a hunting property where in 1983 or 1984, the N-word was found painted on a rock, and never mind it was the Rick Perry family that covered it with white paint. Reporter Stephanie McCrummen could conjure up a virtual Klan hood on Perry's head. "As recently as this summer, the slablike rock—lying flat, the name still faintly visible beneath a coat of white paint—remained by the gated entrance to the camp."

Near the end, she underlined it again: "In the photos, it was to the left of the gate. It was laid down flat. The exposed face was brushed clean of dirt. White paint, dried drippings visible, covered a word across the surface. An N and two G's were faintly visible." [16]

Three thousand words they spent on this.

The *Post* was throwing the biggest rock they could at a

Republican—racism, as in casual acquiescence to the N-word—without telling the public who was behind the accusation. They quoted seven sources, but six of them remained anonymous. Were some Obama supporters or financial backers? Naturally, when some readers protested, *Washington Post* ombudsman Patrick Pexton declared, "If the seven sources the *Post* relied on for this article are truthful, then Perry is lying or is badly misinformed about when the rock was painted." [17] Pexton also insisted that the Perry camp's failure to protest more fiercely made him look guilty. Damned if you do, damned if you don't.

Would the *Post* use six anonymous sources to push a three-thousand-word story on the front page trashing Barack Obama for something some people said anonymously that he did or said in the 1980s? Radio host Hugh Hewitt put it best: "It is a drive-by slander." [18]

Two days after the rock "scoop," a *Post* front-page article by Amy Gardner found Perry's record on race was "complicated" . . . by the facts. Perry "appointed the first African American to the state Supreme Court and later made him chief justice" and oh yes, "One chief of staff and two of his general counsels have been African American." But "minority legislators" complained he used "racially tinged" tactics. Guess what was listed first? "Black lawmakers have been particularly troubled by Perry's recent embrace of the Tea Party movement."

CAIN. Herman Cain was exactly the kind of candidate liberals fear: a successful, dynamic black Republican with a solid record of business success. Liberal journalists couldn't abide the idea that someone of his ilk could ever pretend to be president. *Washington Post* writer Tim Carman made him sound like a mobster: "One of his primary credentials for the job involves his nearly miraculous healing of the once-moribund Godfather's Pizza, as if America were a midgrade Midwestern chain whose many problems could be solved with a few deaths in the family (read: store closings) and a tough-talking thug in a pin-stripe suit and fedora."[19]

When Cain ascended to the top of the Republican polls, it wasn't proof that the Tea Party conservatives were suddenly or temporarily not racists. It was time for another "investigative" takedown. On the night of Halloween, the liberal newspaper *Politico* first reported that when Cain headed the National Restaurant Association, it settled two sex harassment lawsuits. Citing unnamed sources, *Politico* reported two unnamed women had alleged Cain was guilty of "conversations allegedly filled with innuendo or personal questions of a sexually suggestive nature," and also "descriptions of physical gestures that were not overtly sexual" but made women uncomfortable.[20]

"Another high-tech lynching," said Ann Coulter on Fox News.[21]

Even Stephen Engelberg, a former *New York Times* reporter at the investigative journalism shop ProPublica, found it underbaked. "If the facts as published were part of a memo to *Politico*'s editors they would amount to a first-rate tip on a story . . . in this case, it remains unclear whether this was merely a great tip or an actual bombshell."[22]

But the networks were thrilled. "This morning, bombshell blast," announced ABC's George Stephanopoulos hours after the story broke, reporting a "bimbo eruption" of the kind he used to keep out of the news for a paycheck from the Clintons. NBC's Matt Lauer gloated that Cain was "finding out the hard way about the attention that goes along with being a front-runner."[23]

In the first week of the scandal, ABC, CBS, and NBC combined for eighty-four stories on Herman Cain's alleged impropriety with women—before the media would or could identify an accuser with a name and a face.[24] By contrast, eight days into Bill Clinton's sexual harassment scandals with publicly identified accusers Paula Jones and Kathleen Willey and adding even the rape allegation of Juanita Broaddrick, there were eight reports on the three named Clinton accusers combined.[25]

The network story count was almost 100 before a real name emerged, a television avalanche. The networks hurled 117 stories at Cain in the first ten days. Not only that, ABC's Brian Ross suggested Cain's backers were thugs, since one accuser "hired a security team to guard her home outside Washington." Ross added that the accusers might appear together "so they can all tell their stories of Herman Cain, with the sense of safety in numbers."[26]

On November 28, Ginger White told WAGA, the Fox affiliate in Atlanta, that she had a thirteen-year adulterous affair with Cain. All three networks reported it almost simultaneously with the Atlanta story. This is not the way allegations against a Democrat are handled. Ginger White makes an adultery charge against Cain and she's on the *NBC Nightly News* within hours. But when Juanita Broaddrick in a 1999 *Dateline NBC* interview accused Bill Clinton of raping her, then-anchor Tom Brokaw never allowed one single second of her voice to break into his evening newscast.[27]

If only Herman Cain were a Democrat. By the next morning, Cain was dismissed as a political corpse, or a ghost. On ABC, anchor Robin Roberts suggestively asked, "Do [White's] shocking revelations spell doom for his troubled campaign?" On CBS, political analyst John Dickerson proclaimed, "It's hard to see how he comes back from this. . . . At the worst, it's a death blow to the campaign." But NBC's Chuck Todd was the most colorful, citing movies: "Now we're in sort of *The Sixth Sense* mode. Everybody knows this candidacy is basically dead except the campaign."[28]

One day later, Ginger White gave an interview to George Stephanopoulos, a man who would have shredded her reputation and kept her off television if she had claimed an affair with Clinton. The ABC host gloated over Cain's impending doom: "Will our interview spell the end of the one-time front-runner's presidential bid?"[29]

Stephanopoulos was so brazen that he dismissed Cain on character grounds: "There are just too many questions about his honesty, his judgment, his experience, his organization. Even if he stays in [the race], he's not going to be a factor."[30] This from the former official spokesman for Bill Clinton.

Collectively, the media sounded like Yul Brynner playing Pharaoh Ramses in *The Ten Commandments*, shouting, "So let it be written! So let it be done!" Cain soon withdrew.

GINGRICH. Many conservative voters loved the smarts of Newt Gingrich, and loved the way Newt fired away at liberal-media debate moderators—not to mention the idea of him aggressively debating Obama. But seemingly all liberal journalists still carried their 1990s loathing of Gingrich around. NBC anchor Brian Williams announced one night: "The Newt Gingrich that a lot of folks will remember from his speakership days back in the '90s was back on display making statements about controversial issues that left some of his critics slack-jawed."

Chris Matthews recklessly smeared Newt Gingrich, saying, "He looks like a car bomber. . . . He looks like he loves torturing."[31] With a complete lack of awareness of his own incivility, Matthews accused Newt of polluting the civil discourse. "Ever since he appeared on the national scene, politics has been nastier, more feral, too often uglier."[32]

Matthews also declared Gingrich was "a political killer, a gun for hire. . . . That's why they're offering up their partisan souls, why they're ready to bow down before this false god of hatred."

Reporters endlessly cited Gingrich's personal "baggage" in his personal life and public remarks as an impossible obstacle to overcome. Somehow the "baggage" gets lost when the media bellhops are writing about Democrats.

Then again came the Gingrich "investigative bombshell." On the January 19 *Nightline*, days before Gingrich won the South Carolina primary, ABC anchor Terry Moran oozed, "Tonight on *Nightline*, breaking her silence. In an exclusive TV interview, one of presidential hopeful Newt Gingrich's ex-wives speaks out, questioning his moral fitness to be president." Not only was he cheating on her with the woman who would become his third wife, "he was asking for an open marriage."

Brian Ross eagerly prompted ex-wife Marianne Gingrich to tell all: "You know his secrets. You know his skeletons." He boasted to viewers that his scoop could be seen as a "January surprise" to whack Gingrich. Ross implied he shouldn't be considered a conservative, not with his background: "And now, as a candidate for president, Gingrich regularly expounds on family values and the sanctity of marriage between a man and a woman." [33]

What a difference four years makes, especially if the candidate belongs to the other party. At this point in the 2008 campaign, on January 4, Ross was disparaging character attacks on the Democratic contenders. "At grocery store checkout lines, there have been *National Enquirer* headlines, claiming a love child scandal involves Senator John Edwards or a member of his staff, forcing Edwards to issue a strong public denial." Edwards insisted on ABC: "The story's false. It's completely untrue and ridiculous." [34] Ross didn't investigate Edwards for "bombshells" and "skeletons." Ross provided him a national platform to profess his innocence to millions of viewers.

SANTORUM. In November, MSNBC host Rachel Maddow of 2011 laughed at the idea that anyone would ever vote for dark horse former senator Rick Santorum. "Nobody's going to vote for Rick Santorum, come on," Maddow declared, reminding her audience that thanks to far-left sex columnist Dan Savage, when you Google-searched for Santorum, you would find a vulgar definition for the fluid aftermath of anal sex. [35]

MSNBC host Martin Bashir reached for historical smears. "In reviewing his book, *It Takes a Family*, one writer said, 'Mr. Santorum has one of the finest minds of the 13th century.' But I'm not so sure. If you listen carefully to Rick Santorum, he sounds more like Stalin than Pope Innocent III.'"

Santorum reminded former top *New York Times* editor Bill Keller of a radical fundamentalist: "Remember earlier in the campaign when Newt Gingrich was worrying everyone about Sharia law: the Muslims were going to impose Sharia law in America? Sometimes Santorum sounds like he's creeping up on a Christian version of Sharia law."

On January 16, a few days before Santorum's victory in the Iowa caucuses was belatedly announced, the usual "investigative bombshell" landed. *Newsweek* (on its *Daily Beast* website) decided it was "news" to report on Mrs. Santorum's ancient dating history in a piece titled "Before Karen Met Rick." Yes, *before the couple ever met*. The author was Nancy Hass, who a few months before had written a valentine to radical feminist pioneer Gloria Steinem, announcing that Michele Bachmann and Sarah Palin "wouldn't be riling up the Tea Party faithful had Steinem not paved their way out of the kitchen." [36]

Hass wrote that Karen Santorum, the "ultra-pro-life wife," had a dirty secret. "Her live-in partner through most of her 20s was Tom Allen, a Pittsburgh obstetrician and abortion provider 40 years older than she, who remains an outspoken crusader for reproductive rights and liberal ideals. Dr. Allen has known Mrs. Santorum, born Karen Garver, her entire life: he delivered her in 1960." The article featured a picture of young Garver posing with her much older boyfriend as he lounged in a hammock. [37]

It is impossible to imagine a greater personal attack on an innocent wife, and a blameless candidate, than this. Even the networks were a little queasy over this twenty-four-year-old story about a candidate's spouse. CBS brought up the relationship in an interview with Mrs. Santorum in March, forcing her to admit, "I did go through a phase of life where I wasn't living the way I should have been." NBC jumped right on it, though. On the January 21 *Today*, NBC's Michael Isikoff (a *Newsweek* alum) checked the box: "*Newsweek* reported that before she married Santorum, she had a six-year live-in relationship with a Pittsburgh abortion doctor forty years her senior."

In the same story, Isikoff also noted Gingrich's second wife going on ABC and making her "open marriage" allegation. He concluded with the odd suggestion that these personal attacks and ugliness weren't generated by the "objective" media: "All this, political analysts say, is unusual, even by the rough-and-tumble standards of Southern politics. . . . With polls pointing to a close result tonight in South Carolina, personal attacks show no signs of abating as the GOP race continues."[38]

Can you imagine *Newsweek* plotting a hard-hitting investigation of who Michelle Obama dated before Barack? Or who Barack dated before Michelle? Did Mrs. Obama have sex with other men before Barack? Did she have affairs with married men? Those questions would be considered beyond the pale, a repugnant violation of privacy. But somehow, all those niceties did not apply to Mrs. Santorum before she even knew her husband.

At the end of 2004, *Newsweek* proclaimed the arrival of Senator-elect Barack Obama with Jonathan Alter's cover story titled "The Audacity of Hope." In the same issue, there was also a profile of Santorum by Howard Fineman. The contrast was stunning, even by *Newsweek*'s obnoxious standards.[39]

Obama was introduced to the country as the "incredibly pragmatic" soul of civility who is "uniquely qualified to nudge the country toward the color purple" (merging the red states and blue states). He was all about "embracing our hybrid origins and transcending our often narrow-minded past." But Santorum was consistently described with violent undertones. His career was a "bruising crusade" supported by anti-abortion "shock troops." He was a "cultural militant," and a "heat-seeking missile" with a "combatively devout approach."

The photos framing the stories told the tale all by themselves. Obama was shown on a Chicago rooftop with the caption "Skywalker." Santorum was shown in his office next to his picture of "Roman Catholic martyr Thomas More." Captured on his office TV was a Fox News Channel graphic about schools excluding Christ from Christmas. The caption was "Bully Pulpit." No coincidence.

In other pictures, Obama was seen interacting with staff, backslapping with John Kerry, practicing a speech next to Michelle, and kissing his three-year-old daughter, Sasha (to a caption titled "Family Man"). In the only other picture accompanying his profile, Santorum was pictured in the darkened frame of his office door, with the caption underlining his admission that he smoked pot in the 1970s, but adding he is now "in the front ranks of the new faith-based GOP." *Newsweek* had no room for Obama's self-described pot-smoking and cocaine-snorting in their early valentine . . . and no room to acknowledge Santorum was a "family man" with six children.

While Mrs. Santorum was pounded for her ancient romances in 2012, *Newsweek* lauded Michelle Obama in 2004 as a Harvard-trained lawyer with an "innovative nonprofit that provides leadership development." After two of Obama's potential 2004 Senate rivals—Republican Jack Ryan and Democrat Blair Hull—were energetically removed from Obama's path by the gumshoes at the *Chicago Tribune* suing for (and then spilling) their divorce records—Michelle was Obama's character witness. "People always ask, 'What's he got in the closet?' Well, we've been married 13 years, and I'd be shocked if there was some deep, dark secret."

For starters, *Newsweek* could have found the nutty reverend that married them.

Alter even helpfully reported that Mrs. Obama "goes so far as to say" her husband wasn't even a politician. He "is not a politician first and foremost. He's a community activist exploring the viability of politics to make change." Perhaps the most transparently phony thing any reporter could ever write about the news media's "rising star" of liberalism was that he somehow wasn't a politician—a Chicago pol, riding on a shiny rocket of media hype. But Republicans? "Politician" was about the nicest thing said about them.

CHAPTER 2

You're Our Mr. Clean

Obama, "remarkably free of scandal."

There's a corollary to the idea that the first media dirty trick is adjudicating who is dirty. To say the media's rules for what constitutes a scandal are incredibly elastic is an understatement. Journalists who tut-tutted, then declared Herman Cain's campaign deceased for charges of sexual misbehavior were singing a much different tune just thirteen years before. Then faced with far more substantial reports about Bill Clinton's womanizing, they performed great feats of acrobatic journalism telling America we needed to move on.

The double standard could apply to just about anything. They could even treat hurricanes under Democrats as natural disasters and under Republicans as an unethical and racist fiasco. NBC's Brian Williams lectured to Jon Stewart about Hurricane Katrina and how much better the Bush response would have been "if this had been Nantucket."[1] Obama could do a photo-op at Sandy Hook Elementary, then ignore the catastrophe, and still he was viewed as the savior.

An important component in the construction of the image of

perpetually shiny and flawless Obama was the declaration that he had never dirtied himself in the ethical scrapes and scandals that bother and bewilder earthly politicians. The narrative was preposterous, but delivered with a straight face.

On July 17, 2012, *Hardball* host Chris Matthews was in his usual lather on MSNBC, denouncing the "crapola" and "crazy yahoo talk" from Michele Bachmann, Jim DeMint, and Newt Gingrich, as they insisted in turn that Obama was a radical, anti-business, anti-American, and hostile to the Constitution. Those conservative critiques were defensible if not true on all counts.

Matthews couldn't concede even that these charges were grounded in reality. Instead, he addressed them with all the ferocity of someone who's livid that anyone would dare speak against the Great Leader, that anyone would so rebelliously challenge the media cult of personality. "This guy's done everything right! He's raised his family right! He's fought his way all the way to the top of the *Harvard Law Review*, in a blind test becomes head of the *Review*, the top editor there. Everything he's done is clean as a whistle! He's never not only broken any law, he's never done anything wrong! He's the perfect father, the perfect husband, the perfect American!"[2]

This is not journalism. It's the very opposite of journalism. Instead of observing the world as it is and describing it, warts and all, Matthews chose to ignore truth and instead flailed away at Obama's critics, insisting that Obama had no failures, no scandals, no imperfections of any kind. Obama is not just the omnicompetent Alpha and Omega of American politics, but the very essence of goodness. Saintly, even.

Naturally, like a predictable liberal, Matthews concluded these attacks on Obama's radical policy views were . . . racial. Obama was perfect, "and all they do is trash the guy. And it's impossible for me to believe they would have said the same thing about a Walter Mondale or a Jimmy Carter or a Bill Clinton. There's an ethnic piece to this." This "ethnic piece" complaint wasn't lodged by Matthews when his fellow liberals were hunting for scandals in the Justice Department under George W. Bush's friend and U.S. attorney general Alberto Gonzales. Or Clarence Thomas. Or Allen West. Or Herman Cain. Or any Republican of color.

Matthews was not the only pseudo-journalist shredding the rules of his own profession by pushing this zero-scandal myth. On October 27, 2011, former *Newsweek* senior editor Jonathan Alter wrote a column for Bloomberg News headlined "Obama Miracle Is White House Free of Scandal." Alter began: "President Barack Obama goes into the 2012 [campaign] with a weak economy that may doom his reelection. But he has one asset that hasn't received much attention: He's honest." Whether Alter was giggling when he typed those words is unclear.

Alter even bragged: "According to a metric created by political scientist Brendan Nyhan, Obama set a record earlier this month for most days without a scandal of any president since 1977." [3] Nyhan's methodology insisted that a president doesn't have a scandal until there is "a front-page *Washington Post* story focused on a scandal that describes it as such in the reporter's own voice," by using the S-word, as in "the Fast and Furious scandal."

This little trick neatly grants all the power in defining what is or is not a scandal to the Washington media elite. Congress can launch investigations, hold hearings, or otherwise make real news, but journalists hold all the power. It's a scandal when *they* say it's a scandal. Their perpetual pose of ignorance has also helped to keep the Obama scandals from entering the satire stream of late-night comedy shows.

This notion of a scandal-free Obama also emerged occasionally from the print press, the people alleged to obsess about the boring details. *Washington Post* editorialist Jonathan Capehart boasted to

NBC viewers on the October 29, 2011, *Today* program: "We're look-ing at the GOP looking to scratch, trying to find a scandal in an ad-ministration that is remarkably free of scandal."[4]

On June 24, 2012, *Post* columnist Dana Milbank appeared on CNN and acted utterly perplexed at complaints about the media's aggressive scandal avoidance. "I think to say the media isn't interested in scandal is preposterous. We love scandal. I love scandal. That's the thing that really drives us," Milbank chortled. "It's not an ideological thing. I think the media would love to have an Obama scandal to cover."[5]

Clearly, Milbank hadn't checked in with Matthews and Alter. Still, the results were the same: no coverage of scandals. Milbank's *Post* columns brought comfort to Team Obama on Solyndra (one column was headlined "A solar pariah had Republican parents, too") and Fast and Furious ("The Republicans may be furious, but this political scandal is going nowhere—fast").[6]

Skipping Fast and Furious

In 2009, under Barack Obama and Attorney General Eric Holder, the Bureau of Alcohol, Tobacco, Firearms, and Explosives launched "Op-eration Fast and Furious," which allowed licensed gun dealers to sell weapons to illegal straw buyers. Obama's team was hoping to track the guns to Mexican drug cartel leaders, with the hope of following the guns as they were transferred to higher-level traffickers and key figures in Mexican cartels, with the expectation that this would lead to arrests.

But it all went terribly wrong. Mexican gangs shot and killed Bor-der Patrol agent Brian Terry in 2010 (as well as hundreds of Mexican citizens) with guns the ATF allowed to "walk."

A reporter on one network recognized this story as important news. On the February 23, 2011, *CBS Evening News*, Sharyl Attkisson declared : "December 14, 2010: the place, a dangerous smuggling route in Arizona, not far from the border. A special tactical border squad was on patrol when gunfire broke out and agent Brian Terry, shown here in a training exercise, was killed. . . . The assault rifles found at the murder, similar to these, were traced back to a U.S. gun shop. Where they came from and how they got there is a scandal so large, some insiders say it surpasses the shootout at Ruby Ridge and the deadly siege at Waco." [7]

How could this story *not* be news?

On March 23, 2011, three months after Terry's death, President Obama appeared on Univision and spoke about the controversy. He said that neither he nor Attorney General Holder authorized Fast and Furious. He also stated, "There may be a situation here in which a serious mistake was made, and if that's the case, then we'll find out and we'll hold somebody accountable."

Why did it take so long for the president to respond, and why did he think he could play innocent in this scandal?

Because most of the media aren't in the Obama accountability business. While Attkisson was an outlier, with twenty-nine stories on CBS unspooling the scandal, ABC and NBC stayed virtually silent for many months, even as Holder admitted he had misled Congress about when he learned of Fast and Furious, thus also making his boss a dupe, or a liar. So much for scandal-free.

ABC had aired only one brief, on the June 15, 2011, *Good Morning America*. In a bizarre turn, ABC White House correspondent Jake Tapper asked Obama about Fast and Furious in October 2011, but ABC refused to allow any soundbite on that subject to appear on *Nightline*, *World News*, or *Good Morning America* (which all played clips of the interview).

Instead, on *Nightline*, ABC found time to air Tapper and the president playfully discussing children's books and the greatness of

Dr. Seuss. Tapper said, "At the school where we spoke, the president showed off his personal knowledge of children's books." Obama asked Tapper whom he liked in that field. "I'm a big Dr. Seuss guy," said Tapper. "You can't beat Dr. Seuss," agreed the president.[8]

ABC really knows how to make Democrat presidents sweat.

Even Holder's admission on November 8, 2011, that—oops—he may have misled Congress in a May 3 hearing didn't wake ABC and NBC out of their long nap of self-censorship. In May, Holder told Congress he'd learned of Fast and Furious just "a few weeks" beforehand. In November, he admitted "I probably could've said 'a couple of months.'" In fact, he admitted that Senator Charles Grassley (R-IA) had handed him letters in person on the matter in late January. Obama answered Tapper in the unaired ABC interview: "This is not something we were aware of in the White House. And the attorney general, it turns out, wasn't aware of it either."

On the November 8, 2011, *CBS Evening News*, Sharyl Attkisson focused on another deception, this time that Holder claimed in February there was no gun-walking. Holder bizarrely claimed under GOP questioning that the Department of Justice's letter was somehow not false, just inaccurate: "What I said is it contains inaccurate information. . . . I don't want to quibble with you, but 'false,' I think, implies people making a decision to deceive."[9] He was back to the-meaning-of-what-is-is spin.

Why would reporters fail to report on a public official saying it's not a falsehood if it was allegedly *unintentionally* false? Is this the way Bush-whacking journalists treated the case for war in Iraq?

NBC aired absolutely nothing on their morning and evening newscasts. NBC arrived on the story on June 12, 2012—546 days after Agent Terry's shooting. On June 20, the House voted to hold the attorney general in contempt of Congress for failure to provide documents, which caused shameless *NBC Nightly News* anchor Brian

Williams to begin his program by trying to shame someone else: "Washington has blown up into a caustic partisan fight. . . . And for those not following the complexities of all of it, it just looks like more of our broken politics and vicious fights now out in the open."[10]

Williams seemed perturbed that someone would push him to cover this scandal. "Those not following the complexities of all of it" could be defined as anyone who relied on NBC for news on the Obama administration.

To be fair, Chris Hansen, on the April 17, 2011, edition of NBC's magazine show *Dateline*, briefly mentioned that the ATF "as part of an undercover operation, actually allowed hundreds of guns to be smuggled to the Mexican drug cartels." However, Hansen never linked Obama or Holder to the operation or even mentioned Terry's death or name. How could they *not* be part of the story? They were the story.

NBC's failure to mention Terry's name is particularly galling considering that his mother, Josephine, repeatedly demanded Holder apologize for her son's death. After a February 2, 2012, hearing she called Attorney General Holder a "coward politician." Josephine Terry would not be granted one iota of the saint/celebrity status that the networks gave George W. Bush—harassing "peace mom" Cindy Sheehan, whom CBS's Bill Plante called "the red-hot symbol of opposition to the war" and a "magnet for the anti-war movement."[11]

Only CBS put Mrs. Terry onscreen, in a story on *The Early Show* on November 9, 2011: "Brian loved his country. Brian was a true Marine. He was a true American. When Brian was a Marine, he used to always say, you never leave a man behind. And, I think they are leaving my son behind. That's what I think. And I know that would be a disgrace to him."[12]

Even CBS developed cold feet about this scandal as the primaries began. Their first *CBS Evening News* report of 2012 didn't come until

June 20—when Mitt Romney made it an issue. *CBS This Morning* only offered one full story in the first half of the year, on February 3. Sharyl Attkisson had been given other assignments.

No Heat on Holder

The networks offered no brickbats for Attorney General Holder. He submitted himself to zero network TV interviews over the last two and a half years of the first term. But Holder did grant an interview on April 27, 2012, to NPR legal reporter Carrie Johnson. NPR *All Things Considered* anchor Robert Siegel announced "a rare and personal glimpse of the man." Johnson began by observing Holder walk quickly into the Clinton Presidential Library in Little Rock, Arkansas, where she was granted the interview: "Eric Holder is looking back on the arc of his career. After nearly thirty years of government service, he's achieved his highest goal."

NPR listeners were supposed to get a thrill up their legs during rush hour because Holder was attorney general. "The attorney general lingered, wordless over footage of Mr. Clinton's campaign speeches. He had more to say in front of an exhibit of the Little Rock Nine. They were black schoolchildren who tried to integrate Central High School here in 1957, only to be met by violent mobs and soldiers blocking the door." Holder solemnly proclaimed: "These are the folks who make, you know, Barack Obama possible, Eric Holder possible."

The program may be called *All Things Considered*, but one thing wasn't. In the entire seven-minute, thirty-nine-second story, there was absolutely no mention of Fast and Furious. Holder proclaimed, "I serve a president who is among other things a great lawyer. And he spends a great deal of time, great deal of interest focused on the Justice Department, which is a good thing—most of the time."[13] But neither one of them could be blamed for fumbling Fast and Furious? Neither could be challenged to take ownership of what they launched?

There were more important matters to cover. Johnson wasted time ribbing Holder about the Justice Department suing Apple: "So you're hoping you're still on a first-name basis with the guy at the Apple store?" Holder replied they were still happy to see him.

The networks had a chance to revisit Fast and Furious in September. On the 20th, two high-ranking Justice Department officials resigned over the scandal, but as usual, only Attkisson at CBS reported on that. The next day, Obama appeared on the Spanish-language channel Univision for a town-hall interview. Anchor Jorge Ramos asked Obama if Holder shouldn't have known about Fast and Furious, and if not, "shouldn't you fire him?"

Obama's reply was misleading on multiple levels. "I think it's important for us to understand that the Fast and Furious program was a field-initiated program begun under the previous administration." No, it wasn't. While the Bush administration had a version of this, Fast and Furious began in the fall of 2009.

So was *this* now news ? Obama had just pulled a Nixon. The networks noted the Univision interview but ignored Fast and Furious, focusing instead on "tough questions" about the attack on the consulate in Libya, and on the hot concern from the left-wing Democrat base over how (suddenly pandering) Obama admitted his greatest failure of his first term was not fighting harder to pass "immigration reform." Ramos even showed up on ABC's *This Week* roundtable a few days later, and no one brought up Fast and Furious. Again they homed in on the need for amnesty for illegal immigrants.

At the end of September, Univision produced a devastating investigative bombshell on Fast and Furious. Gerardo Reyes and Santiago Wills reported, "Indirectly, the United States government played a role in the massacre" of fourteen Mexican teenagers in a one-story house by "supplying some of the firearms" used in a vicious cartel massacre.[15] In all, Univision claimed that they found fifty-seven additional U.S. government-provided weapons that Congress had not identified.

The same news media that leaped into panic and outrage over mass shootings in Aurora (and after the election, in Newtown) found nothing interesting in fourteen Mexican teens being gunned down with weapons supplied through the Justice Department. They said nothing.

All this was quite a contrast to 2007, when the networks were loaded with hyperbole on the allegedly massive scandal of a smattering of U.S. attorneys fired by the Bush Justice Department. Then–Attorney General Alberto Gonzales—the first Latino attorney general of the United States—tried to put out the blazing story by appearing on five morning-news shows on the same day: March 14, 2007. There were no shootings, no murders. Yet somehow it was worse.

Gonzales was asked forty-two questions by the TV interviewers— and ten of them were repeating demands that he resign, including on the Fox News Channel.[16] NBC's Matt Lauer read from *Washington Post* columnist Ruth Marcus, who accused Gonzales of being "an absentee landlord, chronically clueless." By July 24, 2007, ABC News anchor Chris Cuomo—son of ultraliberal former New York governor Mario Cuomo, and brother of current governor Andrew Cuomo— bluntly asked, "Is Alberto Gonzales out of a job at end of business today?" Cuomo wanted the attorney general professionally whacked, and a month later, got his wish. Gonzales resigned.

Five years later, no one in the media demanded Eric Holder resign. No one even demanded Holder show up at a TV studio for an interview to explain his department's scandalous behavior.

Meanwhile, the Obama Justice Department was working hand in glove with liberal media "watchdogs" to intimidate Attkisson and other outlets like Fox News from covering this story. On September 18, 2012, *Daily Caller* reporter Matthew Boyle uncovered collusion between the Justice Department and the liberal group Media Matters for America, including e-mails back and forth coordinating attacks on conservative media and politicians to contain the damage on Fast and Furious.

For example, in an e-mail on July 8, 2011, Media Matters blogger Matt Gertz wrote to Justice Department spokeswoman Tracy Schmaler asking for her help "debunking what I think is a conservative media myth about Operation Fast and Furious." Gertz told Schmaler that "Xochitl directed me to you as the person to talk to." Gertz was referring to Xochitl Hinojosa, a Justice Department spokeswoman—and former Media Matters staffer.[17]

Another example was a January 31, 2012, e-mail chain titled "per our conversation," in which Schmaler and Gertz were cooperating on an article attacking Representative Darrell Issa (R-CA), chairman of the House Government Reform and Oversight Committee. Schmaler sent Gertz two paragraphs of text from Issa's comments during a House Judiciary Committee hearing on December 8, 2011. Schmaler underlined a portion of the text in those paragraphs in which Issa discussed the differences between Fast and Furious and programs that resembled it in the George W. Bush years. Just hours after Schmaler sent Gertz those blocks of text, they appeared in a Media Matters article titled "Rep. Issa Ties Himself in Fast and Furious Knots."

This kind of partisan media collusion obliterated the old saw that the Justice Department is supposed to be the least partisan outpost in all the cabinet. Only Fox News found this story of collusion worth reporting.

When the networks take months and even years to acknowledge a Democratic scandal exists, it also helps to keep the scandal from entering the satire stream of late-night comedy shows. Obama was a recipient of that journalistic largesse. But when he hosted the White

House Correspondents Association dinner on February 2, 2012, ABC late-night host Jimmy Kimmel mocked Obama from the left: "Even some of your Democrats think you're a pushover, Mr. President. . . . They would like to see you stick to your guns and if you don't have any guns, they would like to see you ask Eric Holder to get some for you."[18]

"It's hard to make fun of Obama in general because he's a cool character," Jimmy Kimmel told Reuters going in, insisting that "outside of his ears, there's not a whole lot" to joke about.[19]

The "Green Jobs" Vanish with Solyndra

On the campaign trail in 2008, Barack Obama painted a picture of five million new "green jobs" created over the next decade, generated by federal government loans of $15 billion annually. The national media have been very generous in evaluating that promise: Reuters said the jobs have been "slow to sprout."[20] That puts it mildly.

The Washington Post to its credit crunched the numbers in September 2011: instead of creating 65,000 jobs, as promised, the $38 billion loan program, which included Solyndra, could only claim 3,545 new jobs, a fraction of a fraction of the presidential promise. But no one on TV was willing to acknowledge this failure, because network coverage of the "green jobs" concept had tilted overwhelmingly in Obama's favor. "We have gotten the message. Green-collar jobs are the wave of the future," cohost Diane Sawyer cheered on ABC's *Good Morning America* on April 15, 2009. MRC's Business and Media Institute found that out of fifty-two network stories that mentioned the administration's "green jobs" program, only four of them (8 percent) bothered to include any critics at all.[21] Not one tilted against the administration.

California-based Solyndra was the first solar company to be awarded a loan from the Department of Energy under President Obama, a cool $535 million in March 2009. Two years later, on August 31, 2011, Solyndra declared bankruptcy and suspended all production, laying off 1,100 employees and sticking the taxpayers with the bill.

Was this news? In the first two months of 2002, the Big Three networks reported a stunning 198 stories on the bankruptcy of Enron, a Houston-based energy company. Enron CEO Ken Lay had been to the Clinton White House, but the networks zoomed in on George W. Bush. They underlined that Bush nicknamed Lay "Kenny Boy." Democrats denounced George W. Bush's "Enronomics" and "Enronizing" of Social Security. In the two months after its August 31 bankruptcy filing, ABC, CBS, and NBC filed a grand total of fifteen stories on Solyndra.[22]

That's an Enron-to-Solyndra comparison of more than 13 to 1. Worse, from the end of that period (Halloween 2011) to Election Day, the networks offered only nine more stories (and six of them were simple anchor-read briefs). The last full story came from CBS on January 13, 2012, ten months before the election. In the election year, there was less evening-newscast time on this scandal than a two-minute commercial break.

"I think the media would love to have an Obama scandal to cover," the *Post's* Dana Milbank told us. Never were more vacuous words ever spoken.

Only ABC (on the October 3, 2011 *World News*) ever ran footage of George Stephanopoulos asking President Obama about Solyndra, despite Obama's casual dismissal about the company's failure. "Do you regret that?" he was asked. Obama said no, that America needed to subsidize "green energy" so American companies "at least have a shot," and blithely admitted "Solyndras would happen." Stephanopoulos followed up: "And you were getting warnings not to back that company up, not to visit?" Obama shot back with annoyance: "Well, you know, hindsight is always 20/20."[23]

On October 7, the same Obama administration that pledged to be the most transparent ever engaged in a late-Friday document dump. The pile included e-mails showing a top Obama fundraiser and Energy Department official, Steven Spinner—who had supposedly recused himself from Solyndra's loan application because his wife worked at a law firm representing the solar energy company—persistently pushing his colleagues to approve the deal.

Spinner sent e-mails demanding to know: "Any word on OMB? I have the O.V.P. [Office of the Vice President] and W.H. [White House] breathing down my neck on this. . . . How hard is this? What is he waiting for?"[24]

Even though these e-mails were sensational enough to make it onto the front page of The New York Times, the networks never found a moment over the long Columbus Day weekend to mention it, never mind investigate the story themselves, just as they skipped the earlier news that Jonathan Silver, who ran the Energy Department loan program that handed more than $500 million in taxpayer money to Solyndra, had resigned.

"Don't ever send an email on DOE email with a personal email addresses," Silver wrote on August 21, 2011, from his personal account to another program official's private account. "That makes them subpoenable."[25] There's nothing innocent in that sentence. Any reporter worth his weight would pound on that lead.

The Washington Post reported then that "Silver repeatedly communicated about internal and sensitive loan decisions via his personal email, the newly released records show, and more than a dozen other Energy Department staff members used their personal email to discuss decisions involving taxpayer-funded loans as well." That was it.

This was a pervasive problem in the Obama administration. Jim Messina, Obama's 2012 campaign manager, used his private AOL account during his time in the White House to make deals with Big Pharma lobbyists to support Obamacare, where they agreed to buy $150 million in ads and lobby for his bill's enactment.[26] This was non-news, but the idea that Alaska governor Sarah Palin used her private e-mail for any public business? That registered as a major scandal to the national press in 2011, when reporters pored over twenty-four thousand Palin e-mails they obtained.

To get traction on the Solyndra scandal, Mitt Romney even made a surprise visit to stand in front of the empty Solyndra headquarters on May 31, 2012. Still, no reaction. The networks only mentioned it in passing, offering no stories explaining Romney's backdrop. CBS reporter Jan Crawford asked Mitt Romney one solitary Solyndra question on *CBS This Morning* on June 1.

When two Solyndra executives took the Fifth Amendment before Congress in September, ABC and NBC skipped that news, too, while CBS offered about twenty-five seconds of coverage. Once he was named Romney's running mate, Representative Paul Ryan briefly mentioned Solyndra in at least two network interviews as an example of "crony capitalism and corporate welfare" by Obama. But the networks weren't following up.

In the vice presidential debate, when Ryan was denouncing the "stimulus" for including "$90 billion in green pork to campaign contributors and special interest groups," Joe Biden interrupted in mid-sentence, as did the debate moderator, ABC's Martha Raddatz, who quickly handed the floor to Biden.[27] They did not want that audience to hear a word about Solyndra.

As former *Newsweek* editor Jonathan Alter predicted in his Obama-miracle article: "Although it's possible that the Solyndra LLC story will become a classic feeding frenzy, don't bet on it. Providing $535 million in loan guarantees to a solar-panel maker that goes bankrupt was dumb, but so far not criminal or even unethical on the part of the administration." [28]

Liberal journalists couldn't even locate anything unethical in awarding campaign donors with federal loan money for a company already in grave danger of collapse. It was a bad call when *McLaughlin Group* host John McLaughlin ended a show in August with this last sentence: "I predict that this will become damaging to Barack Obama's reelection." [29]

Down the Drain with MF Global

On Halloween 2011, MF Global Holdings filed for bankruptcy with a shady mystery: some $1.6 billion was missing from their customers' accounts. Financial analysts blamed the company's CEO, Jon Corzine, a former Democratic U.S. senator and governor of New Jersey, who became the center of an FBI investigation. One TV reporter underlined that this could be a major political problem for President Obama.

Corzine was "one of the leading Wall Street fundraisers for President Obama's campaign and suggested to investors that he might take a top administration post if the President were re-elected. . . . His new legal troubles, sparked by the bankruptcy filing of his investment firm, MF Global, could complicate the President's efforts to raise money from the financial community given Corzine's central role in those efforts. A recent list of top 'bundlers' or elite fundraisers released by Obama's campaign listed Corzine in the highest category—reporting that he had raised more than $500,000 for the campaign." [30]

That TV reporter was Michael Isikoff of NBC News—but his reporting never made it to television. (You'd have to find it on MSNBC. com.) In the upside-down world of Obama "news" judgment, that "leading Wall Street fundraiser for Obama" part seemed to make it *less* newsworthy for NBC and the rest, when it should have made it more so.

Eventually, after several months, the story drew just a few minutes of coverage—six full stories and sixteen anchor briefs on ABC, CBS, and NBC—so it wasn't censored. But nowhere, not once, in this small set of stories was there a single, solitary *whisper* of the name "Obama."

In fact, Jon Corzine's party affiliation was only mentioned once, when Kelly O'Donnell noted it in her December 8, 2011, report for the *NBC Nightly News*. "A fallen Wall Street CEO, personally rich and politically well-connected ... New Jersey's former Democratic Governor and U.S. Senator Jon Corzine under oath ... and under fire," O'Donnell announced.[31] NBC was the only network to notice months later that Corzine may have lied to Congress. Lying to Congress drew only yawns.

ABC's only full story came on the same evening on *World News*. David Muir announced "a former political heavyweight under fire tonight. Jon Corzine, once a U.S. Senator and governor of New Jersey, forced to explain himself to small, everyday investors today. He was testifying on Capitol Hill, saying he has no idea where their billion dollars in investment money went."

On *CBS Evening News*, the network sent correspondent Cynthia Bowers to talk to customers whose money was lost. She asked one man: "So if you could run into Jon Corzine today, what would you say to him?" The man replied: "It would be a bad day for Jon Corzine."[32]

New York Post columnist (and former CNN and Fox anchor) Terry Keenan added, "In what may be the 2011 prize for chutzpah, Corzine made it a point that he would not press for $12.1 million in severance payments from what is now a corpse of a company. Gee, thanks, Jon."[33]

Corzine and MF Global escaped with no federal criminal charges, and liberal journalists who insisted that Mitt Romney would be too friendly to Wall Street didn't care. They were too focused on Romney's tenure at Bain Capital. A few days after the election, Republicans on the House Financial Services Committee issued a report blaming Corzine for the MF Global debacle.[34] Even then, the networks didn't care.

A recent Gallup survey concluded that almost 80 percent of those surveyed do not have confidence in television news.[35] Part of that distrust comes from ideological bias, and part of it comes from the media's ratings-conscious addiction to human-interest stories and celebrity coverage. Those two trends can combine, and demonstrate a media more intensely covering fluff than the stuff of scandal.

As the nonpartisan Tyndall Report found, networks racked up 171 minutes of royal-wedding coverage and 111 minutes of the Michael Jackson wrongful-death trial on the evening news in 2011.[36] Obama scandal news—and hence, any notion the media act as a watchdog or a check on government, during an election year, no less—was nowhere to be found in Tyndall's list of top stories.

CHAPTER 3

Barack Hollywood Obama

The billion-dollar campaign goes populist.

The most effortless dirty trick in the liberal-media playbook in 2012 was painting Mitt Romney anywhere and everywhere as an uptight white gazillionaire, a man who was running for president to boost the profits and ego of his own social class. What really took chutzpah was the other half of the equation: boosting Barack Obama as a populist as he hobnobbed with the richest and most famous elites in Hollywood. Anonymous rich people make better villains than some of the most beloved names in show business.

No pollster ever asks the public if they believe Beyoncé "understands the problems of people like you." In a very real way, it doesn't matter. She's a performer, not a political leader. But in American culture, Hollywood is the closest we'll come to royalty, and where royalty parks its endorsement somehow means something, just as so many Hollywood stars sheers ignorance means nothing. Stars like Beyoncé somehow added glamour and hipness to Obama's aura, transforming his aloof and detached personality into instant populism. And the *Entertainment Tonight* audience willingly, insatiably swallowed the bait.

In keeping with the Obama, "Man of the People" persona, the Obama-Biden campaign was sending its own donors slick "personal" e-mails about how just a tiny three-dollar donation could buy you dinner with the Obamas. This one came with the president's signature attached:

> *Friend—*
>
> *It's not all that often that Michelle and I get to host a casual meal with friends.*
>
> *That's one of the reasons we're both excited about the upcoming dinner with three supporters and your guests.*
>
> *It's the first one we've ever done like this together, and we'd love to have you and whoever you choose to join us.*
>
> *Chip in $3 or whatever you can today—and you'll automatically be entered to be one of our dinner guests.*

Okay, hokey. Staged. Thoroughly staged. But that's politics, and Obama does politics better than anyone. Big deal. But then came the truth-mangling: "We don't take a dime from D.C. lobbyists or special-interest PACs—never have and never will. Instead, we believe in the kind of politics that gives everyone a seat at the table—so we're literally offering these seats at dinner to folks who are willing to step forward and be a part of it." [1]

It was a bold-face lie. Obama has taken untold millions from lobbyists. This is a perfect illustration of how the media couldn't even hold Obama to his own (and their own) liberal ideals. The Romney campaign had no ban on lobbyist donations. It's only the anti-capitalist, Bill Moyers–loving hard-liners in the Democratic base who want to somehow remove the lobbying industry from politics.

So in the same way that Republicans are seen by media liberals as much more hypocritical when they commit adultery, so too phony lobbyist-donation bans and campaign finance scandals should fall much harder on Democrats.

But they don't.

Team Obama defined "lobbyist" with all the sleazy legalistic finesse of Bill Clinton defining "sexual relations." By their definition, if you didn't register as a lobbyist with the federal government, you weren't a lobbyist. Take, for example, David Cohen, the executive vice president for Comcast, which acquired NBC Universal by spreading its influence around the Obama administration in the first term. Cohen was described in the papers as Comcast's "chief of lobbying," but he wasn't registered. He was an Obama bundler, and raised $1.2 million when the president attended a fundraiser at Cohen's glitzy Philadelphia home in June 2011 with about 120 attendees giving at least $10,000.[2] But Obama hasn't taken a dime from lobbyists, "never have and never will."

At the end of 2011, Ed Morrissey at the Hot Air blog mocked the outrage of Obama staffers that they would be typecast as infatuated with big bucks. "You know, nothing says *classy* in a presidential campaign like having to bleep out a word from the national campaign manager in a *prepared video*."[3] Campaign manager Jim Messina told supporters it was "bullshit" that Obama will run a "billion-dollar campaign." Messina sent an e-mail to supporters insisting: "This campaign is funded almost exclusively by more than a million grassroots supporters giving what they can afford—$3 and $10 donations have powered us from the start. . . . We do not and will not have a billion-dollar war chest."

Fast-forward to the website *Politico* on October 25, 2012: "Team Obama raises $1 billion."[4] Reporters Kenneth Vogel and Dan Berman relayed that "Chicago pushed back against the $1 billion figure, saying it really should be $988 million because Obama did not officially declare his candidacy for reelection until April 2011," as if the Obama gang wasn't raising money before then.

Perhaps the most "out of touch" millionaires and billionaires threatening the "common folks" narrative were the entertainment elites in Hollywood and Manhattan. They often had the most elevated—and publicly expressed—opinion of Obama. After the election, on the Soul Train Awards on November 25, actor Jamie Foxx let his adoration hang out: "First of all, give an honor to God, and our lord and savior Barack Obama!"[5]

Barbra Streisand was almost as absurd, claiming on the *Huffington Post* on September 18, 2012, "Compared to George W. Bush and Ronald Reagan, Obama has been more fiscally conservative than any other president in recent history, with the exception of President Bill Clinton."[6] Who has time to notice those unprecedented trillion-dollar deficits? No one in the media raised an eyebrow at that howler.

After the election cycle was over, the Center for Responsive Politics reported that 220 "celebrity" donors had given Obama's campaign $744,857, while only 18 comparable "celebrity" donors gave Romney a total of $60,750.[7] That's a more than 12-to-1 financial disparity.

Through 2011 and 2012, Obama outraised Romney from what the Center called the "TV/Movies/Music" industry, by nearly 5 to 1, with Obama raising $6.39 million to Romney's $1.27 million. These numbers exclude the entertainment industry bundlers who collect money from friends, relatives, and business associates and combine it into one gift. Obama bundlers throwing splashy events included not just movie moguls like Jeffrey Katzenberg and Harvey Weinstein. There was imperious *Vogue* magazine editor Anna Wintour—who inspired the novel and movie *The Devil Wears Prada*—as well as *Glee* creator Ryan Murphy and rock singer Gwen Stefani. Now the Hollywood-generated contributions were in the tens of millions of dollars—and still there was more.

Bill Maher, Super Flack

These figures did not count how Obama's Super PAC "Priorities USA" reveled in three very large Hollywood donations: $2 million from DreamWorks mogul Jeffrey Katzenberg, $1 million from actor Morgan Freeman, and $1 million from Bill Maher, the toxic, atheist bomb-thrower with his weekly *Real Time* show on HBO. Maher didn't just give at "the office" by trashing Republicans on pay-cable TV. He brought a large check onstage during a standup comedy performance in San Jose on February 23—and none of the networks cared.[8] They could ask if Donald Trump was going to embarrass and distract from Romney, but they wouldn't make that connection with a bigot like Maher and Obama.

Just days before, all three networks rang the national alarm bells over how "far to the right" Republicans were tilting when Santorum Super PAC backer Foster Friess had repeated a very old, and equally innocent, joke about Bayer aspirin being used as birth control. Nobody would warn about the Democrats being stuck with a hard-edged atheist image for standing with God-hating Bill Maher, the guy honored for saying "religion must die for humanity to live." But *this* assault on humanity by Friess must be denounced!

On *CBS This Morning*, cohost Charlie Rose demanded that Santorum defend himself over the Friess joke.[9] Nobody at CBS asked Obama about Maher, including Charlie Rose. Indeed, it was worse than that still. A few weeks later, *CBS This Morning* cohost Erica Hill reported that "comedian Bill Maher writes in the op-ed page of *The New York Times*, we've become too sensitive in referring to this year's nasty political campaign. Maher writes, quote, 'When did we get into our heads that we have the right never to hear anything we don't like?'"

The news media were not just shutting out conservative speech or tough questions they didn't like, they were questioning the very right to hear conservative speech.

CBS did not report it when Fox News analyst Kirsten Powers and her friend Penny Lee wrote a letter to the editor published in the *Times* replying to Maher: "We're both women who have worked in Democratic politics and the media for decades and find Bill Maher's misogynist treatment of women candidates deeply disturbing. While others have been held to account for their sexism, Mr. Maher remains unrepentant for his attacks on women in public life. . . . Our message to Mr. Maher and his ilk is: Please *start* apologizing." [10] (Italics theirs)

Maher could start an apology tour by reflecting on all the conservative people he's joked about should be dead.

There's Rush Limbaugh: "Why couldn't he have croaked from [OxyContin] instead of Heath Ledger?"

Dick Cheney when he was vice president: "I'm just saying if he did die, other people—more people would live. That's a fact."

Glenn Beck, when he was a Fox News host: "When we see crazy, senseless deaths like this, we can only ask why, why, why couldn't it have been Glenn Beck?"

Sarah Palin: "Sarah Palin screaming about death panels? You know what, Sarah, if we were killing off useless people, you'd be the first to know."

And Rush Limbaugh again: "Do it [repeal Don't Ask, Don't Tell] because it will make Rush Limbaugh explode like a bag full of meat dropped from a helicopter. Do it because it will make Sarah Palin 'go rogue' in her pants."

Then there was Karl Rove, after Romney lost: "It was a little Hitler's bunker, wasn't it? I wanted to rush in with a cyanide capsule there."

Incredibly, in May, ABC's George Stephanopoulos claimed on his Sunday show *This Week* (over Laura Ingraham's scoffing) that "the President's been held accountable for Bill Maher." [11] In September,

Maher became the star of a strange segment on NBC's *Rock Center* that attacked not Maher, but Maher's critics, including media watchdogs.

We were a bunch of lowlife "gaffe-seekers." Ted Koppel announced, "Comedian Bill Maher has always been a favorite target of Bozell's, but especially since he made a one-million-dollar contribution to a Super PAC supporting Barack Obama." Koppel conjured up the vision of busybodies at groups like the Media Research Center "sitting there with headsets . . . watching television sets . . . waiting for someone to make a misstep." Maher replied: "Gaffe seekers." Koppel injected: "Any little gaffe they can find." [12]

This amazing indictment came after more than a year of liberals leaping on any gaffe or pseudo-gaffe from Republican candidates (and even their donors!) that sounded too conservative, too religious, too Republican, or too rough on Obama. Koppel didn't run any of Maher's gaffes, of course, just one joke: "I love this generation of Republicans. Their approach to a woman's body is the same as their approach to the economy. They have no idea how it works, but they're eager to screw with it anyway."

This was Maher's way of mocking monogamous, married Republicans with children, as opposed to his lifestyle as a childless, lecherous Playboy Mansion regular. Could you label it a joke? Surely. Wishing the deaths of Limbaugh, Cheney, Beck, Palin, and Rove isn't funny. It's a good deal more serious than a "gaffe," too. But it isn't *news*, not to Koppel.

Koppel and the other network stars couldn't even note that this millionaire Maher was beloved by HBO and the rest of the media elite for trashing common Americans in Flyover Country as mouth-breathing idiots. In a *Newsweek* story honoring Maher as a testament to the American Dream, Lloyd Grove noted he "lives like a Reagan Republican in a shining city on a hill—actually a large estate in a rarefied aerie of Beverly Hills." [13] Then Grove told a story of how the uncommonly generous Bill Maher drove his $120,000 electric Tesla roadster downtown and bought Occupy Los Angeles protesters a hundred pairs of dry socks. What a philanthropist! That must have set him back about the cost of dinner at Spago.

The Democrats wanted their candidate to be seen as the embodiment of the "99 Percent." In truth, Obama was the personification of, by, and for the exclusive and ultimate One Percent—the super-rich and super-famous.

Occupy My Heart and Soul

Obama relentlessly attended fundraisers with the Hollywood glitz elite. There was no fear he'd be hounded and accused by fellow liberals in the press because these mansion events with movie moguls and stars are a violation of the left's "Occupy Wall Street" vibe. That short-lived, lawless, and violent protest movement was presented with all the salesmanship and mendacity that only a colluding media can provide.

It served a purpose—making liberalism look populist—and as such it was glorified. But the optics weren't helping. Visuals of violence, of filth, of public urination and defecation by foul-mouthed punks—none of this helped.

The liberal media's apparent ignorance didn't help much, either. ABC *World News* anchor Diane Sawyer looked like a complete idiot by proclaiming this temporary movement had "spread to more than 250 American cities, more than a thousand countries—every continent but Antarctica." That only overstated the number of countries by about eight hundred. Sawyer would later "correct" herself by claiming "more than a thousand *cities* around the world—every continent but Antarctica."[14] That was still exaggerating. If three hoboes showed up with tagboard signs in a town square, that would be included in the ABC count.

When the Occupy movement burst on the scene, in just the first eleven days of October 2011 ABC, CBS and NBC flooded their morning and evening newscasts with a whopping thirty-three full stories or interview segments on the protesters.[15] That was more TV coverage in eleven days than the Tea Party drew in its first nine months swarming in the capital and other cities. By the end of October, the number of stories climbed to eighty-one. A staggering 190 sound-bites (80 percent) were given to those who were in favor of the Occupiers; only 10 soundbites (four percent) featured those who were critical of the movement, a 19-to-1 tilt.[16]

Throughout the weeks of Occupy protest coverage, network anchors and reporters largely avoided the question of how this movement's violence and radicalism might affect President Obama and the Democrats at the polls. They only used the word "liberal" once, and never "radical" or "left-wing." Instead of considering this movement as a political drag, on October 16, NBC's David Gregory touted that these encampments were "going to dovetail nicely into a big message that the President's selling, which is that the wealthy should pay more."

NBC Nightly News anchor Brian Williams led off one newscast: "We begin tonight with what has become by any measure a pretty massive protest movement." In the first week of coverage, Williams already decided they had more staying power than the Tea Party. It "could well turn out to be the protest of this current era." When it faded away after being evicted by big-city Democrat mayors, the anchors turned down their volume buttons on the topic without acknowledging how emphatically they had oversold it.

To demonstrate their slogan that "We Are the 99 Percent," these protesters staged a "Millionaires March" in New York City, parading to the homes of wealthy citizens such as Fox News owner Rupert Murdoch and Tea Party funder David Koch. But Occupy organizers conveniently ignored the massive wealth of celebrities within their own ranks—super-rich Hollywood leftists like Michael Moore. On CNN, Moore disingenuously denied that he qualified financially to be in the dreaded "one percent," as conservative bloggers displayed his multimillionaire's lakeshore mansion in northwestern Michigan.[17]

The Occupiers never showed up to protest Brian Williams (or his two General Electric CEO neighbors) outside his apartment in the glass-encased Bloomberg Tower in midtown Manhattan, thirty-four stories above the tony restaurant Le Cirque. They somehow avoided Diane Sawyer's homes with film director Mike Nichols, including the Fifth Avenue penthouse they bought from Robert Redford for $11 million. The whole movement was a smelly Potemkin village of propaganda.

Obama Boogies Down to Tinseltown

In late September, just days before "Occupy Wall Street" became the latest media fad among liberals, President Obama landed in Southern California for three events: one at the ritzy La Jolla home of Elizabeth and Mason Phelps; a gay event at the House of Blues in West Hollywood with ABC *Modern Family* star and gay activist Jesse Tyler Ferguson; and then a $17,900-a-plate dinner with one hundred top Hollywood bigwigs at Fig & Olive restaurant on Melrose Place, including Jack Black, Judd Apatow, Quincy Jones, Danny DeVito, and Rhea Perlman.[18] This was Hollywood's One Percent, wealthier and far more famous than most of Romney's corporate one-percenters. So how was Obama not at least as elitist as Romney?

On October 24, 2011, Obama warned guests at a $35,800-a-person

Hollywood fundraiser (including actor Will Smith and former NBA star Magic Johnson) stating that "[t]he election will not be as sexy as the first one." In 2008, "everybody loved the Hope posters and all that, but this time, we've got to grind it out a little bit."[19] The same night, Obama grinded it out at a $5,000-per-ticket fundraiser at the home of Melanie Griffith and Antonio Banderas.

On the twenty-fifth, *The Hollywood Reporter* relayed the president had a "secret meeting" with "some of Hollywood's power players," including studio mogul Harvey Weinstein, *Modern Family* creator Steve Levitan, Atlantic Records chairman Craig Kallman, actor and onetime Obama White House staffer Kal Penn, and others. It was reported to be a "casual affair with 'influencers' who could help the president's reelection campaign."[20]

Then he flew to San Francisco for a $7,500-a-head fundraiser with entertainment by mellow pop singer Jack Johnson. Interestingly, about a hundred protesters from Occupy Wall Street and other leftist causes like medical marijuana and "peace" marred the event—they apparently were not buying this populist nonsense—but the national media didn't notice. Only Fox News reported how the *San Francisco Chronicle* published a surprising staff editorial protesting the tight leash on the media, using the darkest left-wing bugaboo, Nixon: "If anything, there's almost a Nixonian quality to the level of control, paranoia, and lack of credibility this White House has demonstrated on the issue of media access to President Obama's fundraisers."[21]

But the Obama-loving media, always slashing the unfavorable news out of their scripts, ignored this. That morning, NBC news reader Tamron Hall reported only that the president "continues his West Coast swing with a fund-raiser tonight in San Francisco. On Monday in Las Vegas, he unveiled his plan to help struggling home-owners modify their mortgages and avert foreclosure."[22] Obama the Populist marched on.

* * *

On the next morning came a doozy. After showing clips of Obama joking around with Jay Leno, NBC *Today* cohost Ann Curry somehow turned this glitz-elite fundraising venture into a populist campaign in a question to David Gregory: "Why is the president making this populist effort now out West, on Leno, reaching out to college graduates, and will it give him the momentum he needs?" Gregory reassured her Obama was leading every Republican contender.[23]

In mid-February, Obama attended a $35,800-a-person fundraiser at the home of Bradley Bell, who produces the CBS soap opera *The Bold and the Beautiful*, with more middle-class guests having an option to attend a Foo Fighters concert in Bell's backyard early in the day for $250. The location was in the Holmby Hills, which local real estate agents tout as "perhaps the most spectacular and luxurious in all of Beverly Hills."

Again, there were Occupy protesters, this time at Will Rogers Memorial Park. The Patch.com website in Beverly Hills quoted the outrage of Nicole Steiner of Occupy Los Angeles: "That money could be spent far better on the human needs of the 99 percent instead of allowing one-percenters to buy a dinner with the president." Steiner complained that for the nearly $36,000 donors were bringing to Obama they could buy dinners for seventeen thousand people at area food banks.[24] A story for an Internet blog—okay. A national television or print story? Forget it.

On *CBS This Morning*, reporter Bill Plante obediently omitted the CBS-soap-mogul details: "His Republican rivals are continuing their long drawn-out battle much to the delight of the President's campaign folks. And the President today heads out to do a little fundraising. Now, this comes just a week after his campaign reversed course and said that it would encourage those large unlimited donations to a Super PAC."[25] Then Plante added that the White House was delighted with the latest CBS poll numbers.

"A little fundraising." That's like saying Michelle does "a little vacationing."

That evening, NBC anchor Brian Williams put more emphasis on Obama's attempt to link himself with economic success stories: "President Obama was in the Midwest today, as well, visiting a Master Lock plant in Wisconsin that has brought some overseas jobs back to the United States. The president pitched his ideas for tax cuts for manufacturing businesses and penalties for companies that move jobs out of the country." The glitzy fundraisers were a tiny footnote, an afterthought: "Tonight he's on a fundraising tour of the West Coast, eight separate events from L.A. to Seattle." [26]

On May 10, the Obama campaign raised $15 million in a fundraiser at George Clooney's mansion. This occasion drew network attention, but it wasn't negative. ABC's Jake Tapper called it "Starmageddon." [27] NBC anchor Brian Williams said Obama hoped "to capitalize on the history he made yesterday" by announcing his support for gay marriage. [28]

Over on CBS, reporter Bill Whitaker turned the event around on Romney: "A-list actors and producers arrived in style," he announced, and interviewed director Rob Reiner. "He says Hollywood progressives who helped put Mr. Obama in the White House, grew disillusioned with him for too often buckling under Republican pressure—but turned off by the hard-right rhetoric of Republican Mitt Romney, and turned on by the President's endorsement of same-sex marriage, Hollywood's excitement has been rekindled." [29]

It's amazing that TV reporters can let Hollywood liberals attack moderates like Mitt Romney as the "hard right." Where does that put Rob Reiner on the American ideological spectrum? This denounce-the-extremes tactic was a habit of Reiner's: on HBO's *Real Time with Bill Maher* in 2010, he complained, "My fear is that the Tea Party gets a charismatic leader, because all they're selling is fear and anger and that's all Hitler sold." [30]

The CBS morning show also ran a clip from *The Daily Show*, in which Jon Stewart asked if the mood was positive at Clooney's house. Jason Jones replied: "Has it been positive? President Obama is at a giant Hollywood party the night after he came out for gay marriage. This is like going to Israel after you kill Hitler."[31]

That evening, CBS anchor Scott Pelley was joyous: "Well, there are no money troubles in the presidential race. Last night President Obama raised a record $15 million at a fund-raiser at the Los Angeles home of actor George Clooney." All this came in the same news cycle in which Romney was fending off the prep school anti-gay/bullying/haircut non-story published by *The Washington Post*. Any elitist overtones of Clooney's event were lost in the shuffle.[32]

On June 6, a Beverly Hills fundraiser drew famous faces from CBS: Les Moonves, the company CEO, and his second wife, Julie Chen, who was a CBS morning news host from 1999 to 2010. Moonves told a reporter for the *Los Angeles Times* of his respect for Obama, who he said "has shown great leadership"—by bringing his support for gay marriage out of the closet.

Moonves stated "I run a news division. I've given no money to any candidate," which is misleading at best. He made a very public appearance at a fundraiser for the DNC's LGBT Leadership Council, although it's unclear exactly whether he or his network made the DNC donation. He didn't contribute directly. But the DNC certainly gave to candidates. Then Moonves dared to admit the obvious: "Ultimately, journalism has changed . . . partisanship is very much a part of journalism now."[33]

Moonves was acknowledging reality, for once. His industry was in the Obama-reelection business.

Just for yuks, Byron York of the *Washington Examiner* asked CBS spokesman Dana McClintock whether Moonves was referring to CBS News. McClintock sent back a four-word response: "No he was not."[34] Obviously, CBS newscasts didn't report its own boss was clinking glasses with the president in Beverly Hills.

Later that night, Obama moved on to a $25,000-a-head event at the nearby home of *Glee* creator Ryan Murphy and his "fiancé," David Miller. Murphy was the "pioneering" TV producer who stated he wanted his legacy to be that he "made it possible for somebody on broadcast television to do a rear-entry [sex] scene" on national TV. The Obama fans attending included movie stars Julia Roberts and Reese Witherspoon, *Glee* star Jane Lynch, and HBO's president of programming, Michael Lombardo.

The media also avoided the European phase of Obama's fund-raising campaign, which began in Paris on July 4 with a reception organized by various fundraising heavy-hitters. Independence Day fundraisers in Paris—somehow the irony of that wasn't noticed. The Obama campaign also hosted events in Geneva, Switzerland, in August as part of their "European outreach effort." George Clooney headlined a fundraiser there for Americans Abroad for Obama that raised an estimated $625,000.

The Associated Press reported without any ironic overtones that Obama "says Clooney is low-maintenance and doesn't take advantage of their friendship. He says Clooney keeps his distance so Mr. Obama won't be criticized for hanging out with Hollywood celebrities."[35]

Mild-Mannered with Manhattan Moneybags

The New York–based national media also went radio-silent on Obama while he raised millions just blocks away from their studios in Manhattan. For days, the media elites incessantly reminded the little people that Obama suavely sang six words of Al Green's soul classic "Let's Stay Together." That came at the Apollo Theatre in one of several Big Apple fundraisers. The *Today* show hyped Obama as "Crooner-in-Chief" onscreen, as weatherman Al Roker oozed "he could be on *The Voice.*" News anchor Natalie Morales added, "Sign him up."[36]

That same night, Obama held a $35,800-per-ticket fundraiser at the Upper East Side brownstone of director Spike Lee, who was infamous in the Bush era for suggesting, in a reckless conspiracy-theory HBO documentary, that the federal government dynamited the levees to drown black people in New Orleans after Hurricane Katrina. Obama patronized the director by claiming his wife and he went on their first date to see Lee's movie *Do the Right Thing,* which ends with a fiery race riot.

All the networks skipped that event, and even *The New York Times* barely mentioned it at the very bottom of its story on Obama's travels that day, even though *Times* reporter Jackie Calmes was present at Lee's place on behalf of other media outlets in the White House reporter pool.

But on July 9, Mitt Romney held a fundraiser out on Long Island, in the Hamptons, and suddenly the class-war negativity was unleashed. Michael Moynihan, a summer substitute for Jennifer Rubin at the "Right Turn" blog for *The Washington Post,* noticed an aggressive anti-Romney trend.[37]

The Associated Press argued "Romney may have unintentionally helped the Obama campaign. Mercedes, Bentleys—and, in one case, a candy red 2013 Ferrari Spider crowded into a series of closed-door Romney fundraisers" in the "weekend playground" of the Wall Street elite.

The New York Times also spotted "a line of gleaming Bentleys, Porsches and Mercedes-Benzes waiting to deposit guests paying up to $25,000 a head" who dined on "prosciutto-covered melon balls." The *Los Angeles Times* noted a "line of Range Rovers, BMWs, Porsche roadsters and one gleaming cherry red Ferrari."

AP spoke with an investment banker who "chewed a cigar in his black Range Rover." The AP also distributed a photo of leftist protesters "from MoveOn.org, the Occupy Movement and the Long Island Progressive" with a banner that read "Mitt Romney Has a Koch Problem." [38] Obama admitted snorting coke, but he never suffered a Coke Problem.

The New York Times also carried a photo of the protesters with the "Koch problem" banner and began its story: "A woman in a blue chiffon dress poked her head out of a black Range Rover here on Sunday afternoon and yelled to an aide to Mitt Romney. 'Is there a VIP entrance? We are VIP!'" The fundraising lunch was held at Ron Perelman's house. "Widely described as the largest estate in East Hampton, when last advertised in the early 1990s, the house was said to have 40 rooms, 9 fireplaces and a mile of frontage on Georgica Pond." [39]

The *Los Angeles Times* insisted without an ounce of disdain that the MoveOn and Occupy protesters "posed with a flag in the style of the Marines at Iwo Jima." [40]

It wasn't the same when Obama had two New York fundraisers less than a week later on June 15 with stylist actress Sarah Jessica Parker and *Vogue* magazine editor and diva Anna Wintour.

The New York Times didn't mention anyone's Bentleys or real estate values in a story simply headlined "Obama Visits New York for Star-Studded Fundraisers." [41] Two days later, Wintour was puffed in a *Times* piece headlined "Power Is Always In Vogue." [42] The *Los Angeles Times* offered no story.

The networks were indifferent. CBS barely noticed at all (with one brief mention of Parker and Wintour on *CBS This Morning* on June 15 in their quick-edit "Eye Opener" feature). NBC passed it along a few times, as Chuck Todd breezily reported on that same morning, "Well, it wasn't quite Bieber fever last night at Sarah Jessica Parker's house, but the president again found himself rubbing elbows with a bunch of celebrities as he tries to rake in as much cash as he can at a couple of fundraisers last night."[43]

Only ABC's Jake Tapper and Terry Moran briefly broke the mold and audibly pondered that the images might not look good in hard economic times. Previewing the events on the June 4 *Nightline*—airing in the East at 11:35 P.M.—Moran said "there just seems to be something tone deaf about the Obama campaign's decision at the very moment unemployment is again on the rise to enlist Madame Wintour as one of the hostesses of his fundraiser."[44]

Unlike their anti-Romney piece, the AP turned the Obama fundraisers into a debate. They quoted Obama spokesman Jay Carney firing back about the super-rich events: "Two words. Donald Trump. Next question?" AP acknowledged "Obama has surrounded himself with blockbuster names lately . . . who make more in one year than most people do in a lifetime," but coolness had to be acknowledged: "Obama played basketball with a Batman (Clooney) and a Spiderman (Tobey Maguire), all in one game."

The story also included this Obama quote to his donors: "You're the tie-breaker. You're the ultimate arbiter of which direction this country goes."[45] Liberal journalists hate the idea that super-rich capitalists are the "ultimate arbiters" of the country's direction—but not so for super-rich actors and fashion magazine editors.

The trend resurfaced on September 18 with a $40,000-a-plate dinner for one hundred people at rap star and former drug dealer Jay-Z's 40/40 Club in Manhattan. *The New York Times* couldn't even put this story in the paper. Online, their report began, "On a day when Mitt Romney's videotaped remarks at a Republican fund-raiser dominated the campaign, President Obama attended two fund-raisers of his own in New York City, one hosted by the music super-couple Beyoncé Knowles and Jay-Z."

They let Obama lecture Romney on populism, reporting that Obama appeared on the Letterman show on CBS and argued, "My expectation is, if you want to be president, you've got to work for everybody, not just for some." Later, he added, "What I think people want to make sure of is, you're not writing off a big chunk of the country." [46]

The *Times* did not report on Jay-Z's prize attraction. His nightclub features a champagne tower of 350 bottles of $300-a-bottle Armand de Brignac Brut Gold, worth $105,000.[47] Try imagining Obama and Jay-Z in front of that spectacle while Obama tells Letterman you can't just work for the rich people.

AP shamelessly distributed a story headlined "Obama: As President You Represent Entire Country." Matthew Daly reported: "Rebuking Mitt Romney, President Barack Obama said Tuesday that Americans are not 'victims' and that voters want to make sure that their president is 'not writing off big chunks of the country.'"[48] With zero sense of irony, Daly began a perfunctory recap of the Jay-Z fundraiser at paragraph 16, with no word of a champagne tower. ABC, CBS, and NBC never mentioned this clash of opulence and "populism."

Obama could campaign comfortably in the knowledge that he didn't really have to worry that the press would report the screaming contradiction between his mansion-hopping opportunism and his left-wing anticapitalist ideals. As Jason Mattera concluded in his book *Hollywood Hypocrites*, Obama's celebrity backers are "the perfect embodiment of all that is wrong with the Left's ideas and policies. Not only do their progressive ideas fail, but they are so bankrupt that even their loudest adherents live lives that stand in direct opposition to their ideology."[49]

CHAPTER 4

The Audacity of Myth

Obama sounded "like great fiction"—and that's what he wrote.

The media's sneakiest dirty trick in the book is bias by omission, because it is so hard to find, when journalists decide "what the people don't know won't hurt them," or more precisely, "what the people don't know won't hurt our candidate."

Back in 1992, CBS correspondent Betsy Aaron made a blunt statement at a journalists' conference. "The largest opinion is what we leave out," she said. "I mean, it sounds simplistic, but I always say worry about what you're not seeing. What you are seeing, you can really criticize, because you're smart and have opinions. But if we don't tell you anything and leave whole areas uncovered, that's the danger." [1]

In Barack Obama's case this omission emerged in 2012 over his biographical narrative: his 1995 memoir *Dreams from My Father*, which became a huge bestseller as he prepared to run for president and enriched him with an estimated $1.3 million in royalties (not to mention almost $4 million for his campaign book *The Audacity of Hope*), and that's just through 2007.[2]

Reporters loved this book. In an October 23, 2006, cover story in *Time* magazine, Joe Klein oozed about Obama's parentage: "He told the story in brilliant, painful detail in his first book, *Dreams from My Father*, which may be the best-written memoir ever produced by an American politician."[3]

Chris Matthews was even more effusive, to the point of slobbery, on MSNBC, which is to say, typical. The book was "unique because he's a politician and not since U.S. Grant has a politician written his own book, and that is refreshing." It was great literature. "It's almost like Mark Twain. It's so American, it's so textured. It's so, almost sounding like great fiction because it reads like us. It's picturesque. Is that the right word, 'picturesque'? I think it's got that quality."[4]

Matthews was exactly right. It sounded like great fiction because so much of it was fictionalized. The warning was right there in the preface to his 1995 memoir, where Barack Obama admitted the chapters to come were taking liberties with the truth: "Although much of this book is based on contemporaneous journals or the oral histories of my family, the dialogue is necessarily an approximation of what was actually said or relayed to me." Even the people weren't entirely real: "For the sake of compression, some of the characters that appear are composites of people I've known, and some events appear out of precise chronology."[5]

Ask a journalist if he supports the notion of a president whose life story is one part mythology, like George Washington and the cherry tree. Some media people have been stunned when they are told of this paragraph, as if they never read this book, or skipped the preface. But that has never nicked the larger legend that's been created. The nation's so-called guardians of factual accuracy don't even expect honesty from Obama on *his own life story*.

Liberal journalists—especially hacks like Matthews at MSNBC—

routinely disparage conservatives for the "birthers" and their conspiracy theories that Obama couldn't be president because he wasn't
born in the United States. They enjoyed the circus around Donald
Trump's demands for Obama's birth certificate as proof that conservatives can't accept a black man as president. When Romney clinched
the Republican nomination in late May, NBC's Matt Lauer wondered on the *Today* show, "will his ongoing relationship with Donald
Trump overshadow his big moment? As Trump plays the birther card
once again."[6]

But the public should see the entire national media as a pack
of "mythers"—people who blithely accepted Obama's concocted
life story without challenging the factual reliability of any of it. It
should be called *Fever Dreams from My Father.* Or *Day Dreams From
My Father.* Anything to underscore that this should *not* be seen as a
biography.

Instead, Obama was *honored* for his narrative-mangling skill. In
2008, *New York Times* reporter Janny Scott oozed, "Senator Obama
understands as well as any politician the power of a well-told story.
He has risen in politics less on his track record than on his telling of
his life story—a tale he has packaged into two hugely successful books
that have helped make him a mega-best-selling, two-time Grammy-
winning millionaire front-runner for the Democratic presidential
nomination at age 46."[7]

Liberals occasionally tried to preserve a fraction of their dignity
as journalists with a few uncomfortable facts. But they were quiet
about it.

For example, on July 13, 2011, in a story published on page 16,
New York Times reporter Kevin Sack explained, "The White House on
Wednesday declined to challenge an account in a new book that suggests that President Obama, in his campaign to overhaul American
health care, mischaracterized a central anecdote about his mother's
deathbed dispute with her insurance company."

The headline said the book "challenges" the Obama story, and in the story they used the word "mischaracterized." It was a whole lot more misleading than that.

That new book was titled *A Singular Woman: The Untold Story of Barack Obama's Mother*. The author was Janny Scott, the same *Times* reporter who was so impressed with Obama's storytelling in 2008. But she found holes in the narrative. Scott quoted from correspondence from Obama's mother, Ann Dunham, to assert that the 1995 dispute concerned a Cigna disability insurance policy. Her actual health insurer had reimbursed most of her medical expenses without argument. The *Times* noted that although candidate Obama often suggested Dunham "was denied health coverage because of a pre-existing condition, it appears from her correspondence that she was only denied disability coverage."[8]

So he was lying. Indeed, reporters could have held Obama accountable for lying repeatedly on his way to his first presidential victory and beyond, obscenely using his own deceased mother as a prop:

- He lied to an entire stadium of supporters in his August 28, 2008, convention speech. "As someone who watched my mother argue with insurance companies while she lay in bed dying of cancer," he announced, "I will make certain those companies stop discriminating against those who are sick and need care the most."

- The same lie was repeated in the October 7, 2008, presidential debate, carried live from coast to coast by all the networks, like the convention speech. "For my mother to die of cancer at the age of 53 and have to spend the last months of her life in a hospital room, arguing with insurance companies because they're saying that this may be a preexisting condition and they don't have to pay her treatment, there's something fundamentally wrong about that."

- He lied as president in a town-hall-style meeting in Portsmouth, New Hampshire, in August 2009. "I will never forget my own mother, as she fought cancer in her final months, having to worry about whether her insurance would refuse to pay for her treatment."

Obama also mentioned her in a 2007 campaign TV ad: "In those last painful months, she was more worried about paying her medical bills than getting well. I hear stories like hers every day."

Kevin Sack of the *Times* turned to liberal Harvard professor Robert Blendon to pronounce the obvious: if Obama's phony story line had been discovered during the 2008 campaign, "people would have considered it a significant error." But it was not an error. It was a bald-faced lie, repeated over and over.

Blendon added: "I just took for granted that it was a pre-existing condition health insurance issue." So did the entire American news media.

But the suppressing media not only failed to find this deception in 2008. They ignored it when it was exposed in 2011. Network coverage of this new jaw-dropper on ABC, CBS, and NBC? Zero in 2011, and zero in 2012.

This suppression of Janny Scott's most damaging anecdote was even true for the *Times* itself. When the paper first ran an excerpt of her book in their Sunday magazine on April 24, 2011, it came with a cover photo of Barack as a preschooler in a pirate costume standing by his mother. The article was a flowery bouquet of prose about "the stout, pale-skinned woman in sturdy sandals, standing squarely a half-step ahead of the lithe, darker-skinned figure to her left. His elastic-band body bespoke discipline, even asceticism . . . he had the studied casualness of a catalog model, in khakis, at home in the view-finder."[9]

This is the same set of newspapers and networks that had devoted multiple heavy-breathing stories to "correcting" noncandidate Sarah Palin's historical knowledge of Paul Revere or mocking Michele Bachmann for confusing the birthplace of John Wayne. But Obama didn't stumble, and wasn't confused. He lied repeatedly about his mother—a shameless, pandering appeal to emotion, using his mother to enact socialized health care, and the media—how can we deny this?—deliberately abetted that dishonesty.

After Obama was safely reelected, David Axelrod insisted that the voters prized Obama's authenticity and disdained Mitt Romney's apparent plasticity. "Barack Obama's very authentic. They knew what drove him. They were comfortable with him."[10] Authenticity was hardly Obama's strong suit, but how could voters know otherwise when the national media were censoring news?

Obama's "Composite" White Women

David Maraniss of *The Washington Post* was another reporter flying all over the world trying to separate the real Obama from the phony memoir of *Dreams*—but in the friendliest possible way. Maraniss told *Vanity Fair* that Obama's memoir had value despite its pack of lies: "I say that his memoir is a remarkably insightful exploration of his internal struggle, but should not be read as rigorous factual history. It is not, and the president knew that when he wrote it and knows it now."[11]

This was a bombshell. Maraniss had spent months exploring Obama's past and held a prestigious editor's post at the dominant paper in the nation's capital, and was overseeing campaign coverage as Obama faced a difficult reelection. But the bombshell never exploded.

In mid-June, his book *Barack Obama: The Story* came out. On June 5, deep inside the paper, *New York Times* reviewer Michiko Kakutani noticed several factual problems with Obama's memoir. She called the book a "forensic deconstruction" of Obama.[12]

For example, Obama wrote about "a woman in New York that I loved." But while the physical description of this character closely resembles a white Obama girlfriend named Genevieve Cook, Maraniss wrote Obama "distorted her attitudes and some of their experiences, emphasizing his sense that they came from different worlds." Maraniss relayed that during an interview at the White House on November 10, 2011, Obama acknowledged his description of his New York girlfriend was actually a "compression" of events "that occurred at separate times with several different girlfriends."[13]

Obama didn't just dump his old girlfriends. He then added insult to injury by blurring them into a fictional composite. If a memoir can't be honest about something as trivial as " a woman in New York that I loved," how can it be considered accurate with matters that are profound?

The glossy magazine *Vanity Fair* published an excerpt from Maraniss but didn't focus very seriously on the "compression." They were fascinated by excerpts from Cook's diary, and letters Obama wrote to another white girlfriend, Alex McNear. On May 2, ABC anchor Diane Sawyer swooned as she quoted Obama's letters, and pretended it was somehow a "peril" for ABC to discover them and praise them.

"One of the perils of being President: Everything you ever wrote will become public. And today, Barack Obama, age 22—long before he met Michelle—new letters and diary entries revealed in *Vanity Fair* from a biography out soon," Sawyer announced.

"He had college girlfriends, two women . . . Genevieve Cook and Alex McNear. And in a love letter to McNear, the President writes adoringly about life in New York. Quote, 'Moments trip gently along over here. Snow caps the bushes in unexpected ways. Birds shoot and spin like balls of sound. My feet hum over the dry walks.' Oh, we were all so romantic when we were young. The book relies on a trove of letters and journal entries that Obama and his friends created during the 1980s." [14]

So much for "peril." Sawyer and ABC never showed the slightest interest in Obama compressing and mangling his college sweethearts in his book.

There was more distortion. One weekend, Cook and Obama took a bus to her stepfather's country estate in Norfolk, Connecticut. He described it this way: "The family knew every inch of the land. They knew how the hills had formed, how the glacial drifts had created the lake, the names of the earliest white settlers—their ancestors—and before that, the names of the Indians who'd once hunted the land." Obama's point was "I realized that our two worlds were as distant from each other as Kenya is from Germany," and "I was the one who knew how to live as an outsider."

This Obama passage had one factual error: the estate didn't belong to Cook's father, but to her stepfather, Phil Jessup. That can be overlooked as an innocent mistake. Less innocent: Cook complained to Maraniss that the notion that the Jessups had been among the earliest white settlers and that they knew the names of the Indians was a "gross exaggeration." Cook also felt Obama misled readers in that she felt just as alienated from the place—and the old-money establishment—as Obama claimed he did, and then, "The ironic thing . . . is he moved through the corridors of power in a far more comfortable way than I ever would have." [15]

Obama also told a story about taking a girlfriend to a "very angry play" by a black playwright and she came out "talking about why black people were angry all the time. I said it was a matter of remembering—nobody asks why Jews remember the Holocaust, I think I said—and she said that's different, and I said it wasn't, and she said that anger was just a dead end. And we had a big fight, right in front of the theater."

Again, Maraniss reported, "None of this happened with Genevieve." She said they attended the theater just once together, to see the British actress Billie Whitelaw performing from the work of the Irish playwright Samuel Beckett. The one time they were in the midst of a black audience was a trip to the movies in Brooklyn to see Eddie Murphy in *Beverly Hills Cop*. Cook told Maraniss, "I was the only white person in the audience," and "It was such a wonderful, uplifting, mind-blowing experience."

There was no fight. There was no crying in the car (neither person had a car). There was no scene where Obama's girlfriend asked about angry black people.

Maraniss asked Obama about this at the White House. Obama acknowledged the scene did not happen with Cook. "That was not her," he said. "That was an example of compression. I thought that was a useful theme to make about sort of the interactions I had in the relationship. And so that occupies, what, two paragraphs in the book? My attitude was it would be dishonest for me not to touch on that at all." [16]

Stop. Rewind. He's saying "it would be dishonest of me" *not* to make up a story about a black-white lovers' quarrel? To Obama, real life was merely raw material for manufacturing the "larger truth" of his mythology. His story was false—period.

In another stunning passage from the same chapter of the Maraniss book, a passage that *Vanity Fair* did not excerpt—perhaps because it wasn't about Obama's love life—Obama describes his brief tenure after graduation from Columbia at a place called Business International, which produced newsletters and updates for corporations seeking to do business abroad. Obama boasted, "I had my own office, my own secretary, money in the bank. Sometimes, coming out of an interview with Japanese financiers or German bond traders, I would catch my reflection in the elevator doors—see myself in a suit and tie, a briefcase in my hand—and for a split second, I would imagine myself as a captain of industry, barking out orders, closing the deal, before I remembered who it was that I wanted to be and felt pangs of guilt for my lack of resolve."

Maraniss found these recollections were "seen as distortions and misrepresentations by many of the people who had worked with him." They said Obama had no secretary, and his office was the size of a cubicle, barely large enough to fit a desk. The dress code was informal and people in his position rarely wore suits. "He dressed like a college kid," said his supervisor Lou Celi.

Ralph Diaz, the company's vice president for publications, thought Obama was embellishing his role for dramatic effect "in a book that reads more like a novel." He said "Obama worked at a very, very low position there. . . . The part about seeing his reflection in the elevator doors? There were no reflections there. . . . He was not in this high, talking-to-Swiss-bankers kind of role. He was in the back rooms checking things on the phone."

Another colleague characterized it with equal distaste: "He retells the story as the temptation of Christ . . . the young idealistic would-be community organizer who gets a nice suit and barely escapes moving into the big mansion with the white folks."[17]

In an interview with *Vanity Fair*, Maraniss admitted that he bent his usual rules to make his interview with the president more advantageous. What's the harm in a little collusion?

"I did something I rarely do: I gave him a copy of the introduction to the book so he would understand its parameters. I also gave him the table of contents, knowing that some of the chapter titles, such as 'Genevieve and the Veil,' would mean something to him but not to his staff. The interview was scheduled for 45 minutes. It went on for more than an hour and a half. He answered all of my questions, sometimes took issue with my interpretations, but was fairly forthright." [18]

Here's how he was forthright. When Maraniss was interviewed on NBC's *Today* on June 18, 2012, substitute host David Gregory noted, "You point out inconsistencies. You talk with greater depth and detail about his pot smoking as a young person. You unearth letters from former, you know, loves. Genevieve Cook. How did he react to all of that?"

Maraniss: "Well, he's a writer himself. When I first interviewed him, he said, 'David, your introduction'—[which] I let him read—'is interesting, but you called my book fiction.' And I said, 'No, Mr. President, I complimented it. I called it literature.' There's a big difference between memoir and biography. And it wasn't that I was trying to fact-check everything that he wrote in his biography, but I just wanted to get the story right. So, he didn't—he didn't really fight with me about it. But it was an interesting conversation."

In the book's introduction, after he praised *Dreams* as "unusually insightful," Maraniss wrote that "it is important to say it falls into the realm of literature, and not of history and autobiography, and should not be read as a rigorously factual account." [19]

Gregory asked, "Was he forthcoming about these additional details?" Maraniss understood Gregory's roundabout inquiry and said Obama didn't put up a fight to the charge he'd mangled his own life story:

"In most cases he said, you're probably right. You know, a lot of the mythology of the family was passed along to him that he didn't check. Like, that his step-grandfather in Indonesia he thought died fighting the Dutch in the anti-colonial war. In fact, the man died of a heart attack falling off an ottoman changing the drapes in his living room. You know, that sort of story is something that the president did not check. And when I told him the reality of so many of those things he said, you're probably right." [20]

These "journalists" were tying themselves into pretzels to avoid calling this a fabrication.

Maraniss faced a tension between his self-perceived role as a historian versus his role as a journalist. The historian wanted to present with some objectivity and detachment a reliable record for the ages. The journalist living in the present was much more circumspect about his findings.

The Punahou Hoops Scoop

Here's the most remarkable discovery of media omissions on Obama's behalf: *The Washington Post,* the journalistic home base of Maraniss, never touched on the memoir lies. *All these passages on Obama's self-made mythology were never republished in the newspaper.*

The *Post* ran massive exposés trying to ruin first Rick Perry, then Mitt Romney, but published nothing about Obama's blatant myth-making. Instead, on June 5, the *Post* published a rave review of the Maraniss tome on the front page of the Style section, headlined "A masterful portrait of a guarded politician."

Shamelessly, *Post* reviewer author T. J. Stiles oozed, "Every biographer knows how difficult it is to render an actual human being with the depth of a fictional character. . . . A character should be capable of surprises without seeming inauthentic or arbitrary." [21] But Stiles never mentioned Maraniss exposing Obama's fictionalizations. He even wrote Maraniss "makes the fringe skepticism of Obama's birthplace seem even more ridiculous, if possible," but utterly ignored how the *Post* editor found Obama lied about his mother's almost-immediate departure for the homeland after his birth.

What did Maraniss think of this whitewash? Maraniss didn't mind. He linked to the rave review on Twitter, with the words: "TJ Stiles says 'no review can convey this book's breadth and depth,' but his review of Obama: The Story not 2 shabby."[22] Not shabby? Stiles had ignored the most damaging part of the book's depth.

After running very large investigative pieces on the front page trashing Rick Perry and Mitt Romney, Maraniss and the *Post* provided the perfect contrast of anti-Republican bile with pro-Obama goo. The only Maraniss book excerpt appearing in the newspaper was placed at the top of the Sunday sports section on June 11. The 5,500-word excerpt carried the headline "President Obama's Love for Basketball Can be Traced Back to His High School Team." The story took up two whole pages inside the sports section.[23]

The *Post* apparently found nothing about Obama's life more illuminating or substantive for readers than repeating that Obama loved basketball—about which Maraniss had also written syrupy passages in 2008. As always with Maraniss, it was all about lovingly toying with Obama's racial identities:

"To say that President Obama loves basketball understates the role of the sport in his life," the excerpt began. "He has been devoted to the game for 40 years now, ever since the father he did not know and never saw again gave him his first ball during a brief Christmastime visit. Basketball is central to his self identity. It is global yet American-born, much like him. It is where he found a place of comfort, a family, a mode of expression, a connection from his past to his future. With foundation roots in the Kansas of his white forebears, basketball was also the city game, helping him find his way toward blackness, his introduction to an African American culture that was distant to him when he was young, yet his by birthright."

All this because Obama likes basketball.

Strangely, the excerpt wrapped up with Maraniss laboring to suggest Obama's use of marijuana in high school was very typical for the Disco Era. "If there is a representative teenager's life, Barry Obama lived a version of it in Hawaii in the late 1970s. Several things stood out—he went to a prestigious school, he lived with his grandparents, his father was gone, his mother was infrequently present, he was a *hapa* black in a place where most people were a lighter shade of brown—and those traits helped shape his particular character, but they did not make his life odd or mysterious. He smoked pot with his Choom Gang and goofed around outside the classroom, where he came across as smart and mature if not notably studious, but the central activity of his high school life was basketball."

The "choom" in "Choom Gang" was a verb meaning to smoke pot. Maraniss found Obama was an enthusiastic pot smoker, but it was mentioned in passing in the *Post*. This paragraph was lifted out of a chapter that began with Maraniss reporting the future president and his friends believed in "TA," or "total absorption," as in "[w]asting good bud smoke was not tolerated." Barry championed "roof hits," that when they were pot-smoking in the car, all the windows had to be rolled up, and when the pot was gone, they tilted their heads upward to suck in the last bit of smoke from the ceiling. Barry was also known for "intercepting" the rotating joint.[24]

Try not to be shocked. Those evocative details were left out of the 5,500-word basketball excerpt.

Maraniss and the *Post* also milked the hoops angle to sell Obama in 2008. As might be expected, a Nexis search of the words "Obama" and "Punahou" brings out mostly laudatory references to his high school basketball career. The seven stories in the sample offered zero criticisms of young Obama, but plenty of oozing sympathy for his fatherless plight. Here are the headlines, to give you a flavor:

1. "A Rusty Toyota, a Mean Jump Shot, Good Ears" (Outlook section collection of positive quotes from friends and classmates, February 11, 2007)

2. "The Ghost of a Father" (December 14, 2007)

3. "BARACK OBAMA WAS DRAWN TO BASKETBALL AS A KID, AND HE HAS NEVER LET IT GO" (same day, December 14, 2007)

4. "For Obama, the Sport Is Much More than a Game" (Sports, April 16, 2008)

5. "Though Obama Had to Leave to Find Himself, It Is Hawaii That Made His Rise Possible," by David Maraniss (August 24, 2008)

6. "Obama Visits Grandma Who Was His 'Rock'; Candidate Hopes She Will See Election Day" (October 25, 2008)

7. "What School Sports Taught These Political Contenders" (Sports, October 30, 2008)

That last story before the election, by Preston Williams, made sure to throw in some negativity toward opponent John McCain: "Obama was sometimes called 'Barry Obomber,' even though the left-handed small forward was known more for his long arms and quick first step on slashes to the basket than for his shooting touch. He favored a street-ball style; Coach Chris McLachlin preached fundamentals." [25]

But for the Republican, "McCain, a self-described rabble-rouser at Episcopal, at the time an all-male boarding school, was one of the smaller boys on campus—he wrestled in the 127-pound class as a senior. But he was also one of the feistiest, earning such nicknames as 'McNasty' and 'The Punk.'"

In 2008 as in 2012, the *Post* would strongly suggest the Republican challenger was a teenaged bully.

Slouching Toward Selma

There's another example that demonstrated that the major media never cared about Obama's reckless disregard for the truth, especially when he was pandering to black voters. Maraniss reported that Obama's account of being separated from his father when he was two was "received myth, not the truth." Maraniss explained Obama's father was "married in name only. Within a month of the day Barry came home from the hospital, he and his mother were long gone from Honolulu," as Ann Dunham returned to the mainland to attend the University of Washington.

In Obama's mythical version, "the family breach did not occur until 1963, when his father left the island. That version of events is inaccurate in two ways. The date: his father had gone from Hawaii in June 1962, less than a year after Barry was born, not 1963. And the order: it was his mother who left Hawaii first." [26]

No one reported on this, or questioned Maraniss about it, never mind questioning Obama himself. Five years before, on March 4, 2007, Obama made a speech saluting the 1965 civil rights march in Selma, Alabama, and claimed his parents were inspired by Selma before he was born. "There was something stirring across the country because of what happened in Selma, Alabama, because some folks are willing to march across a bridge. So they got together and Barack Obama Jr. was born. So don't tell me I don't have a claim on Selma, Alabama. Don't tell me I'm not coming home when I come to Selma, Alabama." [27]

This is a pretty bizarre claim for a man who was born in Hawaii and whose parents never had a real marriage, and were literally on different continents by the time of the Selma march of 1965. Selma didn't bring his parents together; they were officially divorced in 1964, and Obama's father left Harvard in 1964 and returned to Kenya with another white American woman, named Ruth Baker, and they married there in 1964. His mother married Lolo Soetoro in 1965. The real story in no way resembled Obama's mythical narrative that Selma inspired two people to fall in love and conceive a future president.

Obama had no claim on Selma, Alabama.

Obama was never mocked for his shameless attempts at burnishing his legend. NBC anchor Brian Williams could devote attention on three straight nights in June 2011 to how noncandidate Sarah Palin's account of Paul Revere's ride allegedly "differs with history,"[28] but with candidate Obama in Selma, NBC's Andrea Mitchell used this uncorrected clip: "Don't tell me I don't have a claim on Selma, Alabama. Don't tell me I'm not coming home when I come to Selma, Alabama."

On ABC, John Cochran said Obama "seemed to address accusations that he is not black enough because of his mixed ancestry," and used the same clip. ABC's Jake Tapper repeated the tactic in the morning, adding some gush: "Obama's eloquent piety is seldom received better than in a church full of Democrats, especially black ones."

On CBS, correspondent Gloria Borger at least made a small nod to reality, without correcting Obama. "In March of 1965, Barack Obama was just three years old. Even so, he says, he's still the product of Selma."[29] Then came a clip of Obama: "This is the site of my conception. I am the fruits of your labor. I am the offspring of the movement."

CBS This Morning offered a warm anniversary story from Selma on March 4, 2012, but no one explored Obama's absurd claims of 2007. On the day of Obama's second inauguration, the *Post* published a special inaugural section, where *Post* reporter Wil Haygood highlighted quotes from Obama's Selma speech again—including "My very existence might not have been possible had it not been for some of the folks here today"— a claim now clearly debunked. It was only one of several "cultural touchstones related to African-American history" greeting Obama's second term, like the anniversary of the Emancipation Proclamation and the new movie on Lincoln.[30]

Daily Fake Campaign Anecdotes

Obama has never stopped using poetic license when telling his life story. So where are the reporters to point out where he doesn't tell the truth? Let's take just one typical Obama stump speech, on July 5, 2012, in Sandusky, Ohio, and identify the fibs and stretches. They're not hard to find.

There are tall tales about his ancestors. He claimed, as he has many times, "My grandfather fought in Patton's army." In 2009, AP's Nancy Benac noted that the president's grandfather, Stanley Dunham, was in a supply and maintenance company, not in combat. That's noble work, but "fought in Patton's army" implies something else. Moreover, Benac reported Dunham's company was assigned to Patton's army for two months in 1945, and then quoted Obama's own self-boosting memoir: "Gramps returned from the war never having seen real combat." Why was Benac alone in exploring this blatant exaggeration?

There were also myths about Obama's campaigns. Obama bizarrely told the crowd in Sandusky that "back in 2008, everybody said we couldn't do it because we were outspent, we weren't favored." Did Obama mean in the primary race? By a slim margin, he outraised Hillary Clinton, who was the early favorite. But this spin is comical if it refers to the general election, where Obama outraised McCain $779 million to $347 million.

Then Obama added: "That first race that I ran as a state senator, Michelle and I, we were going around knocking on doors, passing out leaflets. Nobody gave us a shot. Everybody said, 'Nobody can pronounce your name, how are you going to win?'" But Obama *ran unopposed* in 1996 in both the primary and the general election.[31]

At first, state senator Alice Palmer urged Obama to replace her since she was going to run for Congress. But she lost that race to Jesse Jackson Jr. and then turned around to seek reelection. In a burst of Chicago-style politics, Obama removed *three* primary opponents (including Palmer) from the ballot by challenging their signatures. A bitter Palmer refused to endorse Obama in the primary or the fall election. To the gut-punchers in Chicago, it meant Obama had arrived. But none of the networks have ever breathed Palmer's name.

Obama's years in the Illinois Senate, from 1997 through 2004, were a part of his life story the national media never found interesting. It was a bit shocking that CBS reporter Steve Kroft would pile up five friendly interviews with Obama on *60 Minutes* before the 2008 election, and two more right after the victory, and yet completely, shamelessly avoid Obama's record in Illinois. It might seem less surprising that his Chicago past didn't come up in the seven interviews Obama gave to Kroft since becoming president. Kroft has never asked about his radical Chicago friends like the Pentagon bomber Bill Ayers and his anti-American minister Jeremiah Wright.[32]

It's not really unusual for CBS to catch up on ancient controversies in a presidential reelection campaign . . . or at least it wasn't when the president was George W. Bush. In 2004, CBS spent untold hours, days, weeks, months, chasing a story about George Bush and the Alabama Air National Guard in 1973 because that was important. But Obama palling around with terrorists, associating with hate-mongers? No one at *60 Minutes* cared what Obama did when he was in his mid-twenties. He was "finding himself."

The liberal assumption was that everything on George W. Bush's résumé was handed to this lightweight by Daddy. This is never a problem when your last name is Kennedy, only if you're an Old Money Republican. Obama, on their other hand, was their poster child, their heavyweight champion—sympathetic, cosmopolitan, progressive, racially mixed, and eternally conflicted about it. Every prize and privilege handed to Obama—including a contract to write a semifictional memoir fresh out of Harvard Law School—was somehow owed to him, a small fraction of America's racial sins being cleansed.

Steve Kroft did find one Obama scandal figure back on April 23, 2008—Tony Rezko, a Syrian-born housing developer, when he was on trial for corruption in Chicago. But CBS never mentioned Obama in the piece. Instead, Kroft was doing a story on how the Bush administration was implicitly allowing corruption in Iraq, and how the former Iraqi electricity commissioner's name came up in Rezko's corruption trial.[33]

Kroft mustered no mention of Rezko's contributing and bundling hundreds of thousands of dollars in campaign financing for Obama, or his scandalous help in helping the Obamas as they bought a fancy six-thousand-square foot Georgian Revival house with seven bathrooms for $1.65 million in June 2005. (Rezko's wife, Rita, bought an adjoining parcel to the Obamas for $625,000, and both sales closed on the same day.) At the time, Rezko was already being investigated for bribery and fraud. Obama later told the *Chicago Tribune* the deal was "boneheaded," but the national media weren't repeating that.

The Rezko scandal even emerged again during the Republican primary season. On November 22, 2011, as the networks were pounding away on Herman Cain's treatment of women, Rezko was sentenced to ten and a half years of prison time for corruption and extortion. ABC, CBS, NBC, MSNBC, NPR, and PBS said absolutely nothing. CNN offered one sentence to Rezko on this day, as John King ironically announced the "news you need to know."

USA Today and *The Washington Post* both reported the news briefly inside their papers, listing Rezko in their headlines as an ally of corrupt governor Rod Blagojevich—not Obama. The Associated

Press headline also touted "Blago ally Rezko." Obama's name came up just once, in paragraph 21.[34]

This was merely the latest proof that even on the most personal matters, Barack Obama could count on the media to act like another set of corrupt business partners. Team Obama could make fun of John McCain's seven homes or Mitt Romney's car elevator and chuckle in the knowledge that Obama's "news" buddies would never mention his Rezko-assisted home purchase. After all, he was perfect.

CHAPTER 5

Richie Rich Romney

Don't vote for a "predatory capitalist" stereotype.

Have you ever noticed the media's dirty trick about multimillionaires in politics? If you're a Democrat named Kennedy or Rockefeller, who inherited millions, or have a habit of marrying women with millions (think John Kerry), or made your millions chasing ambulances (Edwards), it couldn't possibly put a wrinkle in your populist image. As long as you favor every redistribution scheme that the Ivy League economists can muster, your riches aren't disqualifying. They can even add glamour to your aura.

But if you're a Republican with a gleam in your eye toward tax cuts and deregulation, then it doesn't matter whether you're Old Money or New Money or even No Money. You will be deemed an "economic royalist," as Franklin Roosevelt put it.

When ABC anchor Diane Sawyer interviewed Mitt Romney on April 17, 2012, she casually announced "the Obama campaign is working overtime to paint the portrait of a man whose riches have put him out of touch." She then offered Romney the Obama spin:

"The speaking fees, the Cadillacs, the story out now that there's an elevator for your cars in the new house you're planning in La Jolla. Are you too rich to relate?"[1]

There's an obvious answer that Romney did not give. "Diane, you make $12 million a year. The ritzy Manhattan penthouse, the wealthy movie director husband, the estate on Martha's Vineyard. Does that make you too rich and elitist to relate to your audience?"

Romney's actual answer wasn't bad. "We don't divide America based upon success and wealth and other dimensions of that nature. We're one nation under God. We come together. This is a time when people of different backgrounds and experiences need to come together."

The Obamas, like most liberals, loved to talk a good game about national unity, but in the political wars, talk is cheap. They have always preferred, and benefited from, the divide-and-conquer basics of class warfare. In his post-election interview at the University of Chicago, Obama strategist David Axelrod expressed amazement that Romney and his campaign team never sold his life story aggressively. "I don't think they fleshed him out enough," he said. "People need to know who you are, they need to be comfortable with who you are. . . . Whatever message you build has to be built around your biography, and it has to be compelling."

Obama had a biography that journalists never failed to recount and find compelling, even if, as we've discussed, so much of it was the president's own mangled memoir myths and stump-speech whoppers, augmented by apple-polishers like Chris Matthews who found him perfect in every way.

Axelrod and Team Obama obviously preferred to have Obama evaluated as a compelling historical figure, and not so much as a policy architect. They wanted him painted as above the grubby fray of everyday politics. Obama's policies were always secondary, and necessarily so, given their abject failure. Even policy statements could be better understood as empathetic personal poses for the lower- and middle-class voters that said "I understand you, I'm like you . . . unlike that out-of-touch Richie Rich over there with his car elevator."

Axelrod professed amazement that Romney spent at least 90 percent of his primary money on negative ads against his Republican opponents instead of defining himself. After he won the primary, "we thought the first thing they would do would be to do that, and just create a stronger sense among the American people of just who he was." Axelrod was happy that Romney skipped it: "That of course left an opening for him to be defined around some of his business practices that have become well-known now." [2]

Team Obama knew what it was doing. Team Bain Capital didn't have a clue. The Obama campaign and its "unaffiliated" Super PACs were merciless in attacking Romney as the worst kind of financial assassin and tax cheat. Reporters covering the campaign didn't protest. They did not like Romney. He lacked personal warmth. His way of speaking was too crisp and efficient, his hair too tidy. He was a soulless robot. Romney felt compelled to add the word "human" to his campaign speeches, but it did no good. He was a rich Republican capitalist. Strike One, Strike Two, and Strike Three.

For example, on July 17, the very same day that Chris Matthews described Obama on *Hardball* in utopian terms as "the perfect father, the perfect husband, the perfect American," on the very same channel *New York Times* columnist Charles Blow offered MSNBC's dystopian take on former Massachusetts governor Mitt Romney on *The Last Word*. Romney would abandon every liberal position he ever took in Boston to win the White House—as if Obama had never flip-flopped on anything in 2008, or once he was inaugurated—so he had no soul.

"This is the kind of man that Mitt Romney is. This man does not have a soul. If you opened up, you know, his chest, there's probably a gold ticking watch in there and not even a heart. This is not a person.

This is just a robot who will do whatever it takes, whatever he's told to do, to make it to the White House. And he will take whatever push in the back from whatever nasty person is pushing him and move him further in that direction."[3]

The media staunchly resisted any attempt to humanize Romney because it didn't help Obama. In both of his two campaigns for president, Mitt Romney told the heartwarming story of closing down Bain Capital in 1996 to hunt for the missing daughter of a co-worker, fourteen-year-old Melissa Gay, who disappeared after going to a "rave party" and was found the next day. That story even was published that year in *The New York Times*—although Mitt Romney's name wasn't mentioned, just Bain Capital.[4] But her name hasn't been mentioned in the *Times* since then. Her name never came up in either election on ABC, CBS, CNN, MSNBC, or NBC. Republicans like Romney have to pay for *advertisements* to make themselves look human. The networks did that on a daily basis for Obama, free of charge.

The Haircut Bully

In May, after the media had helped eliminate all Romney's conservative challengers, it was Romney's turn to be the object of an attack piece. With exquisite timing, *The Washington Post* suddenly found their latest "investigative" hit piece on Republicans.

Reporter Jason Horowitz penned a 5,400-word "expose," a bombshell. Mitt Romney may have pinned a boy down and cut his hair in 1965. *Nineteen sixty-five.* That's almost a half century ago. Even if every detail in this hit piece was accurate—and they weren't—how is it relevant? The same journalists who couldn't find anything relevant in the mistresses Bill Clinton or John Edwards were "romancing" in the risky present of their presidential campaigns could somehow find something more compelling—a haircut—in the yellowed past of Mitt Romney's high school career. The *Post* carried several full pages of breathless prose under the big headline "Romney's pranks could go too far."[5]

The *Post* reported that Romney's Cranbrook schoolmate John Lauber was "perpetually teased for his nonconformity and presumed homosexuality," and that he screamed for help as a brutish Romney held him down and forcibly hacked off his hair. Another student, David Seed, told the *Post* he ran into Lauber three decades later at an airport and apologized for not doing more to help him. Seed claimed Lauber said, "It was horrible. . . . It's something I have thought about a lot since then." The paper recounted another incident in which Romney allegedly once shouted "atta girl" to a different student at the all-boys' school who, years later, came out as gay.

This story was neatly paired with President Obama announcing the end of his completely insincere opposition to gay marriage. Even centrist *Post* columnist Kathleen Parker could see the way the major media wanted this to unfold: "One, Barack Obama is an evolutionary, 21st-century hero who supports equality for all. Two, Mitt Romney is a gay-bashing bully mired in the previous century who also supports a war on women and, oh yeah, hates dogs."[6]

So what did the alleged victim of the Romney rampage have to say? The family of John Lauber, who died of liver cancer in 2004, issued a statement saying "the portrayal of John is factually incorrect and we are aggrieved that he would be used to further a political agenda." One sister said, "If he were still alive today, he would be furious" about the story.[7] Yet none of this slowed down the *Post* one bit, nor kept everyone else in the national media from rushing to repeat the story.

ABC anchor Diane Sawyer hyperbolically found a firestorm in this tiny tale: "Five of Romney's former classmates have come forward to tell the same story, accusations creating a firestorm and Romney is forced to respond."[8] CNN anchor Soledad O'Brien called it a "pretty harrowing story" from the *Post*. "They talked to several people who recall with great detail and what sounds like a tremendous sense of guilt about that attack on this kid."[9]

"Creating a firestorm." The media create it, and then announce it's created.

After readers complained, *Post* ombudsman Patrick Pexton touted this "scoop" as a "deeply reported story" that "holds up to scrutiny." They claimed the paper "received no specific complaint of inaccuracy from the Lauber family." Note the word-parsing. The Lauber family certainly did complain. But it wasn't a *specific* complaint, so it didn't count. Pexton then turned to national editor Kevin Merida, who insisted, "We stand by the story. It's a full portrait. It's the story of Mitt Romney's years at Cranbrook. . . . Our intention with this story and future stories about both Mitt Romney and President Obama is to give people the fullest possible portrait of the men who are running for president."[10]

Pexton did not explain to readers that Merida is no objective editor. He is a black journalist who wrote a critical biography of Clarence Thomas, called *Supreme Discomfort*, and penned captions for a coffee-table book for Obama-loving liberals titled *Obama: The Historic Campaign in Photographs*. He was named the *Post*'s national editor during the Obama transition. When *Washingtonian* magazine asked him at the time how he would run the national desk, he said, "We're witnessing the rebirth of the country. We have to ask ourselves, 'What did we produce to help people understand the moment of great change?'"[11] It would be safe to assume he didn't want the "moment of great change" to be ended by a President Romney. After the election, Merida was promoted to managing editor, the number-two job.

This story was certainly not a "full portrait," as Merida claimed. It was a hit piece that helped liberal journalists, talkers, and bloggers assault Romney as someone who "tortured gay kids" for fun. Leftists like Joan Walsh of Salon.com had a field day. Her story was titled "Mitt the Prep-School Sadist."

Pexton admitted the *Post* timed this story precisely to echo on the day after President Obama's big pro-gay announcement. They actually waited a day longer than planned to let Obama have the front page to himself when he was being "historic." Merida told Pexton they didn't want the bully story clashing with the Thursday Obama-now-favors-gay-marriage story. In truth, they wanted each story to dominate the front page, not share it. So the Romney hit piece was published online late Thursday morning and was splashed on the front page on Friday.

The "reader's advocate" agreed with this politicized news judgment, implying the *Post* rushed the piece a little once they heard Obama's "history" was coming. "Do I think *The Post* took advantage of the timing? Yes. Vice President Biden had telegraphed the president's position on gay marriage just days earlier," Pexton allowed. "If I were an editor I might have sped it up a little, too, to take advantage of the national discussion on gay marriage. Does that mean *Post* editors are timing stories with the White House? I hope not, and I doubt that is the case."

Post executive editor Marcus Brauchli eventually sent an outraged e-mail to Pexton (which was posted online) strongly denying any hint of collusion, declaring "there was no collusion or coordination between *The Post* and the White House over the Romney story. The notion is 'absurd and the implication is outrageous,'" Brauchli relayed. Pexton added, "I believe him, and based on my time here in the past 14 months I have not seen this kind of collusion or coordination."

Merida made the amazing claim that the story had to be rushed because they are a "competitive news organization." But that never moved the *Post* to action when its investigators worked on the Clinton sex scandals. In 1994 the *Post* delayed for three months the story of Paula Jones claiming sexual harassment, until Clinton hired a defense lawyer. They published the Juanita Broaddrick rape story only after the Clinton impeachment trial had concluded and the president's tenure was safe. They are experienced practitioners of politicized story timing.

The *Post* knows full well that they never did this kind of "investigation" of Barack Obama in 2008. Take Obama's admissions in his memoirs of teenaged marijuana and cocaine use. Did the *Post* send a reporter to find out from Obama's classmates how often he used illegal drugs, and where he purchased them? And did he in turn distribute them?

No. The *Post* tried to assert these troublesome admissions wouldn't matter. In a front-page story published on January 3, 2007, five weeks before he announced he was running, they rushed to the story—a year before the first primary election—and then failed to investigate if Obama's memoirs were accurate.

Reporter Lois Romano's story was headlined "Effect of Obama's Candor Remains to Be Seen; Senator Admitted Trying Cocaine in a Memoir Written 11 Years Ago." It took Romano twenty-four paragraphs to include the actual passage from *Dreams from My Father*: "Pot had helped, and booze; maybe a little blow when you could afford it. Not smack, though."

"Presidential aspirants tend to write more sanitized books for use as campaign tools," Romano claimed. Then she dismissed it as a potential cause of damage: "Obama's partisan opponents and experts said it is too early to know whether the admissions will be a liability because the public seems to be enthusiastically embracing his openness at this point." [12]

Do you think that if Romney had written in a memoir openly professing that he bullied kids in high school, the media would report "the public seems to be enthusiastically embracing his openness"? As for the openness, it was very limited. White House spokesman Robert Gibbs tried to spin it as a positive that Obama admitted cocaine use: "I believe what the country is looking for is someone who is open, honest and candid about themselves rather than someone who seems endlessly driven by polls or focus groups." The next sentence in the Romano story undercut the embracing-openness narrative: "Gibbs said yesterday that Obama was not available for an interview." [13]

Romney and the Dog on the Roof

While stories like Obama's drug use were smothered in his first campaign for president and were considered forgotten in 2012, liberal journalists continued to embarrass Romney on old stories that emerged in his first presidential campaign. In 2007, *Boston Globe* reporter Neil Swidey reported that on a family vacation in 1983, Romney had put his Irish setter, Seamus, in a cartop carrier for a trip to Canada. The dog was apparently frightened enough to suffer from diarrhea, which rolled down the back window. Romney then pulled over to a gas station, cleaned the dog off with a hose, and put him back on top and drove on.

It was a profoundly *nothing* story, but that of course doesn't matter. The Obama people loved it, and would tweak Romney with it. On January 30, 2012, Obama strategist David Axelrod drew a wave of Internet attention when he tweeted a photo of Obama riding inside his car with his dog Bo with the caption, "How loving owners transport their dogs." CNN's Political Ticker blog wrote it up under the title "Axelrod's tweet worse than his bite." [14]

Predictably, some liberal journalists descended into wretched excess. On the January 13, 2012 edition of the public-radio show *On the Media*, distributed across America by NPR, host Bob Garfield interviewed Swidey. "So back in 2007, you surely knew that this story would not be taken only at face value, that it would mutate," Garfield declared, "and it would be used as ammunition by those who would portray Mitt Romney as the Michael Vick of presidential candidates. It still wound up as your lede. You feel any compunction about that at this stage?" [15]

The better question is why Garfield didn't have any compunction comparing Romney's alleged mistreatment of a pet with Michael Vick, who pled guilty to hanging or drowning six to eight dogs. Garfield's program boasts about its own civility on its website: "While maintaining the civility and fairness that are the hallmarks of public radio, *OTM* tackles sticky issues with a frankness and transparency that has built trust with listeners." [16] This would be true if your listeners were limited to liberals who loved this story like David Axelrod did.

No one embraced this story more feverishly than *New York Times* columnist Gail Collins, who served as the paper's editorial page editor for most of the Bush years. Collins worshipped Obama so much that she wrote a column just before Thanksgiving in 2008 with this request: "Thanksgiving is next week, and President Bush could make it a really special holiday by resigning. Seriously." [17] Like many other journalists, Collins was so desperately pro-Obama she wanted him inaugurated in November.

How obsessed as this woman with the silly dog story? Clay Waters of the TimesWatch blog counted that since her first 2007 column on the anecdote, headlined "Haunted by Seamus," Collins had mentioned "Crategate" in twenty-eight columns from 2007 through November 2011. "Every column that mentioned Romney during that span has included the dog story." [18]

The pattern continued from December 2011 through Election Day, with another thirty columns pounding away at the story. On January 3, Collins urged New Hampshire voters to write in the dog: "Did I ever mention that Romney once drove to Canada with the family Irish setter strapped to the roof of the car? The dog's name was Seamus. New Hampshire Republicans, if you can't think of anybody to vote for on Tuesday, consider writing in the name Seamus when you go to the polls. Maybe we can start a boomlet. Makes as much sense as the Newt Gingrich moment." [19]

Collins wrote a whole column on the subject headlined "Dogging Mitt Romney" on March 8. "People, does any of this sound appealing? Elect Mitt Romney and he will take the nation on the road to the future. Some of us will be stuck on the roof. The rest of us will be inside singing camp songs and waiting for the day when the master plan lets us stop to visit the bathroom. Plus, anybody who screws up on the way to the future gets the hose." [20]

CBS and David Letterman liked this story, too, so Collins appeared with late night's most devoted Obama fan on March 20. Letterman told Collins he adored her obsession: "I so loved the fact that this happened to this guy, and I loved the fact that you more than any single journalist that I know, has promoted it. Tell us how you know about it." When she described it, Letterman added, "I mean, as silly as this all might be, I'm told that later upon arriving in Toronto, the dog left, hitchhiked back, he had somebody, took him over the border, and they never saw him again." Collins added to the joke: "He asked for amnesty."

Then Letterman grew angry and said People for the Ethical Treatment of Animals wanted to shut down his "Stupid Pet Tricks" segments. "Now why haven't they been up Mitt's nose about the dog episode?" he demanded.

Letterman admitted that he certainly can't say he hasn't shown poor judgment in his personal life—having reckless sex at the office with the staff like he's Bill Clinton—but insisted this was different because he wasn't running for president. As for Romney, "This is a guy in the Oval Office, the most powerful position in the world, he's a guy we want with crystal-clear judgment, maybe shaded a little bit one way or the other, but by God we don't want a guy deciding 'Let's put the dog on the roof and drive to Canada.' I mean, I'm right about something there." Collins added, "There was a survey done this week in which I think most Americans said they would rather not have a dog on the roof under any circumstances."

Letterman asked the Seamus-obsessive journalist if this was important. "But am I on to something here about this suggests a greater wrinkle of the fabric than just something stupid he did on vacation?" Of course, she replied. "I think pet transport is not a major issue probably in the campaign. But there is something about it, it's sort of like Imelda Marcos and the 2,700 shoes, it just kind of tweaks some feeling people have about Mitt Romney right now, that does make them kind of, you know, 'What was he thinking?'"

Letterman shot back: "Well, yeah, tweaked, but I'd like to see the guy arrested." [21]

In April, Jim Treacher of the *Daily Caller* pulled out a story from Obama's memoir, *Dreams from My Father*, which told of his first months in Indonesia with new stepfather Lolo Soetoro. "With Lolo, I learned how to eat small green chili peppers raw with dinner (plenty of rice), and, away from the dinner table, I was introduced to dog meat (tough), snake meat (tougher), and roasted grasshopper (crunchy)." [22]

Romney misplaces dogs. Obama eats them. How can the former be news—big news—and the latter not be any news at all? To this argument, Collins lamely replied that "eating dog meat when you are a child in Indonesia is not the same thing as driving to Canada with the family Irish setter strapped to the roof of the car when you are 36." [23] That's true. In one case, the dog is dead. Or as Treacher put it, "Say what you want about Romney, but at least he only put a dog on the roof of his car, not the roof of his mouth."

Romney Versus the "Complicit News Media"

The New York Times didn't just crusade for Obama on the editorial page. Two days after Collins appeared with Letterman, in the midst of 8.2 percent unemployment and four-dollar-a-gallon gas prices, the *Times* printed a front-page story headlined "Obama Seizes Chance to Score As an Everyman." The paper stooped to giving Obama and Axelrod credit for exploiting the *Times* along with the rest of the "news" media.

Political reporter Mark Leibovich proclaimed how "Mr. Obama's team has proven effective in exploiting each gaffe" Romney made. He reported that Axelrod's Seamus-mocking Twitter post came a few days after the president's reelection campaign created a "Pet Lovers for Obama" group on Facebook. Leibovich was also strangely impressed that Axelrod mocked Romney's clumsy claim that "the trees are the right height" in Michigan (Axelrod's tweet: "So Mitt wins Guam, where the Sea Hibiscus are just the right height!").[24]

Leibovich even slavishly paid tribute to Axelrod on Twitter: "@davidaxelrod you ate your tweeties today, Axe. Impressed."

The story grew weird as Leibovich quoted "Romney loyalist" Mike Murphy complaining about pro-Obama bias: "How hard is it to cash a lottery ticket?" Leibovich wrote that Murphy "added that Mr. Obama had benefited from a complicit news media that loves to point out Mr. Romney's perceived screw-ups. This in turn makes the Romney campaign—and candidate—overly self-conscious, prompting more gaffes." Murphy said, "I think Governor Romney knows that he's now trying to feed a dog that's trained to bite him." The *Times* surely appreciated another chance to push Romney as hostile to dogs.

Leibovich's story and pictures all sold Obama as a man of the people, touting the president's NCAA basketball tourney talk and his hot-dog chomping at a game alongside British prime minister David

Cameron: "It is the latest iteration of the Obama-Just-Folks offensive, and one that coincides—not by accident—with some particularly clumsy efforts by the Republican front-runner, Mitt Romney, to shed the stereotypical airs of a super-rich guy." [25]

Inside, there were large photos of Obama at the basketball game with the prime minister. Only in media-elite circles is it considered a "just-folks offensive" to fly Air Force One to Kentucky with the British prime minister for a photo op at a basketball game. Obama loves basketball! Who knew?

We were told about Obama boasting he knew about Jeremy Lin of the New York Knicks before the rest of the sports world did. Leibovich forwarded Axelrod making fun of Romney's decision to avoid making NCAA picks. "They asked Mitt if he was filling out his brackets," Axelrod had tweeted, "and he said, 'No I have my accountants to do that.'" They also thoughtfully included a photo of Obama crouching down for a face-to-face meeting with his dog Bo.

The *Times* even made hay with Romney's Mormon devotion to alcohol abstinence. "While office seekers always strain to be the proverbial 'candidate you'd rather have a beer with'—and such contests will never favor a teetotaling Mormon—the president has been laying it on as thick as the Guinness he sipped at a Washington bar on St. Patrick's Day."

Then they turned to the wives: "Michelle Obama went on the *Late Show with David Letterman* on Monday and reminded everyone she went shopping at Target last year (Mr. Letterman helpfully flashed a photo of the outing). It goes without saying that Target is not the kind of store one might envision, say, Ann Romney pulling up to in one of the Cadillacs that her husband says she drives. Or that the Obamas have been playing up their folksiness at a time when Mr. Romney has proven rather butterfingered with his common touch."

The *Times* failed to note that neither the Associated Press nor the White House would comment on how exactly it came to pass that

AP photographer Charles Dharapak was the only news photographer present at the Target store just south of the Pentagon in Alexandria, Virginia, to capture Mrs. Obama's strange shopping excursion.

"All I can say is that it was the result of good source work on his part," AP spokesman Paul Colford said, declining to elaborate on the sources or the work involved. This was a brush-off, not an answer.

Washington Post media reporter Paul Farhi explained what the *Times* ignored—that conservative media had been "sniping" at Mrs. Obama "when she appeared at a fundraiser in New York wearing $40,000 worth of borrowed diamond jewelry," so the Target run looked like a political stunt, and one way to make it look less political was to get the AP involved. If the White House itself issued a photograph of the First Lady at Target, the media would be reluctant to spread it around. But if it emerged from the nation's preeminent wire service, then it would be "news." Farhi implied this stunt also required the corporate cooperation of Target, which usually refuses any attempt at news photographs inside its stores.[26]

NBC best demonstrated its servility in one of its regular Michelle-boosting *Today* segments. A soundbite was featured of *Post* gossip columnist Amy Argetsinger touting the "wow factor" of the First Lady going to the discount department store. Later, NBC's Kelly O'Donnell declared: "Doing ordinary things in tough economic times can be good for a public image." A soundbite followed from left-wing *Huffington Post* politics editor Howard Fineman: "It's great PR for them, because they can say, 'Look, on this trip and others, we know what's going on outside the gates of the White House.'"[27]

It's great PR because the "news" media so shamelessly bought into it. Journalists favored Obama so shamelessly that his transparent manipulation *of* them was praised *by* them as proof of his political skill.

Ann and the Horse

Mitt Romney's wife, Ann, was the kind of aspiring First Lady that liberal journalists cannot fathom: the stay-at-home mom. Feminists say they believe in women making choices, but cannot understand why they would ever make the choice to stay home. Unless—aha!— they are the greedy rich. Now, Michelle Obama could wear $42,000 in diamond bracelets or $500 sneakers from hip fashion designers and draw a pass. It didn't hurt John Kerry to have a wife as wealthy as Teresa Heinz Kerry in 2004. They were liberals and therefore automatic heroines with a right to their wealth, and media swoons were mandatory. Ann Romney, like Cindy McCain in 2008, would be mocked for her money.

Fox News analyst Juan Williams displayed this contempt after Mrs. Romney spoke at the Republican convention: She "looked to me like a corporate wife. . . . The stories she told about struggles—ah, it's hard for me to believe. I mean, she's a very rich woman. And I know that, and America knows that." [28]

Hollywood displayed this contempt, too. As Comedy Central roasted the "legendary" pig Roseanne Barr in August, actress Katey Sagal joked: "Roseanne, I feel honored that you and I broke new ground as TV moms who didn't cook, didn't clean, and didn't make any money. In the '90s that made you a bad mom, but today it makes you Mitt Romney's wife." [29] Neither woman was in a lower tax bracket than Ann Romney.

This hostility came through loud and clear when the media took exception to Mrs. Romney's affection for horses and her involvement in the Olympic equestrian competition known as dressage. This is clearly an enthusiasm for people of wealth, in political terms the very opposite of a populist chomping on pork rinds at the rodeo. Wealthy liberal anchormen and comedians and newspaper editors socked it to the Romneys without any reservation.

Leading the horse-whipping was *The New York Times,* which published a 2,300-word front-page Sunday story on May 26 by Trip Gabriel that reminded everyone that the Romneys are really, really rich. The headline: "In Rarefied Sport, a View of the Romneys' World." The Republican nominee's wife was involved in dressage, "in which horses costing up to seven figures execute pirouettes and other dancelike moves for riders wearing tails and top hats." [30]

Just as with Gail Collins and David Letterman, liberal comedy and journalism worked in tandem. Trip Gabriel whacked Romney by quoting the fake-conservative comedian Stephen Colbert, who "ribbed the sport's fussy, elitist image." In a June 17 story, he quoted Colbert's attack: "The image of Romney as a privileged princeling ends today, because now Mitt is just your average blue-collar fan of dressage."

Gabriel warned, "As millions tune in to the Olympics in prime time this summer, just before Mr. Romney will be reintroducing himself to the nation at the Republican convention, viewers are likely to see 'up close and personal' segments on NBC about the Romneys and dressage, a sport of six-figure horses and $1,000 saddles. The Romneys declared a loss of $77,000 on their 2010 tax returns for the share in the care and feeding of Rafalca."

Gabriel wrote the Romneys didn't really want to talk about this because they "may also have been wary of the kind of fallout that came after Mr. Romney's mention of the 'couple of Cadillacs' his wife owned and the disclosure of plans for a car elevator in the family's $9 million beach house in California, which prompted criticism that Mr. Romney was out of touch with average Americans." He concluded by painting Mrs. Romney as "she mingled casually outside and in the V.I.P. tent, where the dress code included white pants for men and women, with various breeds of small dogs as popular accessories."[31]

This Thurston Howell III routine came from the family newspaper handed down to Arthur "Pinch" Sulzberger Jr., and from a reporter with the first name of "Trip." As a reader might suspect, Gabriel was actually born with the name Bertram Gabriel III, in 1955, and attended Phillips Academy in Andover, Massachusetts, and Middlebury College in Vermont, where he earned a bachelor's degree in philosophy. His father, Bertram Gabriel Jr., was a real estate developer in Santa Fe, and before that was president of Gabriel Brothers Inc., a New York toy company.[32] Before covering politics for the *Times,* Gabriel was an editor for what *The New Republic* dismissed as the paper's "luxury porn" sections, the ones dedicated to the tastes of conspicuous consumers whose idea of a cheap timepiece is an $890 watch from Prada.[33]

It's nice to know that *The New York Times* is looking out for the little guy.

"Imagine the Neighbor from Hell"

The *Times* stooped low enough to survey Romney's neighbors at his new vacation home in suburban San Diego. Political reporter Michael Barbaro rounded up the liberals in a splashy Home section feature titled "The Candidate Next Door." The accompanying text box established the theme: "On a cul-de-sac in La Jolla, residents are not happy about their new neighbor's renovation plans—or his entourage."

Barbaro began: "On Dunemere Drive, it seems as if just about everyone has a gripe against the owners of No. 311. . . . Bellyaching over the arrival of an irritating new neighbor is a suburban cliché, as elemental to the life on America's Wisteria Lanes as fastidiously edged lawns and Sunday afternoon barbecues." But this time, it was Romney, whose presence was "deeply polarizing."

Romney was crass enough to want to expand his home to fit more children and grandchildren, and "many of the residents of this exclusive tract in La Jolla say they are rankled by what they see from their decks and patios as the Romneys' blindness to their impact on the neighborhood. And personal politics is fueling their frustration as much as anything else, several days of interviews with about a dozen residents suggest." [34]

When liberals are unhappy, their disgruntled partisanship only makes them more newsworthy. "It turns out that Mr. Romney—who has likened President Obama's policies to socialism, called for cutting back on federal funding to PBS and wants to outlaw same-sex marriage—has moved into a neighborhood that evokes *Modern Family* far more than *All in the Family*. (There are six gay households within a three-block radius of his house, neighbors said.)"

The stars of the story (with two photos, one on the front page of the section, and one inside) were Randy Clark and Tom Maddox, who wanted to organize an Obama fundraiser in the neighborhood just to stick it to the new neighbor. The inside caption was a doozy: "CONCERNED: Randy Clark, right and Tom Maddox are among those who say they want to protect the tight-knit neighborhood." From Republicans, apparently.

They weren't alone. James Geiger was half of another gay couple. Barbaro added, "Chatting with Mr. Maddox and Mr. Clark a few weekends ago, Mr. Geiger playfully proposed hanging a gay-pride flag from the Italian stone pine tree in his yard 'so that Romney's motorcade has to drive under it.'"

There were more Democrat neighbors to interview. Mark Quint hated the "McMansions" that were being built, like Romney's. "The only thing he wants small is government and taxes," Mr. Quint said. "He likes big houses, big families and big religion."

Barbaro added, "For partisan candor it was hard to top Karen Webber, who lives several blocks away and dislikes the heightened security measures. 'If this were Obama,' she said, standing near bright orange barriers restricting access to Dunemere, 'I'd probably be fine with it.'"

This story suggests a good slogan for *The New York Times*: All the "partisan candor" that's fit to print.

Anti–"big religion" Quint helped spread the story that the intolerant Romneys—think "uptight Mormons"—discouraged pot smoking on the beach. "A young man in town recalled that Mr. Romney confronted him as he smoked marijuana and drank on the beach last summer, demanding that he stop."

MSNBC's Lawrence O'Donnell lunged at this story hours later and interviewed Maddox and Clark. "Imagine the neighbor from Hell," he unsubtly began. Both neighbors touted the "freedom to marry" whoever you want. "We look at our family [as] no different than he and Ann," Tom Maddox declared. O'Donnell wanted to get back to trashing Romney, bringing up the *Times* claim that Romney admonished pot smokers on the beach: "It looks like he's a candidate for Neighborhood Watch there. Are the neighbors talking about this Romney as Local Cop stuff?" Clark admitted, "Well, we do joke about that."[35]

When the primary season ended, *Washington Post* political writer Chris Cillizza suggested Romney's general-election strategy should start with getting a "positive first introduction" to voters through the liberal media because "only the national media can provide that megaphone and serve as a sort of validator for him."[36]

How hard did he laugh after he wrote that?

CHAPTER 6

The War on the Religious Right

Outdated haters don't deserve to be heard.

In every electoral cycle since 1980, when the Reaganites demonstrated their hold on the Republican Party by expunging from the party platform's support for the feminist Equal Rights Amendment to the Constitution, coloring the Republicans as extremists on the "social issues" has been a favorite media dirty trick.

Anyone following the tone of the news media at home might be puzzled at this treatment of the ideological spectrum. The conservative position is automatically "far right," and the liberal position is always moderate. Conservatives are out of the mainstream, extremists usually. Liberals are the essence of common sense. This constantly tells the audience that they must aspire to be a good liberal.

Opposing abortion for any reason is a fanatical extreme. Supporting abortion for any reason is somehow firmly in the mainstream. Opposing the clamor for "gay marriage" and other items on the LGBT agenda isn't just extreme and outdated, but carries the flavor of "hate speech." Favoring everything on that agenda makes you the

Wave of the Future. Opposing untrammeled immigration or asking when the "affirmative discrimination" of ongoing racial quotas is no longer needed is extreme, and racist to boot. Favoring them is the only way to embrace the dreams of the American people.

To follow the Obama campaign narrative, Romney and the Republicans weren't just losing an appeal to women. They were conducting a "War on Women." They weren't just having trouble attracting minorities in competing with the first black president. They were badly disguised crypto-racists.

Obama strategist David Axelrod felt that women and minorities were the key to the president's reelection. In his post-election remarks at the University of Chicago, he explained, "Our country's becoming more diverse. That every election, that diversity becomes more prominent, more Latino voters represented, African-American voters. Women voters would vote in larger numbers than men, and often in a different way.

"We mapped out a plan, a strategy, to make the case strongly to those constituencies that while Governor Romney was separating himself in many ways from those constituencies. We worked very hard to develop and burnish our support there, which was strong to start with."

Romney was "separating himself" from women and minority voters? That was coded language for shoring up his conservative pro-life base by trying to make everyone forget his pro-abortion stance when he ran statewide in Massachusetts. "Mitt Romney made a series of Faustian bargains" to get the nomination, Axelrod said, as if the Democrats had no corresponding liberal base to please. The Republican "gravitational pull was against immigration reform, was against choice [abortion], gay marriage"; they "were running against the demographic and social trend."[1]

This was the political agenda of a well-oiled and radicalized political machine. It was and continues to be the worldview of our national "news" media. It is impossible to locate where leftist political activism ends and journalism begins. It is one and the same.

The results of the 2012 election caused a wave of liberal triumphalism about how the growing diversity of America's population would spell doom for the White Male Republican Party. The favorite sport of liberal journalists might be Pin the Tail of Racism, Sexism, and Homophobia on the Elephant.

For women voters, in the Axelrod narrative, the 2010 wave election, both in the House and in the states, ushered in social conservatives who would push back against the abortion lobby, especially for government support for Planned Parenthood, by far the nation's largest corporate provider of abortions.

For the press it was no different. The media's feminist mind-meld with Planned Parenthood was demonstrated, for example, by the abortion conglomerate's 2011 "Maggie Awards for Media Excellence," honoring the most pro-abortion reporters. The ceremony was hosted by Liane Hansen, an anchor for twenty-two years for NPR's *Weekend Edition Sunday.*

Hansen proclaimed her fervor toward abortion: "As a reporter, I am committed to journalistic excellence, and I am also deeply invested in the protection of women's reproductive health care. I am delighted to be able to honor my colleagues who share both commitments. Through their intelligent investigative work, they have educated the American public and lawmakers alike on these important issues." [2]

She wasn't the only journalist "deeply invested" in abortion. A House investigation into Planned Parenthood business improprieties spurred the Susan G. Komen Foundation to announce on February 1, 2012, that it would no longer be donating to the abortion giant. The outrage boiled over as ABC, CBS, and NBC rushed to play defense. Over the course of about sixty hours, the Big Three emphasized the controversy with thirteen morning and evening news stories on how "women's groups" spurred "outrage and disappointment engulfing the Internet." The soundbite count was loaded: 76 percent of the quotes came from supporters of Planned Parenthood. Only eleven clips or statements came from Komen representatives or their new (very temporary) pro-life allies.[3]

On ABC's *World News* on February 2, correspondent Claire Shipman concluded that the apparent outrage at the breast cancer charity "shows the passion in this country among women on the issue of women's health care, access to services. I think we're going to hear a lot more of that over this campaign year."

Shipman surely knew about what to expect in the coming campaign talking points. Her husband is White House press secretary Jay Carney.

Within days, Komen snapped like a toothpick, reinstalling its Planned Parenthood donations and accepting the resignation of its pro-life vice president, Karen Handel, who was blamed for this "mistake." After the abortion giant crushed Komen on the PR front, MSNBC host Lawrence O'Donnell saluted Planned Parenthood boss Cecile Richards in a tone of deep reverence. "You now have my nomination for America's ambassador to the United Nations," he oozed to her. "Your artful diplomacy and how you have handled yourself in this relationship with your former partner who is now again your partner, the Komen foundation, has been something to behold."[4]

This was classic liberal back-scratching. O'Donnell was one of the "deeply invested" liberal hacks whom NPR's Liane Hansen honored with a "Maggie Award" in the summer of 2011 for his coverage of government attacks on Planned Parenthood. *You are wonderful. No, you are wonderful.*

Obamacare Versus Catholic Religious Freedom? Yawn

The code words were "access" to "health care." Many medical providers shrink from the idea that elective abortions for convenience, or even to eliminate children with disabilities like Down syndrome, could be defined under the Hippocratic oath as "health care." Abortionists don't "cure" women of a fatal disease. They stop them from being "punished with a baby," as Barack Obama so aptly defined it for the left.

"Access" to abortion is one issue. Federal subsidies—taxpayers' funds—to pay for it were something else entirely. Federal funding of abortion was banned by the Hyde Amendment in 1976. But liberals agitating for taxpayer-subsidized abortions have blurred the distinction between access and funding, purposely. In 2012, liberals brought the same confusion to contraceptives. Absolutely no one in this "sex-positive" America of the twenty-first century has proposed a ban on contraceptives. But liberals wanted someone else other than the sex partners to pay for the "protection," whether it was the government or private insurers. To oppose this was to oppose "access" to birth control. That was their game.

Senator Kirsten Gillibrand (D-NY) exemplified the liberal blur that suffused the media narrative, pretending that this new feminist offensive was some kind of lurch backward in time: "I'm dumbfounded that in the year 2012, we still are fighting about birth control."[5]

The Obama administration announced on January 20 that it was giving religious institutions one year to comply with a mandate for insurance coverage of sterilization, abortion-inducing drugs, and contraception in their health plans without a copay. "The government should not force Americans to act as if pregnancy is a disease to be prevented at all costs," insisted then-archbishop (now cardinal)

Timothy Dolan of New York, head of the U.S. Council of Catholic Bishops. "Historically, this represents a challenge and a compromise of our religious liberty."[6]

The same networks that were outraged and scandalized by Komen's temporary cutoff of Planned Parenthood now couldn't find any newsworthy angle.

No member of Congress had voted for this policy—in fact, pro-life Democrats like Representative Bart Stupak of Michigan voted for Obamacare only after they were assured by the White House there would be no taxpayer funding of abortion as written into the Hyde Amendment in 1976. Amazingly, the major media found nothing newsworthy, never mind historic about this. ABC, CBS, CNN, and NBC all ignored it when the story broke. NPR covered it—ready for this?—with a positive tone. The headline on their website: "Administration Stands Firm on Birth Control Coverage."[7]

CBS waited ten days to *mention* it on *This Morning* and provided no subsequent coverage. CNN briefly mentioned the rule when it was announced on January 20, then didn't bother to mention it again for ten days. ABC and NBC waited sixteen days to cover the anti-Catholic ruling, finally citing the new rule on *This Week* and *Meet the Press* on February 5. Only conservative outcry for some media fairness after their Komen feeding frenzy forced the subject to the surface.

After Komen knuckled under to fierce media pressure, the networks mustered a few stories on how the mandate was causing Obama some political heartburn, even including liberal Catholics like Mark Shields panning the president's mandate. Only CBS offered Cardinal Dolan (or any Catholic clergyman or spokesman) an interview to make an argument for the Catholic Church position.[8]

But when the White House announced a "compromise"—never agreed to by the Catholic Church—on February 10, the networks fell back in line. CBS anchor Scott Pelley declared Obama's decision was "one part Solomon, one part semantics." ABC assured viewers that "both the Catholic Health Association and abortion rights groups approved" of the new rules—without noting the CHA was a liberal group not in line with the Catholic Church on abortion that supported Obamacare and wanted to stay on Obama's good side. When the Catholic bishops that night declared the "compromise" was unacceptable, ABC and CBS at least briefly noticed the change. NBC, under bright-eyed Obama fan Brian Williams, never did.

Intolerance when practiced by liberals isn't "news." Across the country, Democrats were pushing Catholic social workers out of helping government social services. In Massachusetts, Illinois, and the District of Columbia, Democrats have insisted on forcing Catholic Charities to quit its longtime assistance in providing adoption and foster-care services because they refused to place children with homosexual couples. The Conference of Catholic Bishops lost a federal contract to aid survivors of sex trafficking because Obama's bureaucrats at the Department of Health and Human Services (HHS) objected that contraceptive and abortion referrals would not be provided.[9]

Do you recall any news coverage of this assault on religious liberty? The colluding media never wanted to concede that Obama was hostile to Catholics. Far better to print the Catholic Church in the kind of negative light that would make opposition a positive exercise. So journalists routinely implied the bishops were sexless old fuddy-duddies who didn't really know their flock or represent their cultural views. The priests only have some of these people's attention for an hour on Sunday, and then Catholics can safely return to the twenty-first century, while the priests return to their pedophiliac ways.

The attacks have been vicious, and effective in demonizing the Catholic Church. But they have not succeeded in squashing opposition to this administration's assault on religious liberty.

Reaffirming the fact that the president's statement was more a PR stunt than an actual compromise, Nebraska and six other states filed suit on February 23, saying that the HHS regulations violated the First Amendment and were an "interference with religious liberty." Incredibly, the networks again ignored this action.

On May 21, forty-three Catholic dioceses and organizations sued the Obama administration over its very narrow idea of how a "religious institution" can be defined under the Obamacare law. This registers as the largest legal action in American history in defense of religious liberty, and against a sitting president. As a news story, it doesn't get more major than this. It was truly jaw-dropping that ABC and NBC completely ignored this action on their evening newscasts, while CBS devoted just nineteen seconds that night to this historic event.[10]

Which isn't to say that the media were uninterested in the Catholic Church. On May 23, *CBS Evening News* anchor Scott Pelley began his newscast by going back to the story of clerical sexual abuse: "Tonight, the Monsignor takes the stand. The highest ranking Catholic Church official ever charged in the child abuse scandal blames a higher power, the former cardinal of Philadelphia."[11]

This is how the media wanted to define the church hierarchy: archaic, tone-deaf, and corrupt.

Then, on May 25, the networks all jumped on a story that the pope's butler was hiding confidential Vatican documents at his house. They offered thirteen stories in five days proclaiming "another black eye for the Vatican" and alleged "corruption at some of the highest levels."

All three networks used highly charged language to portray the church as some sort of criminal enterprise.

NBC's Jim Maceda was happy to wonder out loud about whether "the man closest to the pope may have lifted another veil on the secretive and perhaps illegal activity inside the Vatican itself."[12] The networks had no suspicion that the Obama people had done anything "secretive and perhaps illegal" in rewriting Obamacare. By their measurement, one can conclude that Obama is less ethically suspicious than the pope.

All Women Are Flukes

Barack Obama was portrayed as the knight in shining armor for the damsel in distress named Sandra Fluke. Democrats intended her to be their star witness at a House Oversight and Government Reform Committee hearing on February 16. They wanted her on the first panel of a religious-liberty hearing along with a Catholic bishop, a Jewish rabbi, the president of the Lutheran Church–Missouri Synod, and an evangelical professor.[13]

Representative Darrell Issa explained that he accepted Democrats' late application for Barry Lynn, head of the leftist Americans United for Separation of Church and State, but dismissed Fluke as an expert. She was merely a student at Georgetown Law School. It didn't matter. The Democrats wanted this painted as a Clueless White Guy panel and knew the media would swallow it whole. Representative Carolyn Maloney (D-NY) asked: "Where were the women?"[14] That question echoed throughout the media—without an obvious rebuttal. Two women spoke on the committee's second panel of the day, but the media found that an inconvenient truth.

With the liberal spin established, a week later, the Democratic Steering Committee invited Fluke to be the star witness at a staged press event. If the Republicans had tried something this partisan— and fabricated—the networks would not have sent a camera, not in a thousand years. But the Democrats could always manufacture "news" when the partisan event favored their allies in the press.

Fluke was celebrated by the liberal media as a perfect representative of All Women: a law school student protesting that the oppressive, intolerant Catholic administrators of Georgetown University must look beyond their ancient and patriarchal views and fund contraceptives for their employees through their insurance plan, as Obamacare intended.

The suggestions was that this poor student spending thousands of dollars annually on her schooling somehow couldn't muster the fifteen or twenty dollars at CVS for her monthly birth control, and someone else should come to the rescue, except somehow the Catholic Church was preventing it. The villain in this tale was Rush Limbaugh, who reacted to Fluke's demand for subsidized contraception by laughing at this nonsense, but then mocked her as a "slut" and a "prostitute." Limbaugh admitted later this was an inappropriate use of words and apologized. This naturally did nothing to assuage a furious press that said absolutely nothing when these words were wielded against conservative women, like when Bill Maher called Sarah Palin a "dumb twat,"[15] or MSNBC's Ed Schultz called Laura Ingraham a "talk slut."[16]

They all failed to report—or even consider—that while many taxpayers would oppose subsidizing birth-control pills on religious grounds, many others would also find that subsidizing contraceptives for people engaging in casual sex makes as much sense as subsidizing their X-rated movies or negligees.

Sensing the opportunity created by the press, President Obama called to offer public support to Fluke, which became another celebrated media event. Fluke went on Andrea Mitchell's afternoon show on MSNBC to thank the president: "He encouraged me and supported me and thanked me for speaking out about the concerns of American women, and what was really personal for me was that he said to tell my parents that they should be proud."[17] The networks replayed that and added that Democrats were gleefully exploiting their outrage in fundraising appeals. *Thank you, Sandra, Thank you, Mr. President!* [All caught on tape, lovingly.]

Conservative Georgetown women were shut out. Andrea Morabito wrote, "Funny how the same side that cries 'Get your rosaries off my ovaries' is the same side saying, 'on second thought . . . please pay for me to have all the sex I want!' The people who espouse 'pro-choice values' are the same people who say religious institutions have no right to choose.

"It costs over $23,000 for a year at Georgetown Law. Sandra, are you telling us that you can afford that but cannot afford your own contraception?"[18]

CNSNews.com reported that despite Fluke's claim that pills cost $3,000 a year, "a Target store only three miles from the law school currently sells a month's supply of birth control pills for only $9 to people who do not have insurance plans covering contraceptives." Even Planned Parenthood's website tells women, "Birth control pills may be purchased with a prescription at a drugstore or clinic. They cost about $15–$50 a month."[19]

Fluke was never portrayed as a radical. Indeed, that's why she was a victim: she was just your normal, everyday student holding normal views. Really? Conservative blogger Stephen Gutowski found that Sandra Fluke advocated that insurance policies shouldn't pay just for contraceptives, but also for sex change operations as well. In a journal article, she complained: "A prime example of direct discrimination is denying insurance coverage for medical needs of transgender persons physically transitioning to the other gender. . . . Transgender persons wishing to undergo the gender reassignment process frequently face heterosexist employer health insurance policies that label the surgery as cosmetic or medically unnecessary and therefore uncovered."[20] Liberal media coverage? Zero.

The Democrats even brought Fluke to their convention in Charlotte, North Carolina, where as a pure partisan hack, she should have lost any claim on victimhood. Sounding like Ted Kennedy's scabrous "Robert Bork's America" speech in 1987, Fluke claimed that in Mitt

Romney and Paul Ryan's America, "It would be an America in which you have a new vice president who co-sponsored a bill that would allow pregnant women to die preventable deaths in our emergency rooms."[21]

As usual, Fluke and her feminist allies were taking a rhetorical flamethrower to the simple notion that taxpayers shouldn't have to fund abortions, a position Ryan supported in the Protect Life Act of 2011. Do you recall a single news report pointing that out?

Keep Your Probe out of My Virginia

The so-called War on Women reared its ugly head again when the state of Virginia considered requiring women to see an ultrasound image of their unborn child before an abortion. For early pregnancies, this would require a transvaginal probe, not the traditional abdominal ultrasound. Faced with a storm of liberal media outrage, Virginia governor Bob McDonnell said he would support only an abdominal ultrasound.

The leftist assault compared a vaginal ultrasound to rape, and media outlets obediently repeated that. On February 21, *New York Times* editorial page editor Andrew Rosenthal argued that "since most abortions take place in the first 12 weeks of pregnancy, most women will be forced to submit to trans-vaginal ultrasounds, a coerced penetration that in other circumstances would constitute rape under Virginia state law."[22]

Unsurprisingly, the women on ABC's *The View* came unglued on February 16. Whoopi Goldberg complained, "Women will be required to undergo sonograms, ultrasound when they are about to have an abortion and the other one is that if a heartbeat isn't detected, then they will get a trans-vaginal ultrasound which is basically going into the vagina and very intrusive." To ABC's daytime hosts, a transvaginal sonogram before an abortion is intrusive . . . but a transvaginal abortion is not.

Joy Behar then screeched: "It's like, what are we?! What is this, the Taliban now?! What are we, in Afghanistan?! Where are we exactly in this country?" When the panel's Republican-leaning Elisabeth Hasselbeck said the government should never intrude on a woman's body, Goldberg insisted there is no Republican or Democrat stance on this bill, only the "human stance."[23]

The people who wanted a woman *not* to see her unborn baby before killing it were somehow advocating the "human stance."

On MSNBC on February 23, anchor Luke Russert—whose Catholic father, Tim Russert, used to regale audiences about his meetings with and great reverence for Pope John Paul II—allowed pro-lifers to be trashed as rapists. Even the traditional abdominal ultrasound was somehow still a "sex crime" in the war-on-women frenzy at MSNBC. Russert asked liberal Virginia delegate Charniele Herring: "You said the original procedure was akin to rape. Uh, where is this new procedure, do you feel? Is the new procedure still, do you feel, a sex crime, in the sense that it's so invasive?"

Then he asked another War on Women softball. "Was this policy really done backdoors by mainly all males on the Republican side? That seems to be what some reports out of Virginia suggest." Herring replied, "I believe it was. I don't know if a woman was at the table."[24]

In prime time on February 24, MSNBC host Rachel Maddow mocked Governor McDonnell in an interview with Karen Finney: "I know as the Democrats' communications director you'd never call anybody Gov. Vaginal Probe." Finney replied, "I never would, honestly Rachel, I never would have thought that we would be in a position to actually call someone Gov. Vaginal Pro—, Transvaginal Probe. I mean, did you ever think you would be having this conversation on your show?" Maddow replied, "Never. Never in my life. Never, not just in my show, never in my world!"[25]

So at MSNBC, if you stand in the way of government-funded abortions, you hate women. Like Fluke, Finney cast Republicans as literal lady-killers: "I think they're also not paying attention to the fact that women have very much been awakened over the last several months. Again, look at these Republican legislatures and these sort of anti-women bills, you know, having to prove that you were raped in order to, you know, use Medicare, Medicaid, to have an abortion. I mean, some of the, you know, redefining rape, letting women die."

What Shooting at the Family Research Council?

The liberal media were so unsympathetic to social conservatives in 2012 that they didn't even find it newsworthy when they were shot. Floyd Corkins, a volunteer in the first half of 2012 at the D.C. Center for the LGBT Community, marched into the Family Research Center on August 15 with a 9mm SIG Sauer pistol, denounced FRC's policy positions, and shot a security guard in the arm before being subdued. In his bag, police found fifty rounds of ammunition and fifteen sandwiches from the Chick-fil-A restaurant, which had been treated as notorious by secular leftists for donating to "anti-gay" Christian groups like the FRC and the Fellowship for Christian Athletes.[26]

A "hate crime" to be covered, anyone? Not when the crime was launched against perhaps the preeminent pro-family organization in America. ABC led *World News* with the story on the FRC shooting and saluted the heroic security guard for saving the FRC from a mass shooting in their offices. They were the exception.

CBS gave the story twenty seconds. NBC spent seventeen seconds.[27]

As usual, what helped Obama was news, and what made Obama's side look bad was deemphasized. On both CBS and NBC, the tiny FRC brief was followed by a full story promoting President Obama's new deferral program for illegal alien "Dream Act" students. NBC gave that two minutes, CBS two minutes and fifty seconds.

The newspapers had the story, but some found it equally boring. *USA Today* gave it ninety-eight words on page 3A, beneath other brief items such as "Dallas Gets Tough on West Nile Virus."

Our taxpayer-funded media were silent. *PBS NewsHour* offered nothing. It did have time to announce, "About four million Bumbo baby seats are being recalled because infants can fall out of them." NPR offered no story on *All Things Considered* that night but did find time to report on cheating at a national Scrabble tournament. NPR also skipped it on the next morning's *Morning Edition*, but covered the riveting story of "inter-tribal cattle violence" in South Sudan.

MSNBC's prime-time lineup, starting with Chris Matthews, said nothing about the shooting at FRC—except for Rachel Maddow, who offered a slightly longer brief than Brian Williams. This is the same network that went over the top and around the bend over the fact that someone at a Tea Party rally was peacefully carrying a weapon. So why couldn't they produce one full story on an actual shooting at a conservative office, with the intent to commit mass murder?

CNN covered it, but within twenty hours of the shooting, CNN morning anchor Zoraida Sambolin was unsympathetic enough to argue with a conservative guest, Brian Brown of the National Organization for Marriage, insisting that the left-wing lobby the Southern Poverty Law Center (SPLC) had somehow accurately categorized the FRC as a "hate group." The CNN anchor read from an old pamphlet and insisted the FRC was guilty of "spewing hate" about gay activists, but Brown replied, "By no means can you say just because of a statement like that this is the same as the KKK or the Aryan Brotherhood. That's totally unacceptable." [28]

On the morning after the shooting, the network pattern continued: ABC offered another full story (adding the LGBT-center volunteer connection). By contrast, NBC offered a tiny anchor-read update.

CBS aired nothing, but did find the time for a story on the fortieth anniversary of the movie *Deliverance*. Burt Reynolds in make-believe is somehow more newsworthy than a left-winger aiming to massacre an office of conservative Christians.

Imagine this situation in reverse: a volunteer for the Family Research Council marching into some gay group's headquarters with a gun, and after shouting his opposition to the homosexual agenda, opening fire and wounding a guard before being subdued. Never mind the evening news. This would be "Breaking News!" and for days there would be endless coverage of ongoing conservative hatred and violence.

Instead, this became grounds for liberal humor. On the FX comedy show *Totally Biased with W. Kamau Bell*, the host joked, "Yesterday the Family Research Council, a conservative think tank, was shot up by Floyd Corkins, a liberal protester. Don't worry, nobody was killed. Why? Because it was shot up by a liberal protester. [Laughter] That's not our thing. Our thing is more blogging."

Once the initial shock wore off, new details in the Corkins case still didn't cause one ripple of disturbance in the liberal media. In October, Corkins was indicted on terrorism charges, with no liberal media notice (save a few paragraphs for the locals in *The Washington Post*).

But the story took a deeply disturbing turn on February 6, 2013, when Corkins pled guilty to three charges, including the terrorism charge. Corkins declared in a statement that he "intended to enter the FRC that day to kill as many people as possible and smother Chick-fil-A sandwiches in their faces." How was that not inflammatory enough for news coverage?

Then add this. Corkins explained he used a "hate map" by the SPLC to find his targets, a map showing the locations of groups SPLC designated as "hate groups" that were somehow comparable to the Ku Klux Klan because they were "nationally recognized advocacy groups that openly identify themselves as having socially conservative agendas," especially opposition to gay marriage. It wasn't just the FRC, but also the Traditional Values Coalition and Public Advocate of the United States.

In 2011, the liberal media insisted that Sarah Palin somehow played a role in the shooting of Representative Gabby Giffords by putting a target on her district. But no one would touch the Corkins story and dare to connect the SPLC to the FRC shooting in the very same way they had slammed Palin. CNN, whose anchor protested that the SPLC was right to smear the FRC as a "hate group," only announced beforehand (in a fifty-eight-word news brief) that Corkins would appear in court. There was no report after the outrageous new information that Corkins took the SPLC's map as he planned a killing spree of conservatives.[29]

Unsurprisingly, a Nexis survey found there was no Corkins report on ABC, CBS, NBC, MSNBC, NPR, or PBS. *The New York Times* disposed of it with a 145-word Reuters dispatch on page 17. *USA Today* and the *Los Angeles Times* couldn't find an inch of space for it.

Washington Post reporter Ann Marimow relayed late in her story: "At the time of the shooting, conservative commentators also accused media outlets of giving the shooting less coverage than other gun crimes because the perpetrator was a liberal. Those accusations resurfaced Wednesday."[30] Those weren't accusations. They were the unavoidable facts.

Hate has always been a conservative quality. It could never be located inside Obama's liberal base. They aren't haters, just bloggers.

CHAPTER 7

The Gaffe Patrol

Only Republican misstatements are a media target.

One of the most obvious tricks of the media is how they declare themselves to be entirely objective when deciding which statements by politicians and their campaign aides qualify as "gaffes" and which do not. Gaffes, as everyone knows, can be dangerous, sometimes extremely so, when they can easily be used to cause a candidate to lose an election. *Gaffes* strengthen media caricatures in the public mind, creating character sketches in twenty-five words or less, whether it's Dan Quayle's misspelling of *potato* or Sarah Palin's alleged remark that she could see Russia from her house (something uttered not by Palin, but by her *Saturday Night Live* impersonator, Tina Fey).

The best gaffes are those that entertain, which makes them easy to spread. They are also a handy pretext for the howls of liberal outrage (and laughter) that resound throughout the media echo chamber. The manufacture and promotion of alleged gaffes by conservative candidates is therefore one of the main tricks liberal journalists use to shape and influence public opinion, and ultimately, tilt elections.

The shamelessness of the media's decision-making process was displayed after the 2008 election, when *The New York Times* ran a story on the Obama campaign unironically headlined "Near-Flawless Run Is Credited in Victory." [1] Reporters uniformly thought the Democrat campaign was superbly managed, but check out this sentence below the headline: "And they played it safe when they could, as in the selection of Senator Joseph R. Biden Jr. of Delaware as his running mate."

Biden? As everyone knows, Joe Biden was the Senate's leading gaffe machine, with a long history of embarrassing statements to his credit. In June 2006, he asserted: "You can't go to a 7-Eleven or a Dunkin' Donuts unless you have a slight Indian accent." During the campaign itself, Biden delighted conservative radio hosts by praising Obama as "bright, clean, and articulate." He was a caricature, a massive liability. Then again, Democrats know they can count on their friends in the press to ignore or excuse any embarrassing misstatements by their candidates. They could turn a gaffe machine into something bright, clean, and articulate. All it takes is an airbrush with whitewash.

Liberal journalists have a repetitive tendency to praise their favorite candidates as incredibly skilled campaigners. Ultimately, they are congratulating themselves for keeping the Democratic campaign humming. Exhibit A is Bill Clinton's national career, from Gennifer Flowers forward. Journalists have continuously oohed and aahed that Clinton is a masterful politician, even as they were crushing information about the latest bimbo or intern, or campaign donors from China and Indonesia. Would they really give Bill Clinton a pass with his sexual affairs if he had an *R* on his résumé?

But to read *The New York Times*, you would think the media had nothing to do with Obama looking like a champion and McCain or Romney being shrouded in gloom. For example, in that same 2008 *Times* story, the "paper of record" expressed amazement that John

McCain would bungle so badly in declaring, right as the economic crisis began on September 15, 2008, "the fundamentals of the economy are strong." How could a credible candidate say such a thing? Was he completely clueless? Out of touch? What planet was he living on? The Obama machine quickly turned this supposed howler into a barrage of free advertising, and the colluding media turned it into "news."

What the *Times* story papered over were McCain's contextualizing remarks: "People are frightened by these events. Our economy, I think still, the fundamentals of our economy are strong. But these are very, very difficult times. And I promise you we will never put America in this position again. We will clean up Wall Street. We will reform government. And this is a failure."

But never mind the nuance. Chris Matthews began his *Hardball* broadcast: "Why is John McCain talking like Herbert Hoover? Depression or just depressing?"[2] NBC anchor Brian Williams relayed that "a Democratic politico said to me this week, if the Democrats do their job, they'll make this 'fundamentals of the economy' quote to McCain what 'mission accomplished' was to President Bush."[3]

After the media pounding was done, the *Times* wrote that this episode proved, self-fulfillingly, "the McCain campaign team often seemed to make missteps and lurch from moment to moment in search of a consistent strategy and message, while the disciplined and nimble Obama team marched through a presidential contest of historic intensity learning to exploit opponents' weaknesses and making remarkably few stumbles. The story of Mr. Obama's journey to the pinnacle of American politics is the story of a campaign that was, even in the view of many rivals, almost flawless."

This kind of thing would never happen to Obama. Consider how the press handled his statement in a press conference on June 8, 2012, in the midst of a heated reelection campaign, that "the private sector is doing fine." There was no kinder context. It was a whopper of a gaffe. This came at a time when there was still 8.2 percent unemployment and a falling median household income, housing was still in the tank, and monster deficits looked like a wrecking ball on the national economy. Conservative media had a field day. Rush Limbaugh said Obama couldn't possibly believe that, unless his idea of "doing fine" was building up government programs like food stamps.[4]

In response, the Obama media closed ranks around their candidate. NBC morning anchor Ann Curry played defense with her guest, MSNBC leftist Chris Hayes: "He [Obama] is right in saying that the private sector is doing better than the public sector, is he not? And so that was his point, that this comment was taken out of context."[5]

Felicia Sonmez of *The Washington Post* asked, "Should out-of-context statements be out-of-bounds in campaigns?"[6] *New York Times* reporter Jackie Calmes also felt the need to explain what President Obama meant, and specifically ruled out comparisons to McCain's similar gaffe four years before: "McCain ... spoke in September 2008 as the financial system was already imploding, and his comment underscored his well-known and self-acknowledged unfamiliarity with economic policy." Yet Calmes complained, "for the day at least, the damage was done, as Republicans hijacked the news cycle with their barrage against Mr. Obama's six words in a professorial 29-minute exchange."[7]

So there you have it: When Obama loses his natural media advantage, it's not because he erred or misspoke; it's Republicans "hijacking the news cycle."

Romney Lives Up to "Predatory Capitalist" Stereotype

On January 9, 2012, Mitt Romney told an audience that his health-care plan would allow them to choose and dismiss insurers and health-care providers. "I want individuals to have their own insurance. That means the insurance company will have an incentive to keep you healthy. It also means if you don't like what they do, you can fire them," he said. "I like being able to fire people who provide services to me."

It fit their stereotype. Liberal reporters leaped at the chance to play up the cartoon of Romney as a greed-head venture capitalist. All the networks reported the story, and many of them publicly donned caps as informal campaign advisers. *Washington Post* columnist Dana Milbank had an idea: "one of President Obama's first reelection ads." ABC's David Muir reported "Mitt Romney is getting grilled over his own words in the last 24 hours. At one point telling an audience he understands what it feels like to worry about losing your job. At another rally today, he said he likes being able to fire people." Muir added, "The Obama campaign's senior strategist quickly calling Romney's words a 'rare moment of candor.'"[8] David Axelrod's Twitter account set the narrative: the words "Rare moment of candor" appeared onscreen.

Face the Nation host Bob Schieffer eviscerated Romney on *CBS This Morning.* Apparently the incompetent Romney was "looking for every way he can try to lose and drive down his percentage of victory. . . . I guess the only thing worse you could say, in a time like this, when people are out of work is that Herbert Hoover is my hero or something like that. It just boggles the mind."[9] This is one of those dirty tricks, building a sense of hangman's gloom under the guise of "objective" psychoanalysis and commentary on campaign strategy.

On NPR's *Morning Edition,* reporter Ari Shapiro insisted that putting the statement in context wouldn't help: "Never mind that he was talking about insurance companies. The quote played right into the stereotype of Romney as a predatory capitalist, who made his fortune ruining people's lives."[10] As we'll soon see, NPR's Snidely Whiplash spin here was the polar opposite of the way the taxpayer-subsidized reporters handled gaffes that played into what could be called "the stereotype of Obama as an arrogant socialist elitist, who built his political career on trashing job-creating business executives as predatory capitalists."

But the context was plain: Romney was simply saying if someone fails to provide a satisfactory service, it's nice to have the freedom to fire them, instead of being stuck with a badly performing provider—especially with your health care. Liberals who expect people to put up with government bureaucrats no matter how badly they perform were never going to grant a point on this one.

The same maneuver was repeated on February 1 when Romney said on CNN, "I'm in this race because I care about Americans. I'm not concerned about the very poor. We have a safety net there. If it needs repair, I'll fix it." CNN morning anchor Soledad O'Brien, a very aggressive Obama supporter on-air, used a quote from columnist Kathleen Parker to double-bash Republicans, asserting that Romney couldn't connect with people while the "far less perfect Newt Gingrich can attract support against all reason."

ABC's David Muir used the clip to do a "greatest gaffes" package of recent vintage. "He again said, if the safety net for the poor has holes in it, he would work to repair them. But it comes after a string of moments, critics say, [that] make Romney seem un-relatable. 'Corporations are people, my friend.' Betting Rick Perry '10,000 bucks.'" Add the "I like being able to fire people" rerun.

Muir even added a radio clip of Rush Limbaugh on the air: "He makes himself a target with this stuff. He comes across as the prototypical rich Republican. It's gonna make it harder and harder and harder to go after Obama." Limbaugh was right—making our point, not theirs.

On CBS, Jan Crawford recycled three Romney gaffes: the "very poor," the "10,000 bucks" bet, and the "fire people." On NBC, Peter Alexander noted "[a]ll this dragging Romney off message on a day he intended to enjoy as a victory lap." It's typical for liberals to proclaim Republicans are being dragged off message at the very moment they're doing the dragging. Alexander then added a clip of his MSNBC colleague Chris Matthews: "It is not a good life to be poor. And anybody who thinks so is oblivious."

Alexander saved his greatest-gaffes reminders for the next morning on NBC: "And as for those gaffes it's not the first time for Mitt Romney. Remember that he said corporations are people, or there was the $10,000 bet during the debate, and that's part of the problem. Just one more item that could go onto the president's re-election campaign team's Greatest Hits reel against Romney."

The networks were always eager and willing to put Obama's favorite clips into heavy rotation.

"You Didn't Build That"

On July 14 in Roanoke, Virginia, President Obama told overheated people in the crowd to make way for "paralegals," not paramedics. Then he made a statement that shocked anyone who has built a business, large or small. He arrogantly proclaimed that no one is really responsible for growing their own companies. The credit should go elsewhere, especially to government:

"If you were successful, somebody along the line gave you some help. There was a great teacher somewhere in your life. Somebody helped to create this unbelievable American system that we have that allowed you to thrive. Somebody invested in roads and bridges. If you've got a business, you didn't build that. Somebody else made that happen."

How was this not a gaffe of monstrous proportions? Fox News and conservative talk radio aggressively reported the damaging remark, yet ABC, CBS, and NBC failed to mention it for four days—and then only after Romney made it the centerpiece of a campaign speech.[11]

Romney responded sharply: "The idea to say that Steve Jobs didn't build Apple, that Henry Ford didn't build Ford Motor, that Papa John didn't build Papa John Pizza, that Ray Kroc didn't build McDonald's, that Bill Gates didn't build Microsoft, you go on the list, that Joe and his colleagues didn't build this enterprise, to say something like that is not just foolishness, it is insulting to every entrepreneur, every innovator in America, and it's wrong."[12]

ABC, CBS, and PBS all avoided this eloquent and devastating rejoinder, and NBC ran only a few words of it before interrupting. On the July 18 *Today*, NBC viewers heard, "To say that Steve Jobs didn't build Apple, that Henry Ford didn't build Ford Motor, that Papa John didn't build Papa John Pizza," and then reporter Peter Alexander stopped in mid-sentence like he had a bad case of attention-deficit disorder. He switched to a soundbite of Romney spokesman John Sununu saying Obama needed to "learn how to be an American," followed by an outraged Obama campaign attacking Sununu for attacking the president's patriotism. Romney couldn't be allowed to go on offense for more than ten seconds before being slapped right back into a defensive crouch.

Then consider the print press. *The Washington Post*, *USA Today*, and *Los Angeles Times* couldn't locate Romney's best attack. *The New York Times* must have inspired NBC by running the Romney quote alongside Sununu. Reporters Trip Gabriel and Peter Baker even insisted Team Romney lost the day: "The off-message moments blew a bit of fog over what the Romney campaign had intended to be a coordinated series of sharp attacks on Mr. Obama over free enterprise."[13]

On the July 26 *CBS This Morning*, cohost Charlie Rose was in full damage-control mode, claiming the president was misunderstood.

"But the President was saying, if you look at the full context of that, he was talking about building roads to these businesses, and they didn't build the roads; where the Romney campaign seems to try to indicate that he was saying, they didn't build the businesses." CBS political analyst John Dickerson replied, "Exactly, and what the President was saying, is it takes a village." [14] This is a little like claiming Obama could have never been elected president without the highway system. They'd laugh at that in a liberal newsroom.

But it was NPR that took the prize. On the July 25 *All Things Considered*, they revisited the controversy by offering listeners a whopping seventy-second soundbite of Obama in Roanoke. But first, anchor Audie Cornish turned to NPR White House correspondent Scott Horsley, who spent ninety seconds explaining that the businesses the Romney campaign was using to rebut Obama's remark were all beneficiaries of government largesse. This claim was especially egregious: "There's Applegate Insulation in Michigan. They note on their website that customers may be eligible for tax incentives if they install their product." That, to liberals, is a government grant to business.

This was exactly the attack Democrats at the Center for American Progress were promoting on their blog, Think Progress. Horsley never told his listeners where he received these talking points. [15]

When Obama said, "Look, if you've been successful, you didn't get there on your own," he knew whereof he spoke. Everything he's gained in politics has been granted to him by an adoring news media.

"Mitt the Twit" Gets Heckled (by Media) Abroad

On May 28, President Obama infuriated the leaders of Poland while honoring the late Jan Karski with the Medal of Freedom. He said that Karski had smuggled himself into a "Polish death camp" in order to witness the Holocaust. (It was a German Nazi death camp *located* in Poland.) The Polish government demanded an apology and this stirred in the European papers and on the Agence France-Presse wire. Despite the international incident, ABC, CBS, and NBC aired nothing on the gaffe. Instead, ABC's *Good Morning America* and NBC's *Today* both found "news" in the microscopic scoop that the Romney campaign had misspelled "America" in an iPhone app.[16] Omissions like these helped Obama preserve his reputation as (a) intelligent about history and (b) not a jerk who sticks it to our allies.

Nor was it a story in the fall of 2011 that after endless reports about George Bush's low standing in the Arab world, the Arab American Institute found that Barack Obama, who allegedly was taking the globe by storm, was now viewed even more unfavorably than Bush was at the end of his tenure.

But when Mitt Romney traveled to Europe and Israel in late July, the long knives were out. NBC anchor Brian Williams sat down with him in London on July 25 and they talked about the Summer Olympics there. Noting Romney's role in bringing the Winter Olympics to Salt Lake City in 2002, Williams asked, "And in the short time you've been here in London, do they look ready to your experienced eye?" Romney calmly replied that it was hard to know. "There are a few things that were disconcerting, the stories about the private security firm not having enough people, the supposed strike of the immigration and customs officials, that obviously is not something which is encouraging."

This was the NBC anchor's gentlest question in a hostile interview, and it matched what Williams reported the week before: "Today, the man whose company was hired to provide security at all the Olympic venues admitted his company screwed up." A member of Parliament told NBC it was a "humiliating shambles for the company." The word "fiasco" also came up in reports on ABC and CBS.

But Romney's remarks—a mild-mannered echo of the network's

own reporting—still became an international scandal. On July 27, NBC's Peter Alexander was holding up *The Sun* of London, owned by Rupert Murdoch: "Here is a headline from one London tabloid. It reads 'Mitt the Twit.'"[17] Alexander deemed the comments a "political firestorm" and played a clip of an unidentified British reporter snidely noting, "If he's here to make friends, he has got a funny way of showing it."

Over on CBS, Jan Crawford eagerly held up the same tabloid and asked, "Can you see it? 'Mitt the Twit.' That's not the type of headline you want." Crawford labeled Romney's remarks "a storm in the tea cup [that] started a trans-Atlantic war of words."

On *Good Morning America*, George Stephanopoulos played up Romney's "stumble out of the gate." ABC's David Muir insisted that the "Brits are boiling." CNN reporter Jim Acosta's online piece was headlined "Romney Trip Begins in Shambles." Acosta did a roundup: "He's the 'Party Pooper' in the *Daily Mail*, 'Nowhere Man' in the *Times* of London and 'Mitt the Twit' in *The Sun*."

The Washington Post was especially harsh. "Someone should have told Mitt Romney that they still speak English in England," lectured *Post* political reporter Chris Cillizza as he awarded Romney the "Worst Week in Washington" award that Sunday.[18] "Romney's 'performance' could well be forgotten by the time his European trip concludes with visits to Poland and Israel. But a headline that reads 'Mitt the Twit' (as *The Sun*'s did) probably isn't a good thing for a presidential candidate." Which is precisely why it received so much play in the liberal press.

As Romney's trip continued, so did the negative spin from the evening newscasts. Despite pressing economic and foreign policy problems, both ABC and CBS on July 27 highlighted trivial details such as Romney's motorcade in London getting stuck in traffic—which underlined the candidate's warning about the Olympics.

On July 29, *CBS Evening News* correspondent Jeff Glor piled on:

"After a rough first stop on his seven-day overseas trip, Mitt Romney was hoping Israel would go better than Britain. The day was not error-free," for Romney "had to back off an aide's suggestion he supports an Israeli strike against Iran's nuclear program."

The same abuse erupted in Poland. Romney tried to avoid the press, so they yelled at him . . . about their gaffe story line. The questions could have passed for heckling, like "What about your gaffes?" and "Do you feel that your gaffes have overshadowed your foreign trip?" A Romney aide then admonished reporters to "show some respect" for the "holy site for the Polish people" and cursed at them. CNN reporter Jim Acosta lectured the aide in his report. "[P]eople get tired, people get testy, but you also have to keep your cool at the same time." [19] Reporters can heckle and scream at Romney, but the candidate's team had to "keep cool."

Media Research Center analysts examined all twenty-one ABC, CBS, and NBC evening news stories about Romney's trip to London, Israel, and Poland between July 25 and July 31. Virtually all of these stories (eighteen, or 86 percent) emphasized Romney's "diplomatic blunders," from his "golden gaffe" at the Olympic games to "missteps" that offended the Palestinians.

Over seven days, Romney netted fifty-three minutes' worth of stories from the three networks. In comparison, Obama's 2008 tour through the Middle East and Europe resulted in ninety-two minutes over eight days. In July 2008, Barack Obama's international tour took him to Israel, where, in an attempt to show toughness over Iran, the then-senator incorrectly told reporters that he was a member of the Senate Banking Committee. But no one at the networks noticed any "gaffes" or "missteps" there.

In fact, NBC's Brian Williams could hardly contain himself in Berlin. On the July 24, 2008, *Nightly News*, he trumpeted, "the man from Chicago, Illinois, the first ever African-American running as presumptive nominee of the Democratic Party, brought throngs of people into the center of Berlin, streaming into this city, surging to get close to him, to hear his message."

On the same program, Andrea Mitchell was beside herself, marveling at the large crowds: "It's hard to figure out what the comparison is. What do you compare this with?"

Then–*CBS Evening News* anchor Katie Couric couched the visit in the most favorable terms, hyping, "Barack Obama extends the hand of friendship to Europe." Mark Phillips insisted, "They've been calling this the Obama show in Berlin, his appeal here part exotic politician, part rock star. And a rock-festival-sized crowd of more than 200,000 gathered to see him."

At the end of Romney's tour, Brian Williams summed up the week as concluding "with controversy, some hurt feelings, and some raw tempers." Obama was always a "rock star," and Romney's visit was always "marred by missteps." Conservative columnist Charles Krauthammer blasted the news coverage, calling the trip "a major substantive success" that was wrapped "in a media narrative of surpassing triviality." [20]

No Chains for Joe Biden

Joe Biden can put Dan Quayle to shame in making mindless statements. He is a walking embarrassment to Barack Obama, to the point where there was open speculation about replacing him on the ticket. But the press corps continually covered for him, hailing Biden for his "candor" and "authenticity," which are positive spin for "a ticking talk bomb."

On August 14, 2012, Biden implied to a mostly black audience in Virginia that by pushing deregulation and spending reductions, the Republicans somehow favored reinstituting slavery for blacks: "Look at what they [Republicans] value, and look at their budget. And look what they're proposing. [Romney] said in the first 100 days, he's going to let the big banks write their own rules—unchain Wall Street. They're going to put y'all back in chains."

This was more than a gaffe. It was an insult of the highest order, a crass attempt to fuel the flames of racial animosity against the GOP.

There were only three full stories on ABC, CBS, and NBC, and nine other mentions in passing.[21] *The New York Times* buried the fuss on page A14 in a five-paragraph story under the soporific headline "A Metaphor Draws Notice."[22]

While pundits on MSNBC argued Biden was "almost gaffe-proof" because everyone expected him to bumble, CNN's Soledad O'Brien pushed Representative Emanuel Cleaver (D-MO) to admit the obvious: "You cannot tell me that if in fact we were talking about Mitt Romney saying a line like that . . . that people would not be going crazy and crying about race-baiting and talking about tone and tenor and coded language. I think we would, wouldn't we?"[23] In fact, many reporters were furious and charged racism when Newt Gingrich insisted (accurately enough) that Obama was the "food stamp president."

Biden was so gaffe-prone reporters might be excused for missing some of them. In the same speech, Biden urged the Danville, Virginia, crowd, "With you, we can win North Carolina again!" Only ABC noticed this . . . in one brief mention. Meanwhile the networks all ignored Biden's claim to still be living in the last century: "Folks, where's it written we cannot lead the world in the 20th century in making automobiles?"

On NBC's *Meet the Press*, former GOP speechwriter Peggy Noonan complained, "If it had been a Republican vice presidential candidate who had made those gaffes . . . the subject today of the panel would be: 'How stupid is this person, can this person possibly govern?'"

But reporters had a pattern of either ignoring Biden's gaffes or declaring them lovable burps. In 2008, Biden turned to wheelchair-bound Missouri state senator Chuck Graham and told him to "stand up, Chuck, let 'em see ya."[24] This should have been heavily played by any TV show that wanted an entertaining gaffe clip. Unquestionably, it would have, had it come from Paul Ryan. But it was never aired. In October of that year, Biden said: "The No. 1 job facing the middle class . . . is a three-letter word: Jobs. J-O-B-S, jobs." Again, zero coverage. As vice president, that skip-or-excuse tendency remained:

- On March 17, 2010, Biden mistakenly told Irish prime minister Brian Cowen that his mother had passed away. "His mom lived in Long Island for ten years or so. God rest her soul. And—although, she's—wait—your mom's still—your mom's still alive."[25] (In 2012, Biden mocked Paul Ryan for quoting his father, without really noticing that Ryan's father had died when he was a teenager.) Network coverage? Zero.

- Later in 2010, Biden turned to President Obama as he prepared to sign the Affordable Care Act (Obamacare) and on live national television whispered, "This is a big fucking deal." Had he ever noticed a big live microphone before? But the Democratic National Committee made T-shirts, and the media papered it over. It received just four network stories and came with excuse-making spin. ABC's Bill Weir smiled and said, "Joe Biden gives us another gem." Since the official story line was that Biden was a gaffe machine, none of his individual misstatements were held against him. ABC's Juju Chang confirmed this view: "I think a lot of people are giving Joe Biden some slack on this." Her colleague Robin Roberts added: "He's been known to kind of let things fly a little bit."

- In October 2011, Biden told *Human Events* editor Jason Mattera that if Republicans didn't pass the White House jobs plan, "Murder will continue to rise, rape will continue to rise, all crimes will continue to rise." Broadcast network coverage? Zero, except one brief mention by Jonathan Karl on ABC's *This Week*. CNN's Kate Bolduan showed the exchange and called it a "fiery, unscripted moment."[26]

- In October 2012 at a rally in La Crosse, Wisconsin, Biden claimed Planned Parenthood "under law cannot perform any abortions."[27] In reality, the organization is the largest abortion conglomerate in the country, performing more than 333,000 "terminations" a year in 2011, about one every ninety-four seconds. Network coverage? Zero. But just two days earlier, these programs devoted a combined five minutes to Mitt Romney's statement to *The Des Moines Register* that "there's no legislation with regard to abortion that I'm familiar with that would become part of my agenda."

Despite all this, reporters poured sugary prose on Biden. On August 17, *Politico*'s Jonathan Martin mourned "a media culture that implores politicians to seem authentic but is ready to punish them when they really are—but the challenge is especially exquisite in Biden's case."

Martin wasn't kidding about being in awe. "He is an irrepressible, garrulous and emotive politician, who's flourished and fumbled through 40 years in national office by practicing politics the old-fashioned way—from the gut and without much script. He's as fine a one-on-one politician of any officeholder of his generation, a talent especially prized because it is not a particular gift of Obama's."[28]

On October 8, former *Newsweek* reporter Howard Fineman oozed at the *Huffington Post* that "what Biden lacks in academic chops he more than makes up for in street smarts; genetic political talent (his Secret Service code name is Celtic, enough said); an eye for and an ability to earn the loyalty of brilliant, dedicated staffers; an instinct for the jugular; and a thirst for political combat." [29]

After the election, *New York Times* reporter Mark Leibovich—the one that marveled "You ate your tweeties" to Obama strategist David Axelrod—wrote an article headlined "How This Got to Be a Biden Moment—In a few short months, the vice president has become a star."

Leibovich wrote: "In a few short months, the motor-tongued, muscle-car-loving heartbeat-away hell raiser has been transformed from gaffe-prone amusement to someone whose star shines as brightly as his teeth." [30]

Who was responsible for this transformation? Reporters not only protected him, they argued that Biden was a tremendous asset to the White House, not a "gaffe-prone amusement"—just as the White House would want it.

Akin to Hurt Republicans on Abortion

On August 19, 2012, Representative Todd Akin, Missouri's GOP nominee for the U.S. Senate, appeared on the Fox station in St. Louis with Charles Jaco, a leftist and former national reporter for CNN and NBC. (This is a man who had attacked conservative bloggers as lacking "opposable thumbs." [31]) Jaco asked a series of pointed questions about what he felt were Akin's extremist conservative stands, including on abortion. When Jaco asked Akin if he supported abortion after a rape, Akin replied, "First of all, from what I understand from doctors, that's really rare. If it's a legitimate rape, the female body has ways to try to shut that whole thing down." [32]

The answer was plain stupid. The phrase "legitimate rape" is politically insensitive, if not monstrous, and the notion that the female body can prevent pregnancy from a rape is just medically wrong. But notice what started a national media feeding frenzy: a former national reporter pushing Akin on the toughest abortion decisions. Did Jaco ever try this with the incumbent, Senator Claire McCaskill?

Here's your answer. After boasting that his Akin interview had "created worldwide headlines," Jaco asked McCaskill two weeks later, "Would it be unfair to describe you as pro-choice?" No, she said. "So when you heard Congressman Akin's comments, were you taken aback, or how did it strike you?"[33]

Jaco also described McCaskill on air as a "centrist Democrat." In reality, McCaskill failed to cast a single pro-life vote in her first term in the Senate, earning a perfect 100 score from NARAL Pro-Choice America and a perfect zero from the National Right to Life Committee. She voted for everything the left wanted, from embryo-destroying stem-cell research to UN funding for communist China's forced one-child policy.

But the national media leaped all over Akin's medical gaffe. The ABC, CBS, and NBC evening newscasts and morning shows offered a massive ninety-six minutes (and forty-five segments) of coverage over three and a half days.[34] The disparity between Akin and gaffe-prone Vice President Biden's "chains" controversy from the week before was 5 to 1. Biden was excused. Akin was savaged.

For an illustration of liberal-media hypocrisy over the rape issue, consider this. When Juanita Broaddrick appeared on *Dateline NBC* in 1999 and accused President Clinton of raping her in a Little Rock hotel room, providing a friend who shared her hotel room who confirmed her badly swollen mouth and ripped panty hose after her encounter with the then-attorney general of Arkansas. The three networks produced a paltry few minutes of coverage: two news reports, two briefs, and parts of three interviews. They had no ardor for the idea that our president was a rapist.

But they had ninety-six outraged minutes for Akin's inappropriate *comments* on rape.

"Todd Akin sparked a firestorm," reported Natalie Morales on NBC.[35] CBS reporter Nancy Cordes said Akin's comments "caused a firestorm" and added, "National Democrats are already seizing on his comments as they try to push the notion that Republicans are out of touch when it comes to women's health."

National Democrats define national "news." It's all right there in the transcript.

NBC Nightly News anchor Brian Williams piled on with the echo chamber: "Firestorm. A congressman's words about rape rocket across the country ... women's issues are front and center again." Introducing the lead story moments later, Williams announced that Akin's comments "exploded well beyond the borders of Missouri."[36]

Correspondent Andrea Mitchell predicted—promoted?—political disaster: "Republicans fear their hopes for the White House and control of the Senate could turn on what happened at a St. Louis TV station.... In a race where the President had a 15-point advantage with women voters in the last NBC News/*Wall Street Journal* poll, Republicans were reeling."

Days later, Mitchell was still shoveling, as Akin was described as "inflicting unforeseen and great damage on the national party.... [O]nly days before their convention, Republicans remain trapped in a national debate about abortion and rape."

On MSNBC, Chris Matthews began, "Let me start tonight with this right-wing assault on women, this caveman view of the sexes that has now shown its ugly head.... Finally, we meet the missing link, the evidence that the party of Lincoln cannot get in bed with the most freakish elements of the right."[37]

But no one in the media noticed "freakish elements of the left" that defend abortion at any time, for any reason. Instead, consider the hard line of *New York Times* columnist (and longtime reporter) Thomas Friedman, as proclaimed on the September 2 *Meet the Press*.

"I'm a Planned Parenthood Democrat on the issue of choice. And I think that that is where the country should be. That is where many, many women in this country are. And I'm glad there are people running for the presidency who will defend that position. Period. Paragraph. End it."[38]

Somehow, it was not a gaffe in Media Land when Joy Behar, a panelist on ABC's *The View*, implied in a *Boston Herald* interview that the Republicans wanted to kill and destroy the female half of the human race: "People like Akin that think the vagina is some sort of Magical Mystery Tour and men like that are running this country. This is why I took this job. I have a job already at *The View*. But I feel this country is going downhill because of people like Akin and Ryan and Romney. They're trying to kill us and destroy us."[39]

No one should fail to notice that Akin was favored in this race before this imbroglio. *The Rothenberg Political Report* considered the race a toss-up that "tilts Republican" and called McCaskill "the Senate's most endangered incumbent." Akin led McCaskill in eight of nine polls in the year leading up to the gaffe. This answers the question why "national Democrats" would pounce and define it as "news." If McCaskill had been ahead by 15 points, this would never have been covered, even noticed.

Mauling Mourdock, Omitting Obama Abortion Extremism

The same dynamics were in play in Indiana, with conservative candidate Richard Mourdock locked in a tight race with Representative Joe Donnelly. Once again, the local media pounced on the rape exception on Mourdock in an October 23 debate.

"I believe that life begins at conception. The only exception I have for—to have an abortion is in that case for the life of the mother. I just—I struggle with it myself for a long time but I came to realize that life is that gift from God, and I think even when life begins in that horrible situation of rape that it is something that God intended to happen."

A defensible moral argument? Assuredly, and we will defend it as such. A smart political statement? Absolutely not. It was a gaffe. Unlike Akin, Mourdock wasn't asked directly about a rape exception. A consultant might have winced that he would bring it up unprompted or that he would discuss God's will—always a "fruitcake alert" for secular liberal journalists—but it's appalling that Mourdock was punished for sticking up for the humanity of a baby conceived in rape.

Like clockwork, all three networks leaped on the story. On *CBS This Morning*, reporter Jeff Glor spread the Obama spin: "Senior Obama campaign adviser David Axelrod tweeted, 'Mitt's man Mourdock apes Akin in Indiana debate reflecting a GOP that is way out of mainstream.'"[40] Glor made sure to play a soundbite of Akin, to underline Axelrod's tweet.

None of them were going to consider for even two seconds a debate between religious authorities on rape and abortion, or inviting a pro-life speaker who was conceived in rape, like Ryan Bomberger or Rebecca Kiessling.

This is how insular it was. On the October 26 *Morning Edition*, NPR reporter Scott Horsley explained, "The Obama campaign has been reminding women this week about Governor Romney's support for Indiana Senate candidate Richard Mourdock, who sparked controversy when he said that abortion is wrong even in the case of rape, because if a rape victim becomes pregnant, it's what God intended."[41] Obama's campaign then took that audio (starting with "Indiana") and placed it right into a campaign radio advertisement, followed by a man and woman discussing how nutty Mourdock was.[42]

A few days later, reporters were still hounding Romney to distance himself from the apparent slime of Mourdock. On the Bill Press radio show, producer Peter Ogburn reported, "Our friend Sam Youngman from Reuters—who we have on the show as often as we can, because he's on the road. But he was on the road yesterday. He said at a breakfast stop, me and Steve Peoples from Associated Press and Lisa Lerer from Bloomberg asked Romney repeatedly about Mourdock."[43]

Clay Waters at TimesWatch reported a Nexis search found seven *New York Times* stories that allowed Mourdock's Democratic opponents to paint him as "extreme" or "extremist." The photo caption accompanying Mourdock's picture continued that DNC-friendly pattern: "Richard Mourdock's opposition to abortion in cases of rape has given Democrats an opening to paint Republicans as extremist."[44]

On the October 28 CNN show *State of the Union*, anchor Candy Crowley wouldn't ask about Benghazi damage for Democrats, but she pounded Republican National Committee (RNC) Chairman Reince Priebus about damage to those anti-woman Republicans: "Does it hurt the party image to have these issues out there in a way that makes the party or that is portrayed as making the party look unbending and, you know, anti-woman, as is described in the Obama ad?"[45]

Priebus stated the obvious—no party has a monopoly on gaffes—but the network news squashers specialize in ignoring the obvious. Obama and Biden can say the most foolish or obnoxious things, and the networks skip them. None of them, not even Crowley, found it "anti-woman" when Arizona's Democratic Senate candidate Richard Carmona joked during a debate that his male moderator was "prettier" than Crowley.[46]

This is where media bias on deciding what is a gaffe (and what is not) matters. It was never a gaffe when Senate candidate Barack Obama ran in 2004 (and 2008, and 2012) after having voted four times in the Illinois Senate to allow abortions after the "fetus" became a baby outside the womb. Or forbidding medical professionals from saving the life of an aborted baby who survived. More than one nurse has recounted the heartbreaking account of rocking a baby, even hiding in a closet . . . while the little one died. Absolutely nobody with a press pass found that idea ideologically extreme or scientifically bizarre.

The Media Research Center found that from the launch of his candidacy in January 2007 through the end of the primaries in June 2008, just six out of 1,289 network evening news stories about Obama (0.46 percent) mentioned his position on abortion, and none discussed it in any detail. They never devoted one TV story to examining Obama's abortion record.[47] The same thing happened in 2012. Obama and liberal reporters are in complete agreement, so there's nothing objectionable to report.

To any reporter who cared enough to investigate, Obama's record was self-evidently extreme. In one debate in 2002, in a great spasm of ideological ardor, he argued it was unnecessary to add a doctor (other than the abortionist) to evaluate the medical condition of a baby who survived the abortionist's attempt to "terminate the pregnancy." Obama said that was political, not medical: "adding an additional doctor, who then has to be called in an emergency situation to come in and make these assessments, is really designed simply to burden the original decision of the woman and the physician to induce labor and perform an abortion."[48] The Weekly Standard found audio of this debate in August 2012. The network coverage was zero.

CBS briefly covered Obama's remarks to a right-to-life question at Rick Warren's church yet completely ignored his infamous declaration that deciding when life begins is "above my pay grade." They just ran the quote "I am pro-choice. I believe in Roe vs. Wade. And I come to that conclusion not because I'm pro-abortion, but because ultimately I don't think women make these decisions casually."

This is the same Senator Obama who declared in April 2008 that he wouldn't want his daughters to be "punished with a baby" for having premarital sex without contraceptives. CBS ignored that, too, as did ABC. (NBC skipped it except for a clip on *Meet the Press*.) There is apparently nothing harsh Obama can say about babies that will be considered newsworthy by Barack's disciplined message providers in the media.

CHAPTER 8

The Fluff-My-Pillow Interview Tour

One servile interviewer is much better than a rowdy press conference.

One extended dirty trick in the presidential campaign extended far beyond the news media. Time and again, Obama was welcomed (and beloved) on so many soft-soap shows, interviews Mitt Romney wouldn't do. Romney thought it wouldn't be presidential to appear on *Saturday Night Live*, although Obama and McCain both tried that in 2008. A sore-loser Romney fan might suggest that perhaps you should be president before worrying about being presidential.

It is natural for any politician to seek out the media venues that make him look the best, the most personable and appealing and articulate. It's also natural that when Republicans do that, the "objective" media will be slamming the Fox News Channel.

When Vice President Dick Cheney accidentally shot a hunting partner in the face in Texas in 2006, CBS reporter Jim Axelrod announced, "The Vice President chose to make his first public comments on Fox News Channel's *Special Report*, a broadcast Mr. Cheney sees as friendly and has turned to before." That was polite compared to CNN's Jack Cafferty, who lamented, "It didn't exactly represent a profile in courage for the Vice President to wander over there to the F-word network for a sit-down with Brit Hume. I mean, that's a little like Bonnie interviewing Clyde, ain't it?" [1]

This tsk-tsk routine happened in 2012, too. On September 19, 2012, NPR reporter Brian Naylor announced that in the wake of the 47 percent tape, "Mitt Romney went to the friendly confines of the Fox News Channel yesterday afternoon in another round of damage control." But then Naylor turned to Obama: "Last night, at a taping of *Late Night with David Letterman* on CBS, Mr. Obama acknowledged, in his words, 'We all make mistakes.'" [2] The Letterman show wasn't the "friendly confines," even when the host was oozing about the president's weight: "180 sure looks good on you."

Despite the news media's "slobbering love affair" with Barack Obama, he has rarely reciprocated. In August, *The New York Times* hailed Obama as "Avid Reader, and Critic, of the News." Reporter Amy Chozick touted how Obama, a "voracious consumer of news," told columnists in private meetings about the concept of "false balance"—that reporters "should not give equal weight to both sides of an argument when one side is factually incorrect. He frequently cites the coverage of health care and the stimulus package as examples," the sources said. [3]

He actually wanted his most massive government interventions to be chronicled without any "false balance" from the other side.

Chozick cited just one example, a *USA Today* story from 2009 headlined "Traffic Set to Slow as Stimulus Gears Up." How could it be factually incorrect that the "stimulus" meant a boom in road and bridge work in Obama's first summer as president? This wasn't about facts, it was about spin.

As Mitt Romney emerged as his Republican opponent, the thin-skinned president signaled he was interested in coasting to reelection by largely ignoring the "accountability press," the serious, probing, policy-wonkish, pin-down-the-fact kind of reporters. He preferred sappy interviews with late-night comedians and infotainment hosts—and network "news" anchors who achieved the perky, unchallenging wavelength of *Entertainment Tonight* questioners.

On May 4, veteran White House reporter Keith Koffler penned an insightful blog post titled "Obama Abolishes the Press Conference." He noted, "President Obama has held just one full length, multitopic, solo press conference in the last six months, effectively abolishing the most accessible venue for American citizens to observe the thinking and learn the views of their leader." [4]

As the Republican candidates were pounded by Brian Williams or George Stephanopoulos in debates in late 2011 and early 2012, Obama stuck to a few obligatory pressers with foreign leaders—which are often drab affairs for White House reporters. Only four or five questions are allotted, they're usually dragged out by the necessity of translators, and they're split between the two heads of state, and usually focus on the foreign policy matters between the two countries.

And then the stall. Slowly, ponderously, in as boring a fashion as can be mustered, the president takes forever to answer—or not answer—the question.

On May 21, President Obama took questions for 44 minutes in Chicago, and then all that came after that were two tiny opportunities: 25 minutes in Mexico on June 20, and a quick 22-minute briefing room drop-by on August 20. [5]

Three months after the election, *Washington Post* media reporter Paul Farhi underlined that Obama hadn't granted an interview to the *Post* since early in his first year, with the same snub for *The Wall Street Journal* news reporters. The president hadn't spoken with *The New*

York Times since the fall of 2010. *The Boston Globe* and the *Los Angeles Times* never had an interview with Obama as president—and neither did his (supportive) hometown papers in Chicago.

Obama-loving *Post* editor Kevin Merida—whose term as national editor coincided almost exactly with Obama's—pooh-poohed this lack of access. Who needs access to the president when you run a newspaper in the nation's capital? Interviewing the president "isn't essential to what we do day to day. We've demonstrated we can produce great White House coverage . . . without ever getting an interview with the president."[6] After the election, the *Post* promoted Merida again, to managing editor, the number-two slot.

This supine posture was a sharp contrast to the Bush era, when the media subjected itself to a frenzy of self-loathing after the last press conference before the Iraq War on March 6, 2003. They had access to Bush but were far too easy on him, they thought. ABC White House reporter Terry Moran made waves by telling the *New York Observer* that Bush left his journalism colleagues "looking like zombies."[7] *New York Press* columnist Matt Taibbi suggested reporters were routed, like Texans at the Alamo: "The entire White House press corps should be herded into a cargo plane, flown to an altitude of 30,000 feet, and pushed out, kicking and screaming, over the North Atlantic." By October 2003, PBS omnipresence Bill Moyers mentioned Taibbi's gibe to the left-wing website Buzzflash.com and added, "I'd say it was more a collective Jonestown-like suicide. At least the defenders of the Alamo put up a fight."[8]

This was not the way the left described the press and Obama. In fact, Moran marked Obama's arrival in office by gushing to an interviewer that he was "the first President since George Washington to be taking a step down into the Oval Office."[9] When Obama finally held a real press conference after his reelection on November 14, *Nightline* anchor Moran didn't focus on the questioners. He just praised the swagger of the answerer. "But the real takeaway from the White

House today? There's nothing like a re-election to give the President a jolt of confidence. . . . Today, an Obama smackdown."[10]

Moran was the zombie he had warned against.

"Obama the Puppet Master"

On February 18, 2013, the insider newspaper and website *Politico*—another liberal media organ Obama had denied an interview—published a big story by Mike Allen and Jim VandeHei headlined "Obama the Puppet Master." The article began: "President Barack Obama is a master at limiting, shaping, and manipulating media coverage of himself and his White House."

Even when journalists are willingly manipulated, they have to praise the man pulling the strings?

It quickly grew silly when the duo denied the reality that "a liberal press willingly and eagerly allows itself to be manipulated." They argued, "Conservatives assume a cozy relationship between this White House and the reporters who cover it. Wrong. Many reporters find Obama strangely fearful of talking with them and often aloof and cocky when he does. They find his staff needlessly stingy with information and thin-skinned about any tough coverage."[11]

The words to focus on here are "strangely fearful" and "needlessly stingy." Liberal reporters were telling *Politico* that Obama has no reason to fear them and no need to scrimp on information as if they will harm him in the polls. Memo to Obama: *We all voted for you, we're your allies*. But even if reporters were asking serious questions in the briefing room and complaining to the press officers, none of that emerged in what viewers were watching at home.

Some sounded angry. ABC Radio reporter Ann Compton, who has covered every president since Gerald Ford, told *Politico*, "The way the president's availability has shrunk to the press in the last two years is a disgrace." Aides don't explain how big meetings developed policy in secret, and many of them never appeared on his official schedule. "This is different from every president I covered. This White House goes to extreme lengths to keep the press away."

In response to *Politico*, former White House reporter Matthew Cooper penned an online piece for *The Atlantic* titled "Is Obama Too Mean to the Media, or Are Reporters Just Whiny? It's mostly the latter." He claimed every White House grew more protective of its president, and told reporters to "just grow up."[12] Cooper admitted that he worked at *Time* for seven years with Jay Carney, now Obama's press secretary. He got married in 1997 to Mandy Grunwald, one of the original Bill Clinton bimbo-crushers, so Democratic press manipulation wasn't frowned upon when he worked with Carney.

Cooper was not alone. Todd Purdum of *Vanity Fair*, a former *New York Times* reporter who married Clinton press secretary Dee Dee Myers, hit the same note, smacking the "silly season" for the White House press corps. "They contend that White House beat reporters for the major newspapers and networks are most likely to know the issues, ask tough and unpredictable questions, and hold the president to account. Most of these reporters are fine, hardworking journalists, and many are wonderful people; a good number are my friends. But, as a *class,* they are the world's biggest whiners. I know because I was once one of them, and a first-class whiner myself. I don't think their argument holds water."

Purdum noted that Towson University professor Martha Joynt Kumar, who studies the president and the press, counted that Obama consented to 674 one-on-one interviews in his first term, compared to only 217 by George W. Bush.[13] But this misleads. Those Obama interviews routinely went around the briefing-room crowd to supine top anchors and dazzled local-TV hosts. Obama would rather have an interview with Robin Roberts or Diane Sawyer or Barbara Walters, and leave Compton and Jake Tapper on the sideline.

At the end of 2011, with the reelection year approaching, Barbara Walters hosted the president for an hour in prime time. Oh, how the tough questions flew. Like, she asked, "I know that you answer people's letters all the time. And what we thought that we might do, we asked middle school and high school students to throw a few questions. I'd like to read their questions: 'If you were a superhero, and you could have one superpower, what would it be?'"

Obama answered, "You know, I've talked to Malia about this. We both agree that flying seems like it would be a pretty good thing to be able to do."

Walters posed a self-lampooning question about reincarnation to the First Lady: "If you were to die and come back as a person or a thing, what would you want it to be?" This appeared to be too much for Mrs. Obama, as she interrupted mid-question, "Oh, God, Barbara." Then Walters observed, "I'm looking at you. You're holding hands. That's very sweet. How many years married?" The president said "twenty next year." Walters cooed: "And still hold hands?"

Then out came the Babwa Wawa dagger as she told the audience: "The Obamas' marriage has always been a political asset, not so for every politician, like Republican candidate Newt Gingrich, who has had to address questions of whether infidelity is fair game during a presidential campaign." [14]

Not that Walters wasn't capable of hardball interviews. Ask Sarah Palin, who witnessed Walters in a year-end "Most Fascinating People of 2010" interview telling Palin that people find her "scary" and blaming her for Republican Senate losses and repeating Katie Couric's insulting question about whether she was reading anything. [15]

Michelle Obama appeared on ABC's *The View* on May 29, and Walters began by asking her, "There have been rumors—if the president is not reelected [hands raised to mouth, eyes wide as saucers, dramatic 'God forbid!' face]—or that in the future, that you might consider running for political office." Michelle Obama said the rumors weren't hers. Walters insisted, "Would you ever? . . . You would be a very popular candidate." [16]

On September 25, the president and First Lady appeared again on *The View* as Obama avoided Benghazi questions from real journalists, and cohost Sherri Shepherd put them through this gauntlet of inquiries.

1. "President Obama, are you a romantic kind of husband?"

2. "I heard that there's a plaque in Chicago. It marks the site of your first kiss. Tell us about that first kiss."

3. "You guys have a ritual where, now, First Lady, you go to bed at ten in the evening. Your husband comes to bed at one in the morning. But you have a ritual where he tucks you in at night. What is that?"

Here was the toughest question from Barbara Walters: "Would it be so terrible if Mitt Romney were elected? He was governor. He will probably be a little more moderate. . . . My point is would it be disastrous for the country if Mitt Romney were elected?" Obama said no, but he didn't just want the economy to "survive" under Romney, he wanted it to "thrive" under Obama. [17]

Three weeks and a day later, Ann Romney appeared without her husband—no doubt because in September 2008, cohost Whoopi Goldberg asked John McCain about his view of upholding the Constitution: "Do I have to worry about becoming a slave again?" To which Joy Behar joked, "she's picturing herself on the plantation."

Mitt stayed away, and still the difference in aggression was stunning. Barbara Walters asked Mrs. Romney about her husband flip-flopping on abortion. Behar asked, "Do you think that access to contraception and abortion is an economic issue?" Goldberg argued

Mrs. Romney would be "talking to the mothers whose children are coming home in bags, you know, from wars . . . so how will you explain to them that your sons haven't gone?" Whoopi wrongly asserted that Mormons were pacifists who didn't serve in the military. No one asked Obama why he didn't serve in the military. They were too busy asking about plaques honoring the Obamas' first kiss.

Walters even stooped to pushing a Romney son, Josh, sitting in the front row of the audience, if he agreed with his brother Tagg that there are times he feels he'd like to "take a swing" at President Obama.[18]

This underlines the bizarre game of the allegedly softer interview venues. The Obamas could land the safest of softball interviews in TV environments that the Romneys would have to consider potentially devastating booby traps. One couple knew and expected a valentine. The other couple could only imagine the serious potential for hardballs, gaffes, and controversies.

So in the closing days of the fall campaign, Obama would go on Nickelodeon to be interviewed by liberal former TV news reporter Linda Ellerbee, and children. Romney bailed out. Obama would go on MTV to be interviewed by veejay Sway Calloway and college-age voters. Romney would not. Obama was fawned over by David Letterman. *Time* magazine described it as "pretty much like a stump speech with prompts from Letterman and commercial breaks." Romney knew he could not—just remember Letterman expressing his desire for Romney to be jailed for the Seamus-cartop-carrier story.

There was no concept of fair play or equal time in formats where low-information voters were being addressed by Obama. It was a slam dunk for Obama's media advisers as they "microtargeted" their voting blocs, ultraconfident that Obama could use these shows to seem cool, funny, relatable—and Romney could not.

Making Gay "History" with Robin Roberts

ABC went soft on the president when he selected them to make news, an announcement that would thrill Hollywood and many of Obama's most enthusiastic campaign fundraisers: "I think same-sex couples should be able to get married."

The White House handpicked *Good Morning America* cohost Robin Roberts, and cohost George Stephanopoulos led into the interview by praising her: "Boy, do you know how to make a splash. A little news from the President yesterday. And, Robin, what a watershed moment. You know, whatever people think about this issue, and we know it's controversial, there's no denying when a president speaks out for the first time like that, it is history."

Roberts replied: "And let me tell you, George—I'm getting chills again—because when you sit in that room and you hear him say those historic words, it was not lost on anyone that was in the room like that." Would those chills have been there if he had embraced traditional marriage? Reporters get chills when he speaks Liberal.

During the ABC interview, Roberts offered several softball questions, including one about Mother's Day. The closest Roberts came to a conservative viewpoint was mentioning that as Team Obama has criticized Romney for changing positions on social issues, "Do you see where some people might consider that the same thing, being politics?"

Obama stopped short on imposing gay marriage on all fifty states, and Roberts did tone down the goo briefly by insisting, "But Mr. President, it's not been being worked out on the state level. We saw that Tuesday in North Carolina, the 30th state, in essence, to announce its ban on gay marriage."[19] Obama gave very long, "thoughtful" answers uninterrupted by the network.

Media reports were explicit that the Obama White House chose

Roberts because of her reputation for warm and fuzzy news, not to mention her race and even her age. "The White House went with Robin because of her personal rapport, their friendship, the past interviews—but also her race [black], even her age," one producer at ABC said to *Politico* media reporter Dylan Byers. "There is a very strong, very basic connection there." Think Oprah.

Byers added: "By giving the interview to an African-American and Christian—two groups whose opposition to same-sex marriage has been significant—the White House may have been aiming to make Obama's announcement more palatable to groups that differ with his support for gay marriage." [20]

At ABC, Roberts rarely if ever handles political interviews in the morning—George Stephanopoulos hogs them. Roberts offered a "warmer, gauzier" and less combative presence, former CNN White House correspondent Frank Sesno told Paul Farhi at *The Washington Post*. The White House wanted a "conversation across the back of the fence," not a newsmaker interview: "If you're the White House and you have to deal with something this white-hot, do you want to engage this as a news story or as conversation across the back of the fence?"

Gay activists agreed. Fred Sainz, a publicist for the gay-left Human Rights Campaign, also praised the selection to Farhi. "I thought the selection of Roberts was genius," he said. "She comes across as the neighbor you'd be happy to have a cup of coffee with. That's the way to frame this issue, as an ongoing conversation with the American public."

ABC News spokesman Jeffrey Schneider said Roberts had a reputation as "direct but fair." But do the Republicans get to have a "conversation" on ABC when they take on a very controversial social issue?

In the fall of 2007, the Bush White House offered an interview to Juan Williams to mark the fiftieth anniversary of school desegregation in Little Rock, but NPR refused to let the White House pick an interviewer. NPR insisted it would select the reporter—so Williams conducted the Bush interview for Fox News.[21] (This was an early sign that NPR was going to end up firing Williams for being too Fox-friendly.) ABC didn't play by those rules.

It's not surprising that when Roberts interviewed Ann Romney on July 19, she was tougher on the challenger's wife than she was with the president. She toed the Democrat line by expressing dissatisfaction with the Romneys putting out only two years of tax returns: "Both Bushes gave multiple years, ten and 12 years. President Obama gave seven years of tax returns. Your husband has been adamant about only the two years that will be released. Why will he not follow the example of others on both sides of the aisle?"

After Mrs. Romney reiterated that her husband wouldn't release more than two years and that they had nothing to hide, Roberts hectored, "Why not show that then? Why not release the—because then it's a moot point and people move on."[22]

Charlie Rose Calmly Babbles like a Brook

In July, Barack and Michelle Obama sat down with *CBS This Morning* cohost Charlie Rose for an interview on *Sunday Morning*, the placid little magazine show that ends with video of moments in nature like a babbling brook.

One might have expected that CBS would focus on the plight of every family struggling with unemployment or a house that's underwater financially, or facing its loss of religious liberties with a federal government drunk with power. Instead the interview started with "questions" like these from Charlie Rose:

- "It's not a bad place to live. [The White House.] . . . Well, you got a basketball court; you got a tennis court. You have a fountain. You can see the Washington Monument."

- "How are you going to spend your summer? . . . What is summer vacation?"

- "You didn't have all of these important things to do, and you could travel to anyplace in the world, where would you want to go? What would you want to see and experience?"

- "Does this place change you?"

It seemed obvious to the audience that Charlie Rose was channeling his inner Barbara Walters. The "What kind of tree would you like to be?" question was on the tip of his tongue.

Then there was the marriage question to the president. "I read you, though—this, that I found fascinating. You said, 'I trust her [Michelle] completely, but at the same time, she's also a complete mystery to me in some ways. It is that tension between familiarity and mystery that makes for something strong.' Is that even more so now, and in this place?"

Rose said the original quote came from 1996, but its American debut was a *New Yorker* puff piece that coincided with the Obama inauguration in 2009. CBS was sitting down with the Obamas in 2012 and asking a repeat of a stale question used to promote the Obamas at their highest political summit.[23] You can tell where CBS is happiest. It is forever January 2009.

In fact, Rose showed Obama a *Newsweek* cover from the first inauguration: "Take a look at this. That's four years ago. . . . This was also a time of 'Yes, We Can,' 'Hope and Change.' What happened to that, because that's not the narrative today?" Obama lamented, "I haven't been able to change the atmosphere here in Washington, to reflect the decency and common sense of ordinary people—Democrats, Republicans and independents—who I think just want to see their leadership solve problems. And, you know, there's enough blame to go around for that."

Rose followed up: "And do you blame yourself, in part, because, I mean, you had this confidence—that you had the skills that would allow you to bridge the gap." Obama replied: "I think there's no doubt that I underestimated the degree to which in this town, politics trumps problem solving." [24]

That's the sentence CBS plucked out to lead the whole program: Obama, sad that "politics trumps problem solving," as if that kind of behavior never happened among the Democrats. Reread Obama's answers. He blamed everyone for his failures—everyone but himself. That wasn't a takeaway?

In January, Rose's cohost Gayle King had interviewed Michelle Obama on the occasion of a new book simply called *The Obamas*, by *New York Times* reporter Jodi Kantor. Michelle Obama insisted that she got along wonderfully with every staffer in the White House and complained that she was tagged as nosing around in the West Wing policy decisions. "That's been an image that people have tried to paint of me since, you know, the day Barack announced, that I'm some angry black woman," she sniffed.

After the interview aired, Rose noted that "there seems to be a nice chemistry there. I mean, you've known this person for a long time." King acknowledged that, "I think we should say it's no secret here at the table that we're friends."

No one told viewers that on page 42 of Kantor's book, she placed King right in the inner circle on the night of the first inauguration: "At 1:00 am, the Obamas returned to the White House for the real celebration, a private party for their family and closest friends and allies—downstairs, in the entertaining spaces, not upstairs in the home that they still had not really seen that day. Celebrities including Oprah Winfrey and Gayle King mingled with new cabinet officials, the First Lady's relatives from the South Side, and the president's best friends from Chicago." [25] Obviously CBS hired King in part because she was friends with the Obamas. It's what makes that industry and the Obama administration indistinguishable.

NBC Slow-Jams Its News for Obama

When Obama came through the curtain of *The Jimmy Fallon Show* on April 24, the crowd unleashed a screaming standing ovation reminiscent of the Beatles on *The Ed Sullivan Show*. Then they "slow-jammed the news," which was really just Obama making a campaign speech as Fallon's band played bedroom-eyes soul music in the background.

Obama pandered to the young audience by opposing any increase in interest rates on federally supported student loans. "I've called on Congress to prevent this from happening. What we've said is simple: now is not the time to make school more expensive for our young people." Yeah!

Fallon followed up by uttering embarrassing lines in a bumbling Barry White basso profundo like "Awww yeah. You should listen to the president. Or as I like to call him, the Preezy of the United Steezy." Move over, Bill Clinton. Obama is the coolest person in the room.

After Obama attacked Republicans, blaming them for raising interest rates on college students to keep taxes low for billionaires, Fallon added: "Mmm, mmm, mmm. The Barack Ness monster ain't buying it. . . . And the President knows his stuff, y'all. That's why they call him POTUS, which means person on top—what is it?" Obama replied, "Jimmy, POTUS stands for President of the United States." Singer Tariq Trotter then sang in tribute: "He's the POTUS with the mostest!"[26]

Fallon ended this spectacle later by saying, "We don't take sides politically on this show." Few would remember that six months earlier, Congresswoman Michele Bachmann was greeted with the Fallon house band performing an instrumental version of an obscure 1980s tune titled "Lyin' Ass Bitch."[27]

Obama was performing in the place of Fallon's usual slow-jammer, *NBC Nightly News* anchor Brian Williams, who desperately wants people to think he's hip and funny. Williams provided a series of soft-touch interviews with Obama as he prepared for a re-election campaign. The first came on September 11, 2011, the tenth anniversary of the al-Qaeda terrorist attacks. Williams asked how he and Mrs. Obama feel when they walk through Arlington National Cemetery, and he followed up by typically observing, "We caught the president yesterday in an emotional and reflective time." Williams routinely touted Obama as "reflective" maybe because he routinely asked gaseous please-reflect-for-me questions.

When they ran more interview footage on the morning of September 12, the toughest question Williams asked was if Obama remembered he had told NBC's Matt Lauer in 2009 that if the economy didn't turn around he'd be a "one-term proposition." Obama replied that "you know, what we've done is we've been able to stabilize the economy. And, you know, that is an enormous accomplishment." Unemployment stood at 9.1 percent in the August 2011 report, and Obama was bragging. Williams and NBC aired no fact-check or follow-up to that whopper of a lie.

On the September 12 *Nightly News*, Williams suggested Obama's economic poll numbers weren't great—but he also obediently slammed the Republicans. He informed Obama, "Members of your base are asking when are you going to get your Harry Truman on?" That would seem to include his journalistic supporters, like Williams. Then Williams disparaged those Tea Party hard-liners for poisoning the political well:

"All of this, of course, is if you get what you want in a highly toxic atmosphere, and it sure looked to me from the outside like you went into the debt-ceiling fight thinking, 'Surely they will do the statesmanlike thing. Surely they won't go there.' And it seemed to me as if Speaker Boehner was coming to you, saying, 'Look, if it were up to me we would do this, but I've got this membership problem.' And they went there, and now that marks our politics." [28]

Once again, Obama was painted by the networks as the least partisan player in Washington and Republicans as the worst kind of self-interested obstructionists. Just days before, on September 7, 2011, Williams moderated a Republican debate at the Reagan Library in California. He infuriated Republicans with withering questions, such as telling Texas governor Rick Perry, "Your state has executed 234 death row inmates, more than any other governor in modern times. Have you struggled to sleep at night with the idea that any one of those might have been innocent?" [29]

It doesn't matter that Williams works for NBC, which was owned by General Electric, which has donated millions to the Reagan Library. The Republicans had only themselves to blame for selecting him as their moderator.

Team Obama also selected Williams for an interview with the president in May to celebrate the first anniversary of the president's order to kill Osama bin Laden. Williams played up the drama to celebrate the president's bold risk-taking, as if Obama would have been impeached if the mission were unsuccessful: "If this had failed in spectacular fashion, it would have blown up your presidency, I think, by all estimates. It would have been your Waterloo, and, perhaps, your Watergate, consumed with hearings and inquiries. How thick did the specter of Jimmy Carter, Desert One hang in the air here?" Williams had worked briefly in the Carter White House, so he could relate.

The NBC star attempted to feel Obama's pain, that he had to keep the operation quiet: "Keeping this secret also meant going on about the business of the presidency. Touring that awful storm damage in

Alabama while knowing at that very moment U.S. Navy SEALs were already on the move halfway around the world. You had to go to Tuscaloosa. You had to go have fun at the Correspondents' Dinner. Seth Meyers makes a joke about Osama Bin Laden . . . How do you keep an even keel? Even when we look back on the videotape of that night, there's no real depiction that there's something afoot."[30] Williams even labored to confirm on this prime-time program that the White House sacrificially lowered itself to ordering food from Costco to avoid this big mission from being detected.

While the capture or killing of bin Laden was a major objective of American policy for ten years, this Williams interview wasn't a nonpartisan national moment. It was a reelection special, touting Obama's "even keel" and masterful decision-making. In mid-August on *Rock Center*, reporter Natalie Morales interviewed Ann Romney, and both that show and the *Today* show featured Morales grilling her with four argumentative questions on the family tax returns: "A lot of people still are asking why not be transparent and release more than the 2010 and the estimates for 2011." Mrs. Romney responded forcefully: "Have you seen how we're attacked? Have you seen what's happened?"

Morales implied the Romneys resented any questions: "It's been in the press quite a bit. Now are you angry that it's been in the press? I mean, should you not be questioned about your finances?" Romney pushed back: "We have been very transparent to what's legally required of us. But, the more we release, the more we get attacked. The more we get questioned, the more we get pushed."

Morales completely ignored Senate Majority Leader Harry Reid's completely unsubstantiated and false accusation on the Senate floor that Mitt Romney didn't pay any taxes at all. Morales also urged Mrs. Romney to compliment the Obama family: "Clearly the campaign has gotten to be so negative on both sides. Is there a positive that you see in President Obama and the First Lady?" Romney described how she admired Michelle Obama for taking on the obesity issue and the First Family being a "role model" for others.

Apparently that wasn't enough Obama praise for Morales, who demanded more: "What about President Obama? What can you say, a positive that we don't often hear?" Mrs. Romney said, "I think all of us are so proud that America backed him and I think that piece of it is never going to go away that, that America is a place where anything is possible and anyone can dream whatever they want and anyone can accomplish anything they want. And he is the embodiment of that and I think it's a thrill for all of us to have him as a President." [31]

For the media, the thrill of electing Obama was intense and neverending. Even the Republicans were being pressured to agree.

CHAPTER 9

The Convention Curse

Intolerant, fundamentalist racist conservatives versus inspirational centrists.

The national party conventions used to be an enormous four-day roadblock across prime-time television, a major undertaking for network news operations, with squads of reporters spreading across the convention floors. Over the last twenty-five years, the parties have been losing their grip. Increasingly, pompous anchors have openly complained of being manipulated—the most famous being ABC's Ted Koppel leaving the 1996 Republican convention in San Diego halfway through, huffily declaring, "This convention is more of an infomercial than a news event."[1]

The more that party organizers have made conventions staged and milquetoast affairs, the more audience interest has waned. The networks went from granting the parties three hours of prime time, then two, and then one. By 2012, the networks granted only an hour for the nomination on the last hour on Tuesday, Wednesday, and the big acceptance speech on Thursday night.[2] Before the prospect of

Hurricane Isaac ruined the GOP's plans for a Monday night starring the nominee's wife, Ann Romney, the networks all plotted to skip over her speech for reruns of *Castle, Grimm,* and *Hawaii Five-O.*[3]

There's an upside—the decline of air time left a lot less room for Republican-bashing. To put that one in its proper perspective, we counted 125 questions on the networks in four nights about Dan Quayle's draft status or possible adultery at the 1988 RNC convention.[4] But the network tactics and dirty tricks have stayed remarkably consistent.

In every Republican convention we've been studying at the Media Research Center since 1988, no matter whether the candidate was a Reagan conservative or a McCain moderate, the anchors and pundits have scorned the Republicans as ultraconservative, too exclusionary and hostile to women and minorities, too mired in scandal, and too negative in their attacks on Democrats. In short, they were painted as an all-around turn-off to independent voters.[5]

By contrast, at every Democratic confab we've taped and studied, whether the candidate was liberal like Michael Dukakis or more moderate in tone like Bill Clinton, the networks painted the Democrats as almost disturbingly centrist, free of ethical problems, and stuffed full of "inspirational" addresses as speakers slashed the Republicans as—well, ultraconservative and hostile to women and minorities.[6] Their tone was promotional, aiming to help the Democrats build a "bounce" in the polls, and it was usually successful.

The same tactics emerged in 2012. *New York Times* political writer Adam Nagourney performed the quadrennial newspaper ritual with a spin line that media liberals have been using since liberalism consolidated its grip on the Democrats: "Some leaders expressed worry that the turn to contentious social issues in the days leading up to the Republican National Convention, where the party platform is likely to embrace a tough anti-abortion stance and strict curbs on immigration, could undercut the party's need to broaden its appeal.

Many of them said they feared it was hastening a march to becoming a smaller, older, whiter and more male party."[7]

This was also the *Times* spin going into the 2010 midterms. The Tea Party was going to shrink the GOP and make it older, whiter, and more male. Facts never get in the way of a good liberal-media story line. Nagourney merely echoed what then-NBC anchor Katie Couric was pushing on Quayle almost 20 years earlier, in 1992, and which countless journalists have asked countless times since: "Do you think the Republican Party has grown, or become, too exclusionary, too intolerant, and that this kind of rhetoric is divisive and counterproductive?"

Both parties have factions, but Nagourney argued that the divisions in the Republican Party were the worst in (faulty) recent memory. The *Times* headline: "A Party in Principle Fears Danger in Factions." When it ran in the other Times Company–owned paper, *The International Herald Tribune*, the headline was "Republicans Vow Unity; Reality Is Less Tidy."[8]

This is how the *Times* defines "reality." Try putting the words "Democratic Party" within twenty-five words of "factions" in a Nexis search. The results will stun you. Over the last two years, the *Times* has exclusively used these terms only in stories on foreign countries. One editorial briefly referred to "factions" among Democrats . . . referring to the election of 1860.[9]

For the TV stars, CBS's Norah O'Donnell predicted that she and her colleagues would harass Republicans on social issues: "Everybody is going to be asking about Akin, abortion rights, women's rights, et cetera, during the Republican convention."[10] Shortly before the convention opened on Tuesday, Chris Matthews told *Hardball* viewers to "be on the alert for the tribal messages, the war drums of racial division."[11]

No speaker at the Republican convention in Tampa would match the war-drum nastiness of one journalist, David Chalian, a former

ABC and PBS man working for Yahoo! News. The convention was delayed by a day as Hurricane Isaac passed over Tampa, prompting nasty references to Hurricane Katrina. NewsBusters posted video of Chalian cracking into an open microphone about the Romneys: "They are happy to have a party with black people drowning." [12]

Guess how many networks (other than Fox News) covered this gaffe, even after Yahoo quickly fired Chalian, despite his apologies? CNN mentioned it days later on its media-in-review show *Reliable Sources*. The rest of the networks stayed silent, even MSNBC, the ones who were listening intently for conservative "war drums of racial division." Chalian even drew support on Twitter from PBS anchor Gwen Ifill: "One mistake does not change this. David Chalian is God's gift to political journalism." [13]

By contrast, NBC anchor Brian Williams exemplified the network "news" template in a September 6 interview with top Obama aide Valerie Jarrett. He worried out loud that Team Obama was "in for a good savaging" in a forthcoming book by Bob Woodward: "You, I guess, have to play mistake-free ball now for 60 days, hope for nothing but positive coverage. That's a tall order." [14]

It sounded like a tall order that Williams would lunge to fulfill. There was no mention of Woodward's book on the *NBC Nightly News* before the election, and Woodward made no book-promoting appearance on *Today*.

Reading from the DNC Instructions

The network stars were shameless enough to quote Democrats at the Republicans.

In an interview with former Florida governor Jeb Bush, NBC *Today* cohost Matt Lauer repeated shrill attack lines from deputy Obama campaign manager Stephanie Cutter to question the honesty of Paul Ryan's vice presidential nomination acceptance speech: "'Forty minutes of vitriol and half a dozen previously debunked attacks.' Was it an honest speech? Or was it just a campaign convention speech?" [15]

ABC's instant analysis of Paul Ryan's RNC address included former Democratic operative George Stephanopoulos noting "we saw how much this crowd loved it" . . . before immediately adding, "I got an e-mail from a top Democrat saying the speech was audacious in its dishonesty." Stephanopoulos added in his own words that the speech was "brazen in some of these claims." [16]

When *CBS This Morning* interviewed Paul Ryan on the first morning of the Democrats' convention, cohost Charlie Rose quoted Obama: "Here is what the President said in asking the question about fixing the economy. He said what grade he would give himself. He said, 'I would say an incomplete, but what I would say is that steps that we have taken to saving the auto industry, and making sure that college is more affordable, and invest in the clean energy and science and technology and research. Those are all the things that we're going to need to grow over the long term.' That's from the President." (Ryan replied that an "incomplete" was a terrible answer from the president after four years on the job.) [17]

Republicans were constantly on the defensive. When Lauer interviewed New Jersey governor Chris Christie, he asked three consecutive questions about Romney failing to release more than two years of tax returns, and then closed by slamming an offhand Romney joke about not needing to see his birth certificate. Lauer lamented: "Governor Romney made a comment at a rally, I think it was on Friday and he said no one has ever asked to see my birth certificate, an obvious reference to the birther debate. Is it funny—he says it was a joke. Is it funny to, to kind of pay attention to a fringe group and question the very legitimacy of the President of the United States' citizenship?" [18]

Lauer didn't note, and obviously didn't care, that the Obama campaign actually raised money off the birth-certificate issue, selling mugs and T-shirts mocking the conspiracy theory.[19]

But a week later, when Lauer's cohost Savannah Guthrie interviewed liberal Harvard professor Elizabeth Warren, a candidate for the U.S. Senate, there was no tender regard for Romney's biography. Guthrie asked: "Is it your job here, as you understand it, to argue that Mitt Romney is the personification of that Wall Street greed and excess?" Then Guthrie again urged her to bash Romney: "Do you think Romney's Wall Street background disqualifies him from caring about the middle class or knowing what to do about the middle class?"[20]

When *CBS Evening News* anchor Scott Pelley interviewed Romney on the Monday night of the Republican convention, Pelley lectured the nominee about how his moderate-Republican father would be dismayed. "This Republican Party that you're leading is not your father's Republican Party. He opposed Barry Goldwater in 1964, when this car was built. He was for—a passionate advocate for government support for housing for poor people. I wonder how you would explain this Republican Party to your father?"[21] Can anyone imagine Pelley asking President Obama about his late parents without the mandatory handkerchief and dewy eyes?

A week after the Democratic convention closed, Pelley touted his latest Obama interview. "There was a remarkable moment of candor when he told us the sacrifices he makes being President wouldn't be worth it except for one thing. Listen for it!"

Obama boasted that all the lost freedom, of being unable to drive or walk around like a normal citizen, was worth the sacrifice. "What makes it worth it is when you meet some couple that says, 'You know what? Our kid was able to stay on our health insurance plan and it turns out they were just diagnosed with a curable cancer, but if they hadn't stayed on our plan we would haven't caught it.' That's what makes it worth it."[22]

Apparently, it's an outburst of "remarkable candor" to tout your-self as the magnanimous savior of cancer-stricken children. Some might expect that a journalist of Pelley's stature wouldn't be so excit-edly gullible. But that's how collusion works.

One CBS report most effectively demonstrates the old "Tiffany Network" ardor to polish the Democratic diamonds. As Team Obama withdrew the grand notion of the president giving his acceptance speech in 74,000-seat Bank of America stadium, claiming inclement weather that never emerged, CBS made no mention of empty seats or Obama's ego, and Pelley even skipped the stadium's bank name, calling it merely "the massive stadium that is home to the Carolina Panthers." Reporter Byron Pitts relayed that "according to the DNC, 65,000 people would have filled this stadium. Another 19,000 on the waiting list." Pitts could only find delighted Obama devotees who weren't the slightest bit critical of the decision:

BYRON PITTS: For Stacey Tillman of Harrisburg, North Carolina, a suburb of Charlotte, these tickets meant the chance of
a lifetime. Like thousands of others, two weeks ago she waited
in long lines for nearly four hours in 90-degree heat for a
chance at a ticket to hear the president speak in person. What
was your reaction when you heard the news?
STACEY TILLMAN: Disappointing, but at the same time, the
weather's been a concern all week. We've been watching it,
and I think that it was probably a good decision.
PITTS: David Miller of West Virginia says he'll keep his ticket as
a souvenir, and do as the campaign recommended and go to a
viewing party tomorrow night.
DAVID MILLER: Whether we get to see him live or we get
together as a community and get to watch him in our homes
together, the volunteers really support the president no matter
what.[23]

More Ugly Talk of Racist Republicans

When the Republican convention was over, liberal radio host Bill Press laughed at it as "pale, male, and stale."[24] Before it began, *Newsweek* special correspondent Michael Tomasky claimed that the convention would be a "toxic waste dump of hate and lies and race-baiting. . . . [T]his Romney-Ryan campaign is becoming among the most racist we've ever seen."[25]

But the allegedly racist Tea Party had supported a plethora of minority candidates, often against the establishment. In 2010, they backed Marco Rubio in Florida, against moderate Charlie Crist (who later changed parties). They backed Nimrata "Nikki" Haley, an Indian-American with a Sikh background. They loved another Indian-American, Louisiana governor Bobby Jindal, as a policy wonk. They helped elect new Latino governors in 2010 like Brian Sandoval in Nevada and Susana Martinez in New Mexico and black congressmen like Tim Scott and Allen West.

There were so many talented conservative minorities that it made reporters peer into a virtual kaleidoscope of Clarence Thomases. How the national media hated this narrative! It had to be crushed. *The Washington Post* publicized this narrative under the headline, "Incidents on the floor mar GOP's message of diversity." The *Post* reported the Republicans gave "prime speaking slots to Latinos and blacks who have emphasized their party's economic appeal to all Americans. But they have delivered those speeches to a convention hall filled overwhelmingly with white faces, an awkward contrast that has been made more uncomfortable this week by a series of racial headaches that have intruded on the party's efforts to project a new level of inclusiveness."[26]

There is no greater headache, or acid reflux, than the blatantly slanted media narrative on "diversity." In one incident the *Post* was spreading, two apparent GOP convention attendees reportedly threw peanuts at a black CNN camerawoman and told her this was "how we feed the animals."[27] That's the theme the liberal media wanted to keep propagating, twenty-four hours a day.

The *Post* and the networks didn't notice that black female congressional Republican candidate Mia Love had her Wikipedia biography on the Internet defaced as she spoke on August 29, with disgusting slurs like "House Nigger" and "dirty, worthless whore who sold out her soul."[28] The media liberals didn't mention the sale of racial buttons at the Democrat convention like "Once you vote black you never go back. Obama 2012." Former *Newsweek* reporter David Graham showed that button off at *The Atlantic* website as among "[t]he best of the official and unofficial campaign gear on display."[29]

Being a rising minority star in the Republican Party makes you a media target, not a darling like Obama. Take Senator Marco Rubio. On Tuesday night, NBC anchor Brian Williams hammered away at Rubio on rape: "I want to ask you about your party. You, I've watched you on television for days, talking about this gathering and, and being a proud Floridian. Are you happy with the tone and tenor of the conversation, right now? The rape debate got out of control, went several days. Is this where you want it in the big tent business?"[30] (Williams had another version of this hardball pitch to Paul Ryan, asking if he would "own the fact that the platform of this party allows a woman, who has been raped, no exception but to carry that child to term.")[31]

On Wednesday morning, the Rubio pounding continued. On ABC's *Good Morning America,* cohost George Stephanopoulos again quoted from Democrats: "Look at what the chairman of the Democratic convention, the mayor of Los Angeles, Antonio Villaraigosa, said last night. He said you can't just trot out a brown face or a Spanish surname and expect people to vote for your candidate. He was referring to you tomorrow night."[32]

CBS This Morning cohost Charlie Rose expressed grave pessimism at GOP outreach to minorities: "You are a rising star in this party," he said to Rubio. "How is it changing? Because many people worry that people who are Hispanic, African-American and other minorities don't have a place in this party. You're becoming something that is more narrow rather than outreaching."[33]

On Wednesday night's *PBS NewsHour*, anchor Gwen Ifill sympathized with Rubio on illegal immigration but hammered at "hot-button" conservatives opposed to "comprehensive" amnesty: "You have said this. Jeb Bush has said this. John McCain has said this. Yet the party platform uses kind of hot-button trigger terms like 'illegal aliens' and it calls for self-deportation. And that seems to be a gateway issue for a lot of Latino voters."[34]

Later on Wednesday night, as another new GOP star, New Mexico governor Susana Martinez—Hispanic and female—was speaking at the podium, ABC ignored her speech, preferring to interview liberal Univision anchor Jorge Ramos instead, as he shoveled dirt into the GOP's political grave:

"I think Republicans have a real, real challenge trying to get Latinos. Because just a few words in Spanish from Susana Martinez over principle is not enough," warned Ramos while ABC showed video of Martinez speaking. "If they insist on talking about immigration, they're going to lose even more of the Hispanic vote. The last poll that I saw, they don't even get 30 percent of the Hispanic vote. If they can't get 33 percent, 35 or 40 percent, they're going to lose the election."[35]

The others also skipped over Governor Martinez to make room for liberal blather. On CBS, anchor Scott Pelley pounded John McCain: "Mitt Romney has limited experience in foreign policy and, like several recent presidents, he has no experience in the military. Why should he be the next commander in chief?" McCain didn't make the obvious point that Obama had zero military service, and no blow-dried anchorman cared in 2008. He didn't even ask Pelley if he ever served (he didn't). The senator merely said Romney "has the right instincts the way Ronald Reagan did." [36]

NBC had a four-Caucasian conversation during the Martinez speech. Former anchorman Tom Brokaw took a shot at Obama-bashing conservatives in reviewing Condoleezza Rice's speech. "What was so striking to me was one other line that she had: 'It does not matter where you come from. It matters where you are going.' Well to a lot of delegates, on this floor, it does matter where President Obama came from. Because they've been very critical of his Kenyan father, who had a different faith than many of them would embrace, and they've raised lots of questions about where his ultimate loyalty is." [37]

How Brokaw deduced a majority of delegates were birthers is anyone's guess. But it underlines the contempt that media liberals have for the GOP rank and file.

The next morning on NPR's *Morning Edition*, reporter Ted Robbins concluded a story: "For a Republican Party struggling to connect with Hispanic voters, Governor Susana Martinez may be the perfect symbol." [38] *National Journal* reporter Major Garrett declared on CBS: "Another big star last night was Susana Martinez. The reaction on the floor was absolutely sensational. Not too many people have seen her before, heard her before. . . . I think she was a breakout star last night." [39]

The Republicans had a "breakout star" and "perfect symbol" that ABC, CBS, and NBC ignored or avoided.

The Good Wife and the Housewife

Another obvious and routine double standard emerges in the network interviews with the spouses of the candidates. The feminist lawyer spouse gets the softballs, while the traditional "housewife" gets prosecuted.

In 1992, PBS anchor Judy Woodruff famously drew the ire of First Lady Barbara Bush for her double standard. At the Democratic convention, Woodruff repeatedly asked Hillary Clinton unchallenging questions, admitting out loud she was welcoming Democrat talking points: "The Clinton campaign has been saying this is a week that they were trying to tell the American people more about who Bill Clinton really is. What is it that you think the American people should know about your husband that they might not know or might not understand?"

Weeks later, when Woodruff sat down with First Lady Bush on PBS, she hammered her about the GOP convention being too nasty: they questioned the Democrats' patriotism, they weren't welcoming to gays, a speaker "joked that Gov. Clinton is a skirt chaser . . . does that have a place in this campaign?"

Mrs. Bush took Woodruff to task, deliciously: "Look, you're saying nothing nice . . . where were you during the Democrat convention defending us?" Woodruff just kept on hammering about the skirt-chasing jokes, but Mrs. Bush let loose: "You didn't listen to the Democrat Convention I think. . . . Now c'mon, be fair."[40]

There is no greater demonstration of misplaced idealism than a Republican expecting the national media to be fair in a presidential campaign. Two nights later, Woodruff administered the same beating about GOP negativism to the vice president's wife, Marilyn Quayle.[41]

Since the Republican convention came first, Ann Romney wasn't able to critique the double standard. But NBC anchor Brian Williams was strangely offended that Mrs. Romney hailed her husband's presidential potential in her convention address. "Last night, as you wrapped up, you said 'this man will lift up America.' In an interview you did with Natalie Morales for my other broadcast, *Rock Center*, you used different language: 'I believe in my heart that Mitt is going to save America.' And that jumped off the screen to me. Someone who knows you conceded that if Mrs. Obama used words like that—

'Barack was going to save America'—there'd be all kinds of hubbub. What do you mean? Those are powerful words." [42]

This is how shameless (or just clueless) Williams was. In her 2008 convention speech, Mrs. Obama said the same thing, if not stronger. She described her husband's impending ascension to the presidency as the juncture "where the current of history meets this new tide of hope." [43]

So when Williams interviewed her shortly after her convention speech in 2008, the NBC star must have complained about the tone, right? Mrs. Obama repeated her puffery to Williams: "I come here as a wife who loves my husband and believes he will be an extraordinary president."

Instead of expressing umbrage, Williams jumped right back to placing the "hubbub" in its proper perspective: those evil Republicans. "What of the attacks has busted through to you? What makes you angriest at John McCain, the Republicans? What's being said about your husband that you want to shout from the mountaintops as not true?" [44]

This question is so predictable from NBC. It's almost exactly how Jane Pauley interviewed Mrs. Clinton in 1992: "What was the worst thing you've heard said about you? . . . All right, what was the grossest distortion of your record?" [45]

But Williams wanted to break new grounds in servility. For Mrs. Obama in 2008, he asked people to imagine a "bigger picture" of a country that would finally let the descendants of slaves live in the White House that slaves built: "How do you begin to wrap your head around the bigger picture of, if you're successful, you'll move into a house where, when the Adams [family] moved in, slaves were finishing the plaster over the fireplace. How does that work?" [46]

When Williams interviewed Mrs. Obama at the Democrat convention in 2012, he was still aglow. "In your job you get to listen to all of the psychiatrists analyze your husband. Peter Baker, this morning's

New York Times: He's 'a proud yet humbled President, a confident yet scarred President, a dreamer mugged by reality.' Does that resemble the man you know?"[47]

That's not a softball question. That's a spoonful of baby food. He went on to another syrupy question, trying to kiss up to her about how rapidly the First Daughters were growing up.

To be fair, other anchors were also aggressively slanted, pushing around Mrs. Romney and saving their goo for Mrs. Obama. CBS anchorman Scott Pelley reminded Mrs. Obama how "in your speech on the first night of the convention, you said that the presidency 'does not change a person, it reveals the person.'" He added: "And I wonder, has this experience revealed anything to you about your husband that you did not know?"[48]

Then he asked the First Lady "What do you get tired and frustrated about?" She tried to demur, suggesting she was impressed with her husband's focus on moving America forward. Then Pelley ludicrously suggested, "You could have said that persistent questioning by reporters gets under your skin. That's a possibility." She couldn't answer that, either.

She should have burst out laughing. During the Republican convention, Pelley attempted to embarrass Ann Romney with a gotcha question: "The president is starting a tour called the Romney-Ryan Wrong for Women tour. . . . A lot of women look at the Republican platform on abortion, contraception, a number of issues, and ask the question whether Republicans have women's best interests at heart?"[49]

Inclusive Democrats Didn't Include God

Conservative Christians have been scorned as the death of the Republicans at every convention since Ronald Reagan was nominated, but the increasingly secularizing, God-deleting base of the Democratic Party is routinely ignored.

One controversy briefly erupted at the Democratic convention. Republicans discovered the word "God" was nowhere in the official document for the party, the Democratic platform. The 2008 Democratic platform made one reference to God: the "God-given potential" of working people.[50] In 2012, even that paltry phrase was scrapped. GOP vice presidential nominee Paul Ryan launched the Republican critique on *Fox & Friends*: "I guess I would just put the onus and the burden on them to explain why they did all this, these purges of God."[51] Ryan also attacked the platform's failure to affirm Jerusalem as the capital of Israel, which was upsetting to Jewish and Christian voters.

Melanie Roussell, national press secretary for the Democratic National Committee, called the issue a "faux controversy," since the Democrat platform did express support for "faith," just without the G-word.[52] The media largely followed the DNC script, as usual. In the middle of Wednesday, Los Angeles mayor Antonio Villaraigosa quickly held a delegate vote to add those missing words to the platform. The voice vote was obviously, and audibly, split down the middle, if not a little bit against the inclusion of God. The fanaticism of this party was there for all to hear it and Villaraigosa had to know it. So the mayor proclaimed that two-thirds of the assembly had voted yes, which was nonsense and caused booing. Even the pundits on NPR's *Talk of the Nation* agreed the voice vote was split.[53]

"You don't want to put delegates in a position where they're booing God and Jerusalem, especially on videotape. It has to be included in all the coverage of the convention," proclaimed Steve Hayes on Fox's *Special Report*.[54] But Hayes, like Mrs. Bush, was too idealistic.

CBS Evening News was the "toughest" network covering this scandal by giving this controversy fifty-one seconds (with no video), as anchor Scott Pelley announced: "One of the things that these conventions do is write the party platform—a symbolic document that is immediately forgotten." Reporter Nancy Cordes relayed, "the convention chairman came out here and announced that they were adding those two items to the platform despite some pretty loud boos from some of the delegates in this room." There was no reference to a voice vote. This was damage control, not reporting.

NBC Nightly News gave the platform mess a few seconds, but Chuck Todd quickly pivoted to how delegates spent "most of the day basking in the afterglow of last night's rousing convention kickoff."

But ABC's *World News* shamelessly just skipped it. Instead, they devoted twelve minutes—more than half the newscast—to sappy spin on the convention, including three minutes to fill-in anchor David Muir talking to Caroline Kennedy about the tribute to her late uncle Ted Kennedy. Muir asked her, "You wrote that 'I have never had a President who inspired me the way people tell me my father inspired them. But for the first time, I believe, I have found the man who could be that President.' Do you still feel just as inspired by President Obama?" [55]

On the *PBS NewsHour*, they didn't report on the vote, other than a vague mention tossed in by pseudo-conservative analyst David Brooks: "Some of the platform fights, if you have got a problem with people who go to church, don't leave God out of your platform. If you have got a problem with some Jewish voters because they don't think the president is standing with Israel, don't leave Jerusalem out of your platform." [56]

Even the alleged newspapers of record were also treating it like a "faux controversy." *The New York Times* ran a 1,143-word piece on the platforms on Wednesday and never mentioned the lack of the word "God." On Thursday, a story on page 14 was headlined "Pushed by Obama, Democrats Alter Platform Over Jerusalem," with the God controversy popping up very briefly in the fifth paragraph.[57] That was all.

The Washington Post published a 3,594-word front-page story on Wednesday on the history of recent party platforms, but it never mentioned the missing G-word, or Jerusalem.[58] Thursday's paper briefly mentioned the voice vote in the eighth paragraph of a story on page A-8.

On *Fox News Watch*, conservative panelist James Pinkerton guessed just how this would have been reported very differently if the shoe was on the other party's foot: "If it had been a Republican convention, the media would have hauled out acoustical engineers, and sound decibel checks, and they would have proved which was bigger and so on. Those two [protesting] people in the white T-shirts would be household names by now. *The New York Times* would have them on the front page, on the *Today* show, telling their story about how atrocious the Republicans are." [59]

Perhaps the media's double standard on religion was most effectively embodied by Brian Williams and NBC. While he could only spare a few seconds for the "God" gaffe for Democrats, the prime-time NBC magazine show *Rock Center* devoted an hour-long special to the Mormon church.

"Most Americans say they know next to nothing about the Mormon Church. Tonight, a rare look inside the lives of modern Mormon families. . . . A church still dealing with the issue of polygamy. . . . And other issues of inequality."

Williams touted pop culture mocking the faith on Broadway and on TV, starting with a clip of Fox's sleazy cartoon *Family Guy* in which lead character Peter Griffin declares: "I'm going to be a Mormon. . . . Come on, nailing a different wife every night. That's a no-brainer."

After briefly describing the founding of the religion, Williams quickly focused on negative perceptions of Mormonism: "Part of the history of the Church that they can't shake is polygamy. . . . [E]ven though polygamy was officially banned a century ago, it's something the Church still has to deal with. . . . Critics in other religions have openly called them a cult."[60]

The networks could not see how much they looked like an Obama-worshipping cult.

CHAPTER 10

Secret Tapes and the 47 Percent

Only hidden cameras we like make "news."

When it comes to dirty tricks and secret tapes, Americans will harken back to President Nixon and Watergate. It was considered grotesquely paranoid for a Republican president to record conversations with his unwitting aides in the White House. His defenders insisted he was not the first.

They were correct, but it didn't matter. There were secret White House tapes of John F. Kennedy and Lyndon Johnson. But with them, it was different. The surreptitious habits of these liberal Democrats weren't considered sleazy or unethical. They were considered a gift to history.

It's just another day at the Office of Dirty Media Tricks.

On September 17, 2012, Mitt Romney was victimized by a political enemy at a Boca Raton, Florida, fundraiser who recorded his remarks without his consent. What followed was what many liberal journalists insisted was the death blow to the Romney campaign.

Bloomberg's Josh Barro wrote a piece headlined "Today, Mitt Romney Lost the Election."[1]

He was right. The liberals' joy was palpable after the hard-left magazine *Mother Jones* posted a three-month-old secret tape of Mitt Romney talking to donors at the private residence. The headline emphasized: "When he doesn't know a camera's rolling, the GOP candidate shows his disdain for half of America."[2] Romney said he would never convince 47 percent of the electorate to vote for him, since they were dependent on government.

Remember that David Axelrod's case for reelecting Obama relied heavily on convincing voters that while the economic recovery barely had a pulse, they couldn't trust Mitt Romney. After the election, he said at the University of Chicago that he wanted voters to think Romney "was out of touch with their economic experience, and that his fundamental view of the economy was one which didn't incorporate them. And frankly, when that 47 percent tape came out, it was a pretty strong ratification of our view."[3]

Axelrod was more emphatic with *Politico*: "I think that the greatest gift we got may have been that 47 percent tape, which was him [Romney]."[4]

The partisan provenance of the tape didn't matter. It was acquired through James Carter IV, an unemployed grandson of ex-president Jimmy Carter. Later, Jimmy told Piers Morgan at CNN that, "[w]hen James went to meet President Obama, President Obama ran across the room, embraced him, and thanked him profusely for his time."

He should have hugged the networks, too. Over three full days of coverage, on the Big Three evening and morning shows, they devoted almost an hour and a half (1 hour, 28 minutes, 23 seconds) to the Romney tape, which made up all or part of forty-two campaign stories.[5] Team Romney felt this was not a story that deserved eighty-eight minutes of news time, but the Obama administration clearly felt it was as good as eighty-eight minutes of free campaign advertising.

The network carnival barkers erupted with the chants of "bombshell" and "earthquake" on a "seismic day" for the Republican campaign. A viewer might imagine the earth would open up and swallow Romney whole. NBC's Brian Williams proclaimed, "These are tough days for the Romney campaign. Inside 50 days to go now until the election, and they are dealing with something of a public relations disaster."[6]

The networks were right. There was an earthquake—of their own making. *CBS Evening News* anchor Scott Pelley used the usual lingo when the "news" was designed to eviscerate Republicans: "With 49 days to Election Day, a candidate for president doesn't want a distraction from his message, but it's happened in a big way to Mitt Romney."[7]

On CBS, Bob Schieffer was handing out the shovels to dig a grave for Romney. "I just can't think of anything that he could have said that could have hurt his cause more," and "He's got a lot of work to do to dig out of this hole."[8] NBC brought on ersatz-conservative Joe Scarborough to proclaim, "This is one of the worst weeks for any presidential candidate in a general election that any of us can remember."[9]

Among Romney's remarks caught on tape was his accurate observation about the liberal tilt of ABC's *The View*. The show "is high-risk because of the five women on it. Only one is conservative and four are sharp-tongued and not conservative." The conservative on this list had to be Elisabeth Hasselbeck, who came to Romney's defense on the 47 percent remarks. "I think there's a general feeling that, with more and more people becoming dependent on the government, that by next July we could perhaps be celebrating Dependence Day, not Independence Day," she said.

"Oh, Elisabeth," Barbara Walters scoffed off-camera, like an embarrassed mother. "This is not something that I'm just feeling alone," Hasselbeck insisted. "Yes it is," Walters said, to laughter from the audience.[10] Hasselbeck was certainly alone at that table.

Romney told his donors that Obama could count on 47 percent of the voters who will vote for him no matter what, "who are dependent upon government, who believe that they are victims, who believe that government has a responsibility to care for them, who believe that they are entitled to health care, to food, to housing, to you name it." He added: "My job is not to worry about those people. I'll never convince them that they should take personal responsibility and care for their lives."

It was a monumentally stupid remark. That 47 percent of the electorate dependent on the government includes deadbeats—yes. It also includes the United States military. And retired citizens on (their) Social Security. And folks who don't want government largesse, but are struggling. Romney wasn't intending to insult these constituencies—but he did. He rushed to the (public) microphones to correct the record. It did no good.

Reporters knew that this is not the way any candidate would talk in public. A politician should appeal for any and every voter he can attract. This reminded many political junkies of 2008, when a *Huffington Post* journalist, Mayhill Fowler, had a recording of Obama telling donors in San Francisco about working-class Democrats, "It's not surprising, then, they get bitter, they cling to guns or religion or antipathy to people who aren't like them, or anti-immigrant sentiment, or anti-trade sentiment as a way to explain their frustrations."[11]

That bitter-clingers gaffe was reported at the time because 1) Hillary Clinton made it a central thrust of her improbable campaign to be the lunchpail candidate; 2) liberal reporters are more amenable to (mildly) damaging stories in the primaries, with the strategic thought that the Democrat nominee will be forever "inoculated" from the charges in the general election and beyond; and 3) the *Huffington Post* is a liberal website, not a "far right" blog they could reject for baldly ideological reasons.

The liberal media displayed zero interest in revealing anything Obama said and did behind closed doors as he ran for reelection. As sexy as hidden cameras are to journalists, there were no liberal Mayhill Fowlers to expose Obama in 2012, and conservative hidden-camera journalism has been dismissed as too ideological to be trustworthy.

When conservative activists exposed the leftist pro-Obama group ACORN with hidden cameras in 2009, the networks waited for days to touch it and then aired just one solitary story (ABC, CBS) or three (NBC) as Congress defunded them.[12] When the pro-life activists of Live Action exposed Planned Parenthood clinics advising a "pimp" on how to evade the law with underage prostitutes, these three networks simply put their heads in the sand and pretended it didn't exist, even as CNN and Fox aired the video.[13]

But somehow, *Mother Jones* was the gold standard for quality, nonideological reporting . . . or liberals are just brazen enough to think the only criterion that matters is political usefulness.

No Time for Romney Points on Obama's Economy

Something Romney said actually caused a thrill up the leg of Chris Matthews. On MSNBC, he took to bad singing: " 'If I were a rich man, Yubby dibby dibby dibby dibby dibby dibby dum.' Dumb. It's one thing to be rich and have the majority of voters convinced you're out to help the rich. Is there anything dumber, though, to be caught pandering to your fellow rich?"[14]

Speaking of dumb, the media seemed deaf and dumb to Obama's flaws on the economy. The media elite's incessant hammering on the

"47 percent" tape underlined just how eager they were to avoid conservative arguments that would put a dent in Obama's image as an economically competent president. Consider the network suppression of these matters:

The So-Called Stimulus. A January 2009 report from Obama's economic team suggested that massive new "stimulus" spending would stem the rising unemployment rate at about 8 percent.[15] Signing the $787 billion package on February 17, 2009, Obama proclaimed this marked "the beginning of the end" of America's unemployment woes.[16] At that time, unemployment was at 8.3 percent. It rose above 9 percent by May, and peaked at 10 percent in October. The official rate stayed above 9 percent through October 2011, and then above 8 percent until September 2012.[17]

This was the worst bout of high unemployment since the Great Depression, but during the entire 2012 campaign, ABC, CBS, and NBC never mentioned that Obama's economists predicted that passing the "stimulus" would keep unemployment below 8 percent. On May 25, 2012, the Congressional Budget Office estimated the cost of the "stimulus" was higher ($831 billion) and estimated the "increased number of people employed by between 0.2 million and 1.5 million."[18] That computes to between $540,000 and $4.1 million per job. Network coverage? Zero.

The Deficit. Would the average voter remember that Obama promised in early 2009 he would "improve" on the Bush fiscal record? He could not have been more public and unequivocal. The president held a nationally televised "Fiscal Responsibility Summit" at the White House on February 23, 2009, and boldly promised, "Today, I'm pledging to cut the deficit we inherited by half by the end of our first term in office."[19] He repeated that pledge before a joint session of Congress.[20]

It was a powerful statement. Maybe that's why ABC, CBS, and NBC all reported on this. ABC's Jake Tapper stated, "The president says he plans to cut the $1.3 trillion in half by the end of his first term. He says first term, knowing that whether or not he gets a second term depends on how he delivers on all of these big ambitious promises." [21]

Notice that Tapper (as did NBC's Savannah Guthrie) accepted Obama's goal of cutting in half the deficit estimate for fiscal year 2009, which was not yet half elapsed. The deficit for the last full fiscal year of President Bush, fiscal year 2008, ending on September 30, was only $438 billion, which itself broke the historic record. It may be polite to say Obama "inherited" the spending of his first year in office, even if he was president for the last seven months of it. But Obama voted in the Senate for the massive increase in spending— the Troubled Assets Relief Program—in 2008, and he was planning a dramatic multi-year increase in spending through the "stimulus," so his intentions of expanding the deficit were quite clear to journalists.

Under Obama, the deficits stayed Empire State Building high, from $1.4 trillion in fiscal 2009, to $1.3 trillion in fiscal 2010 and fiscal 2011, to $1.1 trillion in fiscal 2012. Three years after his pledge, Obama told an Atlanta TV station, "Well, we're not there because this recession turned out to be a lot deeper than any of us realized." [22]

So was the president held accountable for his own pledge? This old promise was either ignored or barely noticed by the network evening news shows. Only ABC's Tapper—a man with a tendency to be an outlier and break from the pack occasionally—returned to a video clip of the original 2009 promise and explained—once, on February 13, 2012—that this was a "broken promise for President Obama." [23] On October 19, CBS reporter Jan Crawford reran a soundbite from Mitt Romney from the first debate: "He said that he'd cut in half the deficit. He hasn't done that, either. In fact, he doubled it." [24]

Brian Williams and the *NBC Nightly News* never located any troublesome deficit-promise soundbites.

On November 13, 2011, very early in the election cycle, NBC's

Meet the Press did—sort of. They played a 2008 clip of candidate Obama: "The problem is, is that the way Bush has done it over the last eight years is to take out a credit card from the bank of China in the name of our children, driving up our national debt from $5 trillion for the first 42 presidents, number 43 added $4 trillion by his lonesome. That's irresponsible. It's unpatriotic."

If Bush's deficits made him irresponsible and unpatriotic, what did Obama's make *him*?

Without underlining that Obama had added more than $5 trillion to the debt in only one term, David Gregory pressed Democratic Party chair Debbie Wasserman Schultz: "That's his rhetoric. Should it not be turned on him now?" Schultz dodged the question and changed the subject: "What we should be turning on is that Mitt Romney, for example, who purports to be the alternative to President Obama, would've allowed Detroit to go bankrupt, would've allowed more than a million jobs in the pipeline to just, just evaporate. We wouldn't have had an American automobile industry." Gregory allowed her to filibuster and get away with ignoring the issue: "We're going to leave it there." [25]

None of the network evening shows replayed that "unpatriotic" charge back at Obama. There's another standard dirty-trick double standard: Democrats are allowed to call Republicans pretty much anything.

Poverty. In September 2011, the Census Bureau reported there were 46.2 million Americans defined as living in poverty—the highest number in the fifty-two years the bureau has been publishing figures. The census report the next year found the same number. [26] That's 6.4 million more people than at the end of the Bush era, in 2008, for an increase of 16 percent. [27]

The U.S. Department of Agriculture reported that the number of Americans using food stamps rose to almost 47 million before Election Day. That's a dramatic increase from 31 million in November 2008, when Obama was first elected president.[28]

Of the evening newscasts, the *CBS Evening News* was the leader mentioning the data on poverty and/or food stamps. On the 310 evenings from January 1 up to Election Day, they filed five stories. *NBC Nightly News* aired two.

ABC's *World News* never cited this data, although they aired two Romney soundbites mentioning high rates of Americans in poverty, once about single mothers, once about Hispanics. On September 17, as David Muir talked up "withering criticism" of the GOP nominee from inside his own party, Romney told the Hispanic Chamber of Commerce, "Over two million more Hispanics are living in poverty today than the day President Obama took office." [29]

After several stories on the Benghazi attack on September 12, NBC anchor Brian Williams turned to the home front: "The Census Bureau, the folks who count us all, are tonight out with a look at who we are these days. And their numbers on the economy and poverty in America are both stunning and sad, especially what they say about the once-great American middle class." Williams and his correspondent, Chris Jansing, never uttered the name "Obama" or made any kind of political connection.[30] It was somehow just a sociological accident, and Obama's economic policies were somehow utterly unconnected to it.

Obamacare. Despite Republican fury against Obamacare during the primaries, where every candidate pledged to repeal it, the network evening news shows contracted a severe case of apathy as bad numbers started arriving and Obama's plan cratered. Before he won the White House in 2008, Obama had promised to sign a "universal health care bill into law by the end of my first term as president that will cover every American and cut the cost of a typical family's premium by up to $2,500 a year." [31]

They called their bill "The Affordable Care Act," because they believed nationalizing the system would lower consumer costs. When he signed the bill in 2010, Obama repeated: "This legislation will also lower costs for families and for businesses."[32]

But in September 2012, the annual health benefits survey of the Kaiser Family Foundation—a longtime backer of socialized medicine—showed average premiums rising again. From 2009 through 2012, they rose by an average of $2,370 per family.[33] Costs were going in the exact opposite direction of what had been promised. It was now clearly the Unaffordable Care Act. Network coverage of the Kaiser survey? Zero.

That wasn't the only problem. Liberals always insist that the number of Americans without health insurance is a national scandal, and push government schemes with the ideal of leaving no one uninsured. That was the driving justification for nationalizing one-seventh of the economy. But a March 2012 analysis by the Congressional Budget Office estimated that even with all the new taxes, subsidies, and regulations implemented by 2016, about 26–27 million Americans would remain uninsured.

The news only got worse. Despite Obama's promise that if you like your health-care plan, you can keep it, the same CBO report determined that 3–5 million fewer people would have coverage through an employer "compared with the number under prior law."[34] In March, there was heavy TV coverage of Obamacare as its constitutionality was argued before the Supreme Court—but there was not a single word about the millions who would lose their employer-based insurance, or the tens of millions who would remain uninsured despite the passage of Obamacare.

The wheels had come off this colossus but the American people were being kept in the dark.

There was a mention of the CBO report on ABC's *World News* on March 26, the day the Supreme Court heard oral arguments, but it was used in Obama's favor, not against him. If the court struck down the individual mandate, correspondent Terry Moran insisted, "the Congressional Budget Office estimates that 16 million fewer Americans would have health insurance. So the stakes are very high."[35] ABC left the impression that Obamacare was fairly close to providing insurance for all, so it should be untouched by the Court. It just wasn't true.

In July, about a month after the Supreme Court decision, the CBO revised its estimates upward, predicting 30 million would remain uninsured and 4–6 million would lose their employer-based health care.[36] Network coverage of that increasingly dour scenario? Again, still zero. Zippo.

What about the Republican argument that small businesses would resist expanding beyond fifty employees, the level at which they would be forced to provide expensive health-care coverage or be fined under Obamacare? The negative effect on small businesses and job creation were all but omitted in 2012. There were just two pieces of stories focusing on the small-business impact on the evening newscasts on June 28, the day the Supreme Court upheld Obama's scheme.

ABC's David Muir offered fifteen seconds to pessimistic small businessman Jorge Lozano, and NBC's Anne Thompson devoted forty-six seconds to a small businessman, Joe Olivo, who would delay hiring new employees or instead find part-time workers to avoid Obamacare, a "potential unintended consequence of a law aimed at expanding health care."[37]

CBS never focused on the potentially damaging effects on small business and their hiring patterns. Total network coverage? Sixty-one seconds.

Keystone Pipeline. A Gallup poll in March 2012 found that 57 percent of Americans favored the Keystone XL pipeline, which would run from Canada to the Gulf of Mexico. Only 29 percent were opposed.[38] On January 18, 2012, President Obama pleased the radical environmentalists on the left by denying a permit to the pipeline proposal. Republicans were disgusted. On NBC, Newt Gingrich declared, "This is a stunningly stupid thing to do. And there's no better word for it. These people are so out of touch with reality it's as though they were governing Mars."[39]

But the media weren't exactly in touch with the majority on this proposal, either. All three networks aired full stories on the Obama decision that night. CBS anchor Scott Pelley said "election-year politics is far from over," and NBC anchor Brian Williams predicted "you can be sure, as the campaign season enters the home stretch, we'll be hearing a lot more about this long stretch of pipe."[40]

Not really. After that one night of coverage, the networks virtually buried the story and tried to make people forget one of Obama's more unpopular decisions. There were only seven mentions on the three networks through the rest of the campaign, and a grand total of *one* additional full story—a March 22 *CBS Evening News* piece about an Obama photo op underlining his support for the southern leg of the pipeline, from Oklahoma City to the Gulf of Mexico, a part of the project that didn't require Obama's approval.

"It was a day when both parties played a bit loose with the facts," insisted CBS correspondent Norah O'Donnell. She pointed out Obama didn't note that only the northern part of the project required his approval. Speaker John Boehner then said, "So the president can take credit for having nothing to do with the bottom half of this pipeline, and the fact is, there's only one permit that requires his approval because it crosses our national boundaries."

O'Donnell suggested Boehner somehow played loose with the facts because Obama blocked it after "the Republican governor of Nebraska, Dave Heineman, asked the president to reject it because of environmental concerns."[41] Two days after Obama's second inauguration, Heineman approved the pipeline with an altered route.[42] The networks skipped over that, too.

It didn't matter to the networks that many Democrats and labor unions favored the pipeline project. What mattered was the president making an important concession to radical environmentalists to keep them energized and not protesting in the streets before the election.

What Outrageous Obama Clips?

The media were very skilled at diagnosing Romney's problems over hours of "news" coverage, but they could easily swerve to change the subject away from Obama problems or gaffes—if they had to acknowledge them at all. So Republican operatives went looking for Obama video snippets to fire back at the *Mother Jones* salvo.

Through the Drudge Report, the Romney camp tried to shift the campaign conversation away from the "47 percent" hype by directing the networks to a 1998 tape of Obama at Loyola University, where he professed his love for redistributing other people's money, solidifying the socialist worldview Obama has so zealously denied. "I think the trick is figuring out how do we structure government systems that pool resources and hence facilitate some redistribution because I actually believe in redistribution, at least at a certain level to make sure that everybody's got a shot."[43] The networks gave this real bombshell six and a half minutes of attention. That's "fairness" to these TV people, a 13-to-1 advantage for Obama.

NBC and MSNBC waited to "verify" the old Obama video before airing it and dispatched someone to the university for the full videotape. On her MSNBC daytime show, reporter Andrea Mitchell insisted that "because we have not independently at NBC News and MSNBC authenticated it, we're not airing it. But the basic issue is, they're accusing President Obama, as John Sununu said to me yesterday, of class warfare, that is trying to change the subject."[44] NBC really wanted to keep the negative focus on Romney.

Mitchell did not explain why there was no NBC delay in airing the *Mother Jones* video while they verified it. They began replaying it within twelve hours. There was no delay to see if Romney's tape was out of context, although Romney complained that the tape was only "snippets" of his remarks. The magazine then posted the "complete" video in two parts, except it wasn't. Conservative bloggers discovered the tape had a Nixon-like two minutes edited out of it in the middle. By then the networks had already hammered the anti-Romney message home.

Two weeks later, on October 2, the Drudge Report featured another video as a forthcoming Fox News scoop—a June 5, 2007, Obama speech before black ministers at Hampton University, touted as "Obama's other race speech." The networks quickly disposed of the story on the next morning. NBC's Chuck Todd barely mentioned it. ABC's Jake Tapper reported: "Conservatives are calling it explosive. The Obama campaign is calling it a desperate attempt by Romney's allies to change the subject." At least he threw in a clip from that speech with Obama extolling his "friend and great leader" Rev. Wright.[45]

On CBS, reporter Jan Crawford threw it in briefly at the end of her story, and then CBS demonstrated Team Romney wanted nothing to do with these clips. Cohosts Charlie Rose and Norah O'Donnell asked Romney aide Kevin Madden three times for his opinion on this story, and he avoided the subject like he was being asked to swallow poison.

Then O'Donnell turned to Obama spokesman Robert Gibbs: "I want to give you an opportunity to respond to that tape that was aired by Fox, the President talking about what happened in New Orleans. Does the President believe the Bush administration did not help the victims of Hurricane Katrina because of their race?" CBS had just aired a clip from the tape of Obama slamming the Bush response as "colorblind in its incompetence," so Gibbs repeated that sentiment. Then he shamed CBS for echoing Sean Hannity: "I have to say I'm a little amazed that, as you mentioned, a widely-covered speech, likely by people at your network, has somehow caused a ker-fuffle five years later because somebody like Sean Hannity decided to re-air what was covered extensively." Cohost Charlie Rose obediently replied, "Let me move on." [46]

It was a trick perfected by Bill Clinton: confront an allegation by declaring it Asked and Answered, an old story already covered, when in fact it had barely been touched. Many liberal journalists dismissed the Hampton speech tape as old news in 2012, something that was already covered as news in 2007. In reality, at that time, the coverage of the speech to black ministers was sparse. It drew an anchor brief on ABC and NBC, and nothing on the newscasts of CBS, PBS, and NPR. *The Washington Post* barely managed a paragraph on it.

But journalists will be bored by anything Obama said in public, no matter how odd. Obama began the speech by saying he attended a service in Los Angeles to "commemorate the anniversary" of the Los Angeles riots of 1992, as if the rioters had been engaged in a noble cause. Obama's language of "quiet riots" caused by American neglect of poverty isn't seen as controversial language by liberals, just as the word "redistribution" makes them smile, not gag.

On the other hand, Romney saying that a large chunk of Obama's voters are dependent on government was treated as a disastrous outburst.

There's another reason the networks could have ignored the old June 2007 speech. It was almost exactly the same as an Obama speech on May 5, 2007, to the National Conference of Black Mayors.[47] Asked and Answered. Time to move on. Once they've decided a speech isn't newsworthy, into the shredder it goes.

Rev. Wright Hush Money?

What was new in the Hampton speech was Senator Obama's tribute to "my friend and great leader" Rev. Jeremiah Wright, and the notion that "[o]ur God is big enough" for liberal programs like "affordable health care for every American." Rev. Wright's noxious sermons became the most threatening scandal of Obama's first campaign for president—but too late in the primaries to really stop him. The networks fervently came to his defense and were thoroughly enraptured by the "race speech" designed to end the scandal. Videotapes showed that Wright screamed "God damn America!" from the pulpit and suggested America deserved 9/11, that the attacks on New York and Washington, D.C., were America's chickens "coming home to roost."

In May, author Ed Klein revealed that for his new anti-Obama book, *The Amateur*, he taped an interview with Rev. Wright, who had told him, "After the media went ballistic on me, I received an e-mail offering me money not to preach at all until after the November presidential election. . . . It was from one of Barack's closest friends."[48] The liberal media never "went ballistic" on Wright, unlike the conservative media. They defended him while Obama defended him, and dropped him when Obama dropped him.

On Fox News on May 17, Klein told Sean Hannity that the friend Wright implicated was Eric Whitaker, a personal friend of Obama's from Harvard days who had replaced Michelle Obama in running the Urban Health Initiative at the University of Chicago Hospital. He routinely vacationed with the Obamas and golfed with the president in the first term.

Hannity asked, "Do you think it's possible that Whitaker could have made that offer just independently on his own?" Klein said no, "Because I don't think Whitaker would have done something as important as that without—first of all, he was a confidante of Barack

Obama's. I mean, they were as close as brothers could be. And I don't think he would have done something as dramatic as offering a $150,000 bribe without checking with his pal, Barack, and saying, 'maybe we should do something about silencing this minister.'"[49] Network coverage? Zero.

Eric Whitaker was and continues to be a complete nobody as far as the media is concerned. NBC never mentioned the name before Obama's reelection. CBS mentioned him once, and ABC's Diane Sawyer called him "one of Obama's closest friends from Chicago" on Inauguration Day in 2009. On his "Political Punch" blog at ABCNews.com, Jake Tapper reported Whitaker's brief denial: "I have received your message asking whether I'd offered any sort of a bribe during the 2008 campaign. The answer is no." Wright declined to comment to Tapper.[50]

In her book on the Obamas, *New York Times* reporter Jodi Kantor asserted that Whitaker and Marty Nesbitt were assigned by Obama to "keep him normal while in office. . . . Nesbitt and Whitaker were so close with the president that they did not wait for invitations to visit the White House; they just sent him a message they were coming."[51]

The two Obama buddies "had shared too many basketball games with him to count, so close to the president they earned inauguration seats right near Jill Biden, the vice president's wife." They also served this function during the campaign, Kantor added. "It wasn't the first time they had served a protective function: during the painful fracas over provocative statements made by their pastor, the Rev. Jeremiah Wright Jr., during the campaign, they had rotated, along with Valerie Jarrett, traveling with the candidate, so he would never be without a friend close by."[52]

For her part, Kantor had a different tale about who hushed Wright: a man who would later be honored with a show on MSNBC, Rev. Al Sharpton. "It was Sharpton who finally convinced him to quiet down."[53]

Perhaps this hush-money story is too inflammatory to accept from such a disgruntled source. After all, Rev. Wright also repeatedly charged that AIDS was concocted by the U.S. government. But these same networks have been eager to welcome authors with all kinds of harsh allegations about Republican presidents.

For example, in 2004, NBC's Matt Lauer welcomed Kitty Kelley for three days of interviews to unload personal allegations against George W. and Laura Bush.[54,55] In 2000, CBS put an anti-Bush author on *60 Minutes* claiming Bush had been arrested for cocaine possession in 1972.[56] That anti-Bush author, J. H. Hatfield, had been convicted in 1988 of paying a hit man five thousand dollars to murder his former boss with a car bomb.[57] The Bushes denounced the book as untrue, and St. Martin's Press recalled 70,000 books. CBS put his claims on the air anyway.

The networks wouldn't touch allegations of a Wright hush-money offer. But CBS and NBC each briefly sprung into action on Wright at the whisper of a chance—exposed by *The New York Times*—that a Republican Super PAC might run an ad against Obama using Rev. Wright.

On the May 22 *CBS This Morning*, Bob Schieffer expressed happiness that this plot was foiled: "You know, we saw this week, Charlie, we saw Republicans roundly denounce a plan that some Republicans had to launch this race-baiting campaign tied—trying to tie the president once again to Jeremiah Wright. Now we're seeing people on the Democratic side denouncing this, saying, wait a minute, this has gone too far."[58]

Republican "race-baiting" is deplored, even, as in the case of the *New York Times* story, it has yet to display itself. By contrast, Obama's racial appeals about rioters aren't "news."

CHAPTER 11

The Fractured Fall Debates

When will the Republicans stop accepting a quadruple thumping?

There are few things that Republican presidential contenders control more than the choice of debate venues and debate moderators. It's also apparently a memo they've never read. Every election cycle, they choose liberal media moderators who then act like media liberals and Republicans are . . . astonished. The 2012 cycle demonstrated once again the perils of primary debates with "objective" media anchors like Brian Williams and George Stephanopoulos whacking away at GOP candidates. The price of admission to their networks is too high and the potential for damage is too great, but Republicans don't get it.

Republicans did finally make some movement in the right direction, having debates hosted by conservative organizations, allowing networks to come along and cosponsor events if they wished. These debates let the actual Republican primary voters set the agenda, as opposed to debates allowing Stephanopoulos to ask six questions implying Republicans wanted the government to limit access to condoms and birth control pills.[1]

Unfortunately, the Republican Party establishment once again made no serious attempt to balance the slate of moderators for the presidential debates in the fall, with enormous audiences of around 60 million people. In every tedious cycle at the Commission on Presidential Debates, it looks like it begins by Republicans waving a white flag and welcoming another potential quadruple thumping by liberal media-elite moderators.

They never insist that one of the four questioners come from Fox News, precisely because the Democrats feel about Fox the same way that conservatives have always felt about every other TV news network.

As Bill O'Reilly complained on *CBS This Morning* to cohost Charlie Rose: "CNN gets in; Fox—nobody would touch with a ten-foot pole. That's what gets disturbing, because there are serious journalists at Fox News that can moderate these debates, starting with Bret Baier." Baier even delighted media liberals during the primaries by asking if Republicans would raise their hands if they would accept a deal of ten dollars in spending cuts for a dollar in tax hikes, and the hands didn't go up.

O'Reilly said he prefers a tough-as-nails moderator, who would "come in with a *60 Minutes* mentality and ask questions and get answers." This, of course, ignores how *60 Minutes* has bowed deeply to Obama at every opportunity, as well as the fact that moderators are not the debaters. They are called moderators for a reason. Their job is to ask good questions, and get out of the way.

It is what made the late Tim Russert the gold standard in his field.

Charlie Rose insisted to O'Reilly, "you sound like you want the presidential debate to be a cable news program."[2] But maybe that could be fun, too. Two moderators who would each purposely, by design, debate one of the candidates, like CNN's *Crossfire* in its heyday. O'Reilly or Sean Hannity could interview the Democrat from the right, and they could recruit Bob Beckel or Hannity's old partner

Alan Colmes to interview the Republican from the left. Why not? Presidential candidates in both parties have been far too risk-averse to bite on the kind of format that risks a balance of hardballs.

The most fraudulent debate format is the phony "town hall" Potemkin villages that are routinely slanted against the Republicans. Either the "undecided voters" should be selected without the moderator knowing precisely what they're going to ask, or they should load the "town hall" audience instead with committed partisan voters and let them question the opposing candidates, like Question Time in the British Parliament. At least in this format both sides would take hardball questions.

Then there's the question of the media bias surrounding the debates. Over and over, liberal journalists will crown the Democrat the winner unless it cannot plausibly be declared, and even then, someone will try. For example, before the 2012 debates, the Media Research Center documented how, in eight out of the last nine general election presidential debates, George Stephanopoulos proclaimed a win for the Democratic candidate. (That's every debate since he joined ABC News right out of the Clinton White House in 1997.)[3]

While Team Obama tried to lower expectations before the first debate—standard political posturing—journalists weren't as shy. Carole Simpson, a longtime ABC reporter who moderated the town-hall debate in 1992, told CNN this would be no charisma contest. "Romney is practicing zingers. He's not very funny," Simpson said, saying she saw him bomb before voters in Iowa. But Obama? "He's been on Letterman. He's been on Leno. He's been on *The View*. They're doing all of these shows and I think he's much more comfortable in his skin."[4]

That's not the way it turned out, and the media were furious.

First Debate: Obama Clobbered in Colorado

Nothing seemed to cause as much media angst about Obama's re-election as the first fall debate. At age seventy-eight, retired *PBS NewsHour* anchor Jim Lehrer was talked into his eleventh appearance as a moderator by the Commission on Presidential Debates. (He moderated all three presidential debates in 2000.) To his credit, Lehrer played it straight down the middle, taking his title seriously. He rejected the "gotcha" brand of journalism.

Lehrer asked the blandest of questions, merely seeking the differences between the candidates, as in "What are the major differences between the two of you about how you would go about creating new jobs?" and "What are the differences between the two of you as to how you would go about tackling the deficit problem in this country?"[5]

Obama performed badly enough that Bill Maher was mocking him on Twitter by mid-debate,[6] and Chris Matthews came out angry. "I don't know what he was doing out there," he raged. "I don't know how he let Romney get away with the crap he threw out tonight."[7]

As even former NBC anchor Tom Brokaw acknowledged the next day, liberal journalists were loaded and ready to pronounce this election over and Romney's campaign dead after the first debate: "If it had been Romney performing like the president last night, it would have been over."[8] But the thumping Obama received was so complete that virtually no one denied it.

But how did they report Obama lost? Therein lies the rub: journalists as well as Democratic operatives attempted the spin that this was all about style and presentation. Obama was "flat," "lackluster," "not himself," and "not firing on all cylinders." In other words, Obama wasn't Glorious Obama. Many went further, pushing the Matthews narrative that Romney was somehow mean-spirited and even deceptive in his presentation.[9]

Lehrer was also blamed. Former *Newsweek* reporter Howard Fineman complained on MSNBC that "Jim Lehrer was practically useless as the moderator. It was criminal negligence not to follow up on the question—Mr. Romney specifically what tax loopholes or deductions do you want to get rid of—he didn't ask it." [10]

Fineman thought Lehrer should have taken Obama's argument and repeated it. The president strangely suggested that his New Math said Romney wanted "a $5 trillion tax cut, on top of $2 trillion of additional spending for our military, and he is saying that he is going to pay for it by closing loopholes and deductions. The problem is that he's been asked over 100 times how you would close those deductions and loopholes, and he hasn't been able to identify them." [11]

Liberal journalists think their fellow journalists are supposed to underline Obama's "best" lines, repeat them, and help them sink into the minds of the voters.

On Current TV, leftist talk-show host Stephanie Miller spoke for many in comparing PBS star Jim Lehrer to Lance Ito, the feckless judge in the O. J. Simpson murder trial. Apparently, that makes Romney the wife-killer in this metaphor: "Almost everything Mitt Romney said was a lie which the fact-checkers had talked about today already, and Jim Lehrer was like the Judge Ito in my opinion, he just let Romney, I mean, it's just like, it's filibuster, right? He just kept talking." [12]

Strangely, Team Obama and the media then jumped on Romney for his talk of cutting off PBS funding. "I'm sorry, Jim, I'm going to stop the subsidy to PBS," he said, during the debate. " I'm going to stop other things. I like PBS, I love Big Bird. Actually I like you, too. But I'm not going to—I'm not going to keep on spending money on things to borrow money from China to pay for." [13]

The point was obvious: PBS isn't a pressing need worth throwing on the mountain of national debt. But the networks pounced anyway. The next day, *CBS This Morning* cohost Norah O'Donnell lectured: "This may have been the first time in a presidential debate that Big Bird was mentioned. It seems kind of like a silly thing to bring up."[14] When CNN asked about it, Representative Mario Diaz-Balart (R-FL) grew angry: "I think focusing on a light moment, which was clearly what it was, is doing a disservice to the people of America who are struggling," he bellyached. "That's the best you can come up with from this debate?"[15] CNN also brought on PBS president Paula Kerger to boast about what a great value PBS is for the taxpayers.[16]

On Friday morning, CNN's Soledad O'Brien also turned to PBS *Reading Rainbow* host LeVar Burton, who laid into Mitt Romney for attacking . . . children? "I was outraged. I couldn't believe the man actually fixed his mouth to say that. I interpreted it as an attack on children, Soledad." CNN's headlines onscreen were "Save Big Bird!" and "Romney Takes Aim at Big Bird."[17]

By Friday night, NBC's Brian Williams filed an entire pro-PBS story—with the exception of that one Romney soundbite, now re-packaged as a self-inflicted wound. It starred Obama joking, "He'll get rid of regulations on Wall Street, but he's going to crack down on *Sesame Street*. Thank goodness somebody's finally cracking down on Big Bird."[18] NBC was doing Obama's nightly messaging and passing it off as journalism, again.

The Vice Presidential Debate: Raddatz Singles Out Ryan

The moderator of the vice presidential debate, ABC correspondent Martha Raddatz, was a fresh face, but any Republican trying to pick moderators would have known she displayed the typical pro-Obama tilt in her reporting with the slightest research. The president's sending General David Petraeus to oversee the war in Afghanistan was a "great save." It was "truly historic" when Obama's Joint Chiefs chairman backed gays in the military. Obama accomplished "another huge victory in the War on Terror" when a drone attack killed radical jihadist/American citizen Anwar al-Awlaki. She described the secretary of state like this: "Let's face it. Hillary Clinton is cool, and trending." [19] But in 2009, when thirteen Americans lost their lives in a mass shooting at Fort Hood in Texas, it wasn't a loss for Team Obama. Raddatz notably lamented that she wished the killer didn't have a Muslim name, perhaps because Americans were so hopelessly Islamophobic: "As for the suspect, Nidal Hasan, as one officer's wife told me, 'I wish his name was Smith.'" Diane Sawyer quoted Raddatz again the next morning. [20]

Raddatz had several too-close associations with the Democrats. One was old: Barack Obama was a guest at her marriage in 1991 to Julius Genachowski. This came right after Obama graduated from Harvard Law School, where he was classmates with Genachowski, who would later become Obama's chairman of the Federal Communications Commission. (He and Raddatz divorced in 1997.)

One was much newer. Raddatz attended a Women's History Month reception in March 2012 at the vice presidential mansion. About 110 guests mingled in the foyer of the veep's residence with Biden and his wife, Jill, including not only Raddatz but CBS's Erica Hill and CNN's Gloria Borger, as well as Democratic luminaries like top Obama aide Valerie Jarrett and former secretary of state Madeleine Albright. [21]

Do you think Ann Coulter was invited?

When the debate began in Danville, Kentucky, Raddatz started by asking about the September 11 attack that killed four Americans (including the U.S. ambassador) at our consulate in Benghazi, Libya. Between the attack and this debate, Team Obama strangely attempted to characterize the attacks as not a terrorist attack, but a spontaneous response to a "very offensive video" on YouTube mocking the prophet Muhammad.

That spin had completely collapsed as unfactual. The day before the debate, the State Department disowned this spin line: In a conference call to reporters, senior officials argued, "That was not our conclusion. . . . That is the question you'd have to ask others."

So Raddatz began: "The State Department has now made clear, there were no protesters there. It was a pre-planned assault by heavily armed men." But this didn't acknowledge that Susan Rice's Sunday-show talking points said the exact opposite. Instead, she asked: "Wasn't this a massive intelligence failure, Vice President Biden?"

Biden declared it a "tragedy" and risibly added, "we will get to the bottom of it, and whatever—wherever the facts lead us." Ryan strongly attacked when the question turned to him, questioning Rice's truthfulness and Obama's continued blame on the YouTube video.

Then Raddatz repeated the liberal media spin that Romney and Ryan were uncivil for this critique based on what had become the established facts: "Right in the middle of the crisis, Governor Romney—and you're talking about this again tonight—talked about the weakness, talked about apologies from the Obama administration. Was that really appropriate right in the middle of the crisis?"

This amounted to a softball for Biden when it was his turn to reply. Raddatz did ask a follow-up: "Why were people talking about protests? When people in the consulate first saw armed men attacking with guns, there were no protesters." Biden blamed the "intelligence community."[22] There was no ownership of the fiasco. Saying "the intelligence community" was like saying "someone from the Congo." The White House knew it was a terrorist attack within twenty-four hours—yet continued, for days, blaming a silly video no one had ever seen. And they got away with it.

It's amazing that liberals insisted during the Bush years that the president was the dimmest of dimwits yet was also responsible for every foreign policy mistake. Now the geniuses Obama and Biden could claim complete ignorance when our diplomats die. In the Bush years, bad intelligence was pinned squarely on Bush as commander in chief. In the Obama years, claims of faulty intelligence somehow absolve everyone on his team.

Overall, the Media Research Center scorecard was mixed. Raddatz balanced her questions in the foreign policy section—eight pro-Romney, seven pro-Obama (not counting neutral questions). But on domestic policy, especially on Ryan's area of greatest expertise, that of taxes and spending, she practically joined Biden in trying to damage Ryan, with a dozen questions that incorporated liberal campaign themes, compared to just four from the Romney viewpoint, a 3-to-1 tilt.[23]

It was beyond annoying watching her interrupt Ryan just when he was going to land a punch. Take green jobs. Ryan charged: "The vice president was in charge of overseeing this. Ninety billion dollars in green pork to campaign contributors and special interest groups. There are just at the Department of Energy over 100 criminal investigations that have been launched into just how stimulus—"[24] Biden interrupted, and Raddatz gave Biden the floor.

Washington Post writer Dan Zak penned a TV review of the debates that bragged "only Vice President Biden acted as though he could sit at the desk in the Oval Office and have his feet touch the ground." In the paper, he began with "A pro debated a novice," but on Twitter, Zak previewed he would write: "A man debated a boy Thursday night."

But Zak acknowledged the truth about Raddatz: "Fairly or not, she reserved most of her skepticism for Ryan." Even Zak found it obvious: "'No specifics then?' she asked about his ticket's tax plan. 'Can you guarantee this math will add up? . . . How do you do that? . . . I wanna know how you do the math.'"[25]

ABC showered their own colleague with praise. They exclaimed "Martha Raddatz for President!"[26] This only underlined why the moderator shouldn't be the star of the show.

The Town-Hall Debate Tilts Left—Again

CNN's Candy Crowley seemed like the most promising of the moderators to press both sides for answers, but that's not how it turned out at all. Crowley ended up being the worst of the four in tilting the debate toward the president. Even Frank Fahrenkopf, the cochair of the Commission on Presidential Debates, admitted error three months after the election: "We made one mistake this time: Her name is Candy." [27]

The viewing public might think a "town hall" debate is the most freewheeling populist forum of all the debates. That has never been the case. In reality, the citizen questioners are selected from a Gallup survey of self-declared "undecided voters," but that often strains credulity. The questioners are more carefully selected for the questions they're bringing to the table. [28] Usually that means that the moderators tilt the "real people" to match their liberal bias.

In advance of the debate, Media Research Center analysts reviewed every town-hall debate from 1992 to 2008 and discovered that the citizen questions selected by media moderators slanted by a margin of 2-to-1, with 28 liberal questions and just 14 conservative questions. [29]

The same tilt happened again in 2012. Crowley organized six pro-Obama/liberal-themed questions, versus three pro-Romney questions, and two others scored as neutral. After the debate, she suggested she had wanted to throw in more liberal questions, like "climate change—I had that question, for all you climate change people." [30]

To many conservatives, the most jaw-droppingly partisan question came from Susan Katz, who lectured Romney: "I attribute much of America's economic and international problems to the failings and missteps of the Bush administration. Since both you and President

Bush are Republicans, I fear a return to the policies of those years should you win this election. What is the biggest difference between you and George W. Bush?"[31]

The idea that Katz brought no bias to this debate was obliterated the next morning, when she appeared on CNN. Anchor Carol Costello asked if she was now decided. Katz replied to Costello that she voted for Obama in 2008 and planned to do so again because "I saw in President Obama someone who has ripened with time who deserves another four years to see his vision through."[32]

Katz wasn't alone in showing a bias. On feminism, Katherine Fenton stood and asked Obama: "In what new ways do you intend to rectify the inequalities in the workplace, specifically regarding females making only 72 percent of what their male counterparts earn?"[33] Later, Fenton told the liberal website Salon that she was passionate about "women's equality in the workforce" and "I'm very protective of my reproductive rights." Her "gut" told her Obama would be better for women.[34] No kidding.

On immigration, Lorraine Osorio asked: "Mr. Romney, what do you plan on doing with immigrants without their green cards that are currently living here as productive members of society?"[35] Osorio, the daughter of Salvadorans, told ABCNews.com that "actions speak louder than words," and that Obama's policy deferring deportations demonstrated his commitment to young immigrants.[36] Did that sound undecided?

On gun control, Nina Gonzalez asked Obama: "During the Democratic National Convention in 2008, you stated you wanted to keep AK-47s out of the hands of criminals. What has your administration done or planned to do to limit the availability of assault weapons?"[37]

The New York Times editorial page was delighted: "It took an ordinary citizen, Nina Gonzalez, to stand up at the presidential debate on Tuesday to raise what has been a phantom issue on the campaign trail: the lack of effective gun controls."[38]

NBC correspondent Chuck Todd summed up Wednesday morning: "The President also benefitted from many questions posed by the *so-called undecided voters*, covering issues near and dear to his liberal base." Even NBC was acknowledging the dishonesty of the town hall–style debate.[39]

Candy Crowley Backs a Lie

Of the three questions that could be considered as coming from the Republican perspective, the toughest question for Obama was the one about his administration's obvious failure to provide necessary security for the Libyan consulate, which was attacked on September 11. A man named Kerry Ladka asked: "The State Department refused extra security for our embassy in Benghazi, Libya, prior to the attacks that killed four Americans. Who was it that denied enhanced security, and why?"

After the president and Romney each answered the question, Crowley then recalled that Secretary of State Hillary Clinton took responsibility for the deaths in Benghazi, and asked the president, "Does the buck stop with the Secretary of State?" Obama said the buck stopped with him, but he laid into Romney, whose suggestion, Obama said, that "anybody on my team would play politics or mislead when we've lost four of our own, Governor, is offensive." That came right after he claimed "the day after the attack, I stood in the Rose Garden and told the American people and the world that we are going to find out exactly what happened, that this was an act of terror. . . ."

Barack Obama had lied. He hadn't labeled the Libya attack an act of terrorism. The look on Romney's face said it all: Mr. President, here comes checkmate.

Romney wanted Obama to clarify: "You said in the Rose Garden the day after the attack, it was an act of terror? It was not a spontaneous demonstration, is that what you're saying? . . . [Speaking to Crowley:] I want to make sure we get that for the record because it took the president 14 days before he called the attack in Benghazi an act of terror." [40]

What came next was the most stunning and disgraceful single example of moderator malpractice in the history of televised presidential debates. Crowley allowed Obama to lie to the American people about his administration's Libya cover-up. Even worse, she then validated this lie of extraordinary magnitude by certifying it as honest, and by attacking Mitt Romney when he pressed the president on his administration's cover-up. Crowley robbed tens of millions of Americans of the truth on national prime-time television. Real journalists—especially those who were fed the Obama administration's Libya lies for more than two weeks—should have been furious.

Crowley jumped in to assert to Romney: "He did, in fact, sir . . . call it an act of terror." Obama crowed triumphantly: "Can you say that a little louder, Candy?" Crowley repeated: "He did call it an act of terror." [41]

No, he did not. Not according to the transcript from the White House, which has Obama only speaking generically about how "no acts of terror will ever shake the resolve of this nation," not assigning that label to the violence in Benghazi. [42] Among many others, the official *Washington Post* fact-checker, Glenn Kessler, pointed out the obvious: "He [Obama] did not say 'terrorism'—and it took the administration days to concede that it [was] an 'act of terrorism' that appears unrelated to initial reports of anger at a video that defamed the prophet Muhammad." [43]

Here's where Crowley's fractured "fact check" makes no sense. Back on September 30, on her CNN Sunday program *State of the Union*, she hit Obama strategist David Axelrod on exactly this point: "Why did it take them [the White House] until Friday [September 28], after a September 11 attack in Libya, to come to the conclusion that it was premeditated and that there was terrorists involved? John McCain said it doesn't pass the smell test, or it's willful ignorance to think that they didn't know before this what was going on."[44]

Of course, Axelrod shot back that Obama in the Rose Garden called it an "act of terror." By her very question to Axelrod, she knew this answer wasn't truthful. It was actually a ridiculously dishonest answer. If he meant to blame the terrorists for their attack on the consulate, why not just say so? Instead of the nebulous "no acts of terror will ever shake the resolve of this nation," he would have said, "This act of terror will never shake the resolve of this nation."

And his secretary of state would not have made pious public statements apologizing for a video that never caused anything. And his representative to the United Nations would not have traveled to five major network shows in one day to blame that video.

Axelrod was lying. Crowley knew the Obama administration initially tried to deny the Libya attack was terrorism. But all that disappeared when it truly mattered, on a debate stage with more than 60 million Americans watching. She now defended his lie as the truth.

How does Crowley square her October 16 performance with her September 30 performance? Try this theory: after liberals savaged Jim Lehrer as "useless" for somehow allowing Obama's first-debate fiasco, they'd successfully worked the refs, both Crowley and Raddatz, to push back at the "lies" of the Republicans. Crowley was "useful"—in denying the facts. And a hit with her peers. Quite possibly she saved the Obama campaign.

That night on PBS, John Heilemann of *New York* magazine thought Crowley's tilt to Obama was decisive: "The worst hand that the administration and President Obama have to play in this debate was on Benghazi, and because particularly of Candy Crowley's follow-up on that question, it allowed Barack Obama to win an exchange that I didn't necessarily think it was possible for him to win."[45]

The next morning, even Current TV host Eliot Spitzer acknowledged the truth, telling fellow host Bill Press that Crowley caused the "emotional highlight of the night" by declaring Romney was wrong. "I think that really deflated what otherwise should have been on the Benghazi issue a moment when Romney could have hit it out of the park. But instead he took the step too far. Crowley came in as sort of the voice of neutrality and took the victory away from Romney."[46]

It was precisely because Crowley was the so-called voice of neutrality who moderated a very tilted panel of so-called undecided voters that Obama was awarded a dirty-trick win.

On ABC the morning after, former Bush pollster Matthew Dowd taunted Crowley's critics as losers and implied the facts were somehow not worth considering: "I think what this may lead to is a bunch of conservatives and Republicans attacking Candy Crowley, and when that happens, that is a sure sign that President Obama won this. When you start attacking the ref, or start attacking the umpire, it means you left a lot of plays on the field, and when you see that, you know they know they lost."[47]

The networks settled on another Romney gaffe as well, that Romney said he had "binders full of women" when he was choosing female appointees for his state government in Massachusetts. Despite Romney's record of appointing women to his administration, liberals went nuts on that phrase on Twitter, and the liberal media followed obediently.[48]

The Big Three networks gave the faux-furor over the "binders" comment a whopping twenty-two mentions from Tuesday night through Friday morning. Yet when Vice President Joe Biden, on that Thursday, told an audience member that Republican "young guns" like vice presidential nominee Paul Ryan had "bullets" aimed at him, the networks delivered just a scant two total mentions, one each on CBS and NBC. ABC skipped the gaffe entirely.[49]

On the morning after the debate, ABC's Elizabeth Vargas, on *Good Morning America*, singled out the binders: "You remember the Big Bird line that dominated the conversations online and around the water cooler, in essence, after the first debate? Last night, it was another Romney comment, 'binders full of women' that caused the heat to turn on." [50]

In a forum with former CBS reporter Marvin Kalb after the election, with three of the moderators (which Crowley missed), Bob Schieffer said the town-hall format should be dumped. "It just seems not to work in my view as well. It gives them a chance to put too much show business into it. You know, you get the candidates kind of performing and walking over and getting in the other guy's space sometimes." [51]

The Final Debate: Everyone Shrinks from Libya

The last presidential debate was moderated by Bob Schieffer, a forty-three-year veteran of CBS News who was chosen to moderate for the third election cycle in a row. Both the moderator and the candidates in this foreign policy debate were clearly affected by Candy-gate.

Schieffer's first question was on Benghazi, but it was directed at Romney and not at President Obama. It refrained from any finding of fact to the killers: "Questions remain. What happened? What caused it? Was it spontaneous? Was it an intelligence failure? Was it a policy failure? Was there an attempt to mislead people about what really happened?"

Romney, after suffering from Crowley's fractured "fact check," barely touched on Libya. Now it was his camp's turn to be stunned in disbelief. After a half minute of thank-yous and courtesies, he asserted that "terrorists" caused the murders, and moved on to Mali and other hot spots. Schieffer didn't ask Obama about Susan Rice bizarrely blaming a YouTube video on five Sunday news shows, including his own *Face the Nation.* He merely tossed the question to him with a "Mr. President?"

The only utterance of Benghazi came when the president boasted about the end of Libyan dictator Muammar Qaddafi: "Got rid of a despot who had killed Americans and as a consequence, despite this tragedy, you had tens of thousands of Libyans after the events in Benghazi marching and saying America is our friend. We stand with them." [52]

Overall, Schieffer stuck to a Jim Lehrer formula, keeping questions brief and letting the candidates be the main focus. But on this first round, Schieffer made no real attempt to advance the Benghazi story or hold the president accountable for Susan Rice's fake claims. Schieffer's restraint in the final debate also included failing to ask the president about his promise to end the custody of terrorist suspects at Guantanamo Bay in Cuba.

On June 9, 2005, on MSNBC's *Imus in the Morning,* Schieffer had raged, "This isn't just a boil. It's a cancer. This thing is not doing anybody any good." On June 19, 2006, he led off the *CBS Evening News* with angry editorializing: "Has the U.S. prison for terror suspects at Guantanamo become more trouble than it's worth? Even those who created it have to be asking that question tonight." [53] But Schieffer failed to sustain that outrage and ask a single Gitmo question to Obama in this debate.

Some Obama fans in the liberal media were crowing about an Obama win. When Romney charged "our Navy is smaller now than at any time since 1917," Obama shot back, "Well, Governor, we also have fewer horses and bayonets, because the nature of our military's changed." NBC anchor Brian Williams was especially fond of that line: "David Gregory, we always try to look for the phrase or expression that will live forever out of these. Tonight has to be 'horses and bayonets.' . . . A very sharp comeback from the President." [54] This, obviously, quickly became false. When President Obama traveled to Norfolk, Virginia, in February to dramatize the damage a sequester would cause the military, Williams and everyone else failed to remember the president's mockery of the decline of navy ships.

But just before that quip from Obama, he uncorked this lie about the sequester: "First of all, the sequester is not something that I've proposed. It is something that Congress has proposed. It will not happen."[55]

In his book *The Price of Politics*—published on September 11, six weeks before the October 22 debate—Bob Woodward reported that Obama personally approved of a plan for his chief of staff Jack Lew and congressional liaison Rob Nabors to propose the sequester to Senate Majority Leader Harry Reid.[56] Team Obama never protested Woodward's account. But now he was claiming before before 60 million people that his team never proposed the sequester. Unless he was playing Bill Clinton word games—see, *he* didn't propose the sequester, but his aides did. Nobody in the media—including Woodward—seemed to notice this before the election.

CHAPTER 12

Backing Away from Benghazi

Pay no attention to the failures and lies before you vote.

The media could never believe Ronald Reagan won because people agreed it was time to try conservative ideas. Over time, they all became enamored with the "October Surprise" conspiracy theory to explain why Jimmy Carter lost the 1980 election. Somehow, Carter didn't lose because he was inept in dealing with the economy and inept in ending the Iranian hostage crisis. He must have lost because Reagan's campaign made a dastardly attempt to delay the release of the hostages who had been held in Iran since November 1979. This conspiracy theory was never substantiated, no matter how hard the likes of ABC's Ted Koppel tried to prove it.

In every election cycle, the media have tried to focus their persuasive powers in the last weeks of a campaign on preventing an "October surprise" that would hurt Democratic incumbents (or challengers). On the other hand, if they could unleash or abet a dirty-trick last-minute surprise on the Republican incumbents, they have done so with impunity. Ends justify means.

So when seventeen American sailors died from an al-Qaeda suicide-bomb attack on the USS *Cole* in Yemen on October 12, 2000, the media labored mightily to disassociate the incident from President Clinton and Vice President Al Gore, the Democratic nominee for president. Conversely, in the fall of 2004, the media worked hard to find scandals that would ruin Bush's standing as commander in chief and prevent his reelection, starting most notoriously in September with Dan Rather's bumbling reliance on phony National Guard documents to suggest the president's Vietnam-era evasion of military service.

In the last week, they were still pushing new story lines attempting to dent the Bush advantage. On October 24, the front page of *The New York Times* pushed the headline "Huge Cache of Explosives Vanished from Site in Iraq." The story was dutifully pushed to the top of the three broadcast network evening newscasts. Dan Rather trumpeted at the start of the *CBS Evening News*: "Eight days to go till America elects a president, and disturbing news from Iraq is again dominating the campaign. The White House acknowledged today that a huge stockpile of ultra-high explosives is inexplicably missing from an Iraqi weapons site. Senator John Kerry called this a quote, 'great blunder' by President Bush and his administration." [1]

The next night, CBS reporter John Roberts noted the story had Team Bush "way off message today and losing in the headlines, and in danger of losing momentum at the worst possible time." In contrast, after running four soundbites from what CBS's Byron Pitts described as Kerry's "impassioned critique" of Bush policy, Pitts relayed: "said one [Kerry] aide today, 'The headlines this week are in our favor, and for now the wind is at our back.'" [2]

The *Times* was spooked into publishing this "early," since they were working with the *60 Minutes* crew at CBS, which wanted to break this story on the night of Halloween, just two days before the election. (Ironically, this worked in reverse with Rathergate: the National Guard story was scheduled to land on the eve of the election but CBS was concerned its partner, *The New York Times*, was going to skunk the network, so CBS rushed it out early.)

That malodorous last-minute media sandbag would not be dropped on the Obama administration when the U.S. consulate in Benghazi was attacked on September 11, 2012. A large group of terrorists armed with rocket launchers murdered U.S. Ambassador Chris Stevens and State Department officer Sean Smith at the consulate. Ty Woods and Glen Doherty later died defending the CIA annex after it came under attack from the same terrorists.

When that terrible day began, *CBS This Morning* brought on former *New York Times* reporter Kurt Eichenwald to pounce on. . . . George W. Bush. Eichenwald was promoting his book *500 Days*, accusing the Bush administration of ignoring warnings about a possible terrorist strike as early as May 2001. Eichenwald claimed that "the CIA did a spectacular job. . . . [T]he White House and others said, 'Well, they didn't tell us enough.' No, they told them everything they needed to know to go on a full alert, and the White House didn't do it."[3]

The New York Times didn't put the 9/11 attacks back on its front page but it gave its old reporter a pathway to CBS with an op-ed titled "The Deafness Before the Storm," a stale rerun blaming Bush for ignoring the warning contained in his August 6, *2001*, presidential daily briefing that Osama bin Laden might be readying an attack on the United States.[4]

On September 12, 2012, as the bad news of the Benghazi massacre streamed in, the *Times* suggested it had a different sense of holding Obama accountable. While Benghazi and other Mideast unrest was published on page A4 the day after the attack, this was on page A1: "Dissecting Romney's Vietnam Stance at Stanford." Reporter Michael Wines found that in November 1965, young Romney and his friends cared more about college spirit than geopolitics, as he "stayed true to his chinos and the Vietnam War." [5]

In the first hours after the Benghazi attack news broke, incredibly, it was Romney who was placed in the media spotlight, and it was harsh. On the 9/11 anniversary, the U.S. embassy was breached in Cairo, and Republicans were buzzing about the State Department's astonishing response: "The Embassy of the United States in Cairo condemns the continuing efforts by misguided individuals to hurt the religious feelings of Muslims—as we condemn efforts to offend believers of all religions." After the embassy's invaders pulled down the U.S. flag and put up an Islamic flag, the embassy said on Twitter, "This morning's condemnation (issued before protest began) still stands. As does our condemnation of unjustified breach of the Embassy." (The tweet was later deleted.)

This spurred Romney to put out a statement that evening around 10:30 Eastern time: "I think it's a terrible course for America to stand in apology for our values. That instead, when our grounds are being attacked and being breached, that the first response of the United States must be outrage at the breach of the sovereignty of our nation. An apology for America's values is never the right course." [6]

Romney was entirely correct in his broadside against the administration for its gutless response to an attack against Americans on American soil. Obama's allies in the press knew the embassy's response was preposterous and indefensible. How then to turn this segment against Romney? The answers came a few hours later.

News of four Americans dying in Benghazi came out around 7 A.M. the next day, so Romney decided to hold a brief press conference to comment on his Cairo-embassy statement in light of the new information. Reporters weren't looking for information. They wanted Romney to apologize for daring to play politics with the government response in Egypt and the charge that President Obama's team showed weakness. *"How could he be so heartless while Americans are dying in Benghazi?!"*

The Right Scoop website posted video with an open microphone that showed the liberal reporters on the Romney beat boldly, if quietly coordinating their line of questions to attack Romney. They were seeking a rhetorical retreat:

> JAN CRAWFORD, CBS: That's the question. . . . Yeah that's the question. I would just say "Do you regret your question?"
> ARI SHAPIRO, NPR: "Your question?" Your statement?
> CRAWFORD: I mean "your statement." Not even "your tone," because then he can go off on—
> SHAPIRO: And then if he does, I think we can just follow up and say "but this morning your answer is continuing to sound"—

Then the feed is cut off. Moments later, Crawford adds, "No matter who he calls on, we're covered on the one question." A man (not Shapiro) utters, "Do you stand by your statement or regret your statement?" [7]

There's nothing undemocratic or even unprofessional about journalists working together if the goal is to arrive at the most appropriate line of questioning. But that story line can turn out to be a very biased, politicized line—one designed to trip, to embarrass, to hurt the target. That is unethical. Reporters sometimes mock the idea of a media "conspiracy." This was not a conspiracy. It was open collusion.

Romney's Manners Were the Big Scoop

The perversity of this situation was that Romney was attempting to be forthcoming. He called a press conference in the morning and took questions. And was hammered for it. Should he have behaved like Obama? The president of the United States made a statement without taking questions and hopped on a jet for a fundraiser in Las Vegas. "Mr. Obama and his team have learned from experience that the political costs of campaigning amid crises can be minimal," reported Jim Rutenberg in *The New York Times*.[8] The optics might have seemed terrible, but the president had confidence that the network spinners would take care of him. And did they ever. While the commander in chief palled around with his rich friends, the "news" media pounced on Romney.

On that Benghazi-dominated first night of evening news coverage, a Media Research Center analysis found the rude-Romney angle received nearly ten minutes of coverage on the Big Three newscasts (9 minutes, 28 seconds), versus just 25 seconds questioning Obama's Middle East policies.[9] Time spent covering Obama's shameful fundraising during a national crisis? Zero.

NBC's Brian Williams spoke for the media in pronouncing that Obama's line of national unity would win the spin cycle: "Romney is taking fire tonight for the way he went on the attack politically. . . . Somehow [Romney] wanted today to be about America apologizing for its values, even after it became clear today was about the death of an American ambassador and others in one of two attacks on American interests on 9/11, no less. And instead of backing away, Romney doubled down on his position."

This might sound shameless—that this was supposed to be a day of national unity and mourning, while the president flew to Las Vegas for a whoop-whoop campaign rally. (Only NBC's Chuck Todd even briefly mentioned Obama had an event in Vegas.) But the networks were true to Obama, cuing up this Obama lectured to Romney from an interview Obama granted that day to Steve Kroft of *60 Minutes*, one of his favorite softball specialists.

"There is a broader lesson to be learned here. You know, Governor

Romney seems to have a tendency to shoot first and aim later. And as president, one of the things I have learned is you can't do that. That it is important for you to make sure that the statements that you make are backed up by the facts and that you have thought through the ramifications before you make them." [10]

(If Obama were a Republican, Kroft might have mocked him for using "shoot first" language after the administration failed to offer military assistance of any kind to the scattered security personnel in Benghazi. But Obama isn't a Republican.)

CBS added a few more seconds, with Kroft following up with the typical softball, asking for Romney to feel shamed: "Do you think it was irresponsible?" Obama replied: "I'll let the American people judge that." [11] He'd let the people decide—after the networks had driven home his narrative. For her story, Jan Crawford displayed exactly what she wanted, Romney defending himself against a series of reporters demanding that he apologize for being inappropriate:

> CRAWFORD: Do you think, though, coming so soon after the events really had unfolded overnight, was appropriate? To be weighing in on this as this crisis is unfolding in real time? . . .
>
> UNIDENTIFIED FEMALE: What did the White House do wrong, then, Governor Romney, if they put out a statement saying they disagreed with it? . . .
>
> UNIDENTIFIED MALE: You talk about mixed signals. The world is watching. Isn't this itself a mixed signal, when you've criticized the administration at a time that Americans are being killed? Shouldn't politics stop for this? [12]

But on that first night, CBS reporter David Martin, one of the few serious and knowledgeable journalists left in the business, set down a marker: this was a terrorist attack. "U.S. officials say this was not an out-of-control demonstration, but a well-executed attack by a well-armed band of thugs." After listing all the (belated) military deployments, he concluded his report: "Bottom line: This is a terrorist hunt."[13]

But by Friday the fourteenth, press secretary Jay Carney shifted the White House line into blaming "protests . . . in reaction to a video that had spread to the region," a cheesy, amateurish YouTube video slamming the prophet Muhammad called "The Innocence of Muslims." "We have no evidence of a pre-planned attack," claimed Carney.[14] (Candy Crowley, call your office.) On that day, President Obama and Secretary of State Hillary Clinton welcomed the caskets of the four lost Americans at Andrews Air Force Base. For media liberals, this became another chance to celebrate these two liberal leaders, formerly at loggerheads in the 2008 primaries, grieving for America.

On MSNBC's *Hardball,* Chris Matthews was tingling away. It was an "amazing ceremony," he insisted. After an Obama clip, he said "there was a moment in American history right there. Last week, when Obama spoke at the Democratic National Committee down in Charlotte, he said, 'I am the president.' Well, this week, he showed what it means to be president." He told Willie Brown, the former mayor of San Francisco and Speaker of the California State Assembly, "The wonderful moment when the secretary of state reached over to grab his hand after those remarks, it is something else. I am a sentimentalist, I will admit it. But I can't think of a better way to celebrate our Americanism than the way we did it just then."[15]

If George W. Bush had been president, the arrival of these four caskets would have been painted as a sickening sign of failure and incompetence, of public servants needlessly losing their lives because the White House couldn't piece together their intelligence reports. Matthews would have railed against the Bush people for failing to protect their diplomats in unstable Arab nations. Now it was time to tingle over the unified Democrats instead.

NBC Nightly News made no mention of Romney or Republicans.

NBC's Andrea Mitchell properly celebrated the men who died as "idealists" who "loved service and thrived on adventure." Then their haloes were rubbed on Team Obama. Mitchell ran long, loving soundbites from Hillary describing the good qualities of the deceased. NBC ran a quote of the president quoting from the gospel of John that "greater love hath no man than this, than a man lay down his life for his friends." Like a good publicist, Mitchell added that "U.S. officials insist there was no prior intelligence about the attack in Libya." [16]

Two days later, the administration sent out its ambassador to the United Nations, Susan Rice, to enunciate the same line on five networks, like this on *Meet the Press*: "This is a response to a hateful and offensive video that was widely disseminated throughout the Arab and Muslim world. . . . This is a spontaneous reaction to the video." [17]

Unlike the furor over Romney, the network response was muted, neither endorsing nor attacking the new Obama blame-the-video line. But that narrative began collapsing within days. On September 20, Jay Carney conceded the assault on the U.S. consulate was a "terrorist attack." Even then, network reporters seemed to want to spread confusion. NBC's Mitchell began that night by announcing, "Tonight, the White House confirmed the attack was an act of terror," and then reported that Carney conceded during a flight on Air Force One, "I think it's self-evident that what happened in Benghazi was a terrorist attack." But she also showed Obama failing to concede that day: "What we do know is that the natural protests that arose because of the outrage over the video were used as an excuse by extremists to see if they can also directly harm U.S. interests." Faced with this double-talk, Mitchell concluded, "U.S. officials say that this could have been a long-planned attack, taking the opportunity of a protest, or no protest at all. They are now investigating all possibilities." [18]

On *Face the Nation* on September 23, a week after the Susan Rice Sunday show tour, CBS News political director John Dickerson could see trouble brewing for Team Obama—but not from the media. It was a refreshing moment of candor. "Well, now they are calling it a terrorist attack. 'What went wrong there?' 'What did you get wrong in the first place?' 'Why weren't you securing the embassy the way you should have been?' These are points that a Republican could make, that Mitt Romney needs to make, because he knows the press isn't necessarily going to make that case for him."[19]

One of the reasons the networks may have been restrained is that President Obama himself was so slow to give up the unfactual line that a YouTube video caused the Benghazi attack. He unspooled it on the Letterman show on September 18, repeated it on a Univision town hall on September 20, and he also declined to call it a terrorist attack on ABC's *The View* on September 24.

The anchors of ABC and NBC each were granted an interview with Obama, and neither was interested in asking more than a single question about it for the public. On the October 10 *World News*, ABC's Diane Sawyer began her interview with four solid minutes of channeling liberal angst over his lackluster performance in the first debate. She also allocated more than a minute to encouraging Obama to denounce a lawyerly Mitt Romney utterance that he planned on abortion legislation if he were elected. Sawyer prompted Obama with a harsh assessment of Romney: "Is it a lie?"

The word or concept of "Libya" was not even uttered in the Sawyer-Obama segment. Viewers had to wait until the next story, by Jake Tapper, on a House committee hearing that laid out the administration's failures to provide security for the diplomats in Libya. ABC viewers got a whopping twenty seconds from the White House interview—more than half of that consumed by Obama's defense and assurance he'll "fix" anything that wasn't done properly.

> TAPPER: Diane Sawyer asked the President about the White House's initial claims that the incident began with a protest against that anti-Muslim video.

OBAMA: As information came in, information was put out. The information may have not have always been right the first time. . . . Look, Diane, these are people I know. And if there's something to be fixed, it'll get fixed.[20]

Notice there's no room in this clip for an actual Sawyer question, so viewers didn't see her purported angst over four dead Americans. But they did see her upset over Obama's blown debate.

Two weeks later, on October 24, *NBC Nightly News* anchor Brian Williams aired a taped interview with the president. These are the questions the public was supposed to find most newsworthy.

First, "How is it that with—what, 13 days to go, you're fighting for your life in a 47/47 [percent, tied] race?" Williams was shocked it wasn't a landslide yet.

Second, on the same theme, "So after the excitement of '08, given the power of incumbency, you got bin Laden, you did not expect to be sitting on a more substantial race than we are as we sit here today?"

In an interview segment aired on Wednesday night and again on Thursday morning, Williams also wondered: "What's the dynamic like between you and Mitt Romney? . . . You don't appear to like each other very much." Despite his campaign's particularly nasty attacks on Romney, Obama replied: "I don't think that any relationship between me and Mitt Romney is different from previous presidential campaigns."[21]

Then on Thursday's *Nightly News*, Williams touted Obama's endorsement for the second time by former Bush secretary of state Colin Powell, as if a second endorsement somehow rises to the level of national news. He then took the familiar route of challenging Obama to be more boldly liberal. "Mr. President, the subject of rape has been in the public discourse this campaign year unlike any time I can remember it in American public life. You were asked about it last night, you've inserted a line in your speech, I noted, about women's health. Is that as far as you're comfortable going for now?"

Williams also lamented the election process and imagined Obama as a benevolent despot: "If you could fix either the Electoral College or the fact that we're going to spend a billion dollars electing a president, and Lord knows what cancer cure that might have started us down the road on, which would you do most urgently if you had unlimited powers?"

In none of these programs did Williams raise Libya. During a twenty-minute interview with President Obama aired on the October 25 *Rock Center*—a show in the 10 P.M. Eastern time hour that drew 3.7 million viewers—Williams devoted a total of one minute and thirty-six seconds to the subject of the terrorist attack in Libya—and used it as an opportunity to shield his hero from blame. He treated President Obama as a victim of faulty intelligence work:

"Have you been happy with the intelligence, especially in our post 9/11 world? The assessment of your intelligence community, as we stand here, is that it still was a spontaneous terrorist attack and were you happy with what you were able to learn as this unfolded? It went on for several hours."

Obama replied with the usual still-waiting-for-answers spin: "Well, as I've said, Brian, we're going to do a full investigation. Obviously, when four Americans are killed, you know, you have to do some soul searching in terms of making sure that all our systems are where they need to be. And that's what we are going to find out."[22]

Williams was letting Obama imply he was curious for new information. Neither of them was. Williams completely ignored a breaking story two nights earlier, wherein CBS reporter Sharyl Attkisson reported on e-mails sent directly to the White House and other government agencies in real time as the Benghazi consulate came under attack from armed jihadists. It underlined that Team Obama wasn't as confused about YouTube-inspired killers as he—and Williams—wanted people to believe.[23]

✴   ✴   ✴

Even on CBS, the Attkisson report was treated as completely irrelevant to voters evaluating the honesty of Obama. The same CBS newscast featured reporter Nancy Cordes showing Obama drawing cheers in Florida as he "relentlessly stayed on offense," saying Romney was an untrustworthy flip-flopper: "The person who leads this country—you've got to have some confidence that he or she means what he or she says. . . . Florida, you know me! You can trust that I say what I mean!"[24]

Then came more information. On October 26, Fox News reporter Jennifer Griffin dropped a Little Boy atomic bomb. She reported that "sources claim officers at the nearby CIA annex in Benghazi were twice told to stand down when they requested to help those at the consulate. They later ignored those orders. Fox News was also told that a subsequent request for back-up when the annex came under attack was denied as well."[25]

In apparent defiance of these orders, two former Navy SEALs left the CIA annex to rescue several Americans from the consulate. Ty Woods and Glen Doherty later died defending the CIA annex. The administration had turned its back on its own consulate and four men, including a U.S. ambassador, had died as a result. The networks ignored this story.

Not every reporter avoided it. On the same day that Fox relayed this shocking new development, a local reporter in Denver, Colorado, named Kyle Clark did manage to ask President Obama about it during a campaign stop on October 26. "Were the Americans under attack at the consulate in Benghazi, Libya denied requests for help during that attack, and is it fair to tell Americans that what happened is under investigation, and we'll all find out after the election?" Imagine the president's shock that a local reporter would be so impertinently substantive.

Obama responded that "the minute I found out what was happening, I gave three very clear directives. Number one, make sure that we are securing our personnel and doing whatever we need to. . . . I guarantee you that everyone in the State Department, our military, the CIA, you name it, had number one priority making sure that people were safe." [26] Yet Fox's report—that help was requested and denied—clearly contradicted that claim.

The networks had no interest in testing Obama's claims—questionable (at best)—and ignored the Denver interview. The only coverage of these claims came when Republican guests mentioned them on the October 28 Sunday shows. Former CEO and Republican Senate candidate Carly Fiorina slammed Obama's Libya response ten minutes into NBC's *Meet the Press*: "That attack went on for seven hours . . . [with the] Secretary of Defense saying he denied requests for help over that seven hours." Gregory cut her off: "We'll get to Libya a little bit later." Unsurprisingly, NBC never did. Fiorina's brief mention was the last word on Libya during the hour-long program. [27]

On ABC's *This Week*, Newt Gingrich harped on Secretary of Defense Leon Panetta's failure to send any help to Benghazi and whacked at Obama scheduling choices: "He's canceling trips over the hurricane [Sandy]. He did not cancel trips over Benghazi." ABC host George Stephanopoulos changed the subject. [28]

On the October 28 *Fox News Sunday*, Brit Hume commented that "the mainstream organs of the media—that would be after this like a pack of hounds, if this were a Republican President—have been remarkably reticent. . . . A lot of the media, who are a combined potent force, have not done their job." [29]

Unlike their thrill over televising self-described "grieving Gold-Star mother and militant activist" Cindy Sheehan in 2004 as she protested President Bush for months, the networks were not interested in interviewing relatives of the Benghazi victims. Ty Woods's father, Charles, appeared on Fox News Channel's *Hannity* on October 29. He pleaded: "There are people in the White House—whoever it was—that [were] in that room watching that video of my son dying, their cries for help. Their order, 'Don't help them at all, let them die,' whoever that might be, it might be numerous people—you have the blood of my son. You have the blood of an American hero on your hands. I don't know who you are, but one of these days, the truth will come out. I still forgive you, but you need to stand up." [30]

It was heartbreaking.

The last outrage of Benghazi interviews surfaced very quietly on the Sunday before the election. The chronology here is very important. On September 12, the first day after the attack, Steve Kroft had interviewed the president about Libya, and CBS offered a soundbite that allowed Obama to trash Romney for shooting first and aiming later, with Kroft asking Obama if Romney was irresponsible.

Fuller interviews with Obama and with Romney aired on September 23. But only on November 4, almost two months after Benghazi, did the *60 Minutes* website post new video of Kroft asking directly if it was a terrorist attack. [31] Remember that CBS reported later they knew in real time that a terrorist group was responsible:

> STEVE KROFT: Mr. President, this morning you went out of your way to avoid the use of the word "terrorism" in connection with the Libya attack. Do you believe that this was a terrorism attack?
>
> PRESIDENT OBAMA: Well it's too early to tell exactly how this came about, what group was involved, but obviously it was an attack on Americans. And we are going to be working with the Libyan government to make sure that we bring these folks to justice, one way or the other.
>
> KROFT: But there are reports that they were very heavily armed with grenades; that doesn't sound like your normal demonstration.
>
> OBAMA: As I said, we're still investigating exactly what happened; I don't want to jump the gun on this.

Wait a minute. As was reported on October 20, fifteen days before this interview surfaced, and reported by CBS's own Sharyl Attkisson, Team Obama knew in real time on September 11 that Benghazi was most certainly a terrorist attack. So for the commander in chief to declare to Kroft the next day, "We're still investigating exactly what happened, I don't want to jump the gun on this" shows an astonishing detachment and an administration that was beyond inept—or the president was lying again. Either way, releasing that exchange the day after the Candy Crowley debate on October 17 would have displayed how Obama and his advisers were trying to rewrite history.

It could have been huge news and absolutely devastating news for the Obama campaign. Instead, CBS sat on it for another two weeks, while ABC and NBC also refused to call the president out for his misstatement.

It bears repeating. That quiet little release was only online. It wasn't even on the air. It didn't hit the air until the *CBS Evening News* on November 16—ten days after the election. During a story about ex-CIA director David Petraeus testifying that he never doubted that the attack was an act of terrorism, correspondent David Martin added: "Yet President Obama refrained from calling it a terrorist attack when he spoke with Steve Kroft of *60 Minutes* that afternoon."

They had successfully submerged Benghazi from emerging as a defining moment for judging Obama's competence or honesty. Compare that contrast—wanting to crush Bush's reelection on the Sunday before the 2004 election, to delaying, delaying, and then almost imperceptibly releasing information that underlined Obama's deceit on a national debate stage. They had turned a checkmate for Romney into a checkmate against him.

EPILOGUE

Some Steps to Combat and Persuade the Media

Did the national media deliver the election to Barack Obama? The question invites a level of analysis that is admittedly subjective in nature. What cannot be denied is their bias and their political agenda. As we've documented, it is there, unequivocally and overwhelmingly. Any journalist denying this is flirting with felony ignorance. The real question drills deeper and is more debatable: Were they believed? Did the media succeed in selling this bill of goods called "objective" "news" "reporting"—or did the public see through the charade?

The polling data point to a public that has grown skeptical, to say the least.

On September 21, just two months shy of the elections, the Gallup organization released some remarkable findings. They asked a simple question of the public: *How much trust do you have in the mass media—such as newspapers, TV and radio—when it comes to reporting the news fully, accurately and fairly—a great deal, a fair amount, not very much, not at all?* The results were eye-opening. A full 60 percent of the public has little or no trust in the news media, the highest negative on this question ever recorded by Gallup. Conversely, only 8 percent had a "great deal" of trust in the press.

On Election Night, at our behest, the McLaughlin Associates polling firm asked some questions along these lines in their omnibus survey.

The first question we wanted answered was the degree to which the public believed the news media had helped to reelect Barack Obama versus those who believed they were helping elect Mitt Romney. Take out those who believed the press was neutral, or who had no opinion and you're left with: *Obama 84.8 percent, Romney 15.2 percent.*

Did they succeed? We wanted to know—remember, we were anticipating a GOP victory—if the media might have cost Romney the election, had the public believed them. We asked Romney voters this: *"If you had accepted the liberal media's news reporting as factual, truthful and objective, would you have voted for Barack Obama?"*

The numbers stunned even veterans like us. A full 22.8 percent of Romney voters acknowledged they would have voted for the incumbent had they believed the liberal press. Another 6 percent stated they *might* have.

What, exactly, do those numbers mean? We conducted an exercise that, admittedly, is not entirely scientific, but it's proximate enough to make the necessary point. We took that 22.8 percent number out of the Romney camp and moved it into the Obama total, in every state.

On Election Night, Obama won with 51.4 percent of the popular vote, winning 28 states and registering a 332–206 electoral vote margin of victory.

Now, give him another 22.8 percent and his vote total would have risen by 13 million, to 62.5 percent. He would have won all but five states (Idaho, Wyoming, Utah, Oklahoma, and Arkansas). He would have captured 512 electoral votes. It might have cost the Republicans the three Senate seats they did finally manage to pick up. If so, the new total would be 58 Democrats, 42 Republicans, an insurmountable 16-seat advantage. The House? That may have tipped to the Democrats.

It would have been a Democrat landslide of epic proportions. Obama would declare a national mandate for his socialist transformation. His Democratic majorities would support it, and there's not a bloody thing Republicans could do to prevent it.

So, was this doomsday scenario avoided because the public didn't believe the news media? Because of this educated electorate, was the end of Western Civilization prevented? An exaggeration? Assuredly. What cannot be dismissed, however, is that 22.8 percent number. No matter how it ultimately might have been distributed, that vote switch would have been enormous. It is absolutely unquestionable that those who fought to expose the political agenda of the liberal press, be they organizations such as the Media Research Center, or conservative voices like Limbaugh, and Hannity and Levin, had a significant impact leveling the playing field.

But it is fanciful, even preposterous, to suggest the news media had *no* impact. It is far more reasonable to conclude they provided four points for Obama—his margin of victory.

In this book, we have provided you with hundreds of examples documenting the liberal bias that permeated the 2012 election cycle. Clearly there are thousands more.

These were the endless anecdotes—the sentence here, the phrase there—advancing the righteousness of Obama and/or the failings of Romney et al.

It was the constant, infuriating examples of the soft voice, the look of awe, reverence even, just being in the presence of Obama; the harsh, accusatory question, the piercing look of disbelief, even the guffaw, as the Romney camp was summarily dismissed, time after time.

It was the focus on the positive, always the positive regarding the Obama message, even if that message was incorrect, incoherent, or as was so often the case, dishonest. It was the obsession with the negative, always the negative aimed at Romney, savaging his message as incorrect, incoherent, or as so often the case, dishonest.

Most important, it was the deliberate decision to downplay, even withhold from the public the kind of news and information that might harm the reelection prospects of the incumbent, no matter how newsworthy and, ultimately, necessary for the electorate to make an informed decision: Fast and Furious, Benghazi, the assault on religious freedom, the monumental and disastrous debt created, the wasted trillions, the corruption, the handouts of billions of federal dollars in questionable (at best) federal contracts to contributors. The arrogance, the opulence, the hypocrisy, the lies.

And with the challenger? They made things up.

Obama was the most vulnerable incumbent in modern times. His performance on the economy was (and continues to be) disastrous, by any objective measurement. The United States is on the precipice of a fiscal and monetary collapse. He has done nothing to arrest, even slow the slide. Indeed, because of his excesses the country seems primed to go over the cliff. On social policy he declared war on everyone of faith with his (anti-)religious mandate, while advancing the most radical policies on key issues, from abortion to gays. On foreign policy, after being touted as the necessary antidote for the worldwide damage caused by the anti-Bush poison, he turned out to be even *less* popular.

Barack Obama was a disaster.

And he won reelection, handily.

The media's determination to project the false image of Barack Obama and his potential successor to the presidency as competent and honest public servants was underlined after the election, when the CBS *60 Minutes* butler Steve Kroft was summoned to a "historic joint interview" with Obama and Hillary Clinton. Obama announced he had commanded this airspace on CBS to thank Mrs. Clinton for her diligent service. Dutifully, the network complied.

All of that classic *60 Minutes* aggression was conserved for the next segment, directed at the competitive bicyclist Lance Armstrong. At the end of that piece, Armstrong's fiercest critic, Trevor Tygart of the U.S. Anti-Doping Agency, suggested this was Armstrong's plan: "Cheat your way to the top, and if you get too big and too popular and too powerful—if you do it that well, you'll never be held accountable."

Obama's reliance on the performance-enhancing media is like doping in politics. Kroft & Co. helped Obama cheat his way to the top, and after he reached that pinnacle of power, they never held him to account for his actions.

Liberal media bias is not new. The press has tilted liberal for decades, has it not? Yes, but never have the news media performed as they did in 2012, and if conservatives don't recognize this and commit themselves to changing the equation, they will not win again—at least not any time soon. With the real possibility that the days are numbered for this country's freedoms, it is not just a problem, it is a crisis.

Let's go back a second in time, just thirty-five years ago, and examine the media landscape then. There were the three broadcast networks along with PBS. All were liberal. There were three major magazines, *Time, Newsweek*, and *U.S. News & World Report.* Two were decidedly liberal, the third a fraction less so. There was a vibrant newspaper business; every publication with a national audience was liberal. There were two wire services; both were liberal. Liberals had a complete monopoly on the national news business in America.

Conservatives had no news outlets. Their commentary outlets were almost nonexistent as well. They had no Fox, no political talk radio, and no Internet. Conservatives controlled a handful of polemical publications, but all registered comparatively minuscule audiences. Bill Buckley could challenge liberals on his *Firing Line* show on PBS, but it was watched only by intellectuals, a fraction of a fraction of the population. Conservatives had no outlet for mass communications. Our Pony Express in the world of communications was direct mail, one step more advanced than smoke signals.

The news media were dominated by the Walter Cronkites, Dan Rathers, Peter Jennings, Tom Brokaws, Ed Bradleys, Mike Wallaces, etc.—all liberals, all routinely denounced by the right for their excesses. Entire movements were launched to stop them, with organizations formed exclusively for the purpose. We hit them for their leftist ideology, their support of centralized government and opposition to the free enterprise system; for their embrace of international leftism and rejection of American exceptionalism; for their promotion of a libertine, morally relative culture at the expense of a moral code grounded in Judeo-Christian values.

And we'd give anything to have them back.

Yesterday's journalists were liberals, not today's radical leftists, much in the same vein that their political standard bearers, like George McGovern, were several degrees to the right of the socialist presently occupying 1600 Pennsylvania Avenue. Yesterday's journalists attempted, at least on some level, sometimes, maybe once every solar eclipse or so, to strive for objectivity. Today's journalists make no such effort. They reject a code of ethical conduct if it interferes with their political mission. Yesterday's journalists by and large were educated, not just in the liberal arts, but in journalism. Today's journalists make a mockery of the word. They are naive, even sometimes downright stupid. They are undisciplined, not just in the preparation but in the delivery of news. They cannot, or just will not distinguish between news and information. They are pawns for misinformation and practiced in disinformation. They are loud, condescending, arrogant, dishonest, foolish, incompetent, mean-spirited—and dangerous.

How can this problem, this epidemic of unfairness in the national media, be cured? Let's be blunt. In a clinical sense it can't. It's a free country—at least, for now, mostly—and the national news media have the freedom to present Obama as the finest naked emperor that's ever lived. We must also salute that freedom, and defend it always. Any attempt to control the news media through government fiat must be resisted, fiercely. It is a direct challenge to democracy.

But how ironic that the opposite is equally true. A "free press" controlled by a special interest in furtherance of an agenda which necessitates public support, which support can be achieved only through the practice of censorship, of planted obfuscation and outright distortion, is in equal measure a threat to democracy and should be resisted with similar fervor.

Conservatives must put an end to this. It can be done.

How critical is this to conservatives? There is nothing more important. The 2012 cycle was not an aberration, it is the new normal. It is now an established reality that the "news" media will do anything and everything to distort and discredit any conservative imperative that challenges leftist orthodoxy. Unless and until this situation is corrected, not only will conservatives be thwarted, they will continue to lose ground as their policy prescriptions are ever more vilified. If this isn't a top-shelf concern for a conservative leader or organization, he is condemned to political death and—frankly, at some point we must say it—deservedly so.

Ironically, in a very real way they need us more than we need them. Theirs is an industry in an audience free fall, victims of technological advances, competition, and their own biases. Their monopoly is shattered. The conservative movement has virtually unlimited options now.

The broadcast networks have lost more than half their audience since 1980. The Pew Research Center's Project for Excellence in Journalism found the network newscasts drew 52.1 million viewers per night when Reagan was running against Carter. In the November 2012 sweeps period, the networks attracted just 24.1 million viewers. The contrast is starker when you consider population growth. In 1980, the networks captured 52.1 million out of an American population of 227 million, around 23 percent. In November 2012, the networks grabbed 24.1 million out of almost 314 million Americans—down to 7.6 percent.

CNN, once a serious source of news, is now an Anderson Cooper–Kathy Griffin–Eliot Spitzer–Soledad O'Brien–Piers Morgan laughingstock. The "stars" come, they go—and no one cares. *Time* magazine is on life support. *The New York Times* is gasping for breath. *Newsweek* is gone. Meanwhile, conservative talk radio continues as strong as ever, new television outlets like Fox News provide a balanced approach, and the Internet is ablaze. It is this last item that trumps all others. The Internet is the future, like it or not. The era of news is giving way to the information age. Journalism is no longer a prized endeavor for the privileged and trained few. In the era of blogging, everyone is a pamphleteer.

Conservatives must become far more educated about the industry, selective in their choices, and confrontational when attacked. And they must learn to park their publicity-seeking egos in the garage.

The research is there for anyone to recognize who will and won't be fair, and how he should be treated. Piers Morgan is not going to conduct a civilized interview and with his minuscule audience is irrelevant. So why consent to be interviewed and give him oxygen? *The New York Times* is going edit mercilessly in order to present you in the worst possible light. Why expect otherwise? Conservatives are ammo for Bill Maher, Jon Stewart, and Stephen Colbert. Why agree to be made a fool? There is nothing, absolutely nothing of value on MSNBC for a conservative. Why on earth does anyone accept any invitation for any show for any reason?

There is a world of difference between the taped and live interview. The former lends itself to shenanigans; with the latter, it's more difficult. Conservatives should always insist on a live format, if at all possible, and if in the process the interviewer pulls a fast one, with either incorrect statements, or some other exercise in Gotcha Journalism designed to embarrass the guest, the guest should pounce, and hit right back. It's national television, it's live, and they can't stop you. Embarrass them this way, and Brian Williams & Co. will never try that again. If it's taped and later manipulated, the conservative should publicly denounce the network or print outlet, fully discredit the entity, and refuse ever to participate again unless a clarification, correction, or apology—whatever the offense called for—is issued.

Conservatives should understand there are outlets that aren't biased against them and generate major audiences, even larger ones than most liberal entities. Through conservative talk radio they can reach tens of millions—daily. There is Fox, and *The Wall Street Journal* and other sources that may not be conservative, but aren't activist liberal, either. And then there's the mother lode: the Internet.

Conservatives must understand that in the information age the cultural trumps the political. It is a lesson learned by the left years ago, and one they've perfected, projecting their vision to tens of millions of people daily, nightly, using entertainment television, movies, music, digital media—all the media formats where celebrities they've recruited, not politicians, champion the cause *du jour*. They are our society's royalty. They are the Pied Pipers and their legions of adoring fans will follow blindly, but obediently. When the culture is changed, the political battle is a mop-up operation, simply codifying the new cultural norm into law. They've succeeded with gay rights, made critical advances with environmental issues, reignited momentum for abortion, created a new national outcry for immigration "reform," and now are using it to go for the political Holy Grail, gun control.

Why conservatives ignore the popular culture is puzzling, to say the least. Naïveté? Laziness? Intimidation? Arrogance? Take your pick—but until they focus their energies on the cultural media, where many, many times more people can be found than in the public policy arena, and make their voice heard loudly in the popular culture conversation, they will never succeed. The opposite also holds true: should conservatives choose to enter this arena, the results could be electrifying.

Which is not to say they haven't. Think about the hundreds, the thousands of discussions surrounding Jesus Christ. Now remember the movie, *The Passion of the Christ.* Which had a greater impact? Think about all the dissertations on liberty. Now watch *Braveheart.* Which resonated more? Flawed as he was, Mel Gibson understood that there is no reason, none whatsoever, that conservatives can't be as successful as liberals, more so even when you consider the logical footing on which the conservative argument rests.

Finally, conservatives must commit to devoting the necessary resources to the technologies of the future. Social media is here to stay and the right has been AWOL. What do Facebook, Twitter, Tumblr, Pinterest, and so many other formats have in common? They are interactive, they are enormously popular, and, most important for this discussion, they are free, absolutely free of liberal control. Conservatives can now communicate directly, instantaneously with millions upon millions of people, directing their messages, their way, when they want, where they want, and with whom they want. And by this time next year there will be a half-dozen new vehicles to transport our ideas.

The work of winning hearts and minds for America's original constitutional recipe is a daily grind, and there are few final victories.

But we have no choice if we wish to transmit the spirit of 1776 to a tercentennial celebration, and beyond. A free and balanced media is crucial to the health of this country. Journalists should feel the duty—as outlined in the Society of Professional Journalists' Code of Ethics—to "distinguish between advocacy and news reporting," that "[a]nalysis and commentary should be labeled and not misrepresent fact or context." They pledged to further democracy by "seeking truth and providing a fair and comprehensive account of events and issues." But any honest examination of the national media in 2012 would say these trampled and forgotten pledges of professionalism should be stowed away in Washington, D.C., as an educational artifact in the "Newseum."

NOTES

Chapter 1

1. Alexander Burns, "Barack Obama's 2012 plan: 'Kill Romney,'" *Politico*, August 9, 2011, http://www.politico.com/news/stories/0811/60929.html.
2. Lawrence O'Donnell, on *The Last Word with Lawrence O'Donnell*, MSNBC, August 9, 2011.
3. "President Obama Job Approval," realclearpolitics.com, http://www.realclear politics.com/epolls/other/president_obama_job_approval-1044.html.
4. Tim Graham, "Thomas Friedman Says GOP Looking for Someone as 'Smart and Mellifluous' as Obama," NewsBusters, December 27, 2011, http://newsbusters .org/blogs/tim-graham/2011/12/27/thomas-friedman-says-gop-looking-some one-smart-and-mellifluous-obama.
5. Scott Whitlock, "NYT's Joe Nocera Spews Venom at 'Terrorist' Tea Partiers for Strapping on 'Suicide Vests,'" NewsBusters, August 3, 2011, http://newsbusters .org/blogs/scott-whitlock/2011/08/03/nyts-joe-nocera-spews-venom-terrorist -tea-partiers-strapping-suicide.
6. Rich Noyes, "Latest Notable Quotables: Deriding the Tea Party as Terrorists 'Strapped with Dynamite,'" NewsBusters, August 8, 2011, http://newsbusters .org/blogs/rich-noyes/2011/08/08/latest-notable-quotables-deriding-tea-party -terrorists-strapped-dynamite.
7. Jack Cafferty and Nancy Gibbs, quoted in "Bloodthirsty GOP No Longer the 'Party of Life'?," Notable Quotables (October 3, 2011), http://www.mrc.org/ node/8742.
8. Scott Whitlock, "Chris Matthews: Southern 'Secessionists' Want to 'Kill' Obama . . . 'Politically,'" NewsBusters, August 3, 2011, http://newsbusters.org/ blogs/scott-whitlock/2011/08/03/chris-matthews-southern-secessionists-want -kill-obamapolitically.
9. Transcript, "One on One with Bill Maher," *Piers Morgan Tonight*, CNN, July 15, 2011.

10. Brent Bozell, "Bozell Column: Airing Anti-Palin Bilge at NBC," NewsBusters, September 20, 2011, http://newsbusters.org/blogs/brent-bozell/2011/09/20/bozell -column-airing-anti-palin-bilge-nbc.

11. Noel Sheppard, "ABC World News Investigates Bachmann Clinic: 'Where You Can Pray Away The Gay?,'" NewsBusters, July 11, 2011, http://newsbusters.org/blogs/ noel-sheppard/2011/07/11/abc-world-news-investigates-bachmann-clinic -where-you-can-pray-away-g.

12. Brent Bozell, "Bozell Column: Fear and Loathing of Bachmann," NewsBusters, August 16, 2011, http://newsbusters.org/blogs/brent-bozell/2011/08/16/bozell -column-fear-and-loathing-bachmann.

13. FunnyorDie.com, http://www.funnyordie.com/slideshows/65c6b11c2e/alternate -michele-bachmann-newsweek-covers#slide7.

14. Rich Noyes, "MRC's Notable Quotables: Slashing Rick Perry, 'the Human Tor- nado,'" NewsBusters, August 22, 2011, http://newsbusters.org/blogs/rich-noyes/ 2011/08/22/mrcs-notable-quotables-slashing-rick-perry-human-tornado.

15. Matthew Balan, "CBS Uses Cartoon to Spread Liberal Anti-Perry Talking Points," NewsBusters, September 13, 2011, http://newsbusters.org/blogs/matthew-balan/ 2011/09/13/cbs-uses-cartoon-spread-liberal-anti-perry-talking-points.

16. Brent Bozell, "Bozell Column: Rick's Rock vs. Reverend Wright," NewsBusters, October 4, 2011, http://newsbusters.org/blogs/brent-bozell/2011/10/04/bozell -column-ricks-rock-vs-reverend-wright.

17. Tim Graham, "WaPo's Ombudsman Makes Excuses for Very Anonymously- Sourced 'N-head' Scoop on Rick Perry," NewsBusters, October 10, 2011, http:// newsbusters.org/blogs/tim-graham/2011/10/10/wapos-ombudsman-makes -excuses-very-anonymously-sourced-n-head-scoop-rick.

18. Hugh Hewitt, "Washington Post's Drive-By Slander of Rick Perry," Real Clear Pol- itics, October 2, 2011, http://www.realclearpolitics.com/2011/10/02/washington _post039s__drive-by_slander_of_perry_264625.html.

19. Tim Graham, "WaPo Slams Herman Cain As a Store-Closing, 'Tough-Talking Thug,'" NewsBusters, October 19, 2011, http://newsbusters.org/blogs/tim-gra ham/2011/10/19/wapo-slams-herman-cain-store-closing-tough-talking-thug.

20. Brent Bozell, "Bozell Column: Herman's High-Tech Lynching," NewsBusters, November 3, 2011, http://newsbusters.org/blogs/brent-bozell/2011/11/03/bozell -column-hermans-high-tech-lynching.

21. Noel Sheppard, "Ann Coulter Calls Politico's Herman Cain Hit Piece 'Another High-Tech Lynching,'" NewsBusters, October 31, 2011, http://newsbusters.org/ node/51414.

22. Tom Blumer, "Leftist ProPublica Questions Politico's Decision to Publish Cain Allegations," NewsBusters, October 31, 2011, http://newsbusters.org/blogs/tom -blumer/2011/10/31/leftist-propublica-questions-politicos-decision-publish -cain-allegations.

23. Kyle Drennen, "Networks Pile On Cain: Will 'Bizarre' Response to Harassment

Claims 'Derail' His Campaign?," NewsBusters, November 1, 2011, http://news
busters.org/blogs/kyle-drennen/2011/11/01/networks-pile-cain-will-bizarre
-response-harassment-claims-derail-his-.

24. Scott Whitlock, "Defensive Networks Devote 84 Stories to Herman Cain Scandal,
Hit Him for 'Lashing Out,'" NewsBusters, November 7, 2011, http://newsbusters
.org/blogs/scott-whitlock/2011/11/07/defensive-networks-devote-84-stories
-herman-cain-scandal-hit-him-las.

25. Scott Whitlock, "Network Deluge: 99 Stories on Cain Harassment Charges in
Less than Nine Days," NewsBusters, November 8, 2011, http://newsbusters.org/
blogs/scott-whitlock/2011/11/08/network-deluge-99-stories-cain-harassment
-charges-less-nine-days.

26. Scott Whitlock, "Networks Hit Cain with 117 Stories; ABC: Accusers Seek 'Safety in
Numbers' From Cain," NewsBusters, November 9, 2011, http://newsbusters.org/
blogs/scott-whitlock/2011/11/09/networks-hit-cain-177-stories-abc-accusers
-seek-safety-numbers-cain.

27. Brent Bozell, "Bozell Column: Herman's High-Tech Lynching," NewsBusters,
November 3, 2011, http://newsbusters.org/blogs/brent-bozell/2011/11/03/bozell
-column-hermans-high-tech-lynching.

28. Brent Bozell, "Bozell Column: Let's Kill Cain's Campaign," NewsBusters,
November 29, 2011, http://newsbusters.org/blogs/brent-bozell/2011/11/29/bozell
-column-lets-kill-cains-campaign.

29. Scott Whitlock, "Stephanopoulos Gloats: Will My Interview with New Accuser
'Spell the End' for Cain?," NewsBusters, November 30, 2011, http://newsbusters
.org/blogs/scott-whitlock/2011/11/30/stephanopoulos-gloats-will-my-interview
-new-accuser-spell-end-cain.

30. Scott Whitlock, "Irony Alert: Ex-Clinton Operative Stephanopoulos Attacks
Cain's 'Honesty' and 'Judgment,'" NewsBusters, November 30, 2011, http://news
busters.org/blogs/scott-whitlock/2011/11/30/irony-alert-ex-clinton-operative
-stephanopoulos-attacks-cains-honest.

31. Geoffrey Dickens, "Matthews Rages: Newt Gingrich Looks Like a 'Car Bomber'
Who 'Loves Torturing!,'" NewsBusters, March 2, 2011, http://newsbusters.org/
blogs/geoffrey-dickens/2011/03/02/matthews-rages-newt-gingrich-car-bomber
-looks-he-loves-torturing.

32. RealClearPolitics.com, "Matthews: Gingrich Has Made Politics 'Nastier, More
Feral' And Uglier," November 29, 2011, http://www.realclearpolitics.com/video/
2011/11/29/matthews_gingrich_has_made_politics_nastier_more_feral_and
_uglier-co mments.html.

33. Scott Whitlock, "Smarmy Brian Ross Touts His 'January Surprise,' Eagerly Digs
for Gingrich's 'Skeletons,'" NewsBusters, January 20, 2012, http://newsbusters
.org/blogs/scott-whitlock/2012/01/20/smarmy-brian-ross-touts-his-october
-surprise-eagerly-digs-gingrichs-.

34. Transcript of Brian Ross, "Tricky Business," ABC's 20/20, January 4, 2008.

35. Tim Graham, "Rachel Maddow Slams Newt by Comparing Him to 'Google Santorum' Smear," NewsBusters, November 13, 2011, http://newsbusters.org/blogs/tim-graham/2011/11/13/rachel-maddow-slams-newt-comparing-him-google-santorum-smear.

36. Tim Graham, "The Same Newsweek That Trashed Bachmann Puffed Gloria Steinem as Florence Nightingale," NewsBusters, August 11, 2011, http://newsbusters.org/blogs/tim-graham/2011/08/11/same-newsweek-trashed-bachmann-puffed-gloria-steinem-florence-nightingal.

37. Nancy Hass, "Before Karen Met Rick," thedailybeast.com, January 16, 2012, http://www.thedailybeast.com/newsweek/2012/01/15/mrs-santorum-s-abortion-doctor-boyfriend.html.

38. Tim Graham, "Fox's 'Special Report' Passes Along MRC Finding: OWS-Loving Networks Again Skipped 'March for Life,'" NewsBusters, January 27, 2012, http://newsbusters.org/blogs/tim-graham/2012/01/27/foxs-special-report-passes-along-mrc-finding-ows-loving-networks-again-s.

39. Brent Bozell, "Newsweek's Senators to Watch," MRC.org, January 5, 2005, http://www.mrc.org/node/4200.

Chapter 2

1. Brent Bozell, "Bozell Column: Brian Williams, from Musketeer to Mouseketeer," NewsBusters, August 31, 2010, http://newsbusters.org/blogs/brent-bozell/2010/08/31/bozell-column-brian-williams-musketeer-mouseketeer.

2. Noel Sheppard, "Chris Matthews: 'Obama Is the Perfect Father, the Perfect Husband, the Perfect American,'" NewsBusters, July 17, 2012, http://newsbusters.org/blogs/noel-sheppard/2012/07/17/chris-matthews-obama-perfect-father-perfect-husband-perfect-american.

3. Jonathan Alter, "Obama Miracle Is White House Free of Scandal," Bloomberg.com, October 27, 2011, http://www.bloomberg.com/news/2011-10-27/obama-miracle-is-white-house-free-of-scandal-commentary-by-jonathan-alter.html.

4. Kyle Drennen, "WaPo's Capehart on NBC's 'Today': Obama Administration 'Remarkably Free of Scandal,'" NewsBusters, October 31, 2011, http://newsbusters.org/blogs/kyle-drennen/2011/10/31/wapos-capehart-nbcs-today-obama-administration-remarkably-free-scandal.

5. Brent Baker, "WashPost's Milbank Claims: 'Media Would Love to Have an Obama Scandal to Cover,'" NewsBusters, June 24, 2012, http://newsbusters.org/blogs/brent-baker/2012/06/24/washpost-s-milbank-claims-media-would-love-have-obama-scandal-cover.

6. Dana Milbank, "Fast and Furious: The scandal Republicans have been waiting for?," washingtonpost.com, November 8, 2011, http://www.washingtonpost.com/

opinions/fast-and-furious-the-scandal-republicans-have-been-waiting-for/
2011/11/08/gIQAk1Q32M_story.ht ml.

7. Tim Graham and Geoffrey Dickens, "The Media's Obama Miracle: How Journalists Pretend There Aren't Any White House Scandals," MRC.org, August 8, 2012, http://www.mrc.org/node/40820.

8. Ibid.

9. Ibid.

10. Ibid.

11. "The Liberal Media's Newest Hero," Notable Quotables newsletter, August 29, 2005, http://www.mrc.org/node/8595.

12. Graham and Dickens, "The Media's Obama Miracle."

13. Carrie Johnson, "Holder: 'More Work to Do' Before Term Is Over," NPR.org, April 27, 2012, http://www.npr.org/2012/04/27/151529652/holder-more-work -to-do-before-term-is-over.

14. "Transcript: President Obama's Remarks at Univision Town Hall, Fox News Insider, September 20, 2012, http://foxnewsinsider.com/2012/09/20/transcript -president-obamas-remarks-at-univision-town-hall/.

15. Geoffrey Dickens, "ABC, CBS & NBC Blackout! Major New Findings in Fast & Furious Scandal Ignored," NewsBusters, October 1, 2012, http://newsbusters.org/ blogs/geoffrey-dickens/2012/10/01/abc-cbs-nbc-blackout-major-new-findings -fast-furious-scandal.

16. Tim Graham, "Mass Amnesia Over Mass Clinton Firings," Media Reality Check newsletter, March 14, 2007, http://archive.mrc.org/realitycheck/2007/fax 20070314.asp.

17. Matthew Boyle, "Emails Reveal Justice Dept. Regularly Enlists Media Matters to Spin Press," Daily Caller, September 18, 2012, http://dailycaller.com/2012/09/18/ emails-reveal-justice-dept-regularly-enlists-media-matters-to-spin-press/.

18. Mary Chastain, "At Least Jimmy Kimmel Gets What DC Elite Forgets: Fast & Furious Scandal," Breitbart.com, April 30, 2012, http://www.breitbart.com/Big -Hollywood/2012/04/30/At-Least-Jimmy-Kimmel-Gets-What-DC-Elite-Forgets -Fast-and-Furious-Scandal.

19. Brent Baker, "Correspondents' Dinner Headliner Kimmel Insists: 'It's Hard to Make Fun' of 'Cool Character' Obama," NewsBusters, April 25, 2012, http://news busters.org/blogs/brent-baker/2012/04/25/correspondents-dinner-headliner -kimmel-insists-it-s-hard-make-fun-cool-.

20. Andy Sullivan, "Analysis: Obama's 'Green Jobs' Have Been Slow to Sprout," Reuters.com, April 13, 2012, http://www.reuters.com/article/2012/04/13/us-usa -campaign-green-idUSBRE83C08D20120413.

21. Julia Seymour, "Networks Hardly Criticize Obama Green Jobs Flop," NewsBusters, August 22, 2011, http://newsbusters.org/blogs/julia-seymour/2011/08/22/net works-hardly-criticize-obama-green-jobs-flop.

22. Graham and Dickens, "The Media's Obama Miracle."

23. Ibid.

24. Eric Lipton and John M. Broder, "E-Mail Shows Senior Energy Official Pushed Solyndra Loan," *New York Times*, October 7, 2011, http://www.nytimes.com/2011/10/08/us/politics/e-mail-shows-senior-energy-official-pushed-solyndra-loan.html.

25. Carol D. Leonnig and Joe Stephens, "Energy Dept. Loan Chief Warned Staff That Personal E-mail Could Be Subpoenaed," *Washington Post*, August 14, 2011, http://articles.washingtonpost.com/2012-08-14/politics/35490043_1_personal-e-mail-e-mails-email.

26. Brent Bozell, "Bozell Column: Transparently Biased Against Disclosure," NewsBusters, October 9, 2012, http://newsbusters.org/blogs/brent-bozell/2012/10/09/bozell-column-transparently-biased-against-disclosure.

27. Transcript of the vice presidential debate, Commission on Presidential Debates, October 11, 2012, http://www.debates.org/index.php?page=october-11-2012-the-biden-romney-vice-presidential-debate.

28. Alter, "Obama Miracle."

29. Noel Sheppard, "John McLaughlin: New Solyndra Revelations 'Will Become Damaging to Obama's Reelection,'" NewsBusters, August 5, 2012, http://newsbusters.org/blogs/noel-sheppard/2012/08/05/john-mclaughlin-new-solyndra-revelations-will-become-damaging-obamas.

30. Michael Isikoff, "Corzine, Top Obama Fundraiser, Under FBI Investigation," NBC News.com, November 2, 2011, http://firstread.nbcnews.com/_news/2011/11/02/8599414-corzine-top-obama-fundraiser-under-fbi-investigation?lite.

31. Graham and Dickens, "The Media's Obama Miracle."

32. Ibid.

33. Terry Keenan, "Corzine Shows There's No Justice on Wall St.," *New York Post*, May 26, 2012, http://www.nypost.com/p/news/business/corzine_shows_there_no_justice_on_EdUwVFlpOR4966IyltGvBN.

34. Jamila Trendle and Aaron Lucchetti, "House GOP Raps Corzine Over MF," *Wall Street Journal*, November 14, 2012, http://online.wsj.com/article/SB10001424127887324735104578119103238887208.html.

35. Lymari Morales, "Americans' Confidence in Television News Drops to New Low," Gallup.com, July 10, 2012, http://www.gallup.com/poll/155585/americans-confidence-television-news-drops-new-low.aspx.

36. "Top Twenty Stories of 2011," Tyndall Report, undated, http://tyndallreport.com/yearinreview2011/.

Chapter 3

1. Tim Graham, "Team Obama Cries 'Bull(bleep)' Against Billion-Dollar Campaign Estimates," NewsBusters, December 31, 2011, http://newsbusters.org/blogs/tim -graham/2011/12/31/team-obama-cries-bullbleep-against-billion-dollar-cam paign-estimates.
2. Tim Graham, "Comcast Employees Top Donors to Obama and 'Victory Fund,'" NewsBusters, August 26, 2011, http://newsbusters.org/blogs/tim-graham/2011/ 08/26/abc-tattles-nbc-comcast-top-corporate-donor-obama-victory-fund.
3. Ed Morrissey, "Obama Campaign Manager: Billion-Dollar Campaign Is BS," Hot Air, December 29, 2011, http://hotair.com/archives/2011/12/29/obama -campaign-manager-billion-dollar-campaign-is-bs/.
4. Kenneth P. Vogel and Dan Berman, "Team Obama Raises $1 billion," *Politico*, October 25, 2012, http://www.politico.com/news/stories/1012/82909.html.
5. Noel Sheppard, "Jamie Foxx: 'Our Lord and Savior Barack Obama,'" NewsBusters, November 26, 2012, http://newsbusters.org/blogs/noel-sheppard/2012/11/26/ jamie-foxx-calls-obama-our-lord-and-savior.
6. Barbra Streisand, "Obama vs. Romney: A Clear Choice," *Huffington Post*, September 18, 2012, http://www.huffingtonpost.com/barbra-streisand/obama-vs -romney-a-clear-c_b_1894001.html.
7. "Contributions from Celebrities," Open Secrets, http://www.opensecrets.org/ pres12/celebs.php.
8. Noel Sheppard, "Bill Maher Gives $1 Million to Obama Super PAC," NewsBusters, February 24, 2012, http://newsbusters.org/blogs/noel-sheppard/2012/02/24/bill -maher-gives-1-million-obama-super-pac.
9. Matthew Balan, "Santorum Fires Back at CBS's 'Gotcha;' Raises Rev. Wright Double Standard," NewsBusters, February 17, 2012, http://newsbusters.org/blogs/ matthew-balan/2012/02/17/santorum-fires-back-cbss-gotcha-raises-rev-wright -double-standard.
10. Tim Graham, "Kirsten Powers Rebuts Maher's NY Times Op-ed: 'Please START Apologizing,'" NewsBusters, March 24, 2012, http://newsbusters.org/blogs/ tim-graham/2012/03/24/kirsten-powers-rebuts-mahers-ny-times-op-ed-please -start-apologizing.
11. Noel Sheppard, "Laura Ingraham Schools George Stephanopoulos: 'Did Obama Give That Money Back to Bill Maher?,'" NewsBusters, May 20, 2012, http://news busters.org/blogs/noel-sheppard/2012/05/20/laura-ingraham-schools-george -stephanopoulos-did-obama-give-money-bac.
12. "Meet the Gaffe Seekers: Inside the Political Industry Built on Blunders," Rock Center, September 14, 2012, http://rockcenter.nbcnews.com/_news/2012/09/14/ 13866355-meet-the-gaffe-seekers-inside-the-political-industry-built-on -blunders?lite.

13. Tim Graham, "Newsweek Hails Bill Maher, Testament to the American Dream," NewsBusters, November 18, 2011, http://newsbusters.org/blogs/tim-graham/2011/11/18/newsweek-hails-bill-maher-testament-american-dream.

14. Brent Baker, "Sawyer's Flub: Claims Wall Street Protests Have 'Spread to More than a Thousand Countries,'" NewsBusters, October 11, 2011, http://newsbusters.org/blogs/brent-baker/2011/10/11/diane-sawyer-claims-wall-street-protests-have-spread-more-thousand-coun.

15. Geoffrey Dickens, "A Tale of Two Protests: Media Cheer Wall Street Occupiers but Jeered Tea Partiers," MRC.org, October 13, 2011, http://www.mrc.org/media-reality-check/tale-two-protests-media-cheer-wall-street-occupiers-jeered-tea-partiers.

16. Geoffrey Dickens, "Occupier Outrages Omitted," MRC.org, November 7, 2011, http://www.mrc.org/media-reality-check/occupier-outrages-omitted.

17. Noel Sheppard, "OWS Supporter Michael Moore Lies on National Television About His Wealth: No I'm Not Worth Millions," NewsBusters, October 26, 2011, http://newsbusters.org/blogs/noel-sheppard/2011/10/26/ows-supporter-michael-moore-lies-national-television-about-his-wealth.

18. Brent Bozell, "Bozell Column: Obama Courts the Glitz Elite," NewsBusters, February 4, 2012, http://newsbusters.org/blogs/brent-bozell/2012/02/04/bozell-column-obama-courts-glitz-elite.

19. Tina Daunt, "Obama Addresses Hollywood: Reelection Won't Be as Sexy as His First Campaign," Hollywood Reporter, October 24, 2011, http://www.hollywoodreporter.com/news/obama-reelection-will-smith-james-lassiter-magic-johnson.

20. Tina Daunt and Matthew Belloni, "President Obama Holds Secret Meet-and-Greet with Hollywood Execs and Influencers (Exclusive)," Hollywood Reporter, October 25, 2011, http://www.hollywoodreporter.com/news/president-obama-hollywood-meeting-253151.

21. "Obama White House on Press Access: A Nixonian Quality," San Francisco Chronicle, October 25, 2011, http://www.sfgate.com/opinion/editorials/article/Obama-White-House-on-press-access-a-Nixonian-2325483.php.

22. "President Obama Continues His West Coast Swing," Nexis transcript of NBC's Today show, October 25, 2011.

23. Kyle Drennen, "Network Morning Shows Tout 'Comedian in Chief' Obama Mocking GOP on Leno," NewsBusters, October 26, 2011, http://newsbusters.org/blogs/kyle-drennen/2011/10/26/network-morning-shows-tout-comedian-chief-obama-mocking-gop-leno.

24. Marie Cunningham, "With Obama in Town, Protestors Rally to Fight Big Money in Politics," Culver City Patch, February 15, 2012, http://culvercity.patch.com/articles/protesters-rally-wednesday-to-fight-big-money-in-politics.

25. "For February 15, 2012, CBS," Nexis transcript of CBS This Morning, February 15, 2012.

26. "Obama on Fundraising Tour of West Coast," Nexis transcript of *NBC Nightly News*, February 15, 2012.

27. "Your Voice Your Vote: Fundraising with the Stars," Nexis transcript of ABC *World News*, May 10, 2012.

28. "President Obama arrives in Seattle for three big-ticketfundraisers with donors in favor of his announcement in support of same-sex marriage," Nexis transcript of *NBC Nightly News*, May 10, 2012.

29. "For May 11, 2012," Nexis transcript of *CBS This Morning*, May 11, 2012.

30. Brent Baker, "On Maher, Rob Reiner Equates Tea Party to Hitler: 'All They're Selling Is Fear and Anger and That's All Hitler Sold,'" NewsBusters, October 23, 2010, http://newsbusters.org/blogs/brent-baker/2010/10/23/maher-rob-reiner-equates-tea-party-hitler-%E2%80%98all-theyre-selling-fear-and-.

31. Jordan Zakarin, "'The Daily Show' Spoofs President Obama–George Clooney Hollywood Fundraiser (Video)," *Hollywood Reporter*, May 11, 2012, http://www.hollywoodreporter.com/live-feed/daily-show-riffs-president-obama-clooney-gay-marriage-fundraiser-323480.

32. Brent Bozell, "The Washington Post Bullies Romney," NewsBusters, May 15, 2012, http://newsbusters.org/blogs/brent-bozell/2012/05/15/bozell-column-washington-post-bullies-romney.

33. Noel Sheppard, "CBS President Says at Obama Fundraiser 'Partisanship Is Very Much a Part of Journalism Now,'" NewsBusters, June 7, 2012, http://newsbusters.org/blogs/noel-sheppard/2012/06/07/cbs-president-says-obama-fundraiser-partisanship-very-much-part-journ.

34. Brent Bozell, "Partisanship Reigns at CBS," NewsBusters, June 12, 2012, http://newsbusters.org/blogs/brent-bozell/2012/06/12/bozell-column-partisanship-reigns-cbs.

35. "Obama: George Clooney a 'Good Friend,'" CBSNews.com, August 20, 2012, http://www.cbsnews.com/8301-207_162-57496165/obama-george-clooney-a-good-friend/.

36. Kyle Drennen, "Today Show Groupies Fawn over 'Crooner-in-Chief' Obama: 'He Could Be on The Voice,'" NewsBusters, January 29, 2012, http://newsbusters.org/blogs/kyle-drennen/2012/01/20/today-show-groupies-fawn-over-crooner-chief-obama-he-could-be-voice.

37. Michael Moynihan, "Ribbing on Romney's Rich Donors," *Washington Post*, July 9, 2012, http://www.washingtonpost.com/blogs/right-turn/post/ribbing-on-romneys-rich-donors/2012/07/09/gJQAielDYW_blog.html.

38. Associated Press, "Democrats Want Romney to Explain Offshore Accounts," Foxnews.com, July 8, 2012, http://www.foxnews.com/us/2012/07/08/democrats-want-romney-to-explain-offshore-accounts/.

39. Michael Barbaro, "Romney Mines the Hamptons for Campaign Cash," NYTimes.com, July 8, 2012, http://www.nytimes.com/2012/07/09/us/politics/romney-mines-the-hamptons-for-campaign-cash.html.

40. Maeve Reston, "Protesters Raise Cloud of Sand as Romney Raises $3 Million in N.Y.," LATimes.com, July 8, 2012, http://articles.latimes.com/2012/jul/08/nation/la-na-romney-protests-20120709.

41. Jeremy W. Peters, "Obama Visits New York for Star-Studded Fundraisers," NYTimes.com, June 14, 2012, http://www.nytimes.com/2012/06/15/us/politics/obama-visits-new-york-for-star-studded-fund-raisers.html.

42. Jeremy W. Peters, "Power Is Always in Vogue," NYTimes.com, June 16, 2012, http://www.nytimes.com/2012/06/17/fashion/for-anna-wintour-power-is-always-in-vogue.html.

43. Scott Whitlock, "ABC, NBC Tout 'Star-Studded' Obama Fund-Raisers for 'Prez in the City,'" NewsBusters, June 15, 2012, http://newsbusters.org/blogs/scott-whitlock/2012/06/15/abc-nbc-tout-star-studded-obama-fund-raisers-prez-city.

44. Tim Graham, "Hollywood Worries Obama's 'Increasing Reliance on Stars' Could Backfire," NewsBusters, June 22, 2012, http://m.newsbusters.org/blogs/tim-graham/2012/06/22/hollywood-worries-obamas-increasing-reliance-stars-and-celebrity-contest.

45. Ben Feller, "Obama to Celebrities: 'You're the Ultimate Arbiter of Which Direction This Country Goes,'" Associated Press, June 14, 2012, http://cnsnews.com/news/article/obama-celebrities-youre-ultimate-arbiter-which-direction-country-goes.

46. Mark Landler, "Beyoncé and Jay-Z host Obama Fund-Raiser," *New York Times*, September 18, 2012, http://thecaucus.blogs.nytimes.com/2012/09/18/beyonce-and-jay-z-host-obama-fund-raiser/.

47. Toby Harnden, "Speaking to the 47%: The $105,000 Champagne Tower Featured at Obama Fundraiser Hosted by Jay-Z and Beyoncé," *London Daily Mail*, http://www.dailymail.co.uk/news/article-2205541/280-000-champagne-tower-Obama-fundraiser-Jay-Z-Beyonce-Manhattan-night-club.html.

48. Matthew Daly, "Obama: As President You Represent Entire Country," Associated Press, http://bigstory.ap.org/article/obama-responds-romneys-victims-comments.

49. Jason Mattera, *Hollywood Hypocrites* (New York: Threshold Editions, 2012), p. 223.

Chapter 4

1. Brent H. Baker, *How to Identify, Expose, & Correct Liberal Media Bias* (Alexandria, VA: Media Research Center, 1994), p. 25.

2. Walter Hickey, "How Barack Obama Made His Fortune," Finance.yahoo.com, September 11, 2012, http://finance.yahoo.com/news/how-barack-obama-made-his-fortune.html.

3. Joe Klein, "The Fresh Face," Time.com, October 15, 2006, http://www.time.com/time/magazine/article/0,9171,1546362-3,00.html.

4. Geoffrey Dickens, "Chris Matthews Compares Obama to Mark Twain," News-Busters, March 13, 2008, http://newsbusters.org/blogs/geoffrey-dickens/2008/03/13/chris-matthews-compares-barack-barack-obama-mark-twain.

5. Barack Obama, *Dreams from My Father* (New York: Crown, 2007), p. xvii.

6. Kyle Drennen, "NBC Decides Trump Has 'Overshadowed' Romney Clinching GOP Nomination," NewsBusters, May 30, 2012, http://newsbusters.org/blogs/kyle-drennen/2012/05/30/nbc-decides-trump-has-overshadowed-romney-clinching-gop-nomination.

7. Janny Scott, "The Story of Obama, Written by Obama," *New York Times*, May 18, 2008, http://www.nytimes.com/2008/05/18/us/politics/18memoirs.html.

8. Brent Bozell, "Bozell Column: Obama Lies About His Mom, Networks Yawn," NewsBusters, July 20, 2011, http://newsbusters.org/blogs/brent-bozell/2011/07/20/bozell-column-obama-lies-about-his-mom-networks-yawn.

9. Janny Scott, "Obama's Young Mother Abroad," NYTimes.com, April 20, 2011, http://www.nytimes.com/2011/04/24/magazine/mag-24Obama-t.html.

10. David Axelrod's appearance at the University of Chicago Institute of Politics.

11. Jack Deligter, "David Maraniss on Interviewing Obama—and Bringing Up the President's Ex-Girlfriend—for His New Biography," VanityFair.com, May 2, 2012, http://www.vanityfair.com/online/daily/2012/05/david-maraniss-barack-obama-genevieve-cook.

12. Michio Kakutani, "The Young Dreamer, with Eyes Wide Open," NYTimes.com, June 5, 2012, http://www.nytimes.com/2012/06/05/books/barack-obama-the-story-by-david-maraniss.html.

13. David Maraniss, *Barack Obama: The Story* (New York: Simon & Schuster, 2012), footnote on page 603.

14. Scott Whitlock, "Networks Hype 'Steamy' Details from Obama's Ex-Girlfriend, Downplay False 'Composite' Relationship," NewsBusters, May 3, 2012, http://newsbusters.org/blogs/scott-whitlock/2012/05/03/networks-hype-steamy-details-obamas-ex-girlfriend-downplay-compressi.

15. Maraniss, *Barack Obama,* pp. 499–501.

16. Ibid, p. 499.

17. Ibid., pp. 484–85.

18. Jack Deligter, "David Maraniss on Interviewing Obama."

19. Maraniss, *Barack Obama*, p. xx.

20. "David Maraniss Discusses New Book 'Barack Obama: The Story,'" transcript from Nexis of NBC's *Today*, June 18, 2012.

21. T. J. Stiles, "A Generational Biography in 'Barack Obama: The Story,' by David Maraniss," WashingtonPost.com, June 4, 2012, http://www.washingtonpost.com/opinions/a-generational-biography-in-barack-obama-the-story-by-david-maraniss/2012/06/04/gJQAnLnGEV_st ory.html.

22. David Maraniss's Twitter account, June 5, 2012, https://twitter.com/davidmaraniss/status/210009320857939969.

23. Noel Sheppard, "Washington Post Publishes 5,500 Word Front Page Sports Story on 'Obama's Basketball Love Affair,'" NewsBusters, June 10, 2012, http:// newsbusters.org/blogs/noel-sheppard/2012/06/10/washington-post-publishes -5500-word-front-page-sports-story-obamas-ba.

24. Maraniss, *Barack Obama*, pp. 293–94.

25. Tim Graham, "WashPost 2007–08 Coverage of Obama's Punahou School Years? Mostly Gooey Basketball Patter," NewsBusters, May 11, 2012, http://news busters.org/blogs/tim-graham/2012/05/11/washpost-2007-08-coverage-obamas -punahou-school-years-mostly-gooey-baske.

26. Maraniss, *Barack Obama*, p. 175.

27. Lynn Sweet, "Obama's Selma Speech. Text as Delivered," suntimes.com, March 5, 2007, http://blogs.suntimes.com/sweet/2007/03/obamas_selma_speech_text_as _de.html.

28. Rich Noyes, "For Third Straight Weeknight, NBC Continues to Obsess Over Sarah Palin's Revere Tale," NewsBusters, June 7, 2011, http://newsbusters.org/ blogs/rich-noyes/2011/06/07/third-straight-weeknight-nbc-continues-obsess -over-sarah-palin-s-revere-.

29. Rich Noyes, "Obama's Margin of Victory: The Media," MRC.org, August 20, 2008, http://www.mrc.org/special-reports/obamas-margin-victory-media?page=4.

30. Wil Haygood, "Inauguration Will Cement Ties Between Obama, Martin Luther King Jr.," WashingtonPost.com, January 15, 2013, http://articles.washingtonpost .com/2013-01-15/politics/36385982_1_civil-rights-bill-inauguration-day-presi dent-barack-obama.

31. Brent Bozell, "Bozell Column: Obama's Stump Speech Myths," NewsBusters, July 10, 2012, http://newsbusters.org/blogs/brent-bozell/2012/07/10/bozell -column-obamas-stump-speech-myths.

32. Tim Graham, "Syrupy Minutes: How CBS's 60 Minutes Works Overtime for the Obama Left," MRC.org, September 23, 2010, http://archive.mrc.org/special reports/2010/SyrupyMinutes/ExecSum.aspx.

33. "State of Corruption; Iraq's Main Corruption Fighter, Judge Radhi al-Radhi, Forced to Leave Iraq," CBS transcript of *60 Minutes*, April 13, 2008.

34. Noel Sheppard, "Rezko Sentenced to 10½ Years, Media Ignore It and/or His Ties to Obama," NewsBusters, November 23, 2011, http://newsbusters.org/blogs/ noel-sheppard/2011/11/23/rezko-sentenced-10-years-media-ignore-it-andor -his-ties-obama.

Chapter 5

1. Brent Bozell, "Diane Sawyer vs. 'Too Rich' Romney," NewsBusters, April 17, 2012, http://m.newsbusters.org/blogs/brent-bozell/2012/04/17/bozell-column-diane -sawyer-vs-too-rich-romney.

2. Michael Walker, "A Conversation with David Axelrod," University of Chicago, November 26, 2012, http://uchicagopolitics.tumblr.com/post/37412938570/a-conversation-with-david-axelrod.

3. Noel Sheppard, "Charles Blow: Mitt Romney 'Is Not a Person'—'Just a Robot' with 'Not Even a Heart,'" NewsBusters, July 18, 2012, http://newsbusters.org/blogs/noel-sheppard/2012/07/18/charles-blow-mitt-romney-not-person-just-robot-not-even-heart.

4. Charisse Jones, "Volunteers Search for Missing Girl, 14, in Party Underworld," *New York Times,* July 12, 1996, http://www.nytimes.com/1996/07/12/nyregion/volunteers-search-for-missing-girl-14-in-party-underworld.html, and "Missing Teen-Ager Found in New Jersey," *New York Times,* July 13, 1996, http://www.nytimes.com/1996/07/13/nyregion/missing-teen-ager-found-in-new-jersey.html.

5. Jason Horowitz, "Mitt Romney's Prep School Classmates Recall Pranks, but also Troubling Incidents," *Washington Post,* May 10, 2012, http://articles.washingtonpost.com/2012-05-10/news/35456919_1_school-with-bleached-blond-hair-mitt-romney-george-romney.

6. Kathleen Parker, "A Gay Marriage Proclamation? Bullying? Much Ado About the Wrong Things," *Washington Post,* May 11, 2012, http://articles.washingtonpost.com/2012-05-11/opinions/35457918_1_gay-marriage-equal-marriage-rights-mitt-romney.

7. Joe Newby, "Family of Alleged Romney Bullying Victim Says Portrayal Is 'Factually Incorrect,'" Examiner.com, May 11, 2012, http://www.examiner.com/article/family-of-alleged-romney-bullying-victim-says-portrayal-is-factually-incorrect.

8. Scott Whitlock, "ABC Breathlessly Hypes Romney's 'Troubling' Teenage Bullying'; Did he Go 'Too Far?,'" NewsBusters, May 11, 2012, http://newsbusters.org/blogs/scott-whitlock/2012/05/11/abc-breathlessly-hypes-romneys-troubling-teenage-bullying-did-he-go-.

9. Matt Hadro, "Should Romney Issue Bigger Apology for 'Harrowing' Prep School Incident, Asks Soledad O'Brien," NewsBusters, May 11, 2012, http://newsbusters.org/blogs/matt-hadro/2012/05/11/soledad-obrien-asks-if-romney-should-issue-bigger-apology-harrowing-prep.

10. Tim Graham, "WashPost Ombudsman Upholds Romney Hair 'Scoop' as Paper Shamelessly Admits Pro-Obama Story Timing," NewsBusters, May 12, 2012, http://m.newsbusters.org/blogs/tim-graham/2012/05/12/washpost-ombudsman-upholds-romney-hair-scoop-paper-shamelessly-admits-pr.

11. Harry Jaffe, "Merida on Obama: Both of Us Are New at This," *Washingtonian,* February 11, 2009, http://www.washingtonian.com/blogs/capitalcomment/post-watch/merida-on-obama-both-of-us-are-new-at-this.php.

12. Lois Romano, "Effect of Obama's Candor Remains to Be Seen," *Washington Post,* January 3, 2007, http://www.washingtonpost.com/wp-dyn/content/article/2007/01/02/AR2007010201359.html.

13. Tim Graham, "Did the WashPost Report a 5,000-Word Expose on Obama's

Cocaine Use in the Last Cycle? Of Course Not," NewsBusters, May 10, 2012, http://newsbusters.org/blogs/tim-graham/2012/05/10/did-washpost-report-5000-word-expose-obamas-cocaine-use-last-cycle-cours.

14. CNN Political Unit, "Axelrod's Tweet Worse than His Bite," January 30, 2012, http://politicalticker.blogs.cnn.com/2012/01/30/axelrods-tweet-worse-than-his-bite/.

15. Tim Graham, "NPR Host Smears Romney as 'Michael Vick of Presidential Candidates,'" NewsBusters, January 15, 2012, http://newsbusters.org/blogs/tim-graham/2012/01/15/npr-host-smears-romney-michael-vick-presidential-candidates.

16. On The Media, "About" page, http://www.onthemedia.org/about/.

17. Gail Collins, "Time for Him to Go," New York Times, November 22, 2008, http://www.nytimes.com/2008/11/22/opinion/22collins.html.

18. Clay Waters, "Crate-Gate Continues; Collins Calls Cain, Other GOP Candidates 'Nutjobs,'" Times Watch, December 1, 2011, http://www.mrc.org/articles/crate-gate-continues-collins-calls-cain-other-gop-candidates-nutjobs.

19. Gail Collins, "The March of the Non-Mitts," New York Times, January 5, 2012, http://www.nytimes.com/2012/01/05/opinion/collins-the-march-of-the-non-mitts.html.

20. Gail Collins, "Dogging Mitt Romney," New York Times, March 7, 2012, http://www.nytimes.com/2012/03/08/opinion/collins-dogging-mitt-romney.html.

21. Clay Waters, "NYTimes Columnist Gail Collins Takes Her 'Seamus' Obsession to Letterman Show," NewsBusters, March 22, 2012, http://newsbusters.org/blogs/clay-waters/2012/03/22/nytimes-columnist-gail-collins-takes-her-seamus-obsession-letterman-sho.

22. Jim Treacher, "Obama Bites Dog," Daily Caller, April 17, 2012, http://dailycaller.com/2012/04/17/obama-bites-dog/.

23. Gail Collins, "Obama's Wonderful Town," New York Times, May 5, 2012, http://www.nytimes.com/2012/05/05/opinion/collins-obamas-wonderful-town.html.

24. Tim Graham, "NY Times Lays It on Thick: Obama as 'Everyman,' Romney as Mr. and Mrs. Cadillac," NewsBusters, March 24, 2012, http://newsbusters.org/blogs/tim-graham/2012/03/24/ny-times-lays-it-thick-obama-everyman-romneys-mr-and-mrs-cadillac.

25. Mark Leibovich, "Obama Seizes Chance to Score as an Everyman," New York Times, March 22, 2012, http://www.nytimes.com/2012/03/23/us/obama-seizes-chance-to-score-as-an-everyman.html.

26. Paul Farhi, "Michelle Obama's Target Trip: Critics Take Aim," Washington Post, October 2, 2011, http://www.washingtonpost.com/lifestyle/style/michelle-obamas-target-trip-critics-take-aim/2011/10/02/gIQATrMLGL_story.html.

27. Kyle Drennen, "NBC's Today Swoons Over Michelle Obama Shopping at Target," NewsBusters, September 30, 2011, http://newsbusters.org/blogs/kyle-drennen/2011/09/30/nbcs-today-swoons-over-michelle-obama-shopping-target.

28. Matthew Balan, "Juan Williams Blasts Ann Romney as a 'Corporate Wife' on Fox News," NewsBusters, August 29, 2012, http://newsbusters.org/blogs/matthew-balan/2012/08/29/juan-williams-blasts-ann-romney-corporate-wife-fox-news.

29. Noel Sheppard, "Katey Sagal AKA Peggy Bundy Trashes Ann Romney: Mom That Doesn't Cook, Clean or 'Make Any Money,'" NewsBusters, August 13, 2012, http://newsbusters.org/blogs/noel-sheppard/2012/08/13/katey-sagal-aka-peggy-bundy-slams-ann-romney-mom-doesnt-cook-clean-or.

30. Trip Gabriel, "In Rarefied Sport, a View of the Romneys' World," New York Times, May 26, 2012, http://www.nytimes.com/2012/05/27/us/politics/ann-romneys-hobby-spotlights-world-of-dressage.html?pagewanted=all&_r=0.

31. Trip Gabriel, "Romney Horse Wins Spot on Olympic Dressage Team," New York Times, June 16, 2012, http://www.nytimes.com/2012/06/17/us/politics/horse-co-owned-by-ann-romney-earns-a-spot-on-the-olympic-dressage-team.html.

32. "Alice Elizabeth Simon Is Married to Trip Gabriel," New York Times, June 30, 1985, http://www.nytimes.com/1985/06/30/style/alice-elizabeth-simon-is-married-to-trip-gabriel.html.

33. Michelle Cottle, "The Gray Lady Wears Prada," New Republic, April 17, 2006, http://www.newrepublic.com/article/books-and-arts/the-gray-lady-wears-prada#.

34. Clay Waters, "NYT Devotes Front of Home Section to Romney-Bashing from the Candidate's Snotty Liberal Neighbors," NewsBusters, June 7, 2012, http://newsbusters.org/blogs/clay-waters/2012/06/07/nyt-devotes-front-home-section-romney-bashing-candidates-snotty-liberal.

35. "Mitt Romney's Neighbors Tell All," NBCNews.com, June 7, 2012, http://www.nbcnews.com/id/45755883/ns/msnbc-the_last_word/vp/47731177#47731177.

36. Chris Cillizza, "Mitt Romney Is the Republican Nominee. Now What?," Washington Post, April 9, 2012, http://www.washingtonpost.com/blogs/the-fix/post/mitt-romney-is-the-republican-nominee-now-what/2012/04/09/gIQAN6fU6S_blog.html.

Chapter 6

1. Axelrod at the University of Chicago's Institute of Politics.

2. "Lawrence O'Donnell and the Plain Dealer's Connie Schultz Among Planned Parenthood's 2011 Maggie Award Winners for Media Excellence," Planned Parenthood.org, July 15, 2011, http://www.plannedparenthood.org/about-us/newsroom/press-releases/lawrence-odonnell-plain-dealers-connie-schultz-among-planned-parenthoods-2011-maggie-award-winn-37323.htm.

3. Matthew Balan, "Study: Media Go to Bat for Abortion Giant, Ignore Catholics vs. Obama Controversy," NewsBusters, February 6, 2012, http://newsbusters.org/

blogs/matthew-balan/2012/02/06/study-media-go-bat-abortion-giant-ignore
-catholics-vs-obama-controver.

4. Brad Wilmouth, "MSNBC's O'Donnell: Planned Parenthood Head Should Be Ambassador to U.N., Komen May Not Survive," NewsBusters, February 7, 2012, http://newsbusters.org/blogs/brad-wilmouth/2012/02/07/msnbcs-odonnell
-planned-parenthood-head-should-be-amassador-un-komen-.

5. MSNBC.com staff, "Catholic TV Network Sues US over Birth Control Mandate," NBCNews.com, February 9, 2012, http://usnews.nbcnews.com/_news/
2012/02/09/10365739-catholic-tv-network-sues-us-over-birth-control-mandate
?lite.

6. Brent Bozell, "Bozell Column: Obama vs. Catholics," NewsBusters, January 24, 2012, http://newsbusters.org/blogs/brent-bozell/2012/01/24/bozell-column
-obama-vs-catholics.

7. Julie Rovner, "Administration Stands Firm on Birth Control Coverage," NPR .org, January 20, 2012, http://www.npr.org/blogs/health/2012/01/20/145535551/
administration-stands-firm-on-birth-control-coverage.

8. Matthew Balan, "CBS Turns to Top Catholic Bishop on ObamaCare Mandate Scandal, ABC Punts," NewsBusters, February 9, 2012, http://newsbusters.org/
blogs/matthew-balan/2012/02/09/cbs-turns-top-catholic-bishop-obamacare
-mandate-scandal-abc-punts.

9. Joan Frawley Desmond, "HHS Ends Contract with Church Program for Trafficking Victims, Stressing Need for Contraception," *National Catholic Register*, October 17, 2011, http://www.ncregister.com/daily-news/hhs-ends-contract-with
-church-program-for-trafficking-victims-stressing-nee/.

10. NB Staff, "Fury Spreads: Catholic Leaders Join MRC Outrage over Network Silence on Catholics vs. Obama Lawsuit," NewsBusters, May 23, 2012, http://
newsbusters.org/blogs/nb-staff/2012/05/23/fury-spreads-catholic-leaders-join
-mrc-outrage-over-network-silence-cathol.

11. Tim Graham, "CBS Leads Evening News with Catholics—The Accused Abusers, Not the Obama Litigants," NewsBusters, May 24, 2012, http://newsbusters.org/
blogs/tim-graham/2012/05/24/cbs-leads-evening-news-catholics-accused-abusers
-not-obama-litigants.

12. Kyle Drennen, "After Spiking Catholic Lawsuit Against Obama, Networks Unleash Avalanche of Stories Hyping Vatican 'Scandal,'" NewsBusters, May 31, 2012, http://newsbusters.org/blogs/kyle-drennen/2012/05/31/after-spiking-catholic
-lawsuit-against-obama-networks-unleash-avalanch.

13. House Committee on Oversight and Government Reform, "Lines Crossed: Separation of Church and State. Has the Obama Administration Trampled on Freedom of Religion and Freedom of Conscience?," Oversight.house.gov, February 16, 2012, http://oversight.house.gov/hearing/lines-crossed-separation-of-church-and
-state-has-the-obama-administration-trampled-on-freedom-of-religion-and
-freedom-of-conscience/.

14. J. Lester Feder, "Carolyn Maloney, Eleanor Holmes Norton Walk out of Contraception Hearing," *Politico*, February 16, 2012, http://www.politico.com/news/stories/0212/72971.html.

15. Brent Baker, "Bill Maher Slurs Sarah Palin as a 'Dumb Twat,'" MRCTV.org, March 6, 2012, http://mrctv.org/videos/bill-maher-slurs-sarah-palin-dumb-twat.

16. Tim Graham, "Will MSNBC Suspend Ed Schultz for Calling Laura Ingraham a 'Right-Wing Slut' and 'Talk Slut,'?" http://newsbusters.org/blogs/tim-graham/2011/05/25/will-msnbc-suspend-ed-schultz-calling-laura-ingraham-right-wing-slut-and.

17. Jenna Johnson, "Georgetown President Defends Sandra Fluke, Blasts Rush Limbaugh," WashingtonPost.com, March 2, 2012, http://articles.washingtonpost.com/2012-03-02/local/35447751_1_sandra-fluke-rush-limbaugh-health-insurance.

18. Angela Morabito, "Sandra Fluke Does Not Speak for Me," *College Conservative*, March 2, 2012, http://thecollegeconservative.com/2012/03/02/sandra-fluke-does-not-speak-for-me/.

19. Gregory Gwyn-Williams, Jr., "$9: Price for a Month's Supply of Birth Control Pills at Target 3 Miles from Georgetown Law," CNSNews.com, March 5, 2012, http://cnsnews.com/news/article/9-price-months-supply-birth-control-pills-target-3-miles-georgetown-law.

20. Stephen Gutowski, "Sandra Fluke, Gender Reassignment, and Health Insurance," MRCTV.org, March 5, 2012, http://www.mrctv.org/blog/sandra-fluke-gender-reassignment-and-health-insurance.

21. Susan Jones, "Sandra Fluke: Paul Ryan 'Would Allow Pregnant Women to Die in Our Emergency Rooms,'" CNSNews.com, September 6, 2012, http://cnsnews.com/news/article/sandra-fluke-paul-ryan-would-allow-pregnant-women-die-our-emergency-rooms.

22. Clay Waters, "NYT's Rosenthal Compares Pre-Abortion Ultrasound to Rape, but It's the Counterarguments That Are 'Deranged'?," NewsBusters, February 23, 2012, http://newsbusters.org/blogs/clay-waters/2012/02/23/nyts-rosenthal-compares-pre-abortion-ultrasound-rape-its-counterargumen.

23. Scott Whitlock, "Liberal Joy Behar Trashes Virginia: State's Abortion Law Is like 'the Taliban,'" NewsBusters, February 16, 2012, http://newsbusters.org/blogs/scott-whitlock/2012/02/16/left-wing-joy-behar-smears-va-states-abortion-law-taliban#ixzz2NbyfbQ2P.

24. Ken Shepherd, "MSNBC's Luke Russert Asks Democratic State Legislator: Are Mandated Abdominal Ultrasounds a Sort of 'Sex Crime'?," NewsBusters, February 23, 2012, http://newsbusters.org/blogs/ken-shepherd/2012/02/23/msnbcs-luke-russert-asks-democratic-state-legislator-are-mandated-abdo#ixzz2Nbz2a6jJ.

25. Jack Coleman, "Liberal Shill Jumps Shark, Hypervents That GOP Favors 'Letting Women Die,'" NewsBusters, February 27, 2012, http://newsbusters.org/blogs/

jack-coleman/2012/02/27/liberal-shill-jumps-shark-hypervents-gop-favors-letting
-women-die#ixzz2Nc0mGZUU.

26. "Accused Gunman Ripped Family Research Council Policies Before Opening
Fire, Sources Say," Foxnews.com, August 16, 2012, http://www.foxnews.com/
us/2012/08/16/alleged-gunman-in-family-research-council-shooting-expected
-in-court-thursday/#ixzz2Nc2qhp9w.

27. Tim Graham, "Only ABC Offers Full Story on Shooting at FRC; CBS, NBC Blow
It Off With Tiny Reports," NewsBusters, August 15, 2012, http://newsbusters.org/
blogs/tim-graham/2012/08/15/only-abc-offers-full-story-shooting-frc-cbs-nbc
-blow-it-tiny-reports.

28. Matt Hadro, "It Took Only 20 Hours: CNN Upholds 'Hate Group' Label
for FRC," NewsBusters, August 16, 2012, http://newsbusters.org/blogs/matt
-hadro/2012/08/16/it-took-only-20-hours-cnn-upholds-hate-group-label-frc.

29. Katie Yoder, "Networks Ignore FRC Shooter's Use of SPLC 'Hate Map,'" News-
Busters, February 7, 2013, http://newsbusters.org/blogs/katie-yoder/2013/02/07/
networks-ignore-frc-shooter-s-use-splc-hate-map.

30. Ann E. Marimow, "Family Research Council Shooter Pleads Guilty to Three
Felonies," WashingtonPost.com, February 6, 2013, http://articles.washingtonpost
.com/2013-02-06/local/36940774_1_firearm-sales-floyd-lee-corkins-ii-ammu
nition-across-state-lines.

Chapter 7

1. Adam Nagourney, Jim Rutenberg, and Jeff Zeleny, "Near-Flawless Run Is
Credited in Victory," New York Times, November 5, 2008, http://www.nytimes
.com/2008/11/05/us/politics/05recon.html.

2. Geoffrey Dickens, "Matthews: McCain Sounds like Herbert Hoover," News-
Busters, September 15, 2008, http://newsbusters.org/blogs/geoffrey-dickens/
2008/09/15/matthews-mccain-sounds-herbert-hoover.

3. Brent Baker, "NBC Raises 9/11 & Pushes Quote to Hurt McCain, ABC Ties in
Iraq," NewsBusters, September 19, 2008, http://newsbusters.org/blogs/brent
-baker/2008/09/19/nbc-raises-9-11-pushes-quote-hurt-mccain-abc-ties-iraq.

4. Rush Limbaugh, "Obama: 'The Private Sector Is Doing Fine,'" transcript on rush
limbaugh.com, June 8, 2012, http://www.rushlimbaugh.com/daily/2012/06/08/
obama_the_private_sector_is_doing_fine.

5. Kyle Drennen, "NBC's Curry Argues Obama's 'Fine' Gaffe 'Taken Out of Context,'" NewsBusters, June 11, 2012, http://newsbusters.org/blogs/kyle-drennen/
2012/06/11/nbcs-curry-argues-obamas-fine-gaffe-taken-out-context.

6. Felicia Sonmez, "White House on 'Private Sector Is Doing Fine': We're for 'Good
Reporting Filled with Context,'" Washington Post, June 11, 2012, http://www

.washingtonpost.com/blogs/post-politics/post/white-house-on-private-sector
-is-doing-fine-were-for-good-reporting-filled-with-context/2012/06/11/gJQA
rdxUVV_blog.html.

7. Jackie Calmes, "Six Words From Obama, and a Barrage in Return From the
G.O.P.," *New York Times*, June 8, 2012, http://www.nytimes.com/2012/06/09/us/
politics/six-words-from-obama-and-a-barrage-from-republicans.html.

8. Transcript of *World News with Diane Sawyer*, January 9, 2012.

9. Matthew Balan, "Schieffer on CBS: Romney Firing Remark Just Shy of Saying
'Herbert Hoover Is My Hero,'" NewsBusters, January 10, 2012, http://m.news
busters.org/blogs/matthew-balan/2012/01/10/schieffer-cbs-romney-firing-re
mark-just-shy-saying-herbert-hoover-my-.

10. Ari Shapiro, "Romney Tries to Dig Out from 'Poor' Comment," NPR, February 2, 2012, http://www.npr.org/2012/02/02/146265419/romney-tries-to-dig-out
-from-poor-comment.

11. Geoffrey Dickens, "ABC, CBS & NBC Wait Five Days to Report Obama's 'You
Didn't Build That' Attack on Business," NewsBusters, July 18, 2012, http://news
busters.org/blogs/geoffrey-dickens/2012/07/18/abc-cbs-nbc-wait-five-days
-report-obamas-you-didnt-build-attack-bu.

12. Ed Morrissey, "Videos: Romney on the Attack After Obama's 'You Didn't Build
That' Remark," Hot Air, July 17, 2012, http://hotair.com/archives/2012/07/17/
videos-romney-on-the-attack-after-obamas-you-didnt-build-that-remark/.

13. Trip Gabriel and Peter Baker, "Romney and Obama Resume Economic Attacks,
Despite a Few Diversions," *New York Times*, July 17, 2012, http://www.nytimes
.com/2012/07/18/us/politics/romney-and-obama-resume-economic-attacks
.html.

14. Matthew Balan, "CBS Defends Obama's 'You Didn't Build That' Remarks; Invokes
'It Takes a Village,'" NewsBusters, July 26, 2012, http://newsbusters.org/blogs/
matthew-balan/2012/07/26/cbs-defends-obamas-you-didnt-build-remarks
-invokes-it-takes-village.

15. Tim Graham, "NPR Puts Obama's 'You Didn't Build That' in 'Context'—With
Think Progress Anti-Romney Spin," NewsBusters, http://newsbusters.org/blogs/
tim-graham/2012/07/26/npr-puts-obamas-you-didnt-build-context-think
-progress-anti-romney-spin.

16. Tim Graham, "Networks Bury Obama's 'Polish Death Camp' Gaffe, but ABC and
NBC Find Time to Mock a Romney Misspelling," NewsBusters, May 31, 2012,
http://newsbusters.org/blogs/tim-graham/2012/05/31/networks-bury-obamas
-polish-death-camp-gaffe-abc-and-nbc-find-time-mock-.

17. Scott Whitlock, "Networks That Fawned over Obama's World Tour Mock Romney's International 'Blunders,'" MRC.org, August 2, 2012, http://www.mrc
.org/media-reality-check/networks-fawned-over-obamas-world-tour-mock
-romneys-international-blunders.

18. Chris Cillizza, "Who Had the Worst Week in Washington? Mitt Romney," *Washington Post*, July 27, 2012, http://articles.washingtonpost.com/2012-07-27/opinions/35486280_1_romney-campaign-mitt-romney-worst-week.

19. Matt Hadro, "CNN Absurdly Claims Romney Aide's Outburst Was 'Sort of' 'Unprovoked,'" NewsBusters, July 31, 2012, http://newsbusters.org/blogs/matt-hadro/2012/07/31/cnn-absurdly-claims-romney-aides-outburst-was-sort-unprovoked.

20. Charles Krauthammer, "Romney's Excellent Trip," *Washington Post*, August 2, 2012, http://articles.washingtonpost.com/2012-08-02/opinions/35492000_1_romney-gaffe-rick-gorka-mitt-romney.

21. Geoffrey Dickens, "ABC, CBS and NBC Bury Bumbling Biden's Most Embarrassing Moments," MRC.org, September 4, 2012, http://www.mrc.org/media-reality-check/abc-cbs-and-nbc-bury-bumbling-bidens-most-embarrassing-moments.

22. Rebecca Berg, "The Caucus; On the Trail: A Metaphor Draws Notice," *New York Times*, August 15, 2012, http://query.nytimes.com/gst/fullpage.html?res=9D02E6DA173BF936A2575BC0A9649D8B63.

23. Randy Hall, "CNN's O'Brien Continues Challenging Attempt to Spin Away 'Chains' Controversy," NewsBusters, August 16, 2012, http://m.newsbusters.org/blogs/randy-hall/2012/08/16/cnns-obrien-continues-challenging-attempt-spin-away-chains-controversy.

24. "Top Ten Biden Gaffes: A 'Stand Up' Slip-Up," Time.com, http://www.time.com/time/specials/packages/article/0,28804,1895156_1894977_1841630,00.html.

25. Ed Morrissey, "Biden Spreads His Own Special Kind of St. Paddy's Day Cheer," Hot Air, March 18, 2010, http://hotair.com/archives/2010/03/18/biden-spreads-his-own-special-kind-of-st-paddys-day-cheer/.

26. Madeleine Morgenstern, "'Don't Screw Around with Me': Biden Defends 'Rape' Comments, Gets into Heated Exchange with Reporter," *The Blaze*, October 19, 2011, http://www.theblaze.com/stories/2011/10/19/dont-screw-around-with-me-biden-defends-rape-comments-gets-into-heated-exchange-with-reporter/.

27. Matthew Balan, "Nets Punt on Biden's 'Planned Parenthood Cannot Perform Any Abortions' Gaffe; Played Up Romney 'Shift,'" NewsBusters, October 12, 2012, http://newsbusters.org/blogs/matthew-balan/2012/10/12/nets-punt-bidens-planned-parenthood-cannot-perform-any-abortions-gaff.

28. Jonathan Martin, "Mission Impossible: Managing Joe Biden," *Politico*, August 16, 2012, http://www.politico.com/news/stories/0812/79776.html.

29. Howard Fineman, "Obama Needs the Merciless Joe: Countdown Day 29," *Huffington Post*, October 8, 2012, http://www.huffingtonpost.com/howard-fineman/barack-obama-joe-biden-2012_b_1947146.html.

30. Clay Waters, "New York Times' Mark Leibovich Eagerly Embraces the 'Biden Moment,'" NewsBusters, January 30, 2013, http://newsbusters.org/blogs/clay-waters/2013/01/30/new-york-times-mark-leibovich-eagerly-embraces-biden-moment.

31. Tim Graham, "Charles Jaco Goes Wacko," NewsBusters, August 19, 2005, http://newsbusters.org/blogs/tim-graham/2005/08/19/charles-jaco-goes-wacko.

32. Charles Jaco, "Jaco Report: Full Interview with Todd Akin," Fox2Now.com, August 19, 2012, http://fox2now.com/2012/08/19/the-jaco-report-august-19-2012/.

33. Charles Jaco, "The Jaco Report: Senator Claire McCaskill," Fox2Now.com, September 9, 2012, http://fox2now.com/2012/09/09/the-jaco-report-sept-9-2012/.

34. Scott Whitlock, "Media Obsession with Akin Hits Overdrive: 96 Minutes in Just Three and a Half Days," NewsBusters, August 23, 2012, http://newsbusters.org/blogs/scott-whitlock/2012/08/23/network-obsession-over-akin-hits-overdrive-96-minutes-just-over-thre.

35. Kyle Drennen, "NBC Hypes GOP in 'Hot Water' with 'High-Profile Distractions,'" NewsBusters, August 20, 2012, http://m.newsbusters.org/blogs/kyle-drennen/2012/08/20/nbc-hypes-gop-hot-water-high-profile-distractions.

36. Kyle Drennen, "NBC Declares: 'Women's Issues Are Front and Center Again' and GOP Is 'Reeling,'" MRC.org, August 21, 2012, http://www.mrc.org/node/40962.

37. Scott Whitlock, "Howard Fineman: 'Todd Akin Is the Paul Ryan of Missouri,'" NewsBusters, August 20, 2012, http://m.newsbusters.org/blogs/scott-whitlock/2012/08/20/howard-fineman-todd-akin-paul-ryan-missouri.

38. Brent Baker, "'Fed Up' Gingrich Calls Out Media Refusal to Discuss Extremism Among Democrats,'" NewsBusters, September 2, 2012, http://newsbusters.org/blogs/brent-baker/2012/09/02/fed-gingrich-calls-out-media-refusal-focus-extremism-democratic-platfor.

39. Noel Sheppard, "Joy Behar: People like Romney and Ryan Are 'Trying to Kill Us,'" NewsBusters, August 29, 2012, http://dev.newsbusters.org/blogs/noel-sheppard/2012/08/29/joy-behar-people-romney-and-ryan-are-trying-kill-us.

40. Scott Whitlock, "All Three Networks Hype 'Controversial' GOP Senate Candidate and His 'Ties' to Romney," NewsBusters, October 24, 2012, http://newsbusters.org/blogs/scott-whitlock/2012/10/24/all-three-networks-hype-controversial-gop-senate-candidate-and-his-t.

41. Scott Horsley, "President Obama Stops in Chicago to Vote Early," NPR, October 26, 2012, http://www.npr.org/2012/10/26/163687995/obama-stops-in-chicago-to-vote-early.

42. Alexander Burns, "Obama Airing Mourdock-Themed Radio Ads," Politico, November 1, 2012, http://www.politico.com/blogs/burns-haberman/2012/11/obama-airing-mourdockthemed-radio-ads-147956.html.

43. Tim Graham, "Liberal Radio Hosts Cheer On Tough Questions from Reporters—to Romney About Mourdock," NewsBusters, October 27, 2012, http://newsbusters.org/blogs/tim-graham/2012/10/27/liberal-radio-hosts-cheer-tough-questions-reporters-romney-about-mourdoc.

44. Clay Waters, "New York Times Eager to Paint Mourdock Rape Comment as 'Dilemma' Making It 'Difficult' for Romney," NewsBusters, October 25, 2012, http://

newsbusters.org/blogs/clay-waters/2012/10/25/new-york-times-eager-paint
-mourdock-rape-comment-dilemma-making-it-diff.

45. Brent Bozell, "Bozell Column: The News Squashers," NewsBusters, October 30, 2012, http://newsbusters.org/blogs/brent-bozell/2012/10/30/bozell-column-news
-squashers.

46. Matt Hadro, "Dem Senate Candidate Insulted CNN's Candy Crowley, but CNN Hasn't Reported It," NewsBusters, October 25, 2012, http://newsbusters.org/
blogs/matt-hadro/2012/10/25/dem-senate-candidate-insulted-cnns-candy
-crowley-cnn-hasnt-reported-it.

47. Matthew Balan, "Mainstream Media Ignore Obama's Radical Abortion Record," NewsBusters, October 10, 2008, http://newsbusters.org/blogs/matthew-balan/
2008/10/10/mainstream-media-ignore-obama-s-radical-abortion-record.

48. John McCormack, "Audio: Obama Says 'That Fetus or Child' Was 'Just Not Coming Out Limp and Dead,'" *Weekly Standard*, August 23, 2012, http://www
.weeklystandard.com/blogs/audio-obama-says-fetus-or-child-was-just-not
-coming-out-limp-and-dead_650611.html.

Chapter 8

1. "We're Not Biased, Fox News Is," Notable Quotables, February 17, 2006, http://www.mrc.org/notable-quotables/notable-quotables-02272006.

2. Tim Graham, "NPR Claims Romney Seeks 'Friendly Confines' of Fox, but Obama's Comedy Show Was Not 'Friendly,'" NewsBusters, September 19, 2012, http://newsbusters.org/blogs/tim-graham/2012/09/19/npr-claims-romney-seeks
-friendly-confines-fox-obamas-comedy-show-was-not.

3. Clay Waters, "NYT Cheers 'Media Critic in Chief' Obama as He Complains About 'False Balance,'" NewsBusters, August 8, 2012, http://newsbusters.org/blogs/clay
-waters/2012/08/08/nytimes-nods-along-media-critic-chief-obama-excoriates
-press-false-bala.

4. Keith Koffler, "Obama Abolishes the Press Conference," White House Dossier, May 4, 2012, http://www.whitehousedossier.com/2012/05/04/obama-abolishes
-press-conference/.

5. Authors' review of White House website section on press briefings, http://www
.whitehouse.gov/briefing-room/press-briefingswhitehouse.gov.

6. Paul Farhi, "Obama Keeps Newspaper Reporters at Arm's Length," Washington post.com, February 10, 2013, http://www.washingtonpost.com/lifestyle/style/
obama-keeps-newspaper-reporters-at-arms-length/2013/02/10/3638c5ae-7082
-11e2-ac36-3d8d 9dcaa2e2_story.html.

7. Brent Bozell, "White House Press Zombies," MRC.org, March 13, 2003, http://
archive.mrc.org/BozellColumns/newscolumn/2003/col20030313.asp.

8. Tim Graham and Rich Noyes, "Still Liberal, Still Biased: How Big Media Helped the Left and Hurt the Right in 2003," MRC.org, January 2004, http://archive.mrc .org/specialreports/2004/report0104_p2.asp.

9. Scott Whitlock, "ABC's Terry Moran: For Obama, Presidency Is a 'Step Down,'" NewsBusters, February 20, 2009, http://newsbusters.org/blogs/scott-whitlock/ 2009/02/20/abcs-terry-moran-compares-visionary-obama-george-washington.

10. Scott Whitlock, "ABC's Terry Moran Raves Over President's Press Conference: 'An Obama Smackdown,'" NewsBusters, November 15, 2012, http://newsbusters.org/ blogs/scott-whitlock/2012/11/15/abcs-terry-moran-raves-over-presidents-press -conference-obama-smackd.

11. Jim VandeHei and Mike Allen, "Obama the Puppet Master," *Politico*, February 18, 2013, http://www.politico.com/story/2013/02/obama-the-puppet-master-87764 .html.

12. Tim Graham, "Pro-Carney Reporter Asks: 'Is Obama Too Mean to the Media, or Are Reporters Just Whiny?' He Picks (B)," NewsBusters, February 22, 2013, http://newsbusters.org/blogs/tim-graham/2013/02/22/pro-carney-reporter-asks -obama-too-mean-media-or-are-reporters-just-whin.

13. Todd Purdum, "Next Question? The silly season doesn't usually come in February, but complaints by the White House press corps about lack of access miss the point," *Vanity Fair*, February 2013, http://www.vanityfair.com/politics/purdum/ 2013/02/president-obama-white-house-reporters-access.

14. Scott Whitlock, "Barbara Walters' Slobbering Interview with Obama: What Super Power Do You Want?," NewsBusters, December 23, 2011, http://newsbusters.org/ blogs/scott-whitlock/2011/12/23/barbara-walters-slobbering-interview-obama -what-super-power-do-you-w.

15. Scott Whitlock, "Barbara Walters Slams 'Uninformed' Sarah Palin: Many Find the Idea of You as President 'Scary,'" NewsBusters, December 9, 2010, http:// newsbusters.org/blogs/scott-whitlock/2010/12/09/barbara-walters-slams-unin formed-sarah-palin-many-find-idea-you-pres.

16. Tim Graham, "Barbara Walters Pushes Michelle Obama to Run for Office: 'You'd Be a Very Popular Candidate,'" NewsBusters, May 29, 2012, http://newsbusters .org/blogs/tim-graham/2012/05/29/barbara-walters-pushes-michelle-obama -run-office-youd-be-very-popular-ca.

17. Ryan Robertson, "ABC's 'The View' Crew Had Some Puffy Questions for Obamas," NewsBusters, September 26, 2012, http://newsbusters.org/blogs/ryan -robertson/2012/09/26/abcs-view-crew-piled-puffy-questions.

18. Tim Graham, "ABC 'View' Crew Went Soft on Obamas, but Thumped Ann Romney with Abortion, Contraception, and Draft Evasion," NewsBusters, October 18, 2012, http://newsbusters.org/blogs/tim-graham/2012/10/18/abc-view -crew-went-soft-obamas-thumped-ann-romney-abortion-contraception.

19. Scott Whitlock, "Robin Roberts Awed by Obama's Gay Marriage Stand: I

Get 'Chills' When I Hear It," NewsBusters, May 10, 2012, http://newsbusters
.org/blogs/scott-whitlock/2012/05/10/abcs-robin-roberts-awed-obamas-gay
-marriage-stand-i-got-chills-when-.

20. Tim Graham, "ABC Admits Team Obama Picked Robin Roberts Due to Her
Race, Age, and Previous (Soft) Interviews," NewsBusters, May 10, 2012, http://
newsbusters.org/blogs/tim-graham/2012/05/10/team-obama-says-out-loud-it
-picked-abcs-roberts-due-her-race-age-and-pre.

21. Tim Graham, "NPR Snubs Interview with the President, So It Airs on Fox
News," NewsBusters, September 26, 2007, http://newsbusters.org/blogs/tim
-graham/2007/09/26/npr-snubs-interview-president-so-it-airs-fox-news.

22. Scott Whitlock, "Robin Roberts, Who Got 'Chills' From Obama, Pushes Ann
Romney: 'Why Not Release' Taxes?," NewsBusters, July 19, 2012, http://news
busters.org/blogs/scott-whitlock/2012/07/19/robin-roberts-who-got-chills
-obama-pushes-ann-romney-why-not-release.

23. Brent Bozell, "CBS: Still Lazy with the Obamas After All These Years," News
Busters, July 18, 2012, http://newsbusters.org/blogs/brent-bozell/2012/07/18/
bozell-column-cbs-still-lazy-obama-after-all-these-years.

24. Matthew Balan, "Charlie Rose Boosts 'Enormously Successful' ObamaCare in
Softball Interview of President, Mrs. Obama," NewsBusters, July 16, 2012, http://
newsbusters.org/blogs/matthew-balan/2012/07/16/charlie-rose-boosts-enor
mously-successful-obamacare-softball-intervie.

25. Jodi Kantor, *The Obamas* (New York: Little, Brown, 2012,), p. 42.

26. Brent Bozell, "David Limbaugh's Devastating Book," MRC.org, June 5, 2012,
http://www.mrc.org/bozells-column/david-limbaughs-devastating-book.

27. Noel Sheppard, "Michele Bachmann Greeted with 'Lyin' A—B—ch' by Jimmy
Fallon's Band," NewsBusters, November 22, 2011, http://newsbusters.org/blogs/
noel-sheppard/2011/11/22/michele-bachmann-greeted-lyin-b-ch-jimmy-fallons
-band.

28. Brent Baker, "After Hitting GOP Candidates from Left, NBC's Williams Presses
Obama from Left," MRC.org, September 13, 2011, http://www.mrc.org/bias
-alerts/after-hitting-gop-candidates-left-nbcs-williams-presses-obama-left.

29. Brent Baker, "NBC Debate Moderators Pepper Republicans with Questions from
the Left," MRC.org, September 8, 2011, http://www.mrc.org/bias-alerts/nbc
-debate-moderators-pepper-republicans-questions-left.

30. Kyle Drennen, "NBC's Williams in Awe of Obama's 'Even Keel' During Bin
Laden Killing," NewsBusters, May 3, 2012, http://newsbusters.org/blogs/kyle
-drennen/2012/05/03/nbcs-williams-awe-obamas-even-keel-during-bin-laden
-killing.

31. Kyle Drennen, "NBC's Morales Demands Ann Romney Be 'Transparent' and Release More Tax Returns," NewsBusters, August 16, 2012, http://newsbusters.org/
blogs/kyle-drennen/2012/08/16/nbcs-morales-demands-ann-romney-be-trans
parent-and-release-more-tax-re.

Chapter 9

1. James Bennet, "'Nightline' Pulls the Plug on Convention Coverage," *New York Times*, August 15, 1996, http://www.nytimes.com/1996/08/15/us/nightline-pulls -the-plug-on-convention-coverage.html.

2. Keach Hagey, "Online Media Will Star at the Conventions," *Wall Street Journal*, August 19, 2012, http://online.wsj.com/article/SB10000872396390444233104577 597870434505042.html.

3. Margaret Hartmann, "Ann Romney's Speech Bumped for Hawaii Five-O Rerun," *New York*, August 23, 2012, http://nymag.com/daily/intelligencer/2012/08/ann -romneys-speech-bumped-for-hawaii-five-o.html.

4. "Coddling Democrats & Discrediting Republicans," MediaWatch, September– October 1988, http://archive.mrc.org/mediawatch/1988/watch19880901study.asp.

5. Rich Noyes, "The Media vs. the GOP: Intolerant, Anti-Women, and Always Too Conservative," NewsBusters, August 27, 2012, http://newsbusters.org/blogs/rich -noyes/2012/08/27/media-vs-gop-intolerant-anti-women-and-always-too -conservative.

6. "Network TV Convention Disparities," MediaWatch, September 1992, http:// archive.mrc.org/mediawatch/1992/watch19920901.asp#Study.

7. Adam Nagourney, "A Party of Factions Gathers, Seeking Consensus," *New York Times*, August 26, 2012, http://www.nytimes.com/2012/08/27/us/politics/repub licans-worry-about-keeping-factions-reined-in.html.

8. Brent Bozell, "Republicans, Torn Apart in Factions?," NewsBusters, August 28, 2012, http://newsbusters.org/blogs/brent-bozell/2012/08/28/bozell-column-repub licans-torn-apart-factions.

9. Ibid.

10. Scott Whitlock, "Frenzied Media Give Four Times More Coverage to Akin Flap than Biden's 'Chains' Smear," NewsBusters, August 22, 2012, http://newsbusters .org/blogs/scott-whitlock/2012/08/22/frenzied-media-give-four-times-more -coverage-akin-flap-bidens-chains.

11. David Bauder, "Chris Matthews Took Home Trophy as Most Over-the-Top Pun- dit," Associated Press, September 1, 2012, http://cnsnews.com/news/article/chris -matthews-took-home-trophy-most-over-top-pundit.

12. Matthew Sheffield, "Yahoo Bureau Chief David Chalian: Romneys 'Happy to Have a Party with Black People Drowning,'" NewsBusters, August 29, 2012, http://newsbusters.org/blogs/matthew-sheffield/2012/08/29/abc-news-romneys -happy-have-party-when-black-people-drown.

13. Matthew Sheffield, "Gwen Ifill Stands Up for Fired David Chalian: 'God's Gift to Political Journalism,'" NewsBusters, August 29, 2012, http://newsbusters.org/ blogs/matthew-sheffield/2012/08/29/liberal-pbs-journo-gwen-ifill-stands-dis graced-david-chalian.

14. Geoffrey Dickens, "Brian Williams to Valerie Jarrett: Positive Media Coverage for Obama Will Be a 'Tall Order,'" NewsBusters, September 7, 2012, http://news busters.org/blogs/geoffrey-dickens/2012/09/07/brian-williams-valerie-jarrett -positive-media-coverage-obama-will-.

15. Kyle Drennen, "NBC's Lauer Cites Obama Flack to Question if Paul Ryan Gave an 'Honest Speech,'" NewsBusters, August 30, 2012, http://newsbusters.org/blogs/ kyle-drennen/2012/08/30/nbcs-lauer-cites-obama-flack-question-if-paul-ryan -gave-honest-speech#ixzz2Nj0pDiZf.

16. Matt Hadro, "George Stephanopoulos Relays E-Mail from 'Top Democrat' Ripping Ryan's Speech," NewsBusters, August 30, 2012, http://newsbusters.org/blogs/ matt-hadro/2012/08/30/george-stephanopoulos-relays-e-mail-top-democrat -ripping-ryans-speech.

17. Transcript of *CBS This Morning*, September 4, 2012.

18. Kyle Drennen, "NBC's Lauer: Romney Questioned 'The Very Legitimacy of the President of the United States's Citizenship,'" NewsBusters, August 28, 2012, http://newsbusters.org/blogs/kyle-drennen/2012/08/28/nbcs-lauer-romney questioned-very-legitimacy-president-united-statess-.

19. Jake Tapper, "Obama Campaign Uses Romney 'Birther' Joke to Raise Funds, Question GOPer's Fitness for Office," ABCNews.com, August 24, 2012, http://abcnews .go.com/blogs/politics/2012/08/obama-campaign-uses-romney-birther-joke-to -raise-funds-question-gopers-fitness-for-office/.

20. Kyle Drennen, "NBC's Guthrie Invites Elizabeth Warren to Label Romney 'Personification' of 'Wall Street Greed and Excess,'" NewsBusters, September 4, 2012, http://newsbusters.org/blogs/kyle-drennen/2012/09/04/nbcs-guthrie-invites -elizabeth-warren-label-romney-personification-wal.

21. Brent Baker, "CBS's Pelley Presses Mitt Romney: 'I Wonder How You Would Explain This Republican Party to Your Father?,'" NewsBusters, August 27, 2012, http://newsbusters.org/blogs/brent-baker/2012/08/27/cbs-s-pelley-presses-mitt -romney-i-wonder-how-you-would-explain-republi.

22. Brent Baker, "Pelley Trumpets Obama's 'Remarkable Moment of Candor' in What Makes the 'Sacrifices Worth It,'" NewsBusters, September 15, 2012, http:// newsbusters.org/blogs/brent-baker/2012/09/15/pelley-trumpets-obama-s -remarkable-moment-candor-what-makes-sacrifices-.

23. Transcript of *CBS Evening News*, September 5, 2012.

24. Tim Graham, "Bill Press Hails Democratic 'Truth' Convention, Compared to 'Pale Male Stale' GOP Convention of 'Lies,'" NewsBusters, September 7, 2012, http://newsbusters.org/blogs/tim-graham/2012/09/07/bill-press-hails-demo cratic-truth-convention-compared-pale-male-stale-go.

25. Matt Vespa, "Daily Beast's Tomasky Calls 2012 RNC Convention Racist," NewsBusters, August 28, 2012, http://newsbusters.org/blogs/matt-vespa/2012/08/28/ daily-beasts-tomasky-calls-2012-rnc-convention-racist.

26. Rosalind S. Helderman and Jon Cohen, "As Republican Convention Emphasizes Diversity, Racial Incidents Intrude," *Washington Post*, August 29, 2012, http://articles.washingtonpost.com/2012-08-29/politics/35490241_1_latino-voters-convention-stage-party-with-black-people.

27. Ibid.

28. FoxNews.com staff, "Mia Love Wikipedia Page Vandalized with Slurs," FoxNews.com, August 29, 2012, http://www.foxnews.com/politics/2012/08/29/mia-love-wikipedia-page-vandalized-with-slurs/.

29. David A. Graham, "Charlotte Swag: 'Once You Vote Black You Never Go Back' and More," *The Atlantic*, September 4, 2012, "http://www.theatlantic.com/politics/archive/2012/09/charlotte-swag-once-you-vote-black-you-never-go-back-and-more/261934/.

30. Geoffrey Dickens, "NBC's Brian Williams Obnoxiously Presses Rubio About GOP's 'Rape Debate,'" NewsBusters, August 28, 2012, http://newsbusters.org/blogs/geoffrey-dickens/2012/08/28/nbcs-brian-williams-obnoxiously-presses-rubio-about-gops-rape-deba.

31. Brent Baker, "Chuck Todd: 'Technically Factual' Ryan 'Distorted the Truth,'" News-Busters, August 30, 2012, http://newsbusters.org/blogs/brent-baker/2012/08/30/todd-claims-ryan-distorted-truth-must-concede-ryan-technically-factual-.

32. Scott Whitlock, "Networks Pound Rubio on Anti-Hispanic GOP, Deride Paul Ryan," NewsBusters, August 29, 2012, http://newsbusters.org/blogs/scott-whitlock/2012/08/29/networks-pound-rubio-anti-hispanic-gop-paul-ryan-hitting-mitt-romney.

33. Ibid.

34. *PBS NewsHour* transcript, August 29, 2012, http://www.pbs.org/newshour/bb/politics/july-dec12/rubio_08-29.html.

35. Matt Hadro, "ABC Hosts GOP-Bashing Univision Anchor Over Airing Susana Martinez's RNC Speech," NewsBusters, August 29, 2012, http://newsbusters.org/blogs/matt-hadro/2012/08/29/abc-hosts-liberal-univision-anchor-over-airing-susana-martinezs-rnc-spee.

36. Transcript of CBS News live convention coverage, August 29, 2012.

37. Geoffrey Dickens, "On NBC: Williams and Brokaw Use Condi Rice Speech to Depict Republicans as Narrow-Minded," NewsBusters, August 30, 2012, http://newsbusters.org/blogs/geoffrey-dickens/2012/08/30/nbc-williams-and-brokaw-use-condi-rice-speech-depict-republicans-n.

38. Ted Robbins, "GOP Rising Star: Gov. Martinez Is a Former Democrat," NPR.org, August 29, 2012, http://www.npr.org/2012/08/29/160227100/gop-rising-star-gov-martinez-is-a-former-democrat.

39. Transcript of *CBS This Morning*, August 30, 2012.

40. "Woodruff vs. First Lady," MediaWatch, September 1992, http://archive.mrc.org/mediawatch/1992/watch19920901.asp#FiveB.

NOTES

41. "Team Clinton: The Starting Line-Up of the Pro-Clinton Press Corps," Media Research Center, August 1, 1996, http://archive.mrc.org/specialreports/1996/clinton/woodruff.asp.

42. Brent Baker, "Brian Williams Reprimands Ann Romney for Saying Mitt Romney 'Is Going to Save America,'" NewsBusters, August 29, 2012, http://newsbusters.org/blogs/brent-baker/2012/08/29/brian-williams-reprimands-ann-romney-saying-mitt-romney-going-save-amer.

43. Michelle Obama Democratic National Convention speech, *Chicago Sun-Times*, August 26, 2008, http://blogs.suntimes.com/sweet/2008/08/michelle_obama_democratic_conv.html.

44. Scott Whitlock, "Brian Williams to Michelle Obama: 'What Makes You Angriest' at GOP?,'" NewsBusters, August 28, 2008, http://newsbusters.org/blogs/scott-whitlock/2008/08/28/brian-williams-michelle-obama-what-makes-you-angriest-gop.

45. Tim Graham, "Jane Pauley's 'Unusual Empathy' for Liberals," MRC.org, February 20, 2003, http://www.mrc.org/media-reality-check/jane-pauleys-unusual-empathy-liberals.

46. Whitlock, "Brian Williams to Michelle Obama: 'What Makes You Angriest' at GOP?".

47. Brent Baker, "Pelley and Williams Zinged Mrs. Romney from Left, but Avoid Contentious Politics with Mrs. Obama," NewsBusters, September 6, 2012, http://newsbusters.org/blogs/brent-baker/2012/09/06/pelley-and-williams-zinged-mrs-romney-left-avoid-contentious-politics-m.

48. Ibid.

49. Brent Baker, "Pelley Pushes Ann Romney on 'Whether Republicans Have Women's Best Interests at Heart?,'" NewsBusters, August 28, 2012, http://newsbusters.org/blogs/brent-baker/2012/08/28/pelley-pushes-ann-romney-whether-republicans-have-women-s-best-interest.

50. 2008 Democratic National Party Platform, http://www.presidency.ucsb.edu/ws/index.php?pid=78283.

51. Julien Pecquet and Pete Kasperowicz, "After Three Votes, Dems Put Jerusalem, God Back into Party Platform," TheHill.com, September 5, 2012, http://thehill.com/video/campaign/247747-dems-reinstate-language-on-jerusalem-god-in-their-party-platform.

52. Lauren Markoe, "Dems Under Fire for Removing 'God' from Platform, but 'faith' Is Named 11 Times," *Salt Lake City Tribune*, September 5, 2012, http://www.sltrib.com/sltrib/lifestyle/54835555-80/platform-god-faith-democratic.html.csp.

53. "Revised Platform Elicits Boos at DNC in Charlotte," NPR, *Talk of the Nation*, September 6, 2012, http://www.npr.org/2012/09/06/160686513/revised-platform-elicits-boos-at-dnc-in-charlotte.

54. Brent Baker, "ABC Spikes Democrats Forced to Make Embarrassing Platform

Fixes, Celebrates Michelle Obama's Twitter Popularity," NewsBusters, September 5, 2012, http://newsbusters.org/blogs/brent-baker/2012/09/05/abc-spikes -democrats-forced-make-embarrassing-platform-fixes-celebrates.

55. Ibid.

56. "Shields and Brooks Discuss Democratic Party Unity," *PBS NewsHour*, September 5, 2012, http://www.pbs.org/newshour/bb/politics/july-dec12/shields brooks2_09-05.html.

57. Mark Landler, "Pushed by Obama, Democrats Alter Platform over Jerusalem," September 5, 2012, http://www.nytimes.com/2012/09/06/us/politics/pushed-by -obama-democrats-alter-platform-over-jerusalem.html.

58. Tim Graham, "WashPost Found 'Strong Shift to the Right' in GOP Platforms—But Democrats Achieved 'Balance,'" http://newsbusters.org/blogs/ tim-graham/2012/09/05/washpost-found-strong-shift-right-gop-platforms -democrats-achieved-balan.

59. Brent Baker, "Pinkerton's Amusing Take on How Media Would Have Reacted if GOP Had Platform Dispute," NewsBusters, September 9, 2012, http://news busters.org/blogs/brent-baker/2012/09/09/pinkerton-s-amusing-take-how -media-would-have-reacted-if-gop-had-platfo.

60. Kyle Drennen, "NBC's Mormon Hit Piece: 'A Church Still Dealing with the Issue of Polygamy . . . Inequality,'" NewsBusters, August 24, 2012, http://newsbusters .org/blogs/kyle-drennen/2012/08/24/nbcs-mormon-hit-piece-church-still-deal ing-issue-polygamyinequality.

Chapter 10

1. Josh Barro, "Today, Mitt Romney Lost the Election," Bloomberg.com, September 17, 2012, http://www.bloomberg.com/news/2012-09-17/today-mitt-romney -lost-the-election.html.

2. David Corn, "SECRET VIDEO: Romney Tells Millionaire Donors What He REALLY Thinks of Obama Voters," *Mother Jones*, posted September 17, 2012, http:// www.motherjones.com/politics/2012/09/secret-video-romney-private-fund raiser.

3. "A Conversation with David Axelrod," video posted at UChicagoNews, November 26, 2012. http://news.uchicago.edu/webcast/conversation-david-axelrod.

4. Quoted by Mike Allen in "Politico Playbook," *Politico*, November 11, 2012, http:// www.politico.com/playbook/1112/playbook9441.html.

5. Geoffrey Dickens, "ABC, CBS, NBC Hype Romney Hidden Camera Tape, Bury Obama's 'Redistribution' Clip," Media Reality Check, September 21, 2012, http:// www.mrc.org/media-reality-check/abc-cbs-nbc-hype-romney-hidden-camera -tape-bury-obamas-redistribution-clip.

6. "Crushing Mitt Romney with Media-Generated 'Earthquake,'" Notable Quot-

ables, October 1, 2012, http://www.mrc.org/notable-quotables/crushing-mitt -romney-media-generated-earthquake.

7. Transcript of *CBS Evening News*, September 18, 2012.

8. Matthew Balan, "Schieffer Hypes Romney Video: 'Extraordinary Moment'; 'Seems to Confirm . . . He Is Out of Touch,'" NewsBusters, September 19, 2012, http://newsbusters.org/blogs/matthew-balan/2012/09/19/schieffer-hypes-rom ney-video-extraordinary-moment-seems-confirmhe-out.

9. Kyle Drennen, "NBC's Scarborough Rants: Romney Having 'One of the Worst Weeks of Any Presidential Candidate,'" NewsBusters, September 18, 2012, http:// newsbusters.org/blogs/kyle-drennen/2012/09/18/nbcs-scarborough-rants-rom ney-having-one-worst-weeks-any-presidential-.

10. Tim Graham, "On The View, Barbara Walters Disses Hasselbeck as All Alone in Backing Romney's 47 Percent Talk," NewsBusters, September 18, 2012, http:// newsbusters.org/blogs/tim-graham/2012/09/18/view-barbara-walters-disses -hasselbeck-all-alone-backing-romneys-47-perc.

11. Mayhill Fowler, "Obama: No Surprise That Hard-Pressed Pennsylvanians Turn Bitter," *Huffington Post*, April 11, 2008, http://www.huffingtonpost.com/mayhill -fowler/obama-no-surprise-that-ha_b_96188.html.

12. Tim Graham, "Omitting for Obama: How the Old Media Censored New Media Scoops in 2009," Media Research Center, January 25, 2010, http://www.mrc.org/ special-reports/omitting-obama?page=4.

13. Brent Bozell, "Planned Parenthood, Spiked," Media Research Center, February 8, 2011, http://www.mrc.org/bozells-column/bozell-column-planned-parenthood -spiked.

14. Scott Whitlock, "Multi-Millionaire Chris Matthews Mocks Mitt Romney by Sing- ing 'If I Were a Rich Man,'" NewsBusters, September 18, 2012, http://newsbusters .org/blogs/scott-whitlock/2012/09/18/multi-millionaire-chris-matthews-mocks -mitt-romney-singing-if-i-were.

15. Christina Romer and Jared Bernstein, "The Job Impact of the American Recovery and Reinvestment Plan," January 9, 2009, http://www.ampo.org/assets/library/ 184_obama.pdf, p. 4.

16. Josh Gerstein, "Obama: The Beginning of the End," *Politico*, February 18, 2009, http://www.politico.com/news/stories/0209/18958.html.

17. Data retrieved from the U.S. Department of Labor, Bureau of Labor Statistics, March 2013, http://data.bls.gov/timeseries/LNS14000000.

18. "Estimated Impact of the American Recovery and Reinvestment Act on Employ- ment and Economic Output from January 2012 Through March 2012," Congres- sional Budget Office, May 2012, http://www.cbo.gov/sites/default/files/cbofiles/ attachments/05-25-Impact_of_ARRA.pdf.

19. Remarks delivered at "Fiscal Responsibility Summit," February 23, 2009, and quoted in a White House report issued March 20, 2009, http://www.whitehouse .gov/assets/blog/Fiscal_Responsibility_Summit_Report.pdf, p. 1.

20. Address to a Joint Session of Congress, February 24, 2009, http://www.white house.gov/the_press_office/Remarks-of-President-Barack-Obama-Address-to -Joint-Session-of-Congress.

21. ABC *World News with Charles Gibson*, February 25, 2009.

22. John Merline, "Weak Recovery Driving Deficits; Recession in the Past; Obama's Own Budgets Disprove His Claim That Slump Still to Blame," *Investor's Business Daily*, February 17, 2012.

23. ABC *World News with Diane Sawyer*, February 13, 2012.

24. *CBS Evening News*, October 19, 2012.

25. *Meet the Press* transcript for November 13, 2011, NBCNews.com, November 13, 2011, http://www.nbcnews.com/id/45276821/ns/meet_the_press-transcripts/t/ meet-press-transcript-november/#.UUO2_VeiHws.

26. News release from the United States Census Bureau, September 12, 2012, https:// www.census.gov/newsroom/releases/archives/income_wealth/cb12-172.html.

27. News release from the United States Census Bureau, September 10, 2009, http:// www.census.gov/newsroom/releases/archives/income_wealth/cb09-141.html.

28. Data from the U.S. Department of Agriculture's Food and Nutrition Service monthly program, retrieved March 2013, http://www.fns.usda.gov/pd/34SNAP monthly.htm.

29. ABC *World News with Diane Sawyer*, September 17, 2012.

30. *NBC Nightly News*, September 12, 2012.

31. Remarks in Hartford, Connecticut, June 23, 2007, as noted in "Promise Audit: Tracking President Obama's Progress on Campaign Promises," *National Journal*, http://promise.nationaljournal.com/health-care/provide-universal-health-care/.

32. Remarks by the President and Vice President at Signing of the Health Insurance Reform Bill, March 23, 2010, http://www.whitehouse.gov/the-press-office/ remarks-president-and-vice-president-signing-health-insurance-reform-bill.

33. Quoted by John Merline, "Health Premiums Up $3,065; Obama Vowed $2,500 Cut; ObamaCare Adds to Woes; 2008 Campaign Pledge Relied on Ignoring History, Optimistic Assumptions," *Investor's Business Daily*, September 25, 2012.

34. "Updated Estimates for the Insurance Coverage Provisions of the Affordable Care Act," Congressional Budget Office, March 2012, http://www.cbo.gov/sites/ default/files/cbofiles/attachments/03-13-Coverage%20Estimates.pdf.

35. ABC *World News with Diane Sawyer*, March 26, 2012.

36. "Estimates for the Insurance Coverage Provisions of the Affordable Care Act Updated for the Recent Supreme Court Decision," Congressional Budget Office, July 2012, http://cbo.gov/sites/default/files/cbofiles/attachments/43472-07-24 -2012-CoverageEstimates.pdf.

37. *NBC Nightly News*, June 28, 2012.

38. Elizabeth Mendes, "Americans Favor Keystone XL Pipeline," Gallup.com, March 22, 2012, http://www.gallup.com/poll/153383/americans-favor-keystone -pipeline.aspx.

39. *NBC Nightly News*, January 18, 2012.

40. *CBS Evening News*, January 18, 2012; *NBC Nightly News*, January 18, 2012.

41. *CBS Evening News*, March 22, 2012.

42. Art Hovey, "Heineman Says OK to Pipeline," *Lincoln (Nebraska) Journal-Star*, online article posted January 22, 2013, http://journalstar.com/news/local/govt -and-politics/heineman-says-ok-to-pipeline/article_5e1ec510-4e49-5e72-8ddf -34392cb4c475.html.

43. Speaking at Loyola University, October 19, 1998, http://www.youtube.com/ watch?v=ge3aGJfDSg4.

44. Jeffrey Meyer, "Andrea Mitchell Inadvertently Admits Double Standard at MSNBC: Chuck Todd Remains Silent," NewsBusters, September 19, 2012, http:// newsbusters.org/blogs/jeffrey-meyer/2012/09/19/andrea-mitchell-inadvertently -admits-double-standard-msnbc.

45. Scott Whitlock, "Unlike NBC, ABC's Jake Tapper Highlights Reverend Wright in New Video," NewsBusters, October 3, 2012, http://newsbusters.org/blogs/scott -whitlock/2012/10/03/unlike-nbc-abcs-jake-tapper-highlights-reverend-wright -new-video.

46. Matt Hadro, "Robert Gibbs Mocks CBS's Coverage of Obama Tape, Charlie Rose Changes the Subject," NewsBusters, October 3, 2012, http://newsbusters.org/ blogs/matt-hadro/2012/10/03/roberts-gibbs-mocks-cbss-coverage-obama-tape -charlie-rose-changes-subjec.

47. Remarks to the National Conference of Black Mayors in Baton Rouge, Louisiana, March 5, 2007, http://www.presidency.ucsb.edu/ws/index.php?pid=77001.

48. Ed Klein, "The 'Bribe' to Silence Wright," *New York Post*, May 12, 2012, http:// www.nypost.com/p/news/national/the_bribe_to_silence_wright_io9jneobl3 fUF0cb7LpcNM.

49. Tim Graham and Geoffrey Dickens, "The Media's Obama Miracle: How Journal- ists Pretend There Aren't Any White House Scandals," MRC.org, August 8, 2012, http://www.mrc.org/node/40820.

50. Tapper, Jake, "Obama Friend Whitaker Denies Wright Allegation of Bribe," http:// abcnews.go.com/blogs/politics/2012/06/obama-friend-whitaker-denies-wright -allegation-of-bribe/.

51. Jodi Kantor, *The Obamas* (New York: Little, Brown, 2012), p. 193.

52. Ibid., p. 43.

53. Ibid., p. 203.

54. NBC *Today*, September 12, 13, and 14, 2004.

55. Kitty Kelley, *The Family: The Real Story of the Bush Dynasty* (New York: Double- day, 2004).

56. "CBS Plugged Fortunate Son," Cyber Alert, MRC.org, http://archive.mrc.org/ cyberalerts/2000/cyb20000214.asp#2.

57. Pete Slover, "Publication Halted on Bush Biography; Records Indicate Author Is Felon," *Dallas Morning News*, October 22, 1999.

58. Matthew Balan, "Bob Schieffer Scorns 'Race-Baiting' Rev. Wright Attack; Obama Not a 'European Socialist,'" NewsBusters, May 22, 2012, http://newsbusters.org/blogs/matthew-balan/2012/05/22/bob-schieffer-scorns-race-baiting-rev-wright-attack-obama-not-europea.

Chapter 11

1. Scott Whitlock, "ABC's GOP Debate Questions 6 to 1 Liberal, 25% on Contraception, Gay Rights," NewsBusters, January 9, 2012, http://newsbusters.org/blogs/scott-whitlock/2012/01/09/abcs-gop-debate-questions-6-1-liberal-25-contraception-gay-rights.

2. Brent Bozell, "Bozell Column: Say No to Feisty Liberal Moderators," NewsBusters, October 23, 2012, http://newsbusters.org/blogs/brent-bozell/2012/10/23/bozell-column-say-no-feisty-liberal-moderators.

3. Rich Noyes, "ABC's Stephanopoulos Leads Post-Debate Media Spin for Democrats," NewsBusters, October 2, 2012, http://newsbusters.org/blogs/rich-noyes/2012/10/02/abcs-stephanopoulos-leads-post-debate-media-spin-democrats.

4. Matt Hadro, "Liberal Journalist Carole Simpson Laughs at Romney, Praises Obama on CNN," NewsBusters, October 2, 2012, http://newsbusters.org/blogs/matt-hadro/2012/10/02/liberal-journalist-carole-simpson-laughs-romney-praises-obama-cnn.

5. Commission on Presidential Debates, October 3, 2012, http://www.debates.org/index.php?page=october-3-2012-debate-transcript.

6. Andrew Kirell, "Bill Maher Rips Obama's Performance Via Twitter: 'Looks Like He Does Need a Teleprompter,'" Mediaite, October 4, 2012, http://www.mediaite.com/tv/bill-maher-rips-obamas-performance-via-twitter-looks-like-he-does-need-a-teleprompter/.

7. Matthew Sheffield, "Chris Matthews Blasts Obama for Debate Performance, Urges Him to Get Talking Points from MSNBC," NewsBusters, October 3, 2012, http://newsbusters.org/blogs/matthew-sheffield/2012/10/03/msnbc-hosts-stunned-lackluster-obama-debate-performance.

8. Noel Sheppard, "Tom Brokaw: If Romney Performed like Obama Did Last Night 'It Would Have Been Over,'" NewsBusters, October 4, 2012, http://newsbusters.org/blogs/noel-sheppard/2012/10/04/tom-brokaw-if-romney-performed-obama-did-last-night-it-would-have-bee.

9. Brent Bozell, "Obama Lost So Badly Media Couldn't Spin It. . . . But Guess What's Next," NewsBusters, October 4, 2012, http://newsbusters.org/blogs/brent-bozell/2012/10/04/obama-lost-so-badly-media-couldnt-spin-itbut-guess-whats-next.

10. Matt Vespa, "Liberal on Liberal Violence: MSNBC's Fineman Slams 'Useless' Jim Lehrer," NewsBusters, October 4, 2012, http://newsbusters.org/blogs/matt

-vespa/2012/10/04/liberal-liberal-violence-msnbcs-fineman-calls-lehrer-use less.

11. Commission on Presidential Debates, October 3, 2012, http://www.debates.org/index.php?page=october-3-2012-debate-transcript.

12. Tim Graham, "Liberal Radio Has the DNC Song Sheet: Romney Only Won Because He's a 'Pathological Liar,'" NewsBusters, October 6, 2012, http://news busters.org/blogs/tim-graham/2012/10/06/liberal-radio-has-dnc-song-sheet -romney-only-won-because-hes-pathologica.

13. Commission on Presidential Debates, October 3, 2012, http://www.debates.org/index.php?page=october-3-2012-debate-transcript.

14. Matthew Balan, "Norah O'Donnell Jabs Romney on Big Bird Line: 'Silly Thing to Bring Up,'" NewsBusters, October 4, 2012, http://newsbusters.org/blogs/matthew-balan/2012/10/04/norah-odonnell-jabs-romney-big-bird-line-silly -thing-bring.

15. Matt Hadro, "GOP Congressman Lays Into CNN for 'Doing a Disservice' to Struggling Americans," NewsBusters, October 4, 2012, http://newsbusters.org/blogs/matt-hadro/2012/10/04/gop-congressman-lays-cnn-doing-disservice -struggling-americans.

16. Noel Sheppard, "PBS Strikes Back: 'Romney Does Not Understand the Value the American People Place on Public Broadcasting,'" NewsBusters, October 4, 2012, http://newsbusters.org/blogs/noel-sheppard/2012/10/04/pbs-strikes-back -romney-does-not-understand-value-american-people-pla.

17. Matt Hadro, "CNN Keeps Hyping Romney's Proposed PBS Cuts, PBS Host Calls It 'Attack on Children,'" NewsBusters, October 5, 2012, http://newsbusters.org/blogs/matt-hadro/2012/10/05/cnn-keeps-hyping-romneys-proposed-pbs-cuts -pbs-host-calls-it-attack-chil.

18. Brent Baker, "Journalists Decry 'Threat' to PBS from Romney for 'Targeting' Big Bird, Rally to Defense of PBS Subsidy," NewsBusters, October 8, 2012, http://newsbusters.org/blogs/brent-baker/2012/10/08/journalists-decry-threat-pbs -romney-targeting-big-bird-rally-defense-pb.

19. Tim Graham, "Will Moderator Martha Raddatz Bring Her Biased 'Budget Slasher' Talk to Paul Ryan Tonight?," NewsBusters, October 11, 2012, http://newsbusters .org/blogs/tim-graham/2012/10/11/will-moderator-martha-raddatz-bring-her -biased-budget-slasher-talk-paul-.

20. Ibid.

21. Tim Graham, "ABC's Raddatz Attended Women's Event at Biden's House—With Other Female TV Journos," NewsBusters, October 12, 2012, http://newsbusters .org/blogs/tim-graham/2012/10/12/abcs-raddatz-attended-womens-event -bidens-house-other-female-tv-journos.

22. Commission on Presidential Debates, October 11, 2012, http://www.debates.org/index.php?page=october-11-2012-the-biden-romney-vice-presidential-debate.

23. Rich Noyes, "Debate Moderator Favors Biden; ABC Colleagues Cheer: 'Martha

Raddatz for President,'" NewsBusters, October 12, 2012, http://newsbusters.org/blogs/rich-noyes/2012/10/12/debate-moderator-tilts-obama-abc-colleagues-cheer-martha-raddatz-preside.

24. Commission on Presidential Debates, October 11, 2012, http://www.debates.org/index.php?page=october-11-2012-the-biden-romney-vice-presidential-debate.

25. Tim Graham, "Smug WashPost TV Reviewer: Raddatz Favored Biden, Ryan Was Juvenile and an 'SVU' Pervert?," NewsBusters, October 12, 2012, http://newsbusters.org/blogs/tim-graham/2012/10/12/smug-washpost-tv-reviewer-raddatz-favored-biden-ryan-was-juvenile-and-sv.

26. Noyes, "Debate Moderator Favors Biden."

27. Matthew Sheffield, "Presidential Debate Co-Chair Admits Picking Candy Crowley Was 'Mistake,'" NewsBusters, February 20, 2013, http://newsbusters.org/blogs/matthew-sheffield/2013/02/20/presidential-debate-co-chair-admits-candy-crowley-was-mistake.

28. Brett LoGiurato, "Here's How the Undecided Voters Were Selected to Ask Obama and Romney Questions at Tomorrow's Debate," Business Insider, October 15, 2012, http://www.businessinsider.com/obama-romney-town-hall-debate-how-voters-were-selected-2012-10.

29. Rich Noyes, "MRC Study: By 2-to-1 Margin, Journalists Favor Liberal Questions at Town Hall Debates," MRC.org, October 16, 2012, http://www.mrc.org/node/41520.

30. Rich Noyes, "Candy Crowley Aids Obama with 2-to-1 Liberal Agenda & Validation of Libya Falsehood," MRC.org, October 17, 2012, http://www.mrc.org/node/41544.

31. Commission on Presidential Debates, October 16, 2012, http://www.debates.org/index.php?page=october-1-2012-the-second-obama-romney-presidential-debate.

32. Brent Baker, "NBC Nightly News Showcases 'Undecided Voter' Trashing Romney Hours After She Declares for Obama," NewsBusters, October 18, 2012, http://newsbusters.org/blogs/brent-baker/2012/10/18/nbc-nightly-news-showcases-undecided-voter-trashing-romney-hours-after-.

33. Commission on Presidential Debates, October 16, 2012, http://www.debates.org/index.php?page=october-1-2012-the-second-obama-romney-presidential-debate.

34. Irin Carmon, "Wage-Gap Debate Questioner Katherine Fenton 'Absolutely Not' a Feminist," Salon.com, October 17, 2012, http://www.salon.com/2012/10/17/wage_gap_debate_questioner_katherine_fenton_absolutely_not_a_feminist/.

35. Commission on Presidential Debates, October 16, 2012, http://www.debates.org/index.php?page=october-1-2012-the-second-obama-romney-presidential-debate.

36. Cristina Costaniti, "Meet Lorraine from the Presidential Debate—Or Was It

Lorena?," ABCNews.com, October 17, 2012, http://abcnews.go.com/ABC_Univi
sion/News/meet-lorraine-osorio-presidential-debate-lorena/story?id=17501899.

37. Commission on Presidential Debates, October 16, 2012, http://www.debates
.org/index.php?page=october-1-2012-the-second-obama-romney-presidential
-debate.

38. "The Issue That Goes Ignored," *New York Times*, October 18, 2012, http://www
.nytimes.com/2012/10/19/opinion/the-issue-that-goes-ignored.html.

39. Noyes, "Candy Crowley Aids Obama."

40. Commission on Presidential Debates October 16, 2012, http://www.debates
.org/index.php?page=october-1-2012-the-second-obama-romney-presidential
-debate.

41. Ibid.

42. White House Transcript, September 12, 2012, http://www.whitehouse.gov/the
-press-office/2012/09/12/remarks-president-deaths-us-embassy-staff-libya.

43. Glenn Kessler, "Fact Check: Libya Attack," *Washington Post*, October 16, 2012,
http://www.washingtonpost.com/blogs/post-politics/wp/2012/10/16/fact-check
-libya-attack/?wprss=rss_campaigns.

44. Brent Baker, "Candy Crowley Not in 'Cahoots' with Obama; He and Axelrod
Used Her," NewsBusters, October 20, 2012, http://newsbusters.org/blogs/brent
-baker/2012/10/20/candy-crowley-not-cahoots-obama-he-and-axelrod-used-her.

45. Brent Bozell, "Candy Crowley Self-Destructs," NewsBusters, October 18, 2012,
http://newsbusters.org/blogs/brent-bozell/2012/10/18/bozell-column-candy
-crowley-self-destructs.

46. Ibid.

47. Scott Whitlock, "On ABC, Matthew Dowd, Donna Brazile Target Conservatives:
Attacks on Crowley 'Sure Sign' Obama Won," October 17, 2012, http://news
busters.org/blogs/matthew-balan/2012/10/17/abc-matthew-dowd-donna
-brazile-target-conservatives-attacks-crowley-s.

48. Scott Whitlock, "Desperate ABC Hypes Romney's 'Binder Blunder'; Will It 'Halt'
GOP Gains?," NewsBusters, October 18, 2012, http://newsbusters.org/blogs/
scott-whitlock/2012/10/18/desperate-abc-hypes-romneys-binder-blunder-will
-it-halt-gop-gains.

49. Geoffrey Dickens, "Study: ABC, CBS & NBC Hype Romney's 'Binders' over
Biden's 'Bullets' by 11 to 1 Margin," NewsBusters, October 19, 2012, http://news
busters.org/blogs/geoffrey-dickens/2012/10/19/study-abc-cbs-nbc-hype
-romneys-binders-over-bidens-bullets-11-1-ma.

50. Ibid.

51. Kalb Report, January 28, 2013, https://research.gwu.edu/sites/research.gwu.edu/
files/downloads/DemocracyInAction_Transcript.pdf.

52. Commission on Presidential Debates, October 22, 2012, http://www.debates
.org/index.php?page=october-22-2012-the-third-obama-romney-presidential
-debate.

53. Tim Graham, "Will Schieffer Ask Obama About That 'Cancer' Called Guan-tanamo?," NewsBusters, October 22, 2012, http://newsbusters.org/blogs/tim-graham/2012/10/22/will-schieffer-ask-obama-about-cancer-called-guanta namo.

54. Geoffrey Dickens, "NBC's Williams: Obama's 'Horses and Bayonets' Zinger Will 'Live Forever,'" NewsBusters, October 23, 2012, http://newsbusters.org/blogs/geoffrey-dickens/2012/10/23/nbcs-gregory-obamas-horses-and-bayonets-zinger-was-line-night#ixzz2NpxtHJSK.

55. Commission on Presidential Debates, October 22, 2012, http://www.debates.org/index.php?page=october-22-2012-the-third-obama-romney-presidential-debate.

56. Deroy Murdock, "Obama Caught Lying About Sequester," NationalReview.com, February 26, 2013, http://www.nationalreview.com/corner/341553/obama-caught-lying-about-sequester-deroy-murdock.

Chapter 12

1. Brent Baker, "Nets Follow NY Times and Kerry, Hype Missing Explosives Cache," Cyber Alert, October 26, 2004, http://www.mrc.org/biasalerts/nets-follow-ny-times-and-kerry-hype-missing-explosives-cache-10262004#1.

2. Brent Baker, "Like with Forged Memos, CBS Plows Forward with Explosives Story," CyberAlert, October 27, 2004, http://www.mrc.org/biasalerts/forged-memos-cbs-plows-forward-explosives-story-10272004#1.

3. Matthew Balan, "On 9/11 Anniversary, CBS Promotes Vanity Fair Editor's Blame Bush Tome," NewsBusters, September 11, 2012, http://newsbusters.org/blogs/matthew-balan/2012/09/11/911-anniversary-cbs-promotes-vanity-fair-editors-blame-bush-tome.

4. Kurt Eichenwald, "The Deafness Before the Storm," NYTimes.com, September 10, 2012, http://www.nytimes.com/2012/09/11/opinion/the-bush-white-house-was-deaf-to-9-11-warnings.html.

5. Tom Blumer, "NY Times Puts Coverage of Cairo, Benghazi Attacks on Page A4," NewsBusters, September 12, 2012, http://newsbusters.org/blogs/tom-blumer/2012/09/12/nyt-puts-story-about-cairo-benghazi-attacks-page-a4.

6. Louis Jacobson, "Did the U.S. Embassy in Cairo Make an Apology?," Politifact.com, September 12, 2012, http://www.politifact.com/truth-o-meter/article/2012/sep/12/romney-says-us-embassy-statement-was-apology-was-i/.

7. "EXCLUSIVE: Open mic captures press coordinating questions for Romney 'no matter who he calls on we're covered,'" Right Scoop, September 12, 2012, http://www.therightscoop.com/exclusive-open-mic-captures-press-coordinating-ques tions-for-romney-no-matter-who-he-calls-on-were-covered/.

8. Jim Rutenberg, "Despite Libyan Crisis, Obama Campaign Plans to Stay on

Schedule," *New York Times*, September 12, 2012, http://thecaucus.blogs.nytimes
.com/2012/09/12/despite-libyan-crisis-obama-campaign-plans-to-stay-on
-schedule/.

9. Rich Noyes, "The Media's Coverage of the Libya Attacks: From Slanted to Suppressed," NewsBusters, November 2, 2012, http://newsbusters.org/blogs/rich
-noyes/2012/11/02/media-s-coverage-libya-attacks-slanted-suppressed.

10. Transcript of *NBC Nightly News*, September 12, 2012.

11. Transcript of *CBS Evening News*, September 12, 2012.

12. Ibid.

13. Ibid.

14. "Press Briefing by Press Secretary Jay Carney, 9/14/2012," Whitehouse.gov, September 14, 2012, http://www.whitehouse.gov/the-press-office/2012/09/14/press
-briefing-press-secretary-jay-carney-9142012.

15. Brent Bozell, "Bozell Column: NBC and MSNBC, Networks of Wusses," September 18, 2012, http://newsbusters.org/blogs/brent-bozell/2012/09/18/bozell
-column-nbc-and-msnbc-networks-wusses.

16. Ibid.

17. "September 16: Benjamin Netanyahu, Susan Rice, Keith Ellison, Peter King, Bob Woodward, Jeffrey Goldberg, Andrea Mitchell," *Meet the Press* transcript, September 16, 2012, http://www.nbcnews.com/id/49051097/ns/meet_the_press
-transcripts/t/september-benjamin-netanyahu-susan-rice-keith-ellison-peter
-king-bob-woodward-jeffrey-goldberg-andrea-mitchell/.

18. Transcript of *NBC Nightly News*, September 20, 2012.

19. Scott Whitlock, "CBS Concedes: Romney Better Push Libya Because the Press Won't 'Make the Case for Him,'" MRC.org, September, 2012, http://www.mrc
.org/node/41332.

20. Brent Baker, "Sawyer Spends 4 Minutes Channeling Liberal Angst over Obama's Debate Performance; 20 Seconds on Libya Dissembling," NewsBusters, October 10, 2012, http://newsbusters.org/blogs/brent-baker/2012/10/10/sawyer-spends
-4-minutes-channeling-liberal-angst-over-obama-s-debate-pe.

21. Kyle Drennen, "NBC's Williams Can't Understand Why Obama Isn't Winning by a Landslide," NewsBusters, October 25, 2012, http://newsbusters.org/blogs/
kyle-drennen/2012/10/25/nbcs-williams-cant-understand-why-obama-isnt
-winning-landslide.

22. Brent Baker, "Incredibly, in Prime Time Interview Brian Williams Treats Obama as a Victim of Bad Intelligence on Benghazi," NewsBusters, October 26, 2012, http://newsbusters.org/blogs/brent-baker/2012/10/26/incredibly-prime-time
-interview-brian-williams-treats-obama-victim-bad-.

23. Matthew Balan, "Libya E-mails Break; Morning Shows Minimize Pressure on Team Obama," NewsBusters, October 24, 2012, http://newsbusters.org/blogs/
matthew-balan/2012/10/24/libya-e-mails-break-morning-shows-minimize
-pressure-team-obama.

24. Transcript of *CBS Evening News*, October 23, 2012.

25. Noyes, "The Media's Coverage of the Libya Attacks.

26. Ibid.

27. Brent Bozell, "Bozell Column: The News Squashers," NewsBusters, October 30, 2012, http://newsbusters.org/blogs/brent-bozell/2012/10/30/bozell-column-news -squashers.

28. Noyes, "The Media's Coverage of the Libya Attacks."

29. Ibid.

30. Ibid.

31. Matt Vespa, "On Eve of Election, CBS News Finally Releases Libya Excerpts of Obama Interview," NewsBusters, November 5, 2012, http://newsbusters.org/ blogs/matt-vespa/2012/11/05/eve-election-cbs-news-finally-releases-libya -excerpts-obama-interview.

INDEX

INDEX

ABOUT THE AUTHOR

L. Brent Bozell III is the president of the Media Research Center, the leading right-wing media watchdog. Whenever the media behaves badly, Bozell and the MRC are the "go-to" group for Fox News and conservative commentators, from Rush Limbaugh to Mark Levin. They are dedicated to rebutting and forestalling the media from their mission in composing a very slanted "first draft" of history.

Tim Graham is the director of media analysis for the MRC.

29th Edition

Social Security, Medicare & Government Pensions

Get the Most Out of Your Retirement & Medical Benefits

Attorney Joseph L. Matthews

TWENTY-NINTH EDITION   FEBRUARY 2024

Editor   BETH LAURENCE

Book and Cover Design   SUSAN PUTNEY

Proofreader   CATHLEEN SMALL

Index   RICHARD GENOVA

Printing   SHERIDAN

ISSN: 2163-6419 (print)
ISSN: 2325-3800 (online)

ISBN: 978-1-4133-3153-0 (pbk)
ISBN: 978-1-4133-3154-7 (ebook)

This book covers only U.S. law, unless it specifically states otherwise.

Please note

Accurate, plain-English legal information can help you solve many of your own legal problems. But this text is not a substitute for personalized advice from a knowledgeable lawyer. If you want the help of a trained professional—and we'll always point out situations in which we think that's a good idea—consult an attorney licensed to practice in your state.

MH Sub I, LLC dba Nolo, 909 N. Pacific Coast Hwy, 11th Fl, El Segundo, CA 90245

Acknowledgments

Many thanks to Barbara Kate Repa for her considerable and thoughtful input to the content and structure of this book, and for her thorough editorial work on various drafts of the manuscript.

Later editions owe a large measure of thanks to Spencer Sherman, whose ideas for improvements to the book were extremely helpful, and to Ilona Bray, who guided several incarnations into existence with clarity and graciousness. And thanks to Marcia Stewart and Cathy Caputo, who brought fresh eyes, intelligence, and enthusiasm to the major revisions needed for recent editions of the book.

Special thanks go to the National Council of Senior Citizens in Washington, D.C., for many helpful suggestions on the original edition of the book, and to Bruce Campbell, Karen Fuller, and Sue Schwab of the Health Care Financing Administration office in San Francisco for their assistance in sorting out the many state variations in Medicaid.

Special thanks also to the Health Insurance Counseling and Advocacy Program and Legal Assistance for Seniors office in Oakland, California, as much for their example in tirelessly serving the interests of low-income seniors as for their suggestions for improving this book.

Finally, for the most recent editions, a large measure of gratitude goes to Beth Laurence, who not only did assiduous work as an editor but also brought her considerable knowledge and experience to bear on the materials in the book pertaining to disability benefits, and improved them considerably.

About the Author

Joseph L. Matthews has been an attorney since 1971. In the early years of his career, he taught at the law school of the University of California at Berkeley. Mr. Matthews is the author of *Long-Term Care: How to Plan & Pay for It, How to Win Your Personal Injury Claim*, and *The Lawsuit Survival Guide: A Client's Companion to Litigation*, all published by Nolo.

Table of Contents

Your Social Security, Medicare & Government Pensions Companion

Are you approaching retirement, or are you disabled? Do you help support someone who is?

If so, you'll want to get the most retirement and pension income you're entitled to and obtain the broadest medical coverage you can afford. People in their retirement years have access to a wide variety of programs to help with financial support and medical care. But many people are unaware of exactly what those programs are or how they work, and so do not receive all the benefits they could.

This book is intended to help you get all the benefits to which you are entitled: Social Security (both retirement- and disability-based, including for dependents and survivors), Supplemental Security Income, veterans benefits, and civil service benefits.

With regard to medical care, almost everyone is aware that Medicare is available to many people, but few people understand exactly how it works and what it does and does not cover. This book carefully, in plain language, explains Medicare rules and regulations. It also explains how the holes in Medicare can be filled by medigap private insurance, Medicare Advantage health plans, Medicaid (for people with low income), and veterans benefits.

Locating Chapters That Fit Your Needs

Each chapter in this book explains a different benefit program designed to help older Americans. Each chapter explains how the program works and how it may relate to other programs discussed in the book. Not all of these programs will apply to you. But, even if you don't think you're eligible for a particular benefit, take a look at the general requirements discussed in that chapter. You might be surprised to find that a program, or some part of it, applies to you in ways you hadn't realized. Pay special attention to explanations of how your income, or your participation in one benefit program, might affect your rights in another program.

TIP

You have earned these benefits. A key word in this book is "entitled." Almost all of the benefits discussed here are paid to you because you worked for them, paying contributions into the system throughout your working life. If you're an older American facing retirement and a fixed income, these programs provide crucial support. And you are entitled to it.

RESOURCE

Private pensions and 401(k) deferred benefit plans are far more complex than can be covered in this book. We recommend that you consult *IRAs, 401(k)s & Other Retirement Plans: Strategies for Taking Your Money Out*, by Twila Slesnick and John C. Suttle (Nolo).

Depending on your age and stage of life, there are a number of major issues you should consider as you first scan through the book.

If You Are 60 to 62 and Not Yet Retired

- Find out how soon (at what age) you'll become eligible for Social Security retirement, dependents, or survivors benefits. (See "Timing Your Retirement Benefits Claim" in Chapter 2.)
- Learn how much your Social Security retirement benefits will be reduced if you retire early or increased if you retire later. (See "Timing Your Retirement Benefits Claim" and "The Amount of Your Retirement Check" in Chapter 2.)
- Explore when would be the best time to claim your benefits and which benefits to claim. (See Chapter 6.)
- Find out how much income you can earn without affecting your Social Security benefits if you claim them before full retirement age. (See "Working After Claiming Early Retirement Benefits" in Chapter 2.)
- See whether you can claim civil service retirement benefits if you have ever worked for the federal, state, or local government or any public agency or institution—such as a school system, library, or public health facility. (See Chapter 10.)

- Check the rules of your private pension plan—if you worked for a company that had a pension plan or if you belonged to any union—including whether your pension will be affected by your Social Security benefits. (Private pension plans themselves are outside the scope of this book.)

This Book Provides Ongoing Help to Caregivers

People in their 60s must make initial decisions about Social Security, Medicare, and other benefit programs. But over the years, people also have to make new decisions concerning how they receive their Medicare coverage, choose medigap insurance or prescription drug plans, qualify for long-term care insurance benefits, and determine eligibility for Medicaid and other programs for people with low incomes. This book serves as a guide for caregivers, such as adult children, who might not have been involved in original choices about these matters, but who now must help loved ones make ongoing decisions over time.

If You Are Within Six Months of Your 65th Birthday

- If you haven't already claimed retirement benefits, obtain a current estimate of the benefits you could receive from Social Security, your civil service retirement system, the private pension plan of any company where you've worked for at least three years, and the Department of Veterans Affairs, if you're a veteran. (See Chapters 10 and 11.)
- Be ready to claim your Medicare coverage as soon as you become eligible, if you choose to claim benefits at that time. (See Chapter 12.)
- Look into ways to supplement your Medicare coverage, including medigap insurance, a Medicare Advantage plan, or a Medicare drug coverage plan. (See Chapters 12, 14, and 15.)
- If you have low income and few assets other than your home, check into your eligibility to receive assistance with medical bills from Medicaid. (See Chapter 16.)

If You Are 65 or Older

- If you have a low income and few assets, see whether you can get financial assistance from the Supplemental Security Income (SSI) program. (See Chapter 7.)
- Sign up for Medicare, after reading about Medicare rules as well as those of a Medicare Advantage or a medigap insurance plan that fills in holes in Medicare coverage. (See Chapters 13, 14, 15, and 16.)
- If you have low income and few assets other than your home, see whether you're eligible for Medicaid or for expanded Medicare coverage for prescription drugs. (See "Part D Prescription Drug Coverage" in Chapter 12 and see Chapter 16.)
- If you were in the military, see whether you can claim financial or medical benefits from the Department of Veterans Affairs (VA). (See Chapter 11.)

If You Are Within Six Months of Your 66th Birthday

If you haven't already claimed Social Security retirement benefits, obtain a current estimate of the benefits you could receive when you reach full retirement age, which is between 66 and 67 for those born in 1954 or after. (See Chapter 1.)

If You Can Work Very Little or Not at All Because of a Physical or Mental Condition

- Look into whether you might qualify for Social Security disability benefits. (See Chapter 3.)
- If you have low income and few assets, see whether you might qualify for disability benefits through the Supplemental Security Income (SSI) program. (See Chapter 7.)
- If you were in the armed forces and your physical condition is in any way related to your time in the service, investigate the qualification rules for veterans disability compensation and medical care. (See Chapter 11.)

If You Are a Spouse, Minor Child, Surviving Spouse or Child, or Former Spouse of a Worker Who Is Retirement Age or Is Disabled

- Learn whether you're eligible for Social Security or civil service survivors or dependents benefits. (See Chapters 4 and 5.)
- Obtain an estimate of your own retirement benefits, and compare them to estimates of survivors or dependents benefits (you might be eligible for both but can collect only one).
- Check the rules of the pension plan of any company or government entity for which your spouse worked for more than three years. (See Chapter 10 for government pensions.)
- If you, your spouse, or your parent was in the military, look into whether you are entitled to any veterans retirement or disability benefits. (See Chapter 11.)

If You Are Age 60 or Older and Are Considering Getting Married

- Find out what effect marriage would have on your right and your intended spouse's right to collect Social Security retirement, survivors, and dependents or disability benefits, and on the amount of those benefits. (See "The Amount of Your Retirement Check" in Chapter 2, and see Chapters 4 and 5.)
- Determine what effect marriage would have on your and your intended's eligibility for Supplemental Security Income (SSI) and Medicaid. (See Chapters 7 and 16.)

A Note for Same-Sex Spouses

The U.S. Supreme Court has decided same-sex spouses are entitled to federal benefits such as Social Security dependents and survivors payments, veterans spousal benefits, and Medicare, on exactly the same terms as for other spouses. For rules concerning particular benefits for spouses, refer to the chapters in the book that explain those benefits.

Living Together: Unofficial Marriages and Benefit Programs

Your eligibility for certain benefits and the amount of those benefits may depend on your marital status. Social Security and other programs don't provide dependents or survivors benefits for people who live together without being married even if they are registered domestic partners or have entered into a civil union under their state's laws.

Many people who live together believe they have a common law marriage—a legally recognized marriage—even though they never went through a formal ceremony, took out a marriage license, or filed a marriage certificate.

In fact, common law marriages are recognized only in Colorado, the District of Columbia, Iowa, Kansas, Montana, Oklahoma, Rhode Island, Texas, and Utah. And in Alabama, Georgia, Idaho, Ohio, Pennsylvania, and South Carolina, common law marriages are recognized only if they were formed before a certain date. If you don't live in one of these states and meet your state's particular requirements, you don't have a common law marriage and so are not eligible for Social Security or veterans dependents or survivors benefits based on your partner's work record.

If you do live in one of these states and apply for Social Security or veterans benefits based on your partner's work record, you'll be considered to have a common law marriage only if you and another person intend to be considered as married. You can show this in a number of ways—including living together as husband and wife for several years, using the same last name, referring to yourselves as married, having children together and giving them the family name you share, owning property together, and filing a joint tax return. You can even write out an agreement that says you regard yourselves as being in a common law marriage. However, there is no one thing you can count on to absolutely prove the existence of your common law marriage. And nothing guarantees that Social Security or other programs will consider you married when making a decision about your benefits.

Finally, if either you or the person with whom you live is still lawfully married to someone else, there can be no common law marriage.

Online Help on Social Security, Medicare, and Other Government Programs

The internet has greatly increased public access to information about government programs. But not all this information is created equal. Plenty of information on the internet is helpful, but there is also a lot of confusing or misleading material. The government's own websites—like Social Security's www.ssa.gov and Medicare's www.medicare.gov—contain a huge amount of material, but the sites themselves can be hard to navigate.

This book will point you to some of the most useful internet tools and information from government websites covering retirement, pension, and medical benefits programs. If you find information on your own from nongovernment internet sources, make sure to confirm its accuracy on an official site before you use it to make a decision.

Get Alerts About This Book on Nolo.com

If there are critical changes to the information in this book, we'll post an alert online, on a page dedicated to this book:

www.nolo.com/back-of-book/SOA.html

Social Security: The Basics

S ocial Security is the general term that describes a number of related programs—retirement, disability, dependents, and survivors benefits. These programs operate together to provide workers and their families with some monthly income when their normal flow of income shrinks because of the retirement, disability, or death of the person who earned that income.

The Social Security system was originally intended to provide financial security for older Americans. Unfortunately, this goal of providing financial security is today increasingly remote. Benefits have not come close to keeping up with rapidly rising living costs, especially for seniors, which means that the support offered by Social Security is less adequate with each passing year. This shrinking of the Social Security safety net makes it that much more important that you get the maximum benefits to which you're entitled.

This chapter explains how Social Security programs operate in general. It's helpful to know how the whole system works before determining whether you qualify for a particular benefit program and how much your benefits will be. Once you understand the basic premises of Social Security, you'll be better equipped to get the fullest benefits possible from all Social Security programs for which you might qualify, which are explained in detail in Chapters 2, 3, 4, 5, and 6.

History of Social Security

Public images of our society generally make invisible many millions of economically hard-pressed older Americans. The older person with little income and assets is left out of the standard media pictures of two-car, two-kid suburbanites and of wealthy retired couples in gated luxury communities.

During periods of extreme economic crisis, the number of people cast off by the economy spills over the normal lines of invisibility. One such period of extreme economic dislocation was the Great Depression of the 1930s, during which many millions of people were displaced—not only from job, home, and family, but from any hope for a place in the economy. Faced with the crisis of the Depression and with the possibility of massive social upheaval, President Franklin Roosevelt and Congress pushed through a number of

programs of national financial assistance—one of which was a system of retirement benefits called "Social Security," enacted into law in 1935. But these retirement benefits were set at levels that barely kept people above the poverty line.

In 1939, Social Security benefits were extended to a retired worker's spouse and minor children, and in 1956, they were extended to severely disabled workers. While these additions covered more people in need, neither new program deviated from the basic premise of Social Security: Provide just enough to keep starvation from the door, but not enough to guarantee a decent standard of living.

Benefits Now Provide Diminished Security

The economic position of many older Americans today is increasingly precarious. People are living longer, private pensions are disappearing, and Social Security benefits—despite cost-of-living increases in most years—aren't keeping up with their true living expenses.

And now the Social Security system itself is under pressure. Due to longer life spans and an overall population increase, there is a steady increase in the number of people collecting Social Security benefits. If the system continues as is, the total benefits that retirees, dependents, and survivors collect will eventually surpass the amount of taxes paid into the Social Security Trust Fund by younger workers and the interest earned on the fund. So, if the system isn't altered, at some point—although experts disagree about exactly when—the system will no longer be able to pay the full benefits currently promised.

"Saving" Social Security

Clearly, the Social Security system requires adjustment to ensure its continued health. There are simple ways to fix the Social Security system, but they're ignored by some politicians who want nothing less than to end all public pensions and other support systems and force all retirement savings into the stock market. There, people's savings would be bled by the financial institutions and other corporate profiteers that run Wall Street—a happy prospect for the people who bankroll elected national officials, but a disaster for working Americans.

Instead, simple adjustments to the system—none raising the basic Social Security tax rate—could address its financial problems without introducing investment risk or siphoning off funds to Wall Street.

Remove cap on earnings subject to Social Security (FICA) tax. At present, the Social Security system doesn't tax earned income (wages) over $168,600 per year (the amount goes up each year). This makes the FICA (Social Security) tax what's called a regressive tax (a tax that takes a larger percentage of the income of low-income people than of high-income people). For example, someone earning $30,000 per year pays about 6.2% of their income in FICA tax while someone earning $300,000 pays only 3.3% of their total income. The Congressional Research Service has found that removing this cap on taxed income, by itself, would keep the Social Security retirement system solvent for the next 75 years. So far, however, national politicians and their high-income supporters have resisted this change.

Reduction against early benefits for nonearned income. Under current rules, people can claim Social Security retirement or dependents benefits as early as age 62 and survivors benefits as early as age 60. But if someone collects any of these Social Security benefits and continues working, the benefits are partly reduced by income the beneficiary earns over a certain amount. The rule does not apply, however, to income from sources other than current work—such as investments, real estate, trusts, and so on. This rule penalizes those who must continue to work in order to survive, at the same time permitting others to collect their full benefit amount despite any amount—no matter how enormous—of nonearned income. If the same rule were applied to nonearned as well as earned income, the system could save significantly without taking anything away from those who most need benefits.

Delay full retirement age. The original standard age for full Social Security retirement benefits was 65. Congress raised that age for people born in 1938 or later, saving a great deal of money for Social Security. The age at which most people stop working continues to rise, so there's no reason why the full retirement age for collecting Social Security benefits shouldn't also rise again to parallel this changing reality.

Slight reduction in benefits for high-income recipients. Congress could create a yearly reduction in retirement benefits to people who continue to have a high income from work or investments after they claim retirement benefits—in other words, reduced benefits for people who don't need them.

Any one of the adjustments discussed above would make a significant contribution to the long-term stability of Social Security. Several of them together could put the system on sound financial footing for many decades to come.

What You Can Do

In response to this deteriorating situation, anyone facing retirement should take two important steps.

First, understand the rules regarding Social Security benefits. (They're described in Chapters 1 through 5.) That will enable you to plan wisely for your retirement years, including answering the basic questions of when to claim your benefits and how much you can work after claiming them.

And second, become aware and active concerning proposed moves by Congress regarding the Social Security and Medicare programs. Local senior centers and national senior organizations such as the Alliance for Retired Americans in Washington, D.C. (www.retiredamericans.org) are good sources of current information.

If you're even beginning to think about your retirement, it is not too early to begin trying to safeguard it.

Social Security Defined

Social Security is a series of connected programs, each with its own set of rules and payment schedules. All of the programs have one thing in common: Benefits are paid—to a retired or disabled worker, or to the worker's dependent or surviving family—based on the worker's average wages, salary, or self-employment income from work covered by Social Security.

The amount of benefits to which you're entitled under any Social Security program isn't related to your need. Instead, it's based on the income you've earned through years of working. In most jobs, both you and your employer will have paid Social Security taxes on the amounts you earned. You also pay Social Security taxes on your reported self-employment income.

Social Security keeps a record of your earnings over your working lifetime and pays benefits based upon the average amount you earned. But the only income Social Security considers is earned income, from work, on which Social Security tax was paid. Income such as interest or dividends, or income from the sale of a business or stocks or other investments, isn't counted in calculating Social Security benefits.

Four basic categories of Social Security benefits are paid based on this record of your earnings: retirement, disability, dependents, and survivors benefits.

Retirement Benefits

You can choose to begin receiving Social Security retirement benefits as early as age 62. But the amount of your benefits permanently increases for each year you wait after 62, until age 70. Benefits don't increase past age 70, so don't wait until after age 70 to claim benefits.

The amount of your retirement benefits, if taken at full retirement age (currently 66+ years), will be between about 20% of your average income (if your income is high) and about 50% (if your income is low). For a 66-year-old single person first claiming retirement benefits in 2024, the average monthly benefit is about $1,900; $3,000 for a couple.

The highest earners first claiming their benefits in 2024 (at full retirement age) would receive about $3,800 per month; $5,700 for a couple (receiving benefits on one spouse's earnings record). These benefits usually increase yearly with the cost of living. (See Chapter 2 for a full description of retirement benefits.)

Disability Benefits

If you're younger than full retirement age but have met Social Security's work requirements and are considered disabled under the Social Security program's medical guidelines, you can receive disability benefits.

The amount of these benefits will be roughly equal to what your retirement benefits would be if you'd reached full retirement age before claiming benefits. (See Chapter 3 for a full discussion of disability benefits.)

Dependents Benefits

If you're married to a retired or disabled worker who qualifies for Social Security retirement or disability benefits, you and your minor or disabled children might be entitled to benefits based on your spouse's earning record. This is true whether or not you actually depend on your spouse for your support.

A spouse can be awarded retirement or dependents benefits, but not both. When you file a claim for Social Security benefits, Social Security will determine which benefit you'll receive, depending on which benefit is higher. (See Chapter 4 for a full discussion of dependents benefits.)

TIP
Note for same-sex spouses. Married same-sex spouses are entitled to Social Security dependents and survivors benefits on the same terms as other spouses.

Survivors Benefits

If you're the surviving spouse of a worker who qualified for Social Security retirement or disability benefits, you and your minor or disabled children might be entitled to benefits based on your deceased spouse's earnings record. (See Chapter 5 for a full discussion of survivors benefits.)

TIP
You can choose the program from which to claim benefits.
You might meet the eligibility rules for more than one type of Social Security benefit. For example, you might be technically eligible for both retirement and disability, or you might be entitled to benefits based on your own retirement as well as on that of your retired spouse. You can collect whichever one of these benefits is higher, but not both.

Eligibility for Benefits

The specific requirements vary for qualifying to receive retirement, disability, dependents, and survivors benefits. The requirements also vary depending on the age of the person filing the claim and, if you're claiming as a dependent or survivor, on the age of the worker.

However, there's one requirement that everyone must meet to receive one of these Social Security benefits: The worker on whose earnings record the benefit relies must have worked in "covered employment," thereby earning official "work credits," for a sufficient number of years by the time the worker claims retirement benefits, becomes disabled, or dies.

Earning Work Credits

All work on which Social Security taxes are paid is considered covered employment. About 96% of all American workers—around 180 million people—work in covered employment, including self-employment. For each year you work in covered employment, you receive up to four Social Security work credits, depending on the amount of money you've earned. Once you have enough work credits, you and your dependents and survivors can qualify for Social Security benefits.

The amount of work credits you need in order to qualify for specific programs is discussed in Chapter 2 (retirement benefits), Chapter 3 (disability benefits), Chapter 4 (dependents benefits), and Chapter 5 (survivors benefits).

The Importance of Names and Numbers

The Social Security system does everything—records your earnings, credits your taxes, determines and pays your benefits—according to your Social Security number. On every form you fill out or correspondence you have with the Social Security Administration, you must include your Social Security number. You should also use your name exactly as it appears on your Social Security card. This will make it easier for Social Security to track the correct records.

If you've used more than one name on work documents, indicate all names you have used on correspondence with the Social Security Administration. As long as you have used the same Social Security number, your records should reflect all of your earnings.

If you've changed your name and want to ensure that all your future earnings will be properly credited to your Social Security record, you can protect yourself by filling out an Application for Social Security Card. This form allows you to register your new name and match it with your existing Social Security number. You'll be sent a new Social Security card with your new name, but the same number.

To complete this form, you must bring to your local Social Security office the originals or certified copies of documents that reflect both your old and new names. If your name has changed because you married or remarried, bring your marriage certificate.

If your name change is due to divorce, bring the final order of divorce, which includes a reference to the return of your former name.

If you have any questions, particularly concerning the type of documents you can bring to show your old and new names, call Social Security at 800-772-1213.

The Social Security Administration (SSA) keeps track of your work record through the Social Security taxes paid by your employer through payroll taxes and by you through FICA taxes.

The self-employed—that is, people who receive pay from others without taxes being withheld (such as freelancers and consultants) or who take a draw from a self-owned or partnership business—earn

Social Security credits by reporting income and paying tax for the net profit from that income on IRS Schedule SE. Income that isn't reported won't be recorded on your earnings record. Although many people fail to report self-employment income to avoid paying taxes, a long-term consequence is that the unreported income won't count toward qualifying for Social Security retirement or other benefits, and will reduce the amount of benefits for those who do qualify.

Coverage for Specific Workers

There are special Social Security rules for coverage of some workers in certain sorts of employment.

Federal Government Workers

If you were hired as an employee of the federal government on or after January 1, 1984, all your work for the government since then has been covered by Social Security.

If you worked for the federal government before 1984, your work both before and after January 1, 1984 has been covered by the separate federal Civil Service Retirement System. (See Chapter 10 for a full description of civil service retirement benefits.)

State and Local Government Workers

Many state and local government workers aren't covered by Social Security. State government employees are often covered by their own pension or retirement systems, and local government employees have their own public agency retirement system, or PARS.

However, some state and local government employees are covered by Social Security instead of—or in addition to—a state or PARS pension system. If so, these governments and their workers pay at least some Social Security taxes. And workers under these plans are entitled to Social Security benefits if they meet the other regular requirements.

If you're a government employee and aren't sure whether you're covered by Social Security, check with the personnel office at your workplace. And remember, even if your employment at a state or local agency doesn't entitle you to Social Security benefits, any other work you have done during your lifetime can qualify you, if you paid Social Security taxes.

Workers for Nonprofit Organizations

Since 1984, all employment for charitable, educational, or other nonprofit organizations is covered by Social Security. (Some churches and religious organizations, however, are exempt from this rule.)

Members of the Military

Whether your military service was considered by Social Security to be "covered employment" depends on when you served and whether you were on active or inactive duty. From 1957 on, all service personnel on active duty have paid Social Security taxes, and so all active service from that date is covered employment. Since 1988, periods of active service, such as reserve training, that happened while on inactive duty have also been covered.

Household Workers

Household work—cleaning, cooking, gardening, child care, minor home repair work—should be covered by Social Security, like any other paid work. However, many employers don't report their household employees' earnings to the Internal Revenue Service (IRS) and don't pay Social Security taxes on those earnings. Of course, a lot of domestic workers don't want their earnings reported. They are paid so little that they prefer to receive the full amount, often in cash, without any taxes withheld.

A result of this nonreporting is that unreported earnings don't get credited to the worker's Social Security record. So when the worker or worker's family later seeks Social Security benefits, they might have trouble qualifying and, if qualified, will have lower benefit amounts than if the earnings had been reported.

If you want your earnings from household work reported to Social Security, you have several options. If you work for different employers and make less than $1,000 per year from any one of them, you can report that income yourself as self-employment income and pay 15.3% self-employment tax on it in addition to income tax. Paying self-employment tax on federal income tax Form 1040, Schedule SE, credits the earnings to your Social Security earnings record.

If you work for any one employer who pays you a total of $2,400 or more over the course of a year, you can ask that employer to withhold Social Security taxes from your pay, report your income to Social Security, and pay the employer's share of the Social Security tax on that income. The law requires the employer to do so. (See "Employer's Duty to Report Earnings of Household Workers," below.)

Farmworkers

If you do farm or ranch work, your employer must report your earnings and pay Social Security taxes on them. The employer must also withhold your share of Social Security taxes from your paycheck if you earn $150 or more from that employer in one year, or if the employer pays $2,500 or more to all farm laborers, regardless of how much you earn individually. Any amounts you're paid in the form of housing or food don't have to be reported by the employer.

Farmworkers have long faced problems with employers who don't pay their share of the Social Security tax. To make sure your farmwork is counted toward your Social Security record, check your pay stub to see if Social Security taxes—labeled FICA—are being withheld. Also, ask the person who handles payroll to give you paperwork indicating that Social Security taxes are being paid on your earnings. If your employer isn't paying Social Security taxes on your earnings, or you get the runaround and you're unsure what the employer is doing, ask your local Social Security office to find out for you.

If you're worried about your employer finding out that you're checking on this, ask the Social Security field representative to make a confidential inquiry. Social Security can request all of the employer's wage records without letting the employer know which employee in particular has brought the matter to its attention.

Employer's Duty to Report Earnings of Household Workers

If an employer hires a household worker—cleaner, cook, gardener, child sitter, home care aide—who isn't employed by and paid through an agency, and the employer pays that worker a total of $2,400 or more during the year, the employer is required by law to report those payments and pay Social Security taxes on them. This rule exempts any worker who was younger than 18 during any part of the year.

Employers can report these taxes on their own Form 1040 federal income tax returns and pay the Social Security tax obligation along with their personal income taxes. To file and pay these taxes, the employer will need the names of the employees as they appear on their Social Security cards, the employees' Social Security numbers, and the amount of wages paid.

Earning Work Credits

To receive any kind of Social Security benefit—retirement, disability, dependents, or survivors—the person on whose work record the benefit is based must have accumulated enough work credits. The number of work credits you need to reach the qualifying mark—what Social Security calls "insured status"—varies depending on the particular benefit you're claiming and the age at which you claim it.

You can earn up to four work credits each year, but no more than four, regardless of how much you earn. Before 1978, work credits were measured in quarter-year periods: January through March, April through June, July through September, and October through December. You had to earn a specific minimum amount of income to gain a work credit for that quarter, as follows:

- Before 1978, you received one credit for each quarter in which you were paid $50 or more in wages in covered employment, or each quarter in which you earned and reported $100 or more from self-employment.

- Beginning in 1978, the rules were changed to make it easier to earn credits. From 1978 on, you receive one credit, up to four credits per year, if you earn at least a certain amount of money in covered employment, regardless of the quarter in which you earn it. That means that if you earn all your money during one part of the year and nothing during other parts of the year, you can still accumulate the full four credits. The amount needed to earn one credit increases yearly. In 1978, when the new system was started, it was $250; in 2024, it's $1,730.

EXAMPLE 1: In 1975, Ulis was paid $580 between January and March, nothing between April and July when he could not work because of a back injury, $340 in August, and $600 in cash from self-employment in October and November. For the year 1975, Ulis earned three credits: one credit for the first quarter, in which he was paid more than the $50 minimum; nothing in the second quarter, so he got no credit; one credit in the third quarter, because he earned well over the $50 minimum even though he worked only one month; and one credit for the last quarter, because in 1975 self-employment income was covered by Social Security.

EXAMPLE 2: Eve was paid $800 in January 1978 but did not earn anything the rest of the year. Based on the earnings test in effect in 1978, she got three credits for the year—one for each $250 in earnings—based on her earnings for January alone.

EXAMPLE 3: Rebecca was paid $600 a month in 2024 at her part-time job, for total earnings for the year of $7,200. Because her earnings of $7,200 divided by $1,730 (the amount needed to earn one credit in 2024) is more than four, she received the maximum four credits for 2024.

Determining Your Benefit Amount

If you (or your dependents or survivors) are eligible for a Social Security benefit, the amount of that benefit is determined by a formula based on an average of your yearly reported earnings in covered employment since you began working. Social Security adjusts your earnings records every year that you have Social Security-taxed earnings (even after you begin collecting benefits, if you keep working).

How Your Earnings Average Is Computed

Social Security computes the average of your yearly earnings, but places a yearly limit on the amount you can be credited with, no matter how much you actually earned that year. These yearly income credit limits are shown in the following table, "Yearly Dollar Limit on Earnings Credits."

CAUTION

Only employment-related income counts, and you must have paid Social Security taxes on that income. Other income that you might have earned, such as interest, dividends, capital gains, rents, and royalties, won't be considered in calculating your Social Security benefits.

Benefit Formula

Based on a worker's earnings record, the Social Security Administration computes what's called the worker's "Primary Insurance Amount," or PIA. This is the amount a worker will receive in retirement benefits at full retirement age, which is 66 for everyone born in 1943 through 1954. The full retirement age is 67 for those born in 1960 or later. The exact formula applied to each worker's earnings record depends on the year the worker was born.

Yearly Dollar Limit on Earnings Credits

Year	Amount	Year	Amount
1951–1954	$ 3,600	1995	61,200
1955–1958	4,200	1996	62,700
1959–1965	4,800	1997	65,400
1966–1967	6,600	1998	68,400
1968–1971	7,800	1999	72,600
1972	9,000	2000	76,200
1973	10,800	2001	80,400
1974	13,200	2002	84,900
1975	14,100	2003	87,000
1976	15,300	2004	87,900
1977	16,500	2005	90,000
1978	17,700	2006	94,200
1979	22,900	2007	97,500
1980	25,900	2008	102,000
1981	29,700	2009–2011	106,800
1982	32,400	2012	110,100
1983	35,700	2013	113,700
1984	37,800	2014	117,000
1985	39,600	2015	118,500
1986	42,000	2016	118,500
1987	43,000	2017	127,200
1988	45,000	2018	128,400
1989	48,000	2019	132,900
1990	50,400	2020	137,700
1991	53,400	2021	142,800
1992	55,500	2022	147,000
1993	57,600	2023	160,200
1994	$ 60,600	2024	168,600

CAUTION
There is no "minimum" Social Security benefit amount.
If your average earnings were quite low, your check will also be low.

Social Security benefits for a disabled worker (as described in Chapter 3), or for a worker's dependents (as described in Chapter 4) or survivors (as described in Chapter 5), are based on a percentage of the worker's PIA. Social Security can give you an estimate of your future retirement or disability benefits, or those of a worker on whose earnings record you'll receive dependents or survivors benefits.

Veterans Can Receive Extra Earnings Credit

If you're a veteran of the U.S. Armed Forces, you might be eligible for extra earnings credit, including:

- an extra $300 per quarter for active duty from 1957 through 1977, and
- $100 of credit for each $300 of active duty basic pay, up to a maximum credit of $1,200 per year for active duty from 1978 through 2001. No extra credit is given if you enlisted after September 7, 1980 and didn't complete at least 24 months' active duty or your full tour.

Notice that no extra credit is given for active duty after 2001.

Don't be alarmed if you don't see your extra credits reflected on your Social Security statement. They will be added to your record when you actually apply for benefits, at which time you'll have to provide proof of your military service. Active duty earnings from 1968 on should be included in the benefit estimates on your statement, although the extra credit amounts won't show up in the statement's year-to-year list of your earnings.

Taxes on Your Benefits

A certain amount of Social Security benefits might be taxable, depending on your total income. In determining whether you owe any income tax on your benefits, the Internal Revenue Service looks at what it calls your "combined income." This consists of your adjusted gross income, as reported in your tax return, plus any nontaxable interest income, plus one-half of your Social Security benefits. If your combined income as an individual is between $25,000 and $34,000 (or, for a couple filing jointly, between $32,000 and $44,000), you might have to pay income taxes on 50% of your Social Security benefits. If your combined income is more than $34,000 ($44,000 for a couple filing jointly), you might owe income taxes on up to 85% of your benefits. That 50% or 85% of your benefits will be taxed at your personal income tax rate.

Unpaid Student Debt Can Reduce Benefits

More and more people still have student loan debt when they become eligible to collect Social Security benefits. You should be aware that if you've defaulted on federally guaranteed student debt when you begin receiving retirement, disability, dependents, or survivors benefits, the Social Security Administration can reduce the amount of your benefit until the debt is paid off. The size of the benefit reduction depends on the amount of your remaining debt and the amount you're supposed to be paying off monthly. The maximum the government can take is 15% of benefits, and no one's benefits can be reduced to less than $750 per month.

Note: If you're collecting Social Security disability benefits and your disability might be considered "total and permanent" by special Social Security rules, your entire remaining student debt might be discharged (wiped off the books). For a discussion of this discharge of debt, see Chapter 3.

The way to calculate any income taxes you might owe on your Social Security benefits is explained in the instruction booklet that accompanies the Form 1040 federal tax return. The IRS also publishes a free information booklet explaining numerous tax rules pertaining to older people. It's called *Tax Guide for Seniors*, Publication 554. To get the booklet, call the IRS at 800-829-3676 or download it from the website www.irs.gov.

Taxes paid on Social Security benefits go back into the Social Security Trust Fund, not the general fund.

Your Social Security Earnings Record

The Social Security Administration keeps a running account of your earnings record and the work credits it reflects. (It tracks these by using your Social Security number.) Based on those figures, Social Security can give you an estimate of what your retirement benefits would be if you took them at age 62, full retirement age, or age 70. It can also estimate benefits for your dependents or survivors, or your disability benefits, should you need them.

It makes good sense to find out what your Social Security retirement benefits will be several years before you actually consider claiming them. And you want to make sure that all your covered earnings are credited to you.

To check your earnings record and estimate of benefits, go to the Social Security Administration's website at www.ssa.gov/myaccount.

A Social Security statement is supposed to be mailed yearly to everyone age 60 and older who isn't currently receiving Social Security benefits *and* who hasn't signed up to receive a benefit statement online through the Social Security Administration website. If you haven't received a Social Security Statement, or if you have a question about your earnings record, call Social Security at 800-772-1213.

U.S. Citizens' Rights to Receive Benefits While Living Abroad

If you're a U.S. citizen living in another country, you're usually entitled to the same Social Security benefits—to the extent you earned them through work in the United States—as if you lived in the United States. However, your retirement benefits might be reduced if you also receive a pension in the other country. (See "Reductions for Government or Foreign Pensions" in Chapter 2.)

If you're married to someone who isn't a U.S. citizen, and you both live outside the United States, your spouse isn't entitled to Social Security dependents or survivors benefits based on your work record. (Your spouse might still be entitled to Social Security retirement benefits based on their own work performed while living in the United States; see the following section, "Receiving Benefits as a Noncitizen.")

If you live in one of a few particular countries, there are restrictions on the sending of your Social Security benefits. If you live in Cuba or North Korea, a law passed during the Cold War forbids the Social Security system from sending your benefits there. Instead, you would have to have the benefits sent to a bank in the United States or in some third country, and then transfer the money on your own. If you live in Vietnam or Cambodia, or in one of the Central Asian former Soviet republics, you might be able to receive Social Security payments there, but only if you make special arrangements with Social Security and the U.S. embassy in that country.

Receiving Benefits as a Noncitizen

It's increasingly common for people who aren't U.S. citizens to live and work here for long periods of time. This section explains your rights to collect Social Security benefits if you're not a U.S. citizen, whether you're living in the United States now or have since left to live in another country.

Noncitizens Living in the United States

Noncitizens living in the United States are entitled to all the Social Security benefits that they or their spouse or parents have earned—under the same rules as U.S. citizens—if they're lawfully in the United States. For example, you might be able to collect benefits if you:

- were not a U.S. citizen during some or all of the time you or your family member worked in the United States, but have since become a U.S. citizen, or
- are not a U.S. citizen, but are a lawful permanent U.S. resident or have another immigration status permitting you to be lawfully present in the United States.

Non-U.S. Citizens Living Abroad

Many non-U.S. citizens live and work for a time in the United States, paying Social Security taxes and earning enough work credits to qualify for benefits for themselves and their families. However, many of these people ultimately leave the United States. Their ability to collect earned Social Security benefits after departing depends in large part on whether the United States has entered into agreements with their home countries. If you've formerly worked in the U.S., you need to look at three things to figure out your eligibility for benefits, including:

- your country of citizenship
- the country where you're living when you request Social Security benefits, and
- the type of benefit you're requesting.

To find out what your rights are to collect Social Security benefits based on your country of citizenship, your country of residence, and the type of Social Security benefit you're entitled to receive, see the Social Security Administration's publication *Your Payments While You Are Outside the United States*, available at www.ssa.gov/pubs/EN-05-10137.pdf.

Social Security Retirement Benefits

Many people look forward to retirement as a time of contentedness and quiet, a new time for old friendships, a period of calm sufficiency. They imagine they'll be able to do things they always wanted to do but never had time for. While this might prove true for some, others find a far different reality. Reduced financial resources make it tough to cope with a high-priced world, and retirement often becomes just a different round in the battle for survival. For this large group of people, "retirement" means continuing to work to make ends meet. And often they do so at lower-paying work than they had before reaching retirement age.

The Social Security retirement benefit program helps with some of the financial strain of retirement years. But Social Security retirement benefits alone are not sufficient for most people to live at anything near the standard of living they had during their working years.

This harsh reality brings into question both the age at which you retire and whether you'll continue to work after beginning to collect Social Security retirement benefits. Under Social Security rules, "retirement" can be within a range of years between 62 and 70, and it doesn't mean that you have to stop working altogether. It merely refers to the time you claim and start collecting Social Security retirement benefits. If you claim benefits before you reach your full retirement age but continue to work, the amount of your benefits will be reduced if you earn more than a specific amount of income. (See "Timing Your Retirement Benefits Claim," below.) After you reach your full retirement age, however, you'll collect the full amount of your retirement benefits no matter how much you continue to earn.

This chapter explains how Social Security figures your eligibility for retirement benefits, when you can (and when you should) claim the benefits, and what the rules are regarding earnings after you've started to claim your retirement benefits.

Work Credits Required

To be eligible for Social Security retirement benefits, you must have earned at least 40 work credits over all your working years. Social Security refers to this as being "fully insured." See Chapter 1 to review how work credits are earned.

Checking Your Earnings Record

Even if you haven't worked for many years and you didn't make much money in the few years you did work, check your earnings record. You might be surprised to find that you have quite a few credits from years gone by, since it's quite easy to get work credits, especially easy before 1978.

To check your earnings record, go to the Social Security Administration website at www.ssa.gov/myaccount.

If you find that you don't have enough work credits to be eligible for retirement benefits now, you might be able to work part time for a while and earn enough new credits to become eligible. You've got a high incentive for doing this, because once you qualify for retirement benefits, you're eligible to receive them for the rest of your life. That could mean a lot of money over the years to come.

EXAMPLE: As a young woman in the 1970s, Millie had a good-paying job at an insurance company. After several years there, she married and stopped working outside the home. Her husband was quite a bit older and had earlier made money in business for himself, and he supported them both on his investments. After his death in 1980, Millie was able to live carefully on these investments. By the time she was in her 50s, however, Millie found that her assets were dwindling and the monthly income they produced no longer went very far.

When Millie turned 60, she found out from Social Security that she wasn't eligible for survivors benefits based on her husband's work record because he had made almost all his money from his investments rather than from work.

But Millie also checked her own Social Security work record and found that she had 36 work credits from her time at the insurance company many years before. With 36 credits, she needed only four more to be eligible for her own retirement benefits. She was able to get a part-time job at a local restaurant—the pay was low, but the work allowed her to earn her four additional work credits within a few months, qualifying her for Social Security retirement benefits. Even though these benefits weren't that much, when added to her income from savings and investments, they made Millie's life much more comfortable.

Timing Your Retirement Benefits Claim

Two factors determine the amount of your retirement benefits. The first is your earnings record: how much you've earned over your working life. The higher your earnings, the higher your benefits.

The second is the age at which you claim your retirement benefits. You're allowed to claim benefits as early as age 62, but the earlier you claim them, the lower the benefits will permanently be. You maximize your benefits if you wait until age 70 to claim them. This section explains how the timing of your claim affects the amount of your retirement benefits.

If You Claim Benefits Before Full Retirement Age

You're allowed to claim retirement benefits as soon as you turn 62, but if you claim benefits before your "full retirement age," your monthly payment will forever be considerably less than if you wait until full retirement age. Nonetheless, out of financial need or other calculation, more than half of all people eligible for retirement benefits claim them before they reach full retirement age. Also, if you claim benefits before your full retirement age but continue to work, your benefits may be significantly reduced if your earnings are over certain yearly limits. (See "Working After Claiming Early Retirement Benefits," below, for these limits.)

The amount by which your benefits would be permanently reduced if you claimed them early depends on the time between when you claim benefits and when you reach your full retirement age. The reduction is about 0.555% per month, or 6.7% per year, for the first three years of early retirement. Beyond the first 36 months of early retirement, that reduction is 0.415% per month. If you retire a full five years early, the total reduction can be up to 30%. And, remember, the reduction in monthly benefits is permanent. If you claim your benefits early, they don't increase to the full amount when you reach your full retirement age.

Full retirement age is going up gradually, from 65 to 67, for people born after 1937. For these people, early (reduced) retirement benefits will still be available at age 62. As you'll notice on the "Taking Early Retirement Benefits at Age 62" table below, those born in 1960 or later who retire at 62 will see their benefits shrink by as much as 30%.

Your Break-Even Point

Of course, claiming retirement benefits at less than full retirement age means you'll collect benefits for a longer time. But the permanent reduction in the amount of your monthly benefits means that if you live past your early 80s, you'll wind up collecting less in total lifetime benefits than if you had waited until full retirement age. This point in life is referred to by Social Security as the "break-even age." See Chapter 6 to learn more about the break-even point.

The following table, "Taking Early Retirement Benefits at Age 62," illustrates the effect of claiming early benefits. The table assumes a monthly retirement benefit for the worker at full retirement age of $1,000 and shows exactly how much claiming benefits at age 62 would reduce that amount, plus the overall percentage reduction in benefits.

Taking Early Retirement Benefits at Age 62
(based on a $1,000 retirement benefit at full retirement age)

Year of Birth*	Full Retirement Age	Retirement Benefit	
		Amount	Percent Reduction
1943–54	66	750	25.00%
1955	66 + 2 months	741	25.83%
1956	66 + 4 months	733	26.67%
1957	66 + 6 months	725	27.50%
1958	66 + 8 months	716	28.33%
1959	66 + 10 months	708	29.17%
1960 and later	67	700	30.00%

* If you're born on January 1, use the prior year of birth.

TIP

What if you must retire for health reasons? Some people are forced to stop working before full retirement age because of ill health. If you're under full retirement age and in that position, consider applying for Social Security disability benefits rather than early retirement. The reason is that disability benefits are calculated by the same formula as full retirement benefits, but the amount doesn't depend on the age at which you qualify for them. And the "disability freeze," a benefit calculation rule by which Social Security ignores any low-earning years that were caused by your disabling condition, can actually increase your disability benefits and eventual retirement benefits. Be warned, however, that proving you're incapable of doing any sort of work can be a difficult process. (See Chapter 3.)

TIP

Widows and widowers can switch from retirement to survivors benefits. Financial straits force many widow(er)s to claim their retirement benefits at or before full retirement age, even though they would become eligible for a higher monthly retirement amount if they waited longer. Although claiming early retirement benefits permanently reduces their retirement benefits based on their own earnings record, Social Security rules permit widow(er)s who have previously claimed early retirement to switch to full survivors benefits at full retirement age. And, for many people, these full survivors benefits are higher than their own reduced retirement benefits. (See Chapter 5 for a full explanation of survivors benefits.)

The same rules apply to widows as to widowers, although the disparity in earnings between men and women means this ability to switch benefits is used mostly by women.

Full Retirement Age

For a long time, Social Security considered 65 to be full retirement age. Benefit amounts were calculated on the assumption that most workers would stop working full time and would claim retirement benefits upon reaching age 65.

Now that people are generally living longer, the Social Security rules for what is considered full retirement age are changing. Age 65 is still considered full retirement age for anyone born before 1938. But full retirement age gradually increases from age 65 to 67 for people born in 1938 or later. For people born between 1943 and 1954, full retirement age is 66. For people born in 1960 or later, full retirement age is 67.

In addition, to give incentive for people to delay making their retirement claims, Social Security offers higher benefits for people who wait to make their claims until after reaching full retirement age. (See below.)

Full Retirement Age for Those Born After 1942

Year Born	Full Retirement Age
1943–1954	66 years
1955	66 years + 2 months
1956	66 years + 4 months
1957	66 years + 6 months
1958	66 years + 8 months
1959	66 years + 10 months
1960 or later	67 years

If You Claim Benefits After Full Retirement Age

If you wait until after your full retirement age to claim Social Security retirement benefits, your benefit amounts will be permanently higher. Your benefit amount is increased by 8% each year you wait up to age 70. Also, if you delay your benefits claim until after full retirement age, after you die, your spouse's survivors benefits (see Chapter 5) will also be correspondingly higher. This is a particularly good strategy if, financially, you don't need your retirement benefits at full retirement age and you're in good health, expecting to live well past age 70. This means you're likely to collect your higher benefits for many years.

After age 70, there's no longer any age-related increase and so no reason to delay claiming benefits.

 TIP

Everyone can claim some or all Medicare coverage at age 65. Even if you don't claim Social Security retirement benefits when you turn 65, you can be eligible for Medicare benefits and may want to sign up for some or all of them. (Enrolling in Medicare doesn't affect your current or future retirement benefits.) (See Chapter 12 for more information.)

Reversing a Suspension of Benefits

What happens if you delayed collecting retirement benefits when you reached full retirement age, but at some point before age 70, your financial or health circumstances change and you need those benefits right away? You can file papers with Social Security "undoing" your suspension of benefits and begin collecting them at any time. And once you begin collecting them, an eligible spouse (and/or ex-spouse) and child can begin collecting dependents benefits as well. However, benefits you might have collected during those suspended months can't be collected retroactively. You (and your dependents, if any) are only entitled to benefits beginning with the month you file your request to undo the suspension.

The Amount of Your Retirement Check

The amount of your Social Security retirement benefits depends on how much you earned in covered employment over all your working years. Social Security calculates your benefits based on the amounts in your highest-earning 35 years. Then it applies a set of formulas to these earnings; the exact figures depend on the year you were born. For most people, the amounts are less than bountiful. For example, the average retirement benefit for someone who reaches full retirement age in 2024 is about $1,900 per month. The maximum retirement benefit for someone first claiming benefits in 2024 is about $3,800 per month (at full retirement age). Once you claim your benefits, there's a small cost-of-living increase most years.

Under Social Security's benefit calculation system, the lower your average lifetime earnings, the higher a percentage of those earnings you'll receive in benefits. If your earnings have averaged in the middle range—the equivalent of around $30,000 to $40,000 per year in today's dollars—you can expect a retirement benefit of about 40% of your average earnings for the last few years before you reach full retirement age.

Dependents Benefits Don't Affect Amount of Retirement Benefits

The amount of your retirement benefits isn't affected by the fact that your spouse (and/or ex-spouse) or child(ren) are receiving benefits. This is true whether your spouse collects retirement benefits based on their own work record or collects dependents benefits based on your work record. There's a limit on how much all of your dependents can collect based on your work record (see Chapter 4), but this limit doesn't affect the amount you personally receive in retirement benefits.

If your average earnings have been on the low side—less than $30,000 a year in current dollars—then your benefits might be about 50% of your earnings in the years just before you claim retirement benefits.

If your earnings have always been at or near the maximum credited earnings for each year (see Chapter 1), then your retirement benefits might be about 25% of your earnings in the year in which you retire.

But these figures are just rough averages. To get a much more accurate estimate of what your personal retirement benefits will be, you can either phone Social Security at 800-772-1213 or log in to your Social Security account to see your statement. Go to www.ssa.gov/myaccount and sign up if you don't already have a login. Your statement will provide you with an estimate of what your monthly retirement benefits would be if you claim benefits at age 62, at full retirement age, or at age 70. The actual amount you'll receive in retirement benefits will depend on what your actual earnings are in the years between getting this estimate and claiming those benefits. So, the closer you are to actually claiming your retirement benefits, the more accurate this estimate will be.

Increases for Cost of Living

Whatever the amount of your Social Security retirement benefit, you'll usually receive an automatic cost-of-living increase on January 1 of each year. This increase is tied to the rise in the Consumer Price Index: the cost of basic goods and services. In a very few years, when the cost of living has not risen, there's no increase at all. For 2024, the cost-of-living increase is 3.2%.

Increases If You Keep Working After Claiming Retirement Benefits

As explained above, the amount of your Social Security retirement benefits depends on your average qualifying income over your highest 35 years of lifetime earnings. But can your benefit amount go up if you continue to earn and pay Social Security taxes after you claim retirement benefits? The answer is yes. If, after you claim benefits, your earnings in any year raise your earnings average over your highest 35 years, Social Security will raise your retirement benefit amount accordingly. This is true whether you claim benefits early, at full retirement age, or after full retirement age.

Reductions for Government or Foreign Pensions

Many people have earned retirement benefits from work covered by Social Security and also public employee retirement system benefits from working in government jobs not covered by Social Security. Similarly, some people have earned Social Security retirement benefits from work in the United States and also a pension from work in another country.

Social Security artificially boosts the retirement benefits of people who have many years with very low or no Social Security earnings—to make sure people have at least a small amount. But because of a law called the "Windfall Elimination Provision," this artificial benefits raise is eliminated for people who have either public employee system or foreign retirement benefits.

Those Affected

If your age and work history fit certain categories, your Social Security check will be reduced by 10% to 35% because of this windfall. You might be affected by this reduction if you:

- first became eligible for a government pension in 1986 or later, and
- worked fewer than 30 years at jobs covered by Social Security.

Those Not Affected

The windfall reduction doesn't affect you if you:

- only worked for an employer not covered by Social Security before 1957
- only earned a government pension based solely on work for the railroad, or
- were a federal government employee hired on January 1, 1984 or after.

 CAUTION

Government pensioners seeking spouse's benefits may face limits. Another rule limits benefits to people who collect both Social Security spousal benefits (dependents benefits as the spouses of retired or deceased workers) and public employment pensions based on their own work records. (See "Government Pension Offset" in Chapters 4 and 5 for details.)

Working After Claiming Early Retirement Benefits

Because Social Security retirement benefits plus savings and other investments are often not enough to live on comfortably, many people keep working for at least a few years after they claim Social Security retirement benefits. Other people keep their jobs or take new ones to stay active and involved in the world of work. And if you keep working with a high enough yearly income, this may also increase your lifetime earnings average, thereby slightly increasing your benefits for the years to come.

However, if you claim *early* retirement benefits—meaning, after reaching age 62 but before reaching full retirement age— and continue to work, be aware that the money you earn over a certain amount each year will reduce your Social Security retirement benefits (until you reach full retirement age). Such a reduction in benefits applies only to that year. It has no permanent effect on the amount of benefits you'll receive in future years.

Limits on Earned Income If Claiming Early Benefits

Until you reach full retirement age, Social Security will subtract money from your retirement check if you exceed a certain amount of earned income for the year. For the year 2024, this limit on earned income is $22,320 ($1,860 per month). The amount goes up each year. If you're collecting Social Security retirement benefits before full retirement age, your benefits are reduced by $1 for every $2 in any month you earn over the limit. After you reach full retirement age, there's no limit on the amount of money you can earn and still receive your full Social Security retirement benefit.

EXAMPLE: Henry is considering claiming early retirement benefits this year, at age 64. Social Security calculates that if he does so, he'll receive $866 a month (which is about 13% less than if he waited until his full retirement age of 66). But Henry also intends to continue working part time, with an income that would be about $5,000 over the yearly limit on earned income. If he does claim the early benefits and makes that part-time income, Henry would lose one dollar out of two from the $5,000 he earns over the limit, which means $2,500 for the year. Therefore, his $10,392 in yearly retirement benefits would be reduced to $7,892. So, by claiming early retirement and continuing to earn over the limit, Henry incurs a double penalty: His retirement benefits are reduced by 13%, and he loses an additional amount every year, to the extent he earns over the income limit, until he reaches full retirement age.

The amounts of early retirement benefits you lose as a setoff against your earnings aren't necessarily all gone forever. When you reach full retirement age, Social Security will recalculate upward the amount of your benefits to take into account the amounts you lost because of the earned income rule. The lost amounts will be made up only partially, however, a little bit each year. It will take up to 15 years to completely recoup your lost benefits. And remember, none of this readjustment will change the permanent percentage reduction in your benefits that was calculated when you claimed early retirement benefits (look again at the chart "Taking Early Retirement Benefits at Age 62" earlier in this chapter).

Change in How You Report Earnings

The Social Security Administration bases its benefit calculations on earnings reported on W-2 forms and self-employment tax payments. Most Social Security recipients aren't required to send in an estimate of earnings.

But the Social Security Administration does request earnings estimates from some beneficiaries: those with substantial self-employment income or whose reported earnings have varied widely from month to month, including people who work on commission. Toward the end of each year, Social Security sends those people a form asking for an earnings estimate for the following year. The agency uses the information to calculate benefits for the first months of the following year. It will then adjust the amounts, if necessary, after it receives actual W-2 or self-employment tax information in the current year.

When beneficiaries reach full retirement age, Social Security no longer checks their income. Because there's no Social Security limit on how much a person can earn after reaching full retirement age, there's nothing to report.

TIP
You can collect retirement benefits plus unemployment benefits. As this chapter explains, you can continue to work even after you begin claiming your Social Security retirement benefits. If you're working and you lose your job, you can collect unemployment benefits (assuming you otherwise qualify for them), even though you're also collecting your Social Security retirement benefits.

Only "Earned Income" Affects Your Benefits

The rule that reduces your early retirement benefits based on income over a certain yearly amount applies only to what Social Security considers "earned income." Basically, earned income means money you receive during the year for work you currently do. This rule favors the well-to-do who withdraw significant income from sources other than current work.

Earned income does *not* include:

• interest on savings or investments
• capital gains (profits from the sale of stock, property, or other assets)
• IRA or 401(k) withdrawals
• insurance cash-ins
• rental income, or
• private pensions.

Also, money you receive from certain types of sources based on work you performed *before* you claimed retirement benefits—known as "special sources"—isn't counted as earned income. These exempted amounts include:

• bonuses
• accumulated vacation pay or sick leave compensation
• private retirement fund payments
• deferred compensation
• accumulated commissions, and
• payments to the self-employed for work performed before claiming retirement benefits, if they're received more than one year after claiming benefits.

Special Rule as You Approach Full Retirement Age

If you're already receiving your retirement benefits, a special higher earnings limit applies in the calendar year you turn full retirement age. If you'll reach full retirement age in 2024, you can earn up to $4,960 per month during 2024 without losing any of your benefits. For every $3 you earn over that amount in any month, you'll lose $1 in Social Security benefits. Beginning in the month you reach full retirement age, you become eligible to earn any amount without penalty.

If you're self-employed, you can receive full benefits for any month during this first year in which you didn't perform what Social Security considers "substantial services." The usual test for substantial services is whether you worked in your business more than 45 hours during the month (or between 15 and 45 hours in a highly skilled occupation).

Social Security Disability Benefits

About 10 million disabled workers and their families receive Social Security disability insurance (SSDI) benefits. These people developed severe injuries or illnesses when they weren't old enough to collect retirement benefits but Social Security disability benefits provided an answer.

If you find it very difficult to work because of a physical or mental condition that isn't likely to resolve itself within a year—and you're short of retirement age—read this chapter carefully. If you have enough work credits for your age, you might be eligible for monthly SSDI benefits. And if you're eligible to receive disability benefits, your spouse and minor or disabled children may also be eligible to collect benefits. (See Chapter 4 for more information about dependents benefits.)

Who Is Eligible

Social Security disability benefits are paid to workers and their families only when workers have enough work credits to qualify. Work credits for SSDI benefits are calculated in the same way as for retirement benefits, although the number of credits required to qualify for the disability program depends on a person's age. A person can earn up to four work credits per year, and anyone who works part time, even at a very low-paying job, easily accumulates them. (See Chapter 1 for a discussion of how work credits are earned.)

RESOURCE

Learn more about Social Security disability benefits. This chapter will introduce you to Social Security disability benefits, but to learn more, including how to convince the Social Security Administration that a particular disability makes you unable to work, read *Nolo's Guide to Social Security Disability: Getting & Keeping Your Benefits*, by David A. Morton III, M.D. (Nolo). It includes details on whether you might qualify for benefits, how to apply, how to keep existing benefits, and how much you can work and still receive benefits.

Work Credits Required

The number of work credits you'll need to qualify for SSDI disability benefits depends on your age when you become disabled.

The "Work Credits Required to Qualify for Disability Benefits" chart below provides a quick reference to see how many work credits you need to qualify for disability benefits.

There are also rules that make it easier for younger workers and people who become blind to qualify for disability benefits. (See "Young Workers" and "Blind Workers," below.)

Work Credits Required to Qualify for Disability Benefits	
If you became disabled at age:	You need this many work credits:
21 to 24	6
24 to 31	6-18
31 to 42	20
44	22
46	24
48	26
50	28
52	30
54	32
56	34
58	36
60	38
62 or older	40

Help From the Americans with Disabilities Act

A federal law, the Americans with Disabilities Act, or ADA, prohibits employment discrimination on the basis of a worker's disability. The ADA is intended to help people with disabilities who want to work but are frustrated by noncooperative employers.

In general, the ADA prohibits employers from discriminating against disabled people when hiring, promoting, and making other job decisions. It also requires employers to maintain a workplace that doesn't have substantial physical barriers to people with disabilities. Under the ADA, employers must make reasonable job accommodations for qualified workers with disabilities, unless that would cause the employers undue hardship.

Unfortunately, the ADA is full of vague language. Disability rights advocates, lawyers, employers, and courts are still wrangling over precisely what terms like "reasonable accommodations" and "undue hardship" mean. So, there's no simple set of guidelines about how the ADA works in actual practice.

For information about how the ADA is being enforced and where you can go for help in seeking its protection, contact the Office on the Americans with Disabilities Act in the Civil Rights Division of the U.S. Department of Justice at 800-514-0301 (voice) or 800-514-0383 (TDD). The Justice Department also has an ADA website at www.ada.gov.

Requirement of Recent Work

In order to qualify for SSDI disability benefits, you must have earned at least 20 of the required work credits within the 10 years just before you became disabled, unless you qualify under one of the special rules for young or blind disabled workers. In other words, you need to have worked at least 5 of the last 10 years.

EXAMPLE: Monica worked for 10 years before she had children, earning 40 work credits during that time. After her children were in high school, she went back to work. That was in 2019, and, at the end of 2023, she became disabled with a back injury.

Although she had more than the 40 total credits required for disability benefits, she couldn't collect them because she had only worked 4 years—earning 16 credits—within the 10 previous years (2014 through 2023). She would need to work long enough to earn four more credits before she could qualify for disability benefits. In 2024, that means she would need to earn $6,920 during the year (four credits at $1,730 per credit) before she could qualify.

Young Workers

If you were disabled between the ages of 24 and 31, you need only half of the work credits (2 per year instead of 4 per year) that you could have earned between age 21 and the time you became disabled.

If you become disabled before age 24, you would need only 6 credits in the three-year period immediately before you became disabled. These special rules exist because workers who become disabled at a young age obviously don't have the opportunity to acquire many work credits.

EXAMPLE: Boris became disabled at age 29. There were 8 years between when he was age 21 and the time he became disabled. During those years he could have earned 32 work credits: 4 per year. But under the special rule for young workers, Boris needs only half, or 16 credits, to qualify for disability benefits.

Blind Workers

If you're disabled by blindness, you must have the same number of work credits as anyone else your age. However, you don't need to have earned 20 of your work credits within the 10 years immediately

preceding your disability, as required for other workers. Your work credits can be from any time.

For the purposes of Social Security disability benefits, being blind generally means having no better than 20/200 vision in your better eye, with glasses or other corrective lenses, or having a visual field of 20 degrees or less (or a combination of the two). (See "What Is a Disability?" below, for more information on blindness as a disability.)

Disabled Widows and Widowers

If you're a widow or widower age 50 or older and disabled, you might be able to receive SSDI disability benefits even though you don't have enough work credits to qualify. The amount of these benefits would depend entirely upon your deceased spouse's average earnings and work record. Because they're based on your spouse's work record, you would lose eligibility for these benefits if you remarry before age 50.

You must meet a number of qualifications:
- You must be disabled as defined by Social Security rules. (See "What Is a Disability?" below, for more on these rules.)
- Your spouse, at death, must have been fully insured—meaning they had enough work credits to qualify for disability benefits based on their age.
- Your disability must have started no later than seven years after your spouse's death.
- If you already receive Social Security benefits as a surviving widow or widower with children (called "mother's or father's benefits"), your disability must have begun no later than seven years after these benefits ended. (See Chapter 5.)
- If you divorced before your former spouse died, you'll be eligible for these benefits only if the two of you were married for 10 years or more.

Marital Status Does *Not* Affect Disability Benefits Based on Your Own Work Record

If you collect Social Security disability insurance (SSDI) benefits based on your own work history and earnings record, neither your right to collect those benefits nor the benefit amount would be affected if you get married or divorced. Your spouse's prior, current, or future earnings or assets are not considered by Social Security when you apply for or collect SSDI disability benefits based on your own work record.

Note: This is not the case, however, if you're a widow or widower collecting disability benefits based on your prior spouse's work record (see "Disabled Widows and Widowers," above) or disability benefits through the Supplemental Security Income (SSI) program, for which total household income and assets are considered (see Chapter 7).

If you're collecting SSDI benefits based on your own work record, marriage might actually have a positive effect. If you get married and become entitled to Social Security dependents benefits (see Chapter 4) or survivors benefits (see Chapter 5) based on your spouse's retirement or disability, and those benefits would be higher than your own disability benefits, then you can collect the higher amount (but not both). Also, your spouse might be entitled to Social Security dependents or survivors benefits based on your eligibility for Social Security disability benefits. Your spouse getting these benefits wouldn't cause any reduction in your own benefits.

What Is a Disability?

To receive Social Security disability benefits, you must have a physical or mental disability that both:

- is expected to last (or has lasted) at least one year, or to result in death, and
- prevents you from doing any "substantial gainful work."

Of course, several of the terms within these definitions are subject to different interpretations. This section explains some guidelines developed by Social Security and the courts regarding qualifications for Social Security disability benefits.

Conditions That May Qualify

Social Security keeps a list of common conditions it considers disabling. (See "Listed Impairments," below.) But every person's physical and mental state is different, and the human mind and body can be very complex. So you might well have a condition that prevents you from working but is not on the list of common conditions. Don't let that discourage you from filing for disability benefits.

But to get past one of the first steps of the disability determination process, your impairment must be "medically determinable," meaning that it can be discovered and verified by doctors. Your medical records must include evidence that proves you have a loss of function.

If you're considering making a claim for disability benefits, examine the requirement that the disability must prevent you from performing substantial gainful work, as described below. Discuss the matter thoroughly with your doctor or doctors.

Must Be Expected to Last One Year

No matter how seriously disabling a condition or an injury is, it won't make you eligible for Social Security disability benefits unless it has lasted, or is expected to last, one year. The disability will also qualify if it is expected to cause death.

 TIP
You can apply for benefits upon diagnosis or inability to work.
Even though the disability must be expected to last at least a year, you don't have to wait for a year to apply for benefits. As soon as the condition is disabling and a doctor can *predict* that it is expected to last a year, you can qualify. (The application process is described in Chapter 8.)

EXAMPLE: Ladonna fell down some stairs and badly dislocated her hip. She was placed in a body cast and was told by her doctor to stay in bed for three to four weeks. The cast would stay on for two months. After that, Ladonna would need a cane for another two or three months. In six to nine months, she would be walking normally again, although a little bit more cautiously. She would be off work for a total of six or seven months.

Despite the seriousness of her injury and her total inability to work while she recovered, Ladonna will probably not qualify for Social Security disability benefits. The reason is that her disability is not expected to last for a year. However, she might qualify for her employer's disability benefits, if the company provides them, or for unemployment or state disability compensation through her state's employment or disability office.

If, after you begin receiving benefits, it turns out that your disability doesn't actually last a year, Social Security can't ask for its money back. You're not penalized for recovering sooner than expected, as long as the original expectation that the disability would last a year (or result in death) was expressed in writing by your doctor and accepted by the Social Security review process (and there was no fraud involved). However, you do have the obligation to tell Social Security if you return to work so that they can review your situation.

EXAMPLE: Ravi had a stroke, leaving most of his left side paralyzed. He was unable to walk on his own, was unable to speak clearly, and needed help with most simple daily life tasks. He began physical and speech therapy, but his doctors predicted that he was unlikely to recover full use of his left arm and leg. He applied for Social Security disability benefits, and after waiting three months to see if Ravi's condition was likely to improve, Ravi was found eligible for disability benefits because his condition was totally disabling and he wasn't expected to be sufficiently recovered to return to work within a year. However, through hard work, Ravi recovered both his speech and enough of the use of his arm and leg to return to work in 10 months.

Although his disability didn't last the required year, Ravi was able to keep the disability payments he had already received because the doctors had expected that his condition would be totally disabling for at least a year and the Social Security disability review process had accepted that prognosis.

Listed Impairments

To simplify the process of determining whether a disability makes a person eligible for benefits, Social Security has developed a list of common serious conditions that it considers disabling (if your specific condition meets the criteria in the listing). If you prove, through medical records and doctors' reports, that you have one of the listed conditions—paralysis of both an arm and a leg, for example—Social Security will likely consider you eligible for benefits without making you prove that you can't perform substantial gainful work (instead, simply assuming that you can't do substantial work).

Every person's disability claim is considered individually, however, and having a condition on this list doesn't automatically qualify you for SSDI disability benefits. You must have evidence that your condition meets the requirements of the particular "listing." If you do, your application for disability benefits is likely to be approved, unless you've been working since you became disabled. If you have been working, Social Security will determine whether this work disqualifies you from getting disability, or whether instead it can be considered an "unsuccessful work attempt."

A select few of the conditions Social Security lists as being disabilities include the following, simplified for our discussion:

- a disease of the heart, lung, or blood vessels resulting in a serious loss of heart or lung function as shown by X-ray, electrocardiogram, or other tests—and, in spite of medical treatment, causing severe breathlessness, pain, or fatigue
- severe arthritis causing recurrent inflammation, pain, stiffness, and deformity in major joints so that the ability to get about or use the hands is severely limited
- mental illness resulting in the severe limiting of activities and interests, deterioration in personal habits, and/or seriously impaired ability to get along with other people, such that it prevents substantial gainful employment
- damage to the brain resulting in severe loss of judgment, intellect, memory, or communication ability

- cancer that is progressive and has not been controlled or cured (though some serious cancers qualify at any stage)
- Acquired Immune Deficiency Syndrome (AIDS) or its related secondary diseases, with certain severe complications
- a disease of the digestive system that results in severe malnutrition or anemia
- loss of major function of both arms, both legs, or a leg and an arm
- serious loss of function of the kidneys, and
- total loss of the ability to speak in a way that can be heard or understood.

The full listings are found in the Code of Federal Regulations (CFR) Title 20, Part 404, Subpart P, Appendix 1. You can also find the listings on the Social Security website at www.ssa.gov.

Unable to Do Substantial Gainful Activity

To be eligible for Social Security disability benefits, you must be unable, because of your disability, to perform any substantial gainful activity—generally considered to be any work from which you earn $1,550 (in 2024) per month or more.

If your condition doesn't meet the requirements of a listing, Social Security will then consider whether it prevents you from doing the job you had when you became disabled, or the last job you had before becoming disabled.

To determine whether you can do your past job (or other jobs), Social Security will look at your documented symptoms to determine your "residual functional capacity" (RFC). Your RFC is what activities you can still do despite your medical condition. Your RFC will include things like:

- how long you're able to sit, stand, walk, and lift
- how much weight you can carry and how often, and
- whether you can operate heavy equipment or drive.

If your disability prevents you from performing your usual job, Social Security will next decide whether you're able to do any other kind of substantial gainful work.

In determining whether you can switch to a less demanding job, Social Security will assess whether you're able to perform any kind of work (even the simplest, least-demanding job) existing anywhere in the economy, whether or not there are actually any such jobs available close to where you live.

For older applicants, as part of this determination, Social Security considers your education, training, and work experience ("vocational factors").

Social Security realizes that it's more difficult for older workers to find new employment or to retrain for other kinds of work, so the agency approves the disability claims of those older than 50 more readily than those of younger workers. The agency also knows that it won't be committing to as great an outlay of money when it grants disability benefits to people nearing retirement age as it does when it grants them to younger workers (older workers were on the brink of collecting retirement benefits anyway). For older workers without job skills, this means that they might be able to qualify for benefits even if they could do a less demanding job.

Special Rules for Blindness

If your vision in your better eye is no stronger than 20/200 with correction, or if your peripheral field of vision is limited to 20 degrees or less, you're considered blind under Social Security disability rules. (There are a few other ways to qualify for disability for blindness as well.) Assuming that your work credits add up to the required amount for your age, you (and your family) can receive Social Security disability benefits.

Some blind persons are able to continue working, at least part time, while simultaneously collecting disability benefits. If you're blind, you can earn up to $2,590 per month—the amount increases from year to year—before your job is considered "substantial gainful work" that would disqualify you from those benefits.

Applying Protects Your Retirement Benefits

If you're legally blind and earning too much money to qualify for Social Security disability benefits, but also earning significantly less than before your blindness, you might want to apply for disability benefits anyway. Even though you won't receive cash benefits, Social Security can put what is called a "disability freeze" on your earnings record to protect your overall average.

The amount of your retirement benefits, or of your disability benefits if you later qualify, is determined by your average income over the years. (See "Determining Your Benefit Amount" in Chapter 1 for further explanation.) If, because of your disability, you're now making considerably less than you were before, these lower earnings will pull your lifetime average income lower, resulting in a lower ultimate Social Security payment. This special disability freeze provision for blindness permits you to work without having your lower income figured into your lifetime average earnings.

Over 55 rule. If you're over 55 and blind and doing substantial gainful work, you can qualify for a special status with Social Security. In any month you make above the substantial gainful activity amount—that is, earn more than $2,590—you won't receive a disability check, but you will receive benefits for any month that your earnings fall below the limit.

The key is to show that the work you're doing requires a lower level of skills and abilities than what you were doing before you turned 55.

Examples of Disability Determinations

The following examples help illustrate Social Security's reasoning in applying its guidelines and making disability determinations.

Unsuitability for Other Work

EXAMPLE: Arnold has been a longshoreman for most of his life. At age 58, his back has been getting progressively worse. His doctor told him that he could no longer do longshore work and said that sitting for any length of time will aggravate the condition. Arnold applies for disability.

Because there's no question that Arnold's condition will last more than a year, Social Security will next ask whether it prevents Arnold from performing substantial gainful activity. Arnold's back prevents him not only from doing his regular job or other physical labor, but also from sitting or standing for long periods of time. Unless Social Security can describe a job that requires neither physical labor nor sitting, Arnold will probably get disability payments. And because Arnold has done physical labor all his life, he doesn't have the training, work experience, or education to do many other jobs. Considering his age and the difficulty of finding any type of work for which he could be retrained, Social Security will find him eligible for disability benefits.

Two Conditions Combined

EXAMPLE: Ernestine has been a music teacher for many years. She is now 60 years old and is losing her hearing. She has also developed phlebitis, which makes it difficult for her to walk very far or to stand for long periods of time. She has to elevate her legs for a while every few hours. When her hearing loss makes it impossible for her to continue teaching music, she applies for disability benefits.

The combination of her two conditions might make her unable to maintain substantial gainful employment. She would have to find a job that required neither good hearing nor standing, and permitted her to put her legs up for a half hour several times a day. Because such jobs are scarce, Social Security would find Ernestine eligible for disability, particularly in light of her age.

Mild Disability

EXAMPLE: Rebecca is 52 and has an aortic aneurysm. Despite medication, she has intermittent fatigue and shortness of breath, especially at her job as a waitress. Her doctor says that her work is too physically demanding and stressful for her heart. Rebecca applies for Social Security disability benefits.

Although Rebecca's condition—aortic aneurysm—is on Social Security's listing of impairments, she isn't automatically eligible for disability benefits. Her condition has to meet the criteria in the cardiovascular listing; in this case, an aneurysm must be dissecting (that is, separating from the wall of the artery).

If Rebecca's aneurysm isn't dissecting, Social Security would assess her limitations to see if she could do some type of less demanding work. Even if Social Security found she could only do sedentary work, the agency would probably find that she has job skills, such as dealing with the public and taking orders, that could be used at a desk job (called "transferable skills"). She is less likely to qualify for benefits than Arnold and Ernestine in the two prior examples.

Amount of Disability Benefit Payments

Like other Social Security benefits, the amount of your actual disability check is determined by your age and your personal earnings record: your average earnings for all the years you have been working, not just the salary you were making most recently.

Disability benefits are also available for disabled workers' families (spouses and minor or disabled children). The maximum amount for worker and family combined is either 85% of what the disabled worker was earning before becoming disabled, or 150% of what the worker's individual benefit is, whichever is lower.

EXAMPLE: Manu was making $3,200 a month when he became disabled at age 56. At that time, Manu's Social Security earnings record gives him an individual disability benefit of $900 a month. Manu's wife and teenage daughter are also eligible to collect dependents benefits. Theoretically,

they could each collect up to 50% of Manu's benefit ($450), but their amounts will be limited by the maximum family benefit. Together with Manu, the family's total benefits could not exceed 150% of Manu's individual disability benefit, or $1,350.

Estimating Benefit Amounts

There's no simple formula for what your actual disability payments will be. Although some books and magazines print tidy charts matching age and income with disability benefit amounts, more often than not these charts mislead people, causing them to overestimate their benefits. The charts base their figures on your current earnings and assume that you have had a consistent earning pattern during your entire working life. Most people, however, don't have such a perfect curve of earnings, so the estimates the charts give you are bound to be wrong.

However, you can get a general idea of Social Security disability benefits amounts by considering average payment amounts for 2024:

- overall average monthly payment for a disabled individual: $1,540, and
- overall average monthly payment for a disabled individual plus a spouse and children: $2,720.

In addition, it can be helpful to look at averages based on income levels.

Estimated Disability Benefits for 2024

Average Annual Lifetime Income in Current Dollars	Monthly Benefits
$10,000 to $20,000	$600 to $900 (individual)
	$1,020 to $1,260 (couple or parent and child)
$20,000 to $30,000	$850 to $1,210 (individual)
	$1,330 to $1,815 (couple or parent and child)
$30,000 to $40,000	$1,210 to $2,180 (individual)
	$1,480 to $1,780 (couple or parent and child)
$40,000 and up	$1,650 to $2,860 (individual)
	$1,980 to $3,300 (couple or parent and child)

TIP

Check your eligibility for supplemental benefits. If you receive only a small disability benefit, and you have savings or other cash assets of less than $2,000 ($3,000 for couples), you might be eligible for Supplemental Security Income benefits (SSI) in addition to your Social Security disability benefits. (See Chapter 7 regarding SSI.)

Relying on general estimates of disability benefits makes little sense, however, because you can get a very accurate estimate, based on your exact earnings record, directly from Social Security. You can get this estimate when you apply for benefits or by going to http://ssa.gov/myaccount.

Cost-of-Living Increases

As discussed above, monthly disability benefit amounts are based entirely on your personal earnings record, with no consideration given to the minimum amount you need to survive. Whatever your monthly amount, however, there's usually a yearly cost-of-living increase based on the rise in the Consumer Price Index. For a few years, the cost-of-living increase was 5% or more. In most years, however, the increase has been only 1% to 3%, and in some years, there is no cost-of-living increase at all.

CAUTION

Don't expect to start receiving disability benefits right away. Applying for disability benefits and proving your disability can be a slow, sometimes difficult business. You need to organize your paperwork, have the cooperation of your doctors, and be patient and persistent. What to expect in the application process and how best to prepare for it are discussed in Chapter 8.

Student Debt and Disability Benefits

Many people who qualify for Social Security disability benefits still owe money on their federally guaranteed student loans. If you're in

default on any federally guaranteed student loans, the Social Security Administration can deduct an amount from your monthly SSDI disability benefits payment to help pay off this debt. The maximum the government can take is 15% of benefits, and no one's benefits can be reduced to less than $750 per month.

Discharge of Student Loan Debts for Permanent Disability

If you have what is considered "total and permanent disability" (TPD), you can apply to have the entire remaining amount of your federal student debt wiped off the books ("discharged"). In general, a disability is considered total and permanent if it renders you unable to work and the condition is expected to last more than five years (as opposed to the one-year qualifying requirement for collecting Social Security disability benefits). Those who qualify for TPD status include:

- veterans with service-connected TPD, as determined by the U.S. Department of Veterans Affairs (VA) (veterans no longer need to apply; the VA will automatically notify them of the debt discharge)
- someone already receiving SSDI or SSI benefits based on disability (see Chapter 7), whose next scheduled disability review is five years or more from the date of the most recent Social Security disability determination (or from the date of the original approval), or
- someone who is unable to engage in any substantial gainful activity by reason of a physical or mental impairment that can be expected to result in death, has already lasted for a continuous period of at least five years, or is expected to last for a continuous period of at least five years, as certified by the treating physician.

The discharge applies only to the Federal Direct Loan Program, Perkins Loans, the Federal Family Education Loan (FFEL) Program, and TEACH grants. Other loan programs and private loans have their own discharge rules.

To learn more about qualifying for this TPD discharge of debt and about the process for applying, visit the special TPD webpage of the Office of Federal Student Aid, U.S. Department of Education, at www.disabilitydischarge.com.

Collecting Additional Benefits

Because disability payments are often not enough to live on, it's important for you to collect all the other benefits to which you may be entitled. You might also want to try to supplement your income by working a little bit, to the extent you can.

Disability and Earned Income

Your benefit check won't be reduced if you earn a small amount of income while collecting Social Security disability benefits. However, if you regularly earn enough income for your work to qualify as gainful employment, you might not be considered disabled any longer and your benefits could be cut off entirely.

Social Security usually permits you to earn up to $1,550 a month—$2,590 if you're blind—before you'll be considered to be performing substantial gainful work. Also, in deciding how much you're earning, Social Security is supposed to deduct from your income the amounts of any disability-related work expenses, including medical devices or equipment such as a wheelchair, attendant care, drugs, or services required for you to be able to work. It will be up to you to prove the necessity and cost of such expenses.

The $1,550 per month amount isn't fixed. You can't simply keep your income just below this level and expect that your disability benefits will automatically continue. Both your physical condition and the amount of your work will be reviewed periodically. (See "Continuing Eligibility Review," below, regarding periodic reviews.) This review will take into account the amount and regularity of your income, your work duties, the number of hours you work, and, if you're self-employed, the extent to which you run or manage your own business.

If you're working long hours or have significant work responsibility, particularly if you're in business for yourself, Social Security will look hard, during its review of your disability status, at whether the

$1,550 income limit is a true measure of your work. If, for example, family members are suddenly earning quite a bit more than they used to from the business, Social Security might suspect that you're doing the work and simply paying them instead. Or, if you're not getting paid much but you're working long hours for a business in which you have an ownership interest, they might look more closely at whether you're still disabled.

But you are allowed a "trial work period," during which you can test out working without risking the loss of your SSDI benefits. (See below.)

Other Social Security Benefits

You are not permitted to collect more than one Social Security benefit—retirement, dependents, survivors, or disability—at a time. If you're eligible for more than one monthly benefit based either on your own work record or on that of a spouse or parent, you'll receive the higher of the two benefit amounts to which you're entitled, but not both. Supplemental Security Income (SSI) is an exception; you're allowed to collect SSI in addition to any other Social Security benefit. (See Chapter 7 for more on SSI.)

Other Disability Benefits

You're permitted to collect Social Security disability benefits and, at the same time, private disability payments from an insurance policy or coverage from your employer. However, your private disability policy might allow the insurance company to "offset" your Social Security disability payments; that is, to reduce your private disability payments by the amount of your Social Security benefits.

You can also receive veterans (VA) disability compensation at the same time as Social Security disability benefits, and those benefits will not be offset. (See Chapter 11 for a full discussion of VA benefits.)

Workers' Compensation

You can collect workers' compensation benefits—payments for injuries suffered during the course of employment—at the same time as Social Security disability benefits, but those benefits will be offset.

While you're receiving monthly workers' compensation payments, the total of your disability and workers' compensation payments generally can't be greater than 80% of what your average wages were before you became disabled. If they are, your disability benefits or workers' comp benefits will be reduced so that the total of both benefits is 80% of your earnings before you became disabled. If you're still receiving Social Security disability benefits when your workers' compensation coverage runs out, you can again start receiving the full amount of your Social Security benefits.

> EXAMPLE: Maxine became disabled with a back condition while working as a gardener and earning $1,400 a month. Her Social Security disability benefits were $560 a month, and, because her disability was related to her job, she also received workers' compensation benefits of $625 a month. The total of the two benefits was more than 80% of her prior salary (the combined benefits of $560 and $625 total $1,185, and 80% of $1,400 is $1,120), so her Social Security disability benefits were reduced by the extra $65, down to $495 a month.
>
> If Maxine was still disabled when her workers' compensation benefits ended, her Social Security disability benefits would go back up to $560 a month (plus whatever cost-of-living increases had been granted in the meantime).

Medicare

After you've been entitled to disability benefits for 24 months, you become eligible for Medicare coverage. This is true even if you're not age 65, which is otherwise the standard age to qualify for Medicare. Medicare hospitalization coverage (Part A) is free. However, like other Medicare beneficiaries, you must pay a monthly premium if you want to be covered by Medicare Part B medical insurance or by Part D for prescription drug costs. (See Chapter 12 for a full discussion of Medicare.)

Medicaid and SSI

If you have few or no assets other than your home—or your disability and the resulting medical costs deplete your assets and hamper your ability to earn income—you might qualify for Medicaid coverage. Medicaid is a program of government medical coverage available to people based on their low income and assets. You can be eligible for Medicaid coverage as soon as you qualify under its rules, without the 24-month wait Medicare requires. And even when you do qualify for Medicare, Medicaid can continue to pay medical bills that Medicare won't if you continue to be eligible for both programs. (See Chapter 16 for a full discussion of Medicaid.)

Protecting Your Medicaid Eligibility

If your disability was caused by an accident that was someone else's fault, you might have a chunk of money coming to you as the result of an insurance claim or a lawsuit. Receiving that money, however, might disqualify you from Medicaid and eligibility for other benefits, which would mean you'd have to spend your settlement money on future medical bills, with nothing left for other living expenses.

Federal law and the laws of many states address this problem by allowing you to set up a "special needs trust." This permits you to accept accident compensation without losing your Medicaid and other benefit eligibility. With such a trust, instead of the accident compensation going to you in a lump sum, it's held for you by a bank or similar institution and is used to pay only certain types of bills—usually medical and basic living expenses. If your situation requires a special needs trust, consult an experienced estate planning lawyer for help.

In many states, a cheaper and easier alternative to special needs trusts is now available for people who became disabled before age 26. The Achieving a Better Life Experience (ABLE) Act allows for the creation of ABLE savings accounts, special bank accounts for individuals with disabilities. Funds in the accounts don't count as assets for the purpose of Medicaid (or SSI, up to $100,000).

If you qualify for Medicaid assistance, you might also qualify for cash payments from the SSI program, on top of your Social Security disability benefits. Like Medicaid, SSI is intended to assist people with low income and assets. (See Chapter 7 for more on SSI.)

Continuing Eligibility Review

Eligibility for disability benefits is not necessarily permanent. Depending on the nature and severity of your condition, and on whether doctors expect it to improve, Social Security will periodically review your condition to determine whether you still qualify for benefits.

When Your Eligibility Will Be Reviewed

If, when you apply for disability benefits, your doctors and Social Security's medical experts expect that your condition will improve, your medical eligibility will be reviewed 6 to 18 months after you're approved for benefits. If improvement in your condition is theoretically possible but not predicted by the doctors, Social Security will review your eligibility approximately every three years. If your condition is not expected to improve after you apply, Social Security will review your case every five to seven years.

If at any point after you're receiving disability benefits, you earn a steady or frequent monthly income of close to $1,550 (in 2024) per month, Social Security might also call you in for a work review. The agency will determine whether you're actually able to perform gainful employment that would bring you more than $1,550 per month. Social Security will also check to see whether you're arranging to be paid less than $1,550 per month by having someone close to you receive money for your work, or whether you're being paid in some way other than cash wages or salary.

If you're in what's called a "trial work period," however, your benefits won't be terminated if you're doing work that brings your income over the limit (see a "Returning to Work," below).

The Review Process

The first step in a review of your eligibility for disability benefits is a letter from Social Security with a Disability Update Report form for you to fill out. This short form contains questions about how your health has changed, the medical treatment you've received recently, and any work you've done.

Depending on your answers, Social Security might then send you a longer form to fill out, called the Continuing Disability Review Report, which is similar to your original disability application.

The form will ask for the names and addresses of the doctors, hospitals, and other medical providers you have seen since your original eligibility was established, or since your last review. It will also ask you whether you've worked recently.

Social Security will then refer your file to Disability Determination Services (DDS), the state agency that reviews all disability claims.

The DDS will obtain your current medical and employment records and might ask that you undergo a medical consultation or examination. The DDS will make a determination about your continued eligibility based on the medical records and reports and on your earned income. Unless your disabling impairment has substantially improved so that you can now do substantial gainful work, or you've regularly been earning more than $1,550 per month (or are found to be doing substantial gainful employment despite being paid less than $1,550 a month), your benefits will continue.

If your eligibility is terminated, you have a right to appeal that decision. (See Chapter 9 for a full discussion of the appeal process.) And if you lose your eligibility, benefits can continue for an adjustment period of up to three months while you look for work and wait for a paycheck.

Returning to Work

Most disabled people would rather work than not, and many try to find ways of working despite their disabling conditions. Social Security provides various forms of encouragement for people to return to work. For example, it ensures that people will continue to receive their disability benefits during time they spend testing the workday waters. And if, after returning to work, a person later finds that their disability makes the work too difficult, the person's disability benefits can be restarted quickly and easily.

Trial Work Period

Within any five-year period, you can try out some kind of work—and keep any income you earn—for up to nine months while still receiving full SSDI disability benefits. (Your medical condition must still qualify you as disabled during this trial period.) You can try one job for a month or two and, if it doesn't work out, attempt the same or another job sometime later—up to a total of nine months within any five-year period. These nine months don't have to be consecutive.

Any month in which you make more than $1,110 is considered one of the nine trial work months. If you're self-employed, any month in which you work 80 hours or more is considered a trial work month.

After you've worked for nine trial work months, your trial work period is over, and your extended period of eligibility will begin.

Extended Eligibility for Benefits

After you've worked for 9 months—the trial work period— during a 5-year span, Social Security gives you another 36-month period of eligibility during which you can continue to work without necessarily losing your eligibility for benefits. During this time, you'll receive your full disability benefits for any month you don't have "substantial" earnings. Again, earnings of $1,550 per month are considered "substantial"; the amount is $2,590 if you're blind. You don't need to file a new application for benefits or go through an eligibility review.

The first time that you make substantial earnings during this "extended period of eligibility" (EPE), a grace period starts, during which you can receive your full benefits and keep the income you make from work. The grace period lasts three months, after which your benefits will stop.

Quick Restart of Benefits

What if you've finished your trial work period and EPE, your benefits have been stopped because you're working enough to bring in "substantial" earnings, but you again find yourself unable to work? In such a situation, Social Security makes it easy to restart your benefits. For five years after your disability benefits stop, called the "expedited reinstatement" period, you can get an immediate restart of benefits if you again are unable to work, so long as your inability to work is caused by the same disabling condition as before.

You need not file a new application for benefits, although you do need to file a simple form requesting the resumption of benefits.

Social Security will again review your condition to determine whether you're disabled. However, your benefits should be restarted on the first of the month following your request, without waiting for the review to be completed.

> EXAMPLE: Roberta qualified for Social Security disability benefits because of a congenital back condition that worsened so much in her 30s that she could no longer work. After several years, however, a new surgical technique was developed that greatly improved Roberta's condition. Roberta returned to work part time and soon earned a "substantial" income. That meant she no longer qualified for disability benefits. Her back remained strong enough for her to work for two years, but then it began to deteriorate again. Within another six months, she found she could no longer work. Because Roberta's original disability was the same disability that caused her to stop working again, and it was within 60 months after she had returned to work, she regained her disability benefits within a month, simply by applying for reinstatement.

Continuing Medicare Coverage

If you became eligible for Medicare coverage because you qualified for SSDI disability benefits for 24 months, you don't immediately lose that Medicare coverage once you return to work. After you return to "substantial" work for more than 9 months and your disability benefits stop, your Medicare coverage continues for another 93 months.

This is the period between the end of your grace period and the end of your expedited reinstatement period. During that time, your Medicare Part A coverage is free, but you must pay the same premium for Medicare Part B and Medicare Part D (prescription drug coverage) as other Medicare beneficiaries, unless you qualify for a Medicare Savings Program, administered by Medicaid (see Chapter 16).

Social Security Dependents Benefits

A retired or disabled worker with a family obviously needs more money than someone living alone—especially given that Social Security retirement benefits currently average only about $1,900 per month ($1,500 per month for disability benefits). The situation is particularly acute when the retired or disabled worker was the family's primary breadwinner. To help alleviate this problem, Social Security provides dependents benefits to the spouse and minor children of retired and disabled workers.

Who Is Eligible

Certain family members of a retired or disabled worker are eligible for monthly Social Security dependents benefits if the worker has enough work credits to qualify for, and has claimed and actually begun collecting, their own retirement or disability benefits. If a worker delays claiming retirement benefits until after reaching full retirement age, their dependent(s) must also wait to collect dependents benefits until the worker begins collecting. However, a qualifying divorced spouse need not wait until the ex-spouse worker actually claims retirement benefits (see "Effect of Marriage and Divorce," below).

The amount of benefits paid to dependents is determined by the worker's earnings record and, for a spouse, the age at which the spouse claims the benefit.

Although they're called dependents benefits, you don't have to actually depend on the worker for support in order to claim them.

Individuals Who Qualify

To be entitled to dependents benefits, you need to fit one of the following categories:
- a spouse age 62 or older
- a divorced spouse age 62 or older, with certain conditions (see "Effect of Marriage and Divorce," below)
- a spouse (or partner) younger than 62 who is caring for the worker's child who is under age 16 or who became disabled before age 22

- unmarried children younger than 18
- unmarried children up to age 19 if still in high school
- unmarried children of any age if they were severely disabled before they reached age 22, for as long as they remain disabled (see Chapter 3)
- unmarried stepchildren up to age 18 (19 if still in high school) if living with and under the care of the retired or disabled worker, or
- grandchildren of the worker, if they live with and are under the actual care of the worker and the parents are deceased or disabled, or if the grandparent has adopted them.

Effect of Marriage and Divorce

Couples come in many forms: companions who are not married; couples who are divorced; people who were divorced and later married someone else. Each status has some ramifications regarding Social Security dependents benefits.

Married Couples

You're eligible for dependents benefits (often called "spousal benefits") based on your spouse's work record once you reach age 62 and you've been married for at least one year. You must wait to claim these benefits until your spouse begins collecting their benefits.

Divorced Spouses

You're eligible for dependents benefits if both you and your former spouse have reached age 62, your marriage lasted 10 years, and you have been divorced at least 2 years. This two-year waiting period does not apply if your former spouse was already entitled to retirement benefits before the divorce.

You can collect benefits as soon as your former spouse is eligible for retirement benefits at age 62. Your ex does not actually have to be collecting those benefits for you to collect your dependents benefits.

Remarried

If you're collecting dependents benefits on your former spouse's work record and then marry someone else, you lose your right to continue those benefits. However, you might be eligible to collect dependents benefits based on your new spouse's work record.

If you divorce again, you can collect benefits again on your first former spouse's record, or on your second spouse's record if you were married for 10 years the second time as well.

Try to Stretch the Marriage to 10 Years

If you are in the process of getting a divorce and you have been married almost 10 years, try to have your spouse agree—or stall the legal paperwork long enough—that the divorce won't become final until after 10 years. This is the amount of time you must have been married to get Social Security dependents benefits.

Under Social Security rules, the marriage is considered in effect until the divorce legally becomes final, even if you and your spouse have already been living apart, you have separated your property, and one of you has begun paying spousal or child support.

If you anticipate that your spouse might object to the delay, you might remind them that your dependents benefits have no effect on the amount they can collect in retirement benefits. Nor would your benefits affect the amount of dependents benefits your ex's new spouse could collect in addition to yours.

Whether your former spouse remarries does not affect your eligibility. Nor does your collecting dependents benefits through your former spouse affect their new spouse's right to collect benefits. And there is no reduction in either of your benefits when two spouses (current and former) are collecting them.

Dependents Benefits for Same-Sex Spouses

Same-sex spouses are entitled to federal Social Security dependents benefits on the same terms as other spouses. This is true regardless of whether the couple lives in the state where the marriage was performed.

Foreign marriages. A spouse in a same-sex couple who was married outside the United States but now lawfully lives in the United States might be entitled to dependents benefits based on the other spouse's work record in the United States, depending on the status of that marriage in the country where it was performed. Even if you have doubts about your right to dependents benefits as a same-sex spouse, the Social Security Administration encourages you to apply for them so that the agency can determine whether you are eligible.

Retroactivity. Spousal benefits may be retroactive. The Department of Justice and the Social Security Administration have decided in several cases that the right to spousal benefits for a same-sex spouse can apply to someone who applied for such benefits before the Supreme Court's same-sex marriage decision on June 26, 2015. If you were married and applied for spousal benefits before that date but were denied those benefits (because you lived in a state that did not recognize your marriage), reapply to Social Security specifically requesting retroactive benefits back to the date you first applied.

Unmarried Couples

For the most part, Social Security laws don't recognize the relationship between two adults who are not officially married. There are two exceptions.

First, if one person in an unmarried couple adopts the minor child of the other person, that child becomes eligible for dependents benefits based on the adoptive parent's work record. The other person in the couple does not, however, become eligible for Social Security benefits.

Second, if you live in a state that recognizes common law marriage and you qualify under that state's rules for such marriages, you might also qualify for dependents benefits. The states that recognize common law marriages are Colorado, the District of Columbia, Iowa, Kansas, Montana, Oklahoma, Rhode Island, Texas, and Utah. Alabama, Georgia, Idaho, Ohio, Pennsylvania, and South Carolina recognize common law marriages that were formed before certain dates.

The qualifying rules for a common law marriage vary somewhat from state to state, but all require that you have lived together and have represented yourselves as married by such things as using the same name and owning property together.

Mother's or Father's Benefits

If you care for a disabled worker's child who is under 16 or disabled (and became disabled before age 22), you can get dependents benefits whether or not you're currently married to the worker. Social Security calls these benefits "mother's or father's benefits." But you don't need to be the legal mother or father of the child to get this benefit, unless you're divorced from the disabled worker. This benefit can be as much as 75% of the amount that the disabled parent receives in SSDI benefits, but it's subject to the maximum family benefit amount (see below).

Calculating Dependents Benefits

The amount of benefits available to a retired or disabled worker and their dependents is calculated based on the total number of people in the immediate family. Social Security figures that the economies of scale permit two to live more cheaply than one, three to live more cheaply than two, and so on. Therefore, the amount by which benefits increase with each additional dependent is smaller and smaller for each person added.

One Dependent

The basic Social Security benefit for one dependent, whether the dependent is a spouse, divorced spouse, or qualifying child, is 50% of the worker's retirement or disability benefit amount. If a divorced spouse and a new spouse both receive dependents benefits, each receives 50% (with no reduction to the primary worker's retirement or disability benefit amount).

The actual amount of your dependents benefit is based on the earnings record and timing of the retirement benefit claim of the worker on whom you are a dependent. Even if the worker has claimed retirement benefits before full retirement age, dependents benefits will be based upon what the worker would have received at full retirement age.

Some workers delay claiming retirement benefits until after full retirement age, up to age 70, in order to receive higher benefits. If so, the worker's retirement benefits will be higher, but the dependents benefits won't. Dependents benefits are based on what the worker would have received if they had claimed retirement benefits at full retirement age, not on the worker's higher delayed benefit amount.

However, if you are the worker's spouse, the amount of your spousal benefits depends on your age when you first claim the benefits. The amount of a spouse's dependents benefits is permanently lower if the spouse claims them between age 62 and their full retirement age. At each of the ages listed below, a dependent whose full retirement age is 66 receives a benefit as follows:

Dependent Spouse's Age	Percent of Worker's Benefit
62	35.0%
63	37.5%
64	41.7%
65	45.8%
Full Retirement Age	50.0%

The best way to find out the amount of retirement or disability benefits that you and your dependents are likely to receive is to review your official Social Security statement (discussed in Chapter 1).

TIP

Dependent eligible for Medicare at age 65. At age 65, a spouse might be eligible for Medicare coverage based on the worker's earnings record, even if the spouse doesn't have enough Medicare earnings to qualify on their own. In order for a spouse age 65 to qualify for Medicare on the worker's record, the worker must be at least age 62 and personally have sufficient work credits to qualify for Social Security benefits.

Family Benefits

If your family includes more than one dependent—a spouse and one or more children, or no spouse but two or more children—the benefits paid to the worker and the dependents will be calculated according to the "maximum family benefit amount." This amount is less than the total would be if the worker's benefits and individual dependents benefits were paid separately without a family limit.

The maximum family benefit is 150% to 180% of a retired worker's benefits—the precise amount depends on a complicated Social Security formula—or 150% of a disabled worker's benefits. The retired or disabled worker collects 100% of their benefits, and the remaining 50% to 80% is divided equally among the dependents.

EXAMPLE: Chiang-Fa is retired. Alone, he would be entitled to $900 per month in retirement benefits. He and his wife Yoka have a 17-year-old daughter. With no daughter, Yoka would have been entitled to a $450-per-month dependents benefit—50% of Chiang-Fa's $900 retirement benefit.

However, because their daughter is also eligible, the three of them together are limited to a maximum family benefit of 180% of Chiang-Fa's benefit, or $1,620. That amount would be divided as follows: Chiang-Fa, $900; Yoka and the daughter, each $360. Once the daughter reaches age 18, however, she is no longer eligible for dependents benefits, and Yoka would begin to get a full 50% dependents benefit of $450 per month.

If Yoka is entitled to her own benefit (on her own work record), that could lower the portion of Yoka's benefit that counts toward the family maximum and raise the daughter's amount.

Eligibility for More Than One Benefit

Many people are not only eligible for their own Social Security retirement or disability benefits but also for dependents benefits based on their spouses' work records. As with other Social Security benefits, you aren't permitted to collect both but only whichever one is higher.

If your own earnings record is low and your spouse's earnings record high, you might be entitled to higher monthly benefits as a dependent than you would be by collecting your own retirement or disability benefits. You have no choice about claiming one benefit or another. When you claim either your own retirement benefits or dependents benefits, Social Security will "deem" you to have applied for both. You will then collect whichever of the two benefits is higher, but you can't claim one while putting off the other to allow it to grow.

Working While Receiving Benefits

Before full retirement age, a dependent's benefit will be reduced by $1 for every $2 of income earned over the yearly maximum. After a dependent reaches full retirement age, benefits are not reduced, regardless of how much the dependent is earning. (See Chapter 2 for a full explanation of benefit reductions.)

If several dependents are receiving a combined family benefit amount, one dependent's income doesn't affect the amount the other family members receive.

EXAMPLE: Grace and Omar and their teenage son receive combined family retirement and dependents benefits of $1,650 a month. Grace's and the son's portions of the family benefit are $350 each. Grace is offered a job for a year as a substitute teacher at a salary that is $6,000 more than the yearly earnings limit for her age of 63 years old.

Since Grace's benefit amount is reduced $1 for every $2 she earns above the limit, her benefit would be reduced by half ($1 out of $2) of $6,000. That means a reduction of $3,000, or $250 per month. Since her own part of the family benefit is $350, that benefit would be reduced to $100 per month. The rest of the family's benefits—Omar's $950 per month and the son's $350—would not be affected.

Perils of Claiming Early: Reduced Benefits

If you claim retirement benefits before full retirement age, your retirement benefits will be reduced. (See Chapter 2 for details.) And if you later switch to dependents benefits, those benefits, too, will be reduced by the same amount that your retirement benefits were reduced.

EXAMPLE: Clare would have been eligible for retirement benefits of $500 per month at age 66. She decided to claim early retirement benefits at age 62—and received her full retirement amount of $500 less 25%, for a monthly sum of $375. When Clare's husband turned 66, he applied for retirement benefits and received $1,200 per month. At that time, Clare switched from her own retirement claim to dependents benefits, which ordinarily would have been $600, or 50% of her husband's monthly amount. But because Clare had already taken 25% reduced retirement benefits at age 62, her dependents benefits were now reduced by 25%. She ended up getting $450 per month, instead of the $600 per month she would have received had she waited.

Government Pension Offset

Most people who work for a federal, state, or local government or for a public agency are now fully covered by the Social Security system and are also eligible to receive benefits under their agency's public retirement system. But millions of people of retirement age worked for a branch of government—federal, state, or local—or for a public agency, such as a school district, and earned a retirement pension under the Civil Service Retirement System (CSRS) or a similar pension system that paid no Social Security taxes. (See Chapter 10 for more information about the CSRS.) These people might be subject to a reduction in Social Security dependents benefits called the "government pension offset."

The government pension offset applies if you receive Social Security dependents or survivors benefits and also receive a retirement pension (based on your own work record) from the CSRS or another civil service pension system that didn't contribute to Social Security. If you receive this type of pension, your Social Security dependents or survivors benefits are reduced dollar for dollar by two-thirds of the amount of your civil service pension.

The government pension offset does not apply, however, to people who are eligible to receive retirement benefits under the Federal Employees Retirement System (FERS), state or local Public Employees Retirement System (PERS), or any other public employment retirement system that does pay Social Security taxes.

In particular, the government pension offset does not apply to:

- federal employees who pay Social Security taxes on their earnings
- federal employees who switched from the CSRS to the FERS before July 1, 1988
- federal employees who switched from the CSRS to the FERS after June 30, 1988 and worked for at least five years under FERS
- federal Civil Service Offset employees (employees who had at least five years of federal employment under the CSRS, then left federal employment but were rehired after December 31, 1983 following a break of a year or more)
- people whose retirement benefit is based on work for a state or local government or public agency whose pension system paid Social Security taxes at the time they retired (and who retired before July 1, 2004), or
- people who retired on or after July 1, 2004, and whose retirement benefit is based on work for a state or local government or public agency whose pension system paid Social Security taxes during the last five years of employment.

If you're entitled to benefits under any CSRS pension, you should consider this government pension offset when calculating the amount of your combined CSRS retirement pension and Social Security dependents or survivors benefits. This rule might affect which pension benefit you choose to collect.

EXAMPLE: Gina and her husband both worked for the government under the Civil Service Retirement System (CSRS). Her husband also worked in the private sector, paying Social Security taxes on his earnings. Gina is entitled to $500 per month in Social Security dependents benefits, based on her husband's private sector work record. She is also entitled to a CSRS pension of $400 per month (her own retirement pension) and a $250 per month CSRS dependents benefit based on her husband's work under the CSRS.

If Gina claims her own CSRS retirement pension, her Social Security dependents benefits would be reduced by two-thirds of her $400 pension (meaning the amount deducted from her Social Security dependents benefit would be $266). If, instead, she claims her CSRS pension dependents benefits but not her own CSRS retirement pension, her Social Security dependents benefits are not affected. So, she is better off collecting her smaller CSRS dependents benefits ($250) plus her full Social Security dependents benefits ($500), for a total of $750 per month, than she would be collecting her own larger CSRS retirement benefit ($400) with her reduced Social Security dependents benefit amount ($500 − $266 offset = $234), for a total of only $634 a month.

TIP

Private employer pensions are not affected. The pension offset rule does not apply to pensions paid by private, as opposed to government employers. As far as Social Security is concerned, you are entitled to your full Social Security dependents benefits as well as your private pension benefits. However, your private pension plan might require that your pension benefits be reduced by the amount you receive from Social Security.

Social Security Survivors Benefits

T he Social Security laws recognize that a worker's family might need financial support after the worker dies. Even if the surviving spouse has always worked, the loss of the deceased spouse's income will almost surely be an economic blow to the family. And if the surviving spouse didn't work, or earned much less than the deceased spouse, the loss of the deceased worker's income can be financially devastating. Recognizing the family financial burden brought on by the loss of an earner, Social Security provides for what are called "survivors benefits" to be paid to the spouse and minor children of an eligible worker who has died.

Work Credits Required for Eligibility

Surviving family members of a deceased worker are entitled to survivors benefits only if the worker earned enough work credits before dying. Work credits are accumulated based on earnings from employment covered by Social Security. The required number of work credits depends on the worker's age at death. (See Chapter 1 for more on earning work credits.)

The number of work credits on the worker's Social Security record needed for survivors to collect benefits is listed in the "Credits Required on Deceased's Work Record" chart, below.

TIP
Credits earned just before death might make up for a lack of work credits. Even if the deceased worker didn't have enough work credits according to the chart below, benefits might still be paid to the surviving spouse and children if the worker had at least one and one-half years of work in covered employment in the three years immediately before dying.

Credits Required on Deceased's Work Record	
If the worker died or became disabled at age:	Work credits needed:
28 or younger	6
30	8
32	10
34	12
36	14
38	16
40	18
42	20
44	22
46	24
48	26
50	28
52	30
54	32
56	34
58	36
60	38
62	40

Who Is Eligible

Provided the deceased worker had enough work credits, here's who can claim survivors benefits:

- a surviving spouse age 60 or older
- a divorced surviving spouse age 60 or older, if the marriage lasted at least 10 years

Survivors Benefits for Same-Sex Spouses

A same-sex surviving spouse is entitled to federal Social Security survivors benefits on the same terms as any other surviving spouse. This is true regardless of the state in which the same-sex couple lived, if the marriage was lawful in the state where it was performed.

Foreign marriages. The surviving spouse of a same-sex couple who was married outside the United States but who now lawfully lives in the United States might be entitled to survivors benefits based on the deceased spouse's work record in the United States. The right to benefits in this situation depends on the status of that marriage in the country where it was performed. Even if you have doubts about your right to survivors benefits as a same-sex surviving spouse, the Social Security Administration encourages you to apply so that they can determine whether you're eligible.

Retroactivity. These benefits may be retroactive. The Department of Justice and Social Security Administration have decided in several cases that the right to spousal benefits for a same-sex spouse can apply to someone who applied for such benefits before the Supreme Court's same-sex marriage decision on June 26, 2015. If you were married, widowed, and applied for survivors benefits before that date but were denied those benefits (because you lived in a state that did not recognize your marriage), reapply to Social Security specifically requesting retroactive benefits back to the date you first applied.

- a surviving spouse younger than 60, if caring for the worker's child who is younger than 16 or disabled; this benefit, sometimes called the "mother's or father's benefit," can also be paid to a surviving divorced spouse who is taking care of the workers' child if the surviving ex-spouse is the legal mother or father of the child and is unmarried
- a surviving spouse age 50 or older who becomes disabled within seven years of the worker's death (or within seven years after their mother's or father's benefits end); if you were

divorced, you can collect these disabled survivors benefits only if your marriage lasted at least 10 years

- unmarried children younger than 18; benefits can continue to age 19 if the child is still a full-time high school student
- unmarried children of any age who were severely disabled before age 22 and are still disabled, or
- one or both parents of the worker who are at least age 62 and who were dependent on the worker for at least one-half of their financial support. If an unmarried dependent parent remarries after the worker's death, the parent loses the survivors benefits.

Length of Marriage Rule

To collect benefits as a surviving spouse, you must have been married for at least nine months before the worker's death. However, there are some exceptions to this rule. If you're the biological parent of a child with the worker, or you adopted the worker's child or adopted a child with the worker before the child was 18, the nine-month rule doesn't apply.

The rule is also waived if you were previously married to the same person and your first marriage lasted more than nine months. And the nine-month rule doesn't apply if the worker's death was the result of an accident, as opposed to an illness, or occurred while they were on active military duty.

Effect of Remarrying

One of the assumptions behind survivors benefits for spouses is that the majority of surviving spouses are women and that women are financially dependent on their husbands. Although things are changing, the fact that there are still fewer women than men in the workforce and that women still make less than 84 cents for every dollar men earn in wages, in comparable jobs, means this assumption isn't entirely out of date.

Another assumption is that if a surviving spouse—usually a woman—remarries, her need for survivors benefits will end, because there is a new spouse upon whom to depend financially. So a series of qualifying Social Security rules apply to collecting survivors benefits after remarriage:

- A widow or widower who remarries before age 60 loses the right to collect survivors benefits through the deceased spouse, even if they're still caring for the former spouse's children. The children, however, remain eligible for benefits. (However, at age 62, the remarried spouse might be eligible for dependents benefits based on the new spouse's record.)

- If the widow or widower is older than 50 and disabled, getting remarried won't affect the survivors benefits.

- A widow or widower who remarries after reaching age 60 doesn't lose survivors benefits from the deceased former spouse. However, it might make sense to apply—at age 62 or later—for dependents benefits based on the new spouse's earnings record if that benefit would be higher than the survivors benefits. In that case, Social Security would pay a combination of the survivors benefit and the dependents benefit based on the new spouse's record.

- If you were divorced from your now-deceased former spouse, and the two of you had been married for at least 10 years, you're eligible for survivors benefits even if you remarried before age 60 but are again widowed or divorced. After age 60, you can remarry without losing your survivors benefits.

- If you were divorced from your now-deceased spouse, you're older than 50, and you're disabled, getting remarried won't affect your benefits.

EXAMPLE: Akiko and Yosh were divorced 10 years ago, after being married for 25 years. Three years ago, Yosh died. Akiko has a new sweetheart, Ben. They have been together for the past year and are now considering marriage. But Akiko is concerned about the effect their marriage would have on her right to collect Social Security survivors

benefits. Akiko is 59, and next year she would be eligible for survivors benefits based on Yosh's work record because their marriage lasted more than the required 10 years.

If Akiko waits one more year, she and Ben can marry and she will still be able to collect survivors benefits based on Yosh's record. If she marries before reaching age 60, she will lose those benefits.

Amount of Survivors Benefits

Like all other Social Security benefits, the dollar amounts of survivors benefits are determined by the deceased worker's earnings record. In addition, the amount of the survivors benefits depends on whether and when the worker had claimed retirement benefits. If the worker had claimed Social Security retirement benefits before death, the amount of survivors benefits is equivalent to what the deceased worker was receiving. That is, if the worker claimed reduced retirement benefits before full retirement age, the survivors benefits will be similarly reduced. On the other hand, if the worker waited until after full retirement age to claim benefits, and therefore got a higher benefit amount, the survivors benefits will be similarly higher. If the worker died before claiming retirement benefits, Social Security determines what the worker's full retirement benefit would have been and bases the survivors benefits on that amount.

Percentage of Benefits Awarded

Exactly what percentage of the deceased worker's retirement benefit will be awarded to a survivor depends on whether you're the spouse or child of the deceased worker. Also, if you're a surviving spouse, the amount goes up or down depending on the age you first claim benefits.

The amount of the benefit changes between age 60 and "full benefits age." Full benefits age, or the retirement age for survivors, is set by Social Security based on the year of your birth; it's slightly different than the full retirement age set for workers (for those born before 1962).

As with retirement benefits, the full benefits age will be going up in the coming years. The changes are shown on the following chart. The age at which a person can collect full survivors benefits is currently 66—but this will change in the coming years. For people born in 1957 or after, the survivors full benefits age is gradually rising, finally reaching age 67 for those who were born in 1962 or after.

Surviving Spouse at Full Benefits Age

A surviving spouse who waits until the full benefits age to claim benefits will receive 100% of what the deceased worker's full retirement benefit would have been if the deceased worker died before claiming those benefits or if the worker claimed the benefits at full retirement age. But if the deceased worker had claimed retirement benefits early or had deferred payments until after full retirement age, the amount of the survivors benefits will be based on the level of benefits the worker was actually receiving (reduced for an early claim, increased for a delayed claim).

Full Benefits Age for Widow(er)s	
Birth Date	Full Benefits Age
1/2/45–1/1/57	66 years
1/2/57–1/1/58	66 + 2 months
1/2/58–1/1/59	66 + 4 months
1/2/59–1/1/60	66 + 6 months
1/2/60–1/1/61	66 + 8 months
1/2/61–1/1/62	66 + 10 months
1/2/62 and later	67 years

Surviving Spouse Under Full Benefits Age

A surviving spouse who claims benefits at age 60 will receive 71.5% of what the worker would have been receiving (further reduced if the worker claimed early benefits, enhanced if the worker delayed the claim until after full retirement age). Each year a surviving spouse delays claiming benefits after age 60, those benefits will rise 4.1%

to 5.7% per year, depending on the year of birth, until the survivor reaches full benefits age. (A widow or widower who waits until full benefits age to collect survivors benefits will receive 100% of what the worker would have been receiving.)

Delaying benefits until later might be a good idea for survivors who are under full benefits age and who are still working. (See "Working While Receiving Benefits," below, for more information.)

Surviving Spouse Caring for Child

A surviving spouse who is caring for the worker's child, if that child is younger than 16 or disabled, is eligible for benefits regardless of the surviving spouse's age. The amount of benefits will be 75% of what the worker's retirement benefits would have been.

Minor or Disabled Child

A surviving minor (under 18) or disabled child receives 75% of what the worker's retirement benefits would have been. This is over and above what the survivor parent receives. This amount is, however, subject to the per-family maximum discussed in "Surviving Spouse and Children Together," below.

Dependent Parent

A surviving parent who was dependent on a deceased son or daughter for at least half of their financial support might be eligible for 82.5% of what the deceased worker's retirement benefit would have been. If there are two surviving dependent parents, they each get 75%.

Surviving Spouse and Children Together

A surviving spouse and children together are not entitled to the full amount each would get alone. A maximum is placed on the total amount that one family can receive.

The family benefit limit is 150% to 180% of what the deceased worker's retirement benefits would have been. The benefits are divided equally among the surviving spouse and children.

Estimating Benefit Amounts

You can get a general idea of survivors benefit amounts by looking at these recent average figures:

- overall average monthly benefit for surviving spouse: $1,775, and
- overall average monthly benefit for surviving spouse with two children: $3,650.

In addition, it can be helpful to look at averages based on income levels.

Low Income

The survivor of a worker who had low income most of their working life—less than $30,000 per year in current dollars—might receive monthly benefits between $600 and $1,000. If both a surviving spouse and a minor child will be receiving benefits, the monthly total for the two might be between about $1,000 and $1,500.

Moderate Income

The survivor of a worker who had a moderate annual income—around $30,000 to $40,000 in current terms—might receive between $1,000 and $1,500 per month. A surviving spouse and child might receive a total between about $1,500 and $2,000.

High Income

The survivor of a worker who averaged relatively high earnings—$40,000 per year or more in current dollars—can expect between $1,400 and $2,600 per month. The high earner's surviving spouse and child together might receive between $1,600 and $3,900.

Getting an Official Estimate

You can get a very accurate personal estimate of what your family members' survivors benefits are likely to be directly from Social Security or by logging into your Social Security account.

Eligibility for More Than One Benefit

Many surviving spouses are eligible for their own Social Security retirement or disability benefits and also for benefits based on their spouses' work records. However, you're permitted to collect only one type of benefit, whichever is higher. If your own earnings record is low and your deceased spouse's earnings record was high, you may be entitled to higher benefits as a surviving spouse than as a retired or disabled worker.

Even if you will ultimately be eligible for a higher retirement benefit after you turn age 62, you might be able to claim survivors benefits as soon as you're eligible at age 60, and then switch to your own retirement benefits whenever they become higher than your survivors benefits. Claiming survivors benefits before you reach full retirement age doesn't reduce your own retirement benefit.

It also works in reverse: You might be able to claim reduced early retirement benefits—between age 62 and full retirement age—on your own work record, and then switch to full survivors benefits at any later age if those benefits would then be higher. Options for claiming one benefit and later switching to another, and the best time to do so, are explained in Chapter 6.

EXAMPLE: Francesca would be eligible for full retirement benefits of $600 per month at age 66, based on her own work record; at age 62, she is eligible for reduced retirement benefits of $450 per month. At age 66, she would also be eligible for a full survivors benefit of $800 per month based on her deceased husband's work record; at age 62, she is eligible for a reduced survivors benefit of $600 per month.

Francesca has two choices at age 62: She can claim her early retirement amount of $450 per month and then switch to full survivors benefits of $800 per month at age 66. Or she can claim her reduced survivors benefits of $600 per month at age 62 and collect that amount, plus cost-of-living increases, for the rest of her life.

Francesca has to decide whether she can get along well enough with the $450-per-month retirement benefits she would receive for three years until she switched to her $800 survivors benefits. If she can manage, then waiting would be better in the long run. Waiting for the higher survivor benefit makes particularly good sense if she will also be working during those three years, because her benefits might be reduced because of her earnings.

One-Time Payment for Funeral or Burial Expenses

In addition to the monthly survivors benefits to which family members might be entitled, a family can also receive a one-time-only payment—currently $255—intended to defray funeral or burial expenses. A surviving spouse can claim the money if the couple was not divorced or legally separated at the time of death.

If there is no qualifying spouse, the $255 sum can be paid to the surviving minor children, divided equally among them. You must file a claim for the death benefit at your local Social Security office within two years of the worker's death.

Working While Receiving Benefits

Many surviving spouses find that, despite their survivors benefits, they also have to work to make ends meet. How much a surviving spouse earns, however, can affect the amount of survivors benefits if the survivor is less than full retirement age.

The benefit for a surviving spouse who is less than full retirement age will be reduced by $1 for every $2 of income earned over the yearly maximum. (See Chapter 2 for details.) Once a surviving spouse reaches full retirement age, there is no reduction in benefits, regardless of how much is earned.

If a widow, or widower, and children are receiving a combined family benefit amount, the parent's earnings don't affect the amount the children receive.

EXAMPLE: Manjusha and her teenage son receive a combined family survivors benefit of $1,500 a month, or $750 each. Manjusha is taking a job at a salary that is $6,000 more than the yearly earnings limit.

Since Manjusha is 62, her benefit amount is reduced $1 for every $2 she earns over the limit. Her benefits would be reduced by half of $6,000, for a total reduction of $3,000, or $250 per month. Since Manjusha's part of the family benefit is $750, that benefit would be reduced to $500 per month. But her son's $750 would not be affected.

Government Pension Offset

If you worked enough years for a local, state, or federal government or public agency, you might be entitled to retirement benefits from that agency's pension system. You might also be entitled to Social Security survivors benefits based on your deceased spouse's work record. Most people don't have any problem collecting the full amount of both benefits. But people whose government agency work was more than 20 years ago might find themselves subject to a reduction in their survivors benefits. If your government agency work was under the Civil Service Retirement System (CSRS) or another pension system that did not pay into the Social Security system, collecting your own retirement pension might cause you to lose a substantial portion of your Social Security survivors benefits.

This government pension offset rule for Social Security survivors benefits is the same as for Social Security dependents benefits. (For more information, see "Government Pension Offset" in Chapter 4.)

This rule won't only affect how much your combined government pension and dependents benefits are, but it might also cause you to choose to collect your own Social Security retirement benefits, if you

are eligible for them, rather than Social Security survivors benefits. The combination of your CSRS pension and your own Social Security retirement benefits might be more than your CSRS pension and your survivors benefits reduced by two-thirds of the amount of your pension.

EXAMPLE 1: Marta worked for a state government for a number of years, earning a CSRS pension of $690 per month. She is also entitled to a Social Security survivors benefit of $1,400 per month based on her late husband's work in the private sector, for which he and his employers paid Social Security taxes. Because of the public pension offset rule, however, Marta can't collect the full amount of both benefits. Her Social Security survivors benefit will be reduced by two-thirds of the amount of her CSRS pension. So, she collects her $690 per month pension plus a $940 per month survivors benefit ($1,400 − $460 offset [which is two-thirds of $690] = $940).

EXAMPLE 2: Alice is entitled to $500 per month in Social Security survivors benefits based on her deceased husband's nongovernment work record, for which he and his employer paid Social Security taxes. She is also entitled to both a CSRS pension of $400 per month and a $250 per month benefit as a widow based on her husband's public employee retirement record. Ordinarily, she would choose to claim her own CSRS pension rather than the lower public employee widow's benefit.

But if she claims her own CSRS pension, her Social Security survivors benefits would be reduced by two-thirds of her CSRS pension ($400). On the other hand, if she claims CSRS pension dependents benefits, her Social Security amounts won't be reduced at all. She is better off collecting both her smaller CSRS pension dependents benefits ($250) and her full Social Security dependents benefits ($500), rather than her larger CSRS pension retirement benefit ($400) and the reduced Social Security amount, which would be $233 ($500 − $267 offset = $233).

The pension offset rule doesn't apply to pensions paid by private, nongovernmental employers. However, the rules of a few private pension plans provide that your pension benefits will be reduced by what you receive from Social Security. ●

When to Claim Social Security Benefits and Which One to Claim

A s explained in Chapters 1 through 5, the age at which you claim Social Security retirement, dependents, or survivors benefits affects the monthly amount you receive—earlier claims (up to age 70) mean lower monthly benefits. In some situations, an early claim will also reduce how much you will receive if you later switch to a different benefit. Also, the age at which you claim your benefits can affect how much your survivors collect. Altogether, the difference between filing a claim before, at, or after full retirement age can be many thousands of dollars over your and your family's lifetime.

So, how do you choose the best time to claim a Social Security benefit? And which benefit should it be? There is no simple answer, but several factors can help you make a decision that best fits your personal situation. This chapter discusses the factors that apply to everyone and then explains how specific situations—which depend on your family situation and work history—might present you with certain options.

Considerations for All Beneficiaries

You can claim your Social Security retirement or dependents benefits as early as age 62, or your survivors benefits as early as age 60 (or sooner if you're disabled or caring for the deceased worker's child who is younger than 16 or disabled; see Chapter 5).

But the monthly amount you receive—for your lifetime—is reduced for every month before you reach full retirement age that you claim these benefits. (See Chapter 2 to learn about full retirement age.) On the other hand, you can increase your retirement benefit amount for every year past full retirement age (up to age 70) that you wait to claim benefits. Also, by delaying retirement benefits, you increase the amount your surviving spouse can collect.

Your Lifetime Total: The Break-Even Point

Based on the way the Social Security system calculates benefits, if you claim benefits early but you live past a certain age—called your

"break-even point"—you will wind up collecting less in total lifetime benefits than if you had waited to claim them at full retirement age. Similarly, if you wait until full retirement age to claim benefits, or delay them further, but don't live past your break-even point, you will have collected less in total lifetime benefits than if you had claimed benefits early.

Here's how these break-even points work.

Early claim break-even point. For people who claim benefits at age 62, their break-even point is between 75 and 76 years old (the exact point depends on your earnings record and the year you were born). That means that if you claim early benefits but live past that age, your total lifetime benefits will be less than if you had waited until full retirement age to claim them. The longer you live past the break-even point, the more you lose by having claimed early benefits. (Remember, though, that you might want or need to claim early benefits despite this, for other reasons discussed in this chapter.) Because average life expectancy for people age 62 is about 21 years for men and 24 years for women, most people will lose money over their lifetime if they claim benefits at age 62.

Delayed claim break-even point. For most people who delay claiming retirement benefits until age 70, their break-even point is about age 79 or 80. For people who live past that age, after delaying benefits until age 70, total lifetime benefits will be more than if they had claimed them at full retirement age.

Your personal break-even point. Your personal break-even point may differ from the figures above. Your actual break-even point will depend on a combination of factors, including your earnings record and when you were born. However, the figures above will give you a close estimate. To get more specific information about your personal break-even point, you can call Social Security at 800-772-1213 and ask them to do the calculations for you, or go to the Social Security website's page "When To Start Receiving Retirement Benefits" at www.ssa.gov/pubs/EN-05-10147.pdf.

Factors to Consider

Many people jump at the chance to begin collecting benefits as early as possible, regardless of their break-even point. For some, claiming early benefits is a necessary, or at least sensible, financial choice. But for others, it might be a poor decision that can cost them many thousands of dollars over a lifetime. Before you decide whether to claim early benefits or to delay your claim, consider the following factors.

Immediate Financial Need

You might be in a financial situation that leaves you no real choice—you need your Social Security benefits now, even though your monthly benefits will be lower than if you wait, and your total lifetime benefits will probably be lower. For many people in these difficult economic times, the extra income of even a substantially reduced Social Security benefit is what allows them to afford the bare essentials of daily life.

Even if you don't need your Social Security benefit to meet essential daily expenses, you might want to collect a reduced benefit early in order to have a little extra money to make yourself or your family more comfortable. Having the extra money to use now—to do things you might not otherwise be able to afford—might be worth the chance that you will collect less in benefits over your entire lifetime. For example, you might want to use the extra money to do some traveling that you could not otherwise afford or might not be physically able to do later. Or, you might want to use the money to offer financial help to your children or grandchildren at a time when they could really use it. If there's any reason why you feel that using the money now is important to you, you might want to claim benefits early even though, in a purely financial sense, it might not be the best decision.

You Can Undo an Early Claim

Some people claim early benefits because they need the money immediately, but then their financial situation improves. If, after claiming early benefits, you find new work, switch jobs, get a pay raise, or otherwise come into money, your new income or assets might reduce your need for early benefits. Or your income could even wipe out those benefits entirely (if the new money is earned from work you do) because of the earned income offset rule. (For more about this rule, see "Continuing to Earn Before Full Retirement Age," below.)

If you find yourself in this situation, you're not stuck with the decision you made to claim early benefits. You have the following two options.

Suspend benefits. You can ask Social Security to suspend your benefits. This means your benefits will stop until you notify Social Security that you want your benefits to resume. While your benefits are suspended, your lifetime benefits won't suffer the monthly percentage reductions that would have occurred if you had continued to collect early benefits. When you resume collecting your benefits, Social Security will recalculate them, with a reduction based only on those months you actually collected early benefits.

Withdraw claim, repay benefits. Another option is to withdraw your benefit claim. You can withdraw your application within 12 months after first becoming eligible for benefits, if you repay all the benefits you've received so far. Withdrawing your claim would remove all early claim reductions from Social Security's calculation of your benefit amounts, meaning you would be able to claim your full benefit at full retirement age, or a greater amount if you delay your claim even further. To learn more about how to withdraw a claim and what you would have to repay, see Social Security's online information "Cancel Your Benefits Application" at https://www.ssa.gov/manage-benefits/cancel-your-benefits-application.

Continuing to Earn Before Full Retirement Age

Even if you could really use your retirement benefits before you reach full retirement age, it might not make sense to claim them now if you're going to keep working and earning more than a very small income. As explained in Chapters 2, 4, and 5, a Social Security penalty takes $1 from your retirement, dependents, or survivors benefits for every $2 in income you earn over a low, yearly limit (until you reach full retirement age). If you'll be earning only a slight amount over the yearly limit, it might still make sense to claim early benefits if you need the money. But if you'll be working and earning a substantial amount over the yearly limit, claiming your benefits early would be a double mistake: Your immediate benefits would be substantially reduced if not wiped out altogether by the $1-out-of-$2 earnings offset rule, and your lifetime benefits would be permanently lower because you claimed them early.

Life Expectancy

If a health condition makes it likely you won't live past your mid-70s, then claiming early retirement benefits makes sense. You will get to use or save the money, even though it's a reduced amount, for however many years you live.

If, instead, you wait until full retirement age to claim benefits but die within a few years of receiving them, you will have received less in total lifetime benefits even though your monthly benefit amount will have been greater than if you had claimed early benefits.

If, on the other hand, you have no life-threatening medical conditions, your health is generally good, and you have a family history of relatively long life, you might want to delay claiming retirement benefits at least until, and perhaps even later than, full retirement age. With a long life expectancy (likely to live into your 80s), you are more likely to collect greater total lifetime benefits by delaying your benefits claim.

Availability of Other Benefits

Your eligibility for Social Security survivors benefits (see Chapter 5) might allow you to delay claiming your own retirement benefits past full retirement age, making those retirement benefits higher than if you claim them earlier. Claiming early survivors benefits might be a good idea even if those benefit amounts are lower than your early retirement benefits. That's because in the long run, the yearly increase in your unclaimed retirement benefits can make up the difference between lower dependents or survivors benefits you claim now and what your present retirement benefits would be. If you were born before January 2, 1954, you can also claim Social Security dependents benefits (see Chapter 4) early while delaying claiming your own retirement benefits past full retirement age. The scenarios for claiming one benefit while delaying another are discussed in the following sections.

Considerations When You're Entitled to More Than One Benefit

In addition to the factors that apply to everyone (discussed above), if you qualify for more than one type of Social Security benefit, you might want to delay claiming one benefit while you collect another type instead. Whether you're able to do this varies according to your prior and current marital status, the benefits available to you, and, with regard to dependents benefits, the year you were born.

Unmarried, Divorced, or Widowed

If you've never been married, or if you were married but are now divorced or widowed, the best time to claim benefits depends on which benefits you're eligible for and whether you have dependents yourself.

Dependent Children Can Change the Equation

Any decision about when to claim retirement benefits might be a bit different if you have a minor or disabled child who is eligible for dependents benefits (which would pay the child an additional 50% of your retirement benefits). Dependents benefits payable to a minor child last only until the child turns 18, so if your child is already close to that age, the extra benefits wouldn't last long and probably won't affect your decision one way or the other. If, on the other hand, you have a younger child, the total benefits your child could collect until age 18 might make it worth claiming your retirement benefits earlier than you otherwise would.

With No Benefits From Anyone Else's Work Record

If you aren't eligible for dependents or survivors benefits based on the work record of a prior spouse, you probably need to consider only the factors discussed in the previous sections—your immediate financial need, continuing work, and life expectancy— in deciding when to claim your retirement benefits.

With Benefits From a Former Spouse's Work Record

If you were married previously, you might be eligible for dependents or survivors benefits based on your former spouse's work record. (Remember, though, that if you're divorced, you must have been married for at least 10 years to be eligible for dependents or survivors benefits. And a divorced spouse might be able to claim dependents benefits as soon as the former spouse reaches full retirement age, whether or not the former spouse actually claims retirement benefits then; see Chapter 4.) If your survivors benefits are higher than your own retirement benefits, you might be able to claim those instead

of your own benefits. Whether and when to consider such a claim depends on the following rules.

Survivors benefits. A wrinkle in the Social Security laws allows you to claim early retirement or survivors benefits and then switch to the other of these two benefits without the early claim reducing the new benefit amount. It can work in either of two ways:

- You can claim survivors benefits as early as age 60 (or earlier if you're disabled or caring for the deceased worker's child who is younger than age 16 or disabled; see Chapter 5). If you claim survivors benefits before full retirement age, your early claim reduces those survivors benefits but does not affect your own retirement benefits. Your retirement benefit will continue to grow (until you reach age 70) while you're collecting survivors benefits. At any point, you can switch to your own retirement benefits. Given this rule, even if your survivors benefits are somewhat smaller than your retirement benefits, you might want to claim those smaller benefits for several years while your retirement amount grows.

- You can claim your own retirement benefits before you reach full retirement age even if your survivors bencfits would be larger. Why? Because your early retirement benefits claim won't affect your later survivors benefits, which can grow if you delay claiming them. So, you can first take your reduced retirement benefits without affecting your survivors benefits. When you switch to the survivors benefits later, they will be higher for the rest of your life.

Dependents benefits. You can't choose between dependents benefits and your own retirement benefits. When you file for either, Social Security will pay you whichever one is higher. And filing for either dependents or retirement benefits early will cause your dependents or retirement benefits to be reduced by the same percentage.

Married Couples

The rules for married couples allow for some manipulations that can mean higher lifetime benefits for one or both spouses.

If Only One Spouse Is Eligible for Retirement Benefits

Although their numbers are shrinking rapidly, there are still many married women who did not do enough paid work outside the home during their lifetime to have earned Social Security retirement benefits. (This happens with men, too, of course, but the number of men in this situation is smaller, so the discussion here will assume the example of a no-retirement-benefits wife with a husband who has earned retirement benefits.)

A wife in this circumstance is eligible for dependents benefits (spousal benefits) only when her husband claims retirement benefits, and is eligible for survivors benefits when her husband dies. If the wife claims dependents or survivors benefits before her full retirement age, she will get a reduced benefit.

The husband, in this case, is eligible only for his own retirement benefits. He would have no dependents benefits based on his wife's work record, and no survivors benefits if she dies before him.

In addition to a reduction in benefits if the husband starts receiving benefits before reaching full retirement age, a married couple with only one retirement benefit is faced with two Social Security rules:

- If the husband delays his retirement benefits claim until after full retirement age (up to age 70), both his retirement benefits and the wife's survivors benefits (if she outlives him) will go up.
- The wife can't claim dependents benefits (spousal benefits) until the husband claims his retirement benefits.

Early Retirement or Dependents Claim Reduces the Other Benefit for You as Well

You're eligible for a reduced retirement benefit at age 62. If you claim retirement benefits at any time before you reach full retirement age, that early claim permanently reduces those benefits by 0.52% per month (until you reach full retirement age). The same is true for dependents benefits: If you claim dependents benefits between age 62 and full retirement age, those benefits are permanently reduced by 0.52% per month.

Many people don't realize, though, that claiming either early retirement or early dependents benefits also permanently reduces that other benefit for you. You can't claim early retirement benefits and then switch to full dependents benefits, or claim early dependents benefits and then switch to full retirement benefits. As soon as you claim one of those benefits early, the other one is also reduced by the same percentage.

Note: You claiming early retirement benefits does not reduce the amount of your spouse's or child's dependents benefit amount. Nor does your early retirement benefits claim affect the amount of the survivors benefits you can claim based on your spouse's work record when your spouse dies.

Both Spouses Eligible for Their Own Retirement Benefits

In most couples now reaching retirement age, both spouses have earned Social Security retirement benefits. That means that each spouse is also entitled to dependents (and, eventually, survivors) benefits based on the other spouse's work record. As soon as one spouse claims retirement benefits (at age 62 or later), the other (once reaching age 62) can claim dependents benefits (spousal benefits). And when one spouse dies, the other can claim survivors benefits as early as age 60 (or earlier if disabled, or if caring for the deceased spouse's minor or disabled child).

All this operates, though, under one basic principle: You can claim only one benefit (the higher), not both.

There is one exception that allows switching from one benefit to another, resulting in higher lifetime total benefits, and that involves survivors benefits. You can claim early retirement or dependents benefits, then switch to survivors benefits. Ordinarily, at age 62, a spouse might be reluctant to claim reduced retirement or dependents benefits because the reductions are permanent. Plus, an early claim of either of those benefits permanently reduces the other one, too. But the same is not true for survivors benefits; claiming your own early retirement or dependents benefits (while your spouse is living) doesn't affect the amount of survivors benefits you can collect (after your spouse has died). (Note, though, that if your spouse claims early retirement benefits, your eventual survivors benefit on your spouse's record will be reduced.)

So, if you have a considerably older spouse who has a higher earnings record, or your higher-earning spouse is in poor health, you might want to claim your retirement or dependents benefits early (whichever is higher), relying on the fact that you will be able to switch to full survivors benefits in the not-too-distant future.

Worker With Minor Child

A worker approaching full retirement age might want to delay claiming their retirement benefits for a year or more, up to age 70, to get the benefit of a permanently higher retirement benefit amount, and also a higher amount for a surviving spouse. But if the worker has a minor child, the child would be eligible for dependents benefits as soon as the worker claims retirement benefits. This presents a conflict: Either wait to claim retirement benefits and therefore get a higher delayed retirement benefit but no dependents benefits for the child, or get dependents benefits now for the minor child but lose out on the higher delayed retirement benefits.

Supplemental Security Income

Almost eight million people receive monthly benefit amounts from Supplemental Security Income (SSI), a program jointly operated by the federal and state governments and administered by the Social Security Administration. SSI is intended to guarantee a minimum level of income to financially hard-pressed older, blind, and disabled people.

SSI eligibility is based on your age or disability and on financial need, as determined by both your income and your assets. SSI benefits do not depend on how long you've worked or on how much you've paid into the Social Security system.

You must be quite financially needy to qualify for SSI payments; your income and assets must be so low that many people with no income other than their Social Security retirement benefits aren't eligible for SSI. However, others whose Social Security retirement benefit is low, or who aren't receiving any benefits, might receive a small SSI payment.

Despite these tight restrictions, if, after reviewing the rules explained in this chapter, you think you might be close to meeting the requirements for SSI eligibility, it could be worth your while to apply for it. If you qualify for SSI, you could also be eligible for Medicaid (discussed in Chapter 16) and food assistance from SNAP ("food stamps"), as well as free rehabilitation and home care programs, should you need them.

Who Is Eligible

You must meet four basic requirements to be eligible for SSI cash benefits:

- You must be 65 or older, or blind or disabled.
- Your monthly income must be less than a certain minimum amount established by the state in which you live.
- Your assets must be worth less than $2,000, or $3,000 for a couple, although certain items are exempted from this amount—most importantly, your car and home.

- If you're a new applicant for SSI benefits, you must be a citizen of the United States or meet strict requirements for longtime residency, military service, or political asylum or refugee status. Some legal permanent residents of the United States might be eligible for SSI benefits if they're blind or disabled.

 TIP
The rules for each of these requirements are complicated, but the complications almost always make it easier for you to qualify for SSI benefits than you might imagine. Generally speaking, you're permitted to have more income and assets than the initial figures indicate (more on this below).

Blind or Disabled

If you're younger than 65, you might be able to qualify for SSI payments if you're blind or disabled.

You're considered blind if your vision is no better than 20/200 or your field of vision is limited to 20 degrees or less, even with corrective lenses. (There are a few other ways to qualify as legally blind as well.)

You're considered disabled if you have a physical or mental impairment that prevents you from doing any substantial gainful work and that's expected to last at least 12 months or to result in death.

This definition of disabled is the same as the test used for Social Security disability insurance benefits. (See Chapter 3.) But unlike the Social Security disability program, which looks at only the income you currently earn in order to determine whether you're doing substantial work, SSI looks at income from all sources and measures that income in a more complicated way.

Citizens or Longtime Residents

SSI benefits are generally available only to U.S. citizens and longtime legal residents. Noncitizens must fall within one of the narrow categories described below.

The restrictions hit some of the country's neediest people the hardest. These are people, often elderly, who have lawfully immigrated to this country to join their children or siblings, only to be met here by joblessness and poverty.

As a noncitizen of the United States, you qualify for federal SSI benefits only if one of the following applies:

- You have a legal right to live in the United States and you were already receiving SSI benefits on August 22, 1996.
- You were legally living in the United States on August 22, 1996, and you're now blind or disabled.
- You're a lawful permanent resident of the United States (a "green card" holder) and you or your spouse have worked for at least 10 years in this country, having paid at least the minimum Social Security taxes to qualify for 40 quarters of work credits (see Chapter 1 for information about how work credits are earned).
- You're a veteran (honorably discharged) or an active duty member of the U.S. Armed Forces, or the spouse or child of one.
- You have been granted political asylum or refugee status; however, your benefits in this situation will last for only seven years after you've been admitted to the country.

 RESOURCE

For a more detailed discussion of immigrants' eligibility for SSI: See the National Immigration Law Center website at www.nilc.org or contact their Los Angeles office at 213-639-3900.

State Benefits Might Be Available

Nondisabled noncitizens who don't fall into one of the above categories are generally not eligible for federal SSI benefits. But when you reach age 65, your state might provide you with state supplement benefits as well as food stamps. If you don't fall into one of the above categories, you could still apply for both federal and state SSI assistance; you might be entitled to state benefits even if you're denied federal SSI.

Income Limits

To figure out whether your income is low enough to qualify for SSI, you first need to understand that there might actually be two SSI payments:

- the basic federal SSI payment, and
- a state supplemental payment (SSP) in some states. Most states pay an additional amount over and above the federal benefit, and some of these states pay it alone if you qualify for it, even if you don't qualify for the federal payment.

Not all your income is counted when deciding whether you qualify for SSI. In fact, more than half of your earned income—wages and self-employment income—is not counted. And even though you might have income over the allowable maximum for federal SSI payments, you might still qualify for your state's supplemental payment. That's because a few states set a higher income limit than the federal SSI program does, making it easier to qualify for those states' supplemental payment than for the federal one. (See "Benefit Amounts," below.)

The federal SSI limit on counted income is $943 per month for an individual (this means a total monthly earned income of about $1,900), or $2,500 per month for a couple. The exact figure varies

from state to state. In many states, you might qualify for the state's SSI supplemental payment—as well as Medicaid, SNAP food stamps, and other assistance—even if your counted income was too high to qualify for federal SSI.

Income That Is Counted

In general, half of any income you earn in wages or self-employment, plus any money you receive from investments, pensions, annuities, royalties, gifts, rents, or interest on savings is counted toward the SSI limits. Social Security benefits are also considered counted income. In addition, if you receive free housing from friends or relatives, SSI will attribute some value to that housing and reduce your SSI benefit. (See "Reductions to Benefits," below, regarding outside support.)

Income That Is Not Counted

Some specific amounts of money and support are not counted in determining whether you qualify for SSI benefits.

SSI won't count:

- the first $20 per month you receive from any source— except other public assistance based on need, such as General Assistance
- the first $65 per month of your earned income—wages or self-employment
- one-half of all your earned income over $65 a month
- irregular or infrequent earned income—such as from a one-time-only job—if such income isn't more than $10 a month
- irregular or infrequent unearned income—such as a gift or dividend on an investment—up to $20 per month
- food stamps, energy assistance, or housing assistance from a federal housing program run by a state or local government agency
- some work-related expenses for blind or disabled people that are paid for through public assistance
- some other types of one-time payments, such as tax refunds, reimbursement for financial losses such as insurance payments

for medical bills, or compensation for injury to you or your property, or

• up to $100,000 in a special "Achieving a Better Life Experience" (ABLE) bank account, if you became disabled before age 26.

Differences in Local Rules

Keeping in mind that different income limits apply in various states, one general suggestion applies to everyone: If you're age 65, blind, or disabled, and you're living on a small fixed income, and you have relatively few assets, apply for SSI benefits. The local Social Security or social welfare office might consider certain income differently than you do, and you might be pleasantly surprised to gain some help from SSI.

> EXAMPLE: Carmela receives Social Security survivors benefits of $310 a month and a $40-per-month private pension payment, for a total of $350 in regular unearned income. She also receives a quarterly dividend check; the most recent was $15.
>
> The dividend check would not be counted at all, because it's infrequent income less than $20 per month. The first $20 of income from any source isn't counted, so the $350 total of unearned income would be reduced to $330 of countable income.
>
> Carmela also earns $210 a month doing part-time work. Since the first $65 a month of earned income isn't counted, her earned income amount would be reduced to $145; and since one-half of all earned income over $65 a month isn't counted, half of $80 ($145 − $65) wouldn't be considered for SSI purposes.
>
> This leaves Carmela with $105 countable, earned income to be added to the $330 countable unearned income for the month, for a total of $435 countable income. Since this amount is under the basic SSI qualifying limit of $943 per month (in 2023), Carmela would be eligible for a federal SSI payment (though it would be reduced because of her income). Because Carmela lives in New York, where there is a small state supplemental benefit, she might be eligible for that amount as well. (See "States With Federally Administered Supplements," below.)

Asset Limits

In addition to the limits on your income, SSI rules limit the amount of assets and other resources you can have and still qualify. The general limit is $2,000 in assets for an individual, $3,000 for a married couple living together. But as with the rules regarding income, people are actually allowed more assets than these figures seem to indicate (most importantly, your home, household goods, and car—see below).

Assets That Are Counted

The assets or resources that are counted by SSI include money in the bank, investments of any kind, real estate other than a primary residence, and personal property and household goods over certain limits.

SSI also counts any money or property in which you have an interest, even if you're not the sole owner. If you have a joint bank account with someone, SSI will consider that you own the entire account, because you have access to all of it (but if a co-owner of the account also receives benefits, SSI will count only half the account as belonging to you).

Periodic Review of SSI Eligibility

Social Security periodically reviews your SSI eligibility and the amount of SSI you receive. These reviews take place every one to six years. When you receive a notice of review, you will have to produce the same kinds of information as you did for the original application: your income, assets, living arrangements, and, if claiming based on a disability, updated medical information. Often, most of this process can be handled by mail or telephone, although you might have to make a trip to the Social Security office for an interview. However, you do need to regularly report changes that might affect your eligibility, including changes in your income, address, living arrangements, and marital status.

If you hold any property in "joint tenancy" with someone else, SSI will consider that you own the entire properly. If you have only a partial interest in some property—for example, an ownership interest in a family home along with other family members, and you don't hold the property in joint tenancy—SSI will determine how much your individual ownership portion is worth and count that as an asset.

Assets That Are Not Counted

You're allowed to have more property than the $2,000 and $3,000 limits first seem to indicate. Several important categories of assets are not counted in determining your eligibility for SSI benefits. They include:

- your home and the land it sits on, regardless of value, as long as you live in it
- one automobile, regardless of market value
- your personal property and household goods—such as clothing, furniture, appliances, tools, sporting goods, hobby or craft material, and pets
- wedding and engagement rings, regardless of value
- property needed for medical reasons, such as wheelchairs, hospital beds, and prosthetics
- property essential to "self-support"—such as tools and machines used in your trade—up to a value of $6,000
- life insurance policies with a total face value of $1,500 or less per person, and term life insurance policies with no cash surrender value, and
- burial spaces for you and your spouse, plus a specially ear-marked fund of up to $1,500 for funeral and burial expenses.

EXAMPLE: Rose and Peter are living on Peter's Social Security retirement benefits and on Rose's pension. They qualify under SSI income limits and have the following assets: their home; a five-year-old car; $1,500 in savings; stocks worth $500; furniture and electronics worth about $550; Peter's tools, worth about $600; and Rose's jewelry, which, aside from her wedding band, is worth about $200.

Despite the fact that Rose and Peter's house is now worth $120,000, it isn't counted as an asset. The value of their car isn't counted at all. Their personal property and household goods add up to about $1,350, but none of it will be counted.

Their total counted assets would be their savings and stocks worth about $2,000. Since the SSI limit on resources is $3,000 for a couple, Rose and Peter would qualify for SSI benefits.

Selling or Spending Assets

Even if your countable assets appear to be over the limit, you might still qualify to receive some SSI benefits. The Social Security Administration has a special program where you can begin to receive SSI payments if you sell or spend enough property to come under the limits within a certain time period. That time period begins when you apply for benefits and runs nine months for real estate and three months for personal property and liquid assets.

> EXAMPLE: Mariana applies for SSI benefits when she has more than $5,000 in the bank. She's told that she won't be immediately eligible for benefits unless that amount is reduced to $2,000 within the next three months. Mariana had always planned to be buried near her deceased husband, but never got around to making the arrangements. She now buys a burial space for $2,000 in the same cemetery as her husband. Then she puts $1,000 in a special account to cover her funeral expenses. Since funeral and burial amounts aren't counted as assets under SSI rules, and her assets are now down to $2,000 (within three months of her application for SSI), she will begin receiving benefits as of the date she applied.

However, the sale or transfer must be a real one. Simply transferring title on the property to someone else while you keep control or use of it isn't enough; neither is selling something for a small token amount.

If Social Security does find out that you sold or transferred an asset for less than its market value, you could be ineligible for SSI for a certain number of months, depending on the value of the asset (up to a maximum of 36 months). The SSA can look at any asset transfer or sale that's less than three years before the date you apply for SSI.

Benefit Amounts

Because supplement payments vary from state to state, the amount of your SSI check will vary depending on where you live, as well as on the amount of your countable income. The basic federal SSI payment for 2024 is $943 a month for an individual and $1,415 a month for a couple. These figures usually go up on January 1 each year; the amount of increase depends on the rise in the federal Consumer Price Index.

States With Federally Administered Supplements

A number of states pay supplements to the basic federal SSI amount. In some of these states, the supplement is added on directly to the federal SSI payment. This means that a person needs to apply only once, to Social Security, to receive both the basic amount and the supplement. Both amounts are included in one payment, which is administered by Social Security.

The supplement amount might be different for blind and disabled recipients. Also, the amount might vary depending on whether the person receiving SSI lives alone, in the home of a family friend, in congregate living arrangements, or in a nursing facility.

States in which SSI recipients receive a federally administered supplement include:

California	Iowa	Pennsylvania
District of Columbia	Nevada	Rhode Island
Hawaii	New Jersey	Vermont

SSI Might Get You Medicaid

If you're found eligible for SSI benefits, most states will also give you free health coverage through the Medicaid program (called "Medi-Cal" in California). You don't need to qualify for Medicare to get Medicaid. For an explanation of what Medicaid offers, see Chapter 16.

Your enrollment is automatic in many states, including Alabama, Arizona, Arkansas, California, Colorado, Delaware, District of Columbia, Florida, Georgia, Indiana, Iowa, Kentucky, Louisiana, Maine, Maryland, Massachusetts, Michigan, Mississippi, Montana, New Jersey, New Mexico, New York, North Carolina, Ohio, Pennsylvania, Rhode Island, South Carolina, South Dakota, Tennessee, Texas, Vermont, Washington, West Virginia, Wisconsin, and Wyoming.

In other states, you must separately apply for Medicaid after being granted SSI. This usually involves submitting an application to a state social services or welfare office. Some states will automatically enroll you based on your SSI grant. Others have slightly more restrictive eligibility standards and will separately evaluate your Medicaid application.

The states that automatically enroll you after you separately apply for Medicaid are Alaska, Idaho, Kansas, Nebraska, Nevada, Oregon, and Utah. The states that make an independent decision about whether you're eligible for Medicaid are Connecticut, Hawaii, Illinois, Minnesota, Missouri, New Hampshire, North Dakota, Oklahoma, and Virginia.

In addition, Delaware and Montana have federally administered supplements that are available only to people who live in protective care arrangements (Delaware administers the state supplement for all others). Social Security administers the supplement for some SSI recipients in Iowa and Michigan.

States With Their Own Supplements

Most other states provide some kind of supplement to the basic federal SSI payment, but the kinds of supplements and rules for qualifying are administered entirely by the states. You must apply for these state supplements separately, at the social welfare agency in the county where you live.

Your supplement payments might range from a few dollars to a few hundred dollars above the basic federal SSI payment, or include noncash assistance with food, housing, transportation, and/or medical care. The amounts change frequently, based on the willingness of state legislatures to provide for SSI recipients in their state budgets.

Reductions to Benefits

Your maximum SSI benefit amount will be reduced by income you make over allowable countable limits, as dictated by a number of specific rules.

Limit on Earned Income

Your benefits are reduced by one dollar for every two dollars more than $65 per month that you earn in wages or self-employment.

> EXAMPLE: Ronda has a part-time job at which she earns $280 a month. She is entitled to the basic federal SSI benefit of $943 per month, but that amount is reduced by $107.50 because of her earnings. (The total of $107.50 is arrived at by taking the amount of her earned income that is more than $65 ($215) and dividing it in half—$1 out of every $2 over the limit.) Her monthly income would then be her earnings of $280 plus her SSI benefit of $835.50, for a total of $1,115.50.

Limit on Unearned Income

Your benefits are reduced dollar for dollar by the amount of any *unearned* income you receive that is more than $20 a month. This unearned income includes Social Security benefits, pensions, annuities, interest on savings, dividends, or any money from investments or property you own.

> EXAMPLE: Carl lives alone in a home he owns. His only income is his Social Security retirement check of $330 per month. From Carl's $330 Social Security check, $20 is excluded, making his total countable unearned income $310. Since he has no earned income, his total countable income would be the same: $310. In the state in which Carl lives, the basic SSI payment is $1,000 per month. From this, Carl's total countable income of $310 is subtracted, leaving $690 as Carl's monthly SSI payment.

Limit on Outside Support

Your basic SSI payment will be reduced by up to one-third if you live in a relative's or friend's home without paying rent and/or you receive regular, substantial support in the form of food, clothing, and personal items.

> EXAMPLE: Adam lives in his daughter's house without paying rent. His daughter also provides Adam all of his meals. Adam's only income is his $370 per month Social Security check. The basic monthly SSI benefit of $943 in Adam's state would be reduced by one-third ($314) because Adam receives both regular food and free lodging from his daughter. This would leave an SSI amount of $629. In determining Adam's countable income, SSI doesn't count $20 of his $370 Social Security check, leaving a total countable amount of $350. This $350 is subtracted from his reduced SSI benefit, leaving an actual monthly SSI payment to Adam of $279, in addition to his Social Security benefit.

Limit on Working Couples

A final example shows how SSI amounts are figured for a couple, and how SSI payments change when one person takes a job.

EXAMPLE: Beverly marries Carl and together they collect a monthly Social Security check of $755. In figuring Carl and Beverly's SSI payment, $20 would be exempted from the $755 Social Security check, for a total countable income of $735 a month. That $735 would be subtracted from the basic SSI benefit for a couple, which in Carl and Beverly's state is $1,500, leaving a monthly SSI payment of $765.

When Beverly takes a part-time job paying $100 a month, their SSI payment changes. Beverly and Carl's countable unearned income is still the same, $735 a month—their Social Security check minus $20. But now they have an earned income of $100 a month. The first $65 of this $100 is not counted under SSI rules. Of the remaining $35 of earned income, only one-half of it, or $17.50, is considered counted income. Only $17.50 is added to the $735 of counted unearned income, making a total countable income of $752.50 a month.

The basic SSI benefit for a couple in Carl and Beverly's state is $1,500 a month. The $752.50 countable income would be subtracted from this amount, leaving a monthly SSI payment to Carl and Beverly of $747.50. Their monthly income would be their Social Security check of $755, plus their part-time income of $100, plus their SSI check of $747.50.

Applying for Benefits

Once you get an accurate estimate of how much your Social Security benefits will be and decide when it's best to begin receiving them, applying for those benefits is usually fairly simple. For retirement, dependents, or survivors benefits, most people will already have on hand all the documents needed and can complete their application in a single trip to a local Social Security office; some of the work can also be done ahead of time online. Applying for disability benefits is more complex and usually takes longer, but it can also go smoothly if you're prepared with the proper documents. This chapter discusses the application process for each type of benefit and explains how to organize the required documents.

Retirement, Dependents, and Survivors Benefits

The application processes for retirement benefits, dependents benefits, and survivors benefits all involve the same basic documents and procedures. The hardest part is figuring out the best time to claim benefits. For this, you must understand the relationship between your age and the amount you'll receive.

When to Claim Benefits

You might be eligible for different types of benefits at different times in your life—for example, survivors benefits at age 60, based on your deceased spouse's work record, and retirement benefits at age 62, based on your own work record. And you are eligible for increased benefits for every month you wait to claim them up to age 70.

As a result, your decision about which benefits to claim and when to claim them should be based on how much each benefit would be (measured against the earnings limit for your age, if you intend to continue working) and other factors such as life expectancy and your current need for cash. (For reductions due to earnings, see Chapter 2; for reductions for working dependents,

see Chapter 4; for reductions for working survivors, see Chapter 5; and for options about choosing between different benefits and deciding when to claim them, see Chapter 6.)

To see how much each type of benefit would be at different ages, take a look at your Social Security statement, which you can view online (see Chapter 1). You should examine your statement about six months before you might claim any benefit. This will give you plenty of time to decide what's best for you, and to get the process started if you choose to file soon for benefits.

How and Where to File Your Claim

All Social Security claims for benefits can be filed at local Social Security offices. In addition, an application for retirement, dependents, survivors, and disability benefits can be initiated by phone or through the internet (see "Begin your application process online," below). Even online applications often require a visit to a local office to complete, however.

Most sizable cities have at least one local Social Security office, and in major urban areas there are usually several. To find the address and telephone number of the nearest office, go to www.ssa. gov/locator or call the SSA at 800-772-1213.

The following subsections describe how to get personal assistance with and local information about filing your claim.

Help on the Internet

The Social Security Administration now offers a good deal of information and some of its application processes online at www.ssa.gov. Some of the information can be hard to locate, but Social Security is making good progress in helping people to apply for many Social Security benefits online.

You can also find a lot of information to help you with a disability claim at www.disabilitysecrets.com.

ONLINE

Begin your application process online. Social Security allows people to use its website to file many types of claims for benefits, which might save you one or more trips to a Social Security office.

You can file an online application—or at least begin the process—for:

- retirement benefits
- disability benefits
- dependents benefits (spousal benefits only)
- Supplemental Security Income (SSI)
- Medicare Part A and Part B, and
- Extra Help for Medicare Part D.

To learn more about what Social Security allows you to do over the internet, see its webpage "Online Services" at www.ssa.gov/onlineservices.

Help in Person

A Social Security worker in your local office is usually the best source of information and assistance for filing your claim. Face-to-face conversation is almost always more productive than discussions over the phone or via email. And when you're ready to file your application, handing it to a real person is more secure than sending it by mail.

Most offices permit you to phone in advance and make an appointment to speak to someone personally—a good idea, because you might face long lines if you show up unannounced.

Whenever you consult with someone in a Social Security office, write down the person's name and keep it with your other Social Security papers. That way, when you next contact the office, you can ask to speak with the same person, or you can refer to that person if a question arises about what occurred during your previous visit.

When filing papers, make sure the office gives you some proof that you filed—for example, bring along your personal copy of the application and ask them to stamp it "received" with the date.

Help Over the Telephone

Social Security offers advice and help over its toll-free phone line at 800-772-1213. The phone lines are open between 7 a.m. and 7 p.m. local time Monday through Friday. It's busiest at the beginning

of the month and early in each week, so choose your time to call accordingly. While the phone line has long wait times, you can accomplish a great deal over the phone. The Social Security workers can answer your general questions about benefits and rules and tell you how to fill out or submit a particular form. They might also be able to start your claim process for retirement and dependents benefits.

However, the application process can't be completed over the phone. Before your claim can actually be processed, you'll have to sign a written application and bring certain original documents to Social Security (see "Documents You'll Need," below).

For Early Retirement, Sign Up Three Months Before Your Birthday

If you decide to receive a Social Security benefit payment as soon as you reach the youngest eligible age, file your claim three months before the birthday on which you'll become eligible. This will give Social Security time to process your claim so that you'll receive benefits as soon as you become eligible. If you file a claim for early retirement after you first become eligible, you can't get benefits retroactively for the months during which you were eligible but had not applied. (If you file after full retirement age, on the other hand, you can receive six months of retroactive benefits.)

What about Medicare? At age 65, anyone eligible for Social Security benefits is also eligible for Medicare coverage (explained in Chapter 13). Even if you aren't going to claim Social Security benefits by the time you reach age 65, you should sign up for Medicare coverage three months before your 65th birthday. There's no reason to delay signing up for Medicare, and waiting until after your 65th birthday will delay coverage. If you have current health care coverage through your employer when you turn 65, you might want to sign up for Part A only. (See Chapter 12 for more information.)

Getting the Best Results:
Preparation, Patience, Perseverance

Social Security offices are usually understaffed. Although individual Social Security workers are often helpful, polite, and well versed in the various regulations that govern Social Security programs, the maze of rules, when added to normal human fallibility, inevitably makes for occasional delays, misunderstandings, and mistakes.

It's up to you to help yourself. The most important thing is to keep your papers organized. During the benefit application process, you can mail papers and forms to your local Social Security office. However, it's best to deliver important papers—any original document or certified copy—in person. That way, the papers not only will be sure to get to the local office but also will go directly into your file. This will cut some time off the process and will help to avoid the misadventures that sometimes befall papers that go into Social Security's incoming mail stacks. Keep copies of any form or document you submit to Social Security.

If the local Social Security office asks to see the original or a certified copy, it will usually make a copy on the spot and return the original to you. It's also best to keep a copy in your files in case the original gets lost.

Documents You'll Need

Whether you file for a Social Security benefit in person at a local Social Security office or do all or some of it online through the Social Security website, you'll need to have certain personal papers or information. What you need will depend upon the type of benefit you're applying for, as explained below.

Most documents required by Social Security must be originals or certified copies. However, if you want to apply for benefits right away but don't yet have all your documents together, file your claim

anyway—either by phone, on the internet, or by going to your local Social Security office. The Social Security workers will advise you about how to get the documents you need, and, in the meantime, the application process can begin.

CAUTION

Make sure all your papers can be traced to you. On any copy of a document you bring or send to Social Security, write your name as it appears on your benefit application and your Social Security number. If you're filing for survivors or dependents benefits, also include the name and Social Security number of the person on whose work record you'rre claiming benefits. If you bring or send an original document, clip a piece of paper to it with those names and numbers.

When you apply for any type of benefit, bring with you the number of your account at a bank, a credit union, or another financial institution. Social Security will arrange to have your monthly benefit payment directly deposited to your account. Direct deposit is now used for all Social Security and SSI beneficiaries. It saves money for the Social Security Administration and also avoids the problem of lost or stolen checks.

Retirement Benefits

You may need some or all of the following documents or information to apply for retirement benefits:

- your Social Security number. You don't need your actual Social Security card.
- your birth certificate. If you don't have a birth certificate, bring any other evidence of the date of your birth: baptism record, military papers, immigration papers, driver's license, or passport.
- your military discharge papers, if you served in the military, and
- your most recent W-2 tax form or federal self-employment tax return.

Dependents Benefits

You may need some or all of the following documents or information to apply for dependents benefits:

- marriage certificate, if you're applying for benefits based on your spouse's work record
- divorce papers, if you're applying as a divorced spouse, and
- birth certificate of any child claiming benefits. If you don't have a birth certificate, bring other evidence of the date of your child's birth: baptism record, immigration papers, or passport.

Survivors Benefits

You may need some or all of the following documents or information to apply for survivors benefits:

- Social Security number of the deceased person on whose work record you're claiming benefits, and your own Social Security number
- divorce papers, if you're applying as a divorced spouse
- death certificate of your deceased spouse or ex-spouse
- your birth certificate and those of your children who are claiming benefits. If a birth certificate isn't available, bring other evidence of date of birth: baptism record, military papers, immigration papers, or passport.
- if your spouse died within the past two years, the most recent W-2 tax form or federal self-employment tax return of your deceased spouse, and
- if applying as a surviving dependent parent who was receiving support from your son or daughter who died, a recent tax return from your deceased child showing you as a dependent, or proof of expenditures by your deceased child showing how much support was given to you, as well as your own most recent tax returns.

If You Retire From Your Own Business

If you're self-employed and are claiming retirement benefits before your full retirement age, Social Security might require some extra information from you. They'll want to see evidence that you are really giving up full-time work and not merely shifting your pay (in name only) to someone else.

The reason for this concern is the rule that retirement benefits will be reduced if you are under full retirement age and earn income over certain limits. (See Chapter 2 for these limits.) Some people with their own businesses try to get around this rule by continuing to work and paying a relative instead of themselves, or by continuing to run the business but being paid only for reduced work time.

Social Security is likely to ask for information regarding your continuing involvement with your own business if any of the following are true:

- You maintain ownership of the business.
- Other family members are involved in the business and a relative is assuming most of your previous duties.
- You continue to work for the business at lower pay.
- You control the amount you work and how much you're paid, such that you could manipulate either one.
- Your relatives now receive the salary you previously earned.

Social Security might ask for such documents as the business's pay and personnel records, personal and business tax returns, stock transfer agreements, and business expense records. Try to contact your local Social Security office several months in advance, so that you'll learn what documents Social Security wants and have time to gather the documents.

If Social Security determines that you provide services to the business that exceed the amount you're paid—based on the time you spend, the level of your responsibility, and the value of services you provide—the agency might attach a dollar value to those services. If this dollar value exceeds the amount of earned income permitted for early retirement, your benefits might be reduced.

At the Social Security Office

When submitting your claim at your local Social Security office, you'll be interviewed by a case worker. If you haven't already submitted your application form online or over the telephone, the worker will help you fill out the form. The worker will open a file for you, which from then on will contain all of the documents pertaining to your application.

Write down the name of the worker who talks with you, and their direct telephone line if available, so that you can speak with the same person if you need to call in to provide or receive further information. The Social Security worker will make copies of the documents you've brought and will explain what other information is needed to process your application.

If additional documents are needed, ask whether you can mail in copies instead of bringing originals in person.

When you first apply, don't expect to be told precisely how much your benefits will be. Exact benefit amounts are based upon the computerized records kept at the Social Security Administration's national records center. Your precise benefit amount will be calculated there.

Applications take six to eight weeks to be processed, but when you receive your first payment, it will include benefits back to the date you first applied, or to the date on which you're first eligible, whichever is later (except in the case of disability benefits).

Withdrawing a Benefits Application

After you turn in your application for retirement, dependents, or survivors benefits, your work situation might change, altering significantly the amount of benefits to which you're entitled. This might, for example, occur in one of the following situations:
- you're offered a new position, a new job, or an increased salary
- you're not laid off from a job you expected to lose
- you're called back to work after a temporary job loss, or
- you simply change your mind and decide to continue working full time.

In any of these situations, if the income you earn at your continued work significantly exceeds the earnings limit for early retirement, it might eat up your benefits. If so, your decision to claim early benefits might prove to be a poor one, because you'll receive little or no benefit payments while you continue to work, and your benefit amount will be permanently lower than if you had waited to file your claim at a later age.

You can withdraw your application within 12 months after first becoming eligible for benefits, if you repay all the benefits you've received so far, including any Medicare premiums that were automatically paid out of your monthly Social Security payments. You'll also need to get the consent of all dependents who are receiving benefits based on your work record (except for certain divorced spouses). To withdraw your claim, go to Social Security's webpage on canceling your benefits application at www.ssa.gov/manage-benefits/cancel-your-benefits-application, which explains the procedure and also the amounts you will have to repay. You can also make an appointment at a local Social Security office to discuss with a Social Security worker the process and consequences of withdrawing your application.

Disability Benefits

Eligibility for disability benefits depends upon your physical or mental condition, and your inability to work because of that condition. (See Chapter 3 for a more detailed account of the eligibility requirements.) Because the disability determination process involves these qualifying standards, the application requires much more time and effort than other Social Security benefit applications do. You must get and keep your papers organized, and be thorough and persistent in your contacts both with doctors and with Social Security personnel.

RESOURCE

Proving that your particular medical condition makes you unable to work may not be easy. This book provides an introduction, but for more information and specialized advice concerning particular physical and mental conditions, see *Nolo's Guide to Social Security Disability: Getting & Keeping Your Benefits*, by David A. Morton III, M.D. (Nolo).

When to File Your Claim

You won't be paid any disability benefits until you've been disabled for five full months. This waiting period begins with the first full month after the date your disability began. That date is usually the date you stopped working, or significantly reduced your work hours, because of your physical or mental condition.

However, disability claims take two to eight months for an initial decision. So, don't wait for the five months of disability to pass before filing your claim. You don't even need to wait to gather all the necessary information and doctors' reports. You can file the claim as soon as your medical condition forces you off work and the doctors expect that it will prevent you from working for a year or more. You can complete the gathering of necessary documents while the claim is being processed, with the help of your local Social Security office.

Fast Claims for Severe Medical Conditions

The Social Security Administration has created a streamlined disability benefits claims process for people with certain severe medical conditions. For these people, the Social Security Administration will process benefit claims within a few days or weeks of completing the application. There are more than 200 conditions for which this fast application process, called "Compassionate Allowance," applies. To see the list of conditions and to get more information, go to the Social Security website: www.ssa.gov/compassionateallowances.

Documents You'll Need

When you file an application for Social Security disability benefits, whether online or in person at a local Social Security office, you may need some or all of the following documents or information:

- your Social Security number and proof of age (such as a birth certificate) for yourself and any person eligible for dependents benefits

- names, addresses, and phone numbers of doctors, hospitals, clinics, and other health care institutions that might have diagnosed your medical condition and given estimates of the length of time it's expected to keep you disabled, plus the approximate dates of your treatment. Although you're not required to produce medical records of your disability—Social Security can request them directly from doctors and hospitals—you might speed up the process if you bring copies of key medical records you already have.
- a list of where you've worked in the past 15 years and a description of the kinds of work you did
- a copy of the past year's W-2 forms, or your last federal income tax return if you're self-employed
- the dates of any military service
- information concerning any other type of disability payment you're receiving
- if your spouse is applying for dependents benefits based on your work record, the date of your marriage and of any prior marriages. A certified copy of divorce papers will provide this information.
- if you're applying as a disabled widow or widower, your spouse's Social Security number and a copy of the death certificate, and
- if you're applying as a disabled surviving divorced husband or wife, proof that your marriage lasted 10 years. Marriage and divorce papers will serve this purpose.

If you're physically unable to get to a Social Security office in person, or you're unable to complete the forms or meet other filing requirements, your application can be completed by your spouse, a parent, another relative, a friend, or your legal guardian. And once the initial claim has been filed, a service worker in the local Social Security office can assist you by having the Social Security office directly request necessary documents.

How Your Eligibility Is Determined

Applications for disability benefits go through several stages. Initially, you'll fill out an application at a local Social Security office or online and provide documents regarding your age and employment. After that, however, the process becomes more complicated, as Social Security determines whether your condition is actually disabling according to its standards.

Disability Determination Services

When your application has been completed, the local Social Security office will check to see that you're not working a significant amount and you meet all the general requirements regarding work credits for your age (see Chapter 3 for the work credit requirements). Then, the office will forward your claim to a Disability Determination Services (DDS) office in your state. The DDS office will use your medical records and employment history to decide whether you're disabled under the rules of the Social Security law.

The decision at DDS is made by a disability claims examiner with the help of a doctor or psychologist. They examine all of the medical records you provided with your application and might request more information from you, your doctors, and your employers.

Based on these records, the claims examiner and doctor determine whether your disability is expected to last more than one year and whether it's severe enough to interfere with your ability to continue performing any of the work you have done over the past 15 years. If they agree that you can't do your past work, they'll then determine whether your condition is so severe that you can't perform any type of "substantial gainful work." (See "Unable to Do Substantial Gainful Activity" in Chapter 3 for more on how Social Security determines this.)

If your existing medical records show your condition limits you from performing even the easiest type of substantial gainful work, you will be found eligible for benefits. If not, your claims examiner might request further medical records and/or refer you for a consultative physical examination.

Enlisting the Help of Your Doctor

Your medical records will be the biggest factor in the state DDS office's determination of your eligibility for disability benefits. Therefore, what your doctor puts in your records can be all-important.

If possible, discuss the matter with your doctor before you file your application for disability benefits. Inform your doctor that you intend to apply, and ask your doctor to make specific notations in your medical records of how your physical activities—particularly work-related activities, such as walking, sitting, lifting, carrying—are limited or how your mental or emotional condition affects your ability to regularly perform work. Ask also for your doctor to make a note of when your disability reached a point that it likely interfered with your ability to work.

Don't ask the doctor to give an opinion about whether you're disabled according to Social Security guidelines. Doctors will readily describe a specific medical condition, but many are unwilling to give an opinion about your ability to do any work at all. And, in any event, the DDS evaluation team wouldn't accept your doctor's opinion on this ultimate question of eligibility. Instead, the DDS team will base its determination on its own evaluation of your condition and limitations as they appear in your medical records.

In determining the nature and extent of your disability, the DDS will rely most heavily on the opinions of medical doctors, nurse practitioners, physician assistants, and psychologists, as opposed to physical therapists, chiropractors, and other healers. This reflects the fact that physicians, nurses, and PAs have diagnostic tools—such as laboratory tests, X-rays, MRIs, and other procedures—that are not usually available to nonphysician healers.

Medical Examinations

In some cases, the DDS claims examiner may not feel that they can come to a conclusion about your disability based on your existing medical records. They might request further reports from doctors

who have examined or treated you. And they might request that you undergo a medical evaluation called a "consultative examination."

Social Security pays the cost of the additional reports, examinations, or tests. If you must travel outside your immediate area to get to a physical examination, Social Security can pay for the cost of that travel, if you request it.

This extra examination or testing is often done by a physician who has already examined or treated you. This is particularly true if one of your doctors is a specialist in the area of medicine that deals directly with your disability. In other words, if you've seen an orthopedic surgeon for your back problem, Social Security is likely to have that same doctor perform the consultative examination.

However, if you haven't been treated by a specialist in the field—for example, if only your internist or general practitioner has treated you for a particular medical problem—Social Security will probably send you to another doctor for this examination.

Consultative examinations are limited to specific issues the DDS needs to clarify regarding your ability to work. The exam often involves certain kinds of tests that your doctor hasn't recently performed and that give DDS specific information on the extent of your disability. For example, Social Security might order a consultative exam for range of motion tests if your disability involves restricted movement.

The DDS will set up the examination and send the doctor a written request for the information needed and any specific tests it wants performed. The doctor won't conduct a general examination and won't prescribe any treatment for you. On rare occasions, a representative from DDS will attend the examination to record specific test results. The doctor will send a report to DDS describing the results of the examination, but they won't take part in the final decision about whether you're eligible for disability benefits.

Even though you might not like the idea of going through another medical examination, especially if it's by a doctor you don't know, you must cooperate with the DDS to successfully process your disability claim.

Vocational Rehabilitative Services

When you apply for disability benefits, you might be referred to your state's vocational rehabilitation agency for a determination of whether any of its services might be of help to you. These free services can include job counseling, job retraining and placement, and specialized medical assistance. The services can also train you to use devices—such as a modified computer keyboard—that might enable you to work despite your disability.

Supplemental Security Income (SSI)

You can file a claim for SSI benefits at your local Social Security office at the same time you file for disability benefits. (See Chapter 7 for a full discussion of the SSI program.) If you file for SSDI, the claims representative will ask you if you're interested in also filing for SSI.

If you believe you might be close to the qualifying income and asset limits for SSI benefits, go ahead and apply. If your state offers a separate state-administered supplementary payment in addition to the basic federal SSI payment, you might have to apply separately for that supplement at your local county social welfare office.

The process of applying for SSI benefits is very similar to applying for Social Security benefits. You will need to provide the same general documents. (See "Retirement, Dependents, and Survivors Benefits," above, for instructions.) However, unlike Social Security benefit applications, SSI benefit applications also require that you show records of your income and assets.

Proof of Income and Assets for SSI

Regardless of whether you're applying for SSI payments due to disability or blindness or because you're over age 65, you must bring information regarding your income and assets. This includes:

- information about where you live: for homeowners, a copy of your mortgage papers or tax bill; for renters, a copy of your rental agreement or lease and the name and address of the landlord

- documents indicating your current earned income, such as pay stubs and income tax returns
- papers showing all your financial assets, such as bank books, insurance policies, stock certificates, car registration, and
- information about your spouse's income and assets, if the two of you live together.

Even if you don't have all these papers available, you can go to your local Social Security office and file your application for SSI as soon as you think you might qualify for assistance. The Social Security workers can tell you how to get whatever other papers and records are necessary, and in some instances will get copies of the required records for you.

Proof of Age If 65 or Older

If you're age 65 or older, bring your Social Security number and proof of your age, such as a birth certificate. If you don't have a birth certificate, bring other evidence of the date of your birth: baptism record, military papers, immigration papers, driver's license, or passport. If you're already receiving any kind of Social Security benefit, you don't have to bring proof of your age.

Proof of Blindness or Disability

The process for proving that you're blind or disabled for purposes of SSI benefits is the same as the disability determination process when qualifying for Social Security disability benefits. (See Chapter 3 for the medical eligibility requirements.) The information you need to gather and the process of applying for disability benefits is discussed in "Disability Benefits," above.

Proof of Citizenship or Qualifying Legal Residence

For a reminder of what immigration status you must hold in order to qualify for SSI, see Chapter 7.

If you're a U.S. citizen, you'll need to prove your citizenship by showing a copy of your birth certificate, baptismal record, U.S. passport, or naturalization papers.

If you're a noncitizen, bring proof of your qualifications under one of the categories listed in Chapter 7.

For proof of work for 10 years (one way of qualifying for SSI as a permanent resident), bring your legal resident alien card ("green card") and Social Security numbers for yourself and your spouse. The Social Security or local welfare office will use the numbers to check your reported Social Security taxes.

If you seek to qualify as a veteran of the U.S. Armed Forces, bring evidence of honorable discharge from the military. You will also need a copy of your marriage certificate if you're seeking SSI as the spouse of a veteran.

Finding Out What Happens to Your Claim

You won't find out from your local Social Security office whether your claim for benefits has been approved; that word has to come from the Social Security Administration in Washington, D.C.

Notification of Eligibility

Social Security will notify you in writing whether your claim has been approved, how much your benefits will be, and when you will get your first check.

From the time the application is filed, a retirement, dependents, or survivors claim usually takes from four to eight weeks. A disability claim can take up to eight months.

For all retirement, dependents, or survivors claims, you'll receive benefits dating back to the date you first applied, or first became eligible if you applied before you reached an age of eligibility. The timing of Social Security disability payments is discussed below.

SSI benefits based on age usually begin four to eight weeks after you complete the necessary paperwork. If your claim is based on a disability that hasn't already been established for Social Security disability payments, it might take three to eight months. When you do finally get your money, however, it will cover the period from the month after you filed your claim.

If you were unable to work for more than five months before applying for Social Security disability benefits, you could get benefits going back to your application date. You can actually get retroactive benefits going back to 12 months before your application date, if Social Security determines that your disability actually began 17 months before your application date.

If your claim for any Social Security or SSI benefit is denied, the written notice of denial will state the reasons why. You have a right to appeal a denial of your claim. Your appeal must be submitted within 60 days from the date you receive written notice of the denial or other decision. (See Chapter 9 for appeal procedures.)

When You Need Money in a Hurry

It's possible to get some SSI payments even before your claim is finally approved. If you appear to be eligible for SSI and you need immediate cash to meet a financial emergency, the Social Security office can issue you an advance payment. The amount of this emergency payment will be deducted from your first regular SSI check.

Similarly, if you've already qualified for Social Security disability benefits and you appear financially eligible for SSI, you can be approved for and begin receiving SSI benefits immediately.

If you're financially eligible for SSI and appear to meet the disability requirements, but your disability application hasn't yet been approved by Social Security, you might be able to receive SSI payments while your claim is being reviewed by the disability office. These are called "presumptive disability payments," and they don't need to be repaid. You can get up to six months of presumptive payments.

Methods of Receiving Payment

All new beneficiaries receive their Social Security and SSI benefits by direct deposit into their bank accounts or with a Direct Express debit card. It is also possible for a representative payee to receive payments on your behalf. You must indicate on the application which payment option you choose. You can change your method of payment after you begin to receive benefits.

Direct Deposit

Direct deposit has a number of advantages: You don't have to wait for your check to arrive in the mail, nor do you have to travel to your bank to deposit the check. And you don't have to worry about a check being lost or stolen.

When you first sign up for benefits, you'll give Social Security the name and address of your bank branch and the number of the account where you want the funds deposited.

If you change banks—or want to close one account and open another—you can change your direct deposit information online in your Social Security account or by calling Social Security at 800-772-1213. But don't close your old account until you see that your benefit has appeared in your new one. If your benefit continues to be deposited in the old account, contact your local Social Security office.

Debit Card

Some Social Security recipients don't want to receive their payments by direct deposit. For example, you might not want to pay the bank charge to maintain an account. Or, you might be moving and temporarily won't have a local bank account. If, for any reason, you don't want to receive your benefit payment by direct deposit, you can arrange with your local Social Security office to receive your payments via a Direct Express debit card.

Substitute Payee

If you're unable to handle your own banking, you can have a family member, close friend, or legal representative receive your benefit payments on your behalf. That person must spend the money according to your wishes or directions. This can be done informally, by simply adding the other person as a joint account holder on the bank account where Social Security deposits your check. The bank can make this arrangement for you.

If you need some oversight on how that person spends your benefits, you can have this other person officially appointed by Social Security as a representative payee. That person would then personally receive the benefit payments on your behalf. Social Security can also appoint someone to be your representative payee against your wishes if the agency believes you're unable to manage your finances.

Anyone proposing to be your representative payee must bring to the local Social Security office medical proof—for example, a letter from your doctor—that you're unable to handle financial matters for yourself. The representative payee must sign a sworn affidavit at the Social Security office stating that they will use the Social Security check solely for your benefit. The Social Security office will then verify your medical condition and the identity of the representative payee.

If a person has already been appointed by a court to serve as legal guardian or conservator, proof of that court appointment is all that is required to be appointed representative payee. But people who are named to act in powers of attorney don't automatically qualify as representative payees; they must still apply for representative payee status at the local Social Security office.

The rules require that a representative payee deposit and keep the money belonging to the person entitled to Social Security in a separate bank account and periodically file an accounting with Social Security to show how the money has been spent to care for the beneficiary. The representative payee should keep all bills and receipts in a systematic and organized way so they can be produced easily.

Appealing a Social Security Decision

No matter how certain you feel that you deserve Social Security benefits, the agency might have other ideas and deny your claim. Sometimes this is a mere mistake that can be corrected. More often, the decision was a matter of judgment, especially with disability claims, where questions about medical conditions, ability to work, or income levels are subjective and susceptible to different interpretations.

But if your application for benefits is initially denied or is granted but you're awarded less than you believe you deserve, that need not be the end of the matter. Virtually all decisions of the Social Security Administration can be appealed, and many appeals, especially with regard to disability, are successful.

If Social Security has denied a new benefit or reduced an existing benefit, you can appeal the decision as long as you follow some fairly simple rules and are willing to think creatively about how to present your case in a convincing way. You'll need to put yourself into the shoes of the Social Security workers who first denied your claim, try to understand their reasoning, and then provide convincing evidence so that the next person who sees your file during the appeal process won't view your claim in exactly the same way.

This chapter explains the four possible levels of appeal following any Social Security decision. The first level is called "reconsideration"; it's an informal review that takes place in the local Social Security or Disability Determination Services (DDS) office where your claim was filed.

The second level is a hearing before an administrative law judge (an ALJ); this is an independent review of what the local Social Security office or Disability Determination Services office has decided.

The third level is an appeal to Social Security's national Appeals Council in Falls Church, Virginia. And the final level is filing a lawsuit in federal court.

RESOURCE

Get extra advice regarding disability appeals. More than 90% of all Social Security appeals involve claims for disability benefits (including SSI). Most of these appeals revolve around whether the applicant's physical or mental condition actually prevents gainful employment. Proving this requires careful presentation of medical information as well as completing certain special forms. This book will give you an introduction to this process, but for more information and specialized advice for various physical and mental conditions, see *Nolo's Guide to Social Security Disability: Getting & Keeping Your Benefits*, by David A. Morton III, M.D. (Nolo), and www.disabilitysecrets.com.

CAUTION

Beware of the time limit for filing appeals. The same time limit applies to each step of the appeals process. From the date on the written notice of Social Security's decision—whether denying or granting a benefit—you have 60 days to file a written notice that you're appealing that decision to the next stage in the process. If you receive the notice by mail, you have an additional five days to file your notice of appeal.

Reconsideration of Decision

When a claim for any type of Social Security benefits—retirement, disability, dependents, survivors—or SSI is denied, or an existing benefit is ended, or you receive an amount that's less than what you believe you're entitled to, the first step to appeal that decision is to request reconsideration.

If the negative decision involved a denial of Social Security benefits, follow the procedures discussed below. Some additional procedures to follow when appealing denial of an SSI claim are discussed in "Requesting Reconsideration of SSI Decision," below.

Is an Appeal Worth the Effort?

The first question that might occur to you when considering an appeal is whether it is worth the effort.

Let's start with some encouraging numbers: A substantial percentage of decisions are changed on appeal, particularly disability appeals, half of which are favorably changed in the appeal process.

Appealing a Social Security claim need not be terribly difficult. If you properly organized and prepared your original claim, most of your work for the appeal has already been done. In many situations, the appeal will require little more from you than explaining once more why the information you already presented should qualify you for a benefit. In other cases, it will involve presenting one or two additional pieces of information that better explain your situation to Social Security personnel. In all disability cases, you should submit information from your doctor about more recent visits or test results.

A negative Social Security decision can affect your rights for many years. Because it's so important, and because the appeal process is relatively simple, it's almost always worth the effort to appeal, especially for a disability claim.

Requesting Reconsideration of Decision on Initial Benefits Claim

To start the appeal process, you file a written request for review of the decision, called a *Request for Reconsideration* (SSA-561-U2). The form is available online from Social Security's website at www.ssa.gov/forms/ssa-561.pdf. You can also obtain a copy at your local Social Security office or by calling Social Security at 800-772-1213. See a sample of the form below. If you were denied Social Security disability or SSI benefits for medical reasons, you can file a request for reconsideration online.

The printed form comes in duplicate: a top copy for the Claims Folder (the Social Security office's copy) and a bottom Claimant's Copy (for you). You fill in only the top part of the form. The information requested is straightforward: name, address, Social Security number, and type of claim—retirement, disability, dependents, or survivors.

The appeals process is explained in the sections below. Social Security also provides information about the appeals process on its website at www.ssa.gov/benefits/disability/appeal.html.

Completing the Request for Reconsideration Form

The first few lines of the *Request for Reconsideration* form are fairly simple. On the top left, fill in your own name, exactly as it appears on your Social Security card.

On the top right is the box for the Social Security claim number. Copy that number from the written decision about your claim that you received from Social Security.

The most important part of the form follows the words: "I do not agree with the Social Security Administration's (SSA) determination and request reconsideration. My reasons are: …." On those lines, state briefly and simply why you think you were unfairly denied your benefits.

You need not go into great detail, because your entire file will be examined—including any additional materials you want to submit. Your statement should simply identify the problem, such as: "The decision that I am not disabled was based on insufficient evidence about my condition. I am submitting an additional letter from my doctor about my condition." Or: "The DDS evaluation of my disability did not take into account my inability to sit for prolonged periods."

Along with your completed *Request for Reconsideration* form, you need to submit a form called a *Disability Report—Appeal* (SSA-3441-BK) to explain any changes in your condition since you filed your original claim for benefits and tell Social Security about

Form **SSA-561-U2** (10-2022) UF
Discontinue Prior Editions
Social Security Administration

Page 1 of 4
OMB No. 0960-0622

REQUEST FOR RECONSIDERATION

NAME OF CLAIMANT:	CLAIMANT SSN:	CLAIM NUMBER: *(If different than SSN)*

ISSUE BEING APPEALED: *(Specify if retirement, disability, hospital or medical, SSI, SVB, overpayment, etc.)*

I do not agree with the Social Security Administration's (SSA) determination and request reconsideration.
My reasons are:

SUPPLEMENTAL SECURITY INCOME (SSI) OR SPECIAL VETERANS BENEFITS (SVB) RECONSIDERATION ONLY

THREE WAYS TO APPEAL

I want to appeal your determination about my claim for **SSI** or **SVB**. I have read about the three ways to appeal. I have checked the box below:

☐ **CASE REVIEW - You can pick this kind of appeal in all cases.** You can give us more facts to add to your file. Then we will decide your case again. You do not meet with the person who decides your case.

☐ **INFORMAL CONFERENCE - You can pick this kind of appeal in all SSI cases except for medical issues. In SVB cases, you can pick this kind of appeal only if we are stopping or lowering your SVB payment.** You will meet with a person who will decide your case. You can tell that person why you think you are right. You can give us more facts to help prove you are right. You can bring other people to help explain your case.

☐ **FORMAL CONFERENCE - You can pick this kind of appeal only if we are stopping or lowering your SSI or SVB payment.** This meeting is like an informal conference, but we can also get people to come in and help prove you are right. We can do this even if they do not want to help you. You can question these people at your meeting.

CONTACT INFORMATION

CLAIMANT SIGNATURE - *OPTIONAL:*	NAME OF CLAIMANT'S REPRESENTATIVE: *(If any)*
MAILING ADDRESS:	MAILING ADDRESS:
CITY: STATE: ZIP CODE:	CITY: STATE: ZIP CODE:
TELEPHONE NUMBER: *(Include area code)* DATE:	TELEPHONE NUMBER: *(Include area code)* DATE:

TO BE COMPLETED BY SOCIAL SECURITY ADMINISTRATION

1. HAS INITIAL DETERMINATION BEEN MADE? ☐ Yes ☐ No	**FIELD OFFICE DEVELOPMENT (GN 03102.300)** ☐ NO FURTHER DEVELOPMENT REQUIRED
2. IS THIS REQUEST FILED TIMELY? ☐ Yes ☐ No *(If "NO", attach claimant's explanation for delay. Refer to GN 03101.020)*	☐ REQUIRED DEVELOPMENT ATTACHED ☐ REQUIRED DEVELOPMENT PENDING, WILL FORWARD OR ADVISE STATUS WITHIN 30 DAYS
SOCIAL SECURITY OFFICE ADDRESS AND DATE APPEAL RECEIVED:	**SSI CASES ONLY - GOLDBERG KELLY (GK)** **(SI 02301.310)** RECIPIENT APPEALED AN ADVERSE ACTION: ☐ WITHIN 10 DAYS AFTER RECEIVING THE ADVANCE NOTICE; ☐ AFTER THE 10-DAY PERIOD AND GOOD CAUSE EXISTS FOR EXTENDING THE TIME LIMIT ☐ PAYMENT CONTINUATION APPLIES AND INPUT MADE TO SYSTEM

NOTE: Take or mail the **completed original** to your local Social Security office, the Veterans Affairs Regional Office in Manila, or any U.S. Foreign Service post and keep a copy for your records.

Claims Folder

recent medical visits you've had. (You can also submit this form online.) Instructions for completing this form can be found in *Nolo's Guide to Social Security Disability: Getting & Keeping Your Benefits*, by David A. Morton III, M.D. (Nolo). In addition, you can submit a statement describing in more detail why you think Social Security's decision was incorrect.

You should also submit any other relevant materials to the agency, such as recent medical records or a letter from a doctor or an employer about your ability to work. Such new material might be crucial to winning your reconsideration request—government workers have a tendency to believe that their agency was right the first time, unless you give them something new and different to change their minds.

The Importance of Reviewing Your File

Sometimes a Social Security or SSI claim is denied because a document or another piece of information that should be in your file is not there. Or perhaps some information in the file is incorrect or unclear. This happens most often on medical issues, where medical records are missing or the report from the consultative examination includes a mistake based on a misunderstanding with the doctor who did the exam.

The only way for you to find out if such mistakes exist is to look at your file, which should contain all documents related to your claim. After you file your *Request for Reconsideration*, call your local Social Security office to set up an appointment to see your file or have it sent to you on a CD.

If you find a mistake in the file, write a letter to Social Security explaining the situation. Send the letter to your local Social Security office, asking that it be made part of your file for reconsideration. And, as always, keep a copy of the letter.

This additional information does not have to be submitted by the 65th day after the written decision (the date by which the request itself must be filed). But if you're planning to submit it after your *Request for Reconsideration*, indicate this on the form and submit the material as soon as possible. (Use the space where you explain your disagreement with the decisions.)

Be sure to include your Social Security number and your claim number, in addition to your full name (as it appears on your Social Security card) and the date, on all material you send in. And keep a copy for your records.

The Reconsideration Process

Your claim will be reconsidered by someone in the Social Security or DDS office other than the person who made the decision on it the first time around. The claims examiner will consider everything that was in your file when the decision was made, plus anything you've submitted to the office since the original decision.

Generally, you don't appear in person for this review; you don't have the right to speak face to face with the person making the decision, although you can request a chance to do so. But the person doing the review may request more information—from you, your doctors, or your employer—and might ask you to come in for an informal interview.

You will receive a written notice of the decision made on your request for reconsideration—usually within 30 days (except for disability claims). If 30 days go by with no word, contact the local Social Security office and ask about the delay. Reconsideration of a disability claim often takes five to eight months, particularly if new medical information has been provided during the course of the appeal. If several months go by with no contact, you can call the DDS office and ask them about your disability reconsideration.

Once you receive your written decision, you can, if the decision is negative, file a request for an administrative hearing. (See the discussion of administrative hearings, below, for more information.) You must file your request within 65 days of the date of the written decision.

Continuing Your Benefits During an Appeal

In some circumstances, if you've already been receiving Social Security or SSI disability benefits, you can continue to receive them while Social Security is deciding your appeal. You can request this in either of the following situations:

- You've been collecting Social Security disability benefits and you're now appealing Social Security's decision to end your benefits because the agency determined that your condition has improved.
- You've been collecting SSI benefits and Social Security has decided that you are no longer eligible or that you are eligible for lower benefits.

If you want your benefits to continue during the appeal process, you must make the request to your local Social Security office within 10 days of the date you receive a written notice ending or reducing your benefits.

CAUTION

Continued benefits might not be for keeps. If you continue to collect benefits while appealing Social Security's decision to end those benefits, and Social Security denies your appeal, you might have to pay back the benefits you received during the appeal process.

Requesting Reconsideration of SSI Decision

If you request a reconsideration of a decision regarding a claim for SSI benefits, you'll be asked to choose among three possible procedures listed on the *Request for Reconsideration* form. Which one you choose depends upon how and why you were denied:

- **Case Review.** If Social Security denied your claim for SSI because the agency says that you aren't disabled, you're entitled only to what's called a "case review." This means that you won't be permitted to meet face to face with the Social Security examiner deciding your claim. But you can add more documentation to your file to be reviewed.

- **Informal Conference.** If your claim for SSI benefits was denied for nonmedical reasons—such as your income or assets or your immigration status—you can request a case review or an "informal conference." This option permits you to speak with the person reviewing your claim and to show additional documents. You can also bring along anyone you want to help support your argument.

- **Formal Conference.** If you've been receiving SSI benefits but Social Security decides to end or reduce them, you can request a "formal conference." Despite the name, this option is actually an informal meeting at which you can explain your situation in your own words, present written materials, and have people come to the meeting and give information. It is only "formal" in the sense that the Social Security office can issue a legal summons to require people to show up and answer questions if they refuse to come voluntarily. If you want Social Security to force someone to appear, you must notify your local office several weeks before the hearing date.

Informal Meetings During Reconsideration

You might have an opportunity to meet with the claims examiner who is reviewing your file during the initial reconsideration of your retirement, disability, dependents, or survivors claim. Or, you might meet with the examiner during a conference regarding an SSI claim. These meetings are very informal. You will be given the chance to explain, in your own words and in person, why you believe the decision denying or ending your benefits was wrong.

There are several things to bear in mind during one of these meetings:

- Focus on addressing whatever reason Social Security gave (in the notice denying or ending your benefits) to justify its decision. Perhaps it was changes in your condition, your income, or your work hours. Be strong and direct in explaining why the agency's reasoning was wrong. Don't dilute your argument by telling your life story or explaining your whole medical history.

- If, along with your appeal, you submitted material that wasn't in your original file, ask whether the examiner has had a chance to read it. If so, explain how the new material shows that the original decision was incorrect. If not, give the examiner copies of these new materials and ask that they read them before you continue with the meeting.

- There's no need to go over all the documents in your file except to point out what you believe are errors, or to focus on something in a document that you believe is important but that seemed to have been ignored or misunderstood in making the original decision.

- The claims examiner will ask you questions so that they can focus in on what Social Security considers important. Don't dismiss or ignore any question. Try to answer all questions clearly and directly. If there's other information—from your doctor or employer, for example—that you believe might help answer the question, tell the examiner and either direct the examiner to an existing document in your file or ask that you be allowed to provide the information at a later point, but before the examiner makes a decision.

Informal Meetings During Reconsideration (continued)

- Be calm and polite. Social Security employees understand that the denying or ending of benefits is an emotional matter for you, but they did not make the initial decision, and they are human, so you won't do yourself any good by taking out your frustration on them.

Administrative Hearing

If Social Security denies your claim again after reconsidering it, you can request a formal administrative hearing. This hearing will be held in front of an administrative law judge. The people in the office that denied your claim won't take part in the judge's decision. That means you have a good chance of having the denial of your claim reversed at this hearing, even if you have no new information to present.

Requesting a Hearing

As with other steps in the appeal process, you must file a request for this hearing with your local Social Security office within 65 days of the date on the written notice of the decision after reconsideration.

Your request must be filed on a form called *Request for Hearing by Administrative Law Judge* (HA-501-U5), reproduced below.

Along with your completed *Request for Hearing* form, you will need to submit a form called a *Disability Report—Appeal* (SSA-3441-BK) to update your disability information (if disability is the basis of your claim for benefits). This is the same form you used in filing for reconsideration of your original disability claim. Complete instructions for completing this form can be found in *Nolo's Guide to Social Security Disability: Getting & Keeping Your Benefits,* by David A. Morton III, M.D. (Nolo).

SEE AN EXPERT

Consider getting assistance with hearing preparation from an outside professional, such as a lawyer or an advocate specializing in Social Security matters. If the issue is whether your physical or mental condition qualifies you as disabled, it's particularly important to get help, because you'll need to gather and present evidence that's convincing enough to sway a judge's decision. Your best chance of reversing Social Security's decision comes at the administrative hearing, so you'll want to be as well prepared as possible at this stage.

Completing the Request for Hearing by Administrative Law Judge Form

The first three sections of the form are straightforward. Section 4 of the *Request for Hearing by Administrative Law Judge* form asks you to state the reasons you disagree with the determination made on your claim. State your reasons here simply and briefly; for example: "The decision that I am not disabled was based on incorrect statements about the number of hours I regularly work. I am submitting letters from my coworkers explaining that I actually work fewer hours than stated in the decision ending my benefits."

Section 5 includes two boxes to indicate whether you have additional evidence to submit. You should always check the first box—the one that says you do have additional evidence, which will allow you to submit a new written statement to the judge, as well as any letters or documents that weren't already in your file. If it turns out that you don't have any additional letters or documents to submit, at the hearing you can inform the judge that you have no new written materials but would like an opportunity to speak.

After you (and your representative, if you have one) have organized your papers and spoken with your doctor, your employer, or another person who can provide additional or clarifying information about your claim, you (and your representative) should write a detailed statement summarizing and arguing your claim. Send that statement to your local Social Security office to be placed in your

file, and also send it directly to the administrative law judge at the hearing office who will hear your claim.

Do this at least two weeks before your hearing date so that the administrative law judge will have a chance to read the statement before the hearing. If you don't prepare it in advance, bring it with you to the hearing and present it there.

In Section 6 on the hearing request form, you must indicate whether you want to attend the hearing in person. If you don't, the judge will make a decision based solely on the papers in your file. It's almost always to your advantage to be present at the hearing. Your presence puts a human face on your claim and shows the judge that you're truly concerned about the outcome. It also allows the judge to ask you questions that might not get answered if you aren't there.

If you check "I wish to appear at a hearing" in Section 6 but later decide not to attend the hearing, you must notify the hearing judge's office beforehand. If, on the other hand, you checked the box saying that you don't want to attend the hearing but later decide you do, contact the hearing judge's office as soon as you can. The hearing will probably have to be rescheduled to a later date.

Section 8 of the request for hearing form asks for your representative's name and address. If you don't have a lawyer or other representative by the time limit for filing your request for hearing, file the request without naming anyone. If later you obtain a representative, you can supply that information then.

CAUTION

Timing might be important. To make sure that all your evidence gets in your file and to the administrative law judge in time for your hearing, you must submit all new evidence—letters, documents, records that were not previously given to Social Security—within 10 days of filing your request for a hearing. So, even if you are ready to file a request for an administrative hearing immediately after you receive written notice of the reconsideration decision, it is a good idea to wait until you have gathered whatever additional information you want the hearing judge to see. This might delay slightly the date of your hearing, but it will allow you to make sure all your evidence will be considered there.

Preparing for the Hearing

During the time between filing your request for a hearing and the hearing date, you should take several steps. First, discuss your claim with the attorney or representative who will assist or represent you at the hearing. (See "Lawyers and Other Assistance," below, for suggestions on obtaining legal representation.) It's important to make sure that your representative understands what you believe to be the most important part of your claim and that your representative has thoroughly reviewed any documents that you believe support your position.

Second, examine your file, either at your local Social Security office or at the hearing office. This allows you to see that all the papers you have given to Social Security have found their way into your file. It also allows you to review all of the positive and negative information that Social Security has collected, such as a report on your disability from a consultative examination. Call your local Social Security office to see when and where you can examine your file, or if an electronic file can be sent to you or your Social Security account.

Finally, ask for new statements or records from your medical providers or employers that respond to the reasons expressed by the Social Security office or DDS examiners for rejecting your claim. Submit copies to your local Social Security office and directly to the administrative law judge at the hearing office, while keeping the original and at least one more copy.

The Hearing

After you file the request for hearing, you will be notified by mail of the hearing date and place. You'll receive this notice about 75 days before the hearing.

If you can't attend on that date, contact the office of the administrative law judge (ALJ) and arrange for a new date. Act quickly: Most hearing offices are reasonable about rescheduling, but if you wait until the last week to request a change and you don't have a

Form **HA-501** (06-2022)
Discontinue Prior Editions
Office of Hearings Operations

OMB. No. 0960-0269
Page 1 of 2

REQUEST FOR HEARING BY ADMINISTRATIVE LAW JUDGE

*(Take or mail the **completed original** to your local Social Security office, the Veterans Affairs Regional Office in Manila or any U.S. Foreign Service post and keep a copy for your records)*

See Privacy
Act Notice

1. Claimant Name	2. Claimant SSN	3. Claim Number, if different

4. I REQUEST A HEARING BEFORE AN ADMINISTRATIVE LAW JUDGE. I disagree with the determination because:

An Administrative Law Judge of the Social Security Administration's Office of Hearings Operations or the Department of Health and Human Services will be appointed to conduct the hearing or other proceedings in your case. You will receive notice of the time and place of a hearing at least 75 days before the date of hearing from the Social Security Administration, and 20 days before the date of hearing from the Department of Health and Human Services.

5. I have additional evidence to submit. ☐ Yes   ☐ No

Name and source of additional evidence, if not included.

Submit your evidence to the hearing office within 10 days. Your servicing Social Security office will provide the hearing office's address. Attach an additional sheet if you need more space.

6. Do not complete if the appeal is a Medicare issue. Otherwise, check one of the blocks

☐ I wish to appear at a hearing.

☐ I do not wish to appear at a hearing and I request that a decision be made based on the evidence in my case. (Complete Waiver Form HA-4608)

Representation: You have a right to be represented at the hearing. If you are not represented, your Social Security office will give you a list of legal referral and service organizations. If you are represented, complete and submit form SSA-1696 (Appointment of Representative) unless you are appealing a Medicare issue.

7. CLAIMANT SIGNATURE (OPTIONAL)	DATE	8. NAME OF REPRESENTATIVE (if any)	DATE
RESIDENCE ADDRESS		ADDRESS	

CITY	STATE	ZIP CODE	CITY	STATE	ZIP CODE

TELEPHONE NUMBER	FAX NUMBER	TELEPHONE NUMBER	FAX NUMBER

TO BE COMPLETED BY SOCIAL SECURITY ADMINISTRATION- ACKNOWLEDGMENT OF REQUEST FOR HEARING

9. Request received on _____ by: _____

(Date)   (Print Name)   (Title)

_____

(Address)   (Servicing FO Code)   (PC Code)

10. Was the request for hearing received within 65 days of the reconsidered determination? ☐ Yes   ☐ No

If no, attach claimant's explanation for delay and supporting documents if any.

11. If claimant is not represented, was a list of legal referral service organizations provided? ☐ Yes ☐ No

12. Interpreter needed ☐ Yes ☐ No

Language (including sign language):

13. Check one: ☐ Initial Entitlement Case
☐ Disability Cessation Case or ☐ Other Postentitlement Case

14. HO COPY SENT TO: _____ HO on _____
☐ Claims Folder (CF) Attached: ☐ Title (T) II; ☐ T XVI;
☐ T VIII; ☐ T XVIII; ☐ T II CF held in FO ☐ Electronic Folder
☐ CF requested ☐ T II; ☐ T XVI; ☐ T VIII; ☐ T XVIII
(Copy of email or phone report attached)

16. CF COPY SENT TO: _____ HO on _____
☐ CF Attached: ☐ Title (T) II; ☐ T XVI; ☐ T XVIII
☐ Other Attached: _____

15. Check all claim types that apply:
☐ Retirement and Survivors Insurance Only (RSI)
☐ Title II Disability - Worker or child only (DIWC)
☐ Title II Disability - Widow(er) only (DIWW)
☐ Title XVI (SSI) Aged only (SSIA)
☐ Title XVI Blind only (SSIB)
☐ Title XVI Disability only (SSID)
☐ Title XVI/Title II Concurrent Aged Claim (SSAC)
☐ Title XVI/Title II Concurrent Blind (SSBC)
☐ Title XVI/Title II Concurrent Disability (SSDC)
☐ Title XVIII Hospital/Supplementary Insurance (HI/SMI)
☐ Title VIII Only Special Veterans Benefits (SVB)
☐ Title VIII/Title XVI (SVB/SSI)
☐ Other - Specify: _____

medical or another valid emergency, the judge could refuse to post-pone your hearing. In that case, the judge could hold the hearing without you.

The hearing itself is conducted in a style less rigid than in a traditional courtroom. An ALJ presides, and everything said or done is recorded. You can be represented or assisted at the hearing by a friend or relative or by a lawyer or another advocate. (See "Lawyers and Other Assistance," below, for more information about getting legal or other help.)

You need to submit any new evidence, or at least notify the hearing office that you will be bringing new evidence to the hearing, at least five days before the hearing. If you don't, and you don't have a valid reason such as illness or an unavoidable circumstance, the judge does not have to consider the evidence. It's important to submit new, updated medical evidence, such as any recent test results or doctor's notes from recent appointments—the judge will want to see medical evidence from the last 30–60 days, if possible.

You can present the testimony of any witnesses you would like to have help prove your claim. This testimony is informal. The person simply gives information regarding your employment or medical condition to the judge and answers any questions from the judge. The judge will give you an opportunity to explain your claim in your own words, and might also ask you some questions.

The ALJ who presides at your hearing is a lawyer who works for the Social Security Administration. The ALJ didn't take part in the original claim decision or in reconsidering your claim. The judge will follow certain rules of procedure and might ask you questions about your claim that aren't easy to answer. In general, however, the judges try to be as helpful as possible. If you aren't sure how to present certain information to the judge, explain the problem and the judge should help you get the information into the official record of the case.

The judge will issue a written decision on your appeal, usually within four to six weeks of the hearing. You'll receive a copy of this decision in the mail. If your claim has been denied, you will have 65 days from the date on the written notice of the denial to file a further appeal.

If your claim has been approved, you might be entitled to receive benefits dating all the way back to the time you filed your original claim or even earlier.

Appeal to the National Appeals Council

If your appeal has been denied after an administrative hearing, your next step is to file a written appeal with the Social Security Administration Appeals Council. You must file this within 65 days from the date on the written notice of the administrative law judge's decision.

Completing the Form

The form you'll need at this stage of the appeals process is called *Request for Review of Hearing Decision/Order* (HA-520-U5). (Or you can submit this form online at https://secure.ssa.gov/iApplNMD/oao.)

The form is fairly straightforward, asking only that you give a brief explanation of why you think the administrative law judge's decision was wrong. If there's more to say than will fit onto this form, attach a separate piece of paper with the explanation. Also submit any documents that the judge didn't consider but that you believe are important to your claim.

On Question 10 of the form, you'll be asked to check either "Initial Entitlement" or "Termination or other." Initial Entitlement means you were denied after your first attempt to obtain a particular benefit. Termination or other means Social Security decided to end a benefit you were already receiving or to reduce the amount you receive.

Form **HA-520** (10-2023) UF
Discontinue Prior Editions
Social Security Administration

Page 1 of 2
OMB No. 0960-0277

REQUEST FOR REVIEW OF HEARING DECISION/ORDER

(Do not use this form for objecting to a recommended decision.)

See Privacy Act Notice

(Either mail the signed original form to the Appeals Council at the address shown below, or take or mail the signed original to your local Social Security office, the Department of Veterans Affairs Regional Office in Manila, or any U.S. Foreign Service Post and keep a copy for your records.)

1. Claimant Name	2. Claimant SSN	3. Claim Number (If different than SSN)

4. I request that the Appeals Council review the Judge's action on the above claim because:

☐ Please grant me an extension of time to submit evidence or argument.

ADDITIONAL EVIDENCE

You may submit any additional evidence or argument to the Appeals Council. If you have additional evidence that relates to the period on or before the date of the hearing decision, you must inform the Appeals Council about it or submit it, or any other evidence or argument, when you submit this form unless you request an extension of time by checking the box above. This will ensure that the Appeals Council has the opportunity to consider the additional evidence before taking its action. If you have a representative, then they must help you obtain the evidence. In limited circumstances, the Appeals Council may request the additional evidence related to the relevant period. If you submit neither evidence nor a legal argument now or within any extension of time the Appeals Council grants, the Appeals Council will take its action based on the evidence currently in your file.

IMPORTANT: WRITE YOUR SOCIAL SECURITY NUMBER ON ANY LETTER OR MATERIAL YOU SEND US. IF YOU RECEIVED A BARCODE FROM US, THE BARCODE SHOULD ACCOMPANY THIS DOCUMENT AND ANY OTHER MATERIAL YOU SUBMIT TO US.

SIGNATURE BLOCKS: You should complete No. 5 and your representative (if any) should complete No. 6. If you are represented and your representative is not available to complete this form, you should also print their name, address, etc. in section number 6.

I declare under penalty of perjury that I have examined all the information on this form, and on any accompanying statements or forms, and it is true and correct to the best of my knowledge.

5. Claimant's Signature	Date	6. Representative's Signature	Date
Print Name		Print Name ☐ Attorney ☐ Non-Attorney	
Address	City, State, ZIP	Address	City, State, ZIP
Telephone Number	Fax Number	Telephone Number	Fax Number

THE SOCIAL SECURITY ADMINISTRATION STAFF WILL COMPLETE THIS PART

7. Request received for the Social Security Administration on _____ by: _____
(Date)   (Print Name)

_____ (Title)   (Address)   (Servicing FO Code)   (PC Code)

8. Is the request for review received within 65 days of the Judge's Decision/Dismissal? ☐ Yes ☐ No

9. If "No" checked: ☐ (1) attach claimant's explanation for delay; and
☐ (2) attach copy of appointment notice, letter or other pertinent material or information in the Social Security Office.

10. Check one: ☐ Initial Entitlement	11. Check all claim types that apply:
☐ Termination or other	☐ Retirement or Survivors (RSI) ☐ SSI Disability (SSID)
	☐ Disability - Worker (DIWC) ☐ Title VIII Only (SVB)
Social Security Administration	☐ Disability - Widow(er) (DIWW) ☐ Title VIII/Title XVI (SVB/SSI)
Office of Appellate Operations	☐ Disability - Child (DIWC) ☐ Other - Specify:
6401 Security Blvd	☐ SSI Aged (SSIA)
Baltimore, MD 21235-6401	☐ SSI Blind (SSIB)
TAKE OR SEND ORIGINAL TO SSA AND RETAIN A COPY FOR YOUR RECORDS	

Also notice the section in the middle of the form under the heading "Additional Evidence." Any documents you wish to submit to the Appeals Council that aren't already in your file must be either attached to the form or sent directly to the Appeals Council within 15 days after filing your request for review.

> **SEE AN EXPERT**
>
> **If you aren't yet represented by a lawyer who specializes in Social Security matters, hire one now.** The Appeals Council usually reverses an administrative law judge's decision only when a technical argument can be made as to why the administrative law judge made a legal mistake. Simply arguing to the Appeals Council that the judge was wrong in deciding your case won't be enough.

Appeal Procedure

Unfortunately, your appeal to the Appeals Council is not likely to meet with much success. The Appeals Council reviews a case based on the written documents in your file only. If the Appeals Council believes there is merit to the appeal because of an error, it often sends the case back to the administrative law judge with the direction that the judge hold a new hearing and reconsider something the Appeals Council points out in its written decision.

Although the success rate of having claims denials overturned by the Appeals Council is very low, filing an appeal might be important. You're required to file this appeal before you can move on to the next step, which is filing a lawsuit in federal court.

Lawsuit in Federal Court

If your claim has been denied and you have unsuccessfully tried all levels of the Social Security Administration appeals process, you're entitled to bring a lawsuit against the SSA in federal district court.

You must file the initial papers of this lawsuit within 60 days after the Appeals Council's decision is mailed.

A federal court lawsuit is a complicated, time-consuming, and expensive procedure. However, it might be worth it if you have a strong case. When you add up the total amount of benefits you might receive in your lifetime if your claim is approved, there could be a lot of money at stake. If the amount seems worth the time and effort to you, then you might investigate the possibility of filing a lawsuit. Consult with an attorney who specializes in Social Security appeals.

Whether or not you had legal assistance at some earlier stage of the appeal process, you certainly need expert legal assistance to file a lawsuit in federal court. Your odds of winning there depend almost entirely on convincing a court that the administrative law judge who heard your appeal made a mistake in interpreting the Social Security law. Simply asking a court to take another look at the facts of your case is almost never enough to win a federal lawsuit.

The main things you should weigh in deciding whether to file a lawsuit are your chances of winning (as explained to you by an attorney specializing in such cases), the money it will cost you to fight the legal battle, and the amount of money in benefits that you stand to gain. If you balance all these things and it still seems like a good idea to go ahead with the lawsuit, then consider hiring an attorney to help you proceed.

Lawyers and Other Assistance

Under Social Security rules, you have a right to be represented at every stage of the appeal process by someone who understands the Social Security rules. This person can be a lawyer who specializes in Social Security matters, a nonlawyer from one of the many organizations that help people with Social Security claims, or a family member or friend who may be better than you are at organizing documents, writing letters, or speaking.

Deciding Whether You Need Assistance

It's not always necessary to get assistance in preparing or presenting your appeal at the reconsideration stage. But, if your appeal involves medical issues or a hearing, it might be wise to seek help. This assistance can take several forms:

- talking over your appeal with a knowledgeable friend or relative
- having a person who specializes in Social Security problems go over your papers with you, make suggestions, and assist you at hearings, or
- having a lawyer or disability advocate prepare and present the appeal on your behalf.

Deciding whether to hire a lawyer or to seek an experienced nonlawyer representative depends on several things, such as:

- the complexities of your case. The more complicated the issues—particularly those involving a physical or mental condition as it relates to qualification for disability benefits—the more likely that you need expert help.
- how much money is at stake. For example, if your appeal is only about whether your disability began in March or April, it might not be worth hiring an attorney to represent you. On the other hand, if your benefits have been reduced significantly or denied entirely, it's much more likely to be worth it to hire an attorney.
- how comfortable you feel handling the matter yourself. Particularly at the reconsideration stage of the appeal process, many people feel confident obtaining their own records and documents and filing the forms or discussing their claim with a local Social Security office worker. However, many other people are uncomfortable about explaining things convincingly, and so would like assistance at this stage. And most people become uncomfortable at the prospect of an administrative hearing because they've never been through the process before. If so, it's a good idea at least to get some advice, and perhaps representation, before the hearing stage of the appeal process.

What a Representative Can Do to Help

If you decide to have someone represent you during the course of your appeal—either a lawyer or a disability advocate—your representative can handle as much or as little of the process as you want. A representative can:

- look at and copy information from your Social Security file
- file a request for reconsideration, a hearing, or an Appeals Council review, and schedule or reschedule hearings
- provide Social Security with information on your behalf
- accompany you, or appear instead of you, and speak on your behalf at any interview, conference, or hearing, and
- receive copies of any written decisions or other notices sent by Social Security.

Where to Find Assistance

Whether you should seek aid from a lawyer or an advocate depends on whether one or the other is easily available to you, and with whom you are most comfortable. If you reach the stage of considering going to federal court, however, you should consult with an attorney who has federal court experience in similar cases.

 CAUTION

Appointment of a representative must be in writing. Once a person has agreed to become your representative for the appeal, you must provide their name to Social Security on a form entitled *Appointment of Representative* (SSA-1696). The representative will fill out part of the form and sign it, agreeing to serve as your representative. The form is available online (www.ssa.gov) or at your local Social Security office, which is also where the completed form is to be filed.

Hiring Specialists Other Than Lawyers

The first place to inquire about assistance with your Social Security appeal might be Social Security itself. Some denial letters from Disability Determination Services (DDS) are accompanied by a written list of local community groups and legal services organizations— such as disability rights groups, legal aid offices, and senior counseling services—that either assist with appeals or refer claimants to appeal representatives.

Finding someone through one of these groups or organizations doesn't guarantee that you'll want that person to represent you; that will depend on how well you and the person communicate and whether you feel confident in their advice. But finding someone to assist or represent you through one of these organizations at least assures you that the person has experience in Social Security appeals and has backing from a legitimate organization.

Senior centers are good resources, too. Many have regularly scheduled sessions during which trained advocates offer advice on Social Security problems. Whether or not a particular senior center has such a program, it can usually refer you to a Social Security advocacy group whose members are trained to assist in Social Security matters. You can usually make use of these referrals if you have a disability claim, even if you're not a senior citizen.

Also, each state has its own agency or department handling problems of older people, including Social Security disputes. These agencies are usually referred to as the Department of Aging or, variously, as the "office," "bureau," "division," "agency," "commission," "council," "administration," or "center" on aging. In most cases, this state agency will be able to refer you to somewhere near your home that offers assistance in preparing and presenting Social Security appeals. Call your state's agency and explain what you're looking for.

Other sources of assistance with Social Security matters are business and fraternal associations and unions. If you belong to such a group, it might have a referral service that can put you in touch with Social Security advocates.

Although some nonlawyer advocates provide free services, most charge a fee (although the amount is limited by Social Security rules—see below). The time to ask about fees is before you hire someone to assist or represent you. Get any fee agreement in writing.

Hiring Lawyers

If your income is low, a lawyer might be available to assist or represent you through a "legal services" organization that has specialists in Social Security appeals. These are nonprofit organizations that seek funding from outside sources in order to serve low-income people. The first place to look for legal services offices is on the list of references provided by Social Security along with its notice denying your claim. You can also find legal services offices—sometimes listed as "Legal Aid"—online or in your telephone directory.

Be aware, however, that in the steady campaign by the federal government over past decades to slash public services for low-income people, many legal services offices have suffered staff cutbacks, and most of them now charge a fee for handling disability claims (if you win your case). So, it might not be easy to find a legal aid lawyer who can help you for free with your appeal.

You can also find an attorney in private practice. Most private lawyers know very little about Social Security, however; you need to find one who specializes in Social Security claims.

Asking for a referral to a disability lawyer (or Social Security attorney) from someone you trust can be a good way to find legal help. Also, two sites that are part of the Nolo family, Lawyers.com and Avvo.com, provide excellent and free lawyer directories. These directories allow you to search by location and area of law, and list detailed information about and reviews of lawyers. You can visit www.lawyers.com/find-a-lawyer and www.avvo.com/find-a-lawyer to research attorneys.

Your local county bar association will also have a reference list of lawyers who specialize in Social Security appeals. Few lawyers specialize in Social Security appeals, and the few who are experts in the field usually list themselves with the bar association.

Normally, lawyers cost a lot of money. However, Social Security rules strictly limit the amount of money a lawyer or anyone else can charge for a Social Security appeal (which explains why so few lawyers specialize in the field).

Legal Limits on Lawyers' Fees

Whether your representative is a lawyer or an advocate, Social Security rules limit the fees your representative can charge. And not only are fees limited, but they must be approved by Social Security in each individual case.

Fee Agreements

Most lawyers and nonlawyers can charge a fee only if, with their help, you end up being approved for benefits. If you win your appeal at any stage of the process, you might be entitled to benefits from the date you first applied for them (or for Social Security disability insurance, even earlier)—referred to as "past-due benefits." The lawyers take their fees as a percentage of your past-due benefits. Social Security rules say that a lawyer or another representative can take as a fee 25% of your past-due benefits, or $7,200—whichever is less. However, if the lawyer pursues a lawsuit for you in federal court, different limits apply.

Fee Petitions

In some situations, lawyers are allowed to ask Social Security if they can charge more than the $7,200 cap. Social Security has the power to limit how much you are made to pay, however. If you agree to hire a lawyer under such a fee-for-service arrangement, the lawyer can't collect from you until after submitting a kind of bill called a "fee petition" to Social Security for approval.

The petition is filed when the appeal is finished and lists, in detail, each service the lawyer provided for your appeal and the amount of time the lawyer spent on each service. The lawyer must provide you with a copy of the petition. If you disagree with any of the information on the petition, you must notify your local Social Security office within 20 days of the date you receive it.

Social Security will examine the petition and determine a reasonable fee for the lawyer's services. Social Security will send you a written notice of the amount it has approved under the fee petition. The lawyer or other representative can't charge you any more than the fee Social Security decides on, except for out-of-pocket expenses incurred during your appeal (such as costs for photocopying, phone calls, postage, and transportation to and from your hearings).

Get It in Writing

If you come to a fee arrangement with your lawyer or other representative, the representative must put it in writing, you both must sign it, and the representative must submit it to Social Security for approval. This can be done at any time before your claim is approved.

Federal Civil Service Retirement Benefits

More than two million people work as civilian employees of federal government agencies and departments; millions more have previously been employed there. And although the salaries of these government jobs aren't always as high as those in the private sector, a comprehensive retirement system is one of the benefits that makes federal government employment attractive.

This chapter discusses the two different federal retirement systems—the older Civil Service Retirement System, which still includes some current and many former employees, and the newer Federal Employees Retirement System—and explains the benefits available under each.

Employees of State and Local Governments

Each state and many local governments have their own retirement systems for their employees. It isn't possible here to discuss the rules of all these plans, but most of them work very much like the federal government's Civil Service Retirement System (CSRS), described in this chapter.

In these systems, the amount of pension funds to which an employee may be entitled isn't based on total payroll contributions, as with the Social Security system, but on the highest average salary the employee reached and the number of years of employment. The age at which the employee can claim retirement benefits also depends on the number of years of employment.

As of July 1, 1991, employees of state or local governments who aren't covered at all by an employer pension plan became covered by Social Security. These employees are usually part-time, temporary, or probationary workers.

To find out what retirement plan covers your work, contact your personnel or retirement plan office, or the pension office of your public employees' union, if you belong to one.

On request, the pension office should provide you with an estimate of how much your pension benefits would be if you claimed those benefits at the various retirement ages permitted by the plan.

RESOURCE

For information about nongovernment, personal retirement plans. See *IRAs, 401(k)s & Other Retirement Plans: Strategies for Taking Your Money Out*, by Twila Slesnick and John C. Suttle (Nolo).

Federal Retirement Spousal Benefits for Same-Sex Spouses

Same-sex spouses are entitled to federal spousal benefits on the same terms as other spouses. This is true regardless of the state where the marriage was performed.

Foreign same-sex marriages. A spouse in a same-sex couple who was married outside the United States but now lawfully lives in the United States might be entitled to spousal benefits based on the other spouse's federal employment record, depending on the status of that marriage in the country where it was performed. Even if you have doubts about your right to federal spousal benefits as a same-sex spouse, the federal retirement system encourages you to apply for them so that it can determine whether you're eligible.

Retroactivity. The Department of Justice has decided that the right to spousal benefits for a same-sex spouse can apply to someone who applied for such benefits before the Supreme Court's same-sex marriage decision on June 26, 2015. If you were married and you applied for federal spousal benefits before that date but were denied those benefits (because you lived in a state that did not recognize your marriage), you can reapply to the federal retirement system now, specifically requesting retroactive benefits back to the date you first applied.

Two Retirement Systems: CSRS and FERS

There are two entirely separate retirement systems for civilian federal workers, depending on the date the worker was first hired. Until 1984, all federal government workers were part of the

Civil Service Retirement System, or CSRS. Workers covered by CSRS don't receive Social Security benefits for their government employment; CSRS provides the only benefits those workers will receive for their years of federal government employment (though they might qualify for Social Security benefits through other work they have done).

All federal workers hired on or after January 1, 1984 were made part of a different plan called the Federal Employees Retirement System, or FERS. Workers hired by the federal government on or after January 1, 1984 are also covered by Social Security, which means that work for the government simultaneously builds toward both FERS and Social Security benefits.

Employees who were already working for the federal government on January 1, 1984 were given a choice. They could either remain in CSRS or switch over to FERS. For those who switched, their years of employment under CSRS were credited to FERS. Only a small percentage of employees who are still working for the federal government are enrolled in CSRS.

The rules for both systems are quite similar, and both are administered by the federal government's Office of Personnel Management (OPM). Both CSRS and FERS are funded by a combination of automatic payroll deductions from federal employees and contributions made by the employing agencies.

Under both systems, an employee can:
- receive benefits if disabled
- take early or full retirement
- provide for a survivor
- take a lump-sum retirement amount instead of monthly benefits, and
- participate in a special savings program called the Thrift Savings Plan.

Eligibility and benefit amounts for CSRS and FERS are determined in a very different way than under the Social Security system. In particular, benefits are based on the highest average salary for any three years of employment but don't depend on the total amount contributed in payroll deductions. And although benefits can be paid to retirees and to survivors (if the retiree so chooses), they aren't increased if the retiree has dependents.

CSRS Retirees May Face Pension Offset

People who earned a retirement pension under the Civil Service Retirement System or a similar state pension system that didn't pay into the Social Security program, might be subject to a reduction in certain Social Security dependents or survivors benefits because of what's called the "government pension offset." This offset applies if you receive Social Security dependents or survivors benefits and also receive a retirement pension based on your own work record from CSRS. This government pension offset does not apply to people whose own retirement benefit is under the Federal Employees Retirement System (FERS). (For a full explanation of the government pension offset, see Chapter 4.)

Retirement Benefits

Both CSRS and FERS retirement benefits are easy to qualify for and can be paid out in any one of several ways. Both programs also permit retirement benefits to be structured to provide for a survivor after the retired worker has died. And both offer a special savings plan that provides tax benefits and, in the case of FERS, includes contributions by the government.

If You've Left Federal Work, Then Returned

Some people might be entitled to retirement benefits under both CSRS and FERS: those who worked for the federal government before 1984, when CSRS was their only option, and then left but rejoined federal employment after 1984.

If you worked for the federal government for at least five years but left that job before 1984, you can return to CSRS if you start a new job with the federal government. If you choose not to reenter CSRS, you will work under FERS, and you can qualify for retirement benefits under both CSRS and FERS once you have more than five years of employment under each system.

If you left federal employment for at least a year and you choose to reenter CSRS, you will also be covered by Social Security, as are all FERS employees. Once you collect both Social Security benefits and CSRS retirement, your CSRS payment will be reduced by the amount of your Social Security benefits attributable to your federal employment.

This prevents double payment, since most CSRS recipients don't receive Social Security benefits from their federal employment, and the amount of CSRS benefits is calculated as if there were no additional retirement money from Social Security.

Who Is Eligible

If you've worked at least five years for the federal government as a civilian employee, you can qualify for a pension, referred to as a "retirement annuity." In addition, you can get retirement credit for any years of military service if you pay a premium based on the amount of your military pay. (However, you can't get credit for military service if you're also collecting a military retirement pension.) You can also get credit, after paying a small premium, for time you spent in the Peace Corps.

There are two types of retirement annuities under CSRS and FERS: an immediate annuity and a deferred annuity.

Minimum Retirement Age (MRA) by Year of Birth

The following chart tells you when you reach your MRA for FERS, depending on the year you were born.

Birth Year	MRA
1953–64	56
1965	56 + 2 months
1966	56 + 4 months
1967	56 + 6 months
1968	56 + 8 months
1969	56 + 10 months
1970 and after	57

Immediate Annuity

You can retire at age 62 and immediately begin receiving an annuity if you worked for the federal government a total of five years. The years don't have to be consecutive, nor do they have to be for the same federal agency or department. Any combination of federal jobs totaling five years of work will qualify you.

Special rule for 20 years of service. If you have 20 years of service with the federal government, you can claim your immediate annuity earlier, at age 60.

Special rules for 30 years of service. With 30 years of service, a CSRS-covered worker can retire with a pension at age 55.

A worker covered by FERS with 30 years of service can retire with a pension at what is called the "minimum retirement age" (MRA). Your MRA depends on the year you were born (see the chart above).

TIP

Special rules apply to law enforcement personnel and firefighters. Recognizing the high stress of these jobs, the FERS system has set earlier retirement years and lower requirements for years of service for these jobs. If you've been a federal law enforcement officer or firefighter under FERS, you can claim retirement benefits at age 50 with 20 years of service, or at any age once you have 25 years of service.

If You Are Laid Off Before Becoming Eligible for Your Pension

CSRS and FERS rules allow some long-term workers to collect an immediate annuity if they're laid off from their jobs before reaching the normal eligibility age.

Under CSRS, a worker who has been employed for at least one year in the two years immediately before being laid off, and who is either age 50 with 20 years of service or any age with 25 years of service, may be eligible for an immediate annuity.

Under FERS, the eligibility for this immediate annuity is the same, except that you need not have been employed within the past two years.

The amount of the immediate annuity is reduced from its full amount by 2% per year for every year you're under age 55 when claiming this annuity.

There are two circumstances in which you might not be entitled to an immediate annuity after losing your job. The first is if you've been fired for cause: misconduct, delinquency, or poor job performance. The second is if you've been offered another job in the same agency, in the same geographic area, that isn't more than two grades or pay levels below the current job, but you refuse to take it.

Deferred Annuity

If you end your federal employment before retirement age, you have a choice of leaving your payroll contributions in CSRS or FERS, or withdrawing them in a lump sum when you leave employment. If you leave the contributions in the system when you end your federal job, you can claim a retirement annuity at age 62. If you leave the money in the retirement system but later decide you want it without waiting for retirement, you can collect it in a lump sum at any time before you reach age 62.

You might need or want the lump sum immediately upon leaving your job. But if you've worked a long enough time to have reached a relatively high salary, you'll be eligible for a large pension when you reach age 62. Over your lifetime, that pension would probably amount to much more money than the lump sum you could withdraw when leaving your federal job.

Before deciding which course of action to take, find out from the Office of Personnel Management at the agency where you work exactly how much your lump-sum withdrawal would be, and get an estimate of what your annuity would be at age 62, so that you can make an informed choice.

Calculating Benefits

Two factors are used to figure the amount of your federal CSRS or FERS retirement annuity.

The first factor is the number of years you were employed by the federal government and contributed to the retirement fund. This can include years of military service if you also have at least five years of civilian service (unless you're receiving a military retirement pension).

The second factor is your "high-three average salary"—meaning your average salary for the three consecutive years in which you had your highest earnings. For example, if in three successive years

you reached $55,000, $55,000, and $58,000, you would add these together and divide the total by three. (The total would be $168,000, which divided by three equals a high-three average of $56,000.)

Both CSRS and FERS base the retirement annuity on the high-three average, but each computes the resulting benefit differently.

> **TIP**
> **You'll get a cost-of-living increase.** Both CSRS and FERS benefits are increased annually to keep pace with the rising cost of living. As with Social Security benefits, these cost-of-living increases are tied to the rise in the Consumer Price Index, a yearly indicator of the cost of goods and services.

> **ONLINE**
> **You can get benefit estimates online.** The Office of Personnel Management (OPM) operates the CSRS and FERS systems. OPM offers a website with a calculator that will estimate your federal civil service retirement benefits. Go to www.opm.gov and click "Calculators" (under "Retirement"). The calculator, called the Federal Ballpark E$timate, can estimate what your normal, early, or disability retirement benefits are likely to be. However, the accuracy of the estimate depends on how near you are to claiming your benefits—the nearer you are, the more accurate the estimate.

CSRS Benefits

Once your high-three average pay is calculated, CSRS computes your pension benefits by adding:

- 1.5% of your high-three average pay, multiplied by your first 5 years of service, plus
- 1.75% of your high-three average pay, multiplied by the number of your years of employment over 5, up to 10, plus
- 2% of your high-three average pay, multiplied by the number of years of service over 10.

EXAMPLE: John put in 25 years working for a federal government agency. His highest three consecutive years of pay were $57,000, $61,000, and $62,000. That makes his high-three average pay $60,000. After 25 years, John's retirement pension would be figured like this:

- 1.5% of the $60,000 average is $900; that $900 is multiplied by the first five years of service, for a total for the first five years of service of $4,500; plus

- 1.75% of the $60,000 average is $1,050; that $1,050 is multiplied by the second five years of service, for a total for the second five years of $5,250; plus

- 2% of the $60,000 is $1,200; that $1,200 is multiplied by the remaining 15 years of service, for a total for the last 15 years of service of $18,000.

Together, the three parts of John's pension would add up to a yearly benefit of $27,750.

CSRS Benefits and Social Security

If your federal employment is covered by CSRS, it's not also covered by the Social Security system. However, most people who worked for the federal government under CSRS have also worked, or will work, at some other jobs during their lifetimes. If that other work is covered by Social Security and you earn enough work credits from that work to qualify for Social Security retirement benefits, you can collect both your retirement benefits and your CSRS annuity.

Caution: If you receive a CSRS pension and also Social Security dependents or survivors benefits based on your spouse's work record—rather than Social Security retirement benefits based on your own work record—the Social Security dependents or survivors benefits will be severely reduced. This is known as the "pension offset rule." (See Chapters 4 and 5 for further discussion of the offset rule.) If you're receiving a CSRS annuity as the survivor of a CSRS worker, this rule doesn't apply.

CAUTION

Some workers will receive separate CSRS and FERS benefits.
If you had years of service under CSRS, left that job, and later returned
to work for the federal government under FERS, you can receive two
separate annuities, one using your high-three earnings under CSRS and
the other using your high-three earnings under FERS.

FERS Benefits

FERS has several different types of retirement benefits: full benefits,
reduced early retirement benefits, deferred benefits for people who
left their federal jobs before retiring, and a supplement for longtime
employees.

Full retirement annuity. Full FERS pension benefits are figured
by taking 1% of the high-three average and multiplying it by the
number of years of service.

> EXAMPLE: Elvira worked 25 years for the federal government,
> switching to FERS in 1984. Her highest three consecutive years of pay
> were $58,000, $60,000, and $62,000. That makes her high-three average
> pay $60,000. Elvira's retirement pension would be figured like this:
> 1% of $60,000 = $600; $600 x 25 (years of service) = $15,000, which
> would be her yearly pension annuity. And under FERS, Elvira would
> also collect Social Security retirement benefits as soon as she reaches
> an eligible age.

Reduced benefits for early retirement. If you've accumulated enough
years of service under FERS, you can take early retirement with lower
benefits. With 10 years of service, you can take early retirement at
the minimum retirement age (MRA). (See chart above.) Your
benefits will be reduced from the full retirement amount by 5%
for each year under age 62 at which you claim retirement.

Deferred benefits if you leave. If you leave your federal job after at
least five years of service but before reaching retirement status, you

can claim retirement benefits when you reach a certain retirement age, which depends on your years of service. With five years of service, you can claim retirement benefits at age 62. With 10 years or more, you can claim retirement at the minimum retirement age but the benefit will be reduced by 5% per year for every year earlier than age 62 at which you claim benefits.

 TIP

Reduced benefits might make financial sense. Although your deferred retirement benefits will be reduced 5% for every year under age 62 at which you claim them, it might still be to your advantage to claim as early as age 55. Since you aren't adding any more years of service and your high-three salary remains the same, the base amount of your benefit will be the same whenever you take it.

Annuity supplement for long-term employees. A special supplement to the retirement annuity is available at age 55 to people with 30 years' service and at age 60 with 20 years' service. The supplemental amount is based on total earnings and years of service and is figured using a complex set of calculations. To determine how much your annuity supplement would be, contact the OPM office at the agency where you work.

CAUTION

Your supplement might be reduced by your earnings. Unlike the standard FERS annuity, if you're younger than 62, your annuity supplement is reduced by $1 for every $2 that you make over a certain yearly amount in earnings from other employment after you retire from federal government work. This earnings limit rule works the same as the earnings limit for Social Security benefits. (For more information, see "Working After Claiming Early Retirement Benefits" in Chapter 2.)

Survivors Benefits

Unlike Social Security retirement benefits, the surviving spouse or another survivor of a federal CSRS or FERS retiree doesn't necessarily receive survivors benefits after the retiree dies. To plan ahead for this, the federal worker is given several choices at retirement.

The retiring worker can choose to:

- take a full retirement annuity—if so, no benefits will be paid to any survivors after the retiree dies
- elect a full survivor benefit for a current spouse, in which case the retiree's own annuity will be less
- elect to have survivor benefits paid to someone other than a current spouse (which would also reduce the retiree's own annuity), or
- choose to provide a reduced survivor benefit, which means their own annuity will be lower than a full retirement annuity but higher than if a full survivor annuity were provided.

Annuity Without Survivor Benefits

At retirement, a CSRS or FERS employee can choose to take full retirement benefits without any provision for survivors. This makes particular sense if the retiree is unmarried and isn't supporting anyone else financially. It also makes good sense if the retiree, or retiree and spouse, have extremely limited income and immediately need the full retirement annuity to get by. Finally, it might be a wise choice if the retired worker is married but their spouse is not likely to outlive the worker.

A worker who is married at retirement must specifically choose this no-survivor-benefit option by filing a form with the Office of Personnel Management (OPM). The worker's spouse must sign and notarize this form, which acknowledges that the retiree has given up the right to a survivor annuity. If the spouse's whereabouts are unknown, or the spouse is unable to understand the waiver and knowingly sign the form, a petition can be filed with the OPM to waive the requirement of a written consent form.

Annuity With Full Spousal Survivor Benefits

If you're married when you retire from federal employment, and you and your spouse don't waive your right to a survivor annuity, your retirement annuity will be reduced slightly to provide a lifetime annuity for your spouse if you die first.

This full survivor annuity can also be provided for a former spouse, although if the worker has remarried, the current spouse must consent. A survivor benefit ends when the surviving spouse dies or when the surviving spouse remarries before age 55. After age 55, the surviving spouse is free to remarry without losing the survivor annuity.

The amount of full survivor annuity is slightly different for CSRS and FERS employees.

CSRS full survivor benefits. A CSRS retirement annuity is reduced, to provide full survivor benefits, by 2.5% of the first $3,600 per year, plus 10% of any amount greater than $3,600. The surviving spouse's annuity will be 55% of the full retirement annuity—that is, 55% of the amount before the 2.5% and 10% reductions are taken. And the 55% will include any yearly cost-of-living raises the retiree has received since the pension began.

> EXAMPLE: Ethel is eligible to receive a pension of $9,250 a year. She provides a full survivor benefit for Dante, her husband, so her own retirement annuity is reduced.
>
> The first $3,600 is reduced by 2.5%, which means Ethel receives $3,510 of that first $3,600. The remaining $5,650 is reduced by 10%, leaving $5,085. Ethel's total pension is $8,595 a year instead of $9,250, a reduction of $655 a year. For that reduction, Dante is entitled (if Ethel dies) to a surviving spouse's pension of 55% of the original $9,250, which works out to $5,087.50 a year.

FERS full survivor benefits. A FERS full retirement pension is reduced by 10% to provide an annuity for the surviving spouse. The surviving spouse's annuity will be 50% of the retiree's full pension amount—that is, 50% of the amount before the 10% reduction.

A retiring FERS worker can also choose a 5% reduction in their annuity to provide for a 25% annuity for a survivor. The survivor annuity will include any yearly cost-of-living raises the retiree receives after the pension begins.

EXAMPLE: Rigoberto is eligible to receive a pension of $12,000 a year. He provides for a full survivor benefit for Doris, his wife, reducing his own retirement annuity by 10%, or $1,200. So instead of $12,000 per year, Rigoberto receives $10,800—$12,000 minus the $1,200 reduction. In exchange for that reduction, Doris will be entitled, upon Rigoberto's death, to receive a surviving spouse's pension of 50% of the original $12,000, which works out to $6,000 a year.

Survivor Annuity to Someone Other Than Spouse

Both CSRS and FERS provide for a 55% survivor annuity that can be paid to a person other than a current spouse, such as a fiancé, a child, or a sibling. The amount that your own retirement annuity is reduced to pay for this annuity depends on the difference in age between you and the named beneficiary.

If the beneficiary you name is older than you or no more than five years younger than you, your annuity will be reduced by 10%. Your annuity is reduced 5% for every additional five years the beneficiary is younger than you—reduced 15% if 5 to 10 years younger, 20% if 10 to 15 years younger, and so on.

If the person you name as beneficiary dies before you do, you can have your own annuity restored to the full amount for the rest of your life by simply notifying the OPM. Once you've chosen to name a beneficiary, however, you can't change your mind as long as that person lives and restore yourself to a full pension.

Reduced Survivor Benefits

Both CSRS and FERS rules allow a retiring employee to divide up their annuity, taking the full amount of one part and using the rest to set up a survivor annuity. You can split up your annuity into survivor and non-survivor parts in any proportions you want.

For example, if you're entitled to a $10,000-per-year annuity, you can choose to keep $5,000 as fully your own and direct that the other $5,000 be allotted to and reduced for a survivor benefit. That second $5,000 would be reduced by the normal survivor percentages. For CSRS, the reduction would be 2.5% of the first $3,600 and 10% of the remaining $1,400—leaving you $4,770 plus the untouched $5,000. This arrangement would provide a survivor with 55% of the $5,000 you assigned to the survivor annuity, which amounts to a yearly benefit of $2,750 after your death.

Deciding Whether to Reduce Your Annuity

No obvious answer exists regarding whether to take a reduced pension to provide for another person. Retirees and their spouses or other beneficiaries must decide for themselves. It will help to consider the following:

Age. If your spouse or other potential beneficiary is considerably younger than you are and likely to outlive you by many years, taking a reduced pension now probably makes good sense. The 55% pension could go for many years to your beneficiary. On the other hand, if your beneficiary is older than you are, there may be little advantage to reducing your own immediate pension.

Health. If you're in poor health and might not survive for many years, then it's probably important to provide a survivor annuity. Conversely, if your beneficiary is in poor health and not likely to survive you for long, it's probably better for you to take your full pension.

Income. If your spouse or other beneficiary has or will have a substantial retirement pension or other income of their own, there's less need to reduce your own pension to protect your beneficiary. On the other hand, if your beneficiary is working now and earning a salary that will enable you to afford taking a reduced pension, that will permit your beneficiary to count on a survivor annuity after you're gone.

Thrift Savings Plan

In addition to the annuity pension plan to which both the employee and the employer contribute, federal employees have the opportunity to build up tax-deferred retirement savings through the Thrift Savings Plan (TSP). The TSP is similar to 401(k) savings plans made available to some employees in the private sector.

Contributions to TSP Account

The TSP for a CSRS worker is funded solely by the worker; it's a savings account of the worker's own money, which defers tax liability until retirement. For FERS employees, the government also contributes to TSP accounts, so that the TSP is both a tax-deferring savings plan and an additional pension.

CSRS contributions. CSRS-covered workers can put up to 5% of their before-tax wages into a TSP savings account. They pay no income tax on the income, or on interest earned, if they leave the money in the account until retiring from federal service with a CSRS annuity.

FERS contributions. The government automatically contributes an amount equal to 1% of an employee's pay into a TSP account for the employee. A worker who is covered by FERS can also put up to 10% of their pretax wages into the TSP savings account. If the employee makes contributions, the government will match some of the amounts an employee puts in, in addition to its automatic 1% contribution.

The government matches dollar for dollar the first 3% of wages that an employee puts in the TSP account, and matches 50 cents per dollar for the next 2% of pay the employee puts in the TSP account. Employees who leave the money in the account until retiring from federal service won't owe any tax on the money put into the account or on the interest earned until the money is withdrawn at retirement.

Withdrawals From a TSP Account

Employees who retire from federal service with either a deferred or an immediate annuity can take out their TSP money in a lump sum or in payments of equal amounts over time. Employees will owe income tax when the amounts are withdrawn. But a person who is no longer working full time is likely to be in a lower individual income tax bracket and so will owe less in taxes.

A retiring employee also has the option to transfer the money to an Individual Retirement Account (IRA), which continues the money's tax-deferred status. A retiring employee can also use the TSP account funds to purchase an annuity, which is a plan that pays a set amount for life to the retired worker. Some annuities also permit additional payments to the spouse of a retired worker after the worker dies.

An employee who leaves federal service and withdraws the TSP money before being eligible for a retirement annuity will owe a 10% penalty tax on the money in the account. However, the employee has the option of transferring, or rolling over, the money in the TSP account to a nongovernment Individual Retirement Account (IRA), which will maintain the same tax-exempt status and avoid the tax penalty. The normal limit on yearly contributions to an IRA account doesn't apply to this one-time transfer of TSP funds.

CAUTION

There is a time limit for withdrawing your funds from your TSP account. If you leave your retirement money in your TSP account after you stop working for the federal government, you're required to start withdrawing your money by April 1 of the year following either:

- the year you turn age 70½, if you are at that time no longer employed by the federal government, or
- if you continue in federal employment after age 70½, whatever year you end that employment.

Disability Benefits to Federal Workers

Both CSRS and FERS provide benefits for employees who become disabled while working for the government.

Who Is Eligible

If you've worked for the federal government for five years or more under CSRS, you could be eligible for benefits if you become disabled before you reach retirement age. If you're covered by FERS, you need to have been employed for only 18 months.

Definition of Disability

Under both CSRS and FERS rules, you're considered disabled if, because of disease or other medical condition, you're unable to perform your job. In deciding whether a worker is disabled, the OPM determines if all of the following are true:

- The employee can't perform useful and efficient service in the specific job.
- Every reasonable effort to preserve the person's employment, such as making physical modifications to the jobsite, has failed.
- There is no other vacant position that the employee could perform in the same government agency and geographic area, and at the same civil service grade or class as the current job.

It's somewhat easier to qualify for federal civil service disability than for Social Security disability benefits. Under federal civil service rules, you don't have to be so disabled that you're unable to do any sort of paid work. Instead, you can qualify for disability benefits merely because you're unable to work in the same government agency where you already work, doing a job there at the level you had attained when you became disabled. It doesn't matter that you might be able to work at some other job at a different level or outside the government agency.

Proof of disability depends on information from two separate but equally important sources. First, your physician must write a letter to the OPM fully describing your disability and the date it began and explaining why you're unable to perform your job effectively. You can assist your doctor by carefully explaining what your job entails and why your disability prevents you from performing it.

The second source of information is your supervisor at work. Your supervisor must give the OPM a written statement explaining your duties at work, how your disability impairs your job performance, and whether any other job of comparable rank and pay in the same agency is available to you. You can help yourself and your supervisor by pointing out the specific ways in which your disability interferes with your job and by noting when your disability began to make efficient work impossible.

Review of Disability Status

Your disability doesn't have to be permanent for you to receive federal employees' disability benefits. But the government, at its expense, will periodically require that you be examined by a physician to determine whether or not you continue to be disabled.

As with your original claim for disability benefits, during a review it's helpful if your own physician can write a letter detailing the specific ways in which your condition continues to be disabling. The letter will assist the government's doctor—who will probably only see you once, for a brief examination—in understanding why you're still disabled. The best approach is to have your own doctor write to the government doctor directly, so that the explanation of your condition and its limitations will already be in your file when you undergo your examination.

If your disability is found to be permanent, or if you reach age 60 without recovering from the disability, you'll receive permanent disability retirement benefits. You won't be subject to any further government examinations, and you'll receive your disability benefits for life unless you're later considered to have recovered.

You would be officially considered recovered if:

- You voluntarily take any new job with the federal government.
- Your yearly earnings at jobs or self-employment outside the federal government reach 80% of the current pay for your previous government job.
- A medical examination determines you're physically able to perform your job.

If any of these types of recovery occur, your disability payments would end either:

- on the date you begin reemployment with the government
- six months from the end of the year in which you earn 80% of your prior salary, or
- one year from the date of the medical exam that determined you had physically recovered.

Amount of Benefits

The amount of disability benefits is figured differently by CSRS and FERS.

CSRS Disability Benefit Amounts

CSRS disability benefits are the *lower* of either:

- 40% of your high-three average pay (defined in "Calculating Benefits," above), or
- a percentage of the regular pension you would have received if you had worked until age 60. This percentage varies depending on a certain number of years, which is calculated by adding together your years of service plus the number of years remaining until you reach age 60. Your high-three average salary is multiplied by the percentage, depending on the total number of years, to arrive at the disability benefits figure:
  - 10 years total: slightly more than 16%
  - 15 years total: slightly more than 26%
  - 20 years total: slightly more than 36%, and
  - 22 years or more: 40%.

EXAMPLE 1: Henry went on disability at age 55, after 10 years of employment during which he had reached a high-three average pay of $34,000; 40% of his high-three pay would be $14,400. Using the alternate method of computation, the number of years remaining until he reaches age 60 is 5, which would be added to his number of years of employment for a total of 15 years. At 15 years, the high-three average salary is multiplied by a bit more than 26%, for a total of $8,925. Since Henry is entitled only to the lower of the two computations, he would receive $8,925 per year in benefits.

EXAMPLE 2: Alice went on disability at age 50, with 15 years of service. Her high-three average salary was $38,000. She had 10 years until she would reach age 60, which were added to her 15 years of service for a total of 25 years. Because this is more than 22 years, her yearly disability benefit would be 40% of her high-three average salary—which is the same figure as the alternate method of computing benefits—amounting to $15,200.

FERS Disability Benefit Amounts

Benefit amounts under FERS change over time. In the first year after disability, the disabled worker receives 60% of the high-three average pay, reduced by any Social Security disability benefits.

From the second year of FERS disability until age 62, the worker receives 40% of the high-three salary, minus 60% of any Social Security disability benefits. These benefits are increased yearly, based on a cost-of-living formula that is 1% lower than the rise in the Consumer Price Index.

At age 62, the calculation changes. If you have fewer than 20 years of service, your benefit figure is determined by taking 1% of your high-three average salary (plus all cost-of-living increases since going on disability) and multiplying that by the total number of years of employment. That figure will be the yearly disability benefits for the remainder of your lifetime.

If you have more than 20 years of service, your benefits will be equal to 1.1% of your high-three average salary (plus all cost-of-living increases), multiplied by the number of years of employment.

Payments to Surviving Family Members of Workers Who Die While Employed

In addition to their retirement pension programs, CSRS and FERS provide some financial support for the family of a federal worker who dies while still employed by the government.

Who Is Eligible

If a federal worker covered by either CSRS or FERS dies while still employed by the government, the surviving spouse and minor children can receive survivor benefits if the worker was employed by the government for at least 18 months.

Benefits for Spouse

For the surviving spouse to collect benefits, either the couple must have been married at least a year when the worker died, or the surviving spouse must be the parent of the worker's child. The survivor benefit is paid to the surviving spouse regardless of the spouse's age.

Surviving spouses who also work for the federal government can collect both survivor benefits and their own retirement pension.

Benefits for Children

The children of a deceased federal worker also receive benefits until each reaches 18 years of age or gets married. If the child is a full-time high school or college student, benefits can continue until age 22. If a child becomes disabled before reaching age 18, the survivor benefits can continue for as long as the child is incapable of full self-support.

A child of an unmarried deceased worker also qualifies for a survivor annuity. If the unmarried worker was the father, the worker

must have acknowledged the child or a court must have established paternity. Stepchildren can also qualify for benefits if they lived with the worker in a parent-child relationship.

Amount of Benefits

The amount of survivor benefits depends on whether the deceased employee was covered by CSRS or FERS.

CSRS Benefits

If a CSRS-covered worker dies while still employed by the government, the surviving spouse and qualifying children can each receive an annuity.

A surviving spouse's or child's CSRS annuity can be up to 55% of the retirement annuity that the worker earned before dying. The exact amount is determined by whether the worker chose to reduce their own retirement annuity, and by how much, in order to provide for survivors. For details, visit the OPM's website at www.opm.gov/support/retirement/faq/survivor-benefits.

FERS Benefits

FERS benefits payable to a qualified surviving spouse or child are generally the same as for CSRS-covered employees, discussed just above, but the maximum benefit is 50% of the retirement annuity that the worker earned before dying, and the worker must have been employed for at least 10 years.

Also, children's survivor benefits under FERS are reduced by any Social Security survivors benefits the child receives. The spouse's survivor benefits aren't reduced by any Social Security survivors benefits. (See Chapter 5 regarding survivors benefits.)

A surviving spouse can also receive a death benefit of about $30,000 (the figure goes up most years, adjusted for inflation), plus either 50% of the worker's yearly pay at the time of death or 50% of the worker's high-three average, whichever is higher.

Applying for CSRS or FERS Benefits

Decisions about both CSRS and FERS benefit claims are made by the federal government's Office of Personnel Management (OPM). You must file a written application for specific benefits. You can apply at the personnel office within the agency at which you work. If you no longer work for the agency, you can file your application at any OPM office.

You can get general information about benefits, application forms, the application process, and appeals of decisions of the OPM by telephone from the OPM's Retirement Information Office. Recorded information is available 24 hours a day at 202-606-0400. For additional help, call 888-767-6738 (toll-free) or visit www.services online.opm.gov.

To obtain information about the benefits available to you based on your personal employment record, go in person to your agency's personnel office or put your request in writing and send it to:

U.S. Office of Personnel Management
Employee Services and Records Center
Boyers, PA 16017

This is the office where employee records are maintained, and most questions can be answered by the staff there. If there is some complicated question they can't answer, they will forward your inquiry to the Washington office of the OPM, which will respond. ●

Veterans Benefits

In addition to the pensions and benefits that arise from both public and private civilian employment, many older Americans may be eligible for certain benefits based on their military service.

The Veterans Benefits Administration of the Department of Veterans Affairs (VA) operates a number of programs providing financial, medical, and other assistance to veterans. Eligibility for some benefits depends on financial need or time of service. For older veterans, three major benefit programs are of particular value: disability compensation, veterans pensions, and, perhaps most significant, free or low-cost medical care through VA hospitals and medical facilities. This chapter explains some of these benefits.

Types of Military Service Required

Veterans benefits are available only to people who performed active service in a uniformed branch of the military: Army, Navy, Marine Corps, Air Force, Coast Guard, Women's Army Auxiliary Corps (WAAC), or Women's Air Service Pilots (WASP).

Active service is defined as either active duty or active duty for training.

Active Duty

Active duty means full-time service in one of the uniformed branches of the military forces mentioned above. It also includes full-time duty in the Commissioned Officer Corps of the Public Health Service or the National Oceanic and Atmospheric Administration (NOAA). And, under some circumstances, full-time members of the Merchant Marine who served during wartime and wartime members of the Flying Tigers can also qualify.

Any length of active duty can qualify a veteran for benefits, with the exception of pensions for financially needy veterans, which require at least 90 days of active duty service. (See "Pension Benefits for Financially Needy Disabled Veterans," below, for more on need-based pensions.)

Active Duty for Training

Generally, membership in the National Guard or Reserve Corps doesn't qualify a person for veterans benefits. However, if a person in the Guard or Reserves is called up for full-time duty in the armed forces, this period of service is called "active duty for training." Additional duties might fall under "inactive duty for training." A person who is injured or becomes ill during a period of active or inactive duty for training is eligible for veterans disability compensation if the injury or illness leads to a disability.

Compensation for Service-Connected Disability

The VA administers a system of benefits for veterans who have a disability that can be connected in any way to a period of service. More lenient than civil disability benefit programs, a veteran can receive assistance for partial disability, and almost regardless of the cause, as long as the injury or illness occurred during a time when the veteran was on active duty or training for active duty.

Who Is Eligible

Compensation is available for veterans who have a "service-connected disability." "Service-connected" means that they were wounded, injured, or became ill—or aggravated an existing condition—while on active duty, or training for active duty, in the armed forces.

Your condition does not need to have arisen directly from military duties. Virtually all activities—including playing for the base softball team, eating in the mess, traveling to and from training, and going on authorized leave—are considered part of military duties. This standard rules out only injuries sustained while AWOL, engaging in willful misconduct, or committing some militarily punishable offense.

Amount of Benefits

The amount of disability compensation to which you're entitled depends on the seriousness of the disability. When you apply for disability compensation, VA personnel will review your medical records and examine you to assess your disability.

Your disability is given a rating, based on the extent to which it interferes with the average person's ability to earn a living. This rating is expressed in percent of disability—0% to 100% disabled, in increments of 10%.

Unfortunately, this rating system doesn't normally take into account the real effect of your disability on the work you do. Rather, it applies arbitrary percentages—20% or 30% for the loss of a finger or toe, for example—to the theoretical average person's ability to earn a living. Obviously, the loss of a finger affects a piano player much more than it affects an opera singer. But the VA usually applies its fixed schedule of disabilities to common injuries and conditions.

However, if your disability doesn't match any of the simple descriptions in the VA's rating system, the VA will instead consider the effect of your condition on the work you're able to do.

Benefits range from about $170 per month for a 10% disability to about $3,740 per month for total or 100% disability. If you have at least a 30% disability rating, your dependents are also eligible for some minimal benefits.

Eligible dependents include your spouse and your children up to age 18, or age 22 if a full-time student, or any age if disabled. The total amount received depends on the number of dependents and on your disability rating—the higher the rating, the higher the benefits. The additional amounts for dependents range from about $60 to $210 per month for a spouse and $40 to $140 per month for one dependent child, with lower amounts for each additional child.

Disabilities From Agent Orange, Radiation, and Gulf War Syndrome

Because of the military use of chemicals and radioactive materials, many veterans have fallen ill with serious, disabling diseases years after their service ended. These veterans used to have no way to prove their disease was caused by exposure during military service. After sustained pressure from veterans groups, the VA admitted that certain exposure does indeed cause specific diseases. As a result, if a veteran was exposed to Agent Orange or radiation and later is disabled by certain diseases, the disability is *presumed* to be service connected. To a limited extent, the same can be said of "Gulf War Syndrome."

Vietnam and Agent Orange. If you served in Vietnam and have become disabled by certain diseases, you're presumed to have contracted the disease through exposure to Agent Orange and will be eligible for service-connected disability benefits. Diseases include prostate cancer, Hodgkin's disease, multiple myeloma, respiratory cancers (lung, bronchus, larynx, trachea), non-Hodgkin's lymphoma, chloracne, soft-tissue sarcoma, acute/subacute peripheral neuropathy, and more.

Radiation exposure. If your work in the military exposed you extensively to ionizing radiation, you could be eligible for service-connected disability benefits if you've become disabled by most types of leukemia or lymphoma, most types of cancer, brain or central nervous system tumors, thyroid disease, or multiple myeloma.

Gulf War Syndrome. Almost immediately after serving in the Gulf War, many veterans complained about illnesses—joint pain, rash, fatigue, memory loss, intestinal problems—that they didn't have before service in the Gulf. The cause(s) of some of these illnesses haven't been definitively diagnosed, but if a veteran has a chronic qualifying medical condition, that illness can be presumed to be connected to Gulf service. And if the illness results in a persistent disability, the veteran can be eligible for service-connected disability compensation. For information about Gulf War–related illness and compensation, a veteran can call a special Gulf War Veterans Information Hotline at 800-PGW-VETS.

Changes to Your Rating

Although most service-connected disabilities show up during or soon after military service, some conditions might not appear, or might not become disabling, until years after you get out of the service. Regardless of when a condition actually becomes disabling, if it can be traced to injury or illness that occurred while you were in the service, it can be compensated.

> EXAMPLE: Claudio's knee was bashed while serving as a cook at a training camp during the Vietnam War. The knee healed well and Claudio had no serious trouble with it during the war or the years immediately following it. However, as he got older, his knee got steadily worse. His doctor diagnosed Claudio with a serious arthritic condition in the knee, a result of the wartime injury.
>
> Because Claudio's knee condition resulted from his wartime service, he was entitled to claim disability benefits when the knee began to interfere with his normal activities, even though he made no such claim before he was discharged from the service.

Sometimes, a disability that was rated low when it first appeared grows progressively worse in later years. In such cases, veterans can claim disability benefits even if they were previously rated by the VA as not disabled. Or a veteran can apply for an upgrading of an already-existing disability rating if the condition has worsened over time.

> EXAMPLE: Ernie was an M.P. in Kuwait during the Persian Gulf War. While on leave, Ernie picked up a lung infection. The scarring from it, over the years, occasionally gave him minor respiratory difficulty. A few years after his discharge, Ernie applied for a service-connected disability. Although he picked up his illness while on leave, he was eligible for benefits because he had been on active duty during wartime. He was given a 10% disability rating for his labored breathing.

As he got older, Ernie experienced more breathing difficulties, to the point that even mild exertion made his breathing painful and dangerously difficult. His doctor said that poorer circulation with age was making Ernie's lung condition worse. Since his doctor verified that his condition had worsened, Ernie could apply for an increase in his disability rating. The new disability rating was 40%, which meant not only that Ernie's own benefits would be higher, but that his wife was now also eligible for some benefits as a qualifying dependent. (See "Amount of Benefits," above, regarding dependents benefits.)

Pension Benefits for Financially Needy Disabled Veterans

A small monthly cash benefit called VA pension is available to a financially needy wartime veteran who is 100% disabled from causes that aren't service-connected. Unfortunately, the amount is usually extremely low, only enough to bring the veteran's total income from all sources to just above the poverty line.

To qualify for this small cash benefit, the veteran must have had 90 days or more of active duty, with at least one day during a period of war. However, there is no requirement of service in or near actual combat.

These official periods of war include:
- **World War II.** December 7, 1941 through December 31, 1946
- **Korean War.** June 27, 1950 through January 31, 1955
- **Vietnam War.** August 5, 1964 through May 7, 1975, and
- **Persian Gulf War.** August 2, 1990 through a date yet to be set by Congress or Presidential Proclamation.

Note that the periods of time considered part of the Second World War and the Korean War are longer than the time spans normally attributed to those conflicts.

Totally disabled veterans who meet the service requirements are granted an amount that will bring their total annual income—including income from private pensions, Social Security, and SSI—up to a level established by Congress called the Maximum Annual Pension Rate (MAPR). Those levels, however, are extremely low: about $1,400 per month from all sources for a veteran with no dependents, about $1,800 per month for a veteran with one dependent—a spouse, or a child younger than 18, or a disabled child—and slightly higher for each additional dependent.

Some veterans are entitled to a larger benefit if they live in a nursing home, are unable to leave their house, or are in regular need of "aid and attendance." Veterans with out-of-pocket medical expenses are also entitled to a larger benefit.

Limits on Assets

The pension described in this section is not for veterans with savings or other assets that could be used or cashed in for living expenses. (Fortunately, these potential living expense assets do not include the value of a home the veteran lives in.) Even disabled veterans with little or no income won't qualify for the pension benefits if they have assets over about $80,000, depending on the cost of living where the veteran lives and the amount of ongoing medical expenses that the veteran pays out of pocket.

Survivors Benefits

Several VA programs provide benefits to a veteran's surviving spouse, and in some instances to surviving children.

The VA's Definition of Eligible Marriage

To collect benefits as the surviving spouse of a veteran, you must have been married to the veteran for at least one year and be married at the time of their death.

If you were divorced from the veteran, you can't claim survivors benefits. And if you were still married when the veteran died, you lose your survivors benefits if you later marry someone else.

However, if you remarried after the veteran's death but that later marriage has ended, you might again be eligible for survivors benefits through your first spouse's record.

Dependency and Indemnity Compensation

A benefit known as "Dependency and Indemnity Compensation" (DIC) is paid to the surviving spouse of an armed forces member who died either while in service or from a service-connected disability after discharge. However, if the veteran was dishonorably discharged, no DIC benefits will be paid to the survivor.

The amount of the DIC benefit depends on whether the veteran had a service-connected disability at the time of death.

The basic monthly DIC benefit is about $1,615; an additional amount of about $340 per month is paid if the veteran had a 100% disability rating from a service-connected disability during the eight years immediately before their death (amounts go up slightly each year). Additional amounts are paid if the veteran has a minor child or the surviving spouse is in a care facility or housebound or in need of aid and attendance.

For a complete listing of DIC benefit amounts, see the Department of Veterans Affairs website at www.benefits.va.gov/compensation.

VA Benefits for Same-Sex Spouses

Same-sex spouses are entitled to federal spousal benefits, including VA benefits, on the same terms as other spouses. This is true regardless of whether the couple lives in the state where the marriage was performed.

Foreign marriages. A spouse in a same-sex couple who was married outside the United States but now lawfully lives in the United States might be entitled to VA benefits based on the other spouse's military record, depending on the status of that marriage in the country where it was performed. Even if you have doubts about your right to VA spousal benefits as a same-sex spouse, the VA encourages you to apply for them so that they can determine whether you're eligible.

Retroactivity. The Department of Justice has decided that the right to spousal benefits for a same-sex spouse can belong to those who applied for such benefits before the Supreme Court's same-sex marriage decision on June 26, 2015. If you were married and applied for VA spousal benefits before that date but were denied those benefits (because you lived in a state that did not recognize your marriage), reapply to the VA specifically requesting retroactive benefits back to the date you first applied.

Wartime Service Pension

The surviving spouse of a deceased veteran can claim a monthly pension, regardless of whether the death was connected to service, if that veteran would have been eligible for a wartime service pension and wasn't dishonorably discharged. This survivor pension, like the veteran's wartime pension, requires that the survivor be unmarried and have a low income, taking into account money from any other pensions or Social Security benefits the surviving spouse receives.

The amount of a survivors pension depends on the survivor's income and whether or not the survivor also has dependent children,

is housebound, or requires "aid and attendance" (see below). Maximum pensions are between about $925 and $1,700 per month, but these amounts are usually reduced based on the survivor's income.

A veteran's surviving children can also collect a small survivors wartime pension after the veteran's death if they're under 18 (or 22 if in school full time, or any age if disabled before age 18). The child's benefit is only about $235.

Aid and Attendance

The Aid and Attendance (A&A) benefit is a special additional program to assist veterans and survivors who are eligible for DIC benefits and who:
- are living in a nursing facility
- need help at home performing activities like bathing and eating
- are blind or have very low vision, or
- are largely confined to bed because of illness.

If a survivor is in a nursing facility, an A&A benefit can add between about $500 per month onto the VA pension.

The DIC benefit for a housebound (but not in a care facility) survivor with a permanent disability is less, about $200. The amount of the benefit depends on whether the survivor has additional sources of income and on the survivor's medical expenses.

Medical Treatment

One of the most important benefits available to many veterans is free or low-cost medical care. The VA operates more than 150 hospitals throughout the country. In addition, a great number of outpatient clinics provide health care for veterans. Also, specialized care might be available at no charge through a VA hospital, while the same care might be unavailable or beyond a veteran's means in the world of private medicine.

If you had active duty in the military and were discharged under conditions other than dishonorable, you might be eligible for VA health care benefits. You must have served for 24 uninterrupted months to be eligible for health care. This minimum service time might not apply if you were discharged due to a service-connected disability or for hardship.

If you're a member of the National Guard or Reserves, you might qualify if you had active duty by federal order and served for the full period you were called for.

Medicare and VA Medical Treatment

Many veterans who are eligible for VA medical treatment are also covered by Medicare. The general rule is that for any specific medical treatment, you can choose either of the benefits, but not both. This means that if you're charged copayments for treatment at a VA facility, Medicare can't pay for them. However, if you're treated by a private doctor or facility and the VA pays most but not all of the cost, Medicare might be able to pay some of the unpaid amount. However, if you're treated by a private doctor or facility and Medicare covers the bills, you can't submit any unpaid portion to the VA.

There's a significant exception to this rule, which kicks in where the VA covers services that Medicare doesn't, and vice versa. For example, if the VA authorizes you to receive treatment at a private facility but does not cover all the services you receive, Medicare can pay for any of those services that Medicare does cover.

In a few pilot programs at VA medical centers, dependents and survivors of a veteran can also receive some care if they're unable to afford care in the private sector. (But this kind of care for dependents and survivors is rare in a VA medical system heavily stressed by Vietnam, Iraq, and Afghanistan war veterans.) The VA might also

pay for long-term care in certain private facilities for some veterans with serious service-connected disabilities, if there is no space in a local VA facility.

Even if you qualify for treatment at a VA medical facility, however, limited VA medical resources mean that you might not always be able to get the care when you need it, or the treatment might be available only at a VA facility far from your home.

To meet the demand for medical care, and particularly for its limited number of hospital beds, the VA has established a priority system for deciding who gets treatment directly from VA hospitals, clinics, and doctors:

- **Priority Group 1.** Veterans with service-connected disabilities rated 50% or more disabling or as totally disabling based on individual unemployability

- **Priority Group 2.** Veterans with service-connected disabilities rated 30% or 40% disabling

- **Priority Group 3.** Veterans who are former POWs, received a Purple Heart, were discharged for a disability incurred or aggravated in the line of duty, have service-connected disabilities rated 10% or 20% disabling, or were disabled by medical treatment or vocational rehabilitation

- **Priority Group 4.** Veterans who are receiving aid and attendance or housebound benefits (see "Aid and Attendance," above)

- **Priority Group 5.** Veterans with no disability rating but who have income and assets below certain dollar limits, are receiving VA pension, or are eligible for Medicaid

- **Priority Group 6.** Veterans who served at Camp LeJeune or in the Gulf War, veterans with compensable 0% service-connected disabilities

- **Priority Group 7.** Veterans whose income is below certain limits for their area and who agree to a copayment for services, and

- **Priority Group 8.** All other veterans who agree to pay copays.

TRICARE Medical Coverage for Military Retirees and Dependents

A comprehensive and generous system of medical coverage, completely separate from veterans benefits, is available for retired military service members, their spouses, and their children younger than 21. This system is known as TRICARE and is administered by the Department of Defense. People with TRICARE coverage who become eligible for Medicare must be enrolled in both programs. For details on TRICARE eligibility, benefits, and the coordination of TRICARE and Medicare, visit the TRICARE website at www.tricare.mil.

Health Care Coverage for Dependents of Disabled Veterans

The Civilian Health and Medical Program of the Department of Veterans Affairs (CHAMPVA) is the VA's health care benefit for spouses and children of permanently disabled veterans. Children are eligible for CHAMPVA as long as they remain unmarried and, for stepchildren, living in the veteran's home and are:

- under age 18
- under age 23 if they're in school full-time, or
- disabled (and the disability happened before age 18).

Additional Veterans Programs Are Available

This chapter explains the major programs for which older veterans are usually eligible. However, the VA administers many more programs that a veteran might find useful.

The VA provides financial support for education and vocational training, life insurance, home loans and other housing assistance, and a National Cemetery burial program.

Eligibility requirements vary for each of these programs, but either prior active duty or active duty for training are usual requirements. (See "Types of Military Service Required," above, for definitions.)

For information about other services the VA offers veterans and their families, visit the VA's website at www.va.gov.

Getting Information and Applying for Benefits

The VA maintains a website (www.va.gov) with much useful information about the programs discussed in this chapter. The website can be a little overwhelming, but if you're comfortable navigating the internet, you may find the site very useful. You might find it easiest to use the site's search engine by filling in just the specific subject you're interested in, such as disability compensation or Aid & Attendance.

The VA maintains large regional offices in major cities and many smaller offices known as "Vet Centers" in cities both large and small. Although applications are processed and decisions made at the regional offices, the Vet Centers provide information about benefits and claims. The Vet Centers can also provide you with application forms for various benefits, assist you in filling them out, and help you with an appeal if you're denied a benefit.

To find either the regional office or the Vet Center nearest you, look online or in the government pages in your telephone directory under United States Government, Veterans Affairs Department. Or, call the VA's national benefits information line at 800-827-1000, or their health benefits line at 877-222-8387. Also check the VA website at www.va.gov.

When appearing in person at a Vet Center, the veteran should bring discharge papers, medical records if applying for disability benefits, and wage or tax records indicating current income if considering an application for wartime service pension benefits.

A surviving spouse should bring the veteran's discharge or other military papers, marriage certificate, death certificate, recent wage or tax records, and birth certificates for any minor children or surviving children who are disabled or full-time students, plus evidence of their disability or student status.

Requests for medical treatment or admission to a VA medical facility, or VA coverage of medical treatment by a private facility, are usually handled at the admitting office of the VA medical facility or clinic itself. A veteran seeking medical attention at a VA hospital should (after calling to find out its appointment procedures) bring discharge papers and documents indicating that the veteran is receiving VA disability compensation or VA pension.

Medicare

The high cost of medical care and medical insurance, coupled with the lack of a comprehensive health plan available to all, is disappointing in a nation as wealthy as the United States. Yet whenever discussion of this issue makes its way into the political arena, proposals for creating a decent health care system run into dual roadblocks. The first is mounted by heavily bankrolled corporate interests—pharmaceutical, medical technology, and hospital companies; the insurance industry; and most doctors' groups—who fight any limits on their profit making. The second is set up by politicians who refuse to take any steps that might be seen as opposing these corporate interests. Despite this opposition, since 1965, Medicare has been carving an inroad into the mountain of consumer health care costs.

Medicare pays for most of the cost of hospitalization and much other medical care for older and permanently disabled Americans (though for some, it still leaves almost half of all medical costs unpaid). Medicare now provides coverage for more than 65 million people, most of them age 65 and older.

Despite its broad reach, Medicare doesn't pay for many types of medical services, and it pays only a portion of most services it does cover. Although Medicare expanded its coverage in 2006 to include some of the cost of prescription drugs, only recently has it begun to address the overall skyrocketing costs of those drugs.

And while the 2010 Affordable Care Act expanded Medicare coverage of certain preventive screenings and examinations, and slightly improved prescription drug coverage, it didn't otherwise broaden Medicare.

This chapter discusses the Medicare system, what it covers, and how much it pays. Chapter 13 shows you how to apply for Medicare and take full advantage of its benefits.

The chapters that follow present detailed information about how to fill the gaps in Medicare coverage. Medigap supplemental insurance is discussed in Chapter 14, and the various Medicare Advantage plans are sorted out in Chapter 15. If you have low income and few assets, Chapter 16 explains the government Medicaid program, which provides free coverage in place of buying private insurance or a managed care plan.

If You Will Turn 65 Soon

If you're turning 65 soon (and aren't already enrolled in Medicare through disability benefits eligibility), there are several things you need to do to prepare for Medicare.

Find out if your current health insurance will continue when you hit 65 and, if so, how it works in conjunction with Medicare.

See what Medicare supplement ("medigap") insurance policies (Chapter 14) and Medicare Advantage plans (Chapter 15) are available where you live.

Decide whether to enroll in traditional fee-for-service Medicare (this chapter), and whether to add a medigap policy (Chapter 14) to this, or instead to enroll in a Medicare Advantage plan (Chapter 15).

Look into whether you might be eligible for Medicaid (Medi-Cal in California) coverage, or for state assistance with your Medicare costs (Chapter 16).

Learn about Medicare prescription drug coverage and the insurance plans available in your state to deliver that coverage (this chapter).

Speak to your physician about scheduling an initial Medicare physical examination (within six months after first enrolling) and about preventive services covered by Medicare that are appropriate to your physical condition and health history.

The Medicare Maze

There are two different ways that someone eligible for Medicare can receive the program's benefits. The first way is called "traditional Medicare" or "original Medicare," which includes Part A (hospital insurance) and Part B (medical insurance). With this type of Medicare coverage, a beneficiary can receive care from any doctor, hospital, clinic, or other provider who accepts Medicare patients. Medicare pays the provider a fee for each specific service. For services

for which Medicare doesn't fully pay, the patient has several choices. The patient can choose to:

- pay out of pocket
- buy a private supplemental insurance policy—commonly known as "medigap" insurance—that pays much of what Medicare doesn't (see Chapter 14)
- buy a separate Medicare Part D prescription drug coverage insurance plan, or
- apply for Medicaid coverage (Medi-Cal in California), which is a federal program for low-income people that pays almost all of the health care costs that Medicare doesn't pay. Even if you don't qualify for Medicaid, you can apply for subsidized coverage of prescription drugs ("Extra Help") through Medicare Part D.

The second way that people can receive Medicare benefits is through a "Part C" Medicare Advantage plan, offered by private insurance companies. These plans cover everything that traditional Medicare does, plus some services Medicare doesn't cover at all.

Many Medicare Advantage plans also include outpatient prescription drug coverage. And, they eliminate some of the copayments and deductibles required by traditional Medicare.

Medicare Advantage plans are managed care plans similar to HMOs. They're generally less expensive than a combination of traditional Medicare with a medigap supplemental insurance policy. However, Medicare Advantage plans place greater limits on which specific doctors and other health care providers a patient can use, control referrals to specialists, and otherwise sometimes place restrictions on care.

Medicare Advantage plans also make annual changes: Sometimes they increase the copayment amounts they charge enrollees, sometimes they limit or eliminate specific coverage, and sometimes they eliminate coverage entirely in a particular geographic area. (For more information, see Chapter 15.)

Because of its lower cost, over half of Medicare beneficiaries are now enrolled in Medicare Advantage plans, though some of those are required to enroll because of their dual status as enrollees in both Medicare and Medicaid (see Chapter 16).

Medicare Prescription Drug Coverage

Medicare Part D provides some coverage for outpatient prescription drug costs. Unfortunately, Medicare Part D prescription drug coverage leaves many drug costs uncovered. Part D handed its drug plans over to private insurance companies—whose inefficient overhead and enormous profits add to the cost of prescription drugs under Part D. And the program doesn't control the soaring overall costs of prescription drugs. In fact, historically, the law specifically barred the Medicare program from negotiating with drug companies for lower prices on behalf of Medicare patients.

This restriction helped drug prices increase at rates far above the cost of living, which, in turn, placed enormous economic pressure on seniors and the Medicare program alike. Beginning in 2024, the 2022 Inflation Reduction Act allows Medicare to negotiate prices on a limited number of brand-name drugs. How much of the savings will be passed on to beneficiaries remains to be seen.

(Medicare Part D's coverage is explained at the end of this chapter.)

Medicare and Medicaid: A Comparison

People are sometimes confused about the differences between Medicare and Medicaid. Medicare was created to deal with the high medical costs that older citizens face relative to the rest of the population—especially troublesome given their reduced earning power. However, eligibility for Medicare isn't tied to individual financial need. Rather, it's an entitlement program; you're entitled to it because you or your spouse paid for it through Social Security and Medicare taxes.

Medicaid, on the other hand, is for low-income, financially needy people, set up by the federal government, and administered differently in each state.

Although you might qualify for and receive coverage from both Medicare and Medicaid, you must meet separate eligibility requirements for each program; being eligible for one program doesn't necessarily mean you're eligible for the other. If you qualify for both, Medicaid will pay for most Medicare Part A and B premiums, deductibles, and copayments or will offer you enrollment in a managed care plan that provides a combination of Medicare and Medicaid coverage.

Chapter 16 explains Medicaid, and the chart below describes the basic differences between the two programs.

A Comparison of Medicare and Medicaid

Medicare	Medicaid
Who Is Eligible	
Medicare is for almost everyone 65 or older, rich or poor; for people on Social Security disability; and for some people with permanent kidney failure.	Medicaid is for low-income and financially needy people, including those older than 65 who are also on Medicare.
Medicare is an entitlement program; people are entitled to Medicare based on their own or their spouse's Social Security contributions, and on payment of premiums.	Medicaid is an assistance program only for the needy.
Who Administers the Program	
Medicare is a federal program. Medicare rules are the same all over the country.	Medicaid rules differ in each state.
Medicare information is available at your Social Security office or through the Centers for Medicare & Medicaid Services.	Medicaid information is available at your local county social services, welfare, or department of human services office.

A Comparison of Medicare and Medicaid (continued)

Medicare	Medicaid
Coverage Provided	
Medicare hospital insurance (Part A) provides basic coverage for hospital stays, post-hospital nursing facilities and home health care.	Medicaid provides comprehensive inpatient and outpatient health care coverage, including many services and costs Medicare doesn't cover, most notably, prescription drugs, some diagnostic and preventive care, and eyeglasses. The amount of coverage, however, varies from state to state.
Medicare medical insurance (Part B) pays most of basic doctor and laboratory costs, and some other outpatient medical services, including medical equipment and supplies, home health care, and physical therapy. It covers some of the cost of prescription drugs for those who sign up for supplemental drug coverage (Part D).	Medicaid can pay Medicare deductibles and the 20% portion of charges not paid by Medicare. Medicaid can also pay the Medicare premium.
Costs to Consumer	
You must pay a yearly deductible for both Medicare Part A and Part B. You must also pay hefty copayments for extended hospital stays.	In some states, Medicaid charges consumers small amounts for certain services.
Under Part B, you must pay the 20% of doctors' bills Medicare doesn't pay, and sometimes up to 15% more. Part B also charges a monthly premium. Under Part D, you must pay a monthly premium, a deductible, copayments, and all of your prescription drug costs over a certain yearly amount and up to a ceiling amount, unless you qualify for a low-income subsidy.	

Medicare: The Basics

Medicare is a federal government program that assists older and some disabled people with paying their medical costs. Part A is called "hospital insurance" and covers most of the costs of a stay in the hospital, as well as some follow-up recovery costs afterward. Part B, "medical insurance," pays some of the costs of doctors and outpatient medical care. And Part D pays some prescription drug costs.

Medicare Part C refers to separate Medicare Advantage plans, which can replace Parts A, B, and D (see Chapter 15).

Medicare is operated by the Centers for Medicare & Medicaid Services (CMS), part of the Department of Health and Human Services, in cooperation with the Social Security Administration. The Medicare program's daily business, however, is run by private companies, called carriers or intermediaries, operating under contract with the federal government.

Most of a patient's direct contact with Medicare happens with the company—Blue Cross, Blue Shield, or another large insurance company—that administers Medicare or that runs the patient's Medicare Advantage or Part D prescription drug plan.

One of the outrages of the current Medicare system is that giving Medicare administrative monopolies to these private insurance companies drives up costs to the public.

Special Medicare Eligibility for End-Stage Renal Disease (ESRD)

While Medicare coverage is generally reserved for people age 65 or older and people with long-term disabilities, a special Medicare provision provides full Medicare coverage to most people suffering from permanent kidney failure, known as "end-stage renal disease" (ESRD), regardless of their age. The rules regarding eligibility for this coverage and the extent of this coverage are discussed fully later in this chapter.

Health Coverage If You Stop Working Before Age 65

Medicare and Medicare supplemental insurance and Medicare Advantage plans are available to most people age 65 and older. But what if you stop working before age 65—either because you choose to retire, are laid off, or lose your business? Chances are you'll lose your health insurance at the same time. Then the issue becomes finding affordable medical coverage, and a plan that will cover preexisting conditions, to fill the gap until you turn 65.

Here are some ways to try to stretch your medical coverage without turning to the open market for an individual health insurance policy:

- **Take advantage of continued health insurance from your employer.** If you're entitled to retirement benefits from your employer, these might include continued health care coverage. Be aware, however, that your employer is permitted to drop that retiree health coverage once you turn 65 and are eligible for Medicare. Many retiree health plans at least continue coverage for costs above what Medicare pays. If you aren't automatically eligible for retiree health coverage, you might be able to negotiate continued health coverage with your employer as part of your severance package, or with the purchaser of your business as part of its sale price.

- **Convert to individual coverage under an employer-sponsored plan.** Some employer-sponsored insurance plans permit employees to convert their group coverage to individual coverage upon leaving their employment. If your plan allows this, you'll probably have to pay all the premiums—and they might well be higher than when you were part of a group policy. Even if such individual coverage is available to you through your employer, you might want to compare its coverage and cost with individual insurance available through the new federal or state health insurance exchanges (see below).

- **Continue coverage under COBRA.** The federal Consolidated Budget Reconciliation Act (COBRA) mandates a period of continued health care coverage for people who lose or leave

their jobs (unless they're fired for gross misconduct) and their spouses and children. It also applies to employees whose hours are reduced below the number that qualifies them for health benefits. If you qualify for COBRA, you're entitled to buy 18 months of health insurance from the same company following the end of your employer-sponsored coverage. However, the extent of your coverage might be reduced, and you'll have to pay the full premiums—which will probably be higher than what your employer paid for you. (For more information, see *The Essential Guide to Federal Employment Laws*, by Lisa Guerin and Sachi Clements (Nolo), or search "COBRA" on the Department of Labor website at www.dol. gov.) Also, check with the agency in your state dealing with labor and employment—most states have passed their own laws expanding on COBRA's coverage.

• **Find individual health insurance through your state's insurance exchange or the federal insurance marketplace.** Any individual can buy one of these health insurance policies, regardless of their prior medical history. These policies are sold through what is called a "health insurance exchange," or "marketplace," established by the Affordable Care Act. The cost of the health insurance policies depends on your age, the level of coverage you seek, and your income. About half of the states operate state health insurance exchanges on their own or in partnership with the federal government, while residents of the other states are eligible to use the federal marketplace. To find out what's available where you live, go online to the government site www.healthcare.gov.

• **Claim early Medicare based on disability.** If you stop working because of a disability and you qualify for Social Security disability benefits, you'll qualify for full Medicare coverage once you've been entitled to disability benefits for 24 months. (See Chapter 3 for a full discussion of Social Security disability benefits.)

Working After Age 65

If you have current health care coverage through your employer when you turn 65, you might want to continue with it and not sign up for Medicare Part B. (Medicare Part A is free for almost everyone, so there's no reason not to enroll in it after you turn 65, even if you keep your employer-based insurance. See Chapter 13 for more on enrolling for Part A.)

Many people who continue full-time employment after age 65 are enrolled in health insurance through their employer (often along with their spouse) or through their spouse's employer. If it's a large employer (with more than 20 employees), the employee with health coverage (and the Medicare-eligible spouse) can choose to either keep that health insurance or drop it (and its premium costs) and enroll instead in Medicare Part B.

This might also be true for some small employers—those with fewer than 20 employees—who make special arrangements with their health insurance carrier; check with your employer to see if this is the case for you.

As a rule, however, primary coverage by employer-based health insurance does not apply to most employer-based health insurance for current age-65 employees of small employers with fewer than 20 employees or to retiree health insurance. For smaller company employees and for retirees, employer-based coverage automatically becomes "secondary" to Medicare when they turn 65 and will only help pay for costs that Medicare doesn't pay (such as deductibles and copayments). So, these employees and retirees need to enroll in Medicare Part B—or a Part C Medicare Advantage plan (see Chapter 15)—as soon as they turn 65.

If you have the choice to remain enrolled in employer-based health insurance based on your or your spouse's current employment or to drop that insurance and enroll in Medicare Part B, how do you decide? As with most health insurance decisions, compare the costs. Look at the monthly premium, plus the deductibles and copayments, for your employer-sponsored coverage. Then compare that against the monthly cost for Medicare Part B ($175 per month in 2024; more if

you have income over $103,000, or $206,000 as a couple), plus the cost of a medigap supplemental plan (average of $150 to $250 per month for the most common plan—see Chapter 14), and a Part D drug coverage plan (an average of $35 per month). Alternatively, you could enroll in a Part C Medicare Advantage plan, which provides the full coverage of Medicare Part B, a medigap supplement, and Part D drug coverage, for the lower cost of just the Medicare Part B premium plus another $25 per month (on average). Some Part C plans have no monthly premium.

Cost, however, isn't the only consideration. Be aware that not all doctors accept patients who are covered by Medicare as their primary insurance, especially those who have Medicare Advantage plans. So, even if Medicare Part B plus supplementary medigap insurance or a Medicare Advantage plan would be cheaper for you than keeping your employer-based coverage, before switching to Medicare, you need to check whether the doctors you regularly use accept Medicare patients, and a specific Medicare Advantage plan if you're considering one. If one or more of your regular doctors would no longer see you as a patient if you switch to Medicare as your primary coverage, or to a particular Medicare Advantage plan, you have to consider whether being forced to switch to another doctor is worth the money you would save by switching to Medicare Part B or a Medicare Advantage plan.

Employer-Based Health Coverage for Retirees

Once you're Medicare eligible, your retirement health coverage might be cut off. About 12 million Medicare beneficiaries receive some kind of retirement health benefits from their former employers. These benefits often dovetail with Medicare coverage, paying its deductibles and copayments, and covering services Medicare doesn't, including prescription drugs. However, employers are free to reduce that health coverage or eliminate it entirely for retirees age 65 or older—even if they maintain the coverage for younger retirees.

If this happens to you, you'll have to fill in the gaps in Medicare coverage some other way, as described in Chapters 14 through 16.

Part A: Hospital Insurance

Medicare is divided into several parts. Hospital insurance, referred to as "Part A," covers most of the cost of hospital and skilled nursing facility care when you're an inpatient. Doctors' charges and other medical costs are covered, at least in part, by Medicare Part B. And Medicare Part D covers part of your prescription drug costs. If you're enrolled in a Medicare Part C Medicare Advantage plan (see Chapter 15), your hospital insurance is provided by that plan rather than by Medicare Part A.

Who Is Eligible

There are two types of eligibility for Medicare Part A hospital insurance: free and paid. Most people age 65 and older are eligible for free coverage, based on their work records or on their spouse's work records. People older than 65 who aren't eligible for free Medicare Part A coverage can nevertheless enroll in it and pay a monthly fee. (See Chapter 13 for enrollment procedures.)

Free Coverage

The vast majority of people age 65 and older are automatically eligible for Medicare Part A hospital insurance. They don't have to pay any monthly premium for it; the coverage is free.

The two largest categories of people automatically eligible are:

- people age 65 or older who are eligible for Social Security retirement benefits (or have civil service retirement work credits equal to an amount that would make them eligible for Social Security retirement). (See Chapters 2 and 10 regarding eligibility for these two programs.) You're automatically eligible for Medicare coverage even if you don't actually begin collecting your retirement benefits at 65, as long as you could have started collecting them. If you wait to claim retirement benefits until after 65, you can still begin Medicare coverage at 65.

- people age 65 or older who are eligible for Social Security dependents or survivors benefits. This includes same-sex spouses who are eligible for either of these Social Security benefits. Note that people who are age 65 or older and eligible for dependents benefits when a spouse turns 62 are entitled to Medicare coverage whether or not the spouse actually claims retirement benefits at that time.

Some additional categories of people who might also be eligible for free coverage include:

- people of any age who have been entitled to Social Security disability benefits for 24 months
- people with amyotrophic lateral sclerosis (ALS) who have been approved for Social Security disability benefits (no waiting period), and
- anyone who has permanent kidney failure (ESRD) requiring either a kidney transplant or maintenance dialysis, if the person or spouse has worked a certain amount at jobs covered by Social Security. (There's a full discussion of this special ESRD-based Medicare eligibility later in this chapter.)

Paid Coverage

If you're age 65 or older but not automatically eligible for free Part A hospital insurance coverage, you can still enroll in the Medicare hospital insurance program by paying a monthly premium. The amount of your premium depends on how many Social Security work credits you or your spouse have earned, and on how long after your 65th birthday you apply for coverage.

If you aren't eligible for free Part A coverage based on your or your spouse's work record, you can purchase the coverage by paying a monthly premium of $505 (in 2024); if you or your spouse has 30 to 39 work credits, your monthly premium will be $278. Also, if you enroll in Part A coverage more than a year after you turn 65, your premium will be 10% higher than these monthly figures (unless you fit under an exception, such as having had health coverage, up to the point you apply for Part A, through an employer).

CAUTION

Make sure to compare costs. If you're considering enrolling in and paying for Medicare Part A hospital insurance, it might be cheaper for you to do so through an HMO or a health plan. The cost of such coverage will be part of the broader coverage and cost for full participation in the HMO or health plan, which will vary among different plans. Before purchasing Medicare Part A coverage as an individual, compare premiums and benefits of various group plans.

If you enroll in paid Part A hospital insurance, you must also enroll in Part B medical insurance, for which you pay an additional monthly premium. However, you can enroll in Part B without Part A.

Types of Care Covered

Part A hospital insurance pays much of the costs you incur directly from a hospital as part of inpatient care. Under some circumstances, it also covers some of the cost of inpatient treatment in a skilled nursing facility and by a home health care agency. Doctors' bills aren't included in Part A coverage; they're covered under Medicare Part B.

A few basic rules apply to all claims under Part A hospital insurance coverage, whether for inpatient care at a hospital or nursing facility or for home health care.

Doctor-Prescribed Care

The care and treatment you receive must be prescribed by a licensed physician.

Reasonable and Necessary Care

The inpatient care you receive must be medically reasonable and necessary—that is, the type of care that can be provided only at a hospital or nursing facility. If you could receive the particular treatment just as well and safely as a hospital outpatient, at the doctor's office, or at your home, Part A won't cover you if you receive that treatment as an inpatient. Also, Part A won't normally cover the cost of hospitalization for elective or cosmetic surgery—except

for reconstructive surgery after an accident or a disfiguring illness—because these aren't considered medically necessary.

 CAUTION
"Held for observation" is not the same as "admitted."
Medicare Part A hospital insurance kicks in only if someone is actually admitted to the hospital as an inpatient. Many times a patient is held and treated at the hospital—in a bed, in a room for more than 24 hours—but not formally admitted to the hospital. This is known as being "held for observation" and doesn't trigger coverage by Medicare Part A. Instead, Medicare Part B medical insurance (see later in this chapter) would be available to cover the care provided by the hospital and the doctors, and Medicare Part D prescription drug coverage could cover any medications provided.

The problem is that the copayments and deductibles a patient has to pay under Medicare Part B and Part D are generally much higher than under Part A. Also, being held for observation—rather than being actually admitted to the hospital—doesn't trigger eligibility for Part A coverage of follow-up skilled nursing facility or rehabilitation care (see the following section), which is quite common after hospital treatment. This can mean the entire very expensive cost of the nursing or rehab facility care must be paid out of the patient's pocket.

If you or a loved one are taken to the hospital and treated there for more than 24 hours, ask your doctor to have you or the loved one formally admitted to the hospital, rather than merely being held for observation, so that Medicare Part A coverage will be available to cover the stay and any following skilled nursing or rehabilitation facility inpatient care. Be aware that doctors and hospitals usually use Medicare's "Two Midnight" guideline in determining whether a patient is formally admitted as an inpatient. This refers to an expectation by the treating physician that the patient will need to remain in the hospital for at least two consecutive overnights ("two midnights"). However, this is only a guideline, not a hard-and-fast rule, and a doctor can admit a patient as an inpatient even if the doctor isn't certain the patient will need to remain past two midnights, if in the doctor's reasonable opinion an inpatient admission is medically required. Medicare, however, reserves the right to challenge the reasonableness of that decision.

CAUTION

Custodial care isn't covered. Part A hospital insurance covers only skilled medical treatment of an illness or injury. It doesn't pay for a stay in any facility, or for care from a home health agency, when the services are "custodial"—meaning primarily to make life more comfortable—to help with dressing, eating, bathing, or moving around. In reality, distinctions between medical treatment and custodial care sometimes blur, which can result in disputes between Medicare and patients.

Medicare-Approved Facility or Agency

Medicare issues licenses to hospitals, nursing facilities, and health care agencies certifying that they meet its standards for quality of care and staffing. Medicare will cover only care that is provided by facilities it approves.

Find out in advance if the facility to which you plan to be admitted, or the home health care agency you intend to hire, is approved by Medicare and accepts Medicare payment. Check with the facility's admissions services or administrator's office, or with the administrator of the home health care agency.

Nowadays it's rare to find a hospital or skilled nursing facility that isn't Medicare approved. Some home health care agencies, however, aren't Medicare approved. That doesn't necessarily mean that the agency isn't reputable. Under most circumstances, Medicare Part A pays for very little home care, anyway. So if Medicare isn't going to cover much of your costs, you might want to switch to an agency that is good and less expensive, but not Medicare approved, as soon as your Medicare coverage ends.

Facility Review Panel Approval

Each hospital and nursing facility has a panel of doctors and administrators that reviews your doctor's decision to treat you as an inpatient. The panel usually agrees with your doctor's initial decision. And the panel and your doctor usually agree on how long you should remain in the facility. Sometimes, though, the

panel decides you don't need to be an inpatient to receive certain treatment. Or it decides that you could be discharged from the facility earlier than your doctor recommends. The panel and your doctor will then consult with one another. Usually, they reach an agreement.

If, however, your doctor and the review panel don't agree that you require inpatient care, or they differ as to your discharge date, the question of whether Medicare Part A will pay for your inpatient care will be referred to a Peer Review Organization (PRO). (See Chapter 13 for more on the review process.)

> CAUTION
> **Psychiatric stays are limited.** Medicare Part A covers inpatient psychiatric hospital care, but the total number of days covered is limited. (See the "Psychiatric Hospitals" section, below, for details.)

Foreign Hospital Stays

In almost all situations, Medicare doesn't cover hospital stays outside the United States, Puerto Rico, the Virgin Islands, Guam, American Samoa, and the Northern Mariana Islands, even in an emergency. There are, however, three exceptions to this rule:

- If you're in the United States when an emergency occurs and a Canadian or Mexican hospital is closer than any U.S. hospital with emergency services, Medicare will help pay for your emergency care at that foreign hospital.
- If you live in the United States and a Mexican or Canadian hospital is closer to your home than the nearest U.S. hospital, Medicare can cover your care there even if there's no emergency.
- If you're in Canada while traveling directly to Alaska from one of the other states, or from Alaska to one of the other states, and an emergency arises, you might be covered for your care at a Canadian hospital. However, Medicare won't cover you if you're vacationing in Canada.

Some medigap supplemental insurance policies (see Chapter 14) and Medicare Advantage plans (see Chapter 15) offer coverage for foreign travel emergencies, though not for nonemergency care.

> CAUTION
> **Consider buying travel insurance.** Because there is no Medicare protection for you while you're traveling outside the United States, and if you have no other medical insurance that would cover you while traveling, it might be wise to look into traveler's insurance. These short-term policies are available for a one-time-only premium. A travel agent should be able to give you details. If you have a medigap or Medicare Advantage plan, you might not need extra travel insurance.

Skilled Nursing Facilities

A growing number of patients recovering from surgery or a major illness are referred by their doctors to skilled nursing facilities (sometimes also called "rehabilitative care centers"). These provide an important, less expensive alternative to hospitalization. Medicare may cover some of your costs of staying in a skilled nursing facility, but strictly limits how much it will pay. (See "How Much Medicare Part A Pays," below, for details.)

You'll need to make sure your stay will be covered at all. You must meet two requirements before Medicare will pay for any nursing facility care. You must have recently stayed in a hospital, and your doctor must verify that you require daily skilled nursing care.

Prior Hospital Stay

For your stay in a skilled nursing facility to be covered by Medicare Part A, it must begin after you've spent at least three consecutive days, not counting the day of discharge, in the hospital as a formally admitted inpatient—and within 30 days of being discharged. If you leave the nursing facility after coverage begins but are readmitted within 30 days, that second period in the nursing facility will also

be covered by Medicare. (For details, see "Benefit Period or Spell of Illness," below.) Note: If you're enrolled in a Medicare Advantage (Medicare Part C) plan, the rules for skilled nursing facility coverage might be slightly less strict; see Chapter 15.

Hospitals are supposed to provide a written notice to patients who are at the hospital "under observation" for at least 24 hours, explaining whether the patient's stay at the hospital is officially an inpatient stay or an outpatient stay. If the stay was at least partly as an inpatient, the notice should indicate whether the inpatient status was for the three days (not counting the day of discharge) required for Medicare Part A to cover a following stay in a skilled nursing facility. If the stay was strictly an outpatient stay, the notice must also explain why the patient was not admitted as an inpatient.

When a patient seeks admission to a skilled nursing facility following a hospital stay that included a period of "under observation" outpatient status, the skilled nursing facility must give the patient a Skilled Nursing Facility Advance Beneficiary Notice of Non-Coverage (SNFABN) warning that care might not be covered by Medicare Part A.

Requiring Daily Skilled Nursing Care

Your doctor must certify that you require daily inpatient skilled nursing care or skilled rehabilitative services. This care includes rehabilitative services by professional therapists and skilled nursing treatment—such as giving injections, changing dressings, monitoring vital signs, or administering medicines or treatments—that can't be performed by untrained personnel. This daily care must be related to the condition for which you were hospitalized.

If you're in a nursing facility only because you're unable to feed, clothe, bathe, or move yourself, even though these restrictions are the result of your medical condition, your stay won't be covered by Part A.

This is because you don't require skilled nursing care as defined by Medicare rules. However, if you require occasional part-time nursing care, you might be eligible for home health care coverage (described above) through Part A.

Aspects of Inpatient Care Generally Covered by Part A

The following list gives you an idea of what Medicare Part A does—and doesn't—pay for during your stay in a participating hospital. Remember, though, even when Part A covers a cost, there are significant financial limitations on its coverage. (See "How Much Medicare Part A Pays," below, for the dollar figures.)

Medicare Part A hospital insurance covers:

- a semiprivate room (two to four beds per room); a private room if medically necessary
- all meals, including special, medically required diets
- regular nursing services
- special care units, such as intensive care and coronary care
- drugs, medical supplies, and appliances furnished by the facility, such as casts, splints, and wheelchairs; also, outpatient drugs and medical supplies if they permit you to leave the hospital or nursing facility sooner
- hospital lab tests, X-rays, other diagnostic testing, and radiation treatment billed by the hospital
- operating and recovery room costs
- blood transfusions; you pay for the first three pints of blood, unless you arrange to have them replaced by an outside donation of blood to the hospital, and
- rehabilitation services, such as physical therapy, occupational therapy, and speech language pathology services (speech therapy) provided while you're in the hospital or nursing facility.

Medicare Part A hospital insurance does not cover:

- personal convenience items, such as television, radio, or telephone
- private duty nurses, or
- a private room, unless medically necessary.

Levels of Nursing Facility Care

Most nursing facilities provide what is called "custodial care"—primarily personal, nonmedical care for people who are no longer able to fully care for themselves. Custodial care often lasts months or years and isn't covered at all by Medicare. For the most part, custodial care amounts to assistance with the tasks of daily life: eating, dressing, bathing, moving around, and some recreation. It usually involves some health-related matters: monitoring and assisting with medication and providing some exercise or physical therapy. But it's ordinarily provided mostly by personnel who aren't highly trained health professionals, and doesn't involve any significant treatment for illness or physical condition.

A different, short-term kind of care known as "skilled nursing facility care" is covered by Medicare, although there are severe limits. (See "How Much Medicare Part A Pays," below, regarding these limits.) Skilled nursing facility care, which takes place in a hospital's extended care wing or in a separate nursing facility, provides high levels of medical and nursing care, 24-hour monitoring, and intensive rehabilitation. It's intended to follow acute hospital care due to serious illness, injury, or surgery—and usually lasts only a matter of days or weeks.

The nursing facility care and services covered by Medicare are similar to what is covered for hospital care. They include:
- a semiprivate room (two to four beds per room); a private room if medically necessary
- all meals, including special, medically required diets
- regular nursing services
- special care units, such as coronary care
- drugs, medical supplies, treatments, and appliances provided by the facility, such as casts, splints, and wheelchairs, and
- rehabilitation services, such as physical therapy, occupational therapy, and speech therapy, provided while you're in the nursing facility.

Medicare coverage for a skilled nursing facility does not include:

- personal convenience items, such as television, radio, or telephone
- private duty nurses, or
- a private room when not medically necessary.

Home Health Care

The use of paid professional home health care (including part-time nursing care and physical and other therapies), and home health care agencies to provide the care, has increased enormously over the past two decades. The following sections explain Medicare's substantial coverage of home health care. You can also read Medicare's online publication *Medicare and Home Health Care* at www.medicare.gov/pubs/pdf/10969-medicare-and-home-health-care.pdf.

RESOURCE
Learn more about home health care. For a complete discussion of long-term care, particularly for older people, and how to finance it, see *Long-Term Care: How to Plan & Pay for It*, by Joseph L. Matthews (Nolo). For ordering information, visit www.nolo.com.

Coverage Provided

Part A home health care coverage requires a prior three-day hospital stay. Home care without a prior hospital stay might be covered by Part B. If you qualify for Part A home care coverage, Medicare pays for the following services provided by a participating home health care agency:

- part-time skilled nursing care—usually two to three visits per week as part of a plan certified by a physician, and
- physical therapy, occupational therapy, and speech therapy.

If you're receiving part-time skilled nursing care, physical therapy, occupational therapy, or speech therapy, Medicare can also pay for:

- part-time home health aides
- medical social services, and

- medical supplies and equipment provided by the agency, such as a hospital bed, a walker, or respiratory equipment.

However, Medicare won't pay for a number of services sometimes provided as part of home health care, including:

- full-time nursing care
- drugs and biologicals administered at home
- meals delivered to your home, or
- housekeeping services.

Restrictions on Coverage

Despite the obvious financial as well as recovery advantages of home health care, Medicare coverage for it is severely restricted to the following:

- The agency providing the care must participate in Medicare— meaning it must be approved by Medicare and must accept Medicare payment. Not all agencies participate in Medicare, so find out before making arrangements.
- You must be confined to your home by an injury, illness, or other medical condition. If you need nursing care or other medical services but you're physically able to leave home to receive them, you might not be eligible for Medicare home health care coverage.
- You must initially require part-time skilled nursing care or physical or speech therapy. After your home health care coverage begins, Medicare can continue to cover your home care even if you need only occupational therapy—which helps you regain physical skills needed for daily living that you might have lost because of the illness or injury. Occupational therapy alone, however, can't justify home health care coverage in the first place.
- Your doctor must determine that you need home health care and must help set up a care plan in cooperation with the home health care agency. If your doctor has not mentioned home care to you but you feel it would be a good idea, make your wishes known. Most doctors will prescribe home care, can give you a referral to a Medicare-approved agency, and will cooperate with the home health care agency.

Skilled Nursing Home and Home Health Care Even If No "Improvement"

Medicare Part A coverage for inpatient skilled nursing facility care or for home health care is intended for a period of recovery following a hospital stay for an illness, an injury, or surgery. But there can sometimes be a gray area regarding coverage when a patient reaches a plateau of recovery and their condition is no longer improving. In most cases, this is the point at which coverage ends. However, if nursing facility care or home care is necessary to keep the patient's condition from deteriorating, Medicare Part A should continue to cover that care even though the patient is no longer improving.

The question of whether a person's condition continues to justify Medicare Part A–covered skilled nursing care, either in a nursing facility or at home, or instead only requires nonskilled custodial care or nonskilled home care, which Medicare Part A doesn't cover, can sometimes be tricky. If you or a loved one is in a situation in which Medicare is threatening to cut off skilled nursing facility care or home care, your best allies in keeping coverage are your doctor and the facility or agency providing the care. They need to make it clear to Medicare that skilled nursing care is still needed in order to maintain you at a functioning level, even if your underlying condition isn't likely to improve any further.

Hospice Care

Hospice care is home health care provided to a terminally ill patient who is in the last six months (or so) of life, as judged by the patient's treating doctor.

Hospice care focuses not on treating the illness or fostering recovery, but on making the patient as comfortable as possible. Good hospice care can combine the efforts of family, doctors, nurses, social workers, dietitians, and clergy, as well as physical therapists and other trained caregivers.

Medicare Part A doesn't provide 24-hour hospice care, but it does cover visits by health care workers to the patient's home on a regular basis—daily if necessary—including a hospice nurse on 24-hour call. Significantly, and unlike other nonhospital Medicare coverage, Medicare also pays for any medication prescribed by a physician for symptom management and hospice patient comfort.

Medicare might also cover up to five days of inpatient care in a hospital or skilled nursing facility to give the family or other primary caregivers a respite from their duties. If approved by the hospice, this five-day respite care period can be repeated during a patient's care.

The following sections explain how Medicare coverage of hospice works. Medicare's website also provides information about its hospice coverage in the booklet *Medicare Hospice Benefits*, which you can find at www.medicare.gov/Pubs/pdf/02154-medicare-hospice-benefits.pdf.

Hospice Coverage Provided

Medicare Part A can cover nearly the full cost of hospice care. Hospice care covered by Medicare includes:

- physician services provided by a physician connected with the hospice—Medicare Part B will continue to cover services provided by the patient's other doctors
- nursing care
- medical supplies and appliances
- drugs for management of pain and other symptoms
- health aide and homemaker services
- physical and speech therapy, and
- medical social services, counseling, and dietary assistance.

Restrictions on Hospice Coverage

Care must be provided by a Medicare-approved hospice, under a plan developed by the hospice and the patient's attending physician. The patient's doctor and the hospice's medical director must certify that the patient is terminally ill, with a life expectancy of six months or less. And the patient must sign a statement choosing hospice care instead of standard Medicare Part A benefits.

Right to Return to Regular Medicare Coverage

Some people don't take advantage of hospice care, out of a misunderstanding about how it impacts their Medicare coverage. They might mistakenly fear that they'll permanently lose their regular Medicare coverage, won't be covered by Medicare for hospitalizations or other medical care, or will outlive their six-month diagnosis and be stuck without Medicare coverage. The fact is, however, that a Medicare patient can disenroll from hospice care and return to regular Medicare coverage at any time. Also, if the patient's doctor certifies that the six-month life expectancy no longer applies, the patient can "graduate" from hospice and return to regular Medicare.

This sometimes occurs with degenerative diseases, such as congestive heart failure or emphysema; the physician's best time estimate might be off by years. Most people who disenroll do so after the first or second 90-day evaluation period (discussed further in the next section).

How Much Medicare Part A Pays

To understand any Medicare decision about how much of your hospital, nursing facility, or home care bill Medicare will pay, you have to know the basics of Part A payments. Those basics include benefit periods and deductible and coinsurance amounts.

Benefit Period or Spell of Illness

How much Medicare Part A pays depends on how many days of inpatient care you have during what is called a "benefit period" or "spell of illness."

A benefit period or spell of illness refers to the time you're treated in a hospital or skilled nursing facility, or some combination of the two. The benefit period begins the day you enter the hospital or skilled nursing facility as an inpatient—and continues until you've been out for 60 consecutive days. If you're in and out of the hospital or nursing facility several times but haven't stayed out completely for 60 consecutive days, all your inpatient bills for that time will be figured as part of the same benefit period (even if you're readmitted for a different illness or injury).

There's no limit to the number of benefit periods you can have over your lifetime, except for stays in psychiatric hospitals (see below).

Hospital Bills

Medicare Part A pays only certain amounts of a hospital bill for any one benefit period.

The Deductible Amount

For each benefit period, you must pay an initial amount before Medicare will pay anything. This is called the hospital insurance deductible. The deductible is increased every January 1. In 2024, the amount is $1,632.

First 60 Days Hospitalized

For the first 60 days you're an inpatient in a hospital during any one benefit period, Part A hospital insurance pays all of the cost of covered services. You pay only your hospital insurance deductible. If you're in more than one hospital, you still pay only one deductible per benefit period—and Part A covers 100% of all your covered costs for each.

61 Through 90 Days

After your 60th day in the hospital during one spell of illness, and through your 90th day, each day you must pay what is called a "coinsurance amount" toward your covered hospital costs.

Part A of Medicare pays the rest of covered costs. In 2024, this daily coinsurance amount is $408; it goes up every year.

Reserve Days

Reserve days are a last-resort coverage. They can help pay for your hospital bills if you're in the hospital more than 90 days in one benefit period. But the payment is quite limited. If you're in the hospital for more than 90 days in any one spell of illness, you can use up to 60 additional reserve days of coverage. During those days, you're responsible for a daily coinsurance payment. For 2024, the reserve days coinsurance amount is $816 per day. Medicare pays the rest of covered costs.

Two Benefit Spells Might Be Better Than One

You can get more total days of full Medicare coverage during two spells of illness than in just one. As a result, it can be in your financial interest to stretch your hospital or nursing facility stays into two benefit periods, if possible. For example, using home health care might help you stay out of the hospital or nursing facility for 60 days before you must return as an inpatient for further treatment. If the timing of your inpatient treatment could be somewhat flexible, discuss that timing and its effect on Medicare coverage with your doctor.

EXAMPLE: Oscar is in the hospital with circulatory problems, being treated with medication. His doctor recommends surgery, operating on one leg at a time, monitoring the first leg before attending to the second. Oscar and his doctor plan the dates of surgery so that he will be released from the hospital and will convalesce at home, with the help of home health care services, for more than 60 days before he returns to have the second operation.

This way, Medicare will consider the time Oscar spends in the hospital after the second surgery to be part of a new spell of illness, even though it results from the same condition that made the first operation necessary. If there had not been a 60-day break between hospitalizations, Oscar would have been in the hospital a total of more than 60 days and would have had to pay a hefty coinsurance amount for every day after his 60th day in the hospital—up to his 90th day.

You don't have to use your reserve days in one spell of illness; you can split them up and use them over several benefit periods. But you have a total of only 60 reserve days in your lifetime. Whatever reserve days you use during one spell of illness are gone for good. In the next benefit period, you would have available only the number of reserve days you didn't use in previous spells of illness.

TIP

Try to save up your reserve days. Even if you are in the hospital for more than 90 days, you might want to save your reserve days for an even rainier day. For example, you might not want to use your reserve days if you currently have some private insurance, such as from an employer, that can help cover the costs of those extra days of hospitalization, but you might not have that insurance later in life.

EXAMPLE: Bert had a serious stroke, followed by several complications involving kidney failure and pneumonia. For six months, he was in and out of both a hospital and a skilled nursing facility (SNF), for a total of 130 days. Because Bert never spent 60 consecutive days out of the hospital or SNF, all his inpatient treatment was considered part of the same "benefit period." So when his time in the hospital reached 91 days, he had no choice but to begin using up his "reserve days" coverage. He used 20 reserve days during this benefit period, leaving him with only 40 reserve days for the remainder of his lifetime.

If Bert had remained out of the hospital and SNF for 60 consecutive days during any part of this stretch of treatment, he would not have had to use up any reserve days. Or, if his condition had permitted it, he might have been able to receive some care in an intermediate-level or custodial care nursing facility instead of in an SNF. However, this would have been a practical alternative only if he had some supplemental health coverage that would have paid for some or all of this level of care (Medicare doesn't cover it at all).

Or, if Bert's condition had permitted, he might have received some care at home from a Medicare-approved home health care agency. Medicare would have paid the full amount of this care. And it would not have affected his right to receive coverage when he needed to return to the hospital or SNF.

If you want to use your reserve days, you don't have to make a formal request or fill out any form. Medicare will automatically apply them to cover your hospital bills—minus the hefty daily coinsurance you have to pay.

But if you don't want to use those reserve days, or want to use some but not all of them, you must notify the hospital administrator or billing office. Plan ahead: You must submit your notification before the reserve days come up.

Psychiatric Hospitals

Medicare Part A hospital insurance covers a total of 190 days in a lifetime for inpatient care in a specialty psychiatric hospital (meaning one that accepts patients only for mental health care, not just a general hospital).

If you're already an inpatient in a specialty psychiatric hospital when your Medicare coverage goes into effect, Medicare can retroactively cover you for up to 150 days of hospitalization before your coverage began. In all other ways, inpatient psychiatric care is governed by the same rules regarding coverage and copayments as regular hospital care.

There's no lifetime limit on coverage for inpatient mental health care in a general hospital. Medicare will pay for mental health care in a general hospital to the same extent as it will pay for other inpatient care.

> EXAMPLE: During the five months before his 65th birthday, Horace spent 60 days in a psychiatric hospital. Those 60 days are subtracted from Horace's lifetime total of 190 days of Medicare coverage in a psychiatric hospital. It leaves him with only 130 days more coverage under Part A for psychiatric hospitalization.

Skilled Nursing Facilities

Despite the common misconception that nursing homes are covered by Medicare, the truth is that Part A covers only a limited amount of inpatient skilled nursing facility care.

For each benefit period, Medicare will cover only a total of 100 days of inpatient care in a skilled nursing facility. For the first 20 of these 100 days, Medicare will pay for all covered costs, which include all basic services (but not television, telephone, or private room charges). For the next 80 days, the patient is personally responsible for a daily copayment; Medicare pays the rest of covered costs. In 2024, the copayment amount is $204; the amount goes up each year.

Reserve days, available for hospital coverage, don't apply to a stay in a nursing facility. After 100 days in any benefit period, you're on your own as far as Part A hospital insurance is concerned. However, if you later begin a new benefit period, your first 100 days in a skilled nursing facility will again be covered.

EXAMPLE: Bettina was hospitalized for several weeks with a broken hip. Upon leaving the hospital, she was moved to a Medicare-approved SNF for rehabilitation and recovery. She remained in the SNF for 18 days, then went home. However, some setbacks in Bettina's healing forced her to return to the SNF a week later, where she stayed for another 12 days.

Because Bettina's stays in the SNF were not separated by 60 days, they were considered to be within the same "benefit period." Therefore, of her total 30 days in the SNF, Medicare will pay the entire amount of her bills (minus Bettina's phone calls to her brother in New Zealand) for only the first 20 days. For the remaining 10 days, Bettina will be responsible for a copayment of $204 per day, for a total of $2,040.

If Bettina had had a medigap supplemental insurance policy (see Chapter 14) or a Medicare managed care plan (see Chapter 15) that covered Medicare nursing facility copayments, or had she been eligible for Medicaid (see Chapter 16), that insurance, care plan, or government program would have paid all or part of the $2,040. Having no such extra coverage, Bettina will have to pay out of her own pocket.

How Part A Payments Are Figured

To get a picture of how the overall Part A payment scheme works, an example of one person's hospital stay might be useful.

Annika was hospitalized for a week for an intestinal disorder, went home for a week, came back to the hospital for another five days, and then was taken into surgery. Annika spent two days in intensive care and another week in the hospital recovering from the operation. Annika's hospital bill for all her treatment included:

Semiprivate room, 19 days at $1,600 per day	$30,400
Surgery surcharge	3,200
Intensive care unit, 2 days at $3,000 per day	6,000
Laboratory	1,250
Medications	465
Whole blood (6 units at $175 per unit)	1,050
Telephone calls	94
Television (19 days at $12 per day)	228
TOTAL DUE	$42,687

Medicare doesn't cover, and won't pay anything for, the telephone or television ($322) or the first three units of blood ($525), which Annika must pay out of pocket. But Medicare Part A will cover all the other costs, less the $1,632 deductible for Part A, paying a total of more than $40,000.

Remember, though, that Annika will still have to face all her doctor bills, coverage for which she will depend on Medicare Part B and any medigap supplemental insurance she has.

Home Health Care

Medicare Part A pays 100% of the cost of your covered home health care when provided by a Medicare-approved agency—and there's no limit on the number of visits to your home for which Medicare will pay.

Medicare will also pay for the initial evaluation by a home care agency, if prescribed by your physician, to determine whether you're a good candidate for home care.

However, if you require durable medical equipment, such as a special bed or wheelchair, as part of your home care, Medicare will pay only 80%.

Hospice Care

Medicare pays 100% of the charges for hospice care, with two exceptions. First, the hospice can charge the patient up to $5 for each prescription of outpatient drugs the hospice supplies for pain and other symptomatic relief. Second, the hospice can charge the patient 5% of the amount Medicare pays for inpatient care in a hospice, nursing facility, or the like every time a patient receives such respite care.

There's no limit on the amount of hospice care you can receive. At the end of the first 90-day period of hospice care, your doctor will evaluate you to determine whether you still qualify for hospice—meaning your illness is still considered fatal and you're still estimated to have less than six months to live. A similar evaluation is made after the next 90-day period, and again every 60 days thereafter. If your doctor certifies that you're eligible for hospice care, Medicare will continue to pay for it even if it exceeds the original six-month diagnosis. And if your condition improves and you switch from hospice care back to regular Medicare coverage, you can return to hospice care whenever your condition warrants it.

EXAMPLE: Ted is suffering from cancer. His doctors say it will be fatal within six months. Ted chooses to stop his chemotherapy treatment, stay at home, and receive hospice care there. After 90 days, however, Ted has not gotten any worse. His doctors determine that Ted's cancer has not progressed much and that Ted might live for another year or two. So Ted returns to traditional Medicare coverage.

After another nine months, however, Ted's cancer becomes much more aggressive. After Ted undergoes a short course of chemotherapy, his doctor estimates that Ted now has less than six months to live. Ted can now return to hospice care and stay on it for as long as his doctor still believes the cancer will be fatal within six months.

Part B: Medical Insurance

The second part of Medicare coverage, Part B, is medical insurance. It's intended to help pay doctor bills for treatment either in or out of the hospital, as well as many of the other medical expenses you incur when you aren't in the hospital.

Eligibility and Premiums

You're eligible for Medicare Part B medical insurance if you're age 65 or older and either a U.S. citizen or a legal resident of the United States who has been in the country lawfully for five consecutive years. This is true whether or not you're eligible for Medicare Part A. Anyone who wants Part B medical insurance must enroll in the program. (See Chapter 13 for details about enrollment.)

Everyone enrolled in Medicare Part B must pay a monthly premium; if you also are enrolled in a state Medicare Savings Program, administered by Medicaid (see Chapter 16), Medicaid pays your Part B premium.

The Medicare Part B premium is raised almost every year. The amount of your premium depends on which of the following categories you fall into:

- **Basic premium.** If you were not collecting Social Security benefits as of November 2023, or you first enroll in Medicare Part B in 2024, you'll pay a monthly Part B premium of $174.70.
- **Higher income-based premium.** If your adjusted gross income (based on your 2022 tax return) is more than $103,000 (or $206,000 for a couple filing jointly), your monthly Medicare Part B premium for 2024 will be higher than the basic premium, as shown on the chart below. (If, however, in the year since your 2022 tax return, you've become widowed or divorced or had a significant drop in income, you can contact Medicare and request an adjustment of this income-based premium.)

Yearly Income in 2022	Total Monthly Premium
Single $103,001–$129,000	$244.60
Married $206,001–$258,000	
Single $129,001–$161,000	$349.40
Married $258,001–$322,000	
Single $161,001–$193,000	$454.20
Married $322,001–$386,000	
Single $193,001–$499,999	$559.00
Married $386,001–$749,999	
Single $500,000 or more	$594.00
Married $750,000 or more	

Types of Services Covered

Part B medical insurance is intended to cover basic medical services provided by doctors, clinics, and laboratories. However, the lists of services specifically covered and not covered are long, and don't always make a lot of common sense.

Making the effort to learn what is and isn't covered can be important, because you might get the most benefits by fitting your medical treatments into the covered categories whenever possible.

 TIP

Medicare's website has an extended list of Part B covered services. On the following pages you'll find an explanation of many of the most common medical services covered by Part B. For a more extensive list of covered services, see Section 2, Part B, of Medicare's handbook *Medicare & You* at www.medicare.gov/media/10991.

Doctor Bills

Part B medical insurance covers medically necessary doctors' services, including surgery, whether the services are provided at the hospital, at a doctor's office, or—if you can find such a doctor—at home. Part B also covers outpatient medical services provided by hospital and doctors' office staff who assist in providing care, such as nurses, nurse practitioners, surgical assistants, and laboratory or X-ray technicians.

TIP
Medicare pays for a second opinion before surgery. Before undergoing surgery, it's usually medically wise to get a second opinion from another doctor. Second opinions often lead to the decision not to have surgery. Recognizing this and the savings involved, Medicare will cover your obtaining a second doctor's opinion before undergoing any kind of surgery. And if the second doctor's opinion conflicts with the original doctor's recommendation for surgery, Medicare will pay for an opinion by yet a third doctor.

Outpatient Care and Laboratory Testing

Medicare medical insurance covers outpatient hospital treatment, such as emergency room or clinic charges, X-rays, injections that are not self-administered, and laboratory work and diagnostic tests. Lab work and tests can be done at the hospital lab or at an independent laboratory facility, so long as that lab is approved by Medicare.

CAUTION
Beware of outpatient hospital charges. Medicare pays only a limited amount of outpatient hospital and clinic bills. And unlike most other kinds of outpatient services, Medicare places no limits on how much the hospital or clinic can charge over and above what Medicare pays. (See "Different Payment Structure for Hospital Outpatient Charges," below, for details.)

COVID-19 Vaccines, Testing, and Antibody Treatment

If you become ill with COVID-19 or see a medical provider because you think you might have COVID-19, Medicare Part A and B (or Part C, Medicare Advantage—see Chapter 15) will cover your treatment under the same terms as for any other illness. In addition, Medicare Part B or Part C will cover the administration of approved COVID-19 vaccines, testing, and special antibody treatments under the following conditions.

- **Vaccines.** Medicare covers the entire cost of vaccination with any of the FDA-approved COVID-19 vaccines, regardless of where you obtain the vaccination.

- **Testing.** Medicare covers the cost of tests to determine whether you're currently infected with the COVID-19 virus (diagnostic test) or have developed antibodies to the virus because of being previously exposed (antibody test), if you receive the test at a testing site approved by your local health department, but you might have to pay a copay now that the COVID-19 public health emergency has ended.

- **Treatment.** Special monoclonal antibody treatments were developed for people infected with the COVID-19 virus, but many of them are no longer used because they aren't as effective against more recent strains of the virus. Medicare will cover the cost of monoclonal antibody treatments when provided by a Medicare-participating provider if they are still approved for use by the FDA. Medicare Part D may cover newer oral antiviral treatments, subject to your Part D plan's deductible and copayment rules.

Ambulances

Part B medical insurance will cover the cost of transporting a patient by ambulance, if transport by any other means would not have been medically advisable. This can include not only emergencies, but also nonemergency trips following discharge from a hospital—for example, to the patient's home or to a nursing facility. Transporting

residents of nursing facilities to see their doctors may also be covered. However, Medicare doesn't cover ambulance transport for regular visits from a person's home to a doctor's office, if the trip was arranged simply because the person needed some assistance.

If your doctor prescribes an ambulance for you for a trip from home to the doctor's office, Medicare might cover it but isn't required to. Medicare will cover the ambulance trip only if the doctor's communication with Medicare convinces Medicare that the ambulance was medically necessary.

If Medicare covers an ambulance trip, the ambulance company must accept the Medicare-approved amount as full payment for its services. Medicare will pay 80% of the Medicare-approved amount. You, or your medigap insurer or managed care plan (see Chapters 14 and 15 for descriptions of these plans), are responsible for paying the remaining 20%. The ambulance company can't bill you for any amount over that 20%.

If you need help getting to and from doctor visits, but an ambulance isn't considered medically necessary, look into free transportation for seniors in your community. Call your local senior center or the senior information line or elder care locator listed in your telephone directory or look online for these kinds of resources.

Administered Drugs

Drugs or other medicines administered to you at the hospital or a doctor's office are covered by Medicare medical insurance. However, Medicare Part B doesn't cover most drugs you take by yourself at home, including self-administered injections, even if they're prescribed by your doctor. Exceptions to this rule include self-administered cancer medication, antigens, immunosuppressive drugs, and insulin delivered by insulin pump (and the pump itself). Also, a yearly flu shot and vaccines for COVID, pneumonia, and hepatitis B are covered by Medicare. (Note: Most Medicare Part D prescription drug plans also cover other vaccines; see below.)

Medical Equipment and Supplies

Splints, casts, prosthetic devices, body braces, heart pacemakers, corrective lenses after a cataract operation, therapeutic shoes for diabetics, and medical equipment such as ventilators, wheelchairs, and hospital beds—if prescribed by a doctor—are all covered by Part B medical insurance. This includes glucose monitoring equipment for people who have diabetes.

To learn more about the many types of medical equipment and supplies Medicare Part B covers, and how different equipment can be rented or purchased, see Medicare's online publication *Medicare Coverage of Durable Medical Equipment & Other Devices* at www.medicare.gov/media/publication/11045-medicare-coverage-of-dme-and-other-devices.pdf.
To find a Medicare-certified supplier of medical equipment near you, go to the Medicare website home page at www.medicare.gov, and under the "Providers & Services" tab, click "Find medical equipment & suppliers."

Oral Surgery

Some types of surgery on the jaw or facial bones, or on the related nerves or blood vessels, can be covered by Part B medical insurance. However, surgery on teeth or gums, even when related to an injury or a disease that didn't originate with the teeth, is usually considered to be dental work, and so isn't covered by Medicare.

However, even if the work in question is done by an oral surgeon who isn't an M.D., Medicare might cover it if it's the kind of treatment that M.D.s also provide and if Medicare would have covered it if an M.D. physician had performed it. This is particularly true if the treatment involves not only teeth and gums but also the bones, nerves, blood vessels, or tongue. If Medicare is to cover work performed by a nonphysician oral surgeon, that surgeon must participate in—that is, be certified by—Medicare. You should have your oral surgeon's office check with Medicare about coverage before undergoing any procedure.

Outpatient Physical Therapy and Speech Therapy

Part B of Medicare will cover some of the cost of outpatient physical and speech therapy—if it's prescribed and regularly reviewed by a doctor and provided by a Medicare-approved facility or therapist.

However, there are limits on how much Medicare will pay for these therapies.

Medicare covers only therapy that improves a patient's condition or that is needed to maintain—by preventing or slowing a decline in—a patient's condition. Successfully getting Medicare coverage for therapy under this second standard—maintaining an existing condition—can be difficult, with Medicare and the insurance companies that offer Medicare Advantage policies (see Chapter 15) frequently denying such claims. In order to meet this standard, you might need a good written explanation of medical necessity from the therapist and support from your treating doctor.

There are also yearly dollar limits on the amounts Medicare Part B will pay for outpatient therapy. And the amount Medicare pays will be partially determined by who provides you with the therapy services. These limits are explained in "Payments for Outpatient Therapies," below.

Supervised Exercise Therapy for PAD Patients

Peripheral artery disease (PAD) is a condition in which arteries or other blood vessels in the legs become clogged. PAD isn't only painful but also increases the risk of heart attack and stroke.

Researchers have determined that exercise therapy, such as treadmill walking, can significantly reduce PAD without surgery. This exercise therapy is particularly useful if conducted under the supervision of a certified exercise therapist. Medicare Part B will partially pay for a limited amount of such supervised therapy (usually up to only 12 weeks) if it's prescribed by a physician. The patient must pay out of pocket, or through other medical insurance, for any charges that Medicare doesn't pay for.

Home Health Care

The same home health care coverage is available under Part B medical insurance as is provided by Part A hospital insurance. (See "How Much Medicare Part A Pays," above, for information about home health care coverage under Part A.)

If you have both Part A and Part B, Part A will cover your home health care following a hospital stay of at least three days; otherwise, Part B will cover it. There's no limit on the number of home health care visits that are covered, and you aren't responsible for paying your Part B deductible for home health care. Only skilled nursing care or therapy while you're confined to your home is covered, however, and such care must be ordered by your doctor and provided by a Medicare-approved home health care agency.

Part B medical insurance, like Part A coverage, will pay 100% of the approved charges of a participating home health care agency.

Chiropractors

Part B might cover some care by a Medicare-certified chiropractor. Generally, Medicare will cover a limited number of visits to a chiropractor for manipulation of neck or back vertebrae that are out of place.

Medicare won't, however, cover general health maintenance visits to a chiropractor, nor will it usually cover therapeutic manipulation other than that of the vertebrae. And Medicare generally won't cover X-rays or other diagnostic tests ordered or performed by the chiropractor. Instead, your physician normally must order these tests.

If you go to a chiropractor and hope to have Medicare pay its share of the bill, have the chiropractor's office check with Medicare ahead of time about the treatment being proposed. And even if Medicare initially covers the treatment, it might not do so indefinitely. So, if you continue with the treatments, have the chiropractor's office regularly check with Medicare to find out how long it will keep paying.

Preventive Screening Exams

Medicare covers the following examinations to screen for a number of serious illnesses:

- a one-time routine physical exam (sometimes called an "initial wellness exam") within six months of the date a person first enrolls in Part B coverage

- an annual physical exam that includes a comprehensive risk assessment, which might lead to further Medicare-covered testing

- a Pap smear and pelvic exam for women every three years; every year for women at high risk of cervical or pelvic disease; Medicare covers this exam even if you have not yet met your annual Part B deductible

- bone density tests for women at high risk of developing osteoporosis or for anyone who is receiving long-term steroid therapy, who has primary hyperparathyroidism, or who has certain vertebral abnormalities

- blood glucose testing supplies—if prescribed by a physician— for patients with diabetes

- annual prostate cancer screenings for men older than 55

- a positron emission tomography (PET) scan, which is a diagnostic test for certain cancers

- annual eye screening for glaucoma

- blood screening for early detection of cardiovascular disease, if your doctor says you have risk factors

- screening test for diabetes, if your doctor says you're at risk for the disease, and

- PET brain scans for patients with unusual Alzheimer's-like symptoms, if your doctor believes the source might be a different type of brain disease known as "frontotemporal dementia."

Colorectal Cancer Screenings

Different types and levels of colon cancer screenings are covered by Medicare Part B. Your physician, under Medicare guidelines, determines which specific test you should receive. Medicare Part B pays 100% of the costs, except where noted below:

- fecal occult blood test: a lab test, once per year for people 50 and older
- blood-based biomarker test: a lab test, once every three years for people age 50 to 85
- flexible sigmoidoscopy: an outpatient examination performed in a doctor's office, clinic, or hospital outpatient department, once every 4 years if age 50 or older, or 10 years following a colonoscopy, or more often if patient deemed at high risk
- colonoscopy: an outpatient examination (more comprehensive than sigmoidoscopy) performed in a doctor's office, clinic, or hospital, once every 10 years, or 4 years after a sigmoidoscopy (or more frequently if at high risk). Medicare will cover colonoscopy for patients of any age if a doctor orders it. If the doctor removes tissue during the procedure, the patient must pay 20% of the Medicare-approved amount for the doctor's charges as well as a copayment if the procedure is performed in a hospital outpatient setting. (The Part B yearly deductible doesn't apply.)
- barium enema: an alternative to a sigmoidoscopy or colonoscopy; every four years if age 50 or over (or every two years if patient is high risk). The patient must pay 20% of the doctor's Medicare-approved charges and a hospital outpatient copayment if the procedure is performed at a hospital outpatient clinic. (The Part B yearly deductible doesn't apply).

Mammography

Part B covers a yearly mammogram, even if you have not yet met your annual deductible. The mammogram must be performed by a doctor or facility certified by Medicare to perform mammograms.

Podiatrists

Medicare covers podiatrist services only when they consist of treatment for injuries or diseases of the foot. This doesn't include routine foot care or treatment of corns or calluses.

Eye Care and Eyeglasses

Medicare does not cover routine eye examinations, glasses, or contact lenses provided by an optometrist or optician. The only exception is for people who have undergone cataract or other eye surgery. For them, Medicare covers not only the surgery itself but also glasses, contact lenses, or intraocular lenses, as well as the cost of a post-surgical examination by a Medicare-certified ophthalmologist or optometrist. Medicare Part B does cover medical care from an ophthalmologist (an eye doctor with an M.D., not an optometrist) or other medical doctor for illness or injury to your eyes.

Clinical Psychologists or Social Workers

When a doctor or hospital prescribes it in conjunction with medical treatment, Medicare Part B can cover limited counseling by a clinical psychologist or clinical social worker. The practitioner must be Medicare approved. If your doctor suggests a clinical psychologist or social worker to help in your recovery from surgery, injury, or illness, contact the practitioner in advance to find out whether the services will be approved by Medicare.

Day Care Mental Health Treatment

Medicare Part B can, in some cases, cover mental health care, in the form of day treatment—also called "partial hospitalization"—at a hospital outpatient department or community mental health center, if prescribed by a physician. The facility must be Medicare approved and the particular day program certified for Part B coverage by Medicare.

Alzheimer's-Related Treatments

Until recently, Medicare didn't cover various kinds of physical, speech, and occupational therapy, or psychotherapy and other mental health services, for people who had been diagnosed with Alzheimer's disease. Medicare's reasoning was that patients with Alzheimer's were incapable of medically improving, and that the treatment was therefore not "medically necessary."

Medicare has now reversed its backward stance. A patient can no longer be denied Medicare coverage for physician-prescribed therapies or treatments solely because the patient has been diagnosed with Alzheimer's. So, if you or a loved one has Alzheimer's and a physician prescribes a form of therapy or other treatment to counter the effects of the disease, make sure the treatment provider participates in Medicare and will submit its bills to Medicare for payment.

Obesity

Medicare covers various medically approved weight-loss therapies and treatments for obesity, if prescribed by a physician. These range from stomach surgeries to diet programs to psychological and behavior modification counseling.

Not all treatments are covered, however, and not all patients will be eligible for all covered treatments. But if you're undergoing care from a physician for obesity, the physician can recommend specific treatments for you that are covered by Medicare and can submit it to Medicare for coverage approval.

Chronic Pain Treatment

Medicare Part B covers services specifically to treat chronic pain if your doctor verifies that you've been suffering from such pain for more than three months. Treatment for chronic pain is sometimes offered on an outpatient basis at special pain management clinics, often attached to a hospital.

Outpatient Mental Health Services

Medicare Part B will cover outpatient psychotherapy and counseling, individually or in groups, for diagnosed mental health issues such as clinical depression, anxiety, and substance use disorders. These mental health care services can be provided by provided by psychiatrists, clinical psychologists, nurse practitioners, physicians' assistants (PAs), clinical social workers, marriage-and-family therapists, and mental health counselors. Only practitioners who officially participate in Medicare, however, will be reimbursed.

Medicare can cover intensive outpatient program services provided by hospitals, community mental health centers, federally qualified health centers, and Rural Health Clinics. The care can include outpatient "partial hospitalization" services provided by a community mental health center or by a hospital. Partial hospitalization provides rigorous outpatient psychiatric services as an alternative to inpatient psychiatric care.

Services *Not* Covered by Medicare Part B

When you look at the list of what Medicare medical insurance doesn't cover, plus the Medicare deductibles and copayments, it's easy to understand why people with traditional Medicare still wind up personally responsible for half of their medical bills. It also underlines the need for you to consider additional medical insurance, either through private supplemental plans, an HMO or other Medicare Advantage plan, or Medicaid or Qualified Medicare Beneficiary coverage. (See Chapters 14, 15, and 16 for more on these alternatives.)

The categories of medical treatment and services listed below aren't covered by Medicare.

However, not all the noncovered services listed below apply to HMO or other Medicare Advantage plan coverage. Many Medicare Advantage plans include some coverage for a few of these medical services even though Medicare itself doesn't cover them.

Treatment That Is Not Medically Necessary

Medicare won't pay for medical care that it doesn't consider medically necessary. This includes some elective and most cosmetic surgery, plus virtually all alternative forms of medical care such as acupuncture, acupressure, and homeopathy—with the one exception of limited use of chiropractors. This is despite the fact that many people find these therapies more beneficial than traditional forms of medical care.

Vaccinations and Immunizations

Medicare Part B covers a yearly flu shot and pneumonia, hepatitis B, and COVID vaccines (see "Types of Services Covered," above). It doesn't cover other vaccinations and immunizations, such as shingles, RSV, and vaccines taken for travel abroad. An exception is for emergencies in which a vaccination is required because of risk of infection or exposure to communicable disease. However, most Medicare Advantage plans (see Chapter 15) and Part D prescription drug plans (see "Part D: Prescription Drug Coverage," later in this chapter) do cover other vaccinations.

Prescription Drugs You Take at Home

Medicare Part A covers drugs administered while you're in the hospital or in a skilled nursing facility. Part B medical insurance covers drugs that can't be self-administered and that you receive as an outpatient at a hospital, a clinic, or at the doctor's office. (There are a few exceptions for self-administered drugs; see "Types of Services Covered," above.) Potential coverage for all other prescription drugs falls under Medicare Part D (see "Part D: Prescription Drug Coverage," below), which you must enroll in and pay for separately from Parts A and B, or through a Medicare Advantage plan (see Chapter 15).

Medicare Medical Insurance Is Never Enough

Part B Medicare medical insurance is intended to pay for a portion of doctor bills, outpatient hospital and clinic charges, laboratory work, some home health care, physical and speech therapy, and a very few drugs and medical supplies. But as described above, there are heavy restrictions on what is covered, and as the following section explains, there are limits on how much is paid.

Private Medicare supplement insurance—referred to as "medigap" insurance—might help you make up the difference. Instead, some people fill in the gaps in Medicare by joining a Medicare Part C Medicare Advantage health plan that combines basic Medicare-level coverage with supplemental benefits. (See Chapter 14 for a discussion of medigap insurance and Chapter 15 to learn about Medicare Advantage plans.) If you have low income and few assets other than your home, you might be eligible for Medicaid (called MediCal in California), which covers most of the costs Medicare leaves unpaid. (See Chapter 16 regarding the Medicaid program.)

Nonprescription Drugs

Medicare Part B doesn't cover any of the cost of nonprescription ("over-the-counter") medicines, vitamins, or supplements, regardless of whether they provide help with a medical condition, even if they have been recommended by a doctor.

Hearing Exams and Hearing Aids

Medicare Part B doesn't cover routine hearing examinations or hearing aids. However, if your ears or hearing are affected by a specific illness or injury, examination and treatment by a physician might be covered.

General Dental Work

Medicare doesn't cover work performed by a dentist or an oral surgeon, unless the same work is also performed by physicians.

In other words, if the treatment is considered medical rather than dental, Medicare might cover it. Generally, Medicare won't cover treatment unless the problem is unrelated to normal tooth decay or gum disease, and involves either the blood vessels, nerves, or bones of the mouth or jaw.

Long-Term Care

Medicare Part B covers some home health care, as described in the previous section. But that care is always relatively short-term, limited to a period of recovery from an acute illness, injury, or condition, and includes only skilled nursing care and therapy.

Medicare doesn't provide the kind of long-term care, either at home or in a facility, that many older people need because of frailty or other inability to perform, without help, the activities of daily life. Medicaid and long-term care insurance does cover certain nursing home costs. For a complete discussion of coverage for nursing home costs, see *Long-Term Care: How to Plan & Pay for It*, by Joseph L. Matthews (Nolo).

How Much Medicare Part B Pays

When all your medical bills are added up, you'll see that Medicare Part B generally pays for only about half the total.

First, you pay a monthly enrollment fee. Then, Medicare doesn't cover all major medical expenses—for example, it doesn't cover routine physical examinations, over-the-counter medication, glasses, hearing aids, dentures, and some other costly medical services.

And for services it does cover, you must pay a yearly deductible, then Medicare pays only a portion of what it decides is the proper amount—called the "approved charges"—for medical services. In addition, when Medicare decides that a particular service is covered and determines the approved charges for it, Part B medical insurance usually pays only 80% of those approved charges; you're responsible for the remaining 20%.

Also, the approved amount might seem reasonable to Medicare, but it's often considerably less than what the doctor actually charges. If your doctor or other medical provider doesn't accept "assignment" of the Medicare charges (agreement that these charges will be the total that you owe), you're personally responsible for the difference.

Now that you know the worst, you can deal with the details of how much Medicare Part B pays. The rules aren't hard to understand—just hard to swallow.

Deductible Amounts

Before Medicare pays anything under Part B medical insurance, you must pay a deductible, currently $240 per year.

Medicare keeps track of how much of the deductible you've paid in a given year. It generally does a good job of keeping track, but it's always a good idea to keep your own records and double-check the accounting.

80% of Approved Charges

For most services, Part B medical insurance pays only 80% of what Medicare decides is the approved charge. You're responsible for paying the other 20% of the approved charge, called your "coinsurance amount." And unless your doctor or other medical provider accepts assignment (see "Assignment of Medicare-Approved Amount," below), you're also responsible for the difference between the Medicare-approved charge and the amount the doctor or another provider actually charges.

Many Medicare enrollees cover this 20% through a private supplemental "medigap" insurance policy (see Chapter 14), while a large percentage of people avoid the charges by joining a Medicare Advantage managed care plan (see Chapter 15). Lower-income people might have the 20% paid by a state Medicaid or other program (see Chapter 16).

> **TIP**
> **Low-income seniors can receive state help.** Under programs known as "Qualified Medicare Beneficiary" (QMB), "Specified Low-Income Medicare Beneficiary" (SLMB), and Qualifying Individual (QI), Medicare recipients who have low incomes and few assets can receive considerable help with their basic Medicare expenses.
>
> If you qualify as a QMB, your state will pay all Medicare premiums, deductibles, and coinsurance amounts. If you qualify as an SLMB, your state will pay the monthly Medicare Part B premiums, though not deductibles or coinsurance amounts. If you meet the standards as a QI, your state will pay all or part of your monthly Medicare Part B premium, but not any deductible or coinsurance. (See Chapter 16 for a full discussion of options for low-income persons.)

Limit on Charges for Insulin and Pumps

If you take insulin through an insulin pump, both the pump and the insulin are covered by Part B. You pay no more than $35 per month for the insulin, and the normal Part B deductible doesn't apply.

100% of Approved Charges for Some Services

There are several types of treatments and medical providers for which Medicare Part B pays 100% of the approved charges rather than the usual 80%, and to which the yearly deductible doesn't apply. In these categories, you aren't required to pay the regular 20% coinsurance amount. In most of them, the provider accepts assignment of the approved charges as the full amount, so you actually pay nothing at all.

Home Health Care

Whether you receive home health care under Part A or Part B, Medicare pays 100% of the charges, and you aren't responsible for your yearly deductible. However, if you receive medical equipment—such as a wheelchair, chair lift, or special bed—from the home health care agency, you must pay the 20% coinsurance amount for that equipment.

Clinical Laboratory Services

Medicare pays 100% of its approved amount for such laboratory services as blood tests, urinalyses, and biopsies. And the laboratory must accept assignment (except in Maryland, where a hospital lab can bill you, as an outpatient, for a 20% coinsurance amount).

Preventive Care Screenings

Medicare Part B will pay 100% of the Medicare-approved amount for any covered preventive screening examination appropriately prescribed by a physician (see "Types of Services Covered," above).

Flu, Pneumonia, Hepatitis B, and COVID Vaccines

Medicare pays the full 100% of its approved charges for these vaccinations, and the yearly deductible doesn't apply. However, the provider isn't required to fully accept assignment; there might be up to an additional 15% charge on top of the amount Medicare approves.

Payments for Outpatient Therapies

How much Medicare pays for outpatient physical therapy (PT), speech-language pathology (SLP), and occupational therapy (OT) depends on where you receive the therapy.

Therapy received in a doctor's or therapist's office, a rehabilitation facility, or a skilled nursing facility while you're an inpatient. Medicare will pay 80% of the Medicare-approved amount. You or your supplemental insurance or managed care plan remain responsible for the other 20%. There's no cap on the amount Medicare will pay for therapy in these settings. However, once the costs to Medicare reach $2,330 (in 2024), for you to receive more therapy, your therapist will have to provide written documentation to Medicare showing that your care continues to be medically necessary; your physician might have to provide supporting evidence.

Therapy received at home. If you receive therapy at home from a Medicare-certified home health care agency as part of a comprehensive Medicare-covered home health care program, Medicare will pay 100% of the cost. If you receive therapy at home that isn't part of a Medicare-covered comprehensive home health care plan, Medicare will pay 80% of approved charges.

Therapy received at a hospital outpatient department. There are financial advantages and disadvantages to receiving Medicare-covered therapy at a hospital outpatient department instead of in a doctor's or therapist's office, or at home. One advantage is that Medicare Part B pays the full Medicare-approved amount for the therapy, except for a patient copayment for each visit. This copayment is usually less than the 20% of the Medicare-approved amount a patient would be responsible for if therapy were provided in a doctor's or therapist's office, or at home.

The disadvantage is that a hospital outpatient department can charge an unlimited amount above the Medicare-approved amount for the therapy—an amount you would be personally responsible for. Before you begin therapy at a hospital outpatient department, find out whether they will accept "assignment" of the Medicare-approved amount as the total amount of the bill. (For a full explanation, see "Legal Limit on Amounts Charged" and "Assignment of Medicare-Approved Amount," below.) If not, find out in advance how much more than the Medicare-approved amount they will charge. If it's more than you can comfortably afford, you might want to consider getting your therapy somewhere else.

Outpatient mental health treatment. For mental health services provided on an outpatient basis, Part B pays only 80% of approved charges. This is true whether the services are provided by a physician, clinical psychologist, or clinical social worker at a hospital, nursing facility, mental health center, or rehabilitation facility. The patient is responsible for the yearly deductible, for the unpaid 20% of the Medicare-approved amount, and, if the provider doesn't accept assignment, for the rest of the bill above the regular Medicare-approved amount, up to an additional 15%.

Legal Limit on Amounts Charged

By law, a doctor or another medical provider can bill you no more than what is called the "limiting charge," even if they don't accept assignment from Medicare. The limiting charge is set at 15% more than the amount Medicare decides is the approved charge for a treatment or service. That means you might be personally responsible— either out of pocket or through supplemental insurance—for the 20% of the approved charges Medicare doesn't pay, plus any amount the doctor charges up to the 15% limiting charge. Regardless of how much the doctor or other medical provider charges non-Medicare patients for the same service, you can be charged no more than 15% over the amount Medicare approves.

Assignment of Medicare-Approved Amount

In most instances, Medicare pays 80% of the approved amount of doctor bills; you or your private medigap supplemental insurance pay the remaining 20%. However, you can avoid having to pay anything above the Medicare-approved amount if your doctor accepts assignment of that amount as the full amount of your bill.

More than 99% of all doctors who treat Medicare patients accept assignment of the Medicare-approved amount. That is because almost all doctors have signed up with Medicare in advance, agreeing to accept assignment, and so have become what are called "participating doctors." They do this because they get paid by Medicare at a slightly higher rate.

There are still a few doctors, however, mostly specialists, who don't accept assignment. When deciding whether to see a new doctor you've been referred to, check to see whether the doctor accepts Medicare assignment.

TIP

Treating doctors must accept assignment for Medicaid and QMB patients. If you receive Medicaid assistance (called "Medi-Cal" in California) as well as Medicare, or are a Qualified Medicare Beneficiary (QMB), federal law requires that a doctor who agrees to treat you must also accept assignment. (See Chapter 16 for more on the Medicaid and QMB programs.)

Different Payment Structure for Hospital Outpatient Charges

Medicare pays hospital outpatient departments differently from how it pays doctors and other providers. Sometimes, the difference can mean savings for you, but other times it can leave you with a large unpaid bill. Unlike charges for doctors or other providers, Medicare Part B pays 100% of the Medicare-approved amount for services provided by a hospital outpatient department, except that for each service the patient might be responsible for a copayment that varies with the type of service provided. These copayments are usually smaller than the 20% coinsurance amount you would pay if you received the same service at a doctor's office or clinic.

(Note, however, that if a doctor who isn't employed by the hospital outpatient department provides services to you at the hospital, that doctor will bill you separately and Medicare will pay only 80% of the Medicare-approved amount for that bill.)

But there's also some payment risk if you receive care from a hospital outpatient department. As with individual doctors, the hospital doesn't have to accept "assignment" of the Medicare-approved amount as the full charge for a particular service. Unlike doctors who don't accept Medicare assignment, however, a hospital outpatient department isn't restricted in how much more they can charge above the Medicare approved amount. Their charges can go as high as they want, and you would be personally responsible for everything above the Medicare-approved amount.

ONLINE

The Medicare website at www.medicare.gov has two helpful links for information on keeping down your medical costs. The first, a provider search tool, will tell you which doctors and other health care providers in your area will accept assignment on Medicare-covered services. You'll find this directory at www.medicare.gov/physiciancompare/search.html.

The Medicare website also offers a list, sorted by geography, of Medicare-certified suppliers of medical equipment and supplies. These suppliers accept Medicare's approved amount as the limit of what they can charge. To use this directory, go to the Medicare website home page at www.medicare.gov, and under the "Providers & Services" tab, click "Find medical equipment & suppliers." This will take you to Medicare's supplier directory.

There are several ways to respond to the high prices charged by hospital outpatient departments. First, before you receive any care at a hospital outpatient department, ask their financial office whether they accept assignment of the Medicare-approved amount as payment in full (except for your copayment). If so, find out what the copayment is. You'll then know the total amount—that is, the per-service copayment—that you'll have to pay each time you receive the service.

Beware of Huge Outpatient Hospital Bills

There's no limit to the amount a hospital outpatient department can charge a Medicare enrollee above the Medicare-approved amount for a particular service. Because of this loophole in Medicare rules, Medicare patients wind up paying on average almost 40% of the total charges for hospital outpatient department charges. For outpatient surgery, and for outpatient radiology and other diagnostic services, patients end up paying about 50% of total hospital charges. Because of these high costs, you should be wary of receiving medical care at a hospital outpatient department. Be sure to find out the charges *before* beginning treatment.

If the hospital outpatient department doesn't accept assignment of the Medicare-approved amount, find out how much more than that amount they will charge. If it's just a little bit higher, you might want to receive your treatment there anyway, if the care is recommended by your doctor and the facility is convenient for you.

If the hospital's charges will be considerably higher than the Medicare-approved amount, explain the situation to your doctor and ask whether the service could be performed just as well in a doctor's office or at an independent clinic or laboratory. If not, ask whether there's another hospital outpatient department where the service could be performed. If so, find out what that hospital's charges would be.

Private Fee-for-Service Plans Outside Medicare

Some businesses, unions, and other organizations offer general employee health insurance plans—either during employment or after retirement—that accept people eligible for Medicare. A private health insurance plan that accepts Medicare enrollees must offer at least as much coverage as basic Medicare would provide, and most of these plans provide more than that.

If you choose to join or remain with such a health plan once you become eligible for Medicare, the plan—and not Medicare—will make all decisions about coverage for specific services and the amount of payment.

You might be responsible for plan premiums and copayments, as well as the difference between what the plan pays the provider and what the provider actually charges. Unlike regular Medicare, there's no legal limit on the amount a provider can charge you above what the insurance pays.

Part D: Prescription Drug Coverage

Medicare can cover some of the costs of prescription medications you take at home. This Medicare Part D benefit is administered through private insurance companies that offer Medicare-approved prescription drug plans (PDPs), and through Medicare Advantage managed care plans that include a Part D-type drug benefit (MA-PDs).

The Politics of Part D Administration

While Part D undoubtedly saves many people money, drug costs are higher than they need to be because of the program's little-discussed giveaway to two of the country's biggest industries: insurance and pharmaceuticals.

The enormous Medicare hospital and medical programs (Parts A and B) are operated by Medicare's own low-overhead bureaucracy, with only certain administrative tasks run by insurers. Nonetheless, in enacting Part D, Congress handed over almost the entire prescription drug program to private insurance companies. That means the program has to support their notoriously inefficient overhead, plus their profits.

Also, a provision in the original Part D law actually prohibited Medicare from negotiating with pharmaceutical companies for lower drug prices for Medicare beneficiaries. As a huge market, Medicare could have utilized its buying power to get price reductions; the VA, for example, has done this for many years, and its drug prices are half as much as those through most Part D plans. This Part D prohibition on such negotiations amounted to a massive pork barrel for the pharmaceutical industry. The Inflation Reduction Act of 2022 finally begins to make some inroads, mandating rebates from drug companies that raise prices faster than inflation and, beginning in 2024, allowing Medicare to negotiate prices on a limited number of high-cost drugs. How much of the savings from these provisions will actually be passed along to Part D beneficiaries remains to be seen.

Employer-sponsored health plans also frequently offer prescription drug coverage for Medicare beneficiaries; if so, Part D enrollment unnecessary for covered employees if the employer-sponsored coverage is at least equal to the coverage offered by a basic Medicare Part D plan.

For many people, Medicare Part D significantly reduces their out-of-pocket costs for prescription drugs, particularly for people with very high annual drug expenses.

The Basics of Part D Drug Coverage

Medicare Part D provides substantial coverage for the cost of prescription drugs for people enrolled in Medicare. Before you plunge into the details offered in this section, you might want to familiarize yourself with the overall operation of the program by reading through this summary.

Who is eligible? If you're entitled to Medicare Part A or are enrolled in Medicare Part B, you can join a Medicare Part D prescription drug plan. Participation is voluntary for most people. But, if you receive benefits through Medicaid (Medi-Cal in California) you're automatically enrolled in a Part D plan in order to continue receiving drug coverage.

Who runs the program? Medicare operates the overall program, but you must choose one of the specific Part D prescription drug plans offered by private insurance companies in your state. You enroll directly with that insurance company.

What does it cost to participate? Most people pay a monthly premium to the insurance company. The premium can range from $0 to $50 per month—the cost varies depending on the plans available in your town, the particular plan you choose, and your income.

What does it cover? All plans cover some, but not all, prescription drugs in every category of medication. Each plan has a list, known as a "formulary," of the specific drugs it covers. The plan will pay its share only for drugs listed on its formulary and purchased from a pharmacy or another distributor that participates in that plan.

How much does the plan pay? For basic Part D coverage, there are four payment stages (these figures are for 2024):

- **Deductible.** In many plans, you pay for the first $545 per year of the total cost of your drugs. However, some plans reduce this deductible or even waive it entirely.
- **Partial coverage.** Once your total yearly drug expense reaches your plan's deductible (up to $545), and before it reaches $5,030, the plan pays roughly 75% and you pay up to 25% of your drug costs. Your portion comes in the form of a copayment for each prescription (many plans' copays are less than 25%). Your copayment might be higher for brand-name drugs and less for generics, depending on your plan.
- **Coverage gap ("donut hole").** Once your total yearly drug expense reaches $5,030 (and until your total out-of-pocket costs reach $8,000), you must personally pay 25% of your drug costs for both brand-name and generic drugs. This gap in coverage is commonly known as the "donut hole."
- **Catastrophic coverage.** If your total out-of-pocket costs for drugs in one year reach $8,000, after that you'll have no copayment or coinsurance amount for covered drugs.

TIP

Out-of-pocket costs? To determine when you've reached the "catastrophic coverage" threshold, Medicare counts only what it considers your "true" out-of-pocket costs (TrOOP). For generic drugs that you purchase while in the donut hole coverage gap, your TrOOP is only the 25% that you personally pay out of the total actual cost; for brand-name drugs, the TrOOP is 95% of the total actual cost.

How do I choose the right plan? Not all plans are alike, and choosing the best plan for you involves several steps. You must get the widest possible coverage of the drugs you take, with the fewest restrictions on the drugs' availability to you. And you must do so with the lowest overall out-of-pocket cost to you. That doesn't necessarily mean the lowest premium, but instead takes into

account premium, deductible, copayments, availability of generic drugs, and any differences in coverage in the "donut hole" coverage gap. (See "Deciding on a Part D Plan," below, for a step-by-step discussion of choosing the right plan.)

Can I switch plans if I'm not happy with my plan? Anyone can switch Part D plans. People who receive both Medicaid and Medicare benefits, and people who live in long-term care facilities, can switch at any time. Most people, however, can switch only during an open enrollment period from October 15 to December 7 of each year. The rules and procedures for switching plans are explained in Chapter 13.

People With VA, TRICARE, or FEHB Medical Coverage Need Not Join a Part D Drug Plan

If you receive medical coverage through the Department of Veterans Affairs (VA), the Defense Department's TRICARE program, or the Federal Employee Health Benefits Program (FEHB), you do *not* need to join a Medicare Part D plan when you become eligible for it at age 65. You'll continue to receive prescription drugs through your existing program (which provides essentially the same coverage as Part D, but at less cost to you). If for any reason you lose coverage under any of these programs, you have 63 days to join a Medicare Part D plan without a penalty for late enrollment.

Eligibility

Anyone who is entitled to Medicare Part A coverage (whether actually enrolled in it or not) or who is currently enrolled in Medicare Part B can join a Medicare Part D plan. This is true regardless of whether a person's Medicare eligibility is based on age or disability. Except for people who also receive benefits from the Medicaid program (Medi-Cal in California), enrollment in Part D is voluntary. (The enrollment process is explained in Chapter 13.)

If you qualify for Medicaid (see Chapter 16) as well as Medicare, you must enroll in a Medicare Part D plan in order to receive any prescription drug coverage. Medicaid no longer covers any drugs for people who are also eligible for Medicare if those drugs are covered by an available Part D plan. In some states, however, Medicaid continues to cover a few drugs that aren't available under Part D. If you receive Medicaid benefits as well as Medicare, you can enroll in certain, but not all, Medicare Part D plans—but if you don't enroll yourself, Medicare will automatically enroll you in a plan.

Part D Might Not Be Right for Everyone

If you have prescription drug coverage through a Medicare Advantage plan (see Chapter 15) or through employer-based coverage from your or your spouse's current work, you do not also need a Medicare Part D plan. Even if you're not otherwise covered for prescription drugs, enrollment in a Part D plan is voluntary. But program rules (for instance, a penalty on the premium you eventually pay if you later enroll in a plan after not enrolling when you turn 65) put some pressure on you to enroll even if you don't yet need the coverage. To decide whether enrolling is a good idea for you, and when, see "Deciding on a Part D Plan," below.

Premiums, Deductibles, Copayments, and Coverage Gaps

The cost structure of Medicare Part D is complicated. Except for those who qualify for a low-income subsidy, most beneficiaries pay monthly premiums, a yearly deductible, and a copayment for each prescription filled. And there's a coverage gap that affects most beneficiaries, making them personally responsible for a large portion of their drug costs that are above a certain amount but below a "catastrophic" level.

Premiums

Premiums are the monthly amounts you pay directly to your prescription drug plan or managed care plan to enroll you in Part D coverage. These amounts cover only your membership in the plan and don't pay the cost of any drugs, nor do they count toward your deductible or other cost-sharing amounts.

Standard enrollment. Most people must pay a monthly premium for Part D coverage, either for a stand-alone prescription drug plan or as part of the larger premium they pay if they're enrolled in a managed care plan. Monthly premium amounts for basic benefits vary from plan to plan and by geographic region.

High income surcharge. If you have a higher income, you pay a monthly Part D surcharge in addition to your plan's premium.

Officially known as the "income-related monthly adjustment amount" (IRMAA), the surcharge is based on your IRS tax return from two years previously. If you're enrolled in a Part D plan or Medicare Advantage plan with drug coverage, the IRMAA is automatically deducted each month from your Social Security benefits; if you don't collect Social Security benefits, you'll receive a monthly IRMAA bill from Medicare.

Yearly Income in 2022	Part D Surcharge
Single $103,001–$129,000	$12.90
Married $206,001–$258,000	
Single $129,001–$161,000	$33.30
Married $258,001–$322,000	
Single $161,001–$193,000	$53.80
Married $322,001–$386,000	
Single $193,001–$499,999	$74.20
Married $386,001–$749,999	
Single $500,000 or more	$81.00
Married $750,000 or more	

CAUTION

Lowest premiums are not always the best. Finding a plan with a low monthly premium is important, but it isn't the only factor to consider in choosing a plan. A low premium does you little good if the plan doesn't cover some of your medications, or if it covers them but requires much higher copayments than other plans. Also, you might want to pay a higher premium for a plan that offers you first-dollar coverage (no deductible) or lower copayments within the "donut hole" coverage gap. (See "Deciding on a Part D Plan," below, for more information.)

Medicare's "Extra Help" Low-Income Subsidy (LIS). Extra Help is a program that helps people with low income and assets pay their Part D premiums, deductibles, and copays. You'll qualify for Extra Help if you get Medicaid or SSI, are enrolled in the QLB, SLMB, or QI program (see above), or don't quite qualify for these programs but have income and assets below certain levels.

In 2024, you might be eligible for Extra Help if you have yearly income of less than about $22,000 as a single person, or about $30,000 as a married couple (these figures are a bit higher in Alaska and Hawaii). You might qualify if your income is somewhat higher than this if you're still working or you have dependents living with you. And you must have assets (not including your home or household goods) of less than about $17,000 (about $34,000 for married couples living together).

Apply for Medicare Part D's Extra Help Program Before, and Separately From, Enrolling in a Part D Plan

If you think you're anywhere close to qualifying for a Part D Extra Help low-income subsidy, you should apply for it. You apply for an Extra Help low-income subsidy separately from applying for Part D coverage, and applying for an Extra Help low-income subsidy doesn't commit you to join any Medicare Part D plan. If you're accepted for an Extra Help low-income subsidy, your Part D plan premium will be much less expensive regardless of which plan you choose. To learn about applying for an Extra Help low-income subsidy, see Chapter 13.

If you qualify for Extra Help, you'll pay no premium or deductible. And in 2024, you'll pay a copayment of no more than $4.50 for each generic drug and no more than $11.20 for each brand-name drug. But if you also get Medicaid and are in the QMB program, you won't pay more than $4.60 for any covered drug.

Deductibles

The deductible is the amount you must pay out of pocket for covered medications before your Part D plan begins paying any of your covered prescription drug costs.

Standard enrollment. With most plans, a Part D enrollee must pay out of pocket for the first $545 (in 2024) of costs each year for prescription drugs that are covered by the enrollee's particular plan.

But some plans offer a reduced deductible, and others "first dollar" (no-deductible) coverage, meaning the plan begins paying their share of covered drugs for an enrollee's first prescription of the year (see below).

With low-income subsidy. Part D beneficiaries who get Extra Help don't pay any deductible amount.

Waiver of deductible. Some plans offer what is called "first dollar" coverage, which means you don't pay any deductible and the plan begins paying its share of drug costs with your first prescription. These no-deductible plans tend to have higher premiums. The amount you save, if any, will depend on the plan's premium and other cost features. (See "Deciding on a Part D Plan," below, for more information.)

Initial Copayments

After you've reached your deductible amount in out-of-pocket costs for covered prescription drugs, your plan pays most of the cost of a covered drug and you're personally responsible for the remainder, known as a "copayment." This arrangement continues until you and your Part D plan combined reach a specific yearly total of expenditures—the beginning of the "coverage gap"—on drugs covered by your Part D plan.

Standard enrollment. After you pay your deductible for covered drugs, Medicare and your Part D plan pay 75% of the cost for covered drugs (and you pay the remaining 25% out of pocket) until your total covered expenditures have reached the beginning of the year's coverage gap. (Some plans charge you lower copays for certain drugs.) For 2024, the coverage gap begins at $5,030 in total costs for covered drugs.

What Counts as an Out-of-Pocket Cost?

Many of the rules concerning deductibles, copayments, and catastrophic limits revolve around the amount you pay out of pocket for your medications. In calculating these amounts, Medicare considers only what it determines to be a "true out-of-pocket" cost, or "TrOOP."

In order for a prescription drug payment to qualify as a TrOOP, the prescription drug must be:

- a drug prescribed by a physician and covered by the specific plan's formulary, or covered for a particular enrollee through an exception to the formulary, and
- paid for by the beneficiary, a relative, a charity, a church, or a service organization, or the like, but not by another insurance plan.

Also, for generic drugs you buy while in the donut hole coverage gap, your TrOOP is only 25% of the total actual cost; for brand-name drugs in the donut hole, the TrOOP is 95% of the total actual cost. It's important to remember that what you pay for your premium is *not* considered an out-of-pocket cost.

Actual copayments can vary. Your actual copayments for each prescription can vary:

- The total cost of a drug can vary from plan to plan. This is because each plan individually negotiates prices with pharmaceutical companies. So, if your copayment is a percentage of

the drug's total cost, what you pay will also vary. For example, if 30 doses of a medicine cost a total of $80 with Plan 1 and $100 with Plan 2, a 25% copayment would be $20 per prescription with Plan 1, but $25 with Plan 2.

- A plan is permitted to set up a different copayment system—such as tiered copayments for generic drugs and brand-name drugs, or higher copayments for certain drugs but none at all for other drugs—from the standard copayments described above. Plans can change their copayment structure as long as the average copayments for all covered drugs work out to be the same as with the standard copayment schedule. For this reason, before choosing a plan you must find out in advance what the actual copayment is for your specific drugs.

You Pay the Full Cost of Any Drugs That Your Particular Plan Doesn't Cover

It's important to understand that your plan will pay its portion of the costs only for those drugs specifically included on its formulary (a list of the drugs your plan covers), unless you obtain an exception from the plan. Similarly, amounts you personally pay for drugs count toward your deductible and the coverage gap limits only if the drugs are specifically covered by your plan's formulary, or are covered by your plan after you obtain an exception for that drug from your plan. (See "Restrictions on Coverage," below, for a discussion of plan formularies and other plan payment restrictions.)

TIP
Insulin costs are limited. If you participate in a Part D plan that covers your use of insulin, your out-of-pocket copayments for that specific medicine are limited to $35 per month.

Coverage Gap (the "Donut Hole")

Once your out-of-pocket prescription drug costs for the year (in 2024) reach $5,030, and until they reach $8,000, you're in what's known as the "coverage gap" (also known as the "donut hole"). While you're in the gap, you're personally responsible for paying 25% of the cost of both brand-name and generic drugs.

Finding a Plan That Offers Better Coverage in the Gap

If you have high drug costs, look for a plan with extra coverage in the donut hole coverage gap. A few plans pay more of a patient's drug costs within the gap, either reducing the patient's 25% share or shortening the extent of the gap. The premiums for these plans, however, tend to be higher than for standard plans. But the higher premium might be worth it if you expect that your yearly drug costs will extend well into the coverage gap.

Note: No gap with low-income subsidy. There's no difference in copays during the "donut hole" coverage gap for those qualifying for any category of low-income subsidy.

Reducing costs within the donut hole. You might reach the coverage gap but still have months to go before getting to either the catastrophic coverage limit or the end of the year. If so, you might want to consider using one or more of the following strategies for lowering the total cost of your medications, and thus the amount you pay out of pocket, within the gap. For more on finding the programs that might work for you, see "Finding discount programs," below.

The strategies are:

- **State and community assistance programs.** Some states have programs to help older patients pay for prescription medicines that aren't otherwise covered by Medicare or Medicaid. Some of these programs offer across-the-board discounts on all drugs while others provide only limited discounts on certain drugs. Some programs offer special tax credits for prescription drug costs and others limit their prescription drug assistance to

lower-income seniors. Local community-based programs also sometimes provide free or discounted drugs to seniors. To find out about state and community-based prescription drug assistance programs near you, call the Eldercare Locator at 800-677-1116 or go to the official Medicare website listing of state pharmaceutical assistance programs at www.medicare.gov/pharmaceutical-assistance-program/state-programs.aspx. You can also contact the local office of your State Health Insurance Assistance Program (SHIP), discussed at the end of Chapter 13.

- **Veterans benefits.** If you're a veteran, you may be eligible for free or low-cost medical treatment by Veterans Affairs health providers. If so, this can include free (for disabled or low-income veterans) or low-cost prescription drugs, if prescribed by a VA doctor. Even if you normally see a civilian doctor and use Medicare to cover your care, you might want to see a VA doctor to get a prescription for long-term medication that would be expensive if you had to pay for it under Medicare Part D. (For a discussion of medical benefits for veterans, see Chapter 11.)

- **Physician samples.** In an effort to push their particular brands of drugs, pharmaceutical companies give free samples to doctors. The doctors, in turn, distribute those drugs free to patients. Doctors don't normally have enough samples to fill a long-term need for a medication. But your doctor might have enough free samples of your drugs to help lower your out-of-pocket costs while you're within the Part D coverage gap.

- **Switching to generic.** If you've been taking a brand-name medication, you might find that you can obtain the same results at a lower price with its generic equivalent, if one is available, or with a lower-cost drug that treats the same condition. Check with your doctor to see if a generic or another drug is available and whether the doctor believes that it would provide you with the same results. If so, you might want to try it. If you're satisfied with the less-expensive drug, you might save considerable money by continuing to use it because generic drugs are usually quite a bit less expenhsive than brand names.

- **Pharmaceutical company discount programs.** Under pressure from consumer groups, some pharmaceutical companies have created programs to provide certain specific medicines at reduced prices for Medicare patients. Most of these programs are available only for seniors with limited incomes. The programs don't necessarily include every drug manufactured by the company. And the discounts aren't usually very generous. Nonetheless, even a small discount on an expensive drug can amount to significant savings over time. In order to participate in one of these programs, you have to register with the pharmaceutical company. The doctor who prescribes the medication for you might have to fill out enrollment papers for you, too. Some of these programs provide free or discounted drugs only to doctors, who then distribute them to patients. To learn about specific pharmaceutical company programs that might help with the costs of drugs you take, see the official Medicare website's Pharmaceutical Assistance Programs page at www.medicare.gov/pharmaceutical-assistance-program.

- **Nonprofit and retail discount programs.** Several nonprofit and retail organizations, including large chain pharmacies, have set up programs—some through the use of discount "cards"—to provide discounted prescription drug medications, particularly for seniors. These organizations use their large membership's purchasing power to leverage drug companies into offering discounts on certain drugs, passing those savings on to their members. There's usually a membership fee and a copayment or processing fee for each medicine you order. Savings from these programs average less than 10%. For an expensive drug, however, that can still amount to a substantial amount.

- **Medications from Canada.** The exact same prescription drugs for which we pay exorbitant prices in the United States are available for far less—often 50% to 80% less—in Canada. That's because the Canadian public health system limits what pharmaceutical companies can charge for drugs there. (Even at these much-reduced prices, the drug companies profitably continue to sell their wares in Canada.) Because of the huge price differences,

many people in this country have been taking the trouble to buy their prescription medications from Canadian pharmacies, using mail-order and online prescription drug outlets, while others who live near the Canadian border physically travel across to obtain their drugs at Canadian health clinics.

If you choose to explore this option, you might be able to find services providing medicines from Canadian pharmacies by searching on the internet under "prescription drugs Canada." But before using any mail-order or online Canadian drug outlet, ask people you know—or your local senior center—or a SHIP counselor (see Chapter 13) if they know anything about the particular program and the reliability of its services.

Finding discount programs. There are several ways to find out about government, pharmaceutical company, and nonprofit organization discount drug programs available where you live—starting with the four options below. Once you locate a program for which you might be eligible, you or your doctor must contact the program directly in order to enroll.

Some Discount Drug Purchases Might Not Count as Out-of-Pocket Costs

If your out-of-pocket cost for prescription drugs reaches more than $8,000 for the year (in 2024), you'll pass the coverage gap and reach Part D's catastrophic coverage. Once you reach that coverage, your Part D plan will pay all of your drug costs until the end of the year.

But not all of the money you spend out of your own pocket for prescription drugs during the coverage gap will necessarily "count" toward reaching the catastrophic coverage threshold. If you buy discounted prescription drugs through a state or local government-assisted drug program, the amounts you spend out-of-pocket for those drugs might not count. That's because government funding is already supporting the purchase of these low-cost drugs. If you use one of these programs, check with the program staff about whether your out-of-pocket costs for drugs they supply will count toward reaching catastrophic coverage under Plan D.

- **Information from Medicare.** Medicare itself can direct you both to your state assistance program and to pharmaceutical company programs for a particular drug. It can also alert you to local programs in your area and can refer you to nonprofit and retail organizations that offer drug discount cards and other plans.

  Medicare's information is on its website at www.medicare.gov. Under the "Health & Drug Plans" tab, look under "Find & Compare," then click "Find health & drug plans." This page asks you for some personal information—which is strictly confidential—in order to determine which programs you might be eligible for. It then directs you to your state's prescription drug assistance program and to any community-based programs in your area. And it directs you to some pharmaceutical company discounts that might be available for that drug. Finally, the Medicare website lists contact information for some of the nonprofit and retail organizations that offer drug discount cards and similar plans, and explains their basic benefits and eligibility rules.

  You can also get this same information by calling Medicare's toll-free telephone line at 800-MEDICARE and asking about prescription drug assistance programs.

- **State Health Insurance Assistance Program (SHIP) and Health Insurance Counseling and Advocacy Program (HICAP).** Every state has a program to provide free counseling and assistance regarding Medicare, Medicaid, health insurance, and related problems. This program is called the "State Health Insurance Assistance Program" (SHIP) or the "Health Insurance Counseling and Advocacy Program" (HICAP). The program maintains local offices with trained counselors who can help you learn about your state's prescription drug assistance program and other drug discount programs that might be available to you. They can also help you with the enrollment process. Their assistance is free. For more about SHIP and HICAP, see Chapter 13.

- **Area Agency on Aging.** The Area Agency on Aging is a federal government clearinghouse for information about issues relating to seniors. Your agency can provide you with information about your state's assistance program and about community-based drug assistance programs. To find the Area Agency on Aging office nearest you, call their toll-free line at 800-677-1116 or visit https://eldercare.acl.gov.

Waiver or Reduction of Copayments

Under certain circumstances, you might not have to pay the normal copayment for a covered drug. For example:

- If you reside for more than 90 days in a long-term care facility and are enrolled in both Medicare Part D and Medicaid, you don't have to make any copayments for covered drugs.

- Some plans waive or reduce copayments for certain drugs, particularly generic versions, mostly to coax people to join their particular plans. Waiving or reducing the copayment for a particular drug during a period of time, however, doesn't obligate the plan to continue doing so, nor must it continue to waive or reduce copayments on any comparable drug. The plan can change its copayment rules at any time.

- Pharmacies can waive copayments for any enrollee with a low-income subsidy, for any drug. There are no Medicare rules about when pharmacies can do this, except that they aren't supposed to advertise a policy of waivers. So, you might not know in advance whether your pharmacy will waive a copayment for you. If you're a Part D enrollee who receives a low-income subsidy, you should always ask the pharmacy to waive your copayment. You might be pleased to find out that the pharmacy is willing to do so.

- **Drug discount information clearinghouses.** Through several clearinghouses, most of which provide their information on the internet, you can find out about numerous drug assistance and drug discount card and similar programs. One helpful clearinghouse is RxAssist Patient Assistance Program Center (www.rxassist.org). The RxAssist website provides both a direct link to pharmaceutical company drug assistance programs and information about other sites and organizations that can help you apply for assistance, as well as links to nonprofit and retail drug discount cards and similar programs.

Catastrophic Coverage

Once your total expenditures for medications covered by your plan reach $8,000 in a year, the plan will provide "catastrophic coverage" that pays the entire cost of covered drugs for the rest of the year. Your total expenditures are amounts paid by you and your plan combined during any year.

Restrictions on Coverage

Medicare gives the private insurance and Medicare Advantage companies that operate Part D plans a lot of leeway in imposing limits on the coverage they offer. There are a number of different ways the plans can limit coverage, including restricting the specific drugs covered, providing different levels of payment for different drugs, requiring drug regimens such as "step therapy," or requiring prior approval before covering certain drugs.

Formularies

Every Part D plan, and every Medicare Advantage plan with drug coverage, issues a list, called a formulary, of the specific drugs it covers. Medicare requires each plan to include in its formulary at least two drugs in each "therapeutic class"—meaning a group of

drugs used to treat a specific illness or condition. Some plans offer more than two drugs in certain categories. But the availability of coverage for these "extra" drugs might depend on the plan member paying a higher premium or copayment, or having to get prior authorization or another exception from the plan before using the drug.

Certain Drugs Excluded by Law

The Medicare program specifically prohibits Medicare drug plans from covering most medications within certain categories of drugs, even if these medications were lawfully prescribed by your physician.

These categories include:

- barbiturates (certain sedatives and sleeping pills)
- benzodiazepines (certain tranquilizers)
- drugs used for weight loss or weight gain, and
- over-the-counter medications.

Many of these drugs, which the drug plans are required to exclude, are covered by Medicaid (Medi-Cal in California) for people who qualify for that program. But "dual eligible" beneficiaries—those who are eligible for both Medicare and Medicaid (including many nursing facility residents)—are required to get their drug coverage through a Medicare plan. Dual eligible beneficiaries in some states, however, might still get coverage for some of these drugs if the Medicaid programs in their states will allow it. (See Chapter 16 for more information on Medicaid.)

Under Part D rules, if a drug isn't on your plan's formulary the plan won't pay any portion of the cost of that drug, even if a physician has lawfully prescribed it for you (unless you ask for and receive an exception, discussed below). Also, any money you spend out of pocket on that nonformulary drug won't count toward your Part D deductible or the coverage gap and catastrophic coverage limits.

Formulary Changes Might Force You to Change Plans

A Part D plan can also change its formulary whenever it wants, by providing 60 days' notice to Medicare and to plan members. Such changes might include dropping a drug entirely from its formulary, dropping the coverage of a brand-name drug and substituting its generic equivalent, or increasing a patient's copayment for a drug.

- If the plan entirely drops a drug it has been covering for you, it must continue to cover it for you until the end of the calendar year.
- If the plan raises the copayment it charges for a drug, the plan must continue providing it to you at the former copayment level until the end of the calendar year.

However, if the plan switches from covering a brand-name drug to a generic equivalent, it can immediately require you to use the generic or else lose all coverage for that drug.

If you don't want to continue with a plan after it changes its coverage, you can explore switching to a different plan. If you're eligible for both Medicare and Medicaid, or are a resident of a long-term care facility, you can switch plans at any time. If not, you can switch plans only during the annual open enrollment period (starting October each year).

If you don't want to change plans, or you can't find a plan with better coverage, consider asking your physician to switch you from your previous drug to a different, equivalent drug that is on your plan's formulary.

Tiered Copayments

Medicare allows the insurance companies that operate Part D plans to charge different copayment amounts for different drugs within the same class, even if the drugs are "therapeutically equivalent" (meaning they're used in a similar way to treat the same illness or condition). Part D plans can structure their copayments in a number of ways: They might have lower copayments for generic drugs than for brand-name equivalents; there might be no copayments at all for certain generic drugs; or there might be different copayments for different brands within the same class.

Exceptions to Drug Restrictions

Plan formularies and other cost containment restrictions aren't necessarily the last word on coverage for a drug you use or want to use. Every plan is required to have two systems in place to allow you to challenge that plan's listing or decision regarding coverage of your drug.

The first system allows you to file a request for an "exception" to the plan's listing or decision. This means that you ask the plan to provide coverage that differs from its standard formulary. This type of exception usually requires that you and your doctor show some kind of "medical necessity," meaning that the particular drug you want works better for you or has fewer or milder side effects than other drugs in the class.

The second system permits you to appeal a plan's decision. Each plan has its own appeal process, but every plan allows you to ask for an internal review by the plan itself. If an internal review is unsuccessful, you can seek independent review and ultimately take the plan to court, if necessary.

Plans' exceptions and appeals processes are discussed in Chapter 13.

Drug Substitution

The Medicare Part D program allows plans to substitute a generic or another therapeutically equivalent drug instead of the drug you request. That means that although your doctor prescribes a specific drug for you, the plan can have the pharmacy dispense to you a different but equivalent drug. Of course, "equivalence" doesn't mean "exactly the same." You might have better results or fewer side effects with the drug your physician prescribes you. But under these drug substitution rules, a plan can overrule you and your physician and pay only for the substituted drug. In order to overcome such a drug substitution, you must request an exception to the plan's substitution policy. (See Chapter 13 for more information about exceptions and appeals.)

Prior Authorization

A Part D plan can place certain drugs on a restricted list that requires the plan's prior authorization before it will cover the drug. This means that if you and your physician decide you should take any drugs on this restricted list, you must obtain the plan's approval or else the plan won't cover it. The plan might offer less expensive drugs that it considers to be "equivalent," in which case your doctor might need to give a medical reason why you need this particular drug. Or, perhaps the drug you want to use is prescribed only in special situations, in which case your doctor might need to show the plan that yours is such a special case.

Step Therapy

"Step therapy" refers to a treatment structure in which a patient must try a certain drug—one that is less expensive for the insurance company—before the plan will cover a different drug in the same class. If a Medicare Part D plan offers more than two drugs within a drug class, the plan can impose a step therapy requirement for certain drugs in that class. If that happens to you, your doctor must certify that you've tried the lower-tier drug and that it didn't work well for you. Then, the plan will allow you to "step" up your therapy to the next-higher-tier drug.

Supply Limits

You'll pay a copayment for each prescription you fill. So, one way to keep copayment costs down might be to have the doctor prescribe a large supply of a certain medicine so that it will take fewer prescriptions to get the same number of doses. Plans can block this tactic by imposing a supply limit that restricts the number of doses of a drug that can be filled per prescription.

Broader Coverage, But Difficult Access, for Certain Drugs

Medicare requires each Part D plan to cover at least two drugs for each therapeutic category. And for the following six specific categories of drugs, Medicare plans must provide coverage for "all or substantially all" available drugs:

- antidepressants
- antipsychotics
- anticonvulsants (treatment of seizures)
- antiretrovirals (treatment of certain viruses, including HIV)
- immunosuppressants (cancer treatment), and
- antineoplastics (chemotherapy).

Although Part D plans must extend coverage to all drugs in these categories, the plans can restrict access to these drugs (except antiretrovirals) in other ways. Plans are permitted to make obtaining these drugs more difficult or expensive through "management" devices, such as tiered copayments, prior authorization, and step therapy requirements.

Pharmacy Restrictions

Each Part D plan contracts with certain pharmacies to deliver prescription medications. To receive full coverage from your plan, you must get your drugs from a participating pharmacy, which includes large chains, independent drugstores, HMO pharmacies, or mail-order pharmacies. If you fill your prescription at a pharmacy

that doesn't contract with your plan (an "out-of-network" pharmacy), you might have a larger copayment, or you might not receive any coverage at all (depending on the drug and on your plan's rules).

Deciding on a Part D Plan

If you're eligible for Medicare and are also enrolled in the Medicaid program (Medi-Cal in California), Medicare will automatically sign you up for a Part D drug plan. If you aren't enrolled in Medicaid, your participation in Medicare Part D is voluntary. Deciding whether to join a Part D plan, and if so what plan to choose, depends on several factors:

- whether you have other health insurance coverage (through your or your spouse's employer or union) that includes drug coverage
- whether you enroll in a Medicare Advantage (Medicare Part C) managed care plan that includes prescription drug coverage (see Chapter 15)
- whether you're eligible for a low-income subsidy
- your age and health
- the total cost of the drugs you use
- whether your drugs are covered by a particular plan
- how much the plan charges in premiums and copayments, and
- the plan's restrictions on access to drugs.

Should You Participate in Part D?

Medicare Part D is mandatory for people who are also enrolled in Medicaid. For those who qualify for a low-income subsidy, Part D is an attractive low-cost option. And for most other people, Part D is still better than no coverage at all. But for a few people, deciding whether to join a Part D plan is a bit more complicated.

Penalty for Delayed Enrollment. In an effort to encourage everyone to join a Part D plan as soon as they're eligible, Medicare has created a financial penalty for those who delay enrolling (unless enrolled in Medicaid, a Medicare Advantage plan with drug coverage, or employer-sponsored insurance with drug coverage). The penalty takes the form of a rise in premiums of 1% per month—if and when you do eventually enroll in a plan—for every month you delay enrolling after you first become eligible. And that rise is permanent. So, for example, if you wait to join a Part D plan for two years after you're first eligible for Part D coverage, you'll always pay 24% (1% per month for 24 months) more in premiums for any plan you join.

This penalty for late enrollment offers a strong incentive for most people to join a Part D plan as soon as they're eligible. This is true even if you don't presently have many out-of-pocket prescription drug costs and:

- don't regularly take any prescription drugs, or
- take only one relatively low-cost drug.

If you aren't enrolled in an employer-sponsored insurance plan with drug coverage or a Medicare Advantage plan with drug coverage, and you have no or very low regular prescription drug costs, you have the following two options.

Option 1: Not enrolling. You can choose not to enroll in any drug plan for as long as you don't have any significant out-of-pocket drug costs. This means you'll incur the 1% per month penalty on the premium cost of any plan in which you eventually enroll. But that penalty will be partially or fully offset by the fact that you won't be paying any monthly premium for the years you aren't enrolled.

The risk with this approach is that after a few years your drug needs may change and you might then want to enroll in a particular plan that has a high monthly premium. If so, the 1% per month of delay penalty might add up to more than you've saved by not enrolling early. For example, if you delay 36 months before enrolling, then enroll in a plan that has an initial premium of $50 per month, you'll pay an extra $18 per month (36% of $50) in premiums. And these monthly premium amounts go up each year.

No Penalty for Delayed Enrollment If Covered by Equivalent Employer-Sponsored Health Insurance

As explained above, Medicare imposes a financial penalty on people who delay enrolling in Part D coverage. But this penalty does *not* apply if you're covered by an employer- or union-sponsored health plan (for either current employees or retirees) that provides what is called "creditable prescription drug coverage," meaning coverage that is as extensive as a basic Part D plan. When you first become eligible for Medicare, your employer- or union-sponsored plan will notify you whether that plan qualifies as creditable coverage. If your employer-sponsored plan does offer creditable coverage, you can remain in that plan as long as you can and want to, and incur no penalty if you later join a Medicare Part D plan.

If you subsequently lose coverage by a creditable plan, or the plan's drug coverage falls below what qualifies as creditable, then you can enroll without penalty in a Part D plan. You'll pay no higher premium than a person who is first eligible for Medicare as long as you enroll in a Part D plan within 63 days from the date you lose creditable coverage.

If your health plan doesn't qualify as providing creditable coverage, you must join a Part D plan when you first become eligible or else pay the 1% per month premium penalty when you do finally enroll. Even if you join a separate Part D plan, you may want to keep your employer-sponsored coverage instead of relying entirely on Medicare coverage. If your employer-sponsored coverage provides less expensive and/or more complete general health coverage than Medicare Parts A and B do, you might want to retain that coverage even though you also join a Part D plan.

Stand-Alone Drug Plan or Managed Care Plan

Part D drug coverage is available either through a separate, stand-alone prescription drug plan (PDP) or as the prescription drug component (MA-PD) of full health coverage under a Medicare Advantage plan (see Chapter 15). Each type of plan offers a generally equivalent range of available coverage, though each specific plan is slightly different and costs vary.

If you belong to a Medicare Advantage plan that doesn't offer MA-PD drug coverage and you want drug coverage, you must leave your plan and enroll in a stand-alone PDP, which also means returning to regular Medicare coverage (also referred to as "Medicare fee-for-service") as described in earlier sections of this chapter. Or, you can join a different Medicare Advantage plan that does offer MA-PD drug coverage (most do). (Making this choice is discussed in Chapter 15.)

Option 2: Enrolling in a low-premium plan. For many people in the categories above, a better option than not enrolling at all in a plan is to enroll as soon as eligible in a low-premium plan. Several insurance companies offer plans with no monthly premium or a premium under $10. These plans tend to have poorer coverage than plans with higher premiums. But if such a plan is available where you live, it might allow you to enroll in Part D for little or no money as soon as you're eligible, thus avoiding the late enrollment penalty. If and when your drug costs go up and you need better coverage, you can then switch to a more comprehensive plan with a higher premium. (For an explanation of switching plans, see Chapter 13.)

Finding Out About Available Part D Plans

You can enroll only in a plan that operates in the state where you live. There are several ways to find out about the specific Part D plans available to you.

Medicare. The Centers for Medicare & Medicaid Services (CMS) is the federal agency that administers the Medicare program, including Part D prescription drug coverage. It provides personalized help in locating Part D plans. CMS can not only tell you what plans are available where you live, but can also narrow your choice for you according to the medications you regularly take. You can contact CMS by phone at 800-MEDICARE (800-633-4227). Or, you can visit its website at www.medicare.gov and find information tailored to your specific geographic location and medication regimen.

SHIP or HICAP. Every state has a certified program that provides free advice to consumers about Medicare, Medicaid, and other health insurance matters. It's called the "State Health Insurance Assistance Program" (SHIP), or sometimes the "Health Insurance Counseling and Advocacy Program" (HICAP). These programs maintain local offices in most urban areas as well as some central rural locations. Trained counselors in these offices can tell you about all the Part D plans available in your state and can identify the plans that cover the drugs you regularly use. Once you've investigated several plans, the counselors can meet with you in person to help you make a final decision. To find your SHIP or HICAP office, see the contact information at the end of Chapter 13.

State department of insurance. Every state has a government agency that oversees insurance matters. You can contact your state department of insurance for the names, addresses, and phone numbers of every company offering a Part D plan in your state. See the end of Chapter 14 for a website that lists all of the state departments of insurance.

Have Your Information Handy
When You Contact Part D Assistance

In figuring out which Part D plan is best for you, you'll want to consider the medications you regularly use and the pharmacy where you prefer to get your drugs. Before you contact any agency or counselor for assistance in choosing a plan, have the following information handy:

- a list of the specific drugs you regularly use, including the brand (or generic) name, the dose size and frequency, and the current monthly cost
- the name and address of your pharmacy
- whether you currently receive Medicaid benefits, and
- whether you are, or think you might be, eligible for a Part D low-income subsidy.

CAUTION

Get complete information from the plan itself. You can get very helpful information about Part D plans from several sources. But the most thorough information about a specific plan comes from the plan itself. So, before you make a final choice, contact any plan that interests you and ask them to send you a complete description of the plan, including all the matters discussed in this section. You can get the phone number and address of any plan from Medicare itself, or from the other sources discussed above. Make sure to get any important information from the plan in writing. That's because while insurance companies usually have telephone information centers, their phone information tends to be somewhat unreliable. Also, you have no way of forcing the insurance company to abide by what someone tells you on the phone.

Choosing a Part D Drug Plan

Once you decide to enroll in Part D and you find out what plans are available where you live, you must consider several factors in deciding which plan to choose. (When you're ready to join a particular plan, you enroll directly with that plan. The mechanics of enrollment are discussed in Chapter 13.) Here is a step-by-step guide to choosing the plan that's right for you (you can also use the Medicare Plan Finder at www.medicare.gov).

Step 1: List your regular medications and their costs. The first step in deciding on a specific plan is to list the medicines you regularly take, including:

- the brand name and generic name (if there is one) of each drug (if you take the generic version and don't know the brand name, ask your doctor what it's called)
- the dosage you take
- how many doses are in each prescription you fill, and
- how often you fill the prescription.

Step 2: See which plans include your medications in their formularies. The single most important thing to consider in choosing a plan is whether all the drugs you regularly take are included in the plan's formulary. Eliminate from consideration any plan that doesn't include either the brand-name or the generic version of your drugs. Some plans might cover only the generic version of a drug you take, while others might cover both the brand-name and the generic versions. Under any plan that covers a brand-name drug, copayments for the brand-name will be higher than for the generic version.

Step 3: Check with the different plans to see what the total monthly cost of your drugs would be, as well as your initial copayments. For each plan that includes all your drugs on its formulary, ask the insurance company to provide you with an estimate (in writing) of the total monthly cost of each of your prescriptions—taking into account your normal dosage and number of doses. (Total costs differ among insurance companies because each one negotiates different drug prices with the pharmaceutical companies.) Also

ask the plans to tell you what your copayments would be for each prescription during the initial coverage period (prior to the "donut hole" coverage gap).

Step 4: See whether the plan provides "first dollar" coverage. The standard Part D benefit requires each person to pay out of pocket a $545 (in 2024) per year deductible before the plan begins providing any coverage. Some plans, however, provide what is called "first dollar" coverage, meaning that they waive this deductible and begin paying their share from the first dollar you spend on covered medicines. These plans are generally more expensive but might be worth it if your prescription costs are high.

Step 5: Ask whether the plan offers any coverage within the "donut hole" coverage gap. A few plans offer extra coverage within each year's "donut hole" coverage gap, during which most people must pay 25% of the cost of their drugs. If the total cost of your drugs will put you into the coverage gap, this added coverage might be very important. You can determine whether the cost of your drugs will enter into the coverage gap by calculating the total monthly cost of each of your drugs under each plan, multiplying each by 12 (months), then adding them all together.

Step 6: Total the various costs, including the monthly premium. Eliminate those plans that don't cover your particular medications on their formulary. For the remaining plans, use the information you've gathered to determine how much money you would spend each year under each plan you're considering. For each plan, add up:

- the plan's yearly premiums
- your yearly deductible amount (if the plan doesn't provide "first dollar" coverage)
- your copayments for all your drugs during the initial coverage period, and
- how much you would pay out of pocket during the coverage gap (this requires you to figure out how quickly—meaning, with how many monthly prescriptions—you would reach the coverage gap; you do this by adding up the total monthly cost of your drugs under each plan).

Once you've added up all of these items for each plan, you'll be able to compare the annual cost of each plan side by side. Before you make your final decision, though, there's one more step.

Step 7: Look into access restrictions. Though the cost of drugs is important, you should also consider ease of access to your drugs when choosing among plans. This is particularly true if your costs would be nearly the same for two or more plans. Plans restrict access in two different ways. They can place restrictions on coverage—for example, they might require or have drug substitution, prior authorization, step therapy, and supply limits—and they can require you to purchase your drugs from selected pharmacies and other sources. If a plan places a difficult or cumbersome restriction on your access to the drugs you need, you might want to consider a different plan with fewer restrictions at a somewhat higher cost.

Free One-on-One Help in Choosing a Part D Plan

If you have any doubts or questions about choosing a Part D plan, it might be a very good idea to get free personal advice from an expert counselor with SHIP or HICAP near you. These trained counselors are familiar with all the plans offered in your geographic area. They will sit down with you and help you match your needs, preferences, and finances with the available plans. To find your local SHIP or HICAP office, see the contact information at the end of Chapter 13.

TIP

Switching from one plan to another. Enrolling in a particular Part D plan isn't necessarily forever. If you pick a plan that winds up not suiting your needs and you can find a better one, you can switch plans. When and how often you can switch plans depends upon whether you're also eligible for Medicaid, you receive a Part D low-income subsidy, or you reside in a long-term care facility. The options for switching plans are explained in Chapter 13.

Medicare Coverage for People With End-Stage Renal Disease (ESRD)

Most people qualify for Medicare only when they reach age 65 or after they have received Social Security disability benefits for two years. But you might be eligible for a special category of Medicare coverage, regardless of your age or ability to work, if you suffer from long-term kidney failure, known as "end-stage renal disease" (ESRD).

Eligibility for ESRD Medicare Coverage

To be eligible for ESRD-based Medicare coverage, you have to meet two conditions. One is medical—you must be diagnosed with ESRD, as defined by Medicare. The other has to do with the amount of Social Security work credits that have been earned by you, your spouse, or (if you're a minor) your parent.

Qualifying Medical Condition

To qualify for Medicare's special coverage for people with serious kidney disease, your treating physician (usually a nephrologist or other kidney specialist) must diagnose you as having ESRD. Under Medicare's definition, ESRD means that your kidneys have permanently stopped functioning, so that in order to stay alive, you require either long-term dialysis or a kidney transplant. The required dialysis can be either at a medical facility or at home.

Earned Work Credits

Depending on your age, you or your spouse (or one of your parents, if you're a minor) must have earned a certain number of Social Security work credits, also referred to as "quarters of coverage" (QCs), in order to be eligible for ESRD-based Medicare coverage. Workers can accumulate up to four QCs each year, based on their salary or wages and other earned income; the way Social Security calculates these work credits is explained in Chapter 1.

Overall work record. To qualify for ESRD-based Medicare coverage, you must have earned at least one QC for each year after the year you turned age 21, up to the year you were diagnosed with ESRD. Or, you can qualify instead based on your spouse's work record, if your spouse earned at least one QC for each year after turning 21, up to the year you were diagnosed with ESRD (or, up to the year your spouse reached age 62 or died). If you or your spouse were collecting Social Security disability benefits during any year, that year doesn't count in calculating the QCs needed. Regardless of your age, a minimum of six QCs by you or your spouse is required for you to be eligible for ESRD-based Medicare coverage.

Your child who is younger than age 22 can qualify for ESRD-based coverage if you or your spouse:

- have earned at least six credits within the last three years by working and paying Social Security taxes, or
- are getting, or are eligible for, Social Security or Railroad Retirement Board benefits.

Recent work record. Even if the overall number of QCs earned by you or your spouse doesn't meet the standard described above, you can still qualify for ESRD-based Medicare coverage if you or your spouse earned at least 6 QCs over the 13 calendar quarters immediately prior to the onset of your ESRD condition (or prior to the death of your spouse).

TIP

Go to Social Security's website. You can find out how many quarters of work credit you or your spouse have earned by going to the Social Security website at www.ssa.gov/myaccount and creating a personal account.

Medical Care Covered by ESRD Medicare

If you qualify for this special Medicare eligibility for ESRD, Medicare will cover not only costs related to your treatment for ESRD but also costs for *all other medical care normally covered by Medicare.* That means you'll be fully eligible, on the same terms as anyone else, to:

- enroll in coverage for inpatient care under Medicare Part A, outpatient care under Medicare Part B, and outpatient prescription drugs under a Medicare Part D insurance plan (Parts A, B and D are explained in this chapter)
- purchase a "medigap" supplemental private insurance policy to pay some of the costs Medicare doesn't pay (see Chapter 14), or
- enroll in a Part C Medicare Advantage plan, which puts all these coverages into one package (see Chapter 15).

Like anyone else eligible for Medicare, you'll need to choose which parts of the program to enroll in, and will have to pay each part's premiums, deductibles, and copayments, as well as the 20% of most charges that Medicare Part B doesn't pay. The deductibles, copayments, and unpaid Medicare Part B 20% underline the importance of purchasing a medigap supplemental insurance policy, joining a Medicare Advantage plan, maintaining employer-sponsored health coverage, or (if you have low income and few assets other than your home) determining whether you're eligible to enroll in your state's Medicaid program (see Chapter 16).

To receive maximum Medicare coverage for costs specifically related to your ESRD care, you must enroll in both Medicare Part A and Medicare Part B (which charges a monthly premium), or enroll in a Part C Medicare Advantage plan (these plans combine Part A and Part B coverage). Once you're enrolled in Part A and Part B, or in Part C, Medicare will cover:

- dialysis and related services, including the daily room cost if you receive your dialysis while an inpatient in a Medicare-participating hospital
- dialysis and related services if you receive dialysis as an outpatient at a Medicare-approved dialysis facility
- training for self-dialysis, for both you and a person you designate to help you at home with your self-dialysis, if you request self-dialysis and your treating physician approves
- self-dialysis equipment and supplies for use at home, including certain drugs that your doctor might prescribe, or
- services from your physician(s), as well as laboratory and other tests.

CAUTION
Medicare doesn't pay for dialysis assistants at home. While Medicare will pay for the training of a person to assist you with self-dialysis at home, Medicare won't pay for the person's actual services, nor for a professional dialysis aide to help you at home.

Coordination of Medicare With Group Health Insurance Coverage

At the time you become eligible for ESRD-based Medicare, you might already have health care coverage through an employer group health plan, based on your or your spouse's current employment or through a retirement plan. If so, and if you enroll in ESRD-based Medicare, the private insurance will be the primary payer for your health care costs during a "coordination of benefits" (COB) period of 30 months, with Medicare as the secondary payer. This means that for this initial period, Medicare will contribute to payment of costs that your health plan doesn't pay (which can include deductibles, copayments, and sometimes a yearly cap on payments for renal services). The COB begins the first month that you become eligible for ESRD-based Medicare, whether or not you actually enroll at that time. At the end of the 30-month period, the roles are reversed, with Medicare becoming the primary payer and your employer group health plan becoming the secondary payer.

When ESRD Medicare Coverage Begins

ESRD-based Medicare coverage becomes effective at different times, depending on the nature of your treatment.

Hemodialysis provided at a facility. If you receive hemodialysis at a dialysis center or clinic, your Medicare coverage becomes effective on the first day of your fourth month of treatment. If, however, you're resuming dialysis after your ESRD-based Medicare coverage

ended (due to recovery of kidney function following a transplant or dialysis—more on this below), your Medicare coverage can begin again without the three-month waiting period described above.

Home (self) dialysis. If you and your physician decide that you want and are able to perform self-dialysis at home, Medicare coverage becomes effective as soon as you begin treatment—even if you begin treatment at a facility before switching to home—if you complete a self-dialysis training program at a Medicare-certified facility and then perform self-dialysis at home.

Kidney transplant. If you're to receive a kidney transplant, your Medicare coverage begins the month you're admitted to the hospital for the transplant or for medical care preparing you for the transplant. The coverage can extend back to two months prior to the transplant if you're in the hospital that long prior to the surgery.

When ESRD Medicare Coverage Ends

ESRD-based Medicare coverage ends 12 months after you stop dialysis. If you've had a transplant, ESRD-based Medicare coverage stops 36 months after the date of the surgery (unless you're then still on dialysis). However, special rules might permit continued Medicare coverage of immunosuppressive drugs even after other Medicare coverage ends. (See below.)

Applying for ESRD Medicare Coverage

You apply for ESRD-based Medicare coverage through the Social Security system. You can begin this process online at Social Security's website www.ssa.gov or by phoning Social Security at 800-772-1213. (If you phone, there's usually quite a long wait, but the Social Security phone system allows you to leave your name and number and get a return call instead of waiting on the line; this call-back service works well.)

Special Length-of-Coverage Rules for Immunosuppressive Drugs

Very expensive drugs used to stop the body from rejecting a transplanted kidney are often used by transplant patients for months or years following the surgery. Medicare will pay 80% of the cost of those drugs for three years or indefinitely, depending on how you qualify for Medicare:

- If your Medicare coverage is based on ESRD-based eligibility alone, Medicare will cover the drugs for 36 months. After 36 months, you can enroll in special Medicare Part B coverage for these drugs for as long as you need them (until you become eligible for Medicare Part B under standard, non-ESRD eligibility rules). For this special Part B drug coverage, you'll pay $103 per month (in 2024); the premium is higher for those with incomes above $103,000 (individual) or $206,000 (couple). There's also a yearly deductible ($240 in 2024). The coverage is for these drugs only.

- If, before you got ESRD, you were eligible for Medicare because you were age 65 or older or had received Social Security disability benefits for at least 24 months, Medicare will cover the drugs indefinitely.

- If, after you had a transplant that was covered by Medicare, you qualify for Medicare because you're age 65 or older or have been receiving Social Security disability benefits for at least 24 months, Medicare will cover the drugs indefinitely.

Your specialist physician's office can provide initial help and ongoing support for the medical information you'll need to supply with your Medicare application. If you have problems with eligibility, you can also get help from the National Kidney Foundation at 800-622-9010 or online at www.kidney.org. ●

Medicare Procedures: Enrollment, Claims, and Appeals

Chapter 12 described the eligibility rules for Medicare. As you'll remember, most people are eligible for Part A hospital insurance free of charge; if you aren't, you can enroll by paying a monthly premium. Part B medical insurance coverage is available to most people age 65 and older, and everyone covered pays a monthly premium for it. And Part D—which covers some of the cost of prescription drugs you take at home—is available to anyone who is eligible for Part A or B. Everyone who enrolls in Part D pays a monthly premium for prescription drug coverage, except those who are also eligible for Medicaid or who receive a special Part D low-income subsidy.

This chapter explains:

- how to enroll in Medicare Part A and Part B
- how to get Medicare to pay its share of your medical bills once you're enrolled
- what portion of the bill you must pay yourself
- how to read the notice Medicare sends you
- how to appeal a Medicare decision regarding your claim, and
- the separate procedures for enrolling in a Part D plan, switching Part D plans, requesting an exception to a Part D plan's formulary or another access restriction, and appealing a Part D plan's decision.

Enrolling in Part A: Hospital Insurance

Medicare Part A, also called "hospital insurance," covers most of the cost of inpatient care in a hospital. Part A also sometimes covers the cost of inpatient care at skilled nursing facilities and home health care. Most people age 65 or older are eligible for Part A coverage. Some will receive it automatically and free of charge, along with their Social Security benefits. Others will need to enroll and possibly pay a monthly fee.

Those Who Receive Social Security Benefits

If you're under age 65 and already receive Social Security retirement, dependents, or survivors benefits or Railroad Retirement benefits, you don't need to do any paperwork to enroll in Medicare Part A hospital insurance. Social Security will automatically enroll you, and coverage will take effect on your 65th birthday. About three months before your 65th birthday, Medicare will mail you a Medicare card and information sheet.

Since Medicare Part A is free for people age 65 or over who receive Social Security benefits, automatic enrollment provides excellent supplemental coverage even if you have other health care coverage.

CAUTION

No new contributions to health savings accounts. Once you are enrolled in Medicare (Parts A and B, or Part A alone), which you receive automatically once you claim Social Security benefits at age 65 or older, you're no longer allowed to make new pretax contributions to your health savings account (HSA). You can continue to use the funds already in your HSA account, however. This is true even for employees with HSA health plans who continue to work.

If you receive Social Security disability benefits for two years, regardless of your age, you'll be automatically enrolled in Medicare Part A, effective 24 months from the date Social Security declared that your disability benefits should begin. The Medicare card you receive in the mail will indicate that you're enrolled in both Part A and Part B. If you don't want to be enrolled in, and pay the monthly premium for, Part B, there's a form for you to sign indicating your rejection of Part B, which you send to Medicare. If you do want to be enrolled in both Parts A and B, you don't have to do anything. Just sign your Medicare card and keep it handy.

Managed Care Plans Handle Medicare Paperwork

Many people who are about to qualify for Medicare have an HMO or another managed care insurance plan that they intend to keep when they become eligible for Medicare. Other people decide to join a Medicare Advantage HMO or other managed care plan when they first become eligible for Medicare.

If you intend to remain with your current insurance plan when you become eligible, your plan can sign you up for Medicare and switch you to the plan's Medicare coverage. Begin this process two to three months before you become eligible for Medicare.

Similarly, if you decide to join a Medicare Advantage managed care plan for the first time when you become eligible for Medicare, you can sign up for Medicare at the same time you sign up for the plan. Try to get the paperwork started at least two months before your Medicare eligibility begins.

Medicare Advantage managed care plans are discussed in Chapter 15.

If you're receiving Social Security benefits but don't receive your Medicare card in the mail within a month of your 65th birthday, or within a month of your 24th month of disability benefits, contact your local Social Security office or call the national Social Security office at 800-772-1213.

Those Who Don't Receive Social Security Benefits

If you're soon to turn 65 but you're not receiving Social Security retirement, dependents, or survivors benefits, Railroad Retirement benefits, or federal civil service retirement benefits, you must apply for Medicare Part A either online on the official Social Security Administration website at www.ssa.gov/benefits/medicare or at your local Social Security office. If you're going to apply for retirement or other Social Security benefits to begin on your 65th birthday, you can apply for Medicare at the same time, at your local Social Security office.

Your Medicare Card

When you're enrolled in Medicare, you'll be sent a Medicare card that states:

- your name
- whether you have both Part A and Part B coverage or just Part A
- the effective date of your Medicare coverage, and
- your health insurance claim number—also called your "Medicare number."

Always carry your Medicare card with you. You'll be asked to present it when you seek medical treatment at a hospital, a doctor's office, or another health care provider.

Also, you must include your Medicare number on all payments of Medicare premiums or correspondence about Medicare.

If you lose your Medicare card, you can have it replaced by applying in person at your local Social Security office or by calling the toll-free information line at 800-MEDICARE or Social Security's main office at 800-772-1213. Alternatively, you can apply for a new card online at www.medicare.gov.

Who Is Eligible

If you're eligible for Social Security benefits, you can receive free Medicare Part A coverage at age 65 whether or not you actually claim your Social Security benefits.

For example, many people who continue working after reaching age 65 don't claim retirement benefits until later. Still, they can receive free Part A Medicare coverage by applying for it at their local Social Security office.

Also, if you aren't automatically eligible for free Part A coverage, you can purchase it for a monthly premium. The amount of the premium depends on how many work credits you or your spouse have earned. (See "Part A: Hospital Insurance" in Chapter 12 for details.)

When to Apply

Whether you wish to claim Social Security benefits and Medicare, or just Medicare, apply well before you turn 65. You can apply as early as three months before your 65th birthday.

Signing up early is important for two reasons: First, it will ensure that your coverage begins as soon as you're eligible, on your 65th birthday. Second, if you wait more than three months after your 65th birthday to enroll, you won't be allowed to enroll in Part B until the following January 1, and your eligibility won't begin until July 1 of that year. (See "Enrolling in Part B: Medical Insurance," below, regarding delayed enrollment.)

CAUTION
Avoid delays in Part B coverage. If you don't enroll in both Parts A and B during your initial enrollment period, not only will your enrollment in Part B be delayed, but you'll also have to pay a higher monthly premium for it. (See "Enrolling in Part B: Medical Insurance," below, for details.)

When Benefits Begin

If you apply for Part A of Medicare within six months after you turn 65, your coverage will date back to your 65th birthday. But if you apply after that, your coverage will date back only up to six months before the month in which you applied. If your Medicare eligibility is based on disability, however, your coverage will date back up to one year before the date on which you apply.

Appealing Denial of Coverage

Eligibility for coverage by Part A of Medicare depends solely on your age and on the number of Social Security work credits you or your spouse have acquired. (See "Part A: Hospital Insurance" in

Chapter 12 for a review of the eligibility requirements.) You can be denied coverage by Medicare Part A only if there's a dispute about whether you've reached 65, about the number of your or your spouse's work credits, or about the validity of your marriage.

Decisions about these matters are handled not by Medicare but by Social Security. And, like any other decision of the Social Security Administration, a decision denying eligibility for Medicare Part A hospital insurance coverage can be appealed. The appeal process is discussed later in this chapter.

Enrolling in Part B: Medical Insurance

Medicare Part B, referred to as "medical insurance," covers doctors' services plus laboratory, clinic, home therapy, and other medical services you receive—other than when you're an inpatient in a hospital or skilled nursing facility. Most people age 65 are eligible for Part B.

Everyone must pay a monthly premium to enroll, although some people might pay for Part B in the premiums they pay to HMOs or other Medicare Advantage plans (see Chapter 15).

This section explains who is automatically enrolled in Part B, who must take steps to enroll, and when to do so.

Those Who Receive Social Security Benefits

If you're younger than 65 and already receiving Social Security retirement, Railroad Retirement, dependents, or survivors benefits, you'll be automatically enrolled in both Medicare Part A and Part B within three months of turning 65. Your coverage will become effective on your 65th birthday. Near that time, you'll be sent your Medicare card through the mail, along with an information packet. The monthly premium for Part B coverage will be deducted automatically from your Social Security check, beginning with the first month after your 65th birthday.

If you don't want Medicare Part B coverage—perhaps because you or your spouse are still working and you're covered by an employment-related health plan—notify Social Security of that fact on the form that comes with your Medicare card. If you reject Part B coverage when you're first eligible for it, you can enroll in Part B later on, although only during the first three months of any year. And if you enroll later, your premiums might be higher, though not if you've been covered by a comparable employer-sponsored health plan (see "Delayed Enrollment," below).

Those Who Don't Receive Social Security Benefits

If you're turning 65 but aren't eligible for Social Security benefits—or aren't yet going to claim benefits to which you're entitled—you can still enroll in Part B medical insurance either online on the official Social Security website at www.ssa.gov/benefits/medicare or at your local Social Security office.

You can enroll during an initial period of seven months, which begins three months before the month you turn 65 and ends three months after the end of the month you turn 65. For example, if you turn 65 in July, your initial enrollment period starts April 1 and ends October 31. However, the earlier you enroll during this initial period, the better. If you enroll during the three months before you turn 65, your coverage will begin on your 65th birthday. If you enroll during the remaining four months of your initial enrollment period, your coverage might be delayed from one to three months after you sign up, depending on how long it takes to process your application.

Delayed Enrollment

If you don't enroll in Part B medical insurance during the seven-month period just before and after you turn 65, but later decide you want the coverage, you can sign up during any general enrollment period. These are held January 1 through March 31 every year. If you sign up any time during one of these general enrollment periods, your coverage will begin on July 1 of the year you enroll.

Your monthly premium will be higher if you wait to enroll during one of the general enrollment periods instead of when you turn 65. For each year you were eligible for Part B coverage but did not enroll, your premium will be 10% higher than the basic premium.

Free Late Enrollment If Covered by Current Employment Health Plan

If you're covered by a group health plan based on your own or your spouse's current employment, you can enroll in Part B coverage after your 65th birthday without having to wait for the open enrollment period and without any penalty. This exception refers only to a group health plan based on current employment, not to one based on retirement benefits from employment.

If you've delayed signing up for Medicare Part B because you've been covered by a health plan based on current employment, you can sign up for Part B coverage at any time while you're still covered, or within seven months of the date you or your spouse end that employment, or of the date the health coverage ends, whichever comes first.

If you sign up while you're still covered by a group health plan based on current employment, or during the first full month that you no longer have this coverage, your Part B coverage will begin the first day of the month you sign up. You can also choose, instead, to have your coverage (and the monthly premium you must pay) begin with any of the following three months. If you sign up during any of the remaining seven months of your special enrollment period, your Part B coverage will begin the month after you sign up.

To enroll in Part B after age 65 (when you already have Part A), you can fill out an *Application for Enrollment in Medicare Part B* (Form CMS40B) and bring it or mail it to a Social Security office. If for any reason you're not already enrolled in Medicare Part A, you can sign up for both Part A and Part B online at https://secure.ssa.gov/iClaim/rib (you can't sign up online for Part B only).

Medicare's Payment of Your Medical Bills

Medicare doesn't handle day-to-day paperwork and payments with patients and doctors or other health care providers. It contracts out this work to what are called Medicare carriers or intermediaries. These are huge private corporations, such as Blue Cross or other large insurance companies, each of which handles claims for an entire state, and sometimes for more than one state.

The Medicare intermediary in your state receives, reviews, and pays claims. It sends notices that tell you and the medical provider of the amount of benefits paid, the amount of your medical bill that has not been paid, and the amount the health care provider is legally permitted to charge. (See "Your *Medicare Summary Notice*," below, for more on these notices.) And it's with the intermediary that you'll initially correspond if you want to appeal a decision about Medicare coverage of health care charges. (See "Appealing the Denial of a Claim," below, for appeal procedures.)

Medicare intermediaries handle billing for inpatient charges covered under Part A differently from outpatient charges covered under Part B. This section explains the differences in the billing process.

 TIP

HMOs and Medicare Advantage plans do their own paperwork. If you belong to an HMO or other Medicare Advantage plan, the billing office there handles all your Medicare-related paperwork. All you have to do is pay your plan's own monthly premiums and copayments and deal with the plan's paperwork. You don't have to directly handle any Medicare forms and you won't receive any *Medicare Summary Notices*.

Inpatient and Home Care Bills

Medicare Part A covers inpatient care in a hospital or skilled nursing facility, as well as some home health care. (See "How Much Medicare Part A Pays" in Chapter 12 for a review of Medicare Part A coverage.)

Medicare Billed Directly by Facility

When you first check into a hospital or skilled nursing facility, you present your Medicare card to the admissions office and it takes care of the rest. Similarly, when you and your doctor make arrangements for a Medicare-approved home care agency to provide your care, you give the agency your Medicare number and it takes care of all the paperwork. The provider—the hospital, skilled nursing facility, or home health care agency—sends its bills directly to Medicare and to your medigap supplemental insurance carrier, if you have one. You shouldn't have to do a thing to get Medicare (and your medigap insurer) to pay its part of the bill.

The hospital, nursing facility, or home care agency accepts as payment in full the amount the Medicare intermediary decides is the approved charge for those of your inpatient services that are covered by Medicare (but see Chapter 12 for a reminder of what costs are covered). Unlike doctors' bills—for which you might be personally responsible for the difference between Medicare's approved charges and the actual amount of a bill—a hospital, nursing facility, or home care agency is not permitted to bill you for any covered inpatient charges over the amounts paid by Medicare.

The Medicare carrier will also send you a copy of the bills so that you'll know how much has been paid and how much you must cover on your own.

Patient Billed for Some Charges

The hospital, nursing facility, or home care agency will bill you, and your private Medicare supplement insurance company (if you have such insurance), for:

- any unpaid portion of your deductible
- any coinsurance payments—for example, for hospital inpatient stays of more than 60 days, and
- charges not covered at all by Medicare, such as for a private room you requested that was not medically necessary, or for television and telephone charges.

The Medicare carrier will send you a form called a *Medicare Summary Notice* (MSN) that will show what hospital services were paid for and the portion of your deductible for which you're responsible. The hospital or other facility will bill you directly for the unpaid portion of your deductible and for those amounts not covered by Medicare or by Medicare supplemental insurance. (See Chapter 14 regarding supplemental insurance.)

Outpatient and Doctor Bills

How much of your covered doctor and outpatient medical bills Medicare Part B will pay depends on whether your doctor or other medical provider accepts assignment of the Medicare-approved amount as the full amount of the bill. (For more information, see "How Much Medicare Part B Pays" in Chapter 12.)

If the doctor accepts assignment, you—perhaps assisted by private medigap insurance or Medicaid—are responsible only for your yearly Part B deductible, plus the 20% of the approved charges Medicare does not pay.

If the doctor or other provider doesn't accept assignment, then you and your additional insurance might also be responsible for all amounts of the bill up to 15% more than the Medicare-approved amount.

Assignment Method of Payment

If your doctor or other health care provider accepts assignment of your Medicare claim, you're personally responsible for your yearly medical insurance deductible, and then only the 20% of the Medicare-approved amount of the bill that Medicare does not pay. By accepting assignment, the doctor or other provider agrees not to charge you a higher amount than what Medicare approves for the treatment or other covered service you've received.

Catching Overbilling

Medicare does a decent job of catching billing errors and fraud by health care providers. But they're not perfect, so you should still check your bill carefully to determine whether the facility or other provider has billed you for services you did not receive or services that Medicare has paid, or has charged more than once for the same service.

The Medicare intermediary might look closely at the portion of the bill Medicare is supposed to pay, and if you have medigap supplemental insurance, the insurance company will also check the bill. But neither one will carefully examine the amounts for which you're personally responsible.

Check all medical bills to make sure there are no charges for services you did not receive. Then, place the bill from the facility or other provider next to the statement from the Medicare carrier and from your medigap insurance company. Compare them to see whether any amount the facility or other provider has billed you directly has been paid by Medicare or by your medigap insurer.

If so, you must contact the billing office at the facility or other provider, sending a copy of your statement from the Medicare carrier or medigap insurer that shows that the charges have been paid. If the problem is billing for a service you don't believe you received, ask the facility's or provider's billing office to send you a copy of your medical record where the service was recorded.

For more information about how to deal with what you believe are billing errors, go to the Medicare website at www.medicare.gov and look under the tab "Providers & Services," then "Claims & appeals," then click "File a complaint (grievance)."

After you and the health care provider are informed by a *Medicare Summary Notice* form from Medicare how much the Medicare-approved charges are, the provider's office will either bill you directly for the remaining 20% of approved charges or bill your medigap supplemental insurance carrier if you have one.

EXAMPLE: Franco was examined for a painful knee by his regular doctor, who then decided to refer him to an orthopedist. Franco asked his doctor to refer him to someone who accepted Medicare assignment. The orthopedist examined Franco, took X-rays, and prescribed exercises and some medication. Franco's own doctor charged $200 for Franco's original examination. The orthopedist charged $300. Both doctors accepted assignment.

Medicare's approved amount for Franco's regular doctor was $150 and, for the orthopedist, $240. Because Franco had already paid his yearly deductible for Part B, Medicare paid 80% of the approved amount of each doctor's bill: $120 to Franco's regular doctor (80% of $150 = $120) and $192 to the orthopedist (80% of $240 = $192). Medicare sent these amounts directly to the doctors. Franco had to pay only the remaining 20% of the approved amounts.

The following chart shows who paid what amount of Franco's bills in this example.

Payment of Doctor Bills—Assignment Accepted

	Initial exam	Orthopedic exam	Total
Doctors' normal charges	$200	$300	$500
Amount approved by Medicare	$150	$240	$390
Amount paid by Medicare (80%)	$120	$192	$312
Amount patient paid (20%)	$30	$48	$78

Payment When No Assignment

If your doctor or other health care provider doesn't accept assignment of the Medicare-approved charges as the full amount of the bill, you—or you and your medigap supplemental insurance—will owe the difference between what Medicare pays and the full amount of the doctor's bill, up to 15% more than the Medicare-approved amount. You end up having to pay one-third (33.25%) of the Medicare-approved amount, rather than one-fifth (20%) of the approved amount.

Medicare has a complicated way of calculating this. For nonparticipating doctors, Medicare lowers the approved fee to 95% of what it would be for participating doctors. But it allows nonparticipating doctors to charge 15% of this lowered fee to patients, in addition to their 20% copayment.

EXAMPLE: In the example above, Franco's own doctor normally charged $200 for an examination and the orthopedist charged $300. If neither doctor accepted assignment but stuck to their normal fees, the payment amounts would be as follows.

Medicare's approved amount for Franco's regular doctor was $150 and, for the orthopedist, $240. But Medicare will allow only 95% of this fee as the approved fee since the doctor doesn't accept assignment. The doctor can charge 115% of this lowered fee (which works out to an additional 9.25% of the regular approved fee). Medicare will pay 80% of the lowered fee.

The following chart summarizes who paid what amount of Franco's bills in this example. You'll see that his payment is one-third of the regular approved amount.

Payment of Doctor Bills—Assignment Accepted

	Initial exam	Orthopedic exam	Total
Doctors' normal charges	$200.00	$300.00	$500.00
Amount approved for nonparticipating doctors (95% of approved fee)	$142.50	$228.00	$370.50
Total amount doctor allowed to charge (115% of lowered fee)	$163.88	$262.20	$426.08
Amount paid by Medicare (80% of lowered fee)	$114.00	$182.40	$296.40
Amount paid by patient (20% of lowered fee)	$28.50	$45.60	$74.10
Additional amount doctor can charge (15% of lowered fee)	$21.38	$34.20	$55.58
Total amount paid by patient (20% of lowered fee + additional amount)	$49.88	$79.80	$129.68

TIP

Handling Medicare billing paperwork is free. Even a doctor or another health care provider who does not accept assignment must fill in the Medicare paperwork and send it to Medicare for payment—and you can't be charged for processing this Medicare paperwork.

Paying Your Share of the Bill

Doctors and other health care providers must wait to find out how much the Medicare-approved charges are before asking you to pay your share. Until they know what the Medicare-approved amount is, they can't know the legal limit—15% over those approved charges—on how much they can require you to pay.

Following your treatment or other service, the doctor's or other provider's office will submit their bills for payment to Medicare. You don't have to submit the paperwork yourself.

If you have private medigap supplemental insurance that pays your deductible and the 20% coinsurance amount that Medicare does not pay, the doctor's office will send its paperwork to the insurance company as well as to Medicare. The doctor will receive payment directly from both Medicare and the supplemental insurance, after Medicare has determined the approved amount for the care you received.

Every three months you'll receive a form called a *Medicare Summary Notice* that includes the following information about every Medicare-billed service you received during the previous three-month period:

- how much of each bill is Medicare-approved
- how much Medicare will pay the provider
- how much of your deductible has been met, and
- how much must be paid by you or your private medigap insurance.

Your *Medicare Summary Notice*

A form called a *Medicare Summary Notice* (MSN) is sent to you to explain what Medicare Part B is covering of your recent medical services and how much Medicare is paying for those services. You receive such a notice every three months; if you did not have any medical services during those three months, you won't receive an MSN for that period.

Don't Let a Doctor Take More Than the Law Allows

Medicare rules are clear—and every doctor and other health care provider knows them. You can be charged only an extra 9.25% above what Medicare decides is the approved amount for a specific medical service (which is actually an extra 15% of the approved amount for unassigned claims). And the *Medicare Summary Notice* form does the arithmetic for you, stating the amount of the maximum charge.

If a doctor or another provider does not accept assignment and bills you more than the allowable amount, send the doctor's office a copy of your *Medicare Summary Notice* form, underlining the spot where the maximum bill is stated—and keep a copy for yourself. If you already paid the bill, and the amount you paid was more than the allowable Medicare-approved amount plus 15%, you're entitled to a refund.

Again, contact the doctor's or other provider's billing office and request your refund, letting them know the date you paid the bill, the amount you paid, and the Medicare-approved amount. If they won't refund the overpayment, contact the Medicare carrier, which will then contact the doctor or other health care provider directly.

The MSN is not a bill. It simply allows you to check the information Medicare has received from your medical providers and to see how much Medicare will pay and how much is left over to be paid by your supplemental insurance carrier or by you out of pocket. Every time you get an MSN form, you should check it carefully

to see that the information is correct and that you agree with Medicare's decisions. For an example of an MSN, information about what you need to look at closely on the form, and how to challenge any errors you find, go to the special Medicare webpage explaining the latest version of the MSN form: www.medicare.gov/pubs/pdf/ SummaryNoticeB.pdf.

You can also receive your MSNs electronically on your computer rather than on paper through the mail. If you sign up for electronic MSNs, you'll get a monthly MSN rather than one every three months. You can sign up for that service by going to www.medicare. gov/forms-help-and-resources/e-delivery.html.

Appealing the Denial of a Claim

Unfortunately, not every request for Medicare payment runs a smooth course. Occasionally, a Medicare hospital or nursing facility review committee might decide your inpatient stay need not last as long as you and your doctor think, and will recommend ending Medicare Part A coverage. Or, more commonly, the Medicare carrier will deny Part B coverage for what you believe is a covered medical service. Or sometimes it will cover only some but not all of a treatment that you believe should be covered.

You can appeal any of these decisions. This section explains the procedures you must follow.

Decisions About Inpatient Care (Medicare Part A)

Occasionally, disputes arise about whether treatment as an inpatient in a hospital or skilled nursing facility continues to be medically necessary. These disputes often pit the patient and doctor on one side and the facility's Medicare review committee on the other. The review committee might believe that the patient can be moved from the hospital to home or to a nursing facility sooner than the doctor advises, or moved from the skilled nursing facility to a nonskilled

facility or to home care. If this happens to you, there are several steps you can take to convince Medicare to pay for your continued inpatient care.

Help From the State Health Insurance Assistance Program (SHIP) and Medicare Rights Center

Every state has a program to provide free assistance to any person with questions or problems regarding Medicare, medigap supplemental insurance, Medicare managed care, Medicaid, and long-term care. For example, people often have questions about enrollment, paying bills, and filing appeals. The overall program is called the "State Health Insurance Assistance Program" (SHIP), though in your state the program might go by one of several different names—"Health Insurance Counseling and Advocacy Program" (HICAP), "Senior Health Insurance Benefits Advisors" (SHIBA), or something similar. Whatever the name, the program provides free counseling by professional staff plus trained volunteers. The offices are often connected to legal service agencies that can provide free or low-cost legal advice if the matter involves an interpretation of a law or rule, or a legal battle.

SHIP offices are staffed by dedicated people who aren't only knowledgeable and trained to give helpful advice but are also willing to fight for your rights. They sit down with you in person, review your story and papers until they understand your situation, and help you handle the paperwork and telephoning sometimes necessary to make your enrollment or appeal work.

To find the SHIP office nearest you, see the contact information at the end of this chapter.

Help with all sorts of Medicare questions and problems is also available from the nonprofit Medicare Rights Center. Its website, www.medicarerights.org, provides the answers to many common questions about Medicare. And you can call the center toll free at 800-333-4114 to speak, at no cost to you, with a knowledgeable counselor.

Coverage Decisions

Initial Medicare approval of whether your treatment should be as an inpatient is made by the hospital's or nursing facility's Utilization Review Committee (URC), a group of doctors and administrators. The committee makes this determination before you're admitted or within one day of your emergency admission. The URC also periodically reviews your condition and progress in the facility and can decide—after checking your medical records and consulting with your doctor—that you no longer require inpatient care at that facility.

Such a decision does not mean that you'll be kicked out of the facility, but it might mean that the URC will recommend to Medicare that your inpatient stay at the facility no longer be covered by Part A insurance. If you and your doctor believe you should remain in the hospital, there are procedures to follow that might reverse the URC's decision. And even if the decision is not reversed, the process of appealing can give you a bit more time in the facility without being personally responsible for the huge inpatient bills.

Notice of Noncoverage. If the URC decides that your condition no longer requires inpatient care, it will consult with your doctor. If your doctor agrees, the URC will give you a written Notice of Noncoverage stating that your Medicare hospitalization coverage will end on a certain day. If you don't feel that you should be discharged from the hospital at that point, first express your wishes to your doctor. Ask that the doctor request from the URC that a longer period of inpatient care be approved.

If the doctor or ombudsman can't change or delay the URC's decision, or your doctor won't oppose the decision, but you still feel that you should not be discharged, you'll have to file an appeal to protect your right to have Medicare Part A cover your inpatient care.

If your doctor disagrees with the URC opinion that you should be discharged, the URC will either back off its decision and not contest your Medicare coverage—in which case you'll hear nothing about it—or will ask for an opinion from the state's Peer Review Organization (PRO). The PRO is a group of doctors who are paid

by Medicare to review the medical necessity and appropriateness of inpatient care. This is a bit like the foxes guarding the chickens, but the PROs are also medical professionals who respect the opinions of treating physicians. The PRO will review your medical records, the URC's recommendation, and your doctor's position.

If the PRO agrees that your continued stay at the hospital is medically necessary, you'll hear nothing more about the matter and Medicare will continue to cover your inpatient care. However, if the PRO decides that your inpatient care is no longer medically necessary, you'll receive a Notice of Noncoverage stating that your coverage for hospitalization will end as of a certain day.

Immediate Review

If you receive a Notice of Noncoverage, it will contain important information, including when the URC intends to end your Medicare coverage and whether your doctor or the state PRO has agreed with the decision. How you'll obtain immediate review—the first step in appealing the decision—differs slightly depending on whether your doctor agreed with the URC or the decision was made by the PRO over your doctor's objection.

Immediate review of joint URC and doctor decision. If the Notice of Noncoverage states that your doctor agreed with the URC that coverage for your inpatient care should end, you must take some action to get the process moving.

If you're in the hospital, chances are you might have physical difficulty making phone calls and having conversations to get your immediate review started. You can have a friend or relative act on your behalf by making the necessary call requesting review of your case. You can also ask your doctor to initiate the review, even though the doctor initially agreed with the URC's recommendation that Medicare inpatient coverage should end on the specified date. You can also ask to speak with the hospital ombudsman, who can then make your request for immediate review.

Once the PRO has been notified that you're requesting immediate review, it will contact you in order to discuss the matter.

Request an immediate review by the PRO by noon of the first workday after you receive the Notice of Noncoverage. Contact may be made by phone or in writing at the number and address of the PRO given on the notice.

A representative of the PRO will speak with you directly about why you believe you still require inpatient care—and with the doctor who had you admitted to the hospital or with the physician overseeing your care.

Your Doctor Can Be Your Best Ally

The most important element in winning an appeal, particularly for coverage of inpatient care, is gaining your doctor's cooperation. The decision on a Medicare appeal often depends on what the doctor notes in your medical records about your condition and the treatment involved—and on how much assistance you can get from the doctor in providing clarification to the people doing your Medicare review.

The problem is that many doctors view their responsibility to the patient as including only the technical treatment of a medical condition: your body and how it works. Many doctors aren't particularly concerned with how you pay the bill, as long as you pay it. And if it's someone else's bill—the hospital's, for example—the doctor might be even less interested.

If you're fortunate, your doctor will give some attention to your Medicare needs, calling the Medicare appeal personnel and writing a letter, if necessary. If so, you'll find the Medicare appeal process fairly simple. But if your doctor won't take the time to listen to your Medicare problem and help you with the appeal, you might have a frustrating time, which can't help your recovery process. It might also prompt you to consider changing doctors.

TIP

Try again with your doctor. Help from your doctor is the best hope you have of convincing the PRO to approve your continued coverage. Speak with the doctor again about why you think you should have continued coverage. Sometimes a doctor agrees with the URC decision on care without consulting the patient, or based on an expectation of the patient's improvement that has not occurred. Also, there might be more than one doctor treating you. If so, try to enlist the help of your other doctors. Ask them to speak with your admitting physician about your needing more inpatient care.

The PRO will review your case and, within a matter of days, inform you directly of its decision—either by phone or in writing. If the PRO agrees with the facility that your coverage should end, coverage will continue only until noon of the day after you receive notice of the PRO's decision. After that, the facility will bill you for all inpatient costs.

TIP

Your coverage will continue during the review. If you have requested an immediate review of a joint URC and doctor decision, Medicare will continue to cover your inpatient care until the PRO makes a decision.

Immediate review of a URC decision your doctor opposes. If your doctor believes that you need to remain in the hospital but the URC disagrees, the URC will have taken your case to the PRO before you receive a Notice of Noncoverage. And the notice will tell you that the PRO has already agreed with the URC.

You must still ask the PRO for immediate review. But unless you and your doctor can present some strong reasons why the decision should be changed, it will likely remain in effect.

The review process should then proceed as follows:

- Contact the PRO at once by phone or in writing to explain why you believe your continued inpatient care is necessary.
- Ask your doctor—or several doctors if more than one is treating you—to immediately call the PRO to give reasons why your inpatient care continues to be medically necessary. If doctors who are treating you haven't previously been in contact with the PRO regarding your case, they can help immensely now by backing up what your admitting physician has said about your continuing need for inpatient care.
- Within three working days of your request for review, the PRO will notify you in writing of its decision.
- Medicare Part A coverage will end the third day after you receive the Notice of Noncoverage, even if the PRO has not yet decided. If the PRO takes the full three days to decide on your coverage and then agrees with the Notice of Noncoverage, you'll be personally responsible for the full cost of one full day of hospital costs—the day after coverage stops but on which the PRO has not yet decided.

If the PRO upholds the decision that your inpatient coverage should end, that is not the last word on your Medicare coverage. Similarly, if you did not request immediate review, you can still appeal the decision of noncoverage. Several stages of appeal are open to you, as described below.

Have Your Bill Submitted to Medicare

Whether or not you asked for immediate review, you must ask that the hospital or other facility billing office submit the bill to the Medicare intermediary for payment. If you can get strong backing from your doctors, the intermediary might reverse the decision of the URC. Without such support, however, the intermediary will probably uphold the decision of the URC. Either way, if you want to pursue an appeal of the decision, you must have the hospital submit the bill to Medicare. Only by getting a Medicare carrier's decision can you move your appeal to the next stage.

Unfortunately, while the intermediary is deciding on your claim, the hospital or nursing facility might bill you for the uncovered part of your inpatient stay. If you pay the bill and later win your appeal, Medicare will reimburse you.

Reconsideration of Carrier's Decision

If the Medicare intermediary denies the claim for payment of part of your inpatient bill, you have 60 days from the date you receive the denial notice to submit a request for reconsideration. You'll find the address for sending this request on the notice denying your claim.

This reconsideration will be made by what Medicare calls a Qualified Independent Contractor (QIC). The QIC was not involved in the original determination of your appeal.

This request for reconsideration can be made by filing a special *Medicare Reconsideration Request* form. You can find this form online on Medicare's official website at www.cms.gov/Medicare/CMS-Forms/ CMS-Forms/downloads/cms20033.pdf. Or, this request can be made in the form of a simple letter explaining why your stay in the facility continues to be necessary. Once again, however, it's not so much what you say in your letter as whether you have the support of one or more of your doctors. Ask all of the doctors who support your position to send a letter to the intermediary stating their medical opinion, and also to give you a copy. Attach a copy of each doctor's letter to your request for reconsideration, and always keep an extra copy for yourself.

It's sometimes difficult to get a doctor to write a letter on your behalf, even if the doctor supports your position. Sometimes it's simply a matter of the doctor being too busy, or not concerned enough with your financial problem, to speak with you in person before you must send in your request for reconsideration. Other doctors charge a fee for writing any letter that does not involve consultation about treatment— as opposed to payment of bills—and the fee might be too high for you. If you haven't obtained a letter from a doctor who supports your position, at least list your doctor's name and phone number in your request to the QIC. Ask that the QIC contact the doctor before completing its reconsideration.

The QIC will give you a written decision on its reconsideration. If it again denies coverage, you have 60 days to begin the next step in the appeal process.

> **TIP**
>
> **Put everything in writing and keep copies.** Keep copies of all correspondence and other papers concerning Medicare claims and appeals. Also, keep notes on all conversations you have with your doctor, representatives from the hospital, the PRO, and the intermediary. Write down the date of the conversation, the name of the person with whom you talked, and what information was given or taken.

Request an Administrative Hearing

If, upon reconsideration, your appeal is denied by the QIC, you have 60 days from the date on the QIC's written decision to request a hearing by an administrative law judge (ALJ). The hearing is held before an ALJ who is attached to a local office of the Office of Medicare Hearings and Appeals (OMHA). You can ask that an actual hearing be held, which the ALJ will conduct either in person or by telephone. Or you can ask that the ALJ decide your appeal without a hearing, just by reviewing written materials. You can request a decision by an ALJ only if the amount you're contesting is $140 or more.

The form for requesting this administrative hearing is provided online at www.hhs.gov/sites/default/files/omha-100.pdf. For more information about how the hearing process works, you can go directly to the website of the Office of Medicare Hearings and Appeals at www.hhs.gov/omha.

As with every other stage of a Medicare appeal, your doctor's (or doctors') cooperation is the single most important element. Your doctor could appear personally at the hearing and testify on your behalf in front of the judge, but most doctors would charge an arm and a leg to do this. Instead, ask your doctor—or several of your doctors, if possible—to write an explanation of why your medical condition required inpatient treatment. You can then present the written explanation to the judge. Be aware that many doctors charge for writing such a letter, and Medicare laws permit them to do so.

Appeals Council and Federal Lawsuit

If the decision of the administrative law judge goes against you, you can file an appeal to the Social Security Appeals Council. And if that appeal goes against you, you can file an action in federal court challenging the Medicare decision. (See Chapter 9 for more information.)

You can file such a lawsuit only if the amount you're contesting is $1,400 or more. Because of the time and expense involved, it's likely you would file such a lawsuit only if the amount is quite a bit higher than that anyway. If you're considering such a lawsuit at this stage, consult with an experienced attorney. You might be able to get a referral to such an attorney from a SHIP office (see contact information at the end of this chapter).

Payment of Doctor and Other Medical Bills (Part B)

During the course of one or more of your Medicare Part B medical insurance claims, you might disagree with the carrier's decision about whether a particular treatment or service is covered by Medicare. If you find that the Medicare carrier has denied coverage for a certain bill, you have a right to appeal. However, the Medicare Part B appeal process is quite limited, and most people have more success informally contacting the carrier than they do with formal appeals.

Read the *Medicare Summary Notice*

The place to start with a question or complaint about your Medicare Part B coverage of a particular treatment or service is the *Medicare Summary Notice* (MSN) you receive from the carrier. (See "*Your Medicare Summary Notice*," above, for a discussion of the MSN.)

It not only shows whether a health care service is covered but also gives a description of the service, a Medicare code number—called a "procedure code"—for the service, and a limited explanation of why a particular service was not covered.

Certain services might be covered if they're described one way by your doctor's office in the Medicare forms they submit, but not covered if described differently. These problems are sometimes caused simply by a wrongly placed checkmark—for example, indicating

a routine physical exam (not covered) instead of indicating physical examination for a particular patient complaint (covered). Such a mistake could be made by any number of people involved in handling your claim: your doctor, someone in your doctor's office, or someone in the Medicare carrier's vast paperwork machinery.

The MSN might also indicate that you were denied coverage for a particular service because you had the service performed too frequently during a given time. For example, you might have had two mammograms in one year when Medicare normally covers only one per year. However, if the treatment was determined to be medically necessary by your doctor—because, for example, you have a family history of breast cancer, or prior exams have disclosed potential problems—Medicare can and should cover the second mammogram.

In either situation, the next step is to contact your doctor's office to get a letter supporting the medical necessity for the treatment provided.

Check With Your Doctor's Office

If you believe that the MSN incorrectly describes the service or treatment you had, call your doctor's office and ask whether the claim form sent to Medicare had the same information as shown on your MSN. If either the claim form or the MSN had incorrect information, ask that the doctor's office contact the carrier with the correct information.

If coverage was denied because Medicare claims the treatment was not medically necessary or that you received the treatment too often, ask the doctor to write a letter explaining why the treatment was medically necessary. Also, ask that doctor to make a copy of any of your medical records that support this conclusion—and to send the letter and records to you so that you can then deal with the Medicare carrier.

Contact the Medicare Carrier

Most mistakes in billing and coverage are corrected informally, by phone and letter. The Medicare carriers know that mistakes are often made, and they would rather correct them quickly and inexpensively than go through a lengthy and more costly appeal process.

The number to call to reach your carrier is printed in the "Customer Service Information" box in the upper right-hand corner of the first page of your MSN. When you reach your Medicare carrier, give your name, your Medicare number, and the date of the MSN, explaining that you want to discuss coverage of a particular item. Then explain why you believe a mistake was made and describe your doctor's response to the problem. If you have a letter or any medical records from the doctor that explain matters, tell the Medicare carrier what you have. The carrier will either contact your doctor's office or ask you to send in a copy of your doctor's letter, or both.

If this informal contact results in a change in decision by the Medicare carrier, it will send you a revised MSN explaining what the new Medicare payments are and how much you owe. If it does not change the coverage decision based on this informal contact, your next step would be to push on to a more formal written appeal.

Write a Request for Redetermination

If you haven't been able to resolve the coverage question informally, you have 120 days from the date you receive the MSN within which to file a written request for redetermination of the carrier's decision—also called a "request for review." The bottom of the second page of your MSN provides information and a short form to help you appeal the decision.

Make a copy of the MSN, circle the items you want to challenge, sign the back of the copy, and send it to the carrier listed on the front of the form. Although the MSN says you can write your appeal on the form itself, it's better to send along a separate, signed letter with the MSN, stating your reasons for appealing. There's very little space allowed for your statement on the appeal form, usually not enough to explain your reasoning adequately. Or, you can file your request for redetermination on a form provided by Medicare online at www.cms.gov/cmsforms/downloads/CMS20027.pdf, but this form, too, has only limited space to explain your reasons for requesting a change in Medicare's decision.

The letter should include your full name as it appears on the MSN, your Medicare number, the date of the MSN, the date of the disputed medical service, and a brief explanation of why you believe the treatment or other service should be covered. Include any letter or other records from your doctor that support your position.

TIP

Hold on to the documents. Keep copies of all letters and documents you send to or receive from the Medicare carrier and from your doctor. Also, keep notes of every conversation you have with anyone at the Medicare carrier, including the date of conversation, the name of the person with whom you spoke, and any action decided upon in the phone call—such as, you'll send them a letter, they will contact your doctor, or they will call you back within a week.

Time to Seek Assistance

If you're considering a request for a review of your medical bills, or you've completed the written review and are considering a request for a hearing, it might be time for you to get some assistance from a local State Health Insurance Assistance Program (SHIP) office (see contact information at the end of this chapter). This is particularly true if the amount you're contesting would put a sizable hole in your budget.

If you're considering an appeal to an administrative law judge for a hearing, you might want to consider not only help from SHIP but also the assistance of an experienced Medicare lawyer. (See Chapter 9 for tips on finding legal help.) SHIP can also help refer you to such lawyers.

On the following pages are samples of request for redetermination letters to a Medicare carrier. There are no magic words you must include in such a letter, but these examples demonstrate the kind

of simple information required. A letter should include several key points, each of which should be described as briefly and clearly as possible. Keep in mind that the letter is meant merely to point out how and where the error was made and where proof of the error can be found, not to serve as proof itself. Only your medical records and the opinion of your doctors can actually prove anything.

First, you should briefly describe the treatment you received.

Second, you should point out the specific reasons why the intermediary's decision not to cover the treatment was incorrect—for example, you did not have merely a routine physical exam but an exam to determine the cause of a specific problem, or you did not have a dental exam but an examination by an oral surgeon of the nerves in your jaw.

Third, refer to the doctor's letter or other medical records that support your claim.

Notice that at the bottom left of each letter is the notation "cc:" and next to it the name of the doctor. This indicates to the Medicare carrier that you have sent a copy of this letter to your doctor—an action you should take so that the letter goes into your medical file. Sending a copy of the letter to the doctor will help prepare the doctor for a call from the Medicare carrier, and it might remind the doctor to do a better job of explaining the medical necessity of your care the next time you have treatment.

When the carrier reconsiders your claim, it will review your file, check the documents on which the original decision was made, and investigate any new information you've presented or the carrier has obtained by contacting your doctor. You don't have an opportunity at this stage to appear in person and explain things.

If a mistake was made because incorrect or incomplete information had originally been provided to the carrier or someone made a simple clerical error, the carrier is likely to reverse its decision and provide you with coverage. You'll then receive a written notice of its review determination and a new MSN.

Request for Redetermination Letter: Sample #1

Betty Patient
222 Public Street
Consumer, USA 12345
Telephone: 123-123-1234

March 1, 20xx

Transprofit Insurance Company
P.O. Box 123
Moneyville, USA 12345

Re: Request for Review and Redetermination
Medicare Part B
Medicare Number xx-xxx-xxxxA
MSN Notice dated January 2, 20xx

To Whom It Concerns:

    This letter is a request for review and redetermination of a decision made by Transprofit denying coverage of medical treatment I received on November 1, 20xx. A copy of the MSN notice of January 2, 20xx, denying coverage, is enclosed.

    I believe that Transprofit denied coverage of the mammogram I received on November 1, 20xx, from Dr. Alice Well because I had previously had a mammogram in January 20xx, which Medicare covered, and Medicare does not normally cover more than one mammogram per year. However, this second mammogram was medically necessary because I have a family history of breast cancer and because my previous mammogram in January showed some spots of potentially cancerous tissue.

    Apparently the original Medicare claim from my doctor's office did not include this background information. However, I am enclosing a copy of a letter from Dr. Well and a copy of the medical records from my January mammogram to indicate why the second mammogram was medically necessary.

    Based on this information, please reconsider the original decision denying Medicare coverage of the November 1, 20xx treatment.

Yours truly,

Betty Patient

cc: Dr. Alice Well

Request for Redetermination Letter: Sample #2

Andy Q. Everyone
18B Main Street
Anytown, USA 12345
Telephone: 222-222-2222

June 1, 20xx

Ourworld Insurance Inc.
P.O. Box 567
Big Money, USA 12345

Re: Request for Review and Redetermination
Medicare Part B
Medicare Number xx-xxx-xxxxB
MSN Notice dated March 1, 20xx

To Whom It Concerns:

This letter is a request for review and redetermination of a decision made by Ourworld Insurance denying coverage of medical treatment I received on January 10, 20xx. A copy of the MSN notice of March 1, 20xx, denying coverage, is enclosed.

I believe that Ourworld Insurance denied coverage of the eye exam I received on January 10, 20xx, from Dr. Barry Eyesore, because Dr. Eyesore's office mistakenly noted on the Medicare claim form that I underwent a routine eye examination refraction on that date, marking on the form Procedure Code 92015.

This was a mistake. In fact, I had a specific examination and treatment for blurred vision and eye pain that I had been suffering. Dr. Eyesore's records indicate that this was a medically necessary examination for a medical condition, for which he prescribed medication, rather than a routine eye examination. Enclosed is a copy of my medical record from Dr. Eyesore indicating the nature of the exam on that date.

Based on this additional information, please reconsider the original decision denying Medicare coverage of the January 10, 20xx examination and treatment of my eyes.

Yours truly,

Andy Q. Everyone

cc: Dr. Barry Eyesore

If there's a dispute about whether a certain treatment truly was medically necessary, the carrier might well reverse itself at this stage, but it does so less often than in cases of simple clerical errors or missing documentation from the doctor.

Once the Medicare carrier has received your request for redetermination and your supporting documents, someone within the company who was not involved in making the original decision will decide on your request. You'll receive a written response from the carrier, called a *Medicare Redetermination Notice*, about 60 days after you file your request and supporting papers. It will contain information about a further appeal if you're not satisfied with the decision.

Request for Reconsideration by Qualified Independent Contractor (QIC)

If the carrier reviews your file and still refuses to cover your treatment, you can continue your appeal by requesting a reconsideration.

You have 180 days from the date you receive the written notice of determination to request a reconsideration by what's called a "Qualified Independent Contractor" (QIC). A QIC is a company separate from the Medicare carrier itself. The address to which to send your request is printed on the carrier's written notice of determination.

You can file your Request for Reconsideration on a form provided by Medicare online at www.cms.gov/cmsforms/downloads/CMS20033.pdf. However, space on the form is limited, and you might prefer to write a letter request instead, an example of which is shown below (see "Letter Requesting Reconsideration by QIC"). The letter requesting a reconsideration is similar to the letter requesting redetermination, except that you should refer to the date of the carrier's written notice of determination following your request for redetermination in addition to the original MSN.

In separate paragraphs, make the following points:

- Describe the treatment you received and the dates on which you received it. This description should be brief, since the carrier will get its full explanation from your medical records.

- State the specific reasons why the intermediary's initial decision not to cover the treatment was incorrect.
- Refer, by name and date, to your doctor's letter and to the specific medical records that support your claim.

Attach to your request for a reconsideration copies of letters from your doctors and of your medical records, if you have them. Also, call your doctors' offices to request that they send copies of your records to the address you've been given on the notice.

You'll get a written decision, called a *Medicare Reconsideration Notice*, from the QIC within about 60 days after you file your request for reconsideration. If you're not satisfied with this decision, you have 60 days from the date you receive the notice to request a hearing before an administrative law judge.

Hearing Before Administrative Law Judge

If your claim for doctor bill coverage is once again denied after the reconsideration by the QIC, you can request a hearing before an administrative law judge if the amount you're contesting is $180 or more. If the amount in dispute is less than $180, the hearing before the carrier's hearing officer is the end of the line.

You must request a hearing before an administrative law judge within 60 days of the date you receive written notice of the decision by the carrier's hearing officer. (See Chapter 9 for a full discussion of the administrative hearing process.) Medicare provides an online form to request this hearing at www.hhs.gov/sites/default/files/omha-100.pdf.

Medicare Appeals Council Review

If you don't receive a favorable ruling from the administrative law judge, you can appeal the decision to the Medicare Appeals Council. In Medicare Part B claims, the written appeal must be filed within 60 days of the date of the administrative law judge's written decision.

Letter Requesting Reconsideration by QIC

Rosa Albertez
3456 Broadway
Anytown, USA 45678
Telephone: 333-333-3333

June 1, 20xx

Your Money Insurance Co.
P.O. Box 1234
Greentown, USA 12345

Re: Request for Reconsideration by QIC, Medicare Part B
Medicare Number xx-xxx-xxxxC
Notice of Determination After Review Dated May 1, 20xx

To Whom It Concerns:

This letter is a request for a reconsideration by QIC following a determination made on May 1, 20xx. That determination upheld a decision made by Your Money denying coverage of a medical service I received on February 1, 20xx, and laboratory work performed on February 5, 20xx. A copy of the MSN notice of March 15, 20xx, denying coverage, is enclosed. Also enclosed is a copy of the written determination after review, dated May 1, 20xx.

I believe that Your Money denied coverage of the physical examination I received from Dr. Walter Thorough and of laboratory work ordered by Dr. Thorough because Dr. Thorough failed to give certain information to the carrier. The physical and the laboratory tests were not routine examinations but were a response to severe muscle fasciculation and cramping that I had been suffering over the previous several weeks. Dr. Thorough's records indicate that the examination and laboratory tests were medically necessary to diagnose and treat my condition.

I have enclosed a copy of my medical records from Dr. Thorough, as well as a letter from Dr. Thorough, both of which make clear that the examination and laboratory tests were medically necessary and should be covered by Medicare.

Yours truly,

Rosa Albertez

cc: Dr. Walter Thorough

Federal Court Case

It's highly unlikely that a Medicare Part B decision will involve enough money that it would be economically sensible for you—and a lawyer representing you—to file a lawsuit in federal court to challenge a negative decision by the Medicare Appeals Council. However, if your claim is for $1,850 or more, you do have such a right. You must file the lawsuit within 60 days of the written decision by the Appeals Council.

Medicare Part D: Enrollment, Exceptions, and Appeals

How you enroll in a Part D plan will depend on several factors, including whether you:

- receive Medicaid benefits
- live in a long-term care facility
- have had employer-sponsored health coverage that included drug coverage
- qualify for a Part D low-income subsidy, or
- are in none of those categories.

Note that, if you believe you might be eligible for the Part D low-income subsidy, you must file two separate applications—one for Part D coverage, and one for the low-income subsidy (see below).

Once you're enrolled in a Part D plan, your plan's decisions about coverage and costs aren't necessarily final. The plan might exclude one of your drugs from coverage, might require you to jump through hoops to get coverage for a particular drug, or might charge you a higher copayment for your drug than for a generic equivalent. In any of these situations, you have the right to request an exception. And you have the right to appeal the plan's decision.

Enrollment

How and when you enroll in a Part D plan depends on whether you're a Medicaid beneficiary or have been accepted for a Part D low-income subsidy. Regardless of the plan you enroll in or how you're enrolled, your coverage won't begin until the first of the month following the completion of your enrollment.

Applying for Extra Help Paying for Medicare Part D

Medicare's Extra Help program offers assistance (also called a "low-income subsidy") to help pay for the cost of prescription drugs above and beyond what a standard Part D plan pays. (See Chapter 12.) You apply for Extra Help by submitting an application to the Social Security Administration (SSA) rather than to Medicare or to a Part D plan. Contact the SSA to get an Extra Help application and instructions, or to set up an appointment to get help applying. You can reach the SSA toll free at 800-772-1213. Or you can visit the special Social Security webpage called "Extra Help with Medicare Prescription Drug Plan Costs," at www.ssa.gov/medicare/part-d-extra-help, to file an application online. Or, you can also apply for Extra Help at a local county Social Services office or another local government office in your state that processes Medicaid applications.

Free one-on-one help is available at your local SHIP or HICAP office. These programs have trained counselors on staff to help you with your application. To find the office nearest you, contact the SHIP or HICAP program in your state (for details, see the end of this chapter).

If your application for Extra Help is approved, the benefits will be retroactive to the date you first applied. Once approved, your participation in Extra Help will remain in effect for one year. Within the first year of your Extra Help, the Social Security Administration will review your finances to see if you remain eligible. If so, your participation in Extra Help will be automatically renewed. After the first year, SSA will periodically review your Extra Help eligibility.

Enrolling in a Part D Plan

Most people will follow the standard enrollment procedures described below. If you're a Medicaid beneficiary or are qualified for a Part D low-income subsidy, your enrollment procedures will differ slightly (see below).

Standard enrollment. If you're not a Medicaid beneficiary and you haven't qualified for a Part D low-income subsidy, you enroll in Part D by signing up directly with the plan you want to join. Private insurance companies administer each Part D plan using their own enrollment forms and procedures. Some plans might permit you to enroll online, while others might require written forms. You must contact the plan directly to find out the details of their coverage and costs, and to enroll in the plan.

Your Part D plan will cover the cost of your medications only after you've completed enrollment in the plan and your Medicare Part A or B coverage has begun. This means that any drugs you buy while your application is pending won't be covered. It's therefore a good idea to decide on a plan and submit an application in the months before you become eligible for Medicare, so that coverage will begin as soon as you're eligible.

If you don't enroll in a Part D plan when you're first eligible for it, your premiums will be higher when you do finally enroll. Medicare allows the plans to charge an additional 1% for each month you delay enrolling (unless you've been enrolled in a Medicare Advantage or an employer-sponsored plan that covered prescription drugs). So, if you intend to enroll in a Part D plan as soon as you're eligible for Medicare, you should do the paperwork ahead of time. This will ensure not only that your coverage begins immediately, but also that you won't have to pay a higher premium because of a simple paperwork delay.

Medicaid beneficiary. If you're a Medicare beneficiary who is also eligible for Medicaid assistance (Medi-Cal in California), you can enroll in any Part D plan. But in order to get the full benefit of your low-income subsidy, you must enroll in a plan whose premium is at

or below your state's average. If you enroll in a plan with a premium higher than the state average, you'll be responsible for the extra premium cost out of your own pocket.

If you don't enroll in a Part D plan on your own, Medicaid will automatically enroll you in a plan with a premium below the state's average. And if that plan doesn't fit your needs for drug coverage, you can switch plans at any time (see "Switching Part D Plans," below).

Low-income subsidized enrollment. If you're eligible for one of the Part D low-income subsidies but aren't a Medicaid beneficiary, you can enroll in a Part D plan at any time, directly with the plan of your choice. If at any later time, your plan no longer offers you the best coverage, you can switch to another plan (see "Switching Part D Plans," below).

Exceptions

Part D plans use a variety of methods to restrict or control the use of medications by their enrollees. (See "Part D: Prescription Drug Coverage" in Chapter 12.) These restrictions include excluding drugs from coverage, setting higher costs for certain drugs within the same class, substituting one drug for another, imposing a drug supply limit, and requiring you to try a series of other drugs before the plan will cover the one you want.

Medicare gives plans very broad discretion to create and change these coverage restrictions. This means that you might begin coverage with a plan whose restrictions don't seriously affect you, only to find the plan changes its rules later on. You might then find yourself with a restriction on one of your drugs that is financially burdensome, physically discomfiting, or even medically inadvisable. For example, your plan might drop one of your drugs from its formulary and replace it with a drug that the plan considers "equivalent," but this drug might not provide you with the same quality of relief or might have more side effects. Or, your plan might increase the copayment for your drug, costing you more money per prescription.

Eventually, you might be able to switch to a plan with fewer restrictions on your drugs. But until you're able to do so, or if there's no other plan available at the same cost with fewer restrictions, you have a chance to get your plan to lift its restriction in your individual case. You do this by requesting an "exception" from your plan's rules, based on "medical necessity." You make this request to the plan itself, not to Medicare. Each plan has its own rules for handling exception requests, and Medicare requires only that a plan have a formal procedure and make a decision, called a "Coverage Determination," within 72 hours after you file an exception request.

Medical necessity. Your doctor's support is the key to success with any exception request. To convince your plan that you need easier access to your drug, you must show that you have a medical necessity to take that particular drug rather than another drug that the plan considers equivalent. Medical necessity does not necessarily mean that you'll have very serious or dangerous medical consequences if you take the equivalent drug. But it does mean that there will be some change in your physical condition—for example, less effective treatment or more severe side effects—if you take the so-called equivalent drug instead of the one you usually take.

Your chance of convincing the plan of your medical need for a particular drug almost certainly requires an explanation from your doctor. The plan might request a letter from your doctor, or a copy of your medical records demonstrating your complaints to the doctor about the substituted medicine, or simply a phone conversation with your doctor. Whatever form the contact will take, it's important that you prepare your doctor to explain your problem. Meet with or talk to your doctor by phone about the problem and about your exception request. This will allow you to make certain that the doctor understands the full extent of your difficulty with the substituted drug and will give the doctor advance warning that the plan will be requesting information.

Help With Exceptions and Appeals

As discussed in these sections about exceptions and appeals, it's crucial to have your doctor's help in explaining the medical necessity of a particular drug. But your doctor can only do so much—your doctor won't help you fill out request and appeal forms, or write your letters to the insurance company explaining your situation. To get help with the exception or appeal process itself, you might want to contact the counselors at your local SHIP or HICAP office, whose expert advice is free. You can find the local office of these counseling organizations by calling the central office for your state; for contact information, see the end of this chapter.

You can also get free expert counseling from the Medicare Rights Center; contact them through www.medicarerights.org.

If your appeal reaches the later stages, and particularly if you intend to take it to federal court, you'll likely need the assistance of a lawyer experienced in Medicare appeals. (For a discussion of when a lawyer might be needed and how to find one, see Chapter 9.)

If the plan denies your request for an exception, you can file an appeal. Appeals are discussed below. And if your appeal is denied, or if you simply don't want to bother going through the appeal process, you can switch to another plan that offers better coverage of your drug (if you can find one) as soon as you're permitted to switch by Part D enrollment rules (see "Switching Part D Plans," below).

Appeals

Part D plans regularly make decisions and change rules about their drug coverage. But these decisions and rules aren't necessarily the final word about coverage. You can appeal a plan's rule or decision if you find that it forces you to give up, or pay a higher copay for, a drug you and your doctor believe is medically necessary. Appeals initially go to the plan itself. At later stages, an appeal can be considered by independent reviewers outside the plan.

If at any stage of the process an enrollee wins a change in the plan's decision, its effect will be retroactive back to the time the enrollee first challenged the plan's coverage decision. This retroactivity works well when the issue is the amount of money an enrollee has to pay out of pocket. Retroactivity is only cold comfort, however, if the enrollee has been forced to make do with a substitute drug during the time spent on the appeal.

In almost every case, success with an appeal depends on your doctor's presenting a convincing argument that the drug in question is "medically necessary" to you (see "Exceptions," above).

Types of Decisions That Can Be Appealed

Part D enrollees can appeal several types of plan decisions, including a plan's:

- denial of an exception request
- decision not to cover a drug—or to cover it only at a higher copay—because it's not on the plan's formulary or because of some other access restriction (such as step therapy or therapeutic substitution)
- decision not to cover a drug for a particular enrollee because it's not "medically necessary"
- decision not to cover a drug because it's excluded from the Medicare Part D program, and
- decision not to cover a drug—or to cover it at a higher copay—because it was provided by a pharmacy that didn't have a contract with the plan (called an "out-of-network pharmacy").

Appeal Procedure

Each plan determines the details of its appeal procedure. But all plans must follow certain basic rules.

Coverage determination. When a plan makes a decision about coverage or an exception request, it issues a written letter called a "coverage determination." The plan must issue the coverage determination within 72 hours of the enrollee's filling of a prescription, denial of a prescription, or request for an exception.

Redetermination. Once an enrollee receives an unfavorable written coverage determination from the plan, the enrollee has 60 days to request what is called a "redetermination." This second-round decision will also be made by the plan itself, though it might be made by someone within the plan bureaucracy other than the person who made the original coverage determination. From the date the plan receives a written request for redetermination, it has seven days within which to issue its redetermination decision.

Reconsideration. If an enrollee's request for redetermination still does not result in a favorable decision, the enrollee can file a written request for reconsideration by an Independent Review Entity (IRE). This is where an independent arbitrator reviews and considers both the enrollee's request and the plan's reasons for denying the request. An enrollee must file a request for reconsideration by an IRE within 60 days following receipt of the redetermination decision. Your plan will provide contact information for the IRE that will hear your request. Once the IRE receives your written request for reconsideration, it has seven days to make a decision.

Administrative hearing. If the IRE turns down the enrollee's request, the enrollee has 60 days within which to file a request for a hearing before an administrative law judge (ALJ). To have an administrative hearing with an ALJ, the amount in controversy must be at least $180. But unless the drug coverage question for an enrollee involves only a one-time prescription, the ongoing cost of the drug to the enrollee will almost always exceed $180. The ALJ must issue a decision within 90 days from the date of receiving the request.

Medicare Appeals Council. If the enrollee gets a negative decision from the ALJ, the enrollee has 60 days to file an appeal to the next highest level, called the "Medicare Appeals Council" (MAC). The MAC has 90 days to issue its decision.

Federal court. If the MAC denies an enrollee's appeal, and the amount in controversy concerning the drug is at least $1,850, the enrollee can file a claim in federal court. The enrollee has 60 days from the MAC's decision to file the claim in federal court. If your coverage issue involves continuing expensive medication and you believe that appealing your decision to federal court might be worth

the time and expense, you almost certainly will want to consult with an attorney who specializes in Medicare appeals. For more information on hiring an attorney, see Chapter 9.

Switching Part D Plans

The fact that you're in a particular Part D prescription drug plan doesn't mean that you're forever stuck with that plan or with the insurance company that issued the plan. There are several good reasons why you might want to switch from one plan to another. You might want to switch plans in the following cases:

- You begin taking a new medication, and your old plan does not cover that drug or covers it at a higher copayment than offered by another plan.
- Your current plan drops one of your drugs from its list of covered medications.
- Your current plan raises its premiums or changes its terms of coverage, making a different plan a better fit for you.
- A new plan is offered—or you learn about another plan— that would give you better coverage or lower costs than your current plan.

Whatever your reason, you can switch plans—to a different plan offered by the same insurance company or to a plan with a different company—at least once every year. And some people can switch as often as every month.

When You Cay Switch Plans

Monthly switch. People in two different categories can switch from one Part D plan to another as often as every month, with the new plan's coverage beginning on the first of the month following enrollment. "Dual eligibles"—people enrolled in both Medicare and Medicaid (Medi-Cal in California)—can switch plans as often as monthly. And a person who lives in a long-term care facility (if the facility is certified by Medicare or Medicaid) can also switch plans monthly.

Once-yearly switch. Low-income subsidy beneficiaries and standard enrollees (people who don't receive Medicaid coverage and who don't reside in a long-term care facility) can switch plans once a year, but the switch must happen during an open enrollment period (from October 15 to December 7 each year). **Note:** If you are currently enrolled in a Medicare Advantage plan that covers your prescription drugs (see Chapter 15) but you want to drop that plan, switch to original Medicare, and join a stand-alone Medicare Part D drug plan, you can do so between January 1 and March 31, with coverage to begin on the first of the month following enrollment.

Plans You Can Switch To

If you want to switch from one Part D drug plan to another, you can switch to any Medicare-approved plan currently offered in your state by any company. If you're switching during the open enrollment period from October 15 to December 7 of each year, you can enroll in any plan being offered for the following calendar year, to begin coverage on January 1.

Dual eligibles. If you're a dual-eligible beneficiary (Medicare plus Medicaid), the full cost of your Part D premium is paid by Medicare, as long as your plan's premium is less than your state's average for all Part D plans. If you want to continue receiving that full premium payment, you can only switch to a new plan with a premium lower than your state's average premium. If you switch to a plan with a premium above your state average, you must pay the difference between the new premium and the state average.

How to Switch From One Plan to Another

Switching from one plan to another is not difficult, but it does involve several steps.

Step 1: Find a plan in your area. Find out what plans are offered in your geographic area and select a plan that's right for you, using the selection methods explained in "Part D: Prescription Drug Coverage" in Chapter 12.

Step 2: Enroll in the new plan. Once you've found a plan you like, contact the insurance company directly to make sure you're eligible for the plan. If you're eligible, follow the insurance company's directions to enroll in the plan.

Step 3: Cancel your old plan. Once you receive written confirmation from your new insurance company that you're enrolled in your new plan, it's time to cancel your old plan. Notify your old plan—in writing—that you're canceling your policy. Do this even if the new insurance company has told you that it will notify the old company. Make sure that your cancellation becomes effective only after your new plan is in effect.

> CAUTION
>
> **Don't cancel your old plan too soon.** You might be signing up for a new plan to begin the following month or changing plans during the yearly open enrollment period to begin coverage on January 1. In either case, don't cancel enrollment in your current plan until you have written notification of enrollment in your new plan. And make sure you check the date the new coverage begins, so that you don't cancel your old plan before the new one goes into effect. As with any bureaucratic institution, delays and mistakes do occur. You want to avoid having any gaps in your insurance coverage.

Step 4: Don't double-pay. Make sure your old and new insurance policies don't overlap. If you pay for your Part D plan by sending the insurance company a check, this is easy—you simply don't send in any payment to the old company once your new coverage begins. But many people have their Part D premium amount automatically paid (for example, withheld from their Social Security benefit or transferred directly from their bank). If you pay your old Part D plan automatically, you must stop the automatic payment as of whatever date you begin your new plan.

Step 5: Notify your pharmacist. After you receive confirmation of enrollment in the new plan, notify the pharmacists you use about your new plan. This will make things go more smoothly when you fill your prescriptions.

State Health Insurance Assistance Programs (SHIPs)

Every state has a nonprofit organization for consumer counseling about Medicare, medigap, Medicare Advantage plans, and related matters. The organization operates under the general name State Health Insurance Assistance Program (SHIP) or Health Insurance Counseling and Advocacy Program (HICAP), though in some states it has a similar but slightly different name. These central offices can direct you to a local counseling office near you. You can find the phone number and website for your state's SHIP/HICAP office on the SHIP organization website at www.shiphelp.org. You can also find the website for your state's SHIP/HICAP office by going to Medicare's website at www.medicare.gov/talk-to-someone.

Medigap Insurance

Even for people who have coverage from both Medicare Part A and Part B, a serious illness or injury can cause financial havoc because of the bills Medicare leaves unpaid. About a third of all Medicare recipients age 65 and older respond to this risk by buying a private supplemental health insurance policy known as "medigap" insurance.

The term medigap comes from the fact that these insurance policies are designed to cover the gaps in Medicare payments. Unfortunately, even medigap coverage leaves some medical costs unpaid.

As an alternative, a Medicare Advantage plan typically provides broader coverage at slightly lower cost than the combination of traditional Medicare Part A and B plus a medigap policy (see Chapter 15). However, Medicare Advantage plans restrict the doctors and other providers available to you. And in recent years, some Medicare Advantage plans have been raising enrollee costs, reducing coverage, and dropping coverage entirely in many areas, adding an element of risk to the Medicare Advantage option.

Before choosing one type of coverage or another, compare benefits and approaches and measure your preferences against the price you would have to pay for each.

This chapter gives you guidance about the gaps in Medicare that need to be filled, and the types of medigap insurance policies that exist to partially fill them. Chapter 15 covers the various types of Medicare Advantage plans available as alternatives to medigap supplements. Before selecting either a medigap policy or a Medicare Advantage plan, review the advantages and disadvantages discussed in Chapter 15, and use the charts at the end of that chapter to compare the costs of and coverage provided by individual policies and plans.

As with other decisions about Medicare and related insurance coverage, you can get excellent, free counseling regarding medigap insurance from your local office of the State Health Insurance Assistance Program (SHIP), also known in some states as the "Health Insurance Counseling and Advocacy Program" (HICAP).

Insurance From Continuing or Former Employment

Many people who become eligible for Medicare at age 65 continue to work and have health insurance through their employers. Many others have health insurance through a spouse's employer.

And many other people keep their job-related health insurance after they retire, as part of their retirement benefits packages, although they usually have to pay much more than current employees pay.

Most employment-based health plans require you to sign up for Medicare Part A when you turn 65, but cover your hospitalization in conjunction with Medicare. Most plans based on current employment don't, however, require you to sign up (and pay for) Medicare Part B, but many retiree plans do require you to enroll in Medicare Part B. The health benefits or human resources office at your work or union can explain the details of coordinating coverage between the employer's plan and Medicare.

The fact that you're eligible for a work-related health plan, however, doesn't mean that you have to continue with it. Work-related health insurance has become more expensive and less comprehensive for employees—particularly retired employees. You might find that Medicare plus a medigap policy, or Medicare through a Medicare Advantage managed care plan, provides you with as good or better coverage at a better price than your employer-based medical insurance does.

Even if you decide not to participate in the regular health plan offered in your workplace, your employer's insurance company might offer you a different policy with limited coverage for some services Medicare doesn't cover at all, such as prescription drugs, dental care, or hearing aids. Compare such a policy with the medigap policies and managed care plans discussed in this chapter to see which one offers you the best coverage for your money.

Gaps in Medicare

When considering the kinds of supplemental coverage available, keep in mind the specific gaps in Medicare payments that you're trying to fill. Medicare coverage is explained in detail in Chapter 12, but some of the most significant things it doesn't cover, or covers but only partially pays for, are listed below.

Gaps in Part A: Hospital Insurance

Medicare Part A covers almost all the cost of most hospital stays. Its most common gap is the deductible, which everyone must pay before Medicare pays any part of a hospital bill. A much less frequent but much more frightening gap is the daily coinsurance amount for hospital stays of longer than 60 days. All of the gaps are listed below.

Hospital Bills

Medicare Part A hospital insurance doesn't pay the following costs during a hospital stay:
- a deductible for each benefit period—$1,632 in 2024
- a daily coinsurance amount ($408 in 2024) for each day you're hospitalized more than 60 days and up to 90 days for any one benefit period
- a daily coinsurance amount ($816 in 2024) for each day you're hospitalized more than 90 days and up to 150 days for any one benefit period
- anything past a hospitalization of 150 days
- first three pints of blood, unless replaced, or
- anything for medical costs during foreign travel

Skilled Nursing Facility Bills

Medicare Part A doesn't pay the following costs during a stay in a skilled nursing facility:
- a coinsurance amount of $204 per day for each day you're in the facility more than 20 days and up to 100 days for any one benefit period, and
- anything for a stay of more than 100 days.

Home Health Care

Medicare Part A doesn't pay the following costs for home health care:

- 20% of the approved cost of durable medical equipment or approved nonskilled care, and
- anything for nonmedical personal care services.

Gaps in Part B: Medical Insurance

Medicare Part B leaves some very large gaps in the amounts it pays doctors and other outpatient providers, depending on whether the doctors or others accept assignment. Everyone with Part B faces the 20% of the Medicare-approved amount that Medicare doesn't pay. And if your doctor or other provider doesn't accept assignment, you're also responsible for up to 15% more than the amount Medicare approves. (See "How Much Medicare Part B Pays" in Chapter 12 for more on Part B payments.)

Medicare Part B doesn't pay the following costs for doctors, clinics, laboratories, therapies, medical supplies, or equipment:

- a yearly deductible ($240 in 2024)

- 20% of the Medicare-approved amount

- 15% above the Medicare-approved amount if the provider does not accept assignment, or

- 20% of the total charges for some outpatient hospital services.

Standard Medigap Benefit Plans

The federal government regulates Medicare supplement (medigap) insurance policies—and insurance companies can't offer medigap policies that duplicate Medicare's own coverage.

You can choose among the nine currently available standard medigap plans. The standard policies are specifically tailored to Medicare coverage, each one filling a certain number of Medicare's gaps.

Important Changing Landscape for Medigap Policies

As of 2010, new medigap policies in original plans E, H, I, and J are no longer sold, but people with existing policies under those plans can continue them. People who continue with these policies should be aware, though, that their premiums are likely to rise more steeply over the coming years because there will be increasingly fewer people enrolled in these plans.

Also in 2010, policies began to be issued under two new plans, M and N, and a hospice copayment benefit was added to new policies under all plans.

In addition, some of the plans are subject to small changes from year to year. For more information on these changes and the coverage provided under each plan type, see "Descriptions of the Standard Medigap Plans," below.

CAUTION

Delay may limit your choices. Insurance companies would be happiest if they could sell coverage only to healthy people. When you're shopping for a medigap policy, you might find it hard to buy a policy if you're already ill and didn't buy a policy when you first became eligible. (The Affordable Care Act eliminated preexisting condition limitations for regular private insurance, but not for medigap.)

The federal government has, however, established some protections for people buying medigap policies, depending on when and under what circumstances you apply. You'll receive the most coverage options if you apply within the first six months after you begin your Medicare Part B coverage. In a few other circumstances, you might also have options to purchase some, though not all, medigap policies without fear of being turned down because of your preexisting condition. If you wait too long to apply for a policy, however, the insurance companies are allowed to review your medical records and reject you if they consider you a bad "profit risk." (To understand the rules regarding your right to purchase a medigap policy, see "Terms and Conditions of Medigap Policies," below.)

Medigap Does Not Cover Long-Term Care

Many older people fear the possibility of living out the final years of life in a nursing home. The prospect of nursing home life itself provokes distress for many, as does the financial ruin that can be brought about by the cost of long-term care. Unfortunately, neither Medicare nor medigap supplemental insurance nor managed care health plans protect against this potentially enormous cost. Medicare covers only a limited period of skilled nursing facility care and covers nothing of long-term custodial, nonmedical care in a nursing home. Medigap policies and Medicare Advantage plans similarly fail to cover long-term nursing home care.

Long-term care at home is increasingly an option for people who in years past would have been forced to enter a nursing home. More services are available at home, and more agencies and providers offer home care. However, while Medicare and medigap policies cover some short-term home health care, neither covers long-term nonmedical home care.

There's a type of private insurance that can cover some of the cost of long-term nursing home or at-home care. Referred to as "long-term care insurance," it's available in a variety of benefit packages but comes with numerous restrictions and exclusions. The cost of these policies varies greatly, depending on the extent of coverage and the age of the person purchasing the plan. Medicaid also covers long-term care costs.

For a complete discussion of these policies, the kinds of care they cover, and Medicaid coverage for nursing homes, see *Long-Term Care: How to Plan & Pay for It*, by Joseph L. Matthews (Nolo). (Visit Nolo's website at www.nolo.com for ordering information.)

Not every insurance company offers every medigap plan. And only the benefits included in each standard category of plans are standardized. Other important aspects—premium increases and preexisting illness exclusions, for example—vary from policy to policy and require careful comparison shopping.

When you consider medigap policies, your task is to see how many of the gaps in Medicare payments you can fill within the constraints of your budget. The broader the coverage in a medigap policy, the higher the cost.

And the cost of a standard policy can vary widely from company to company. So you must determine not only which standardized benefit plan best suits your needs, but which company offers which plan at the best price. Then examine the other elements of each policy, such as premium increases and preexisting illness exclusions, before making your choice.

Basic Benefits Included in All Medigap Plans

The benefits included in the standard medigap plans and a chart comparing their coverage follow.

All standard medigap policies begin by offering the same basic benefits, including coverage of:

- hospital coinsurance amounts under Medicare Part A (but not necessarily the deductible)
- 365 days of hospital coverage after Medicare coverage ends
- some or all of the cost of covered blood transfusions
- some or all of the Medicare Part B coinsurance amount (the 20% of Medicare-approved amounts that Medicare Part B doesn't pay), and
- some or all of the out-of-pocket cost for hospice care (for all policies issued on or after June 1, 2010).

Notice that these basic benefits are meant to close gaps in Medicare coverage, not to provide separate medical insurance. If a hospitalization or medical treatment isn't covered at all by Medicare, a medigap policy won't cover any of it, either. The exception to this is those medigap policies that cover foreign travel.

Inpatient Hospital Costs

For every benefit period, every medigap plan pays all your Medicare Part A coinsurance amounts through your first 90 days as an inpatient, plus your coinsurance amount for any reserve days. After your

reserve days are used up, every plan pays for the entire Medicare-approved amount of hospital charges for an additional 365 days. All plans pay some amount for the first three pints of blood you receive (Plans A through J pay the full amount; K pays 50%; L pays 75%). All plans except Plan A pay the yearly Part A hospital inpatient deductible (but Plans K and M pay only 50%, Plan L pays only 75%).

Medigap: It Pays to Shop Around

The federal government decides what benefits must be included in standard medigap policies. But it doesn't control prices, which vary widely. Prices vary for different ages and change from state to state, reflecting regional health care costs and level of competition for customers.

But the price for the same policy can vary tremendously even within the same state. Even the most basic Plan A policy can vary in cost by hundreds or even thousands of dollars per year in some states. And the more extensive the plan, the greater the cost disparity among policies from different insurance companies.

Most of the time, there's no basis for the price disparities other than "name" recognition. Don't fall for the first policy that comes along. Even when you've decided what standard policy you want, comparison shop for the best price from several different insurance companies.

Medical Expenses

Every plan pays some of the 20% coinsurance amount that Medicare Part B doesn't pay (except for preventive care copayments, which are covered separately). Plans A through J and Plan M pay the full Part B coinsurance amounts; Plan K pays 50% and Plan L pays 75% of the Plan B coinsurance amounts (up to those plans' yearly caps, after which they pay 100%). And Plan N pays the full Part B coinsurance amount except for a $20 copayment for office visits and a $50 copayment for emergency room visits (which the patient must pay out of pocket).

Only Plans C, F, and J pay the yearly Medicare Part B deductible. And only Plans F, G, I, and J pay the 15% "excess charges" above the Medicare-approved amount that a doctor is allowed to charge a patient if the doctor doesn't accept assignment.

> CAUTION
>
> **Make sure there are limits on premium raises.** It's always important to check the terms under which a medigap insurance company can raise the amount of your premium. And it's particularly important when the initial premium already stretches your budget. (See "Terms and Conditions of Medigap Policies," below.)

Descriptions of the Standard Medigap Plans

Medigap policies are standardized. That means every policy in each lettered plan category must offer the same minimum coverage regardless of which insurance company offers it (though extra coverage can be added, and premiums vary).

As of June 1, 2010, no new policies have been sold in Plans E, H, I, and J. However, people already enrolled in one of those plans' policies as of that date are allowed to continue with it.

Special Rules for Massachusetts, Minnesota, and Wisconsin

If you live in Massachusetts, Minnesota, or Wisconsin, the standard medigap policies are somewhat different from the standard policies offered elsewhere. Each of these three states has a basic plan, plus options. You pay extra for any of the options you choose. The basic benefits in Massachusetts and Wisconsin include some things that the nine standard medigap policies don't. For information on the details of medigap policies in any of these states, call your state's department of insurance. You'll find its phone number and contact information for its website at the end of this chapter.

Standard Medigap Insurance Policies

All plans include these basic benefits:

- Hospitalization: Medicare Part A coinsurance plus 365 days of coverage after Medicare ends.
- Medical costs for outpatients: Some or all of the Medicare Part B coinsurance (the 20% of Medicare approved costs that Medicare Part B doesn't pay).
- Blood transfusions: All plans cover some or all of the first three pints of blood each year.
- Hospice: All plans issued June 1, 2010 or later cover hospice copayments (Plan K 50%, Plan L 75%); for policies issued before June 1, 2010, only Plans K and L provide this coverage.

A bullet below means that the plan covers the item 100%.

	A	B	C[2]	D	E[1]	F[2,7]	G[7]	H[1]	I[1]	J[1]	K	L	M[5]	N[5]
Medicare Part A Deductible		•	•	•	•	•	•	•	•	•	50%	75%	50%	•
Medicare Part B Deductible			•			•				•				
Part B Coinsurance	•	•	•	•	•	•	•	•	•	•	50%	75%	•	$20
Skilled Nursing Coinsurance			•	•	•	•	•	•	•	•	50%	75%	•	•
At-Home Recovery[3]				•			•		•	•				
Blood Transfusion Coinsurance (first three pints of blood)	•	•	•	•	•	•	•	•	•	•	50% of first 3 pints	75% of first 3 pints	•	•
Foreign Travel			•	•	•	•	•	•	•	•			•	•
Preventive Care Coinsurance[3]	•	•	•	•	•	•	•	•	•	•	•	•	•	•
Medicare Part B Excess Charges						•	•[6]		•	•				
Prescription Medicine	No plan offers prescription drug coverage—you'll need to sign up for Medicare Part D to cover your medications (see "Part D: Prescription Drug Coverage" in Chapter 12).													
Cap on out-of-pocket expenses[4]											$7,060 per year (in 2024)	$3,530 per year (in 2024)		

[1] As of June 1, 2010, no new Plan E, H, I, or J policies will be sold. Existing policies can be continued.

[2] As of January 1, 2020, no new policies under Plan C or F will be sold to people newly enrolled in Medicare. Anyone with an existing Plan C or Plan F policy as of January 1, 2020 can keep it, and anyone who was eligible for Medicare before 2020 can buy Plan C or F.

[3] Coverage for preventive care (that isn't covered by Medicare Part B) continues for Plans E and J issued before June 1, 2010.

[4] After the cap on out-of-pocket expenses is reached, the policy will pay 100% of all covered Part A and Part B costs.

[5] Available as of June 1, 2010.

[6] 80% for policies issued before June 1, 2010; 100% for all Plan G policies issued June 1, 2010 or later.

[7] In some states, there are also high-deductible Plan F and Plan G policies in which the insured pays the first $2,800 (2024) out of pocket before the policy pays anything.

The standard plans are summarized in the "Standard Medigap Insurance Policies" chart, above, and are discussed more fully in the subsections that follow, with separate sections on rules for policies issued before and after June 1, 2010.

Medigap Plan A

Policies Issued Before June 1, 2010

Plan A medigap policies include only the basic benefits discussed earlier. (See "Basic Benefits Included in All Medigap Plans," above.) Because of their limited benefits, Plan A policies are the least expensive.

Plan A policies are most useful if the doctors who regularly treat you accept assignment of Medicare-approved amounts, and you can afford to pay for the uncovered costs of doctors who don't accept assignment but by whom you might have to be treated. (See "How Much Medicare Part B Pays" in Chapter 12 regarding assignment practices.) Also, you must be able to afford the Part A hospital insurance deductible, bearing in mind that because there is a separate deductible for each separate hospital stay, you might have to pay it more than once in a year. (See "How Much Medicare Part A Pays" in Chapter 12 regarding Part A coverage.)

If these potential expenses plus the cost of a Plan A policy would put a severe strain on your finances, consider the alternative of a Medicare Advantage plan, which may provide broader coverage for less money. (See Chapter 15 for a full discussion of the Medicare Advantage option.)

Policies Issued June 1, 2010 or Later

Plan A policies issued June 1, 2010 or later also include coverage for hospice copayments.

Medigap Plan B

Policies Issued Pre-June 1, 2010

In addition to the basic benefits, a Plan B policy also pays your Medicare Part A deductible.

If your doctors all accept assignment but your budget would be severely strained by paying more than one hospital deductible in a year, Plan B might be marginally better for you than Plan A. However, if you have to pay more than a few dollars a month more for Plan B than for Plan A, it might be a bad bargain.

Measure the yearly cost of a Plan B against the cost of a Plan A policy. If you're reasonably healthy—meaning you don't expect frequent hospitalizations—and the difference in premiums is more than 25% of the Part A Medicare deductible ($1,632 in 2024), it's probably not worth the extra premium, and you should stick to a Plan A policy.

Policies Issued June 1, 2010 or Later

Plan B policies issued June 1, 2010 or later also include coverage for hospice copayments.

Medigap Plan C

CAUTION

Plan C has limited enrollment. No new Plan C policies are sold to people newly enrolled in Medicare after January 1, 2020. If you already had a Plan C policy as of that date, you can continue it. And if you were eligible for (but did not enroll in) Medicare before 2020, you can still buy Plan C.

Policies Issued Pre-June 1, 2010

Plan C adds three benefits beyond the basic and other benefits offered in Plan B. First, it pays your yearly Medicare Part B deductible of $240. (But because this policy will probably cost you more than $240 per year over Plan A or B, that alone isn't a good reason to purchase it.)

Second, Plan C policies cover the Medicare coinsurance amount for skilled nursing care. Remember that, under Medicare skilled nursing coverage, you're personally responsible for a coinsurance amount ($204 per day in 2024) for stays of 21 to 100 days in a skilled nursing facility. This can add up to a considerable amount of money, but it applies only if you're covered by Medicare for short-term skilled

nursing care in a nursing facility following a hospital stay. (See "Part A: Hospital Insurance" in Chapter 12 regarding Medicare skilled nursing coverage.) If you have a medical condition that puts you in and out of the hospital, this can be a valuable addition to your policy. But the odds are low that most people will be in a skilled nursing facility for more than 20 days more than once or twice in a lifetime.

Finally, Plan C offers some coverage for medical care while traveling outside the United States. For people who travel abroad frequently, this can be a valuable benefit. After you pay a $250 deductible, Plan C pays for 80% of emergency medical costs you incur abroad. For purposes of these policies, "emergency" means any unplanned medical costs; it's not restricted to "emergency room" treatment (as it's called in the United States).

However, there are some restrictions on the coverage. Your emergency medical care must begin within the first 60 days of each trip abroad; if you take long trips, this policy won't protect you after the first two months. And there is a $50,000 lifetime maximum on these foreign travel medical benefits. If you spend a good portion of each year abroad, you might need a separate—that is, non-medigap—travel health insurance policy to cover you fully for treatment received outside the United States.

Remember that your overseas medical care must be emergency care; if you regularly spend time abroad and simply want to be able to see a doctor for ongoing medical problems, this policy won't cover such visits.

The cost for Plan C policies is considerably higher than for Plan A or B but runs about the same as for Plans D and E.

Policies Issued June 1, 2010 or Later

Plan C policies issued June 1, 2010 or later also include coverage for hospice copayments.

Medigap Plan D

Policies Issued Pre-June 1, 2010

Plan D is the same as Plan C, except it doesn't pay the yearly Medicare Part B deductible, but it does cover at-home recovery (home health aide services).

Policies Issued June 1, 2010 or Later

Plan D policies issued June 1, 2010 or later also include coverage for hospice copayments, but don't include at-home recovery.

Medicare SELECT Medigap Policies

In addition to regular fee-for-service medigap policies, there is a category of supplemental insurance that is partly fee for service and partly managed care. It's called "Medicare SELECT." A SELECT policy must provide the same benefits as any of the standard medigap policies, but it has a two-tiered payment system.

If you use hospitals—and under some policies, doctors—who are members of the policy's network, the policy pays full benefits. If you use a provider outside the network, the policy pays reduced benefits. In this way, a Medicare SELECT medigap policy works like a preferred provider organization or an HMO with a point-of-service option, except that those managed care plans usually cover more services than most medigap policies. Because of the provider restrictions, Medicare SELECT policies are somewhat less expensive than regular medigap policies.

Medigap Plan E

CAUTION

Plan E has been discontinued. No new Plan E policies have been sold since May 31, 2010. If you already had a Plan E policy as of that date, you can continue it.

Plan E adds minimal coverage of some preventive care but eliminates Plan D's coverage of at-home recovery. Plan E pays for only $120 per year of such preventive health care and screening, so it's not much of a benefit.

Medigap Plan F

> ### CAUTION
> **Plan F has limited enrollment.** No new Plan F policies are sold to people newly enrolled in Medicare after January 1, 2020. If you already had a Plan F policy as of that date, you can continue it. And if you were eligible for Medicare before 2020, you can still buy Plan F.

Policies Issued Pre-June 1, 2010

Plan F offers the most significant added benefit beyond Plans B, C, D, and E: payment of 100% of what a doctor actually charges you above the Medicare-approved amount. (Remember, doctors who don't accept assignment are permitted to charge a patient up to 15% more than the Medicare-approved amount for any covered service, as discussed in "How Much Medicare Part B Pays" in Chapter 12.) If you receive extensive medical care from doctors who don't accept assignment, that extra 15% mounts up quickly.

Because the extra 15% of medical bills can amount to a lot of money, insurance companies charge higher premiums for Plan F than for the plans discussed previously. If you're in generally good health and the few doctors you see all accept assignment, this higher premium might not be worth the extra coverage. If, on the other hand, you require frequent or extensive medical care and you receive it from doctors who don't all accept assignment, Plan F might be worth the higher premiums.

If you like the coverage offered by Plan F but find the higher premiums too much for your budget, many companies that offer Plan F also offer a high-deductible version of this plan for a much lower premium. These high-deductible plans provide coverage only when your out-of-pocket costs for covered services exceed a certain amount for the year.

Policies Issued June 1, 2010 or Later

Plan F policies issued June 1, 2010 or later also include coverage for hospice copayments.

Medigap Plan G

Policies Issued Pre-June 1, 2010

Plan G is similar to Plan F. However, unlike Plan F, Plan G doesn't cover the Medicare medical insurance deductible. Plan G policies issued before June 1, 2010 cover only 80% of the excess charges some doctors and other providers charge under Medicare Part B.

Policies Issued June 1, 2010 or Later

Plan G policies issued June 1, 2010 or later provide 100% coverage for doctors' excess charges under Medicare Part B and also include coverage for hospice copayments.

Medigap Plan H

CAUTION

Plan H has been discontinued. No new Plan H policies have been sold since May 31, 2010. If you already had a Plan H policy as of that date, you can continue it (though without drug coverage that the policy might have provided you before 2006).

Plan H policies (without the drug coverage provided before January 1, 2006) cover the Part A deductible, Part A skilled nursing facility coinsurance amounts, and some coverage for emergency care while traveling outside the United States. Plan H policies provide the same coverage as a Plan C policy except for the yearly Part B deductible that a Plan C policy covers. If you're considering keeping a Plan H policy, comparison shop with available Plan C policies.

Medigap Plan I

CAUTION

Plan I has been discontinued. No new Plan I policies have been sold since May 31, 2010. If you already had a Plan I policy as of that date, you can continue it.

Plan I policies (without the drug coverage provided before January 1, 2006) cover 100% of doctors' excess charges under Part B, which can be a significant amount if you regularly see a number of doctors or have major treatment in any particular year. It also includes coverage of at-home recovery, in addition to the more commonly covered Part A deductible, skilled nursing facility coinsurance amounts, and emergency care during foreign travel. It's comparable to a Plan F policy, except that Plan F pays the Part B deductible instead of covering at-home recovery. If you can find a Plan F policy for a considerably lower premium than your Plan I policy, it might be worth it to switch.

Medigap Plan J

CAUTION

Plan J has been discontinued. No new Plan J policies have been sold since May 31, 2010. If you already had a Plan J policy as of that date, you can continue it.

Plan J policies (without the drug coverage provided before January 1, 2006) are the luxury model of medigap policies, and also the most expensive. They cover 100% of doctors' excess charges and the Part B deductible, as well as all the other costs covered by any other plan policy.

Medigap Plan K

Policies Issued Pre-June 1, 2010

Plan K policies cover many Medicare gaps but pay only 50% of certain covered costs. Plan K compensates for this partial coverage by providing a cap on an insured person's out-of-pocket expenses. In addition to the standard Part A hospital coinsurance and extra lifetime hospital inpatient coverage offered under all medigap plans, Plan K policies cover 100% of the coinsurance amounts for Part B

preventive care and 50% of the Part A inpatient deductible, Part A coinsurance amounts for blood transfusions, skilled nursing facility stays and hospice care, and Part B coinsurance amounts.

Plan K policies also place a $7,060 per year limit (in 2024) on a policyholder's out-of-pocket costs for covered medical expenses. After the policyholder reaches that amount, the policy pays 100% of all covered Part A and B costs.

Policies Issued June 1, 2010 or Later

There are no changes to Plan K policies issued June 1, 2010 or later.

Medigap Plan L

Policies Issued Pre-June 1, 2010

Plan L policies provide the same coverage as Plan K policies and have the same kind of yearly cap on a policyholder's out-of-pocket expenses. But Plan L policies cover 75% of the Part A inpatient deductible, Part A coinsurance amounts for blood transfusions, skilled nursing facility stays and hospice care, and Part B coinsurance amounts. And Plan L's yearly cap on out-of-pocket expenses is $3,530 (in 2024). Because of this better coverage, Plan L policies are more expensive than Plan K policies.

Policies Issued June 1, 2010 or Later

There are no changes to Plan L policies issued June 1, 2010 or later.

Medigap Plan M

Plan M policies offer the same coverage as Plan D but pay only 50% of the Medicare Part A deductible.

Medigap Plan N

Plan N policies offer the same coverage as Plan D, but you must pay a $20 copayment for each health care provider visit under Medicare Part B and a $50 copayment for an emergency room visit.

Terms and Conditions of Medigap Policies

In addition to comparing the services covered, the amount of benefits, and the monthly cost of different medigap insurance policies, there are several other things to consider before making a final decision.

Look first at how high the company says it can raise its premiums in the years to come—and therefore whether you will still be able to afford the policy when you might need it most. Also important are policy terms that determine whether you're covered for a particular illness during a certain time period after you purchase the policy.

Premium Increases

It's one thing to find insurance coverage you can afford today. It might be quite another to find a policy that you can continue to pay for in the future when your income and assets have decreased and the policy premium has increased. In choosing a medigap policy, consider what the contract says about how much the policy premiums will rise over time. If the current premium will already be a significant strain on your financial resources, consider a less expensive policy, because any policy is sure to get more expensive in the future.

There are several ways insurance companies set up premium increases in medigap policies. Choosing the best premium increase terms—what the insurance companies call "rating" methods—is something for you to consider along with other terms of the policy.

Level Premiums

The best method for the consumer is one called "level premiums." This means that premiums don't go up on your policy as you reach a certain age, but only when the insurance company raises premiums on all medigap policies of the type you have. Of course, the premiums will go up regularly, but the amount they go up will be at least partially controlled by market forces and by your state's insurance commission.

Attained Age

"Attained age" policies base your premium entirely upon your age. The company charges the same premium to everyone of the same age who has the same policy. As you get older, the premiums rise in lockstep, by a set amount. Some policies mandate that your premiums go up yearly; others hike the premiums when you reach a certain age plateau, such as 70, 75, or 80. Attained age policies tend to be cheaper at age 65 than comparable policies. However, once you reach 70 or 75, attained age policies tend to become, and stay, more expensive than other types.

When considering a policy with attained age premium increases, ask to see not only how much it would cost you at your present age, but also the current premium costs at each of the next age levels. That will give you a sense of how high the rates jump for that policy. Figure that your premiums will rise by at least the same percentages, and calculate how much your policy is likely to cost at your next two age levels. Only then will you have a realistic picture of how much this policy will cost.

ONLINE

Medigap information from Medicare's website. Medicare's official website at www.medicare.gov offers a link that can provide you with the names and contact information of insurance companies that offer specific medigap policies available where you live. On the www.medicare.gov home page, click the "Health & Drug Plans" tab, then click "Find a Medicare Supplement Insurance (Medigap) policy." Enter the requested information about your location. It will then provide you with information about specific medigap policies being sold where you live, including what the policies cover and which companies offer each type of policy, with contact information for those companies.

Issue Age

The initial premium for an "issue age" policy is determined by your age when you first purchase it. From then on, as long as you keep the same policy, you pay the same premium as anyone else who buys the policy at the same age at which you bought it.

For example, if you buy an issue age medigap policy at age 65, in five years you will pay the same as a person who first buys the policy at that time at age 65. Your premium will steadily rise, but the increases might be controlled by the insurance company's need to keep the premium competitive to continue signing up new policyholders.

No Age Rating

A few insurance companies sell policies that charge the same amount regardless of age. They base their premiums entirely on the cost of medical care in the geographic area in which you live. (For this reason, these are sometimes referred to as "community-rated policies.") These policies tend to be a bit more expensive than others for people ages 65 to 75 and a bit less expensive for people age 75 and older.

Eligibility and Enrollment

Your ability to purchase the medigap policy of your choice depends on when and under what circumstances you apply for it. The following sections discuss applying:
- during open enrollment periods
- during limited guaranteed enrollment periods, and
- outside these enrollment periods.

Applying During Open Enrollment

You're guaranteed the right to buy any medigap policy sold in your state, without any medical screening or limits on coverage, if you:
- are within your first six months of enrollment in Medicare Part B, or
- leave a Medicare Advantage plan within a year of age 65.

Your First Six Months With Medicare Part B

During the six months after you first enroll in Medicare Part B (see "Enrolling in Part B: Medical Insurance" in Chapter 13 for enrollment procedures), you can buy any medigap insurance policy sold in the state where you live. During this initial enrollment

period, federal law prohibits an insurance company from requiring medical underwriting—that is, prior screening of your health condition—before issuing a policy. Nor can the insurance company delay coverage because of preexisting health conditions. Companies are also prohibited from charging higher premiums based solely on your age or area of residence.

Most people enroll in Medicare Part B as soon as they turn 65. Your six-month open enrollment period for medigap begins on the first of the month during which you reach age 65 and are enrolled in Part B.

If you did not enroll for Medicare Part B on your 65th birthday but enroll during a yearly Medicare general enrollment period (January through March), your six-month open enrollment period for any medigap policy begins on July 1 of the same year. If you did not enroll in Medicare Part B on your 65th birthday because you were still covered by an employer-sponsored health plan, you have a six-month open enrollment period for any medigap policy beginning whenever you enroll in Medicare Part B.

You Leave a Medicare Advantage Plan Within a Year of Age 65

If you joined a Medicare Advantage plan (see Chapter 15) at age 65 when you first became eligible for Medicare, but you leave the plan within a year, you have a guaranteed right to buy any medigap plan sold in your state. This is true whether your Medicare Advantage plan dropped you—perhaps because it stopped doing business in your county of residence or because you moved out of its business area—or you left the plan voluntarily.

However, to protect this guaranteed right, you must apply for a medigap policy within 63 days of the date your Medicare Advantage plan coverage ends. If you're still in the six-month period immediately following your enrollment in Medicare Part B, you have whatever is left of that six-month period within which to apply for a medigap policy, or 63 days from the end of your Medicare Advantage coverage, whichever is greater.

Medigap Coverage If You Move

What happens if you buy a medigap policy while living in one place, then move elsewhere? Because all medigap policies are "guaranteed renewable," your insurance company can't cancel your policy. This is true even if you move to an area where the company doesn't normally sell similar policies. However, the insurance company has a right to increase your premium if you've moved to an area where the costs of medical care are higher. The rates must be approved by the department of insurance in the state to which you have moved.

Applying With Limited Guaranteed Enrollment

You have the guaranteed right to buy a medigap policy if, under certain circumstances, you:

- lose your Medicare coverage, or
- drop medigap, join a Medicare Advantage plan, then leave the Medicare Advantage plan.

You can use this right for any of several standard medigap plans, though not for all plans (see below). For those plans to which you have no guaranteed right, however, you can still purchase a policy if the issuing insurance company approves your application.

You Lose Coverage by a Medicare Advantage Plan or an Employer-Sponsored Policy

Insurance companies are free to drop their Medicare Advantage plans, and they often do so in counties and even entire states in which the companies are unhappy with their profit margins. (See Chapter 15 for details.)

If you've been dropped from a Medicare Advantage plan because the company is no longer operating the plan where you live, you have a guaranteed right to purchase any standard medigap Plan A, B, C, or F policy sold in your state. (In Massachusetts, Minnesota, and Wisconsin, you have a right to purchase a medigap policy with provisions similar to these four standard medigap plans.)

You have the same guarantee if you're losing your Medicare Advantage coverage because you're moving out of your plan's service area.

These rules also apply if you lose employer-sponsored insurance that had operated like a medigap policy, meaning that it paid for some costs your Medicare coverage did not.

If you had a medigap Plan D, E, or G before dropping it to join a Medicare Advantage plan that has now dropped you, you also have a guaranteed right to again purchase that same plan from the same insurance company, if the company still sells the plan in your state.

To take advantage of any of these guaranteed rights, you must apply for a medigap plan within 63 days from the end of your Medicare Advantage or employer-sponsored coverage.

Some States Offer Extra Protection

Some states' laws offer even more protection around your right to purchase a medigap policy than the federal guarantee described in this chapter. These state laws typically give you more medigap plans from which to choose. To find out what extra protection your state might offer, call your state's department of insurance (see contact information at the end of this chapter) or your local SHIP office (see contact information at the end of Chapter 13).

You Dropped a Medigap Policy to Join a Medicare Advantage Plan or a Medicare SELECT Policy, Then Left the New Plan Within a Year

If you once had a medigap policy but dropped it to join a Medicare Advantage plan or to purchase a Medicare SELECT policy (see "Medicare SELECT Medigap Policies," above), you might have a guaranteed right to drop the Medicare Advantage plan and repurchase a medigap plan. However, you must meet two conditions:

- The Medicare Advantage plan or Medicare SELECT policy you drop must be the only one in which you've been enrolled.

- You must leave the Medicare Advantage plan or drop the Medicare SELECT policy within a year of when you joined.

If you meet these two conditions, you can either buy your original medigap policy from the same company (if it's still sold in your state), or buy any medigap Plan A, B, C, or F sold in your state. There's a time limit on applying for the new medigap policy, however. Your guaranteed right to purchase lasts only 63 days from the end of your previous coverage.

Applying Without Guaranteed Enrollment

If you want to buy a medigap policy but have none of the guaranteed rights described above, an insurance company can freely choose whether or not to sell you a policy. Even if the company does offer you coverage, it can attach whatever terms, conditions, and premiums it chooses, as long as the coverage matches one of the standard plans.

In such circumstances, the insurance company is likely to demand that you undergo medical underwriting (screening)—particularly before they'll sell you one of their more desirable policies. The screening will involve a detailed examination of your medical history.

If your history shows a likelihood of extensive or expensive medical treatment in the foreseeable future, the company might refuse to sell you the policy. Or, they might offer to sell it to you at a high premium, perhaps also with limitations on when coverage begins.

Preexisting Illness Exclusion

Most medigap policies contain a provision excluding coverage, for a set time immediately after you purchase the policy, of any illness or medical conditions for which you received treatment within a given period before your coverage began. Six months is a typical exclusion period: These policies provide no coverage, for six months after you buy the policy, for illnesses you were treated for within six months before the policy started. Usually, the shorter the exclusion period, the higher the premium.

If you have a serious medical condition that might require costly medical treatment at any time, and you've been treated for that condition within the recent past, consider a policy with a short exclusion period or none at all.

Discounts for the "Healthy"

Some insurance companies offer extra discounts on medigap policies for people they consider to be better risks than others. For example, women might be offered lower premiums than men because women tend to remain healthier longer, meaning the insurance company collects more premiums before having to pay out on claims. For the same reason, nonsmokers are also frequently offered discounts.

You might also be able to reduce your premiums if you've been free of any serious illness or condition and are willing to prove it by undergoing what is called "medical underwriting"—a screening process during which the insurance company examines your medical history to see whether you're likely to cost them a lot of money in the near future. If the screening shows that you have had no serious illnesses or medical conditions over the previous 10 years, you might be able to purchase the policy at a significantly lower premium than if you had bought it without first being medically screened. Ask the insurance company whether they offer this sort of discount.

Finding the Best Medicare Supplement

Shopping for a medigap policy can be difficult, not only because of the differences in policy terms among the 10 standard policies, but because of the wide spectrum of prices among insurance companies. Near the end of Chapter 15 is a chart to help you do a side-by-side comparison among different medigap and Medicare Advantage plans.

Fortunately, your first step—namely, finding out what medigap insurance policies are available in your state—is fairly simple. Your state department of insurance can give you a complete list of available

policies (see the contact information at the end of this chapter). Be warned, however, that their lists are often a bit stale, so you'll need to follow up with the insurance companies or insurance agents for the latest facts and figures. Many people also use insurance agents to find policies, although you should first read the cautions in "Using an Insurance Agent," below. In addition, some seniors' organizations offer discounts on certain medigap policies.

The Medicare.gov website also has a useful medigap policy finder that lists and compares policies in your area.

Using an Insurance Agent

If you use an insurance agent to present you with a choice of medigap policies, make sure the agent is experienced with the provisions of several different policies from different insurance companies. Insurance agents tend to work with policies from certain companies and might not know of less expensive or less restrictive policies from other companies. So you might want to consult more than one agent.

Even if you arrange to get your insurance through an agent, keep your own ears and eyes open for policies that might fit your needs. Friends, relatives, and organizations to which you belong can all be resources to find out about available plans. And senior organizations can be a good source of information. A good insurance agent should be willing to find out the details of a policy you've located yourself. If the agent can't or won't check on such a policy, it's probably time to find a new agent. Likewise, if an insurance agent is unwilling to sit down with you and compare the coverage and costs of different policies, then you ought to comparison shop for a new insurance agent.

Senior Associations

A number of organizations of seniors or retired people advertise medigap policies. These organizations don't actually act as insurers. Instead, they negotiate deals with insurance companies to offer medigap policies to their members, sometimes at reduced rates.

But some senior organizations act almost as fronts for insurance companies. These organizations might appear to exist for the benefit of older people, offering a number of programs or services for seniors. But many of these alleged benefits are nearly worthless. In truth, these organizations exist to sell themselves through membership dues and products (including overpriced insurance) behind a facade of supposedly protecting senior citizens.

Help With Decisions About Medigap and Medicare Advantage Plans

Each state has a program to assist people with Medicare, medigap supplemental insurance, and Medicare Advantage plans. It's called the "State Health Insurance Assistance Program" (SHIP), although in some states it might have another, similar name, such as "Health Insurance Counseling and Advocacy Program" (HICAP).

SHIP has professional staff and volunteers who are knowledgeable not only about the rules pertaining to Medicare and medigap insurance but also about what policies are available in your state and what Medicare Advantage plans are available in your local area. SHIP staff can look over particular insurance policies and Medicare Advantage plans and help you see the strengths and weaknesses of each.

In larger states there are many SHIP offices, and you can reach the office nearest you by calling the state's general toll-free number. In smaller states there might be fewer offices, and you will be referred to a SHIP program at a local senior center or another nonprofit organization. (See the end of Chapter 13 for contact information.)

The best way to tell whether the policies a particular organization offers are good or bad is to compare their specific terms and prices with those of other policies offered by different insurance companies or health plans. In the final analysis, it's the terms of the policy, not an organization's good intentions or friendly advertising, that determine the quality of your coverage. The insurance company, not the senior organization, determines your coverage and pays your claims.

Beware of Mail-Order and Limited-Offer Policies

Beware of medigap policy offers you receive unsolicited in the mail. Their flashy promises often far outstrip their coverage. If you do become aware of a policy through the mail, and its provisions seem good to you after comparing it with other policies, check the reputation of the company offering the policy. You can get information on the company from your state's insurance department or commission, or from your state or local consumer protection agency.

Also be wary of policies that are offered with short-time enrollment periods. You have likely heard or seen advertisements for insurance that holler: "Limited offer! One month only! Buy now, the greatest offer in years! Once the offer is over, you'll never get another chance at an opportunity like this again! Once-in-a-lifetime offer!"

This is nonsense.

If it's a reputable company with a legitimate policy to offer you, the same or similar terms will be available any time—although you must keep in mind your own six-month open enrollment period after you sign up for Medicare Part B. These advertising slogans are just another way insurance companies have of pressuring you into buying a policy without first carefully considering and comparing its terms.

Most companies permit you to look over your policy and carefully examine its terms for 10 days before you're obligated to keep it. If you decide you don't want the policy—for any reason—you can return it within 10 days to the company or to the insurance agent you bought it from. You'll be owed a refund of all the money you've paid up to that point. And if you're buying a new medigap policy to replace one you already have, you're legally entitled to 30 days to review the new policy to decide whether you want to keep it. You can cancel it without penalty at any time during those 30 days.

Only One Medigap Policy Required

You need only one policy to supplement your Medicare coverage—and it's illegal for an insurance company to sell you any other health

insurance policy that duplicates coverage you already have with a medigap policy.

When you apply for a medigap policy, you will be asked to provide information concerning any health insurance policies you have. This gives written notice to the seller of your policy—insurance agent, broker, or company representative—about your existing insurance so that you won't be held responsible for paying for duplicate coverage if the insurer mistakenly sells it to you.

If you already have medigap insurance but want to replace it with a new policy, some rules help protect you while you make the change.

Replacement Policies

If you're considering replacing your existing policy with a new one, there are a number of things to keep in mind.

First, even if your new policy would ultimately provide better coverage, it might have a preexisting condition exclusion that would deny you coverage for up to six months after you switch policies. If you've been treated in the previous six months for any serious medical condition that might require further treatment in the near future, don't cancel a basically good policy for one that's only slightly better if the new policy has such an exclusion.

Second, unless you're signing up within the first six months following your enrollment in Medicare Part B, the new insurance company from which you applied for coverage might reject you if you have had serious medical problems in the recent past. So, don't cancel your old policy until you've been given written notice from the new insurance company—not just from the agent or broker who sold you the policy—that your new policy is in effect.

When you apply for a replacement policy, you must sign a statement agreeing that you will drop your old policy when the new one takes effect. The law gives you a review period within which to decide between the old and new policies. Once you've received written notice of your acceptance in the new insurance plan, and you've been given a written copy of the new policy, you have 30 days to cancel either the new policy or the old one.

Dread Disease Policies: A Dreadful Idea

A few insurance companies offer policies that don't provide medigap supplemental coverage but provide particularized health coverage that might overlap some with medigap policies and even Medicare coverage itself. Most of these policies cover treatment for a specific disease and are known as "indemnity" or "dread disease" policies. They are often solicited over the phone or by direct mail and are offered at low monthly premiums.

One of these policies might initially sound promising if it covers a particular disease—for example, a specific type of cancer—for which you have a high risk. However, close examination of these policies usually shows them to be a waste of money. They pay only a small, set amount of money for each day you're hospitalized or for each medical treatment for the specific disease, usually far less than the Medicare deductible or coinsurance that a medigap policy would pay.

And because they pay only when you're treated for the specific disease, you wind up needing to carry a medigap policy anyway to cover all medical bills not related to this particular disease. Or if you don't carry a medigap policy, you will be responsible for paying out of pocket for all medical bills not covered by this specific-disease policy. Either way, these policies are a bad investment.

Department of Insurance

You can contact your state's department of insurance to ask for information about medigap insurance policies being sold in your state. To find contact information for your state, see the list of state departments of insurance maintained by the National Association of Insurance Commissioners (NAIC) at https://content.naic.org/state-insurance-departments.

Medicare Part C:
Medicare Advantage Plans

Medicare Part C health plans, referred to as "Medicare Advantage plans," fill gaps in basic Medicare, as do medigap policies. But the two systems operate differently. As explained in Chapter 14, medigap policies work alongside Medicare: Medical bills are sent both to Medicare and to a medigap insurer, and each pays a portion of the approved charges. With a Medicare Advantage plan, on the other hand, enrollees no longer deal with Medicare directly, although enrollees still have to pay their monthly premium for Medicare Part B (see Chapter 12).

A Medicare Advantage plan takes the place of Part A and Part B, and often Part D as well, providing all basic Medicare coverage and often offering extended coverage in addition to basic Medicare. The extent of coverage beyond basic Medicare, the size of premiums and copayments, and decisions about whether a patient's particular treatment should be covered are all controlled by the Medicare Advantage plan, not by Medicare. (See "Comparing Medigap and Medicare Advantage Plans," toward the end of this chapter, to help compare specific policies.)

Medicare Advantage plans come in two basic forms: managed care plans and fee-for-service plans:

- **Managed care plans.** In return for coverage beyond basic Medicare, Medicare Advantage managed care plans charge a low monthly premium—or none at all—and small copayments. But they limit the doctors and other providers from which you can receive care; they cover only services provided by doctors and others who participate in that particular plan. They restrict services as well—placing limits on treatments and the length of hospital stays for managed care patients.

- **Fee-for-service plans.** With these plans, you can receive care from any doctor or other provider who participates in Medicare. But for each service or treatment, the doctor or other provider must accept the Medicare Advantage plan's restrictions and amount of payment. If a doctor or another provider won't accept the plan's restrictions or payment level for a particular medical service, the plan won't cover the patient's care by that provider. In that case, the patient must

either personally pay the provider or seek care from a different provider who will accept the plan's terms.

Most fee-for-service plans also have provider networks. If you receive services from a provider within the network, your out-of-pocket costs will be lower than if you receive services from a provider who isn't in the plan's network.

Medicare Advantage Plan and/or Medicare Part D?

Many Medicare Advantage plans include coverage for prescription drugs, but others offer no such coverage. So, deciding whether to join (or remain in) a Medicare Advantage plan involves comparing the prescription drug coverage offered by that plan with the coverage and cost of drugs under various Part D plans. You can compare the cost of your medications in each plan using Medicare's website at www.medicare.gov/plan-compare.

If a Medicare Advantage plan includes drug coverage, enrolling in that plan means that you don't also enroll in a Part D plan. But enrolling in a plan with drug coverage is a good idea only if that plan covers the drugs you regularly take and offers them at a reasonable copayment without serious access restrictions. (Coverage restrictions are discussed in more detail in Chapter 12. See "Part D: Prescription Drug Coverage.")

If a Medicare Advantage plan doesn't offer drug coverage, you might still want to keep or join that plan if you like its other coverage features and costs. But if you also want prescription drug coverage, you will have to enroll in a separate, stand-alone Part D prescription drug plan.

If your current Medicare Advantage plan offers drug coverage but doesn't cover your specific drugs, or does so with high copayments or access restrictions, consider joining a different Medicare Advantage plan that better meets your needs. Or, leave the managed care system altogether and return to original Medicare coverage under Parts A and B, and separately enroll in a stand-alone Part D prescription drug plan that does a good job of covering your drugs. (See Chapter 12.) If you leave Medicare Advantage altogether, you might also want to take out a medigap supplemental insurance policy to fill some of the gaps in Medicare coverage that your Medicare Advantage plan used to cover. (See Chapter 14.)

If you're considering a Medicare Advantage plan, you must decide whether any of the plans available in your area offer adequate care at an affordable cost. You should evaluate not only the cost of premiums and copayments but also how the plan limits the particular doctors and other providers you can get care from. Despite the lower monthly cost for Medicare Advantage plans, their limitations have resulted in only about half of Medicare beneficiaries choosing to enroll in these plans (others are automatically enrolled in a Medicare Advantage plan as part of their enrollment in Medicaid).

When considering a Medicare Advantage plan, you'll also need to assess the risks of yearly changes—including the chance that a particular plan might drop out of an entire geographic region— associated with these types of plans. In the past several years, many seniors have been dropped from Medicare Advantage plans that stopped serving the areas where they lived and have been forced to find another plan or return to original Medicare coverage. And millions of people have found their premiums shooting up, copayments rising, and coverage shrinking for those services not legally required by Medicare.

Not only do you risk your plan's disappearing or becoming far more expensive (at renewal time), but if you choose to leave a Medicare Advantage plan and return to regular Medicare, your chance to buy a medigap insurance policy (as discussed in Chapter 14) might be much more limited.

To learn what Medicare Advantage plans are available in the area where you live, you can visit the Medicare website at www.medicare.gov. To find out the recent history of a particular Medicare Advantage plan—whether it has dropped patients or hiked costs, for example—call your local SHIP or HICAP counseling office (see the end of Chapter 13 for contact information) or your state department of insurance (see Chapter 14 for contact information). If you're dropped from a Medicare Advantage plan, your alternatives and when you must exercise them are explained in "Your Rights When Joining, Leaving, or Losing a Medicare Advantage Plan," below.

> ### Joining a Medicare Advantage Plan Means Leaving Direct Medicare Protection
>
> If you join a Medicare Advantage plan, in effect you leave the Medicare program. The insurance company that runs the Medicare Advantage plan gets a monthly payment from Medicare on your behalf, but the plan itself then decides what health care providers you can use and approves or denies medical coverage for all of your specific medical care. (When the plan denies coverage, the plan itself handles the your request for reconsideration—the first level of appeal. But if your request for reconsideration is denied, then you're entitled to an independent review, just as in an appeal under original Medicare (covered in Chapter 13). For more information, see Nolo's website article on "How to Appeal a Denial of Medicare.")
>
> If you leave a Medicare Advantage plan, you're permitted to rejoin traditional Medicare. But if you return to Medicare after the first year following your initial Medicare eligibility, you might find that not all medigap supplemental insurance policies will accept you. And you might be able to join another Medicare Advantage plan only during open enrollment. (See "Your Rights When Joining, Leaving, or Losing a Medicare Advantage Plan," below.)

Medicare Advantage Managed Care Plans

Most Medicare Advantage plans are structured as managed care plans. In these plans, a patient's care is managed by the insurance company that issues the plan. The basic premise of managed care is that the member-patient agrees to receive care only from specific doctors, hospitals, and other providers—called a "network"—in exchange for reduced overall health care costs. The patient also agrees that the plan, rather than Medicare itself, will decide whether a particular medical service is covered.

There are several varieties of Medicare Advantage managed care plans. Some have severe restrictions on consulting with specialists or seeing providers from outside the network. Others give members more freedom to choose which doctors they can consult for treatment. Generally, more choice translates into higher cost.

Health Maintenance Organization (HMO)

The HMO is the least expensive and most restrictive Medicare Advantage managed care plan. It's also the most common type of Medicare managed care plan. There are four main restrictions.

Care Within the Network Only

Each HMO maintains a list—called a "network"—of doctors and other health care providers who participate with that HMO. The HMO member must receive care only from a provider in the network, except in emergencies.

If the plan member uses a provider from outside the network, the plan pays nothing toward the bill. And because a Medicare Advantage plan member has withdrawn from traditional Medicare coverage, Medicare itself picks up none of the tab, either. The plan member must pay the entire bill out of pocket.

Because of this restriction, it's very important to find out whether the doctors and other providers you regularly use, particularly your primary care physician, are included in the HMO's network. It's also important to make sure that the hospital in your vicinity, or a hospital you and your doctor prefer to use, is in the network. If all of your doctors and your preferred hospital are in the HMO's network, this restriction might not be as important to you.

However, most HMOs and other managed care plans (except for integrated HMOs like Kaiser Permanente) do sometimes drop doctors and hospitals. And doctors' groups and hospitals leave HMOs that become too stingy in reimbursing for medical care or authorizing services for their patients. If the plan or one of your

providers decides to cut ties, you won't be able to continue seeing that provider. So, even if you begin a managed care plan with all the right doctors and hospital, you might later find yourself searching for new doctors or a new hospital, or leaving your HMO and searching for a new managed care plan or medigap policy.

This instability of many managed care plans makes it important for you to discuss with your doctors any particular HMO you're considering. Ask first whether your doctor participates in that HMO, then whether your doctor has experienced problems with the plan, particularly with approval of treatments, referrals to specialists, or early release from inpatient hospital care.

Some doctors are uncomfortable speaking with patients about insurance companies. But responsible physicians will at least tell you if their offices have had regular, serious problems getting a plan's coverage for their patients, and certainly should tell you if they're considering dropping their contract with a particular plan.

Emergency and Urgent Care Anywhere

Federal law requires that all Medicare Advantage plans cover emergency services nationwide, regardless of restrictions they place on the use of doctors and hospitals for routine care. The law also requires that these plans pay for covered services you receive from a nonplan provider if the treatment was urgently needed while you were temporarily outside the plan's geographic service area. Urgently needed care means care for an unforeseen illness or injury for which a reasonable person wouldn't wait until they could return home to seek medical help.

This required emergency or urgent care coverage doesn't apply to most foreign travel. However, some plans offer such travel coverage on their own. If you travel or live any part of the year outside the United States but aren't covered by your Medicare Advantage plan while abroad, it might be a good idea to buy a temporary travel medical policy covering you for the time you're out of the country.

All Care Through Primary Care Physician

Within an HMO, a member must see their primary care physician before obtaining any other medical services. The member can't see other doctors or providers—even from within the plan's network—or obtain other medical services without a referral by the primary care physician.

This system encourages the primary care physician—who is paid less than a specialist by the plan—to take care of medical problems that don't absolutely require a specialist. Because of the hassle of the extra step, it also discourages the plan member from seeking specialist care.

This restriction is a significant reason why managed care is cheaper for insurance companies—and for the member/patient—than traditional fee-for-service policies are. However, since many seniors regularly require specialist care, this restriction is also a reason why many reject HMO coverage in favor of medigap insurance or less restrictive types of managed care.

Prior HMO Approval of Some Services

HMOs require that your primary care physician or other network physician obtain prior approval from the plan for certain medical services the doctor might want to prescribe. If plan administrators don't believe a service is medically necessary—or believe service from a non-specialist or other less expensive treatment would do just as well—they might deny coverage for that prescribed service.

HMO With Point-of-Service (POS) Option

A few Medicare Advantage HMOs have a significant wrinkle that makes them more attractive—and more expensive—than standard HMO plans. These plans offer what is called a "point-of-service" option. This option allows a member to see physicians and other providers who aren't in the HMO's network and to receive services from specialists without first going through a primary care physician.

Special Needs Plans for Certain Chronic Conditions

In some states, a particular kind of Medicare Advantage plan, called a "Special Needs Plan," might be offered to people with a specific serious chronic or disabling medical condition. Like all other Medicare Advantage plans, these C-SNPs (meaning "Chronic-Special Needs Plans") offer both inpatient and outpatient care at least as broad as Medicare Part A and Part B, plus prescription drugs. Unlike other Medicare Advantage plans, though, a C-SNP is tailored to a specific condition, providing a network of doctors and other providers who specialize in the treatment of that condition, a broad selection of the drugs used to treat that condition, and usually a "care coordinator" who monitors a patient's health status and helps ensure that the patient follows proper care procedures at home.

C-SNPs are offered in only about half of all states, with a total enrollment of only about 0.5% of all Medicare beneficiaries. And almost all C-SNPs (more than 95% of all C-SNPs offered) cover one or more of only three sets of conditions. If your doctor certifies that you have one of these three sets of conditions, you might qualify for a C-SNP that specifically covers your condition and actually find such a policy offered where you live:

- cardiovascular disorders, including chronic or congestive heart failure
- diabetes mellitus, or
- chronic lung failure.

If you have one of the following conditions, technically you might also qualify for a C-SNP, but insurance companies have offered such C-SNPs in only a very few places in the country:

- cancer
- stroke
- alcohol/drug dependence
- Alzheimer's or dementia
- disabling mental health disease
- neurological disorders
- HIV/AIDS
- autoimmune disorders
- end-stage liver or kidney disease, or
- severe hematological disorders.

Special Needs Plans for Certain Chronic Conditions (continued)

In addition to the difficulty of finding a C-SNP for your condition where you live, there's the issue of whether the plan would actually be better for you than other Medicare Advantage plans. In theory, concentrating providers around a single condition and coordinating care should improve care. How a C-SNP plan performs, however, varies from plan to plan.

If you're interested in exploring whether a C-SNP might be right for you, you can find out what plans are available in your area by going online to the government's Medicare Plan Finder, www.medicare. gov/find-a-plan/questions/home.aspx. If you find a plan that interests you, be sure to compare it to what's offered by other Medicare Advantage plans in your area, including asking the insurance company what the plan's "quality measures" ratings are. For help in choosing a plan, you can get free counseling from a local office of the State Health Insurance Assistance Program (SHIP). (See information about SHIP at the end of Chapter 13.) More information is also available from Medicare's webpage on SNPs at www.medicare.gov/health-drug-plans/health-plans/your-coverage-options/SNP.

If you decide that you want to try a C-SNP offered where you live, you can enroll (with your doctor's certification that you have a qualifying condition) or disenroll under the same terms as you could with any Medicare Advantage plan (see "Your Rights When Joining, Leaving, or Losing a Medicare Advantage Plan," below). In addition, you can enroll in a C-SNP anytime you're newly diagnosed with the condition that qualifies you for the plan.

However, if a member does go outside the network or sees a specialist directly, the plan pays a smaller part of the bill than if the member had followed regular HMO procedures. The member pays a higher premium for this option than for a standard HMO plan and a higher copayment each time the option is used.

Preferred Provider Organization (PPO)

Although it has a different name, the PPO works the same as an HMO with a point-of-service (POS) option (discussed above). If a member receives a service from the PPO's network of providers, the cost to the member is lower than if the member sees a provider outside the network.

PPOs tend to be more expensive than standard HMOs, charging both a monthly premium and a higher copayment for nonnetwork services. However, many people find that the extra flexibility in choosing doctors is an important comfort to them, and therefore worth the extra money.

Provider Sponsored Organization (PSO)

The PSO is a group of medical providers—doctors, clinics, and a hospital—that skips the insurance company middleman and contracts directly with patients. As with an HMO, the member pays a premium, as well as a copayment each time a service is used.

PSOs are rare, and you're unlikely to find one where you live. However, if a PSO operates in your area, you might want to consider it as an alternative to other types of Medicare Advantage Plans.

Medicare Advantage Fee-for-Service Plans

Some insurance companies offer what are called "fee-for-service" Medicare Advantage plans that they tout as offering greater enrollee "freedom" in choice of doctors and other providers. Unfortunately, for reasons described below, many people discover that this freedom is mostly illusory. Nonetheless, in some places—particularly in rural areas—these fee-for-service plans are a viable alternative if there are few or no other Medicare Advantage plans available.

How Most Medicare Advantage Fee-for-Service Plans Work

Unlike managed care plans, most Medicare Advantage fee-for-service plans cover care provided by any health care provider that accepts Medicare patients. Also, many of these plans have a cap on the total out-of-pocket payments an enrollee will pay each year for care that is covered by the plan.

Fee-for-Service Plans With Tiered Payment

Most fee-for-service plans maintain provider networks, just like a managed care plan. With these plans, you can receive medical services from any doctor or other provider who accepts the terms of the plan. But if you receive medical services from a provider within the plan's network, your out-of-pocket costs are lower than if you receive services from a provider who isn't in the plan's network.

Disadvantages of Medicare Advantage Fee-for-Service Plans

Fee-for-service plans impose several significant restrictions that might severely limit a patient's choice of doctors and other providers, making such a plan a poor option if other types of Medicare Advantage plans are available. These restrictions are

- **Strict rules for providers.** For any specific medical treatment or service, a doctor or another provider must accept the terms offered by the fee-for-service plan. These terms include the nature and extent of care the insurance company will approve and what the provider will be paid. If the doctor or other provider isn't willing to accept the plan's terms, the plan won't cover the particular care with that provider. In that case, the patient must either personally pay for the care or seek treatment from a different provider.

- **Lack of predictable care.** The fact that a doctor or another provider previously accepted a plan's terms doesn't mean the provider will accept the terms the next time the patient wants care, either for the same or for a different medical service. In other words, if you enroll in one of these plans, you won't know whether care from a particular doctor or other provider will be covered by the plan until the time comes when you need it.
- **Few additional services.** Unlike other types of Medicare Advantage plans, fee-for-service plans usually don't cover many extra services (services not covered by original Medicare Part A and Part B).
- **Extra costs.** In some plans, you might have to pay the doctor or other provider out of your pocket—up to 15% more than the amount the plan pays the provider.

If you're considering a private fee-for-service plan, be sure to carefully evaluate your choices by following the suggestions offered in the rest of this chapter.

Choosing a Medicare Advantage Plan

To evaluate a Medicare Advantage plan of any type, it's important to get a complete written explanation of its coverage, costs, and procedures. These are usually contained in a printed brochure called a "summary of benefits," available from each plan. Also, ask each plan for a chart showing premiums and copayments. Compare that written information with each important category discussed in this chapter.

If you don't understand exactly what the coverage, costs, and procedures are, ask a plan representative to tell you where they're explained in the written information. If you can't get an important piece of information in writing, don't join the plan.

Choice of Doctors and Other Providers

For many people, the most important factor in choosing a Medicare Advantage plan is whether the doctors, hospitals, and other providers they already use and trust are in the plan's network of providers or, in the case of fee-for-service plans, whether those providers regularly accept the plan's terms.

Tracking Membership Satisfaction

Your state department of insurance or department of corporations is charged with monitoring Medicare Advantage plans. And it pays to see whether many members complain about crucial services. Most complaints are based on a plan's having:

- rejected referrals to specialists
- ordered early discharge for hospital inpatients
- dropped coverage in certain geographic areas
- dropped doctors and hospitals from its network
- raised copayments
- switched drugs on the plan's formulary, or
- dropped extra coverage.

An excellent and free source of information about Medicare Advantage plans is the State Health Insurance Assistance Program (SHIP)—in some places called the "Health Insurance Counseling and Advocacy Program" (HICAP). To find your local office, contact the SHIP or HICAP office in your state (for contact information, see the end of Chapter 13).

Managed care plans. If the people and places you prefer for care are in a managed care plan's network, the tight restrictions of HMOs might not have much effect on you, at least for the foreseeable future. But if they're not, you'll have to find new doctors, which is rarely an easy or comfortable process. And you might have to use a hospital that's more distant from your home, leaving you a little less secure.

The problem isn't quite as great with PPOs or HMOs with a point-of-service option. These plans permit you to use providers who aren't in a plan's network. So, if you want to continue with a particular doctor or provider who isn't in the network, you can do so, but with a higher copayment each time you use the nonnetwork provider. If you're frequently treated by nonnetwork doctors, the extra payments might cancel out the cost advantage of managed care.

Fee-for-service plans. Some Medicare Advantage fee-for-service plans don't have a provider network, so there's no simple way to know that the doctors and other providers you use will accept the plan for any particular treatment or service. Before joining one of these plans, it's important to talk directly with your primary care doctor and any other doctor or other provider you regularly receive care from. Ask them whether they have experience with the plan you're considering and, if so, whether they often refuse to accept the plan's terms. If your regular providers have little experience with the plan or regularly refuse the plan's offered terms, joining that plan is probably not a good idea if you want to continue being treated by those same providers.

Help With Medicare Advantage Choices

People finding their way through the Medicare Advantage maze can get help from the State Health Insurance Assistance Program (SHIP), also frequently called the Health Insurance Counseling and Advocacy Program (HICAP). SHIP is funded by a combination of government grants and private donations and has no connection to the health care or insurance industries. SHIP provides free counseling about Medicare Advantage plans and medigap policies. Local staff can help you compare plans and policies. They can also tell you about other people's recent experiences with specific plans and policies.

To find the SHIP or HICAP office nearest you, contact your state's central SHIP or HICAP office (see the end of Chapter 13 for contact information).

ONLINE

Compare plans on Medicare's website. Medicare's official website at www.medicare.gov offers a link that can give you the names and contact information for insurance companies offering Medicare Advantage plans available where you live. On the www.medicare.gov home page, click "Health & Drug Plans." Then look under "Find & Compare" and click "Find health & drug plans." This takes you to a page that asks for your zip code and the type of plan you're looking for. This page can then take you to information about specific Medicare Advantage plans being sold where you live, including basic information about what the policies cover and how to contact the insurance companies offering those plans.

In addition, it offers patient satisfaction ratings and statistics on how many people have left each plan. Be aware, though, that the information on this page is only intended to give you basic information about these health plans. To get the detailed information you need—about costs, networks, and coverage—to make a decision, you must contact the plans themselves. Also, you should always double-check such information with your local SHIP or HICAP office, because some of it might be out of date, and it might not include how many people have been dropped by the plan.

Access to Specialists and Preventive Care

The requirement that you must visit your primary care physician to obtain most referrals to other providers is one of the main customer objections to managed care plans.

Referrals

Your primary care physician refers you for testing, laboratory work, and treatment by most specialists. Speak with your primary care doctor and other providers you see regularly about their experiences with a particular plan. Does the plan often overrule the doctor's recommendation? Has the plan set guidelines for the doctors that might affect their ability to send you for treatment?

Direct Access to Specialists Through Treatment Plans

Medicare rules require managed care plans to develop a specific treatment plan for patients with a complex or serious condition, such as heart disease, cancer, or kidney failure. The treatment plan must outline what specialists you require, and it must allow you to see them without continuing to get referrals from your primary care doctor. If you have a condition that requires regular care by specialists, find out from the plan whether your condition is considered sufficiently serious or complex to permit direct access to those specialists.

Preventive Care Options

Under Medicare rules, a managed care plan must permit members to obtain routine preventive women's health care screening from a gynecologist without first seeing a primary care physician. It must also permit a member to obtain Medicare-covered mammograms without a referral. Find out from a managed care plan how often other preventive care services—such as physical exams, prostate screening for men, cholesterol testing, or hearing exams—are covered by the plan.

Now You Get Coverage, Now You Don't

The government doesn't regulate Medicare Advantage plan coverage except to insist that the plans offer at least basic Medicare benefits. Nor is there any regulation of premiums and copayments. What this means is that Medicare Advantage plans are free to change coverage and charges at renewal time.

Plans might cut back on coverage. In some plans, benefits are shifted from no-premium plans to deluxe plans with a premium. Raising copayments for specific services—particularly prescription drugs—is also common, as is restricting access to certain medications.

But to compete with other insurance plans, your plan might expand coverage. In recent years, for example, short-term custodial care and overseas travel coverage have been added to many plans, although most charge an added premium for these "extras."

Prescription Drug Coverage

Many people get prescription drug coverage through their Medicare Advantage plan, rather than through a separate Medicare Part D drug plan.

If you're thinking about joining a Medicare Advantage plan with prescription drug coverage, it's very important that you examine that coverage closely. Review that coverage just as you would when considering a stand-alone prescription drug plan. (See "Part D: Prescription Drug Coverage" in Chapter 12.) In particular, you must determine whether the plan:

- includes on its formulary (its list of covered drugs) the drugs you regularly take
- charges reasonably low copayments for those drugs, and
- imposes no significant access restrictions to those drugs.

Once you've determined how well various Medicare Advantage plans cover the particular prescription drugs you take, you must weigh that information along with the other aspects of the plans discussed in this chapter. If you use many costly prescription drugs, how well a particular plan covers your drugs should be a major part of your decision. If you use few prescription drugs, then the other aspects of a plan might influence your decision more strongly.

Before you choose any Medicare Advantage plan, be sure to investigate the stand-alone Part D prescription drug plans that are available to you. Then, add the costs of the Part D stand-alone drug plan that best covers your drugs to the costs of a Medicare Advantage plan without drug coverage. It's this combination of costs and stand-alone Part D drug coverage benefits that you should consider when comparing these plans to other Medicare Advantage plans that include drug coverage.

Consider Total Costs, Not Just Premiums

Many Medicare Advantage plans, particularly managed care plans, charge relatively small premiums, often much lower than the combined premiums of a medigap policy plus a Part D drug plan. But premiums don't tell the whole story of what your supplemental Medicare coverage will actually cost you. This is because a Medicare Advantage plan's medical coverage and its prescription drug coverage will both require you to make copayments.

Most Medicare Advantage managed care plans charge a copayment for doctor visits (usually $5 to $20), and many older people frequently consult several doctors. Drug coverage is offered only for drugs on a plan's formulary (see "Part D: Prescription Drug Coverage" in Chapter 12), and copayments vary depending on the type of medication and whether it's a brand-name or generic drug. Within these parameters, Medicare Advantage drug copayments can run up to 25% of the drug's actual retail cost.

By law, there's a limit on out-of-pocket expenses for members of Medicare Advantage plans. For 2024, the maximum out-of-pocket limit is $8,850, not including out-of-pocket costs for prescription drugs. Each plan sets its own limit up to this maximum, with many plans setting a limit well below the maximum.

Only by comparing the copayments and premiums of various plans can you fully understand how much each plan is likely to cost you.

Extent of Service Area

Consider the extent of a plan's service area, particularly if you live in a rural or spread-out suburban area. If the service area isn't broad enough to include a good selection of specialists, you might find your future care choices limited.

Also, find out whether the plan has what are called "extended service areas." Some plans permit you to arrange medical care far from your home if you travel frequently or spend a regular part of the year away from its primary service area. This allows you to take care of nonurgent medical needs even if you're not at your primary residence.

Appealing a Plan's Decision About Your Care

Up to 10% of prior authorization requests for services are denied by Medicare Advantage plans as being medically unnecessary or otherwise not covered. This phenomenon of having an insurance company overruling your doctor can be upsetting, and if it involves a serious condition, the plan's rejection can be devastating, either to your health or to your wallet.

There's a standard process for you to appeal such a denial of coverage. Unfortunately, the first step in the review process is handled by the plan's insurance company itself. The plan will provide you with a written decision denying the coverage, which will also include instructions for filing the initial step in your appeal. This first step is a written request for reconsideration of their decision; you must do so within 60 days of receiving the notice from the plan denying coverage. The plan must then make a reconsideration decision within a set time limit: 30 days for a decision regarding coverage of a service you want to have performed, 60 days regarding payment for a service you've already had.

If the plan doesn't provide the coverage you want after this initial reconsideration, your next step is to appeal to an independent review entity (IRE) that doesn't work for the plan insurance company. At this point, your appeal will follow the same procedures as if you were in traditional Medicare, as explained in Chapter 13.

Other Plan Features

Many Medicare Advantage plans offer a variety of features beyond basic Medicare coverage. The following benefits are either extra services some plans cover or major medical expenses for which some plans pay a portion of the total costs. If you're likely to use any of these benefits, a plan that offers them might be more attractive to you.

Short-Term Custodial Care

Following an injury, a surgery, or a serious illness, you might not be strong enough to take care of yourself, but you might not require skilled nursing care. Instead, you might need what's called custodial care—help with dressing, bathing, eating, and other regular activities of daily living.

Custodial care isn't covered at all by Medicare, unless you're already receiving skilled nursing care or therapy. But some Medicare Advantage plans offer coverage for short-term custodial care, either at home from a certified home health care agency or in a certified care facility.

Such plans usually limit the number of home care visits or days you can spend in a care facility, and charge copayments as well as a separate premium for the coverage. Despite these limitations, this can be valuable added coverage, because many seniors can use this kind of care at some point.

Medical Equipment

By way of reminder, traditional Medicare Part B pays 80% of the amount it approves for most doctor-prescribed medical equipment, such as wheelchairs, hospital beds, ventilators, and prosthetic devices. But the recipient is responsible for 20% of the approved amount, plus anything above that amount if the equipment company doesn't accept Medicare assignment. Some Medicare Advantage plans, on the other hand, pay the full cost of prescribed medical equipment, although it must be purchased or rented from a provider in the plan's network or, if you choose a fee-for-service plan, from a provider that accepts the plan's terms and payment levels.

Chiropractic Care, Acupuncture, and Acupressure

Medicare pays for a very limited amount of chiropractic care and pays nothing at all for acupuncture or acupressure treatment. Some Medicare Advantage plans cover a greater amount of chiropractic care. And a few recognize the value of acupuncture and acupressure and pay for some of the cost.

Treatments must be received from providers in the plan's network or those who accept the plan's terms, and a copayment is almost always charged for each visit. However, if you regularly use one of these treatments and your practitioner happens to be in the plan's network or regularly accepts your fee-for-service plan's terms, this coverage can be a good money saver.

Foreign Travel Coverage

Many people travel abroad to visit family; others hope to do some foreign traveling during retirement. Medicare provides no coverage for medical costs incurred outside the United States, nor do most Medicare Advantage plans. But a few Medicare Advantage plans offer coverage for emergency care while abroad. And some also offer free or low-cost immunizations for foreign travel. If you plan on traveling abroad frequently or for long stays, this coverage can be valuable.

Eye Examinations and Glasses

Medicare covers only eye examinations and optometry services that are necessary because of an eye disease or other medical condition. It doesn't pay for regular vision testing or for eyeglasses or contact lenses, except after cataract surgery. A number of Medicare Advantage plans, however, offer some kind of bonus vision coverage, although none of them pays the full cost of glasses.

Some plans cover an eye examination every two years and offer a set annual amount toward prescription lenses. Instead of a set amount, other plans offer discount examinations, lenses, frames, and contacts from optometrists who participate in the plan's network.

Hearing Tests and Hearing Aids

Some Medicare Advantage plans offer a free regular hearing exam, plus discounts on hearing aids. As with other Medicare Advantage coverage, the care must be obtained from a hearing center that is connected to the plan's network or that accepts the plan's terms and payment amounts.

Dental Work

A few Medicare Advantage plans offer discounts on dental work. The discounts usually include a low copayment for cleaning and examination and up to a 35% reduction in the cost of other services. The networks of dentists are usually quite limited, however. Finding a dentist who participates in the plan—and with whom you're comfortable—is the key to making this extra coverage worthwhile.

After-Hours Advice and Treatment

People don't always become ill during regular office hours. But visiting an emergency room can be a miserable—and often unnecessary—experience. Some Medicare Advantage managed care plans maintain 24-hour phone lines staffed by experienced nurses who can help you stay out of the ER. Other plans—usually provider-sponsored organizations or individual groups of doctors within larger HMOs—maintain evening and weekend clinics. There, you can consult a doctor for a lower copayment and less stress than a visit to an emergency room.

Chronic Disease Management and Wellness Programs

The managed care industry does better than original Medicare in recognizing how much money it saves by monitoring and managing chronic conditions and offering programs to improve general health. As a result, many managed care plans offer free or low-cost educational and monitoring programs to help people with chronic illness keep their conditions under control. Some programs include blood pressure and cholesterol education for heart patients, diabetes

classes to control blood sugar levels, and classes for Parkinson's patients to reduce their risk of falls. Some plans offer programs to help people lead healthier lives, such as nutrition and exercise programs to improve flexibility and cardiac health, to help lose weight, and to help you quit smoking.

Added Services in Some Plans

Some Medicare Advantage plans offer additional services not required by Medicare law. These might include:

- adult day care programs
- in-home aides for nonmedical assistance with the activities of daily living (such as dressing, bathing, toileting)
- palliative care at home for seriously ill patients
- help paying for home safety devices such as grab bars and wheelchair ramps
- transportation to and from medical appointments, and
- special services for chronically ill patients, tailored to their specific needs.

Not all plans will offer all of these new services, and the amount paid will vary from plan to plan. But if any of these are services that are likely to be of use to you, you might want to consider them when choosing a Medicare Advantage plan.

Comparing Medigap and Medicare Advantage Plans

After you've found several medigap (see Chapter 14) and Medicare Advantage plans that seem to fit your needs and budget, the best way to compare them is to view their costs and coverage side by side. Refer to the "Comparing Medigap to Managed Care" chart below for a comparison of the major benefits of medigap and Medicare Advantage plans. Then, use the next chart to help you compare the actual plans you're considering.

Comparing Medigap to Managed Care

	Medigap Plans	Managed Care Plans
Choice of Doctor and Providers	As long as doctor or other provider accepts Medicare, a medigap policy will cover whatever Medicare does.	Choice restricted to doctors and providers in the network. PPO and some HMO options allow nonnetwork providers at higher cost. Fee-for-service plans cover care only from providers who accept a plan's terms.
Access to Specialists	As long as specialist accepts Medicare, a medigap policy will cover whatever Medicare does.	Must get referral from primary care doctor to specialist also in plan's network. Limited direct access available for some serious conditions. In fee-for-service plans, specialist must accept plan's terms.
Premiums	Vary widely, with higher cost for plans with more services. Plan A: $50–$400/month. Plans B–G: $100–$400/month. Plans H–J: $75–$500/month ($150–$500/month for continuing plans with drug coverage). Plan K: $50–$150/month. Plan L: $75–$200/month.	Usually no or low premium for basic HMO that provides coverage equal to traditional Medicare Part A and Part B. Member must pay Medicare Part B premium. Broader coverage or more provider choices might cost between $25–$200/month.
Copayments	No copayments for services except under Plan N policies, which charge a $20 copayment for each doctor's office visit and $50 for each emergency room visit.	Require copayment for most services, generally $5–$25 per visit. In fee-for-service plans, might be responsible for up to 15% more than what plan pays.
Treatment Approval	Automatic if service is covered by Medicare.	Coverage denied if plan decides that treatment is medically unnecessary (perhaps if a different, cheaper treatment is available) or experimental.
Geographic Mobility	Most plans can be used wherever you obtain Medicare-covered services in the United States.	With managed care plans, nonemergency coverage limited to specific geographical area. Some plans offer care away from home. All plans must cover emergency care anywhere in the United States.

Comparing Medigap to Managed Care (continued)

	Medigap Plans	Managed Care Plans
Emergency Care Overseas	Covered by Plans C–J, M, and N.	Some plans cover, but might charge a higher premium.
At-Home Recovery	Covered by Plans D, G, I, and J, but only if also receiving skilled nursing care at home (only if issued before June 1, 2010).	Some plans cover, but for a higher premium and copayment.
Eye Exams and Glasses	No, unless connected to illness or injury.	Most offer limited discounts on exams and lenses.
Hearing Exams and Aids	No, unless connected to illness or injury.	Most offer discounts on exams and hearing aids.
Dental Discounts	No.	Some offer discounts.
Wellness Programs	No.	Many offer a variety of low-cost or free wellness programs, including heart-healthy education, weight loss, quitting smoking, and cholesterol management.
Chiropractic Care	Only if covered by Medicare.	Some offer broader coverage than Medicare.
Prescription Drugs	No coverage (except for some people who had a Plan H, I, or J prior to January 1, 2006 and who keep that plan). Requires purchase of a separate stand-alone Medicare prescription drug plan. Must add the premium cost of the Medicare drug plan to the cost of the medigap policy when comparing costs with a managed care plan. Must also compare the drug copayments of the drug plan against the copayments of the managed care plan.	Some plans offer coverage, with copayments of $0–$25 per prescription. Amount of copay depends on whether you use generic or brand-name medication and your specific plan's formulary list (which might have separate copayment levels for different medications).

Comparing Medigap Policies and Managed Care Plans

		Plan Name	Plan Name	Plan Name	Plan Name	Plan Name
Cost (monthly premium)						
Copayments (amount I must pay per visit)						
Other Medicare gaps left unfilled						
Is there coverage outside the plan?	Yes					
	No					
Cost of care outside the plan						
Dental care covered	Yes					
	No					
Choice of dentists	Yes					
	No					
Short-term custodial care	Yes					
	No					
Eyeglasses	Copayments					
	Visits per year					
Other services:						
Hearing exam	Yes					
	No					
Chiropractic	Yes					
	No					
Foreign travel	Yes					
	No					
Exercise program	Yes					
	No					
Other	Yes					
	No					
Prescription drug coverage (compare Part D drug plans and managed care plans)	Copayments					
	Annual limit					

Your Rights When Joining, Leaving, or Losing a Medicare Advantage Plan

Insurance companies offering Medicare Advantage plans are free to charge whatever they want in premiums and copayments. They alone decide what types of medical care to cover, although they must provide at least the same basic services that Medicare does. Moreover, they might offer a Medicare Advantage plan one year and withdraw it the next—leaving its beneficiaries without coverage. Some Medicare Advantage plans do this region by region around the nation, deciding which spots are profitable enough for them and dropping plans—and the people in them—in places that don't measure up.

Despite this general corporate freedom for Medicare Advantage insurance companies, they must follow a few rules concerning people's rights to join or to leave their plans.

Joining When First Eligible for Medicare at Age 65

When you approach age 65, you have an initial seven-month window in which to sign up for a Medicare Advantage plan (if you're otherwise eligible for Medicare and you sign up for Parts A and B). This seven-month period begins three months before the month you turn 65 and ends three months after the month in which you turn 65. During this period, you can join any Medicare Advantage plan that operates in the county of your primary residence. The plan must accept you, on the same terms and conditions as anyone else of your age, without any medical screening and regardless of your medical history or physical condition (unless you have ESRD and aren't already getting health benefits through the same organization that

offers the Medicare Advantage plan you want to join). If you don't sign up during this initial period, you can join later during a plan's open enrollment period (see below).

Joining During a Plan's Open Enrollment Period

Every Medicare Advantage plan must have at least one month every year of what's called "open enrollment"—meaning that during that time, anyone eligible for Medicare can join the plan regardless of their medical history or condition. Open enrollment is October 15 to December 7 each year, with coverage to begin the following January 1. But some plans also have more open enrollment during other months of the year.

Joining During Extended Open Enrollment Period

There's an extra open enrollment period for Medicare Advantage plans. Anyone already enrolled in a Medicare Advantage plan can enroll in another Medicare Advantage plan or drop an existing Medicare Advantage plan and return to original Medicare, between January 1 and March 31. If you enroll in a plan during this extended enrollment period, your coverage will begin on the first day of the following month. This enrollment period is called the "Medicare Advantage Open Enrollment Period."

TIP

You can switch to a highly rated plan any time. If a Medicare Advantage plan is rated five stars by Medicare, you don't have to wait for an Open Enrollment Period to switch to it. You can switch to a five-star plan any time of the year, except for the first week of December (but you can only use this exception once per year).

Leaving a Medicare Advantage Plan

When you can leave a Medicare Advantage plan depends on how long ago you joined. If you first enrolled in a plan during your initial Medicare eligibility period, you can drop the plan anytime during the first 12 months and revert to original Medicare coverage. If you want to switch to a new Medicare Advantage plan, you can do so during the open enrollment period from October 15 to December 7 each year (for coverage to start the following January 1) or during the extended enrollment period from January 1 through March 31 each year (for coverage to start the first of the following month).

After your first year of membership in a plan, you can leave the plan and join another plan, or return to original Medicare coverage, either during the open enrollment period from October 15 to December 7 each year (for coverage to start the following January 1) or during the extended enrollment period from January 1 through March 31 each year (with coverage starting the first of the following month).

Joining When Dropped From Another Medicare Advantage Plan

If you have been enrolled in a Medicare Advantage plan and that plan notifies you—by October 1—that, at the end of the year, it's dropping the plan in the county where you live, you have several options. You can return to original Medicare Part A and Part B coverage, and you're guaranteed the right to supplement that coverage by purchasing one of several medigap insurance policies. (See "Finding the Best Medicare Supplement" in Chapter 14 for a discussion of choosing a medigap policy.)

Or, you can enroll in any other Medicare Advantage plan being sold in your county, if the plan hasn't reached its membership limit for the year. You have this right to join a new Medicare Advantage plan during a special enrollment period from December 8 through the last day of February.

Joining When Moving to a New Geographic Area

Each Medicare Advantage plan serves only a specific geographic area, often a single county. If you move from the plan's service area, you lose the right to continued coverage with that Medicare Advantage plan.

If you move out of a plan's service area and want a Medicare Advantage plan, you must apply to a plan that serves your new community. If you notify your current plan before you actually move, you have the right to enroll in a new plan (that operates in your new area) beginning the month before the month during which you move, and continuing for two full months after you move. If you don't notify your existing plan until after you move, you have a right to switch plans beginning the month you notify your plan, plus two more full months thereafter. You also have the right to join a new Medicare Advantage plan (one that operates in your new area) during that plan's open enrollment period, which runs from October 15 through December 7, and sometimes longer, each year. ●

Medicaid and State Supplements to Medicare

W hen all types of medical expenses for older Americans are added up, Medicare pays for only about half of them. If you have a low income and few assets other than your home, however, you might qualify for assistance from your state's Medicaid program (called Medi-Cal in California). Medicaid can not only pay Medicare premiums, deductibles, and copayments, it also covers some services Medicare does not.

If you have low income and assets, but either is too high to be eligible for Medicaid, you could still qualify for one of several Medicaid-administered programs to help you meet medical costs: Qualified Medicare Beneficiary (QMB), Specified Low-Income Medicare Beneficiary (SLMB), or Qualifying Individual (QI). (For a discussion of these programs, see "Other State Assistance With Medical Costs," below.)

Medicaid Defined

Medicaid's purpose is to help pay medical costs for financially needy people. The program was established by the federal government and is administered by the individual states. Medicaid operates in addition to Medicare to pay for many of the medical costs Medicare doesn't cover.

The basic difference between Medicare and Medicaid is simple: Medicare is available to almost everyone age 65 or older, regardless of income or assets, while Medicaid is available only to people over 65 or disabled, to families with minor children, and to foster youth and former foster youth until age 26—and in some states, to individuals of any age—who are financially needy. Just how "needy" you must be in order to get Medicaid is up to the state in which you live. (Note: Children with certain disabilities and foster youth and former foster youth until age 26 may be eligible for Medicaid without regard to financial need.)

There are currently almost 50 million adults who receive some form of Medicaid assistance; about 10 million of them are also on Medicare. (For a fuller comparison of the programs, see "Medicare: The Basics" in Chapter 12.)

There are federal guidelines for Medicaid, but within them, each state is permitted to make its own rules regarding eligibility, coverage, and benefits. This chapter explains the basic eligibility and coverage rules of Medicaid and indicates where eligibility standards might be higher or lower than the basic levels.

Who Is Eligible

Generally, states use one of two ways to determine who is eligible for Medicaid. One way is to base eligibility on income and assets alone ("categorically needy"). The other is to base eligibility on income and assets plus medical costs ("medically needy").

Medicaid Eligibility Expanded to People Under 65 in Some States

Under Medicaid rules that have been in effect since the program's beginnings, eligibility has generally been limited to people who are age 65 or older, disabled, or have minor children, if they also met the financial standards discussed in the following sections. However, under the health care reform law passed in 2010, individual states were allowed to expand Medicaid eligibility to financially needy people of any age. Over three-quarters of the states have decided to expand Medicaid under the Affordable Care Act.

Categorically Needy

To qualify for Medicaid as categorically needy, your income and assets must be at or below certain dollar amounts. Some states use the same income and asset limits set by the federal Supplemental Security Income, or SSI, program. Other states establish their own Medicaid limits.

SSI-Based Standards

In most states, you can automatically receive Medicaid if you're eligible for SSI assistance. To be eligible for SSI, you can't earn more than about $1,400 to $2,000 per month, or about $2,000 to $2,900 for a couple with both spouses eligible for SSI, though these amounts can vary depending on your state. Also, you can't possess cash and other assets of more than $2,000 for an individual and $3,000 for a couple.

Fortunately, a number of important assets aren't counted in the SSI eligibility calculation. You can own:
- your own home of any value
- a car (though in some states, only up to a certain market value)
- engagement and wedding rings
- household goods
- life insurance, and
- a burial fund.

(For details of SSI eligibility rules, see Chapter 7.)

State Standards

States have gone in all directions when establishing their own Medicaid standards. In a few states, the standards are slightly less difficult to meet than SSI standards. In some others, the standards are stricter, including a dollar limit on the value of your home and lower limits on the values of your automobile and other property.

To find out your state's standards, contact your local county department of social services or department of welfare. You can also find the basic Medicaid eligibility requirements in your state by visiting the website of your state's Medicaid program. To find that website, go to www.medicaid.gov, to the "Medicaid" tab, and then under "Program Information," click "Medicaid & CHIP Eligibility Levels."

Not all income is counted when Medicaid considers your eligibility, so if you're anywhere close to the eligibility limits in your state, consider applying for Medicaid or a state Medicare supplement (described in "Other State Assistance With Medical Costs," below) as well.

Medically Needy

What if your income and assets are higher than your state's Medicaid limit under the categorically needy standard, but your medical expenses cancel much of this out? You might be what's called "medically needy" and eligible for Medicaid coverage in some states. Medically needy means your income and assets are over the Medicaid eligibility levels for your state but your current or expected medical expenses will reduce your income or assets to eligible levels.

This process of subtracting actual medical bills from income and assets is called "spending down," in Medicaid slang—because medical bills would force you to spend your extra money down to the point that you would meet eligibility levels.

The following states offer Medicaid coverage to medically needy people (but note that income limits vary from state to state, and some states limit benefits to children, people 65 or older, persons with disabilities, and pregnant women):

Arkansas	Louisiana	North Carolina
California	Maine	North Dakota
Connecticut	Maryland	Pennsylvania
District of Columbia	Massachusetts	Rhode Island
Florida	Michigan	Tennessee
Georgia	Minnesota	Utah
Hawaii	Montana	Vermont
Illinois	Nebraska	Virginia
Iowa	New Hampshire	Washington
Kansas	New Jersey	West Virginia
Kentucky	New York	Wisconsin

EXAMPLE: Roberta's income is low, but her savings are $2,000 more than what is allowed to qualify for Medicaid as categorically needy by the rules in her state. However, surgery, home nursing care, physical therapy, and medication have left Roberta with medical bills of almost $3,000 (not paid for by Medicare). Roberta's state offers Medicaid coverage to the medically needy. If she paid her $3,000 medical bills, she would be spending her savings down to a level that would meet the Medicaid standards. Instead of forcing her to spend that money and be reduced to Medicaid savings levels, Roberta qualifies immediately for Medicaid, which will pay the bills.

Medicaid When One Spouse Is in a Nursing Home

The Medicaid rules get a bit tricky when one spouse is in a nursing home paid for by Medicaid while the other spouse remains at home. Some states look only at income in the nursing home resident's name, but other states consider the joint income of both. A monthly income allowance is permitted for the at-home spouse, and some of the nursing home resident's income can be used to support the at-home spouse. At-home spouses are also allowed to keep their homes and to retain between about $30,000 and $150,000 in other assets, depending on the state. These figures go up periodically, usually on January 1 or July 1 of each year.

However, Medicaid can also place a lien on the home or on other assets in an amount equal to the entire amount Medicaid spends on nursing home care for the spouse. When the at-home spouse dies or sells the house, Medicaid will enforce the lien, taking money that the at-home spouse would otherwise be able to spend or leave to survivors.

To take best advantage of Medicaid coverage for long-term care, it is important to understand these rules and also the alternatives to nursing homes that can serve your needs while preserving as much of your savings as possible.

Long-term care and how it's paid for, including a comprehensive discussion of Medicaid nursing home rules, is covered fully in *Long-Term Care: How to Plan & Pay for It*, by Joseph L. Matthews (Nolo).

TIP

If your income and assets are a little too high for Medicaid, the government might help through other programs. If your income and assets are low but slightly too high for you to be eligible for Medicaid in your state, you might still be eligible for state Qualified Medicare Beneficiary (QMB), Specified Low-Income Medicare Beneficiary (SLMB), or Qualifying Individual (QI) benefits. These programs help meet medical costs not paid for by Medicare. You might also qualify for a low-income subsidy to help pay the costs that come with Medicare Part D prescription drug coverage. (See "Other State Assistance With Medical Costs," below, for details.)

Determining Couples' Income and Assets

In determining your eligibility, Medicaid generally considers your income and assets plus those of your spouse, if you live together. If you're divorced or separated and living apart, your spouse's income and assets aren't counted, except to the extent that your spouse is actually contributing to your support.

This rule of considering a spouse's income in determining Medicaid eligibility has had the unfortunate effect of keeping many older couples from marrying. They fear that if they marry, a serious illness could bankrupt both of them before they would become eligible for Medicaid assistance.

If both spouses become eligible for Medicare, however, this loss of Medicaid might not be as serious, and marriage might make financial sense in other ways. For example, when spouses marry, each becomes eligible at age 62 for Social Security dependents benefits based on the other's work record. If one person has earned considerably higher Social Security or civil service benefits than the other, this ability to get dependents benefits might make a considerable difference. (See Chapter 4 regarding dependents and Chapter 10 regarding civil service benefits.) The same is true of Social Security or civil service survivors benefits. Marriage would allow one spouse to claim these benefits when the other dies and to collect them for life (see Chapters 5 and 10 for details).

Financial Help From Friends or Family

The income or assets of your children, other relatives, or friends, even if you live with them, aren't considered in deciding your Medicaid eligibility. However, if you receive regular financial support from a relative or friend—cash or help with rent—Medicaid can consider that assistance as part of your income.

Also, if you're living rent free with children or other relatives and they give you all of your food and clothing, Medicaid could put a dollar amount on that support and count it as part of your income. This doesn't happen frequently. But it is possible that, during the application process, the person reviewing your eligibility could visit your home and determine whether you're receiving substantial, regular income in the form of noncash support.

Medical Costs Covered by Medicaid

Medicaid covers the same kinds of services as Medicare and, in most states, also covers a number of medical services Medicare does not.

One of its best features is that it covers most long-term care, both at home and in nursing facilities. This includes not only long-term skilled nursing care, but also nonmedical personal care—such as adult day care and at-home assistance with the activities of daily living (ADLs).

Medicaid also pays many of the amounts Medicare does not pay in hospital and doctor bills. Specifically, this means Medicaid pays:

- the inpatient hospital insurance deductible and coinsurance amounts that Medicare doesn't pay
- the Medicare Part B medical insurance deductible
- the 20% of the Medicare-approved doctors' fees that Medicare medical insurance doesn't pay (for traditional Medicare), and
- the monthly premium charged for Medicare Part B medical insurance.

Services Covered in Every State

In every state, Medicaid completely covers certain medical services, paying whatever Medicare does not.

These services include:

- inpatient hospital or skilled nursing facility care
- nursing home care in approved facilities
- outpatient hospital or clinic treatment
- laboratory and X-ray services
- physicians' services
- home health care, and
- transportation—by ambulance, if necessary—to and from the place you receive medical services.

Most Prescription Drug Coverage Comes From a Medicare Part D Drug Plan or a Medicaid Managed Care Plan

For people who are eligible for both Medicare and Medicaid (known as "dual eligibles"), Medicaid doesn't provide much prescription drug coverage. Instead, a dual-eligible person must receive most drug coverage through a Medicare Part D prescription drug plan or through a Medicaid/Medicare managed care plan.

People who become dually eligible will be automatically signed up for either a special Medicaid/Medicare managed care plan with drug coverage or a Part D prescription drug plan. A dual eligible who doesn't like the coverage or access to drugs offered by the automatic-enrollment Part D plan can switch plans at any time. Automatic enrollment for dual eligibles and their right to switch plans is explained in the sections that discuss Part D prescription drug coverage in Chapters 12 and 13. If someone is enrolled in a Medicaid managed care plan, you can switch to another plan during certain periods each year.

Medicare Part D provides coverage for most categories of drugs but not all. To fill these gaps, many state Medicaid programs cover some of the drugs, both prescription and over the counter, that Medicare Part D plans don't.

Optional Services

In all states, Medicaid also covers many other types of medical services that Medicare doesn't. However, state Medicaid programs aren't required to cover these optional services, and in some states they might charge a nominal fee for them. (See "Cost of Medicaid Coverage," below.)

Most states provide the following optional medical services commonly used by older people:

- **Prescription drugs.** All states provide Medicaid coverage for prescription drugs, though there might be a small copayment for each prescription filled. For people eligible for Medicare as well as Medicaid (dual eligibles), however, Medicaid no longer covers most drugs. Instead, dual eligibles receive their drug coverage through a separate Medicare Part D plan or a Medicaid managed care plan. In some states, though, Medicaid covers the cost of some prescription and over-the-counter drugs for dual eligibles that Medicare Part D plans don't cover.
- **Eye care.** Standard eyesight exams (every one to two years), plus the cost of eyeglasses.
- **Dental care.** Routine dental care, though the list of dentists whom you're allowed to see might be quite limited; most states also cover the cost of dentures.
- **Transportation.** Nonemergency transport to and from medical care, usually with some sort of van service under contract to the county.
- **Physical therapy.** Some amount of physical therapy beyond the very limited amount covered by Medicare.
- **Prosthetic devices.** All states cover the costs of medically necessary prosthetics beyond what is paid for by Medicare.

The types and amount of coverage for other optional services vary widely from state to state. However, these other optional services often include chiropractic care, podiatry, speech and occupational therapy, private-duty nursing, personal care services, personal care and case management services as part of home care, adult day care, hospice care, various preventive, screening, and rehabilitative services, and inpatient psychiatric care for those 65 and older.

Medicaid Through Managed Care

People who qualify for both Medicaid and Medicare are known as "dual eligibles." Increasingly, Medicaid and Medicare coverage is offered to dual eligibles through managed care (an HMO or similar plan). In some cases, these managed care plans are optional—a dual eligible can choose to receive traditional Medicare Part A and Part B and enroll in a Medicare Part D prescription drug plan, with Medicaid paying for the Medicare premiums and also providing some additional coverage (which varies from state to state). In many geographic regions, though, dual eligibles who want Medicaid coverage are required to enroll in a Medicaid managed care plan.

These Medicaid managed care plans operate like Medicare Advantage plans, explained in Chapter 15. Their advantage for the patient is that all medical care—inpatient and outpatient, and usually prescription drugs—is handled by a single program, instead of the patient having to negotiate both Medicare and Medicaid, and perhaps a private insurance company for drug coverage. However, these plans require that medical care be received only from certain doctors, hospitals, clinics, and other providers, and they control a patient's ability to see specialists.

Some of these managed care plans for dual eligibles are called "Special Needs Plans" (SNPs). These plans are specially designed for people with specific chronic conditions. The major difference between an SNP for dual eligibles and other Medicaid managed care plans is that an SNP has what's called a "care coordinator" or an "interdisciplinary care team" that helps the patient deal with the different medical providers that people with such conditions often see, and tries to help the patient follow all medical instructions and properly take medications. If you're interested in an available SNP for dual eligibles, you can enroll in it at any time of the year.

Medicaid Through Managed Care (continued)

Each participating Medicaid/Medicare managed care plan for dual eligibles operates differently. Your county department of social services (or other department that administers Medicaid in your state) can explain what Medicaid managed care options are available to you. To help compare such a managed care plan with standard Medicare and Medicaid coverage—if your Medicaid program gives you the choice—contact the SHIP office nearest you for free counseling (see contact information at the end of Chapter 13).

CAUTION

Coverage changes frequently. Medicaid coverage for optional services changes frequently, with states adding some services and dropping others. Check with your local social services or social welfare office for the latest. You must also find out the terms on which such optional services are offered. Sometimes you can obtain such services only if the care is provided by county or other local health clinics, rather than from a private doctor or clinic of your choice.

Requirements for Medicaid Coverage

Even if a particular medical service or treatment is generally covered by Medicaid, you must make sure that the care was prescribed by a doctor, administered by a provider who participates in Medicaid, and determined to be medically necessary.

Care Must Be Prescribed by Doctor

The medical service you receive must be prescribed by a doctor. For example, Medicaid won't pay for chiropractic services or physical therapy you seek on your own. And if it pays for certain prescription medications, it might not pay for an equivalent medicine you could buy over the counter.

For services in which a medical doctor is generally not involved—such as regular eye exams or dental care—Medicaid might place restrictions on how often you can obtain the service and who can authorize it. And Medicaid will cover some services for those who qualify as medically needy only if the care is provided by certain public health hospitals, clinics, or agencies.

Provider Must Participate in Medicaid

You must receive your treatment or other care from a doctor, a facility, or other medical provider that participates in Medicaid. The provider must accept Medicaid payment—or Medicare plus Medicaid—as full payment. And if you see a nonphysician, such as a physical therapist or chiropractor, or are visited by a home care agency, that provider must be approved by Medicaid.

Not all doctors and clinics accept Medicaid patients. So, before you sign up with any doctor or other provider, ask whether they accept Medicaid payment.

Treatment Must Be Medically Necessary

All care must be approved by Medicaid as medically necessary. For inpatient care, the approval process is similar to the one used for Medicare coverage. By requesting your admission to a hospital or another facility, your doctor sets the approval process in motion. You won't need to be involved. In fact, you won't even hear about it unless the facility decides you should be discharged before your doctor thinks you should. (See "What to Do If You're Denied Coverage," below.)

Prior approval from a Medicaid consultant is required before you obtain certain medical services. The rules vary from state to state, requiring prior approval for such services as elective surgery, some major dental care, leasing of medical equipment, and nonemergency inpatient hospital or nursing facility care.

If a particular medical service requires prior Medicaid approval, your doctor or the facility will contact Medicaid directly. You might be asked to get an examination by another doctor before Medicaid will approve the care, but this doesn't happen often.

If you have questions about the approval process, discuss it with both your doctor and a Medicaid worker at your local social service or welfare office. Ask what Medicaid considers most important in making the decision about the medical care you're seeking. Relay that information to your doctor, so that the doctor can provide the necessary information to Medicaid.

Cost of Medicaid Coverage

Almost all Medicaid-covered care is free. And Medicaid also pays your Medicare premium, deductibles, and copayments if you're a dual eligible. However, there are a few circumstances in which you might have to pay small amounts for Medicaid-covered care.

No Payments to Medical Providers

Hospitals, doctors, and other medical care providers who accept dual-eligible Medicaid patients must accept Medicare's approved charges—or the amount approved directly by Medicaid if it's not covered by Medicare—as the total allowable charges. They must accept, as payment in full, the combination of payments from Medicare and Medicaid or from Medicaid alone; they can't bill you for the 15% more than the Medicare-approved amount (which they could do if you weren't on Medicaid).

Fees to State Medicaid Agency for Services

Federal law permits states to charge some small fees to people who qualify for Medicaid as medically needy. (See "Who Is Eligible," above, for the definition.) If you qualify as categorically needy, however, states can charge you a fee only for optional covered services. (See "Optional Services," above, for a description of these services.) State Medicaid charges will take one of three forms: an enrollment fee, a monthly premium, or copayments.

Enrollment Fee

Some states charge a small, one-time-only fee when medically needy people first enroll in Medicaid. This fee can't be charged to people who are considered categorically needy.

Monthly Premium

States are permitted to charge a small monthly fee to people who qualify for Medicaid as medically needy. This premium can be charged whether or not Medicaid services are actually used that month. The amounts vary with income and assets, but usually come to no more than a few dollars.

Copayments

State Medicaid programs are permitted to charge a small copayment for each Medicaid-covered service you receive. A copayment can be charged to the medically needy for any service and to the categorically needy for optional services only. (See "Optional Services," above, for a description of these services.)

Medicaid and Private Health Insurance

Insurance companies aren't permitted to sell you a medigap insurance policy if you're on Medicaid. However, you're permitted to have other private health insurance—such as that provided by a retirement program or a policy you purchase to protect against a specific illness—and still qualify for Medicaid.

Medicaid will deduct the amount of your private health insurance premiums from the calculation of your income when determining whether you're under the allowable income levels to qualify.

However, if you do have private health insurance, and a medical service is covered by both your insurance and by Medicaid, Medicaid will pay only the amount your insurance doesn't. If you receive a payment directly from your insurance company after Medicaid has paid that bill, you must return that insurance money to Medicaid.

Other State Assistance With Medical Costs

Many people with low income and assets have trouble paying the portion of medical bills left unpaid by Medicare and can't afford private medigap insurance, but don't qualify for Medicaid. If this is your situation, you might still get help paying Medicare premiums and portions of Medicare-covered costs that Medicare does not pay.

Three cost-reduction programs—called Qualified Medicare Beneficiary (QMB), Specified Low-Income Medicare Beneficiary (SLMB), and Qualifying Individual (QI)—are administered by each state's Medicaid program. They don't offer the extensive coverage beyond Medicare that Medicaid does, but the savings to you in Medicare-related medical costs can be substantial.

You Could Qualify for the Part D Prescription Drug Program's Extra Help

If you qualify for any of the state assistance programs described in this section, you also qualify for a low-income subsidy called Extra Help to help pay the personal out-of-pocket costs that come with Medicare's Part D prescription drug coverage. The Medicare Part D program and Extra Help are explained in Chapter 12. You can apply for the Part D low-income subsidy when you apply for other state assistance programs (discussed below).

Qualified Medicare Beneficiary (QMB)

If you're eligible for Medicare and meet the income and asset eligibility requirements for the QMB program, your state will pay all of your Medicare Part A and Part B premiums, deductibles, and coinsurance. Depending on how much you use Medicare-covered services in a year, this could mean a savings of up to several thousand dollars.

Income Limits

To be eligible as a QMB, your income must be no more than slightly above the Federal Poverty Guidelines (FPG). This figure is established each year by the federal government; in 2024, the income level is about $15,000 per year for an individual and about $20,000 per year for a married couple. These figures are slightly higher in Alaska and Hawaii. Some states, however, allow residents to have higher incomes and still qualify as QMBs, especially for those with income from current work.

It's important to know that certain amounts of income aren't counted in determining QMB eligibility. Particularly if you're still working and most of your income comes from your earnings, you might be able to qualify as a QMB even if your total income is almost twice the FPG. QMB follows the SSI guidelines for countable income, described in Chapter 7. If, after applying these rules, the figure you arrive at is anywhere close to the QMB qualifying limits, it's worth applying for it.

Asset Limits

There is a limit on the value of the assets you can own and still qualify as a QMB—generally, no more than about $9,000 for an individual and about $14,000 for a married couple. However, many assets, such as your house, your car, and certain personal and household goods, aren't part of the resources that are counted. (See "Who Is Eligible" in Chapter 7 for how SSI counts assets.)

Specified Low-Income Medicare Beneficiary (SLMB) and Qualifying Individual (QI)

If your income is slightly too high for you to qualify for QMB benefits, you might still be eligible for one of two other state medical assistance programs: Specified Low-Income Medicare Beneficiary (SLMB) or Qualifying Individual (QI). The resource limits for eligibility are the same as for a QMB, but the income limits are 20% to 80% higher, depending on the program.

If your counted monthly income—after the same adjustments made in calculating income for SSI purposes (see Chapter 7 for these calculations)—is less than $1,500 for an individual, or $2,000 for a couple, you're likely to qualify for SLMB or QI support.

Because the SLMB and QI programs are for people with slightly higher incomes, they have fewer benefits than the QMB program. The SLMB and QI programs pay all or part of the Medicare Part B monthly premium, but don't pay any Medicare deductibles or coinsurance amounts. Nonetheless, this means potential savings of more than $500 per year.

Applying for Medicaid, QMB, SLMB, or QI

Before you can get coverage by the Medicaid, QMB, SLMB, or QI programs, you must file a written application separate from your Medicare application. An application for Medicaid also serves as an application for QMB, SLMB, or QI. If you're found ineligible for one program, you might still be found eligible for one of the others.

This section explains some of the things you'll need to do and documents you will need to gather to file an application for Medicaid, QMB, SLMB, or QI.

Where to File

To qualify for Medicaid or the QMB, SLMB, or QI programs, you must file a written application with the agency that handles Medicaid in your state—usually your county's department of social services or social welfare department.

In many states, if you're applying for SSI benefits at your local Social Security office, that application will also serve as a Medicaid application. You'll be notified of Medicaid eligibility at the same time as you receive notice regarding SSI. (See Chapter 7 for a full discussion of the SSI program.)

If you or your spouse is hospitalized when you apply for Medicaid, ask to see a medical social worker in the hospital who can help you fill out the application.

Required Documents and Other Information

Because eligibility for Medicaid and the QMB, SLMB, or QI programs depends on your financial situation, many of the documents you must bring to the Medicaid office are those that will verify your income and assets.

Although a Medicaid eligibility worker might require additional specific information from you, you will at least be able to get the application process started if you bring:

- pay stubs, income tax returns, Social Security benefits information, and other evidence of your current income
- papers showing all your savings and other financial assets, such as bank books, insurance policies, and stock certificates
- automobile registration papers if you own a car
- your Social Security number
- information about your spouse's income and any separate assets, if the two of you live together, and
- medical bills from the previous three months, as well as medical records or reports to confirm any medical condition that will require treatment in the near future. If you don't have copies of these bills, records, or reports, bring the names and addresses of the doctors, hospitals, or other medical providers who are treating you.

Even if you don't have all these papers, go to your local social services or social welfare department office and file your application for Medicaid as soon as you think you might qualify. The Medicaid eligibility workers will tell you what other documents you need—and sometimes can explain how to get necessary papers you don't have or can help get them for you.

Application Procedure

A Medicaid eligibility worker—or an SSI eligibility worker if you apply for SSI at a local Social Security office—will interview you and assist you in filling out your application. There might be lots of forms to fill out, and you might have to return to the office for several different interviews.

> **TIP**
>
> **Don't get discouraged.** Delays, repeated forms, and interviews don't mean you won't be approved. The state has created procedures that make it difficult for people to get through the qualification process, driving some people to give up on benefits to which they are entitled. Patience is not only a virtue; it's an absolute necessity.

Normally, you will receive a decision on your Medicaid application within a few weeks after you complete the forms and provide the necessary information. The law requires that a decision be made within 45 days. If you don't hear from Medicaid within a month after you apply, call the eligibility worker who interviewed you. Sometimes it takes a little polite pushing to get a decision out of an overworked social services agency.

Retroactive Benefits

If you're found to be eligible and have already incurred medical bills, Medicaid might cover some of them. This retroactive eligibility can go back to the beginning of the third month before the date you filed your application. Make sure to show your Medicaid eligibility worker any medical bills you have from this period.

If you're denied eligibility for Medicaid, QMB, SLMB, or QI, you have a right to appeal (see below).

Review of Eligibility

How long your Medicaid coverage will last depends on your finances and your medical costs. Medicaid eligibility is reviewed periodically, usually every six months and at least once a year.

If, upon review, the Medicaid agency finds that your financial situation has changed to put you over the eligibility limits for your state's Medicaid program, your coverage might be discontinued. Until then, your Medicaid or QMB, SLMB, or QI coverage will continue, even if your income or assets put you over the limits some months before.

Likewise, if you became eligible for Medicaid as medically needy because of high medical costs, but those medical costs have ended, you might be dropped from Medicaid when your review is completed. Until the review, however, you will remain on Medicaid regardless.

If new medical costs arise after your coverage has been ended, you can apply again for Medicaid coverage.

What to Do If You're Denied Coverage

If you're denied Medicaid, QMB, SLMB, or QI coverage for which you believe you're eligible, go immediately to the office where you applied. Ask about the procedure in your state for getting a hearing to appeal that decision.

In some states, if you request a hearing in writing within 10 days after receiving the notice saying that your coverage is going to end, your coverage can stay in effect until after the hearing officer makes a decision.

At an appeal hearing, you'll be able to present any documents or other papers—proof of income, assets, medical bills—that you think support your claim. You'll also be allowed to explain why the Medicaid decision was wrong. If expected medical bills, which you claim will qualify you as medically needy, are the main question concerning your eligibility, then a letter from your doctor explaining your condition and the expected cost of treatment could be important.

The hearing itself is usually held at or near the welfare or social service office. You're permitted to have a friend, relative, social worker, lawyer, or another representative appear with you to help at the hearing.

Getting Assistance With Your Appeal

If you're denied Medicaid, QMB, SLMB, or QI, you might want to consult with someone experienced in the subject to help you prepare your appeal. The best place to find quality free assistance with these matters is the nearest office of the State Health Insurance Assistance Program (SHIP) (see the end of Chapter 13 for contact information).

If there is no SHIP office near you, you might be able to find other assistance through your local senior center or by calling the senior information line listed in your telephone directory.

You can also hire a Medicaid lawyer or health care lawyer to help.

Although the exact procedure for obtaining this hearing, and the hearing itself, might be somewhat different from state to state, they all resemble the hearings given to applicants for Social Security benefits (covered in Chapter 9).

You should be notified of the decision on your appeal within 90 days after the hearing.

For more information, see Nolo's series of articles on Medicaid appeals at www.nolo.com/legal-encyclopedia/medicaid-law.

Index

NOLO **Save 15%** *off your next order*

Register your Nolo purchase, and we'll send you a **coupon for 15% off** your next Nolo.com order!

Nolo.com/customer-support/productregistration

On Nolo.com you'll also find:

Books & Software

Nolo publishes hundreds of great books and software programs for consumers and business owners. Order a copy, or download an ebook version instantly, at Nolo.com.

Online Forms

You can quickly and easily make a will or living trust, form an LLC or corporation, or make hundreds of other forms—online.

Free Legal Information

Thousands of articles answer common questions about everyday legal issues, including wills, bankruptcy, small business formation, divorce, patents, employment, and much more.

Plain-English Legal Dictionary

Stumped by jargon? Look it up in America's most up-to-date source for definitions of legal terms, free at Nolo.com.

Lawyer Directory

Nolo's consumer-friendly lawyer directory provides in-depth profiles of lawyers all over America. You'll find information you need to choose the right lawyer.